Surviving the Storms

Memoirs of David P. Scaer

David P. Scaer
Concordia Theological Seminary
Fort Wayne, Indiana

Surviving the Storms

Memoirs of David P. Scaer

Robert E. Smith, Editor

Luther Academy

© 2018 Luther Academy and David P. Scaer

All rights reserved. Except where cited for the purposes of review, no part of this publication may be reproduced, stored in a retrieval system, or transmitted in any form or by any means, electronic, mechanical, photocopying, recording, or otherwise, without the prior permission of Luther Academy.

ISBN: Hardcover: 978-1-935035-23-7, Paperback: 978-1-935035-24-4
Printed in the United States of America

And I will see to it that after my departure you may be able at any time to recall these things.

∼ 2 Peter 1:15

Μνημονεύετε τῶν ἡγουμένων ὑμῶν, οἵτινες ἐλάλησαν ὑμῖν τὸν λόγον τοῦ θεοῦ, ὧν ἀναθεωροῦντες τὴν ἔκβασιν τῆς ἀναστροφῆς μιμεῖσθε τὴν πίστιν. Ἰησοῦς Χριστὸς ἐχθὲς καὶ σήμερον ὁ αὐτὸς καὶ εἰς τοὺς αἰῶνας.

Remember your leaders, those who spoke to you the word of God; consider the outcome of their life, and imitate their faith. Jesus Christ is the same yesterday and today and forever.

Hebrews 13:7–8, RSV

CONTENTS

Acknowledgements xi
Editor's Preface, Robert E. Smith xiii
Author's Preface: The Storm Petrel xv
About this Book, Robert E. Smith xix

Chapter 1 • The Early Years in New York 3
    Excursus I • Lutherland and the Poconos 13
    Excursus II • Exegetical Theology at Concordia Seminary,
        St. Louis (1955–1974) 21
Chapter 2 • Saint Louis Seminary Days 25
Chapter 3 • Studies in Germany 53
Chapter 4 • Parish Ministry 63
    Excursus III • Working with the Gospels 77
Chapter 5 • The Early Years in Springfield 87
    Excursus IV • College Courses at the University of
        Illinois–Champaign 107
    Excursus V • Lutheran World Federation (LWF) at Évian 121
    Excursus VI • John Tietjen, John Damm and Seminex 129
Chapter 6 • The Schultz Presidency 143
    Excursus VII • Robert David Preus 159
Chapter 7 • Early Years of the Robert Preus Presidency 169
    Excursus VIII • A Tale of Two Dogmatics Series 185
    Excursus IX • Symposia on the Lutheran Confessions 199
    Excursus X • Quest for an Advanced Degree Program 203
Chapter 8 • The Era of Good Feeling 207
    Excursus XI • The Sermon on the Mount: The Church's
        First Statement of the Gospel 241
    Excursus XII • Warren Wilbert 247
    Excursus XIII • Objective vs. Subjective Justification 251
Chapter 9 • The "Retirement" of Robert Preus 259
    Excursus XIV • Waldo Werning 277
Chapter 10 • Interregnum 301
Chapter 11 • The Schmiel Presidency 329
Chapter 12 • The Wenthe and Rast Presidencies 353
    Excursus XV • Commission on Theology and Church Relations ... 357

Glossary 371
Index 375
Bibliography of David P. Scaer by Robert E. Smith 387

CONTENTS (Alternate)

Acknowledgements xi
Editor's Preface, Robert E. Smith xiii
Author's Preface: The Storm Petrel xv
About this Book, Robert E. Smith xix

Chapter 1 • The Early Years in New York 3
Chapter 2 • Saint Louis Seminary Days 25
Chapter 3 • Studies in Germany 53
Chapter 4 • Parish Ministry 63
Chapter 5 • The Early Years in Springfield 87
Chapter 6 • The Schultz Presidency 143
Chapter 7 • Early Years of the Robert Preus Presidency 169
Chapter 8 • The Era of Good Feeling 207
Chapter 9 • The "Retirement" of Robert Preus 259
Chapter 10 • Interregnum 301
Chapter 11 • The Schmiel Presidency 329
Chapter 12 • The Wenthe and Rast Presidencies 353

Excursus I • Lutherland and the Poconos 13
Excursus II • Exegetical Theology at Concordia Seminary,
    St. Louis (1955-1974) 21
Excursus III • Working with the Gospels 77
Excursus IV • College Courses at the University of
    Illinois–Champaign 107
Excursus V • Lutheran World Federation (LWF) at Évian 121
Excursus VI • John Tietjen, John Damm and Seminex 129
Excursus VII • Robert David Preus 159
Excursus VIII • A Tale of Two Dogmatics Series 185
Excursus IX • Symposia on the Lutheran Confessions 199
Excursus X • Quest for an Advanced Degree Program 203
Excursus XI • The Sermon on the Mount:
    The Church's First Statement of the Gospel 241
Excursus XII • Warren Wilbert 247
Excursus XIII • Objective vs. Subjective Justification 251
Excursus XIV • Waldo Werning 277
Excursus XV • Commission on Theology and Church Relations 357

Glossary 371
Index 375
Bibliography of David P. Scaer by Robert E. Smith 387

ACKNOWLEDGEMENTS

What follows on these pages in some way fits the dictionary definition of memoirs as "a historical account or biography written from personal knowledge." What I remembered was supplemented by my notes, the memories of others who had put them to paper, accounts published in books and unpublished documents in the synod, seminary and congregational archives. In pursing the task, all sorts of documents of accounts in which I was a participant began to surface. So many years had passed that in seeing the names on these papers, I could not in some cases attach faces to the names. This was not a case of manuscripts verifying memory, but manuscripts providing data that had been forgotten. In doing his own research Lawrence R. Rast Jr. would come across a document and send it along with a note asking whether this would jar my memory. So memory had to be reconstructed around what the documents reported. Faced with possible removal from the St. Louis seminary during my second and third years, I began writing up accounts of my meetings with fellow students and faculty so that the record could be kept straight.

Shortly after coming to the Springfield seminary, I saw the necessity of acquainting myself with form criticism, first of Martin Dibelius, then Ruldoph Bultmann's demythologizing of the Gospels. This method had been promoted by some in the faculty majority. This led to the walkout in February 1974. Demythologizing left little, if anything, in the Gospels. It did make an attempt, failed as it was, to describe how things that happened in the life of Jesus ended up in the Gospels. This method is no longer seen as relevant, but they were attempts—and important ones—to trace how what happened came to find its way onto the written pages. This is hardly new. Luke in his Gospel lays out how in pursuing his task he actually talked to the apostles of Jesus, whom he calls eyewitnesses of the word, and consulted an available document, which is arguably the Gospel of Matthew. Though translations and commentaries speak of several documents, the Greek here is singular. Luke's Gospel is written no later than thirty years after the life of Jesus. One second-century church father called the Gospels memoirs or reminiscences of the apostles. The Gospels are what the apostles and others remembered about Jesus, what he did and said. All memoirs have a bias in how the events they report were perceived by those who participated in them, saw them and first heard.

I have written about things from different time periods, and I have done the writing at different times. The chapter of my St. Louis seminary days (1955–1960) was written half a century after the events in it happened, and without the aid of notes and documents I would not have remembered them. As the reader will note, I have made use of books by those who did not participate in these events, but who did the research to find out what happened. Things that happened at the Springfield (now Fort Wayne) seminary (1966–1975) were written right after they happened. Some time around my seventieth birthday, I began thinking about putting in place a memoir. With the help of a computer and the WordPerfect program, I was able to sort the events into chapters according to time periods. In order not to interrupt the flow of the narrative—and a narrative is more like a river than still a body of water like a lake—some materials could be reported chronologically, others according to subject matter, and still others according to theological topics.

In the initial stages, Lawrence R. Rast Jr. read the manuscript and provided suggestions and data from the archives as they surfaced. Helping to bring the document to full term was Fort Wayne librarian Robert Smith, who in reading it noted that the same event had been included more than once and took the appropriate surgical action. He also collected loose odds and ends and put them into paragraphs and chapters. In all cases he worked to keep my style intact. Without him the task could not have been done. Just as no one can know his secret faults, so no writer can be his own editor. Since these memoirs have to do with a time period with which many, maybe most, of our readers have no direct experience, birth and death dates have been provided.

Through his contacts with the Concordia Historical Institute, Librarian Robert Smith has done this arduous work. These will help the readers put things in perspective. Attached in an appendix is a bibliography of some length. Dates of publication can be matched up with the narrative to provide an outline of what the theological issues of a particular time were. An index reference will give a bird's-eye view of persons who found a place in this narrative.

Bringing this work to completion was made possible with the aid of Daniel Preus, who headed up Luther Academy for years and served as Missouri Synod vice president. Much of what is here written has to do with his late father, Robert D. Preus, who more than anyone else in the last half of the twentieth was the synod's most significant theologian.

EDITOR'S PREFACE

David Scaer is many things. He is a professor, pastor, mentor, author, exegete, dogmatician, fearless confessor of the faith, son of the Missouri Synod, participant in ecumenical dialogue, to his students a drill sergeant, speaking truth to power, and loyal friend to those who know him well.

Most of all, he is a teacher of the church. Having taught at Concordia Theological Seminary, both in Springfield, Illinois, and then Fort Wayne, Indiana, for more than a half century, over 40 percent of the pastoral roster of the Lutheran Church—Missouri Synod sat at his feet. As a long-serving member of the Commission on Theology and Church Relations, author of over one hundred sixty publications, including several volumes of the Confessional Lutheran Dogmatics series, he has helped shape the doctrine of the Lutheran Church—Missouri Synod as it is believed, taught and confessed today.

Although I am a graduate of the St. Louis seminary, I, too, count myself as his student. As a librarian at Concordia Theological Seminary for the past twenty-five years, I have worked closely with Dr. Scaer, done some editing for him from time to time and count him as a friend. I have learned much from him, especially during the process of shaping this book. It is my prayer that all who read this work will learn much from him as well.

Robert E. Smith
Editor

AUTHOR'S PREFACE

THE STORM PETREL

The storm petrel is a small bird with wide wings that flies far from land and, upon return to land, finds refuge in the jagged and often submerged rocks in the sea. It would fit with the family name Scaer, which, if it is of Nordic origin, comes from the word meaning "an isolated or protruding rock in the sea." This may be symbolic of having gone through tempestuous times not only surviving but, in certain periods, prospering.

At this writing, I have served nearly fifty-seven years in ministry and more than a half century at Concordia Theological Seminary: once in Springfield, Illinois, and now in Fort Wayne, Indiana. Seminary teaching has been more of my life than it has been for any other person teaching at either seminary of the Lutheran Church—Missouri Synod in the last century. Those who served as seminary president during my tenure on the faculty include J. A. O. "Jack" Preus (1920–1994), Lorman Petersen (1915–2009), Richard "Dick" Schultz (1920–2001), Henry "Hank" Eggold (1917–1982), Robert D. Preus (1924–1995), Norbert Mueller (1927–2013), Michael Stelmachowicz (1927–2009) (chief administrator), David Schmiel (b. 1931), William "Bill" Weinrich (b. 1945), Dean Wenthe, and Lawrence R. Rast Jr.

During these years, I taught dogmatics, the Lutheran Confessions, and courses in the Gospels, and served as academic dean, chairman of the department of systematic theology, faculty representative to the synod's Commission on Theology and Church Relations, editor of the *Concordia Theological Quarterly* (formerly *The Springfielder*), and faculty marshal. I was an advisory delegate to the Missouri Synod conventions in 1975, 1989, 2001, 2004, and 2007, and attended with no credentials in 1967 and 1992.

During the administrations of Richard Schultz (Academic Dean Petersen), Norbert Mueller (Academic Dean Walter A. Maier II [b. 1925]), Michael Stelmachowicz, and David Schmiel (Academic Dean Alan Borcherding), punitive measures were taken against me that could easily be interpreted as attempts to remove me. In the midst of my troubles, a dear colleague wrote me a memo saying that I had brought upon myself any misfortune that had come my way. Well, that may be, but the petrel survives the storms and finds refuge in the rocks that bring doom to large ships.

As a young pastor, I found autobiographies of ministers of all Christian denominations fascinating. I still do. Common themes run through the lives of God's servants. It is one story told with different characters. We discover that we are not the first ones to take the roads that sometimes run into threatening situations. Perhaps in the following pages some will find themes of their own ministries.

This is not a history of the Missouri Synod, but it may help those who write these histories to see how one person saw the synod from his particular space and time. Here and there it might provide glimpses of how a Lutheran church body with the most conservative reputation since the seventeenth century reached its current point. Synod president Gerald Kieschnick (b. 1943) said the synod was not his grandfather's church. No church ever is.

In arguing against the privileges Rome claimed because its founders were Peter and Paul, Hermann Sasse (1895–1976) said that in 150 AD the church was not what it was when the apostles were there. A century makes a difference. Pastors and people change; what we speak about changes; how we speak changes. The New Testament is not the Old, and the Gospel of John is not that of Matthew.

Taking a cue from Carl E. Braaten's (b. 1929) *Because of Christ: Memoirs of a Lutheran Theologian*, what follows here is "a theological autobiography... starting where it all began...."[1] What follows in these memoirs comes not only from memory but from memos, letters, and documents of all kinds collected through the years—and, in some places, they provide the perspective and the structure of things happening during these years at Concordia Theological Seminary and in the Missouri Synod.

Reviewing these things occasions sorrow and depression and raises the following question: If I had known the path in front of me, would I have taken another road, or, taking the metaphor of the petrel, flown in another direction? Much of my work received recognition only at the end of my active professional life, those years when others have either retired or are planning to do so. If life's calendar could have been reversed, the pitfalls might have been avoided and laurels appreciated earlier, but that's not how it works. The storm petrel ignores the weather and flies far from the land over rough seas with foaming waves and returns to the jagged rocks. This is what these memoirs are about—a flight over the seas and a return to the rocks.

---

1. Carl E. Braaten, *Because of Christ: Memoirs of a Lutheran Theologian* (Grand Rapids, MI: W. B. Eerdmans Publishing Co., 2010), vii.

Author's Preface

There were some early plumbs along the way. Twice I was awarded the John W. Behnken Post-Doctoral Fellowship by the Aid Association for Lutherans (now Thrivent), but this did not change the course of life. One book collected some of my writings. One volume contains my sermons and another volume my popular articles.[2] My theology has been the subject of five books, three of them doctoral dissertations. Two were less than positive. My *Discourses in Matthew*[3] was featured by the Association of Theological Publishers as one of the best books of 2004. These scholarly reviews of my dogmatical and New Testament writings at least showed that they had roused a few new thoughts in the minds of others.

My theological life has been lived within the borders of a confessional Lutheranism known as the Missouri Synod, but these were not boundaries inhibiting me from going into other places. A festschift entitled *All Theology is Christology*[4] encapsulated what the Bible and theology were all about. Alongside contributors from churches in fellowship with The Lutheran Church—Missouri Synod were Catholics, Anglicans, Reformed, and Evangelical Lutheran Church in America (ELCA) scholars.

In 2000, The David P. Scaer Chair of Biblical and Systematic Theology was established through the generosity of Alma Nielsen and her sister Corrine Nielsen, largely at the recommendation of their brother Paul Nielsen. That's one way to grasp immortality, but soon names attached to campus buildings and endowed chairs and the persons whom the names represent are forgotten. So it must be. Each generation must make its own way. What follows here is an account that reflects what was happening in one corner of the Missouri Synod as it had just passed its centennial mark and was not that far from the end of its second century.

---

2. David P. Scaer, *In Christ: The Collected Works of David P. Scaer, Lutheran Confessor*. Edited by Peter C. Bender (Sussex, WI: Concordia Catechetical Academy, 2004).
3. David P. Scaer, *Discourses in Matthew: Jesus Teaches the Church* (St. Louis, MO: Concordia Publishing House, 2004).
4. Dean O. Wenthe and David P Scaer, *All Theology Is Christology: Essays in Honor of David P. Scaer* (Fort Wayne, IN: Concordia Theological Seminary Press, 2000). There were twenty-four contributors.

ABOUT THIS BOOK

This book is hard to characterize. Like a memoir, it contains the memories of David Scaer. Like a biography, much of the reflections are supported by a documentary corpus assembled by him, primary source material, secondary sources and memoirs of his contemporaries. In some places, he teaches, explaining concepts in the study and teaching of Biblical exegesis and systematic theology. More than anything else, it is the telling of his story—that of a professor of theology during difficult days in the history of the Lutheran Church—Missouri Synod.

So the structure of this book is unique. To read the work like an autobiography, read the sections called chapters and by-pass the ones labeled excursuses. To learn about a specific topic or a significant person in his professional life, read one or more of the excursuses. These are placed within the story where the issue discussed first appear, but covers the topics over time—sometimes over decades. This design is intended to let Dr. Scaer teach and at the same time to witness to events that shaped and still shape his ministry.

Robert E. Smith
Editor

Surviving the Storms

Memoirs of David P. Scaer

Chapter One

THE EARLY YEARS IN NEW YORK

∂♥

FAMILY TIES

Most of my roots were in the soil of Midwestern Missouri Synod families, but my life was formed by being brought up in New York in what was then—and still is—the world's most exciting city. My father, Paul Henry Scaer (1898–1967), graduated in 1922 from Concordia Seminary in St. Louis and pursued a master's degree in English at Columbia University. In August of 1924, he was ordained and installed as pastor of Trinity Evangelical Lutheran Church of Flatbush in Brooklyn, New York, where he spent his entire forty-three-year ministry.

My mother, Victoria Zimmermann (1909–2005), was a member of the congregation and daughter of Lydia (née Trier, 1885–1982) and Gustav Zimmermann (1874–1958). The Zimmermanns were founding members of the congregation. My father met my mother at Trinity and married her on November 28, 1930.

On March 13, 1936, I was born at the Lutheran Hospital in Brooklyn. I was the second of the three children they raised. An older sister, Elizabeth (b. 1931), and a younger one, Jean (b. 1937), were also born in Brooklyn and remained in the East.

Trinity of Flatbush, my father's parish, had been established by Pastor George C. Koenig (1894–1951), a son-in-law of Franz Pieper (1852–1931). The church worshiped at first in a store front on Coney Island Avenue.[1] Brooklyn was once a bastion of Protestantism. At that time, Brooklyn, with its large white Protestant population, enjoyed the title "City of Churches." However, in the intervening years, things have changed, and one church after another has since closed down.[2]

---

1. Theodore Graebner, *Dr. Francis Pieper: A Biographical Sketch* (St. Louis, MO: Concordia Publishing House, 1931).
2. For a general treatment of the issue of Protestant decline, see Walter Sundberg, "Religious Trends in Twentieth Century America," *Word and World* 20 (Winter 2000): 22–31.

The borough had its own day of celebration known as "Brooklyn Day," during which the public schools were closed and the children of the Protestant churches' Sunday schools marched down major boulevards accompanied by bands and flags, ending up at a bandstand from which public dignitaries spoke. On one occasion, President Harry Truman (1884–1972), Governor Thomas Dewey (1902–1971), the mayor, and the president of the borough were present.

On Brooklyn Day, Trinity's Sunday school left the church at East 8th Street and marched up 18th Avenue to join the other Sunday schools in marching along Ocean Parkway towards Prospect Park. A rotation system gave each Sunday school a different parade position each year. The most desirable was first place, which meant that that particular church had the honor of marching along with the band. Hymns were sung by all the churches. "Onward Christian Soldiers" was the finale. Police cars accompanied the marchers.

Afterwards, each Sunday school returned to its own church for ice cream and soda. These Sunday school parades likely ended in the 1960s, long after they were out of touch with the times. Children from the Catholic parochial schools did not participate. Soon, large Lutheran, Reformed, and Congregational churches closed their doors and were replaced by high-rise apartments. Protestantism had lost its hold in Brooklyn.[3]

Like all congregations, Trinity experienced successes and challenges. Soon after my father became its pastor of Trinity, the congregation constructed a church in the mock English Gothic style. Payment of the mortgage, which had been taken out just before the Great Depression, became a challenge for the congregation, whose membership never matched older churches. Still, a mortgage-burning ceremony took place in the church in 1950. Church attendance during World War II was augmented by servicemen from the Midwest on their way to Europe by ship via the Brooklyn Navy Yard. They were often guests in our home for dinner on Sundays after church. Years later, they remembered my mother's generous hospitality, especially at Christmastime.

After the war, my mother, who was active in the Atlantic District zone of the Lutheran Women's Missionary League of the Missouri Synod and even served as its president, regularly provided hospitality to missionaries

---

3. Roman Catholic churches are also feeling the effects of decline. See Jeremy B. White, "Brooklyn's Fading Catholic Churches, and posted May 13, 2011, http://brooklynink.org/2011/05/13/26043-brooklyns-fading-catholic-churches/. See also Eliot Willensky, *When Brooklyn Was the World, 1923–1957* (New York: Harmony Books, 1986).

going to and coming from Africa. Often they lodged in our home, even in the years after she was widowed. Several of our seminary students have since become pastors in the New York area. My father and mother had a big job in holding a Lutheran congregation together. These men have a bigger job in front of them.

Trinity of Flatbush was one of three congregations in Brooklyn that belonged to the English District of The Lutheran Church—Missouri Synod rather than the geographical area jurisdiction of the Atlantic District.[4] For years, my father served as the visitor and counselor for congregations in the New York-New Jersey Circuit of the English District. He was also chairman of its annual pastoral conference, which generally met at Lutherland in the Poconos.[5]

At Trinity, my father also had the major responsibility for secretarial and janitorial work. He typed the church bulletin and ran it off on a mimeograph in our basement. Dad also did all of the mailings. We were conscripted into folding the bulletins and stuffing the envelopes. A snow storm meant shoveling the walk in front of the church. Christmas meant decorating the church. My father had his study at home, and so we really lived right in the middle of the church.

Sometimes I would accompany him on his sick and shut-in calls and would sit in another room as he ministered to his flock. He would take me to get church supplies at Kaufmann's, located on the Manhattan side of the Brooklyn Bridge. In the war years, we took the Coney Island Avenue trolley, which in those days went over the Brooklyn Bridge into Manhattan. Now the bridge is used only for automobile and pedestrian traffic.

This bridge had a special place in my family lore. My grandfather and my great-grandfather, Maximillian Zimmermann, a Civil War veteran, were part of the opening ceremonies for this significant architectural structure and had walked across it on that day. On the day it was opened to the public, several people died as crowds from both sides made their way onto the bridge.[6]

Some Sunday afternoons were spent walking across the bridge. Even today, seeing the bridge means that I am close to home. We reached Man-

---

4. The others were Our Saviour and Good Shepherd. Our Saviour was at 417 W 57th St., and Good Shepherd was at 2139 New York Avenue.
5. For the story of Lutherland, see Excursus I: Lutherland and the Poconos, 13 ff.
6. "Dead on the New Bridge: Fatal Crush at the Western Approach," *New York Times* (May 31, 1883). Available at *https://timesmachine.nytimes.com/timesmachine/1883/05/31/102825484.pdf*.

hattan by going north either on the subway or the trolley. Going south led to Coney Island. After school on the warm June and September afternoons, my mother would take us to the ocean at that famed beach. She had a great love for the water, and she swam up into her mid-80s. This love was contagious, and wherever there is a suitable body of water, I am ready to take the plunge.

The annual church bazaar on the first Thursday and Friday in November was a successful fund-raising event. My father would procure advertisements from local merchants for the church annual, which listed more names than the church probably had members. Dinner was served, and a variety of games of chance were offered. As children, we looked forward expectantly to this event. On Saturday morning, members gathered at the church to take away the tables and disassemble the wooden frames. In my first year at the Bronxville prep school, at age thirteen, I remember my sadness in not being able to come home because I lacked a sufficiently high grade.

Simply put, our family's world was Trinity Lutheran Church of Flatbush. Both my father and I were ordained there, and he was buried from that church in April 1967. For me and my sisters, Elizabeth and Jean, Sundays meant Sunday school and then church. As children, we generally sat with grandparents, who had staked out their position in the fourth row in front of the lectern on the left. My sisters and I sang in the choir.

During my high school years, since I was not there during the week for rehearsals, church organist and choir director Ada Brown tutored me after church. My love of music and ability to read notes did not translate into performance. After the beginning of my high school years at Bronxville, at age thirteen, I began teaching in the Sunday school. I continued to do so until I entered junior college at Bronxville. At that point, I no longer came home on weekends, and my association with Trinity and Brooklyn, apart from school holidays, ended.

In 1938, our family moved from 715 Foster Avenue to 1121 Ditmas Avenue, where my mother lived until 1977. My grandparents, Gustav and Lydia Zimmermann, lived within a forty-minute walk at 966 East 18th Street. Since my grandparents lived within walking distance, I spent many nights there when someone at 1121 had a contagious disease.

I had a special relationship with my maternal grandfather. Due to the fact that he had no son of his own and I was his first grandson, I had the advantage of having him take me on Saturday mornings to his office at Union Square at 14th Street in New York City. He would board the Brighton Beach local at Avenue J, get off at Newkirk Avenue, and go upstairs to pick me up as I waited with my mother. The fare was one nickel. Part of the routine was a shoeshine and lunch with some friends, all probably Jewish, and one of whom was a Communist.

As a boy, my grandfather delivered flowers for Eugene Higgins (d. 1948), one of the wealthiest men of the first half of the twentieth century. He was a bachelor, and when he died in 1948, his estate went to establish the Higgins Trust, which was at that time the eleventh largest of its kind in the United States. Later, Higgins put Gustav Zimmerman in charge of his American properties. For his fiftieth anniversary, Higgins gave him a black tie dinner at the Waldorf Astoria. Higgins was caught in England before World War II and never again returned to the United States. Until Higgins's death in 1948, my grandfather continued on to manage his American properties.

Two assemblies were held for the student body of Public School 217 (P.S. 217) each week: one on Wednesday afternoon and the other on Friday morning. Either the principal or the vice principal would read a portion from either the Old or New Testament. There was a presentation of the American flag with a color guard, of which I was member for a short time, and the Pledge of Allegiance. Mrs. Bilderslee was Jewish. Reading from the Bible or singing hymns, like "Come Thou Almighty King" and at Christmas "The First Noel," was not problematic at all. This was a different age, when a sharp line between the public school and religion had yet to be drawn. "King of Israel" undoubtedly meant different things to different people. On Wednesday afternoons, the students were allowed to attend religious classes at their own churches at two PM.

Confirmation instruction at Trinity lasted for two years and took two hours every Saturday. We were required to know the questions and answers in the synod catechism. Each confirmand was publicly examined on his or her knowledge of Martin Luther's (1483–1546) Small Catechism and Explanation on the Sunday before Palm Sunday. The Rite of Confirmation was administered on Palm Sunday itself, and first Communion followed on Easter. To conserve heating oil (a practice that began in World War II), confirmation classes were held in the basement kitchen next to the boiler room, which was the warmest place in the church. Twice I was expelled by my father for misbehavior—or was it because I thought I knew it all?

Outside of Trinity Lutheran Church, my world was not Lutheran. Ours was one of five large three-story houses on Ditmas Avenue between Strafford Road and Westminster Roads. Three families were Jewish, and one was Roman Catholic. In the course of nine years, I can only recall two Protestant teachers at P.S. 217. Some teachers were Catholic, but the majority of my neighbors were Jewish, as were most of the student body. At some point for some forgotten reason—perhaps it was an essay—I was awarded by P.S. 217 an American Legion medal with a ribbon to be pinned on a jacket. I still have the medal.

Most Catholic children attended the parochial school of St. Rose of Lima, which was at the other end of East 8th Street, south from Trinity. Jewish children were absent on their holidays, which then were not legal ones, and so on these school days I was the only one in class. Growing up in an environment where there were no other Lutherans in my classes or among my friends gave us the sense of being in the minority. To view Christmas decorations, we drove over into the Italian section of Bay Ridge. Summers in Lutherland in the Pocono Mountains of Pennsylvania gave me a chance to mingle with other Lutherans.[7] Otherwise, the world in Brooklyn was mostly Jewish. It took a little bit of adjustment to discover and get used to another world elsewhere.

Still, there was plenty of time for fun. Afternoons and warm summer evenings were spent playing stickball on Strafford Road, with two sewer covers serving as home plate and second base and two lampposts for first and third. Harold Roettger, assistant to Branch Rickey (1881–1965), the president of the Brooklyn Dodgers, rented a room in our house.

For a short time, I worked as an office boy in the downtown Dodgers office for a wage of twenty-five cents an hour, of which ten cents went for the round-trip subway fare. On some Saturdays, I went to Ebbets Field to watch the Brooklyn Dodgers. A seat in the bleachers cost sixty cents—the equivalent of two hours of work. A score card came along with a copy of *The Brooklyn Eagle* for five cents. Ebbets Field was two stops away on the Brighton Beach Express.

The traditional date for the transformation of Brooklyn—some would say its death—is 1957, the year the Brooklyn Dodgers left Ebbets Field for Los Angeles. Whether it was a transformation or a death, Brooklyn had changed, and familiar haunts along Flatbush and Coney Island Avenues today have little resemblance to what they looked like in the middle of the twentieth century.

By 1957, Trinity had already been feeling the pinch. Confirmation classes had dwindled in size. Youth activities were harder to arrange. My sister Elizabeth belonged to a Protestant group at Brooklyn College, which did not meet with the approval of the Lutheran chaplain to New York col-

---

7. See Excursus I: Lutherland and the Poconos, 13 ff.

leges, Richard Klann (1915–2005). He was later one of the minority of five faculty members who did not join the faculty Seminex walkout.[8]

CONCORDIA COLLEGIATE INSTITUTE, BRONXVILLE, NEW YORK

In the 1960s, The Lutheran Church—Missouri Synod modified its educational system, which was modeled after the German gymnasium, to fit the American model. For over a century, students preparing for the seminary studied for six years at one of its regional educational institutions with the equivalency of the American four years of high school and two years of junior college. Since our family lived in Brooklyn, New York, the school of choice was Concordia Collegiate Institute in Bronxville, New York.[9]

Pre-theological curricula in all the synod's schools were nearly identical, with high school students taking four years of German, three of Latin and two of Greek before most of them reached the age of eighteen. For those not heading to the seminary, an academic track was designed, in which the math and science courses were taken instead of the ancient languages. Though all of the students were found in the same classes, the groups were distinct, and those preparing for ministry knew that after the two years of college, they would have another five years at the seminary. Pastors who later took opposite sides on some theological issues and became members of other synods were held together by friendships established in prep schools, as the pre-seminary institutions of the synod were called then.

In the 1960s, when the high school programs were phased out and junior college programs were expanded to a full four years, this all changed. I was brought up under the older model and by pedigree more than upbringing I belonged to old Missouri.

The year 1949, my first year at Bronxville, meant a new way of life. All freshmen were required to attend compulsory study hall in the dining room from seven to nine o'clock PM until they attained an 80 percent overall average. Weekend trips home were allowed on Saturday morning. When students attained an 85 percent average, they were then permitted to leave on Friday afternoon. I accomplished this feat only in the spring of 1950 after the fourth of six terms. Algebra and German presented real obstacles to me until the end of the first semester. My sister, who had

---

8. See Excursus VI: John Tietjen, John Damm and Seminex (129 ff.) and Excursus VII: Robert David Preus, 159 ff.
9. Now known as Concordia College New York.

a gift for math, and my father, who occasionally preached in German, helped me through these.

In my first year in the high school, 1949, Herman Otten (b. 1933) lived in the "suite" next to mine on the first floor of Bohm Hall. While dorm arrangements did not deserve its description, each "suite" had one room with four or five desks for study and a room with beds. Herman thought it was healthy to sleep in a cold room and wake up in a warm one. Shagging, the practice of having students in the lower classes do the will of the upper class men, was the law of the streets in many of the synod's schools, including Bronxville. Often Herman shagged me to get up at five o'clock AM to shut his window. We were on the same campus for the next two years, but the junior college students had little if any contact with high school students.

All aspects of the four years of high school were rigorous. Two years were spent on the synodical catechism. Along with having to know the chief parts of Luther's catechism, we were required to memorize the Bible passages and the questions and answers, which supposedly were written by H. C. Schwan (1818–1905), synod president from 1878–1899.[10]

Harold Haas (1925–2013) was my teacher for the first course in religion. Haas was a St. Louis seminary vicar, who later taught sociology at Concordia Senior College, Fort Wayne. Students entering the high school program in 1951 attended the junior college and then went to the senior college to complete their pre-seminary training. In the old system, students had eleven years between grammar school and graduation from seminary. Now it would be twelve.

Memorable for most pre-seminary students was Carl F. Weidmann (1906–1980), the prep school principal and the teacher of Old Testament, Greek, and Latin. Tests were difficult and the grades accordingly low. So I was as surprised as I was content to get 80 percent in the first term of his Old Testament course in my third year. Whatever I learned after those high school years in these areas was only the growth of what he had planted.

The student body mix in the junior college years was different from the high school. Along with the students heading for the seminary, some were headed for careers as parochial school teachers. It was rare for high school students not heading for the seminary to go into the junior college program. Since the requirements for the ministry and teaching were dif-

---

10. Arthur Christian Repp, "A study of the authorship of Schwan's Catechism." *Concordia Historical Institute Quarterly* 46, no. 3 (September 1973): 106–111.

ferent, we took only a few courses together. Many who later became pastors met their spouses here.

Students who desired to go to the seminary but who had not attended the high school were required to spend three years in the junior college program to learn the languages. One notable exception was Kurt Marquart (1934–2006), whose superior intellect allowed him to finish the work in two years. When I was beginning my first year in the junior college in 1953, he was beginning his second year. We began a friendship that lasted through our days together on the faculty of Concordia Theological Seminary.

Kurt Marquart had enrolled in the junior college division of Concordia Bronxville in 1955, the beginning of my senior year in the high school division. During his second year in the college, I was in my first year. I do not remember that we ever socialized.

Ambivalent feelings accompanied my leaving Bronxville. At nineteen years of age, there would be two more years of college, which were absorbed into seminary training. On the other hand I was ready for something more.

Excursus I

LUTHERLAND AND THE POCONOS

❧

After my grandparents were married in November 1908, they spent summers with my grandmother's parents in Fort Wayne. After my great-grandparents passed away, my grandparents rented a bungalow at Lutherland in the Pocono Mountains of eastern Pennsylvania. Lutherland was a vacation resort intended for Lutherans from the metropolitan area of New York City.[1] Both my father and grandfather were instrumental in its establishment in 1926 and served on its board of directors. In 1930, my grandparents bought a house with a view of Lake Naomi and Locust Knob.

It was here where my sisters and I spent our summers until 1950. At ages fourteen and fifteen, my sister Jean and I were ready to work in one of the three dining rooms in the hotel complex of Lutherland. One summer, I was a bellhop and carried luggage.

Summers in Lutherland were a delight. Church services every day except Saturday were part of the routine. The list of preachers in the early days of Lutherland serves as a "who's who in the Synod." Here, the famous Lutheran Hour preacher Walter A. Maier I (1893–1950) got his start. Others of note included John Behnken (1884–1968), pastor at Trinity Lutheran Church in Houston, Texas, and later president of the synod (1935–1962); O. P. Kretzmann (1902–1975), president of Valparaiso University; O. A. Geiseman (1893–1962), longtime pastor of Grace Lutheran Church in River Forest, Illinois; Oswald Hoffmann (1913–2005), later speaker of the Lutheran Hour; and Adolph Meyer (1899–1988), a Yonkers, New York, pastor and editor of the independent magazine *The American Lutheran*.

My father had his turn, too. For many years, my father held these services, sometimes for a two-week period. When he preached, our family stayed with my grandparents and had our meals in the main dining room,

---

1. Ted Suttmeier, *Lutherland, A Dream Fulfilled and Memories: History of Lutherland-Pocono Crest, 1926–1982* (Pocono Pines, PA: Printing Craftsmen, 2007).

a luxurious experience. After that, it was difficult to get back into the routine of drying the dishes and burning the garbage. For lunch, I would accompany my father to Beaverbrook, a camp for adults, where he would give the same lecture that he had given to the hotel guests at nine-thirty AM.

The name "Casino" was a misnomer. It had nothing to do with gambling but had an assembly hall on the second story for about six hundred people. It also featured a gift shop, a soda fountain, a tea room, a bowling alley, and pinball machines on the ground floor. Until the late 1960s, it was an evening meeting place for hotel guests and cottage owners. Guests had their main meal in the evening. Ours was at noon. After the evening meal, everyone would be properly dressed—men with suit jackets, white shirts and ties—and go to the Casino. Nickel ice cream cones were the standard fare for all. On Thursday nights, the guests and staff of Camp Beaverbrook would give sketches and plays. Saturdays were for square dancing, in which we joined. I still know the steps.

Names associated with Beaverbrook were Rudolph "Rudy" Ressmeyer (1924–2017), longtime camp director and later president of the synod's Atlantic District; Eugene Nissen (b. 1925), professor at the synod's Ann Arbor college; Ted Wittrock (1920–2007), a pastor in the Bronx, who later served as director of the American Lutheran Publicity Bureau; and Walter (b. 1926) and William Schoedel, who played the organ and violin during Sunday services in the Casino.[2] Walter A. Maier I began services there in 1925, and for over forty years the Casino had been used for two Sunday morning services: one for the campers and the other for hotel guests.

In the 1960s, the Lutheran hotel experience that began with such great hopes as Lutherland in 1925 was in decline. Changing the name from Lutherland to Pocono Crest did not reverse the resort's declining fortunes. A resort with three hotels and three camps—one for adults and the two others for the younger set—no longer attracted vacationers who now had an expanding interstate system to travel farther.

In bankruptcy since the early 1950s, Lutherland fell into the hands of Valparaiso University, which assured bondholders that they could deduct

---

2. William "Bill" Schoedel and his brother Walter had been directors of Camp Beaverbrook. With their musical talent, they led the hymn singing in Sunday morning services in the Casino. I accompanied my father in his noon lectures at Camp Beaverbrook, where we ate lunch at the staff table with Bill and Walter. Bill became one of the foremost scholars in early church Gnosticism and assumed a professorship at the University of Illinois (Champaign) while I was teaching there. He has retired as professor of religion at the University of Illinois. At this writing, Walter is a retired pastor in St. Louis.

from their taxes the face value of bonds they donated to the university. Besides the financial advantage, those who had invested in Lutherland were assured or assumed that the Lutheran character of the resort would continue. It didn't.

In the summer of 1964, while I was serving as pastor of Trinity Lutheran Church in Rockville, Connecticut, my wife, Dorothy, and I contracted to purchase a cabin on the Lutherland property. Joining the faculty of Concordia Theological Seminary in 1966, then in Springfield, Illinois, freed us to spend our summers there. With a place in the Poconos, our Eastern connections remained in place.

While Lutheran services were being held in Pocono Crest, the Lutheran Church of Our Savior began holding services in the municipal building in nearby Mount Pocono. Before then, Lutheran services were not provided for permanent residences from September to May, and many of those who were first summer residents and had become year-round residents attended the Methodist church.

After her December 1961 marriage, my sister Jean moved permanently to the Poconos and soon was attending the Mount Pocono church. Its first pastor, Melvin Pingel (1992–1989), conducted the funeral services for her husband, Bob Ervin, who was killed in automobile accident on Christmas Eve in 1964.

As long as services were offered, Dorothy, the children and I attended Lutheran services in the Casino at Pocono Crest. But when they ceased, we alternated between services led by Pastor Alfred Trinklein[3] in the conference room on the hotel property and Our Savior at Mount Pocono. By 1970, we were becoming regular attendees at Our Savior.

At first, Valparaiso University ran a summer drama program there, but after consulting with the east coast districts of the Lutheran Church—Missouri Synod, it concluded that a permanent satellite campus in the Poconos was not feasible. Concordia Collegiate Institute in Bronxville, New York, had upgraded its program to a full college and was hardly a hundred miles away.

The last full year that Valparaiso University had control of the Lutherland property was 1968, and that was also the year that the last officially sponsored Lutheran worship service was conducted in the auditorium of the Casino. The last Lutheran service in the Casino was held on the Sun-

---

3. He was, for a long time, first vice president of the Atlantic District and pastor of St. Matthew's Lutheran Church, where later Lutheran Hour speaker Dr. Oswald Hoffmann served as assistant pastor.

day of Labor Day weekend in 1968. During these years, remaining residents of the Pocono Pines Association (founded by the Reverend Hugh Miller, a Presbyterian minister) were regular attendees of the Lutheran services. Serving as deans for the Lutheran services in 1968 were Adolf F. Meyer and Alfred Trinklein (1902–1993).

Among the ten preachers for the final year were Rudolph Ressmeyer (July 21) and George Loose (1920–2007) (July 28).[4] Preaching for the final service (September 1) was Henry Koepchen (1896–1957) of Messiah Lutheran Church in East Setauket, Long Island, New York.[5] Five and a half years would pass before those who led the Lutheran services in the Casino in the summer of 1968 at Pocono Crest would be players in a disruption of the synod that threatened to bring it to its knees.

In early 1969, Valparaiso University sold Pocono Crest to Sesqui Industries. Even though the Sunday of Labor Day weekend in 1968 marked the last officially sponsored Lutheran worship service in the auditorium of the Casino, services were continued in the conference room of a motel that had been added to the original hotel property during the Valparaiso years. Responsible for these services was Alfred Trinklein, who had moved from Manhattan to take up residence in Pocono Pines. His home is now the parsonage for the Roman Catholic parish of St. Maximillian Kolbe, formerly Our Lady of the Lake.

These ad hoc services attracted up to one hundred persons on a Sunday from the original Lutherland community. In the winter of 1972, water pipes that had been drained broke, and Sesqui Industries abandoned the hotel property and discontinued services.

In the summer of 1972, members of the original Lutherland community began attending the Lutheran Church of Our Savior, and with the influx of summer members, attendances in two services for the years 1972 and 1973 often swelled to one hundred eighty.

In 1974, the differences in the Missouri Synod had come to the attention of the press, and congregations were dividing over this issue. That summer, I received permission from my sister Jean Van Gilder, who had

---

4. He was pastor of Bethel Lutheran Church in University City, Missouri. He was chairman of the board of regents at the time John Tietjen (1928–2004) was elected president of Concordia Seminary in St. Louis.
5. He is now retired. He was pastor of the Stoney Brook congregation. Later he was appointed by J. A. O. "Jack" Preus to take the place of Rudolph Ressmeyer, whom Preus removed as president of the Atlantic District on April 2, 1976. Still later elected to the Synod's board of directors, Koepchen served as its chairman (1989–1992).

leased the motel on the old Pocono Crest property, to make a presentation in that conference room. Ads ran in the newspaper and notices were placed in the local post office. Attendees for the evening numbered about fifty and were mostly members of the Missouri Synod congregations who were longtime summer residents at Lutherland. To a person, those who attended were genuinely concerned about the denials of the miracles in the Bible, a view that was now being allowed by the former St. Louis seminary faculty, which had by then organized into Christ Seminary in Exile, commonly known as Seminex. Just how effective the presentation was is another matter. When the split in the synod came, these Lutherans remained as members of congregations that formed the Association of Evangelical Lutheran Churches (AELC) and would eventually belong to the Evangelical Lutheran Church of America (ELCA).

In 1974, Seminex graduate Dell Schomburg (b. 1948) was introduced during a summer service at Our Savior in Mount Pocono as assistant to the Reverend Lawrence E. Kelm (b. 1939), who had succeeded Pastor Pingel in September of 1969. On the following Sunday, it was announced that he would be the assistant pastor. Normally only after a longer process that allows members to nominate names does a voters assembly elect to choose a pastor. When this happened, our family erected an outdoor altar to conduct services on our Pocono property.

Though Dell Schomburg began helping with church services in the summer of 1974, the official date for his beginning to serve the congregation is listed as November of 1974. Our Savior was asked to take a second fulltime pastor for a ministry to vacationers who even then were less inclined to spend any of their summer holiday time in going to church. Church records indicate that Schomburg was called to minister to them. Though attendances were high in the summers, in the off months from September into the middle of June, the year-round membership was noticeably less and had to devote its full financial effort to support one full-time pastor.

At that time, I did not know the full circumstances of his call. What was happening at Our Savior would only be clarified later. During the summer of 2014, the Mount Pocono congregation celebrated its fiftieth anniversary, and church records provided names and dates. Church records examined in connection with the congregation's fiftieth anniversary year show that the Eastern District promised the church a subsidy of $18,000, a fair amount now and even more so in 1974. The Eastern District president was Herman Frincke (1912–2010), one of the eight district presidents who committed themselves to finding assignment for the Seminex graduates and were willing to designate district moneys to congregations who could not otherwise afford it. Then there is the matter of whether the constitutions and the bylaws of the congregations who took these graduates as pastors were broken. Other congregations who agreed to take a Seminex graduate may have also received similar subsidies. After leaving Our Savior, Schomburg served congregations that later were received into the ELCA. He was received back into the Missouri Synod in the 1980 by colloquy. He is now retired.

An episode from the life of my sister, who was a member of the congregation, shows how a new theology promoted by the former St. Louis faculty was taking hold in the synod's congregations. On a visit to her home, one of the two pastors told her that the virgin birth was a theological but not physical miracle. This was a not-so-clever device that some theologians had used for some time to deceive the people. At that time, this approach had been popularized by the neoorthodox theologians whose views first appeared at the St. Louis seminary in the 1950s.

To assuage her concerns, she arranged a visit with the pastor in his office, in which he told her that the bread and wine of the Lord's Supper were not Christ's body and blood. She had her youngest child with her, William Van Gilder Jr., then a baby, and often she speaks of how upsetting this was. The conversation concluded with the pastor telling her that he hoped that in spite of these differences she would continue to receive Holy Communion at the church. Matters came to a head when the senior pastor learned that the assistant pastor had created a following among the congregation's members, and differences between the two pastors led to the assistant resigning. This led to the senior pastor having a change of heart and his supporting the synod's theology.

In the summer of 1976, the year we moved to Fort Wayne with the seminary, we began attending the Mount Pocono congregation again, and I again began preaching when the pastor was away. Dissident members of Our Savior, who supported the Seminex assistant pastor, became a core group of Faith Lutheran Church located in Blakeslee, fifteen miles from Mount Pocono.

The influence of Rudolph Ressmeyer, long associated with Lutherland Pocono Crest, resulted in members and summer attendees of Our Savior joining the newly formed Blakeslee congregation. He had been a counselor at Camp Chickagami, the boys' camp in the Lutherland complex, and held various positions, including director of the adult camp, Camp Beaverbrook. A charismatic figure in his own way, Ressmeyer was greatly admired and loved by the Lutheran community that survived on and around the old Lutherland/Pocono Crest property.

Since they bought a place there in 1965, the Ressmeyers had been our close neighbors. Less than a half a mile in another direction lived Raymond Schulze (b. 1932), who had taken the Immanuel Church on 88th Street in New York into what is now the ELCA. His wife, Margaret (b. 1935), was the daughter of Richard Caemmerer (1904–1984) and my cousin. Since many of the Lutherland community followed Ressmeyer into what would become the ELCA, tensions existed between them and those that remained with the synod.

The next pastor at Mount Pocono served only a few years and was followed by Louis Meyer, a mission executive with the New Jersey District and, before that, with the Atlantic District. During his ten years at Our Savior at Mount Pocono, guest preachers included Lutheran Hour Speaker Oswald "Ossie" Hoffmann, Atlantic District and then New Jersey vice president Ewald Mueller (1916–1991), and Valparaiso University president Albert Huegli (1913–1998). Well-attended church dinners were held at Mount Airy, a nearby resort, whose owner was a member of the congregation. Marie Otten Meyer was another one of those notable speakers.

On June 2, 2013, the congregation began its yearlong celebration of its fifty years with about the same number of people in attendance as at the first service in 1964. Considering the difficulties the congregation had endured in its half century of existence, it is a miracle of sorts that a confessional Lutheran congregation was still present in the Poconos. Octogenarians, formerly associated with the Missouri Synod, still attend the ELCA congregation in Blakeslee, where the former pastor's wife serves as pastor of a distant congregation and the current pastor is a woman. What happened at Our Savior in 1974 is not even a memory for the current membership. A few from neighboring ELCA churches in desperation have joined Our Savior.

My grandparents' summer house remained in the family until 2000, when my Aunt Florence Kenyon (1921–2005), widowed in September 1950, no longer made the trip from Lantana, Florida. There are now fewer Lutherans in the Poconos, and Lutherland is a fading memory.[6]

---

6. A plaque commemorating Lutherland (1926–1967) was placed in August 2016 on old Route 940 opposite my grandparents' house by the Pinecrest Development Corporation. Noted in the plaque was the desire of metropolitan New York Lutherans to have a place where their Christian faith could be exercised. Funds for the plaque were provided by the Historical Association of Tobyhanna Association, which has a large Jewish membership.

Excursus II

EXEGETICAL THEOLOGY AT CONCORDIA SEMINARY, ST. LOUIS (1955–1974)

❦

In the late 1950s at the St. Louis seminary, faculty theological positions were in a state of flux and it is hard to say how many had put together a unified system of theological thought. Many were attracted to neoorthodoxy as a way to harmonize modern Biblical scholarship with the historic teachings of the Lutheran Church. Neoorthodoxy seemed to be the miracle patent medicine that allowed the older beliefs to exist side by side with the most radical methods that had risen in eighteenth century rationalism and were held by the prince of the nineteenth century, liberal scholar Adolph von Harnack (1851–1930). J. A. O. Preus's uncovering of this double-minded hermeneutic led to the 1974 faculty walkout when all this was clarified. It was not at all clear in 1955 when I entered seminary.

Karl Barth (1886–1968), Emil Brunner (1889–1966), and Rudolf Bultmann (1884–1976) used theological terms in a way that did not correspond with their historic usage and sense. A further disconnect existed between the words and what happened. What was spoken, or more specifically what was written in the Bible, did not have to correspond to what actually happened. To put it another way, what was reported by the authors of the New Testament did not have to have happened in order for the message to be effective and "true."

Trying to determine what Jesus actually did and said in the New Testament had come to be called the Quest for the Historical Jesus. In fact, there now have been three of these quests. German has two words for the English word *history*: *Geschichte* and *Historie*. The neoorthodox used both to convey their views. *Geschichte* was the record of what happened. *Historie* was what actually happened. While past events cannot be replayed in the present, the neoorthodox theologians went so far to say that *Historie* was beyond what could be known with certainty. Only *Geschichte* could be known. Only in this sense could the Bible be taken seriously as the word of God. New Testament scholars are still not agreed about what can be known of *Historie*, a quest I have followed for some time.

Even though the neoorthodox theologians were for all practical purposes agnostic about the past, they were able to produce perceptive theological works. Karl Barth's *Church Dogmatics*[1] and Rudolph Bultmann's *Theology of the New Testament*[2] serve as examples. The neoorthodoxy that was the rage in the mid-twentieth century and that dominated theology at the St. Louis seminary no longer occupies the center stage.

Below are a few examples of how the St. Louis faculty made use of neoorthodox concepts. In 1958, Martin Scharlemann's (1910–1982) "exploratory" essay to the faculty titled "The Inerrancy of Scripture"[3] held that the Bible contained errors while remaining "true." This method, originating with Rudolph Bultmann in its separating the preached gospel from the historical facts, would take hold in seminary classrooms in the 1960s. I am unsure that the essay represents an authentic theological position, but it caused disruption. One evening I passed the room where the faculty was discussing an essay and sensed the tension emitting from the room. Probably Scharlemann's essay was the topic.

This essay came to light in the 1971 faculty interviews conducted by the Fact Finding Committee appointed by synod president J. A. O. Preus. In retrospect, it is amazing that students were knowledgeable about this method. Who knows how many seminary professors in 1954 knew it as well. A good guess is that most were happily naïve; others were at the till, intentionally guiding the seminary into new waters.

Holland "Casey" Jones (1920–2016), who had long presented himself as a Bible-believing Christian, as typical of clergy from the Southern states, explained that the great resurrection text in Job (19:26) really taught the opposite. It was not from his flesh that Job would see God, but without his flesh. I responded that the Hebrew word *min* ordinarily meant "from within." He also held that only those things were the word of God that said they were. For example, in "God said, 'Go to Judea,'" "Go to Judea" was word of God, but not "God said." Perhaps some other

---

1. Karl Barth, *Church Dogmatics* (Edinburgh: T. & T. Clark, 1936).
2. Rudolf Bultmann, *Theology of the New Testament* (New York: Scribner, 1951).
3. A copy of the essay, Martin Scharlemann, "The Inerrancy of Scripture" (unpublished manuscript, February 25, 1958), as cited in Mary Todd, *Authority Vested: A Story of Identity and Change in the Lutheran Church—Missouri Synod* (Grand Rapids, MI: W. B. Eerdmans Publishing Co., 2000), 178, n. 119, is available at Concordia Historical Institute, Martin Scharlemann papers, Supplement III, Box 14.

scholar may have made this distinction, but I have still to come across who that might be.

Gilbert A. Thiele (1910–1983) was a precocious transplant from the Wisconsin Synod who had earned his doctor's degree from the University of Basel for a dissertation on the formation of the Lutheran World Federation. *Concordia Theological Monthly* later published it in part.[4] Oscar Cullmann (1902–1999), a professor at Basel, had written a slender volume entitled *Immortality of the Soul or Resurrection of the Body?*[5] Cullmann argued that the Plato's view of an "immortal soul" must not take the place of the Christian view of the "resurrection of the body." Thiele had interpreted Cullmann's view as an either/or. One must hold to either the "resurrection of the body" or the "immortality of the soul," and Thiele came down on side of the resurrection as opposed to the soul's immortality.

In the same book Cullmann said that the Platonic view that only the soul survived was paralleled with the biblical view that the soul existed after death. Thiele and others seemed to have missed that part of the book. Some older pastors still hold Thiele's view. Though Thiele studied under Karl Barth, he gave no indications that he was a Barthian, a term often synonymous with neoorthodoxy. While Thiele was giving the impression that the soul did not exist after death, Arthur Carl Piepkorn (1907–1973) was promoting prayers for the dead. Later at Springfield a senior colleague Otto Stahlke (1906–1992) liked to tell the story of how he debated Piepkorn at a joint faculty meeting. Prayers for the dead would hardly allow for the non-existence of soul after death, but I am not sure that this argument was ever brought up. Regardless, both in and outside the classroom, I enjoyed and have only pleasant memories of Thiele.

---

4. Gilbert A. Thiele. "The Lutheran World Federation." *Concordia Theological Monthly* 27, no. 6 (1956): 445–71.
5. Oscar Cullmann, *Immortality of the Soul or Resurrection of the Dead? The Witness of the New Testament* (New York: Macmillan, 1958).

Chapter Two

ST. LOUIS SEMINARY DAYS

આ

During my four years of residency at Concordia Seminary (1955–1958; 1959–1960), travel between St. Louis, Missouri, where the seminary was located, and New York was always an adventure. For the first trip to St. Louis in September 1955, I took the train. I still remember seeing my mother and father standing on the platform at the magnificent Pennsylvania Station in New York City as the train pulled out. Though we never shared our thoughts about that day, we were asking ourselves why the Missouri Synod couldn't have had a seminary closer to home. The United Lutheran Church in America (ULCA) had seminaries in Philadelphia and Gettysburg.

Waking up in the morning as the train rolled through Ohio, I knew that I had entered a world quite different from the one I left in New York and the Pocono Mountains of Pennsylvania. As fate would have it, the majority of my years would be spent in the Midwest, but in outlook I wanted to remain an Easterner.

My father's youngest sister, Dorothy (1905–1996), who was married to Richard Caemmerer (1904–1984), the renowned professor of homiletics at Concordia Seminary, met me at St. Louis's Union Station. They helped me adjust to my new surroundings and life and were gracious Sunday-after-church hosts for dinner. Here I became acquainted with Ray Schulze, who in the summer of 1956 married my cousin, Margaret Caemmerer.[1] No seminary student in the incoming class was over twenty and some of us were barely nineteen. It was good to have some family ties at the seminary.

After the first train trip, travel between St. Louis and New York was by car. The Eisenhower Interstate System was only in the planning stage at this point, and so trips took at least twenty-four hours. A driver took four

---

1. During this same period, my cousin Richard R. Caemmerer Jr. (1933–2016), whose reputation as an artist was already established, was stationed at Fort Dix, New Jersey, and was spending weekends with my folks in Brooklyn. He died in 2016.

passengers and took each directly to their homes for between eight and ten dollars. A stop in Pittsburgh made the trip longer. Dual-lane roads were in place in parts of Indiana and New Jersey and on the Pennsylvania Turnpike. US 40 through Illinois was only two lanes. Once, in an attempt to pass, we came face to face with a car whose driver was an airplane pilot who said this was his closest encounter with death. On those day-long trips we hunkered down in our seats and did not even bother to look at our watches.

All entering students already had German, Latin, and Greek, so only Hebrew had to be mastered, which I did with ease. But with others more capable, my "A" performance in Hebrew earned only a "B" from Carl Graesser (b. 1929), who marked on a curve. Life is unfair. We had to take a Greek competency test and those of us who finished with the highest grades took Edgar Krentz (b. 1928), with whom I had four other classes.[2] Charles 'Chuck' Froehlich (b. 1927) took the others through basic Greek.

In an article in *First Things*, Gilbert Meilaender (b. 1946) said the only memorable thing about his seminary days was a comment by George Hoyer (1919–2011).[3] This mirrored my own experience at the seminary. In his address opening the 1955–1956 academic year, seminary president Alfred O. Fuerbringer (1903–1997) noted we had the privilege of working with the word of God—and he was right. I also recall the excessive heat in the fieldhouse where the service was held. As we said the litany, which was longer than any I had ever known before, I prayed that God would deliver us from both the heat and the litany.

Alfred Fuerbringer was a true Missouri Synod blue blood, with a family that traced itself to the Saxon immigration. Even though he was a son of former seminary president, he never impressed me as a scholar. During his presidency, he put in place a theologically progressive faculty, which ultimately supported John Tietjen (1928–2004), his hand-picked successor, as his replacement. Fuerbringer announced his retirement in September 1968, allowing his heir to be in place prior to the 1969 LCMS convention. It was a brilliant move.

Fuerbringer spent his last years of retirement in Norman, Oklahoma, where he was visited by Pastor David Nehrenz. In these conversations,

---

2. Edgar Krentz was a recognized New Testament scholar and was on sabbatical during the 1974 faculty walk out and later joined the Lutheran School of Theology in Chicago. His wife was sister to the wife of Arthur Graf, a professor of evangelism at Springfield when I joined the faculty in 1966.
3. Gilbert Meilaender, "How Churches Crack up: The Case of the Lutheran Church—Missouri Synod," *First Things* 14 (June 1991): 38–42.

he regretted the direction the Lutheran church had taken, when by all accounts he was a major player in recruitment of the faculty that walked out. Without scholarly contributions, just what he knew about the newer theology at the seminary is uncertain, though Tietjen claimed that Fuerbringer was fully complicit in the theological developments.[4]

In my first seminary year, I was not aware that the seminary's theology was in transition. Franz Pieper's three-volume *Christian Dogmatics*[5] was quietly giving way to newer, neoorthodox views associated with the work of Emil Brunner, Karl Barth, and Rudolph Bultmann.[6] These as we later learned, were the major proponents. No attempt was made to blend the older and newer approaches into a unified theology. Two different theological approaches were joined by a common vocabulary.

My first years at the St. Louis seminary were not overly stimulating. Following an almost elementary school procedure, students were assigned classes and were apportioned into two divisions alphabetically. So for the four years I was on campus, I was with students whose surnames began with letters from the lower end of the alphabet. This might not be a bad idea in light of curriculums that allow too many free choices. While such is not the door to creative thinking, it preserves the faith.

Henry Reimann (1926–1963), who would soon pass away, had the students reading Emil Brunner, the great neoorthodox theologian, in the form of his book *The Divine Human Encounter*,[7] along with Pieper's *Dogmatics*, without any explanation of their similarities and differences.[8] Though these theologians may have sounded the same in speaking about the "Word," they were light years apart theologically, something that I discovered in my second year. I have no idea if Reimann knew this, but if he did, he did not bring it to the attention of the students. Failure to note the difference led some students later on as pastors follow the St. Louis professors out of the synod. In their minds these professors held to the traditional Lutheran understanding of the Bible, when they really did not.

---

4. John H. Tietjen, *Memoirs in Exile: Confessional Hope and Institutional Conflict* (Minneapolis, MN: Fortress Press, 1990), 6.
5. Franz Pieper, *Christian Dogmatics* (St. Louis, MO: Concordia Publishing House, 1950–1957).
6. For more detail, see Excursus II: Exegetical Theology at Concordia Seminary, St. Louis (1955–1974), 21 ff.
7. Emil Brunner, *The Divine-Human Encounter* (London: S.C.M. Press, 1944).
8. Later as a graduate student in a course taught by Gilbert Thiele, I learned that Brunner and Barth were as vehemently opposed to Schleiermacher's theology as was Pieper, though this was not pointed out.

Lorenz Wunderlich (1906–1993), one of the "faithful five" that remained with the St. Louis faculty during the 1974 walkout, taught a largely unimaginative dogmatics course. This could also be said for Herbert Bouman (1908–1981), who served as a theological advisor to synod presidents John Behnken and Oliver Harms (1901–1980). They were consistently and uniformly dull and we rarely, if ever, ventured beyond Pieper's *Christian Dogmatics* in the then-recent English translation.

Alfred Klink (1900–1959) had just come from the presidency of Concordia River Forest, then a teachers college, to teach Old Testament. A pleasant man, he had authored a pamphlet-like book of few pages on the Old Testament that was suited for a Bible class but did not engage the burning issues of how the Old Testament books originated.

Teaching New Testament introduction was Frederick Danker (1920–2012), who took over from his faculty colleague William Arndt (1880–1957) the production of the Bauer-Gingrich lexicon of the New Testament.[9] It was then called "BAG" for the initials of its editors. Later Danker's prodigious contributions led to it being called "BAGD."[10] Three books required by Danker represented liberal, middle, and conservative positions on the historical origins of the New Testament—and one view was not favored over another.

Some have suggested that their views, as well as mine, were shaped by Arthur Carl Piepkorn, but in my case this was hardly so.[11] This extremely knowledgeable professor came across to me as somewhat eccentric, though he projected a different image with his colleagues, as I later learned from Donald Deffner (1924–1997) and Robert Preus with whom he was friends.

Students in Piepkorn's courses were assigned to read the Lutheran Confessions in the German, upon which he based his daily true and false quizzes. Few knew more than that the German word for *Confessions* was *Bekenntnisschriften*. We also had to read the introduction to the German

---

9. William F. Arndt, F. Wilbur Gingrich, Frederick W. Danker, and Walter Bauer, *A Greek-English Lexicon of the New Testament and Other Early Christian Literature*, 2nd ed. (Chicago: University of Chicago Press, 1979).
10. Frederick W. Danker et al., *A Greek-English Lexicon of the New Testament and Other Early Christian Literature*, 3rd ed. (Chicago: University of Chicago Press, 2000).
11. For information on Piepkorn's perspective, along with a significant collection of material by and about him, see *https://www.crossings.org/arthur-carl-piepkorn/* For a bibliography, see *http://www.ctsfw.net/media/pdfs/ArthurCarlPiepkornBIBLIOGRAPHY.pdf*.

edition of the confessions, which was also in German. Class time was spent debating the answers, a method later popular with some of my seminary colleagues. To me the method appeared to be an excuse for not preparing a lecture.

During my seminary second year, through the intervention of my uncle, Richard Caemmerer, who was the dean of the chapel, I was given the position of sexton.[12] This meant getting to the chapel before the daily services to make sure everything was in order, including lighting the candles, though I have no memory of what that altar may have looked like. Professors were assigned to preach for an entire week and this usually meant five sermons on one theme.

Alfred Rehwinkel (1887–1979) was the most popular preacher.[13] One time some students put a false front on the clock on the rear balcony. Rehwinkel kept looking up and thinking he had another ten minutes to preach—we all endured the extension. The black preaching gown was then in vogue, with some professors wearing the three-striped version to announce their doctoral status. Surplice and stole had yet to become the norm and the alb was nowhere to be found. Being in the sacristy before the professors of the week arrived to preach, I came to know them and they me. Even those who for me were the most formidable in scholarship and stature suffered a bit of angst before going out into chancel that was really a stage in front of an auditorium. Even for the most seasoned clergy, preaching is never devoid of anxiety.

---

12. James C. Burkee refers to the position as "seminary altar boy," a term that would have been anachronous in a chapel in which Holy Communion was never celebrated. See *Power, Politics, and the Missouri Synod: A Conflict that Changed American Christianity* (Minneapolis, MN: Fortress Press, 2011), 34. One task required changing by hand hundreds of service folders for the funeral of William Arndt. During those first two years Professors Riedel (1921–1956) and Donald Meyer died. Before coming to the seminary Paul Riedel was in the New York-New Jersey Metropolitan Circuit of the English District of which my father was counselor. Meyer was the son of a venerable pastor of an old St. Louis congregation. His widow was sister to Richard Koenig (1927–2011), later editor of *Lutheran Forum* and spokesman for the Seminex cause. A campus pastor in Holyoke, Massachusetts, he was effective in having the college congregation leave the LCMS first for the AELC and now the ELCA. Koenig first accepted and then declined an invitation to lecture at the Symposium on the Lutheran Confessions marking the thirty-fifth year of the St. Louis seminary walkout. Meyer was succeeded by Robert Preus as assistant professor of systematic theology with assignments in philosophy.
13. See Ronald Stelzer, *Salt, Light, and Signs of the Times: The Life and Times of Alfred M. (Rip) Rehwinkel* (New Haven, MO: Lutheran News, 1993).

At this time theology had no special interest for me. That soon changed. In the year before I came to the seminary, 1954–1955, Herman Otten and Kurt Marquart had raised concerns about new directions at the seminary, something confirmed by the account in James C. Burkee, *Power, Politics, and the Missouri Synod*.[14] While neoorthodoxy was an unknown quantity to me and nearly all other students—and who knows how many members of the faculty—Kurt knew exactly what it was. Marquart explained how theologians who belonged to this school of thought, among whom the most prominent were Karl Barth, Emil Brunner, and Rudolph Bultmann, could on one plane develop their theologies with biblical terms that were used also in classical Lutheran and Reformed theologies.[15]

If seminary classes were forgettable, there was a memorable week in January 1956 at the end of the first semester. At that time the first semester for most academic institutions began in September and ended after the second or third week in January. No one thought to ask if a two week Christmas break would hinder students taking their final exams in January after their return. Exams were followed by a week break and a twenty-four-hour car trip back to New York had no appeal.

Conveniently for that lost week in January, Pastor Louis Buchheimer (1897–1988) of Our Savior's Lutheran Church in Detroit issued an open invitation to students of both seminaries to be guests of his church. He was a burly man in whose kitchen in the evenings we would chomp on cold ham from the refrigerator and enjoy good whiskey. His brother, Paul Buchheimer (1915–1999), was a pastor to the Chinese congregation in Manhattan, now called The Church of All Nations, and so he was not a complete stranger to me. Both brothers were known to my father, perhaps one of them from their St. Louis seminary days. During that week we slept on the floor somewhere in the gym that on certain nights was open to community roller skating.

It was an impressive operation. Three Sunday services took care of a still-growing congregation. For the son of a pastor whose congregation was losing more members than were joining, a church with three pastors was astonishing. Serving as an auxiliary pastor in retirement was Ted Daniel (1920–2008), an uncle of the renowned young scholar Jaroslav Pelikan (1923–2006), and then vice president of the Evangelical Synodical

---

14. James C. Burkee, *Power, Politics, and the Missouri Synod: A Conflict that Changed American Christianity* (Minneapolis, MN: Fortress Press, 2011), 31.
15. See Excursus II: Exegetical Theology at Concordia Seminary, St. Louis (1955–1974), 21 ff.

Lutheran Conference.[16] There was a younger pastor on staff, whose name at this writing I do not recall, but have run into him from time to time.

Buchheimer was rolling out the red carpet for us. Among the highlights of the week was a visit with Detroit mayor Albert Cobo (1893–1957) and UAW president Walter Reuther (1907–1970), who, as we learned, was the son of an Evangelical and Reformed pastor. He offered an unforgettable interpretation of the parable of the vineyard: workers in the Lord's vineyard should not throw grapes at one another. Think about it.

A day trip took us to St. Lorenz Church in Frankenmuth, Michigan, one of the synod's founding congregations. We also enjoyed the mandatory chicken dinner at Zehnder's, still a pilgrim destination for Missouri Synod Lutherans. Before the dinner was over, an unstoppable bloody nose landed me in the emergency room of the local hospital. It was astounding to me that so many Lutherans—especially Missouri Synod Lutherans—clustered, almost as majorities, in so many towns and cities. Later I experienced the same in Fort Wayne, Indiana.

Each night Buchheimer gathered us in his study for conversation and one evening he began the event by challenging the seminary students assembled to ask what were the two questions most people asked him. Complete silence. We students numbered about twenty. Because my father knew him and his brother, there was that kind of rapport that let me rise to the occasion to ask if he knew the names of all the members of his congregation. He blew up: "Scaer, you have some nerve!" I do not remember the rest of his diatribe, but he concluded by acknowledging that this was the right question. Then he asked for someone to pose the second most asked question. After a long, repeated silence, I offered the second question—but have forgotten what it was. Buchheimer was consistent in shouting "Scaer" and concluding that this was the right question, whatever that was.

Despite such respites, the bottom line is that, for me, the seminary environment was simultaneously uninteresting and confusing. At the end of the school year, now twenty years of age, I looked forward to what would be the final summer of work at Pocono Crest, as Lutherland was now called.[17]

---

16. The Evangelical Lutheran Synodical Conference was formed in 1872 as an association confessionally committed Lutheran synods in America. The Wisconsin Synod and Evangelical Lutheran Synod broke fellowship with the Missouri Synod in 1961. When the conference dissolved in 1967, only the Missouri Synod and the Slovak Synod (Synod of Evangelical Lutheran Churches) were members.
17. See Excursus I: Lutherland and the Poconos, 13 ff.

A DANGEROUS YEAR

Things began to change in my second year of seminary (1956–1957). I was assigned a room on the first floor in Loeber Hall. It so happened that Kurt Marquart was rooming with Herman Otten on this same floor. There is good reason to doubt Burkee's claims that I introduced Kurt to Herman Otten.[18] Before then my acquaintance with them was tangential. His first year in the college division at Bronxville was my last in the high school. By that time, September 1952, Otten had already left for the seminary.

Kurt Marquart was a remarkable person. Under a lithograph of synod's first president, C. F. W. Walther (1811–1887), Kurt's custom then and throughout his life was staying up to the wee morning hours poring over sixteenth- and seventeenth-century books, some acquired from Arne Pettersen (1911–1999).[19] On Saturday mornings, Kurt and I would often go to the counter at Woolworth's for the ten-cent breakfast of eggs and toast. He often asked that his eggs be fried with onions. It took a while for the server to figure this all out. More importantly, Kurt was helping me overcome the confusion of my first year in which traditional orthodoxy was taught alongside of neoorthodoxy. While we would later come to hold somewhat different theological perspectives, I remain grateful for Kurt's clarity of thought in the even more confusing and turbulent situation in the synod.

At the time, I did not keep a diary of the events or copies of the relevant documents. My goal was ordination into the ministry of the synod. In writing an account of those times from interviews with those involved and the documents themselves, James Burkee has provided a service to me

---

18. *Power, Politics, and the Missouri Synod*, 29. Marquart, Otten and I were not in college at the same time. Otten was in the college 1950–1951, Kurt was there 1952–1954 and I was there 1953–1955. As already noted, Otten was not on the seminary campus during my first year (1955–1956). So only in the school year 1956–57 were we on the same campus at the same time. When claims like this are made solely on the basis of oral interviews, inaccuracies, inconsistent as they may be, are inevitable.
19. Burkee refers [*Power, Politics, and the Missouri Synod*, 30] to Arne Pettersen urging Otten in 1954 to speak to Walter Wolbrecht (1915–1990), the executive director of the Missouri Synod, about his concerns about the St. Louis faculty. Still at Bronxville I was unaware of this. Until he died in 1999, Pettersen, a collector of rare books, was in contact with Marquart. Pettersen had been married in my father's church on June 21, 1941 by Walter A. Maier I. He and his wife, Ingrid, and their family were longtime friends whom we visited into the early 1970s in their summer home at Lake in the Clouds in the Poconos.

in reconstructing some events that are cloudy in my memory, especially in the academic year in the 1956–1957.

In the 1955–1956 academic school year, Herman Otten had been away from the campus on vicarage, but in the previous years, 1954–1955, he and Kurt Marquart had brought charges against William Schoedel.[20] In reconstructing March 1957, Burkee has helped my memory in referring to a meeting in which eight students, of which I was one, were brought before the faculty for having brought charges against other students we thought deviated from church teaching. The accused had been coached in formulating their views by some faculty members who were presenting them in their classroom lectures.[21]

Yet even with Burkee's account, I cannot reconstruct the meeting chaired by Martin Scharlemann.[22] He was a man of heavy temper, and though he presented himself as a scholar, he bucked his opponents. Twice he threw me out of class for asking questions he found inappropriate. He was intimidating. The practical reality at that time that seminary professors were gods in the pantheon of the synod.

According to Burkee's report, Scharlemann pounded his fists on the table and we were threatened with psychological examinations. A mentally imbalanced person could hardly be certified for the ministry. Psychology is a succession of theories open to constant change, and the one found to be unbalanced has limited recourse in showing that he is more mentally fit than the one administering the test. If, as reported, I appeared shaken during the meeting, it makes perfect sense. Our future—my future—was on the chopping block. Another of the students succumbed to the pressure and collapsed in tears, "But all held fast." None would retract. It was encouraging to learn from Burkee's account that none of us backed

---

20. Burkee, *Power, Politics, and the Missouri Synod*, 31.
21. The text of the original charges of May 1, 1957 was reprinted in *State of the Church (Missouri Synod): Book of Documentation*. 1961, 79–81. The response from the accused students, including Arlis Ehlen (1931–2016) (who later served on the faculty of Concordia Seminary, St. Louis, but whose non-renewal of contract in 1972 for some of these same issues was a point of serious contention), may be found on page 82. In it they state: "In view of the content of the New Testament *Kerygma*, we have not placed the Genesis account of the creation on the same level as the witness of the Apostles to the deity of Christ, the redemption effected by our Lord on the cross, His resurrection, or the new life in Christ." No wonder things were confused.
22. Scharlemann also served as a chaplain in World War II and the Korean Conflict. See "Scharlemann, Martin Henry" in *Christian Cyclopedia*, http://cyclopedia.lcms.org/display.asp?t1=S&word=SCHARLEMANN.MARTINHENRY.

down. Scharlemann quickly dismissed the charges, and the controversy ended—for the moment."[23]

One persistent question is whether we seminary students had taken the right steps in bringing charges—might there have been another way to handle this? Because it was rare that seminary students would challenge the orthodoxy of their instructors, there was little precedent to follow.[24] In their classrooms all professors have a functional infallibility. This was more so in a synod that claimed for itself the pure doctrine and a faculty entrusted with determining and preserving it. Scharlemann's blustery response made this evident.

With our backs up against the wall, it was time to walk away from the battle. We were scared, but we still had our lives. In March 1957, when the meeting of the students and the faculty took place, I still had three more years of seminary in front of me. Not only would there be nothing more to gain from this approach, we might no longer find ourselves eligible for calls. At this time I was thinking of a summer vicarage in Wyoming. There more of life in front of me—or so I hoped. At this point I disappear from Burkee's narrative. I played no public part in resolving opposing positions that came to a head seventeen years later in the 1974 walkout of the faculty.[25]

Another confrontation emerged from the 1956–1957 academic year in St. Louis. Horace Hummel had challenged the direct messianic intent of certain Old Testament passages. He claimed the Israelites adopted the coronation rites of the surrounding nations, a view put forth by Sigmund Mowinckel (1884–1965). Challenging a professor's views was to challenge his authority. Hummel's contract was not renewed, and he went on to teach at Wartburg Theological Seminary, then to the Lutheran School of Theology in Chicago and then Valparaiso University, before returning to Concordia Seminary, St. Louis, after the Seminex walkout.[26]

In the end, who or what is "liberal" and who or what is "conservative" is a matter of perspective. In my seminary days, it was generally understood that "liberal" referred to those who followed the views that might

---

23. Burkee, *Power, Politics, and the Missouri Synod*, 32.
24. Even now the positions of its theological icons C. F. W. Walther and Francis Pieper are for some above challenge.
25. See Excursus VI: John Tietjen, John Damm and Seminex, 129 ff.
26. Things have a way of turning around. Some years later as the editor of *The Springfielder*, I obtained for publication Hummel's essays, which was part of a process that returned him to the St. Louis seminary as an honored professor and defender of the church's theology.

be called "neoorthodox," and "conservative" referred to one committed to the synod's position as set forth in *A Brief Statement* and F. A. O. Pieper's *Dogmatics*.[27]

Yet liberal might mean open to new views and conservative might mean maintaining the status quo. Ironically enough, if one accepts this definition of conservative, operations at the St. Louis seminary would have to be described as "conservative." Although President Alfred Fuerbringer was working to bring his faculty theologically up to date, he was determined to keep the old order in place—students should keep their place. In another time and place faculty and students would have sat down and worked things out. Not at this point—the old order still stood. That time did come later, however, during the administration of John Tietjen first at 801 DeMun Ave. (1969–1974) and then at Seminex (1974–1983) when students were regular participants in committees that were once limited to faculty members.

Presently, at the end of each term, students at Concordia Theological Seminary, Fort Wayne are asked—really required—to assess their instructors on such matters as the their knowledge of the topic. That was not the case at Concordia Seminary, St. Louis in the 1950s and had not yet been suggested. So in a way those who had difficulties with what they considered unacceptable views were ahead of their time. But in 1950s their raising concerns was seen as an act of insurrection against the established order.

For years, students at both seminaries could not be married or for that matter engaged. Miraculously many, if not most, were married shortly after graduation and just before ordination. This has been a source of constant amusement for those who worked around these restrictions. By the mid-1950s, with the permission of the dean of students, marriage was allowed, probably after completing the first two years after which a Bachelor of Arts degree was awarded. Three years remained in seminary education. Marriage without permission meant expulsion with not being allowed to continue seminary studies until the class of which the offender had been a member had graduated.

My uncle, Richard Caemmerer, defended the policy with an argument I could not grasp, that since marriage was the original institution, the student should devote himself to it and then continue with his seminary studies. Failure to ask for permission might be seen as disrespect for authority, but such an incident would be open to negotiation. It wasn't.

---

27. *A Brief Statement* may be found online at *http://www.lcms.org/doctrine/doctrinal-position*.

The world of the seminary at that time was lockstep. We all took the same courses, we all sat in assigned seats and we all followed the rules. This was closely related to how church orthodoxy would be maintained. The "no marriage without permission" rule resulted in an embarrassing situation in my first year as an instructor at Springfield. We had gone to dinner at a local restaurant and the waitress was the wife of St. Louis classmate who offended the marriage rule. He was now a student at Springfield studying for the ministry and his wife was supporting him. If the marriage rule had not been in effect in St. Louis during the 1950s, he would have been in his seventh year of ministry.

In September 1957, Robert D. Preus joined the faculty. In him the older theology found an able spokesman who had a firsthand knowledge of new theology from his studies in Edinburgh, Scotland, Basel, and Harvard. This advantage was outweighed by Marquart's leaving the campus for vicarage.

As 1958 dawned, Herman Otten was attending Trinity Lutheran Church in New Haven, Missouri, and was looking forward to completing the requirements for the Master of Sacred Theology degree in time for the spring graduation. At a meeting of the seminary's board of control in January, "Otten spent an hour detailing what he perceived to be the rapid advance of liberalism at Concordia [Seminary, St. Louis], specifically criticizing Horace Hummel."[28] Also present was academic dean Arthur Repp (1906–1994).

Later in 1958, a dialogue on the Lutheran World Federation between John Behnken and Martin Marty (b. 1928) was held on campus. Marty would later make a name for himself as editor of the *Christian Century*.[29] At this event, according to Burkee, I approached Behnken and told him, "Some of us are concerned about is going on here." Burkee goes on to say, "The group soon met with Behnken, who asked the students if they would be willing to share their concerns with the entire faculty. Only Otten agreed."[30]

After sixty years, it is difficult to recall all of the details. Lawrence Rast brought to my attention a letter I wrote that I did not remember.[31] It was written to synod president John W. Behnken, vice president Arthur H. Grumm (1893–1959) and Herman A. Harms (1889–1980). The letter ap-

---

28. Burkee, *Power, Politics, and the Missouri Synod*, 34.
29. Burkee, *Power, Politics, and the Missouri Synod*, 35–36.
30. Burkee, *Power, Politics, and the Missouri Synod*, 34.
31. David P. Scaer, letter to John W. Behnken, May 13, 1958.

pears authentic especially with its obsequious salutation, "Dear Doctors and Fathers in Christ" and signature, "Your son in Christ Jesus, David Paul Scaer." I rarely use my middle name in signatures. Why here? I am not sure. Perhaps I hoped to give it the look of importance.

The letter claims that it was shown to three faculty members before being sent and it contains no information that was not found in papers leading to the March 1957 meeting. The professors may have included Robert Preus, Lorenz Wunderlich, and Albert Merkens (1897–1980). I brought the same concerns to them that I and others had addressed to seminary president Alfred O. Fuerbringer.[32] In a letter addressed to Alfred von Rohr Sauer, Chairman of the faculty committee, we accepted its opinion that the students with whom we were concerned held to the synodical position as outlined in the *Brief Statement*. Later events proved that this was premature.

In 1958, Arthur Simon (b. 1930) was teaching at Concordia Teachers College in River Forest, Illinois,[33] the same views on biblical inerrancy and the historicity of the Genesis creation account that had been raised in the May 1957 letter to Fuerbringer.[34] I and several others wrote again to Behnken about the matter.[35]

I sent a copy of this letter to Kurt Marquart, who did not take very kindly to what I had written and wrote to tell me so. In contacting Behnken about what Arthur Simon was teaching, Kurt called me "Karlstadt." Andreas Karlstadt (1486–1541) was Luther's colleague on the Wittenberg faculty and a radical reformer. I wrote back to Kurt that I had not acted precipitously, since before writing Behnken, I had consulted three professors. My letter to Behnken also requested his intervention in a faculty disciplinary action against Herman Otten for his accusations of false doctrines against some professors. For him the stakes were high and could have repercussions for others including myself.

Both letters, a copy of my letter to Behnken and Kurt's response to it, brought out a side of him I had not seen before. He took exception to my calling the professors appointed to handle our concerns in the spring of 1957 "a kangaroo committee." I probably meant "a kangaroo court," which of course it was, and in any event I was writing Kurt in a personal letter not intended for anyone else. I was not speaking in a public forum.

---

32. David P. Scaer, letter to Alfred O. Fuerbringer, May 1, 1957.
33. Now known as Concordia University Chicago.
34. David P. Scaer, letter to Alfred O. Fuerbringer, May 1, 1957.
35. David P. Scaer, letter to John W. Behnken, May 15, 1958.

Calling the faculty committee a kangaroo court was putting the best construction on a hearing that was typical of how the old Soviet Union administered justice. Before two groups of students met with the faculty committee chaired by Martin Scharlemann, the outcome had already been determined.[36] After the meeting, Martin Scharlemann wrote Arthur Simon a note, "If you are ever challenged I want it known that I consider you to be of sound theological conviction."[37]

By taking the initiative in writing synod president John Behnken and two vice presidents, I had, in Marquart's view, gone "one step further" from what we had done in meeting with the students in 1957. Kurt could be sharp with those who differed with him. He had difficulty in letting others take the lead in theological and procedural matters. In my letter to Marquart, I mention meetings with two other professors, Carl S. Meyer (1907–1972) and Herbert Bouman. In my first meeting with "C. S.," as Meyer was called, I shared copies of papers from Simon's class at River Forest. In our second meeting, he said he had no memory that I had given him these papers.

As a consultant to Behnken and Oliver Harms, his successor as synod president, Bouman was highly placed in synod circles and he served on the 1957 faculty committee that exonerated the students about whom concerns were raised. In seeing the papers from Arthur Simon's class, he became agitated, as I had written to Kurt. In my saying in my letter to Kurt that Bouman's guilty conscience was a "'mode of penance,'" he found reason to censure me again.

In exonerating the students in the March 1957 meeting, Bouman as a member of the faculty committee had acted against what he knew to be true. I wrote to Kurt,

> I certainly did not mean to imply that I played havoc on the man's conscience [sic] by rubbing in the Simon Papers. I mentioned clearly in my letter to you that this man needs the comfort of the Gospel and not the Law." My letter goes on to say, "Seeing that I presented my case in such apparrently [sic] evangelical terms, I am the more [!] amazed that I received

---

36. John H. Tietjen entitled the chapter "Kangaroo Court," in which he described his removal as president of Concordia Seminary, St. Louis. *Memoirs in Exile*, 161–185.
37. Burkee, *Power, Politics, and the Missouri Synod*, 197, n. 89. In May 2016, Concordia Seminary, St. Louis awarded Art Simon the honorary Doctor of Divinity degree for his work with Bread for the World, a charity organization dedicated to stamp out hunger.

such a sharp rebuke from you. As I said before what or who provoked that letter of yours.[38]

The remainder of my letter opens a window into the cloak-and-dagger atmosphere of those days—and so it had to be, since we had been threatened with expulsion from the seminary.

On May 15, 1958, Herman Otten appeared before the faculty's disciplinary committee. When he did not take the opportunity to withdraw his charges made against certain faculty members, he was told by Martin Scharlemann that he could not continue his graduate studies in the seminary's Doctor of Theology program and would not be certified for the ministry of the Missouri Synod.[39] The latter issue remains a thorn under his saddle. This rejection gave rise to *Christian News* in 1962, which publicized the new direction that theology was taking at the seminary. Had Otten been certified, he might not have been able to construct a platform for his views.

Later musing on these matters, Robert Preus wondered whether Otten should have gone to Germany for a degree after the March 1957 meeting. With German-born parents, he was conversant in the language. Upon his return, the matters that had engulfed the seminary campus in 1956–1957 would likely have been defused. Only he knows whether he could have taken that path. Many would say that he simply could not.

One episode recorded in this letter to Marquart is worth telling. A meeting was arranged for me that spring, probably in May since the weather was warm, with Wilhelm Oesch (1896–1982), a professor at our sister church's seminary in Oberursel, Germany at his sister's farm in Illinois. Since I did not own a car and relied on the good will of others and public transportation, I do not know how I traveled there.

This was a hush-hush meeting, so no one on the faculty would know about it. It was like a scene taken out of World War II movie which in the Dutch resistance met secretly at night to avoid detection by the German occupation forces. A bit dramatic, but that's how life at the seminary was. After four years of seminary, Marquart was making a name for himself among those who opposed the direction of the St. Louis seminary and Oesch wanted to meet him.

This was one topic for the meeting on the farm in Illinois. It would be arranged that Oesch would visit Hugo Kleiner (1897–1963), a St. Louis

---

38. David P. Scaer, letter to Kurt Marquart, June 9, 1958.
39. Burkee, *Power, Politics, and the Missouri Synod*, 34.

seminary classmate, to see Niagara Falls. Kleiner was Kurt's vicarage supervisor and president of the synod's English District and by end of Kurt's vicarage year had been alerted to what was happening at the St. Louis seminary. Those who met Oesch would not recognize that he was American born and educated until his mid-twenties and not a native German.

His transformation happened in this way. Serving a German-speaking congregation in London, he was stranded in a visit to Germany at the outbreak of World War II and began serving the independent Lutheran synod there. After the war, he remained and had become a spokesman for confessional Lutheranism against the rising tide of neoorthodoxy, the same affliction that had taken root in the 1950s within the St. Louis faculty. To further his cause, Oesch wanted to establish contacts in America, among whom was not only Marquart but also Martin Naumann (1901–1972), a professor at the synod's Concordia Theological Seminary in Springfield. His goal was establishing a theological journal. Nothing came of this proposal and Oesch continued to edit the *Lutherische Rundblick*.

Arne Petterson, a conservative New York layman, also wanted to meet Kurt, but was hesitant to do so, fearing that he would compromise his conversations with Arthur Repp in helping Herman Otten to be certified for the synod's ministry. If Marquart's name came up in conversation with Repp, Petterson could hardly say that he did not know him. Otten had been lobbying Petterson to have certain papers published in booklet form for limited distribution. I do not think this ever happened.

In my letter to Kurt I gave my prognosis for Otten, even though his fate was inevitable.

> Our good friend Herman Otten has been brought before the committee for Disciplinary Action because he spoke to Dr. Grueber [(1877–1959) a former synod vice president] of Milwaukee. As I understand it from Herman, the administration is calling into question his procedure. If an unfavorable verdict is rendered Herman's status in the seminary and synod would be jeopardy.[40]

Before meeting with the disciplinary committee, Herman had written a letter of apology to synod president Behnken. Since he had not offended Behnken, he may have apologized for his accusations against the faculty. In this letter he said he had visited the faculty members he had accused, supposedly in the meeting with the Board of Control. In each visit he presented a statement on paper of what that professor believed and asked

---

40. David P. Scaer, letter to Kurt Marquart, June 9, 1958.

him whether he had correctly understood him. This did not resemble an apology and could be seen as self-incrimination. It did not work.

Not everyone was of the same mind about what Otten had done. Alfred Rehwinkel and Robert Preus thought by apologizing, Herman had admitted guilt in his accusations against certain professors and that he should not have done it. When seminary dean of students Leonard Wuerffel (1910–1987) saw a copy of the letter sent to Behnken, he was described "as hitting the roof." One suggestion bantered about to resolve the tension was having Otten go on a second vicarage under an older seasoned pastor who could teach him about Christian love, but no guarantee could be given that afterwards he would be certified.

At the conclusion of my letter to Kurt, I expressed how I felt at that time. "Concerning your letter: It was good for me, it made my blood pressure rise. But please dear friend, not too many of those letters, I might die of a heart attack." This evoked a letter of apology from Kurt to which I responded.

> Thank you for your letter. It certainly cleared up a few things. The letter in question is no longer with us. We mourned it soon after its arrival. Let the bloody thing be all forgotten. We have no time to waste on such things when there are larger tasks before us. Your last letter was excellent. At least among us who are of the same mind we should have the unity that the others babble about . . . and we do have the same mind and spirit.

My letter to Kurt had news that affected him directly. He had been the only one who had applied for the editorship of the *Seminarian*, the student theological journal, for the coming academic year (1958–1959), and so it was certain the job would be his. When John Huber (b. 1929) and Robert Wilken (b. 1936) learned of this, they called up Norman Theiss (b. 1934), who also was on vicarage, urging him to apply, and Kurt was denied the position. Theological differences among students and faculty had become the topic of campus conversation and in the *Seminarian* these differences were thrashed out in print. David Joeckel (b. 1933), who as vice president of the student body was also president of the student council, heard about it and wanted to reverse the appointment of Theiss as editor. It was too late. Joeckel was about to graduate and the school year was coming to an end.

I wrote again to Marquart to arrange a meeting with him, Petterson and myself in New York, before I left for my vicarage in Manhattan, Kansas.[41] Otten was running up against a stone wall in getting faculty certification. He had already been rebuffed by Richard Caemmerer, who would not be

---

41. David P. Scaer, letter to Kurt Marquart, June 19, 1958.

satisfied with a written apology but wanted a personal visit. Herman was planning another meeting with Grueber. Should this come to light, still another reason would be found to deny him certification. In July shortly after I arrived in Manhattan, Kansas, Herman Otten and his brother Walter (b. 1934) paid a surprise visit and relayed much of what was happening to Herman to my vicarage supervisor Robert Rosenkoetter (1918–1983).

Life presents certain times for self-appraisal, and the conclusion of three years at the seminary was such a time. At the beginning of the 1956–1957 academic year, I was only twenty years of age, and by my twenty-second birthday I had been involved with those challenging the status quo in the seminary and synod. Those looking in from the outside could consider this madness or courage.

The mid-1960s would soon arrive and protesting students would be heralded as heroes for challenging the status quo. It was the "Age of Aquarius," and the world has never been the same since then. Concordia Seminary students walked out of the campus in support of the dismissed president John Tietjen in 1974, and in support of the students nearly the entire faculty joined the walkout.[42] In the mid-1950s, students with concerns were summarily dismissed, but twenty years had intervened and the world was different.

At the end of the 1950s, some of us recognized that basic Christian beliefs were being undermined at Concordia Seminary, and even without a full philosophical or theological understanding of what was involved, we responded. Some faculty members concurred, the vast majority did not. That majority increased in number and evolved into the St. Louis seminary faculty majority that left their positions in February 1974 to form Seminex, which provided the catalyst for the formation of the Evangelical Lutheran Church in America (ELCA).

A word should be said about my relations with Herman Otten and Kurt Marquart. In entering a theological conversation, Otten's mind was made up and was not going to change. Otten was a self-contained man who was largely immune to influence. I suppose in one way or the other, this is true of each of us. Those who cannot approve of every point on his agenda can admire his courage, but I did not want to tether myself to everything he did and said. I did not want to be responsible for someone's beliefs and actions.

Kurt Marquart was also a man of unmovable conviction and with his expansive knowledge was as close to being a Renaissance man as Leon-

---

42. John H. Tietjen, *Memoirs in Exile*, 186–206. See also Excursus VI: John Tietjen, John Damm and Seminex, 129 ff.

ardo Da Vinci (1452–1519) was. He saw theological truth as a system in which one part was dependent on another, but such is the nature of dogmatic theology. With this I agree, but the truth foundation of Christianity is not derived from how and where a doctrine is placed within a system or how the system is held together.

A danger in any systematized theology or philosophy is that one doctrine or philosophical hypothesis determines the character of the whole, and more often than not those committed to the system do not recognize this. Soon after beginning to teaching dogmatics, I saw that even such a fundamental doctrine as biblical inspiration could not be taught in isolation, but had to be seen as a derivative of the authority of the apostles derived from Jesus. This injected an historical component into how the Scriptures took form. All this was expressed in my *Apostolic Scriptures*,[43] whose publication was arranged by Robert Preus, the foremost exponent of biblical inspiration. As the years passed, I would see theology more from a biblical perspective, and particularly from the Gospels.

When Marquart joined the faculty in Springfield in December 1975, I deferred to him as theological leader, but our methods as well as some of our conclusions were different. Others saw this as did he.

The bottom line is that our expulsion from the seminary was a real possibility. In retrospect, still in my twenties, these challenges could have had dire consequences. Happily that year came to an end quickly. Then it appeared that basic Christian concepts were under attack—and they were—but this does necessarily mean that we fully grasped the new theology. This could hardly be expected of fledgling students, but this did not devalue the validity of our concerns. In any event, the majority of the St. Louis faculty was also in the dark.

A WESTERN INTERLUDE

More of a bread-and-butter issue than a theological issue faced me as that year was concluding. After six summers of waiting on tables in the Poconos and with a Bachelor of Arts degree after two years of seminary, I wanted to do something for which this education had prepared me. Having been brought up in a pastor's home and receiving a synod-sponsored education for eight years, I was ready for the ministry in some sense. My sister Elizabeth was then serving as assistant to the associate general secretary of the National Council of Churches (NCC) in charge of organizational

---

43. David P. Scaer, *The Apostolic Scriptures* (St. Louis, MO: Concordia Publishing House, 1971).

matters. Its offices were on New York's upper west side near Grant's Tomb. Through Warren Ost (1926–1997), associate general secretary of the NCC, she became aware of an opening in the ecumenical ministry in Grand Teton National Park in Wyoming. Travel by train would not be provided, but lodging and food were given to those who worked at the Grand Teton Lodge, owned by a Rockefeller family member who had donated funds to procure the park.

A summer in the great far west was tempting, but I was not sure that I could work all week and have the time and energy to put a sermon together for Sunday. Weighing on my conscience was participating with those of other Protestant faiths in the conduct of worship services. Arthur Strege (1927–2013), the assistant dean of students, counseled me against doing anything against my conscience. For this I remain grateful to him.

Just how the circumstances developed I do not remember, but a summer vicarage was offered by the Northern Nebraska District at Redeemer Lutheran Church in Dubois, Wyoming, which included conducting Lutheran services at Jenny Lake in Grand Teton National Park. Pastor Edward Schmidt (1892–1980), who at sixty-five had retired to Crowheart to work in Indian missions project Oversight, was my supervisor. The National Park Service allowed the NCC to advertise all religious services in the park addition. On posters listing the various services, ours were listed not as "Lutheran" but as "Missouri Synod." In light of my correspondence with the NCC, this was hardly accidental.

It might be thought that a church service listed as "Missouri Synod" would impede attendance. It didn't. For good or for ill, "Missouri Synod" meant something to many people, and our attendances ranged from fifty to a hundred.

My assignment from the Northern Nebraska District included Mt. Calvary Lutheran Church in Dubois, Wyoming, where I preached on Sunday evening after returning from the park. I also was in charge of a weekly Vacation Bible School.

Preaching was central and the Epistle readings from the old series provided the texts. Later I came to hold that Sunday sermons should be based on the words of Jesus from the Gospels and not the teachings of St. Paul, which were intended for those who already knew the rudiments of the faith. Epistles confirmed and defined faith. With an audience unknown in front of me each Sunday, detailed doctrinal expositions from the Epistles were not appropriate.

Once after a sermon on baptism based on Romans 6, I was confronted by two gray-headed Presbyterian ministers, both about fifty years of age.

They challenged what I said about baptism, arguing that they knew Lutherans who had trusted in their baptism and had fallen from grace. At twenty-one years of age I was intimidated by ministers more than twice my age. Since then I have often thought of how I should have responded. One answer might have been that I have known those who made decisions for Christ who have met the same fate, but, of course, this would not have convinced the Calvinist Presbyterians. Better still, this problem might not have come up if I had preached on the appointed Gospel.

Preaching regularly was a new and demanding experience for me. C. H. Dodd (1884–1973), a prominent twentieth-century English scholar, noted that the sermons in Acts had four themes: Christ died for sins, rose from the dead and will return as judge and that he is Lord and Christ. Only after having created this conviction in the heart of the hearers can the preacher go on to such doctrines as baptism, the Lord's Supper, justification, and sanctification.

Sticking to the basics in a sermon to a congregation of unknown religious conviction is still good advice. Having run out of things to preach—and that's the way it often is with doctrinal sermons—I thought the summer could not come to an end too soon. Younger preachers exhaust the whole counsel of God sooner than the older ones do.

VICARAGE AND THE LCMS SAN FRANCISCO CONVENTION

Things were coming together for me after a tumultuous year. I had requested a university campus vicarage and got the best of both worlds at St. Luke's in Manhattan, Kansas. The Rev. Robert Rosenkoetter was my supervisor. Kansas State College, now Kansas State University students were integrated into the congregation, which had special programs for them, among which were a Sunday night supper and a midweek service. Sunday morning attendance was very high, perhaps over five hundred, and often fraternities and sororities would attend *en masse*. That was the custom then. I shared a room with Robert Main, a fourth year college student, for fifteen dollars a month. Leisure time allowed one course in logic and another in French in the spring semester. Additional credit was earned by reading French books.[44]

---

44. This proved to be beneficial in passing the language proficiency requirement for the doctor's degree in the fall of 1962. In June of 2003, I visited St. Luke's and the grounds gave the appearance of not having been kept up. Since then I learned that this once vibrant congregation has suffered a loss in membership and attendance.

To allow Pastor Rosenkoetter a week of vacation, I agreed to stay on into July 1959, until my replacement came. In exchange I was given a week's vacation in June, which allowed me to hitch a ride to the synod's San Francisco convention with Kurt Marquart and Herman Otten. The latter's relatives provided an attic for lodging. Advisory delegates to the 1959 convention included my father's older and younger brothers, Carl Scaer (1896–1983), representing Concordia Teachers College, River Forest, Illinois, and Ernest F. Scaer (1900–1971), representing California Concordia College, Oakland, a longtime professor and its last president.

Of primary interest at the 1959 convention was the status of *A Brief Statement* as a binding, synodically adopted doctrinal statement. Written by Franz Pieper shortly before his death in 1931, *A Brief Statement* set forth the LCMS position on a number of points for negotiations with other Lutheran synods, especially the newly formed American Lutheran Church (ALC, 1930). In the years following its adoption by the synod in 1932 and its reaffirmation in 1947, *A Brief Statement* had become a rallying point for "conservatives" in the face of developments within the synod, especially at the St. Louis seminary in the wake of the Scharlemann papers. What was less clear was its relation to the confessions contained in the *Book of Concord* to which the synod was specifically bound. A resolution was passed that raised *A Brief Statement* to almost the level of the Lutheran Confessions. Some saw this as a change in Article II of the synod's constitution, an issue that would repeatedly come up in the events leading up to the "walkout."

Observing from the visitors' gallery above the convention floor, I recognized certain delegates. Hermann Sasse was there, and although he was regarded as a stalwart defender of the Lutheran Confessions, he was not satisfied with the synod's action on or understanding of *A Brief Statement*.

A perpetual memento of the San Francisco 1959 convention is a photo of me and Kurt Marquart talking to Hermann Sasse, which nearly sixty years later continues to appear in *Christian News*. Sasse autographed my copy of *This is My Body*,[45] which had just been published by Augsburg Publishing House. It laid out the historical circumstances that led Martin Luther to reject Ulrich Zwingli's compromise on the Lord's Supper at Marburg in 1529.

---

45. Hermann Sasse, *This Is My Body: Luther's Contention for the Real Presence in the Sacrament of the Altar* (Minneapolis, MN: Augsburg Publishing House, 1959).

Karl Graesser was also visible from the gallery. He was then an Atlantic District vice president for its New England region. He sat up front on the left. His daughter, Lois Meyer, had been in my class at Bronxville and our parents were often in the same social situations. During the elections, he continually huddled with other delegates. This fit his profile, for it appeared that he and others were seeking to displace Herman Rippe (1896–1969) from the district presidency, and this had been going on without success for some time. In the previous Atlantic District convention, Graesser was unsuccessfully put forward as an alternative to Rippe.

At San Francisco, Rippe was put forward as a vice president of synod. But he was not elected to the synod's praesidium. Finally at the next district convention (1961), Graesser succeeded in garnering a majority of the votes and took Rippe's place. While Rippe had continued to serve as pastor of Trinity in Long Island City, Graesser became that district's first full-time president. From this position he played a key political role in the synod. Along with his son Karl Jr., who served on the St. Louis faculty, Karl Sr. supported the new theological direction of Concordia Seminary, St. Louis. Further, at the same convention in which Graesser was elected district president, Rudolph Ressmeyer was elected first vice president of the Atlantic District. This put him in line for the presidency—a position that he would soon take.

Travel to and from San Francisco had both its benefits and challenges. Whoever the driver was picked me up in Manhattan, Kansas. One night we climbed over a fence to find sleeping quarters in a sheep shed, probably in Utah. Parking and leaving the car in Salt Lake City, we had the good fortune of a flyer placed in the windshield wiper advertising a ninety-nine-cent breakfast. This was close to the sign of the dove leading Brigham Young (1801–1877) to the Mormon Zion. Either coming or going we crossed the Colorado River, which offered an opportunity to swim from one state to another. Sometime in the night we passed through the desert-like country of the Texas panhandle.

Only stopping at a roadside restaurant for breakfast in the morning did we realize that the car had hit a dog, some of whose remains were left on the bumper. As we sat at a table, we could see that a chicken had come to pick at the dog's remains, to which Marquart quipped, "Instant dog." He was always in good form, and his sense of humor was made elegant by an accent soon to be acquired by a call to a congregation in Queensland, Australia.

After the convention and having completed vicarage, I headed off to spend the remaining weeks of the 1959 summer in the Poconos in my grandmother's house, where the extended family often gathered. At the time I was thinking of either graduate studies or serving as an assistant pastor in the New York metropolitan area. Family contacts would have made this possible. John Tietjen, John Damm (b. 1926), and Daniel Reuning, among others, had taken or would take similar paths. Many of the parishioners from my home congregation of Trinity of Flatbush had found their way into Long Island congregations, and it was easy to think of my future in one of them. An assistantship in New Jersey was proposed by a pastor who had longtime associations with my family. My wish for a New York metropolitan-suburban parish came close to coming true when I took the call to become pastor of Trinity Lutheran Church in Rockville, Connecticut, in 1964. But in the summer of 1959 the future was in graduate school. Robert D. Preus had earned a Ph.D. from Edinburgh and older seminary graduates like Robert Schulz, Lowell Green, and Paul Maier (b. 1930) had made their way to the continent. I hoped to follow them. But first there were other matters to which I had to attend.

DOROTHY NEHRING AND THE FINAL SEMINARY YEAR

The year 1959 became particularly important as my relationship with Dorothy Nehring (b. 1931) blossomed. Dorothy was the young widow of Fred Nehring Jr. (d. 1957), whose family had been close Pocono family friends since the founding of Lutherland in the 1920s. Dorothy and Fred's son, Frederick III, was born in 1955. Daughter Pamela followed in 1957, a little more than two months before her father died. Dorothy and I were married in the Village Lutheran Church of Bronxville, New York, on June 18, 1960, with my father officiating and the church's pastor, Howard Halter (1907–1975), assisting.[46]

My seminary roommate, John Puelle (1935–1999), whom I had known since 1949 from Bronxville prep school days until seminary graduation, was best man. He had served his vicarage in Guatemala and was assigned there as a missionary. John would later return as assistant pastor to Trinity Lutheran Church, "the eightth-street church," on Manhattan Island. He left the synod in the wake of the 1974 seminary walkout. In later years he resigned from the ministry and followed in his father's footsteps as a

---

46. During Bronxville prep school and college days (1949–1955) Village Lutheran Church was my church away from home. In 1950 its congregation went from worshiping in a house to a regular church edifice, whose style was copied by other Atlantic District congregations. Its nave and chancel were enlarged before 1960.

banker. After our wedding I saw him only three more times prior to his death shortly before the third millennium dawned.

My final year at the seminary (1959–1960) passed without incident. Dorothy and I were making marriage plans, and I looked forward to studying in Germany. Herman Otten, who did not succeed in gaining membership in the ministerium of the Missouri Synod, ultimately had a large hand in shaping its history. Some of my articles were reprinted in Otten's *Christian News Encyclopedia* without my prior knowledge.

Herman Otten's theology is still left to be analyzed. It may have more Reformed and Evangelical elements than he, others and we were aware, but with the broad appreciation for the evangelist Billy Graham (1918–2018) among the synod's membership, he was certainly not alone. A retired Australian professor once called *Christian News* the Missouri Synod's bulletin board in providing information not available elsewhere, at least until the advent of Facebook. Otten is no longer alone in wanting to be heard. Some used to check it weekly to see who made the pages.

At graduation in June 1960, I was surprised to learn from my uncle Richard Caemmerer, professor of homiletics, that I was one of the better students. There was a lot to suggest otherwise, including a less than stellar performance in the first two years. Loren Kramer (b. 1934), whom I came to know well years later as a member of the Commission on Theology and Church Relations, reminded me of heated confrontations between me and Richard John Neuhaus (1936–2009) and Robert Wilken (b. 1936), both of whom joined the Roman Catholic Church, one as a priest, now deceased, and another as a formidable historian of the early church. These debates and their intensity escape my memory, but putting things together from what others have said, they could be very vocal and public, often in the seminary quad. Neuhaus and Wilken purposed to move the synod in directions that then surfaced in the theological positions leading to the 1974 St. Louis majority walkout. In the passing of the years our theological perspectives were closer together, but this was not the case in seminary days.

Having an uncle on the faculty was awkward. Nepotism means giving favors to one's relatives, especially to one's nephew. Of this I was extremely conscious, and to avoid any appearance of favoritism I took my homiletics courses from George Hoyer, David Schuller (1926–2002), and Alex Guebert (1895–1986), and one was guaranteed an "A" from Guebert, when one's sermon ended with a hymn verse. Already in seminary student days Richard R. Caemmerer Sr. was destined for the faculty on which he became a leading light and was a leader for the faculty at the February 1974 walkout.

During those seminary days when I was beginning to get a handle on neoorthodoxy, Caemmerer's *Earth with Heaven* was published.[47] There is nothing to indicate that at this or any time he was a student of Karl Barth, the great theologian of neoorthodoxy, but in offering his own theology of the "word," similarities were obvious and were confirmed in his interview with Jack Preus's Fact Finding Committee, during which he said that denying the historicity of the raising of Lazarus was not divisive of fellowship. With its battle cry of the "word alone," the synod had opened itself to the "word theology" of neoorthodoxy, and Caemmerer's theology might be viewed as not an unnatural position.

In my joining the Fort Wayne faculty in 1966 we saw each other at joint faculty meetings, and he was always most cordial and kind. As a guest in our home in Springfield, he was careful to avoid topics that would compromise either of us. The founding of Seminex and the AELC created another situation. Richard and Dorothy Caemmerer would visit their daughter and son-in-law, Margaret and Ray Schulze, at their Pocono summer home hardly half a mile from our place. During the first years we kept our distance. Then one day Richard Caemmerer stopped his car as I was jogging, and the ice of those sad days and tragic years dissolved.

After his death, his widow and my aunt, Dorothy Caemmerer, and cousins Richard and Margaret attended a festive celebration of my mother's eightieth birthday in the summer of 1989. Ray and Margaret would come with me to the Royal Choir Festival at St. Stephen's Episcopal Pro-Cathedral in Wilkes-Barre, Pennsylvania. Over a hundred choristers would conclude a week's training session with a grand Evensong on Sunday. At that time Ray and Margaret had joined the Catholic Church. Still, we all enjoyed ourselves.

One question that I personally face is considering and reconsidering my participation in those events. Those who left the synod to form the Association of Evangelical Lutheran Churches (AELC) and then the ELCA have to be asking themselves, if the administration of then seminary president Alfred Fuerbringer and academic dean Arthur Repp had properly handled the students who raised concerns in 1956–1957, would it have come out differently. Theirs was not a theological but an administrative response that the synod structure must remain intact. The synod's infallibility was implied, and this position was officially articulated by the faculty of the St. Louis seminary. Within this rigid frame of reference

---

47. Richard R. Caemmerer, *Earth with Heaven: An Essay in Sayings of Jesus* (St. Louis, MO: Concordia Publishing House, 1969).

there was little room for theological discussion or doing theology. That began to change when Robert Preus joined the faculty in 1957—meaningful theological discussion actually began to take place. In 1974, students raising objections to the status quo were given heroic status. We were not.

In distinction with the rest of the animal creation, human beings have the ability to reflect on the past and plan for the future. We are not able to fully grasp the God who alone is without beginning and end, but we can begin to grasp eternity once we approach the allotted three score and ten. We can question whether we took the right turn at certain divides in life's road. My years at the seminary, especially 1957–1958, were a critical junction not only for me, but for the effects that they would have on the synod. The Missouri Synod would never be the same.

Chapter Three

STUDIES IN GERMANY

During my last seminary year, 1959–1960, wedding and graduate school plans were on my mind. Dorothy and I were engaged at Thanksgiving and made it official at Christmas. Short engagements were still in vogue, and we were married on June 18, 1960. Deciding on graduate school was one thing; choosing the right one is not so easy.

Longtime St. Louis New Testament professor Paul Bretscher Sr. (1921–2016) suggested my studying under Ernst Kinder (1921–2016), a protégé of Werner Elert (1885–1954). So toward the end of July 1960 it was off to Münster, Germany on the SS Statendam,[1] a ship in the Holland-American fleet, sailing from Hoboken, New Jersey. We landed in Rotterdam. As the decade of the 60s waned on, flights across the Atlantic began to take the place of ocean travel, but at the beginning of the decade, passenger ships rolled out of Hudson River ports on both sides. When we returned in March 1962, the SS France[2] was making only its second westward Journey.

Werner Elert and Paul Althaus Jr. (1888–1966), along with Hermann Sasse, had been distinctively Lutheran voices at the University of Erlangen up until after World War II. With Elert's death, Ernst Kinder, who had edited Elert's *Der Christliche Glaube*,[3] was seen as carrying on this tradition, and for this reason Bretscher had recommended his name. Recognizably Lutheran theologians on the Protestant faculty of the University of Münster in 1960 were Kinder and Karl Heinrich Rengstorf (1903–1992), a New Testament scholar, who had served a year's term as university chancellor. As an influential member of the Protestant faculty, Rengstorf had proposed Kinder as a professor of dogmatics. Westphalia—*Westfallen* in German, where the university was located—had

---

1. See *https://en.wikipedia.org/wiki/SS_Statendam_(1956)*.
2. See *https://en.wikipedia.org/wiki/SS_France_(1961)*.
3. Werner Elert, *Der Christliche Glaube: Grundlinien Der Lutherischen Dogmatik*, edited by Ernst Kinder. 3. Und Erneut Durchg. Und Erg. Aufl. ed. (Hamburg: Im Furche-Verlag, 1956).

been absorbed into Prussia, and the Lutheran congregations were incorporated with Reformed ones into the Prussian Union 1817–1830. Together they spawned a hybrid that combined the character of both Reformation traditions.

In leaving his post as the head or abbot of a preacher's seminary in Hannover, a Lutheran territory, Rengstorf had been assured that the churches in Münster followed a Lutheran liturgy. In his receiving the Lord's Supper, Rengstorf listened as the pastor distributing the hosts followed the Lutheran formula, "Take, eat. This is the true body of your Lord and Savior Jesus Christ." The pastor with chalice used the compromising formula used in some Reformed churches, "Jesus said, 'This is my blood of the new covenant.'"

Rengstorf the next day went to the city hall and resigned from the territorial Union church and became a member of St. Thomas congregation, which belonged to the Selbstständige Evangelische-Lutherische Kirche (SELK), the "Independent Evangelical Lutheran Church." In coming to Münster, Kinder, like Rengstorf before him, was automatically enlisted in the territorial church, as is the custom in Germany, but he attended, received communion, and preached at St. Thomas with the understanding that he not participate in the churches of the Prussian Union. Sometime toward the end of 1961, Kinder made a formal break with the St. Thomas congregation. This was a serious matter, since he was a member of the *altlutherisch*, the "Old Lutheran" church, which resisted incorporation into the union church with the Reformed. Even before that, as a professor on the Protestant theological faculty, he preached at the University Church (as perhaps Rengstorf had). Kinder's formal severance from the St. Thomas congregation resulted in a falling out with Rengstorf, who was now left as the only member on the faculty who was a member of an explicitly Lutheran congregation.

Professor Kinder was very gracious in receiving me and suggested a dissertation on the doctrine of infant baptism in nineteenth-century German Protestant theology. During those years, I became acquainted with the Melanchthon scholar Robert Stupperich (1904–2003) and was often a guest in Rengstorf's home with his wife and two daughters.

Our family would spend two Christmases there. Having learned German in Bronxville, I was not at a complete loss in listening to lectures and assimilating materials for the dissertation. Dorothy had an Opel station wagon—ordered in America and picked up in Rotterdam—at her disposal, and for me it was the bike, which I also used to take daughter Pamela to the kindergarten through the city of Münster. With the advent of prosperity, bikes have now given way to cars, but the bike paths along the main thoroughfares made this mode of transportation the easiest and most efficient way of getting around this ancient city.

A number of noteworthy things happened while we were there. Among the more spectacular was the funeral for a Roman Catholic bishop. It featured the papal nuncio and three German archbishops, probably the successors of the Electors of the Holy Roman Empire of Luther's day, along with that country's minor bishops and diocesan priests, all following the coffin on a horse drawn wagon through the city streets. The German army led the procession and the wagon was banked with evergreen branches. Separation of church and state was not a significant issue for them.

Son David was born on June 12, 1961, and my father conducted the Baptism at St. Thomas and I preached. After the service a parishioner asked, *"Was war das für eine Sprache?"* (What kind of language was that?) On that Sunday, the Berlin Wall was erected, an event which suggested to many foreigners that they leave the country.

Speaking German demanded my attention. At first I had to translate the German lectures into English, but as time went on, I began thinking in German. Then there was the matter of becoming accustomed to the German university style of education of either hearing lectures in large halls with hundreds of students or participating in seminars in which minutes of each session were taken and read at the beginning of the next.

Willi Marxsen (1919–1993), who was reputed to be more radical than the great demythologizer Bultmann in separating theology from historical events, was called to Münster while I was there. Rengstorf was highly upset, because Marxsen had been given the New Testament chair Rengstorf held. When we visited Münster in 1986, Rengstorf was still active holding seminars at a dining room table and traveling by train once a week to the University of Osnabrück. Marxsen was in and out of the psychiatric section of the hospital, called in German a *Nervenklinick*. His was not a happy life or ending.

Life in Germany offered a variety of experiences for all of us. Not speaking English at home, we never were assimilated into the German culture, but my German had progressed far enough that at times I was at loss for finding the appropriate English word. Dorothy and I occasionally passed ourselves off to the German employees as British citizens to shop in the store and attend the movie theater for that nation's troops stationed in Münster. Living close to Soviet-occupied East Germany, we appreciated seeing British troops on maneuver. Working with only German sources in preparing a dissertation, I became familiar with German theological vocabulary. A female student in the pulpit for a preaching seminar in the fall of 1960 was a foretaste of women in the ministry, which at that time had not been authorized in Germany. Ten years later women would be preaching in Lutheran churches in America.[4]

Working through how nineteenth-century German theologians handled infant baptism showed that the major issue was how Lutherans wrestled in bringing a real sacramental theology in line with the doctrine of justification by faith. These theologians wanted to return to the classical Reformation theology by moving away from the eighteenth century Enlightenment, yet sought to do so without repudiating the fundamental principle of an individual decision. It simply could not work.

This Reformation revival in the nineteenth century may have been motivated as much by Romanticism in search of authentic German tradition as it was a sincere desire to be guided by the Lutheran Confessions. With the exception of explicitly confessional Lutheran theologians like Wilhelm Löhe (1808–1872) and Friedrich Adolph Philippi (1809–1882) in Germany and C. F. W. Walther in the United States, all of whom accepted Luther's doctrine of infant faith, most of the new "Confessionalists" held to the Rationalistic notion that faith was an intellectual function of which children—especially infants—were incapable. To overcome this deficit, their views resembled Calvin's (1509–1564), which had been taken over into Rationalism. Baptism grafted children into the outward society of the church until they were intellectually mature enough to understand and believe. Others held that Baptism deposited a mystical seed in the child to which an intellectual component was added later. Baptized children were saved without faith, at least a faith that was not present at their baptism, which was seen as a ritual that neither worked faith nor was received in faith, so far as children were concerned.

Kinder's proposal to examine what German theologians thought about infant baptism was related to the interest of German churches at that time in Christian education for the youth. Kinder thought my work would provide a link between the baptism of infants and their further Christian education. My research led me in a different direction. My dissertation, "The Doctrine of Infant Baptism in the German Protestant

---

4. Elizabeth A. Platz was ordained by the Lutheran Church in America on November 22, 1970. See Erin Stybis, "ELCA Celebrates Forty-Five Years of Ordaining Women," *Evangelical Lutheran Church in America*, Nov. 19, 2015, https://www.elca.org/News-and-Events/7798.

Theology of the Nineteenth-Century,"[5] showed that German theologians had compromised the doctrines of grace in baptism and justification by faith.

Kinder and I did not have the same purpose for the dissertation. He wanted an analysis of how the views of these theologians fit into the cultural and intellectual climate of that time—or so he said. With eighteen months under our belts in Germany, it was time to pack up and return to the United States.

Had Kinder showed more enthusiasm in January 1962 for my reworking the dissertation, I would have made a further investment by remaining in Germany. At a Christmas gathering in 1960 at our residence at Erphostrasse 35 in Münster, Kinder gave me a copy of the new edition of Werner Elert's dogmatics that had been published in the same year.

Engaged in going through what the nineteenth-century Lutheran theologians wrote, I did not pay that much attention to what Elert had said about infant baptism. That was a mistake. Kinder had edited a fifth edition of Elert's *Der Christliche Glaube*,[6] which is described as thoroughly reworked and expanded—that meant it most likely reflected Kinder's own views.

In 2011, as I was preparing the manuscript for publication, I belatedly checked on what Werner Elert had to say about infant baptism in his dogmatics. Elert cites no nineteenth-century Lutheran theologians in his discussion of infant baptism, but he holds to their basic premise that faith comes later in life. He repeats the argument of some, that infants cannot reject the divine working in baptism, but never affirms that they can believe.[7] On this point, Elert stood in the tradition of the nineteenth-century Erlangen theologians. Ernst Kinder was Elert's heir, and my dissertation had struck at the heart of their arguments. I did not know that at the time.

By that time, I was coming around to seeing that the sticking point for the Reformed, the eighteenth-century Rationalists and the nineteenth-century Lutherans was the doctrine that infants could not and did not believe at the time of their baptism. This became the more evident in their taking issue with what Luther said, and I was becoming more convinced

---

5. David P. Scaer, "The Doctrine of Infant Baptism in the German Protestant Theology of the Nineteenth Century" (Concordia Seminary, 1963).
6. Werner Elert, *Der christliche Glaube; Grundlinien der lutherischen Dogmatik*, 5, und erneut, Durchgesene und erg. Aufl (Berlin: Furche-Verlag, 1960), 447–452.
7. Elert, 449.

that Luther was right. This became one criterion by which I approached these theologians.

Elert had not specifically denied infant faith, but he presented arguments that the nineteenth-century Erlangen theologians had used to suggest that it could not be proven. Since baptism was a process that embraced one's entire life, attention should not be given to the first days of a person's life. He also adopted the Rationalist view that baptism was an obligation of the church to care for the child and the view of the Erlangen theologians that baptism was a participation in Christ's death. No Lutheran can take issue with this, but all this happened without faith or only in the sense of Calvin, a faith coming into existence in the future. Only later did I realize that in offering a critique of the nineteenth-century theologians, I had taken exception to Elert. Kinder would hardly accept my approach that saw infant faith as both the biblical and Lutheran view, and its critique upon expansion would have included Elert.

His critique, probably prepared by his assistant Klaus Handler, offered no specifics other than saying that I had not seen the nineteenth-century theologians in their theological and cultural milieu. A dissertation in electronic form would have easily allowed for the necessary expansion and alteration. Personal computers still lay in the future. When I saw Kinder in 1969, reasons for not accepting the dissertation did not come up, but they continued to hang over my head.

At my parting visit with Kinder in 1962, I expressed my gratitude to him and left him amazed that I held no regrets. His office was on the third floor of a huge house where I had often gone. We had been guests in each other's homes. He was an energetic and outgoing man, almost in American style, and always good company. Added to complications of our relationship was his dissociation from the St. Thomas church, which even in his own mind led him to question his commitment to Lutheran theology.

Seven years later, in the summer of 1969, I paid him a visit. In the intervening years, before he reached his sixties, he had suffered a stroke and was confined to the first floor. By then I had finished three years as an assistant professor at Concordia Theological Seminary in Springfield, Illinois, and was about to be promoted to associate professor with tenure and had been awarded a fellowship from the Aid Association for Lutherans, now Thrivent. In the intervening years Jobst Schöne (b. 1931), later bishop of SELK, had written his doctoral dissertation for Kinder and is better positioned to narrate his spiritual journey.

Kinder died seven years after my visit, and as with many people taken from this world, a few more prior conversations with him would have opened more windows. The dissertation, however, continued to have a positive impact. First, I submitted a chapter on such confessional Lutherans as Adolph Philippi and Carl Ferdinand Wilhelm Walther to Erwin Lueker (1914–2000), the Concordia Seminary's graduate school head, as partial fulfillment for the Master of Sacred Theology (S.T.M.) degree. Surprisingly, it was not returned. Lueker instead suggested that the rest of the document serve as the Doctor of Theology (Th.D.) dissertation, a proposal to which I readily agreed. It satisfied these requirements, and in 1963, Concordia Seminary, St. Louis, awarded me the Doctor of Theology degree.

That was not the end of the dissertation, however. A forty-year-old carbon copy manuscript resisted being scanned into electronic form, but through the kind services of Trudy Behning, at one time secretary to Robert Preus, the dissertation was put into electronic form, and once updated to show that the views of the nineteenth-century Lutheran theologians were similar to those of the classical Reformed theologians, it was published.[8] Central to the dissertation was that the nineteenth-century Lutheran theologians had discredited such traditional arguments for infant baptism as being commanded by Christ and practiced by the apostles. Universally denied was that infants could believe, the so-called *fides infantium*, and so Lutheran theologians had to offer other grounds for its practice.

Since then, concerns about the practice have come from Roman Catholics, whose Second Vatican Council called for the creation of commissions to prepare new baptismal liturgies called Rites of Christian Initiation. These commissions saw the baptism of adults as its proper New Testament form and only allowed for infant baptism where later Christian education was assured. This had already been proposed by nineteenth-century Lutheran theologians following the lead of Friedrich Schleiermacher (1768–1834).

This dissertation led to the writing of many articles on Baptism and then the Lord's Supper. It provided the motivation and the historical background for my *Baptism* book[9] in the Confessional Lutheran Dogmatics series. My work in the sacraments was a direct result of having seen how the German theologians wrestled to put the doctrines of Baptism and faith, especially that of infants, in a meaningful theological form.

---

8. Published as David P. Scaer, *Infant Baptism in Nineteenth Century Lutheran Theology* (St. Louis, MO: Concordia, 2011).
9. David P. Scaer, *Baptism*, ed. John R. Stephenson, vol. II, Confessional Lutheran Dogmatics (St. Louis, MO: Luther Academy, 1999).

After returning to the States, I came across the dissertation of Karl Brinkel, a German Lutheran pastor in the Soviet zone, entitled *Die Lehre Luthers von der fides infantium bei der Kindertaufe* (1958), "Luther's Doctrine of Infant Faith in Connection with Infant Baptism."[10] This dissertation gave expression to my own conclusions about how Baptism and faith were related. An effort to have Concordia Publishing House publish the book in English translation did not succeed. A letter to Pastor Brinkel received a response from his wife that he had died. Years later I would come across *Baptism in the Theology of Martin Luther* (1994)[11] by Jonathon Trigg, a Church of England vicar serving St. Michael's, a London parish. To both I owe a debt at various points in my life for elucidating the Reformer's teachings. Theologians outside of the Missouri Synod had recognized and preserved the Reformation theology.

RETURNING TO THE UNITED STATES

There were other signs it was time to go home. I had been hit with a debilitating case of pneumonia, which convinced a twenty-five-year-old of his mortality. On a visit to a *Buchhandlung* my bicycle was stolen, apparently by celebrating workers who had put a crown of flowers on the completed rafters of a building across the street. I walked home with the complete edition of Friedrich Adolf Philippi's *Kirchliche Glaubenslehre* (1864),[12] a dogmatics with a clear Lutheran vision and one that still graces my bookshelves.

In early March 1962, we drove our Opel station wagon through Holland and Belgium and by ship crossed the channel to England. Early on the morning of our departure we were awakened by a choir of brass instruments from St. Thomas playing German Lutheran chorales. Hearing the music in the midst of a sound sleep, I thought that we had been taken to heaven—at least it was a foretaste of it. Instead of heaven it was back to America. My obligations were to the Missouri Synod, and so a return stormy trip across the Atlantic in March 1962 was not unwelcome.

We stayed in London with Carl Weidmann, the principal from my Bronxville prep school days (1949–1953), his wife, Cathy, and their family. Weidmann was recovering from the news that the prep school was being

---

10. Karl Brinkel, *Die Lehre Luthers von der fides infantium bei der Kindertaufe*. Theologische Arbeiten; Bd. 7 (Berlin: Evangelische Verlagsanstalt, 1958).
11. Jonathan D. Trigg, *Baptism in the Theology of Martin Luther*, Studies in the History of Christian Thought, 0081-8607; v. 56 (Leiden; E. J. Brill, 1994).
12. Friedrich Adolf. Philippi, *Kirchliche Glaubenslehre*, 2, U. durch Excurse verm, Aufl. Stuttgart: Liesching, 1864.

discontinued to allow the expansion of the junior college division of Concordia Collegiate Institute into a four-year college. Even though seventeen years had passed since the war, fuel was expensive and the house was heated by a coal fire in the kitchen from which burning coals were carried on a shovel to the fireplace in the living room.

On Ash Wednesday, Weidmann took me for matins at Westminster Abbey. An attendant standing at the gate cautioned tourists that a service was about to take place. An Anglican clergyman who was entering at the same time remarked that he thought he would never see people dissuaded from going into a church. Those remarks have a firm place in my memory. Christians are sometimes so embarrassed about the practice of their faith that they do not have the courage to invite others to attend and participate. A group of several hundred school girls dressed in gray uniforms comprised most of the congregation.

The trip home was, like the trip over, by ship. Our car was left with a shipping concern on a side street in London to be transported across the Atlantic to the New Jersey docks on the Hudson River. We took the train to Portsmouth to board the S.S. *France* on its second transatlantic voyage west. It took five days, about half the time that it took on the S.S. *Statendam* in July 1960.

On March 13, 1962, Arthur Nordstrom, a family friend who worked in the shipping industry, arranged to have my twenty-sixth birthday celebration on board the ship *France*. The next day we docked on Manhattan's west side to be greeted by family and friends. We took up temporary residence on the third floor of my parents' home in Brooklyn.

Our stay in Münster gave rise to any number of associations. Victor Pfitzner (b. 1937), later New Testament professor, then principal, of Luther Seminary in Adelaide, Australia, now retired, was sponsor for our son David. John "Jack" Elliott (b. 1935), a classmate from Bronxville prep school and junior college days (1949–1955) through seminary days (1955–1960), arrived at Münster at the same time I did and received a Doctor of Theology degree under Rengstorf for a dissertation on First Peter in which he repudiated the Missouri Synod idea that the ministry could be deduced from the universal priesthood of all believers. Later he supported the Seminex movement, which built its case on theology of C. F. W. Walther that his dissertation repudiated. He stayed long enough in Münster to marry Detlinda Kattenstroph. Upon returning to the States, he became a New Testament professor at the St. Louis seminary, and I last saw him when he visited Springfield. He soon left St. Louis for the University of San Francisco, a Jesuit institution, and made a name for himself in Catholic scholarly circles. Retired from that position, he served as the pastor of University Lutheran Chapel in Berkeley, once a Missouri but now an ELCA congregation, which was established by Don Deffner, who, as a good friend of Robert Preus, became a good friend of ours.

Also in Münster at the time was Paul Jersild, though I do not remember his area of study. He became a professor at Lutheran Theological Southern Seminary in Columbia, South Carolina, now merged with Lenoir-Rhyne University. He was later its president.

In the early 1960s, the war was still a living memory and planes had not replaced travel by ship, so one did not so easily go back and forth across the ocean, as we do now. Pfitzner did not return to his native Australia for all the years he was there, perhaps as many as five. Telephoning from continent to continent required making a reservation at a special location and was financially prohibitive for students. In a situation where one is in touch with the folks at home only by letter, one is quicker to make friends and share meals. Making friends with the American attaché to the British troops allowed us to attend Anglican services on that base. Days in Münster gave me exposure to this language that my American-born faculty colleagues did not have. Another German experience came in the spring of 1969 with a fellowship to Heidelberg. Study abroad had been challenging, but also fulfilling. Now it was time to enter parish ministry.

Chapter Four

PARISH MINISTRY

ঽ✥

GILLESPIE, ILLINOIS

In April 1962, I took the Greyhound bus to St. Louis to be certified for the ministry. Certification was required of seminary graduates who did not take a call right after graduation, which for me had been June 1960. Perhaps there is a record of those professors who took part in the interview, but I do not recall it or them.

After it was completed, it was suggested to me that I would be assigned as an instructor in religion at Concordia Teachers College in River Forest, Illinois, and so I returned that night to the dormitory room with the assurance that this would be my immediate future. The next morning things had changed, and I was assured that I would be assigned to a congregation where I could complete my doctor's degree at the St. Louis seminary. It is not improbable that it was thought I would not fit into the plans for the new directions in which the synod's colleges were going. A phone call from Harry Coiner (1912–1992) on the evening of the day on which calls were assigned to the seminary graduates informed me that I would be going to Redeemer Lutheran Church in Gillespie, Illinois, fifty miles in either direction to St. Louis, Missouri, or Springfield, Illinois.

Redeemer Lutheran Church had been established in 1930. St. John's, a neighboring congregation of the American Lutheran Church, had long since taken Missouri Synod members into its fold before a synod congregation was formed. Our place of worship was formerly an Episcopal church built in the style of its missionary church buildings with a high ceiling and no side aisles. Buildings like this are found throughout the Midwest and West and are easily recognized as being built by Episcopalians. Since the congregation had been established, its membership decreased by one member annually and had never been able to remove itself from subsidy. It contributed as much to missions as it received in subsidy, so in a sense in was self-supporting. The congregation closed its door in 2016.

Ordination was on May 20, 1962, in the regular Sunday morning service at Trinity Lutheran Church of Flatbush. My father was the Ordinator. Fred Hinz (1926–2009), one of my teachers in Greek and Latin at Bronxville, then principal of the Martin Luther High School in Queens, was the liturgist. William "Bill" Scar (1922–2009), husband to my father's sister Margarette (1903–1991) and supervisor of college campus ministries in New England, was the preacher.

On May 22 we left for Gillespie, Illinois, with a two-day stop in Pittsburgh at Dorothy's mother's house on the city's south side. Interstates were just beginning to be built and slow travel required yet another stop in Indianapolis. No arrangements for lodging for our arrival in Gillespie were made, and so we stayed in a motel in Litchfield, about ten miles away. The next day the moving van arrived. There was no enthusiastic welcoming party. One member of the flock, Albert Severn, who lived around the block, came over and informed me that they were not going to taking anything from "a New York City slicker." As firmly and politely as possible, I told him that he would not address any pastor like this again. We soon became good friends and he became more active in the church, even serving as a sponsor for our son Stephen.

Installation was on Sunday afternoon, May 27, with Alfred Buls (b. 1925), recently elected president of the Southern Illinois District, officiating.[1] Henry Peckman (1906–1988) of Zion Lutheran Church in nearby Bunker Hill, the vacancy pastor, preached the installation sermon. At Southern Illinois District convention I signed the synod's constitution probably in Alton, Illinois, around June 1962, in the presence of a synod vice president.

Our Gillespie parsonage was next to the post office, whose employees could peer right into our kitchen. The one-floor parsonage had three bedrooms, a living room, a kitchen-family room and one bathroom located between our bedroom and the one used for the baby. Nighttime visits to the bathroom had to be done with nearly complete silence not to wake the baby, David, age one. In the next year, June 18, 1963, his place at the bottom rung of the family was taken by Stephen (b. 1963), whose birth coincided with our third wedding anniversary. Neither the Catholic hospital nor the Catholic delivering physician charged us. Catholic respect for the ministry is worth emulating.

Rick and Pam Nehring had the large front bedroom, whose glass door facing to the living room made that room inaccessible for late night

---

1. Alfred Buls later became pastor of Bethel Lutheran Church, near the campus of the St. Louis seminary. He was instrumental in leading that church out of the synod. His brother, Harold Buls, came to the Springfield seminary in 1969 and was my colleague until he died in 1997.

visiting. A window air conditioner brought the smoke of the neighbors' burning tomato plants into the house. Our first new accessions to the Redeemer congregation were families of the daughters of these neighbors, who initially thought that our Lutheran congregation were holy rollers. To satisfy their curiosity, they attended with their son's mother-in-law, who had been raised in the Church of England. The Mitchels never joined and were good neighbors, but their married children did.

The first funeral for a young pastor is long remembered. We know the biblical teachings about life and death, but facing those first deaths is where faith works itself out in reality. Each death in that congregation remains with me. In the first instance, death for an elderly gentleman seemed imminent. When I received a phone call about a death in the family, I assumed he had died. When I went to the house, which was in walking distance of the parsonage, I discovered that he was very much alive and that his wife was in fact the one who had died. We sat there in the living room with her body on the couch until the funeral director arrived, and then he proceeded to finish the cooking she had begun.

Another elderly maidenly Sunday school teacher was memorable not only because of her service to the church in her advanced age, but for her appraisal of Genesis as an exciting book with some of the best stories ever told. She was right and she was always a bright light in the congregation. There could hardly have been a more devoted Christian than Andy Ewenson. Born a Presbyterian in Scotland, he plied his trade as an upholsterer. His death and burial coincided almost to the minute with those of John F. Kennedy, days that will be remembered by those who lived through them. In my last visit to Andy in the St. Francis Hospital in Litchfield, he noted that bad weather was on the way and urged me to go home. So we said our farewells. In his last hours Andy was more concerned about me than himself. Here was an expression of faith that is not often found. All these saints passed easily from this life into the next life.

Within an hour of taking over as vacancy pastor at Zion Lutheran Church in Litchfield in June 1963, I received a phone call that a child born during Pastor Edwin Blumenkamp's (b. 1929) final sermon was in critical condition and was on the way by ambulance to a hospital in Springfield. When I arrived at St. Francis Hospital in Litchfield, I learned from the parents that child had died en route and made arrangements with the father for a private service and burial the next morning. When I arrived at the funeral home, I discovered that over one hundred relatives and friends had gathered around an open casket filled with stuffed animals, while children's lullabies were played on the loud speaker. A full service and sermon were expected. Veteran pastors learn to expect the unexpected. At the one-year marker in the ministry, I was just learning. This was the first of several infant burials that later shaped my thinking that the baptism of infants showed the gospel in its purest form.

Gillespie had seen its best days when the coal mines in Benld and Sawyerville, satellite towns, were in full swing. Benld had a main street with shuttered storefronts. Sawyerville was a ghost town whose only inhabitant was one of our members whose son was a pastor. Sunday morning attendance was between sixty and eighty, which by today's standards is good. In the two summers we were there, we had vacation Bible schools with a surprisingly good attendance. Two farming families, the Johnsons and the Alexanders, had dynasty status and were major supporters of the church. Our budget was about five thousand dollars of which four thousand was for my salary. Car allowance was fifty dollars per month. With pork steaks selling at twenty-nine cents a pound, we lived well.

Along with "spiritual" duties I was responsible for most of the "worldly" matters affecting the church. Among these were cutting the grass, shoveling the snow, directing the choir—as much as that was possible—and handling janitorial duties around the church and the attached education unit. Since I was brought up in the home of a pastor who had done precisely these things and was still doing them—at least as much his deteriorating health allowed him in his last years—I knew that all this belonged to the ministry, especially of a small church.

Two items should be recorded for posterity on how people think. Parsonage and church shared one refuse barrel. A voters' assembly decided that since my family was contributing more to the barrel, we should pay for garbage removal. When the garbage removal truck brought us a new barrel, the driver informed me that simply because of my ministerial status, I should not expect to get to get it gratis. Price—fifty cents. Each congregation has its own personality, and the sooner a new pastor recognizes its unique character, the better it will be for him.

Privileges were extended to the local clergy by the Carlinville Country Club, about four miles north on Route 4. In the summer days about four o'clock PM Dorothy and I would pack the kids into the car and head out to its swimming hole with its clear water. When doctoral studies were behind me after June 1963, I would go out on warm fall days to hit the ball around the golf course.

After seminary days I had largely lost contact with Kurt Marquart. Then one day in Gillespie in 1962, I received a phone call from Kurt, who was visiting with Paul Dorn, a colleague from student days who had shared similar concerns about what was being taught at the seminary. Dorn was in the same circuit as I was, and we saw each from time to time.

I did not expect the call from Kurt. Beyond that, though I had known him since 1953 in Bronxville days, I did not recognize him since he now spoke with an accent I did not recognize. Following seminary graduation in 1959, he had gone to Texas, where he met and married Barbara, and in 1961 they left for Queensland, Australia, where they remained until coming to the Springfield seminary in December 1975. Brought up in various places in Europe during and after World War II, he had spent his high school years in Nyack, New York. Then he moved on to Bronxville, St. Louis and Texas. Very precocious, his spoken English in those days did not indicate that he was not American born. Now listening to Kurt after his being Australia for one year, I could not be sure he was the person I had known in seminary days.

Being stationed in Gillespie allowed me to take requisite course work at the St. Louis seminary for which I was awarded the Doctor of Theology degree on June 4, 1963. In the same month, Edwin Blumenkamp left Zion Lutheran Church in Litchfield, a town of less than ten miles from Gillespie, to become an executive secretary of Southern Illinois District, and I became the vacancy pastor. Schedules were arranged so that I could preach one service in Gillespie and two in Litchfield. In a matter of weeks a call was issued to Lawrence Heuchert (1924–2014) of Smithtown, New York, and he was installed in August. Had the call process taken longer, there was a good chance that I would have been the one called. His installation service was followed by a reception that focused on my brief ministry there. In no other place did I experience such wonderful collegiality among pastors as in the Litchfield Circuit of the Southern Illinois District. Our pastoral conferences were full-day affairs with the wives and pre-school children coming along.

My first contact with the Springfield seminary happened in Münster, Germany, where I had met its president, George Beto (1916–1991), who was attending a Reformation conference at the university.[2] He left the seminary presidency to become director of the Texas state penal department and was succeeded by his academic dean, J. A. O. Preus, first as acting and then permanent president with installation in October 1962. Liv-

---

2. David M. Horton and George R. Nielsen, *Walking George: The Life of George John Beto and the Rise of the Modern Texas Prison System*, North Texas crime and criminal justice series, no. 5 (Denton, TX: University of North Texas Press, 2005).

ing less than an hour away, we could conveniently attend. There we met Jack, his wife Delpha (1917–1999), and his mother, Idella (1884–1968), recently widowed from the former Minnesota governor. Donna (1925–2017) and Robert Preus were also there. Hospital visits took me to Springfield and on one occasion I visited Jack and we walked around the campus.

Things could be difficult in Gillespie, and ordinarily an opportunity to accept a call as an assistant pastor to St. Andrew's Lutheran Church, an upscale congregation in Pittsburgh, would be tempting. Pastor August Brunn (1895–1994), a longtime friend of my parents, phoned to offer me the position. Salary, living conditions, and closeness to Dorothy's family were reasons for taking the call, but serving as an assistant pastor with special responsibilities for the homebound and youth did not entice me. Except for one Sunday a month, Pastor Brunn would reserve the pulpit to himself. In Gillespie I was preaching every Sunday, and a new pastor needs an every Sunday preaching experience. In spite of the enticements Pastor Brunn put before me, I turned it down on the spot.

THE ROCKVILLE DAYS

After Christmas services in Gillespie, Illinois, in 1963 we piled the four kids into the Opel station wagon and headed east to visit Dorothy's mother in Pittsburgh and then on to Brooklyn to see my parents. Waiting for me there was a letter from a bank. With a bank logo as the return address, I assumed it was commercial mail and I ignored opening it for a couple of days. It turned out to contain a call document from Trinity Lutheran Church in Rockville, Connecticut. Fred Hallcher (1908–1997), the church president, had used a bank envelope to send the document. This was the introduction to two very happy years.

The next morning we were off to Rockville, a trip of about 150 miles. Entering the Rockville Savings Bank, whose logo was on the envelope, I asked to speak to Fred Hallcher, whose handwriting on the envelope suggested he was the custodian. Out came a slightly built man in a business suit. Mr. Hallcher was the bank president. His wife, Martha (1901–1991), invited us for dinner, and after that brief visit, I was convinced that Trinity Rockville was for me. Such generous hospitality was overwhelming and had not been part of our experience. We returned for another visit to make arrangements and then it was back to Gillespie, Illinois. After stopping in Pittsburgh on the way back, the car's gas line froze up and we spent most of that day thawing it out in an Ohio garage. The children—then ages nine, seven, two and six months—were long-suffering travelers. Uncle Bill Scar tried to dissuade me from taking the Rockville call. Bill thought a possible vacancy in either Nashua or Manchester, New Hampshire, would be better suited for me. In contemplating service in the church, a possible call in the future has no value. Two years later I had another opportunity to ignore Uncle Bill's advice when he urged me not take the call to the Springfield seminary.[3]

Before leaving New York shortly into the 1964 New Year, I was determined to take the call to Rockville, but upon returning to Gillespie a letter under date of January 2, 1964, from Walter E. Mueller (1912–1971), acting academic dean of Concordia Teachers College in Seward, awaited me, asking me to come for an interview for a teaching position that would involve systematic theology and biblical history and interpretation. It looked as if the position was mine for the taking. In December 1963, he had written asking for my academic credentials, and had I not received the call to Rockville, Connecticut, I would have probably accepted. For years in the back of my mind I saw myself as a pastor of a flourishing Long Island church, the kind to which members from my father's congregation in Brooklyn had migrated, and a Connecticut congregation came close to realizing this dream. We left Gillespie on a January day so cold that not a cloud dare blight the pure blue sky. Any number of days stand out as particularly happy, and the day we headed out of Illinois for a place closer to home was one of them.

Since colonial days, the Congregationalists had been virtually the established church in Connecticut. Nineteenth-century Irish and Italian immigration had made Catholicism the majority religion, and each ethnic group formed its own parish. Lutheran presence came with the German migration at the same time. A Lutheran community had been brought together by a synod pastor, Otto Hanser, in 1864. But a split in the congregation over allowing Masons as members gave rise to two congregations: First Lutheran Church, which kept the original articles of incorporation; and Trinity, which continued the succession of LCMS pastors.

The classic wood structure of Trinity Lutheran Church in Rockville, built in the 1880s, was on a hill not far from the center of town; but lack of parking space had become an issue for older members. Connecticut winters brought torrents of snow right up through April.

---

3. Bill was an uncle by marriage to my father's sister Margaret and a third cousin. Scaer and Scar are the same family names spelt differently. Margaret and Bill lived with us in Brooklyn in 1945 while waiting for living arrangements at St. John's Lutheran Church in Staten Island, New York, where he was assistant pastor to Edwin Spruce. Later he became campus pastor for New England. Of my entire father's family we knew them the best.

The installation service was set for January. Atlantic District president Karl Graesser sent his regrets in not being able to attend because of a prior commitment, specifically an occasion honoring Albert Meyer (1905–2000), the president of Concordia Collegiate Institute, Bronxville. Later Fred Hallcher told me that later Graesser phoned to ask him how I had gotten on the call list and was chosen as pastor. The reason was simple. Graesser, who did not approve of my coming to New England, then part of the Atlantic District, had suffered a heart attack, and his responsibilities for the Connecticut congregations were shifted temporarily to the vice president for New England, Norman Kretzmann (1928–1998), pastor in Marblehead, Massachusetts. Norman Kretzmann was also a longtime family friend from Lutherland days and passed my name on to the congregations without objection.[4] The Lord works in mysterious ways.

During my time at Rockville, I corresponded with Graesser but saw him only at the 1964 district convention. When the congregation decided on purchasing property for eventual relocation, I contacted the district office for advice and assistance but none was forthcoming. Even then the district had a variety of executive secretaries who I thought might have expertise in what we intended to do, but I was mistaken. Trinity Rockville had supported the establishment of congregations in Storrs and South Windsor and had transferred some of its members to the latter and was a reason the Rockville congregation suffered attrition. When it was time for Trinity to step out into the light, it had to do it on its own. We had expertise among the members, and property was bought on the Hartford Turnpike in Vernon. A couple of years before I arrived, the Episcopal Church, around the corner from our Prospect Street location, had moved to Hartford Turnpike and had experienced significant growth. The new location contributed to attracting new members, but in not moving earlier it did not have the advantage other churches had. Trinity had missed the wave. Nevertheless, a church edifice was built during the pastorate of my successor, Bruce Rudolf, who invited me to preach the dedication sermon.[5]

When I arrived in Rockville, each of Connecticut's circuits held its own monthly meetings. Shortly thereafter, these circuits including those in central Massachusetts, combined to meet as the Connecticut Valley Pastoral Conference. A favorite meeting place was Westfield, Massa-

---

4. A photo of my installation by Kretzmann along with other pastors present including my father hangs in my son Peter's seminary office.
5. That morning the sermon was delivered by Bertholdt von Schenk (1895–1974), son of a former pastor and longtime pastor of Our Savior's in New York and famed for introducing into the synod a sense of liturgical appreciation.

chusetts, whose ethnic Polish congregation had recently built a beautiful edifice. Liberal/conservative lines, which disrupted the synod in the mid-1970s, were already appearing, but at that time pastors with differing views cooperated with each other.

The first order of business in 1964 was putting in place a Vacation Bible School. This was a major undertaking, given that the VBS attracted over two hundred children, helped the congregation add members, and ultimately was a factor for seeking a more accessible location.

The next time I attended a district convention was for the Atlantic District in Bronxville, New York, in June 1964, at which a replacement for Norman Kretzmann as New England regional vice president was to be chosen. A caucus of New England delegates to select two candidates to be placed on the district ballot was scheduled for six o'clock PM in the nave of the Village Lutheran Church across from Concordia College, where convention deliberations took place. At that time New England was home to over ninety congregations with the total soon to reach near one hundred.

Each congregation had one pastoral and one lay delegate to the convention, and so there were approximately 180 eligible to participate in the caucus for nominating two candidates for the New England regional vice presidency. Names of the two pastors receiving a majority vote from the caucus would be presented to the full convention as the two candidates for the vice presidency. Hardly fifty persons showed up to vote. A six o'clock PM meeting time could have been a factor.

On the first ballot Robert "Bob" Riedel of Bristol, Connecticut, received less than ten votes. But with so few delegates casting votes, on the succeeding ballots this slight advantage turned into a majority. Oscar Milke (1913–1982) of Trinity Lutheran Church in Stanford, Connecticut, a pastor with a more conservative reputation, was chosen as the second candidate, but the election by the full convention went to Riedel.

Upon the breakup of the Atlantic District in 1975, Riedel became the New England District's first president. He was a tall, lanky man with a brilliant mind and was an eloquent speaker. His brother Paul Riedel was my philosophy instructor in my first semester in St. Louis and died around Christmas in that year. As I was home, I accompanied my father, who conducted the funeral in New Jersey. It stuck in my mind how a well-organized group could turn a few votes at a caucus into a majority to elect a district vice presidency that would be transformed into a district presidency.

In the fallout of St. Louis faculty walkout and formation of Seminex and the Association of Evangelical Lutheran Churches, no other district in synod lost proportionately as much as New England. With nearly one hundred congregations, it lost nearly thirty congregations, many of which were the larger ones. Had another vice-presidential candidate been chosen that June 1964 evening, the synod most likely would have maintained its growing position in New England.

In April 1965, my predecessor at Trinity, Erich O. Pieper (1897–1965), passed away. He was the son of the synod's former president and great theologian, Franz Pieper, whose widow spent her last years in the Rockville parsonage. Also sharing the parsonage with Erich Pieper was his sister Emma Schmidt (1889–1972), the widow of a Lutheran pastor who had served Immanuel Lutheran Church 88th Street in Manhattan.

Once a month I visited him and his sister in Bolton Notch, where they lived in an apartment in a house owned by Claire and Adolph Freier, who covered most of the rental costs. During those visits Pastor Pieper did not tell me that he was terminally ill, and he spent his last weeks in a hospital in New York. His death came as surprise.

Taking charge of funeral arrangements, as well as his last hospital days, was his sister, Dr. Irene Koenig, one of the first female physicians in America. His funeral service, for which I was the preacher, brought an array of family and pastors to Trinity, among whom where his nephews, Henry "Joe" Ressmeyer and older brother of Rudolph, then Atlantic District first vice president, who within two years would succeed to the presidency at Graesser's death. Also speaking after the service was Robert Riedel, Atlantic District vice president for New England. After the committal in the Grove Street Cemetery by the Reverend Paul Prokopy (1929–2008), the clergy present for the occasion informed me that hospitality was expected of me.

So into our small living room came Paul Riedel and Fritz Brauer of Holy Trinity in Terryville, Connecticut. One was a liberal and the other conservative—at least in how those terms were commonly used then. Somehow in spite of whatever these differences then represented, we got along splendidly.

Things were going splendidly in Rockville, and I anticipated a long stay. The congregation had agreed to our purchasing our own home, on which we had made a 10 percent down payment of $2400. Complicating matters was a cryptic handwritten note from Robert Preus received in November 1965. In it he noted that the Springfield seminary was looking for a professor in systematics. This left me in a dilemma, and I phoned Robert, who said no call to Springfield would be forthcoming and urged me to complete the purchase of the house. A few months later—early February 1966—I received a phone call from Jack Preus asking me to come to Springfield for an interview on February 11, 1966, for a position in systematic theology and New Testament.

February 11 was Ash Wednesday that year. Dorothy, who was expecting son Peter in May, accompanied me. Present for the interview were Sam Goltermann (1926–2004), Lewis Niemoeller (1911–1999), and Fred Kramer (1902–1991), with Jack Preus present in his office that was part of the library administration building. Goltermann, the assistant executive secretary for synod's board of higher education, was known to belong to what was emerging as the synod's liberal faction, and Niemoeller, president of the Central Illinois District, was a confirmed conservative. Fred Kramer, the academic dean, sat in for synod president Oliver Harms. I had to answer their questions to the satisfaction of all. Interviews of this kind generally last only one hour. Mine was two.

During the interview Jack stepped out of his office and phoned Karl Graesser, president of the Atlantic District, who gave me a positive endorsement. Whatever difficulties Graesser thought he had with me before I came to Rockville were satisfied. That night Jack and his wife Delpha took us out for dinner at The Mill, a restaurant with a lavishly red interior, within walking distance of the president's campus house. Our flight back to Hartford was diverted by a snowstorm to Boston, where we rented a car.

When we returned to Rockville, Jack called to offer a two-year appointment as assistant professor in systematics and New Testament. We were in the kitchen, and on the spot Dorothy said that we would leave Rockville only if the then ordinary four-year initial appointment for assistant professors was offered. Having checked with the electors, Jack called back agreeing to the longer appointment of four years, beginning July 1, 1966, and ending June 30, 1970. The contract was signed by Jack Preus on April 1, 1966, and by me on April 13, 1966.

In my last months in Rockville, the congregation wanted to obtain a pastor and avoid a prolonged vacancy. For my replacement, Jack had promised a Springfield candidate, but since he was away on a trip to the Holy Land, he was not able to fulfill his promise. Instead the congregation received a candidate from St. Louis who would help prepare for the congregation to leave the synod in ten years.

Leaving Rockville was a difficult decision and personally sad for both Dorothy and me. Two things crossed our minds in returning to Illinois to teach in Springfield in 1966. Connecticut, situated between New York City and Boston, offered as much and more in natural beauty, outdoor activities and cultural advantages as any place in the nation. This central

Illinois could not match. Later we thought about this often, particularly when we took drives through the flat land, which boasted a steady continuation of soy beans and corn in the three hundred miles between Chicago and St. Louis.

By having put a down payment on a house, we had planned in spending a good portion of my ministry there. Trinity's members could not have done more for us and they were enthusiastic in outreach into the community. Then there was the fear of what would happen after I left. My second-last sermon was based on Paul's sermon to the elders in Ephesus warning them of future dangers. This sermon was prophetic.

Trinity, the oldest Missouri Synod church in Connecticut, left for the Association of the Evangelical Lutheran Churches, the group that supported the 1974 St. Louis Seminary walkout, and the great Lutheran tradition of that church was lost.

During the two summers I was at Rockville, Trinity hosted two Vacation Bible Schools, which pushed the facilities (which included the other half of our parsonage) to capacity with about 225 children. Half of the white tenement house next to the church served as the parsonage and the rest was available for my study and classrooms. The basement was remodeled into a meeting room, but with so many children, the garage at the back of the church property had to be used. Norm Schmidt put an ad with a coupon for registration in the shopping newspaper for which he worked. This strategy worked and the registrations came pouring in. Prospect Street had never seen such traffic jams as happened at noon during the two-week sessions as the children were picked up by their parents and the school bus we hired.

One day the minister from the First Congregational Church, the prestigious granite church around the corner, phoned to ask what educational tools we were using. Dorothy, who answered the phone, said the Bible. During those summers the First Congregational Church and First Lutheran Church, the Lutheran Church in America congregation, had combined efforts to sponsor a week-long program with horseback riding as an added benefit and attracted seventy-five children. After I left, members told me that my successor found our summer program was divisive of community unity.

He was followed by Don McClean, whom I knew from Bronxville and St. Louis days. After taking Trinity out of the Missouri Synod and into the AELC, he went to Maryland and joined his family boat-building company and retained a formal membership of what would develop into the ministerium of the Evangelical Lutheran Church in America.

In May 2006, two members who were major factors in the success of the Vacation Bible School paid a surprise visit to the Fort Wayne campus. As we reminisced about the Rockville years, he identified himself as the chairman of the meeting at which the congregation voted to leave the synod for Association of Evangelical Lutheran Churches. Now in retirement they belonged to a LCMS congregation in Florida. It was hard for me to continue the conversation. Both husband and wife had deep roots in the congregation's history. In many Connecticut towns there were two congregations, one that allowed lodge members and affiliated in the 1960s with the Lutheran Church in American (LCA), now the ELCA. Rockville had a Missouri Synod congregation and an ELCA one. With Trinity leaving the Missouri Synod, both congregations belonged to the ELCA.

By a strange circumstance, on the day Trinity voted to leave the Missouri Synod, I was lecturing about synod events in Our Savior's in South Windsor or Wapping, as it was called, whose original membership came from the Rockville congregation. Now it is called East Windsor. Members of Trinity who were at my presentations advised me not to attend the meeting. After all, I had not been the pastor for ten years and my presence at the meeting might have made a bad situation worse—who knows? Members in attendance chose to leave the synod.

I am remembered by this congregation as the pastor under whom this church property was purchased. For a few years I received and did not acknowledge invitations to attend Trinity's anniversary celebrations. Others may disagree, but this was the only way to express my dissatisfaction. Many years have passed since Trinity left the Missouri Synod to join a Lutheran denomination which is now in fellowship with the Congregational church which was around the corner from our building on Prospect Street, the church whose minister wanted to know how we had so many children in the Vacation Bible School.

This church, like my father's church where I was baptized, confirmed, and ordained now belongs to the ELCA. Several times in the last forty-some years we have passed through Rockville. On a visit to the edifice on the Hartford Turnpike located on a property purchased during my tenure, the pastor knew who I was and greeted me warmly. The wooden building on Prospect Street still stands. For years it was home to a Pentecostal congregation. Removed from the stained glass window in the front were the letters "U.A.C." for the Unaltered Augsburg Confession. At the time it stood for the German equivalent. On our last visit a white alabaster Buddha statue stood on white stones between the church and the sidewalk that bordered the street. Things change.

Excursus III

WORKING WITH THE GOSPELS

By the time I arrived at the Springfield seminary, Rudolph Bultmann's demythologizing method in reading the Gospels was in decline in Germany, but it was reaching its apex in America. This method was the ultimate theological cause for the St. Louis faculty walkout and formation of Seminex in 1974. It was diametrically opposed to an understanding of verbal inspiration that saw each word in the Bible directly provided by the Holy Spirit to the writer.

Part of Bultmann's program held that episodes from the life of Jesus and his words were preserved by communities, with each adding its own interpretations before passing them on to other communities. So the simple teachings of the rabbi from Nazareth evolved through Jewish communities to Hellenistic ones where they coalesced into our Gospels.

Sharp divisions between Jewish and Hellenistic communities may have never been so distinct, and so the hypothesis for this program was foundationally flawed. During the time of the upheavals some of the St. Louis faculty may not have recognized this. At the University of Münster (Germany), I heard the lectures of Willi Marxsen, who introduced redaction criticism, a method that saw the Gospels as theological compositions. Bultmann's method was theologically unproductive. Marxsen's was not.

As a pastor in Illinois and Connecticut (1962–1966) I did not give much attention to theological developments in the synod. This only happened in my coming to the seminary in 1966. At the time Bultmann had so dominated New Testament studies that it seemed his method would set the tone of biblical studies for years to come, but it gave way to literary redaction and canon criticisms. These methods took more seriously the documents that were in hand and paid less attention to Bultmann's concern of how data about the person of the historical Jesus underwent change in the early Christian communities and found its way into the written Gospels.

Some critics still wrestle with this question of how the words and deeds of Jesus found their way into the Gospels where they were preserved, but more are likely to come to terms with the content without resolving historical concerns about their origins. Some take a completely agnostic view and claim that nothing in the Gospels has anything to do with Jesus, who in their opinion may not have even existed, or at least he is historically irretrievable.

Traditional theology held that the church was created by Jesus. Here the tables were turned, and the earliest communities that came to be known as the church created Jesus. Friedrich D. E. Schleiermacher's view that faith emerged from the community reached an ultimate triumph. Apart from working to determine near-absolute historical certainty, the emphasis in Gospel studies shifted from determining how the events actually happened to how each evangelist handled the data he received to write the Gospels. Each evangelist was a theologian in his own right and each Gospel was a theology. This conclusion stood in sharp distinction to Luther and the classical Lutheran theologians, who saw the Gospels as histories and the Epistles as theologies.

This classical distinction is not without theological problems, because it elevates Paul to the position of the church's chief theologian, even surpassing Jesus. Christianity is cobbled together from Paul's Epistles and the Gospels are relegated to documents providing historical data for his theology. If faith is made the source of what is believed, a position that cannot be granted but must be presented for the sake of argument, then the honor of church's chief theologian should belong to Jesus and secondarily to Paul.

Theological honors belong properly to the evangelists who recorded Jesus' life and deeds. Paul applied the teaching of Jesus to those who did not know him. So Jesus is in the first place, the evangelists in the second place and then Paul. To set the record straight, Luther for the regular Sunday series preached on the Gospels and most often on Matthew and then John. However, in the period of Lutheran Orthodoxy, biblical studies and dogmatics, what is known as theology in the narrow sense, came to be presented as complementary but nevertheless different disciplines.

An argument based on the faith of the community that was classically articulated by Schleiermacher is not entirely without merit or biblical precedence. Along with listing witnesses to the resurrection, Paul argues backwards from justification, i.e., the Corinthians know the forgiveness of sins, to the resurrection. Justification is only possible if Jesus rose from the dead, and the Corinthians were denying the resurrection, but nevertheless understood themselves as justified. Paul's arguments that Jesus could have only been the center of faith in the early Christians communities would make sense only if he had actually existed and risen from the dead (1 Corinthians 15:13–14).

In this sense, Jesus as a figure in history is dependent on faith, i.e., on what the earliest Christians remember and believed about him. Arguing from the conclusion to the premises may present logical problems, but Paul does just this. Scholars, in their search for the Jesus of history, have never been certain about his existence, but rarely have doubts about Paul's existence. However, he was never an object of faith, even among the churches he founded. Contrast this with Jesus, who in the earliest apostolic times was worshiped as God, an honor never given Paul or any of the apostles. Within a church context, Jesus himself is the source and norm of what should be and must be believed including and especially about what he said about himself.

In this scenario, the Gospels are recognized as the source of what is known about him and what should be believed, and they take precedence in church life and theology over all other books, including the Old Testament and the Epistles, all of which, like the Gospels, claim divine origin and authority. So while the term *Christology* is reserved for a particular section in the dogmatic sequence, the term should primarily be used of the Gospels. They are Christologies in the primary sense. All other writings, including the Epistles, as later reflections on the person and work of Jesus are Christologies in a secondary sense. Early Church fathers and dogmatics are still even later reflections on the person of Jesus as the church confronted false teaching.

Like the persons of the Trinity, each Gospel is complementary to another, and though they have the same purpose in creating and confirming faith, yet each does it in a different way. They cannot be shuffled together like the four suits in a deck of cards, but when their divine origin by the Spirit's inspiration was emphasized over their historical origins and first purposes, this is what indeed happened.

The Gospels are complementary but not identical or interchangeable. One can anticipate or rely on another but one cannot replace another. They are not redundant. Such an approach differs from the citation or proof-text method of Bible study where one passage can be substituted for another without attention to the book where it is found or context in which the author put it. Referencing Bible passages without determining the context in which they were written and heard creates an ethereal Christianity in which the lives of Jesus and the apostles are incidental to the theological task and produces a biblicistic Gnosticism in which doctrines need not be anchored in history. However, forming the Gospels happened soon after they were written.

In 1 Timothy 5:18, Paul combined Matthew 10:7 with Luke 10:10 and a citation from Deuteronomy 25:4. Paul saw the unity of what the Gospels said as more important than recognizing how one evangelist was distinct from the other, then went on to place these references from the Gospels on same level as the Old Testament Scriptures. By including the two earlier Gospels in the third Gospel, the third evangelist, whoever he was, saw these documents as authoritative without a sense of obligation in having to preserve their historical context.

On the other hand, coming to terms with the historical origins of the biblical documents without recognizing their theological content and purpose is like dissecting cadavers and never coming to terms with real, live persons. C. S. Mann (1917–1996) compared certain aspects of meetings of the Society of Biblical Literature to a carnival in which each participant hawks his own wares. A Saturday morning flea market might also be an apropos comparison.

Inclusion of a citation in any situation, biblical or not, to address another situation is taking it out of context, but is necessary in advancing an argument, which is what preaching is all about. In jurisprudence, one law or ruling builds upon another. So in theology, there is advancement not only from the Old to the New Testament, but from one book to another, whether that is a Gospel or an Epistle.

This evolutionary scheme is not an excuse for failing to examine a biblical book on its own merits and, in the present discussion, recognizing how one Gospel fits in with the other three. In the proof-text method, the evangelist becomes so anonymous as to lose his personality and lost is his role as a theologian in his own right. David Hengstenberg held to the historical authenticity of the entire Bible, and so he agreed with David Friedrich Strauss (1808–1874) that the Bible was to be treated as a unified whole and not piecemeal.

Biblical studies went through a cataclysmic change in the eighteenth century when scholars put aside the divine origins of biblical writings and concentrated on the historical ones. In the case of some scholars, e.g., David Friedrich Strauss, this led to complete historical agnosticism. Others held to some classical items in the Christian faith, but not others. They did not renounce the faith, but laid the groundwork for others who would.

Rudolph Bultmann had the best of two worlds. Historically, he worked in the world of unbelief and theologically in the world of belief. His scholarship led him to the brink of complete historical agnosticism in regard to the person of Jesus, and at the same time his faith allowed him full participation in the life of the Lutheran church in Germany in which he grew up. His two volume *The Theology of the New Testament*[1] is useful and can be cited with impunity. Some find this kind of intellectual schizophrenia impossible or not worth the mental effort to sort out acceptable articles of faith from historical data they find unconvincing. Rather than denying the necessity of historical criticism, as a strictly verbal inspiration view of the Bible requires, for some, a line should be drawn upwards from the historical to the divine.

History precedes God's speaking to us in our history, and so the incarnation is the necessary prelude to inspiration. When we have moved from the historical to the divine, the motion is reversed so the argument goes from the divine to the historical. Thus being convinced that the claims of the prophets and apostles that they are speaking words of God, we do not in each case have to examine the historical evidences in which these words were first spoken. In some cases, it has to be done, as with Paul's defense of the resurrection with the Corinthians.

Typically dogmatics goes from the divine, with the assumption that the Scriptures are inspired, then to the historical, i.e., if God says it, it must be so. This is true, but this leaves unaddressed the historical context in which that authoritative word of God was spoken. In practice it becomes unimportant. If this is a privately revealed word like a vision or dream, the word is not open to historical inquiry. Without historical context, Christianity is no different from Islam or Mormonism, both of which rely on private revelations to their prophets.

Karl Barth operated from the divine to the historical without placing much, if any, value on the historical context. His oft-quoted phrase that the most important theological phrase was the children's song "Jesus loves me, this I know; For the Bible tells me so" allows no place to the historical context in which the revelation is made. Inspiration replaces incarnation as the foundation of theology.

In response to Barth and inspiration-based theologies, it must be upheld that the *crucifixus sub Pontio Pilato* of the creed does not count for only one thing in Christian theology but for everything. Total commitment to the divine in Barth's word-of-God theology may account for the initial enthusiasm with which it was received by some Missouri Synod theologians who may have already inadvertently absorbed a Protestant fundamentalism into their theologies.

---

1. Rudolf Bultmann, *Theology of the New Testament* (New York: Scribner, 1951).

In reaction to the neglect of the historical aspect of Christian faith, interest in apologetics arose. Since the platforms of Bultmann and Barth did not allow for recovering the past, apologetics presented a method by which the past could be recovered. Leading apologists in the Missouri Synod were John Warwick Montgomery (b. 1931) and Paul L. Maier. Since the practice of biblical criticism can lead to historical agnosticism, the goal of apologetics is to show the certainty of the biblical history. Yet neither method relies on the inspired character of the Scriptures as evidence for its conclusions.

Rather than addressing historical questions as historical criticism, which apologetics attempts to do, many scholars take the Gospels at face value without going back to the events that they report. They look for how one Gospel is related to the other and look for how parts of one Gospel might be incorporated in another. Though the majority of scholars assume the priority of Mark, and with less agreement they place Luke before Matthew.

How the Gospels evolved was not simply a matter of one evangelist looking at the written Gospel of another evangelist and copying it. Most scholars posited a lost document called "Q," the first letter of the German word *Quelle*, meaning source, which Matthew and Luke incorporate in their Gospels. Complicating matters is that some posit that Mark used Q. In addition, each evangelist had access to his own sources in the oral tradition that contained data about Jesus, which at the time of composing a Gospel had not taken written form. It is unlikely that scholars will each arrive at one view of the origins of the Gospels that will be satisfactory to all.[2]

In the post-apostolic world, Matthew emerged as the one authoritative writing to which other writings, including Paul's Epistles, were at best ancillary and secondary sources. Matthew may already have been referenced by Paul, as argued by Bernard Orchard (1910–2006).[3] Classical Lutheran theologians presented their views from passages throughout the Scriptures with special attention to Paul. How the New Testament documents were related to each other was not an issue for them or for others who

---

2. For a near-comprehensive view of current thinking, see P. Foster, A. Gregory, J. S. Kloopenborg and J. Verheyden, eds. *New Studies in the Synoptic Problem*, Oxford Conference, April 2008 (Leuven-Paris-Walpole, MA: Peeters, 2011). The 961 page volume contains thirty-one essays.
3. Bernard Orchard, "Part Two: the Historical Tradition," in Bernard Orchard and Harold Riley, *The Order of the Synoptic Gospels* (Macon, GA: Mercer University Press, 1987), 118–119.

approached the Scriptures from their inspired character. They bolstered their positions with Luther references, the Lutheran Confessions and arguments from classical dogmaticians. Just as each theologian pursues theology his own way, each evangelist produced his own account of the life of Jesus that was uniquely his.

I was drawn to using the Gospels, especially Matthew, as the primary source for theology. This first reputed evangelist thought he was writing the concluding volume to the Old Testament. At the time he wrote his Gospel, he may not have been aware that it was to become the first volume of the New Testament. It is more likely that he thought that his would be the only Gospel.

My first venture into this field was my popularly written *What Do You Think of Jesus?*[4] Not only did I think that this was the most defensible way of doing theology, but this was the best way of bringing believers into a face-to-face relation with the man Jesus in whom they trusted for salvation. In doing this, I attempted to keep in mind that history preceded faith, and even if faith was the goal of the Gospels, it could not be substituted for history. Incarnation took priority over justification.

Bultmann offered a method that placed justification by faith as the foundation, and this eviscerated form of Christianity was hardly more than early church Gnosticism. My interest in the Gospel of Matthew resulted in writing my books *The Sermon on the Mount: The Church's First Statement of the Gospel* and *Discourses in Matthew: Jesus Teaches the Church*,[5] to which the prelude was *James: The Apostle of Faith*.[6] Tackling a verse-by-verse commentary on Matthew seems an improbable task for me at the end of life, but is tempting as long as there is breath in the lungs.

My first formal connection to inclusion in the scholarly discussion on the Gospels came from an invitation from William Farmer (1921–2000) to attend a colloquium at the Perkins School of Theology at Southern Methodist University to respond to Martin Hengel's (1926–2009) study on Mark that appeared in German in 1983 and would soon appear in

---

4. David P. Scaer, *What Do You Think of Jesus?* (St. Louis, MO: Concordia Publishing House, 1973).
5. David P. Scaer, *The Sermon on the Mount: The Church's First Statement of the Gospel* (St. Louis, MO: Concordia Publishing House, 2000) and David P. Scaer, *Discourses in Matthew: Jesus Teaches the Church* (St. Louis, MO: Concordia Publishing House, 2004). See also Excursus XI: The Sermon on the Mount: The Church's First Statement of the Gospel, 241 ff.
6. David P. Scaer, *James, the Apostle of Faith: A Primary Christological Epistle for the Persecuted Church* (St. Louis, MO: Concordia, 1983).

English in 1985.[7] To this day I do not know how I came to Farmer's attention, but my holding to Matthew as the first Gospel corresponded to the Griesbach (1745–1812) hypothesis that the correct order of the Gospels was Matthew-Luke-Mark, a view diametrically opposed to the still near-universally held view that Mark was the first Gospel and that out of it and the hypothetical "Q" document, Matthew and Luke constructed their Gospels. In inviting me, Farmer had several motives, one of which was that since I read German, I could summarize and analyze Hengel's book on Mark. As a Lutheran, I would be ideal in winning Hengel over to Farmer's position on the order of the Gospels, so Farmer thought. So I could spend as much time with him as possible, it was arranged that I would room with Hengel.

Unexpectedly, Hengel had come with his wife, and I was assigned a room with Christopher S. Mann, author of the Mark volume in the Anchor Bible Commentary series. At the symposium, plans were set forth for an international conference on the Gospels in 1984 in Jerusalem at which varying views on the order of the Gospels would be presented by three teams of five scholars each. Farmer said that if he had heard the paper that I delivered in Dallas before invitations were sent out for the Jerusalem conference, he would have included me on his team.

Prominent on that team with Farmer was Bernard Orchard, a Benedictine monk from London, and David L. Dungan (1936–2008). Until the conference took place, I was kept up to date on its planning in case one of its members was not able to attend. Bernard Orchard suffered a heart attack during the conference and returned to England. The meeting in Dallas initiated a friendship with Mann, with our commitment to a project to present the entire New Testament including the Gospels as theological treatises. We offered as the hypothesis that the New Testament books were written as catecheses, treatises for teaching the Christian faith in the church's first years.

Farmer did not think in theological terms, but Orchard did. Both held to the same order of the Gospels, but Farmer dated them after 70 AD and Orchard before that date. I visited Orchard once in London at Ealing Abbey, the farthest stop, on the London Metro.

After Orchard and Farmer died, David L. Dungan led the group that would soon be further diminished by his own death. I saw him at the

---

7. Martin Hengel, *Das Evangelium und die Evangelien* (Tubingen: J. C. B. Mohr (Paul Siebeck), 1983); Martin Hengel, *Studies in the Gospel of Mark*, trans. John Bowden (Philadelphia, PA: Fortress Press, 1985).

San Diego meeting of the Society of Biblical Literature in 2008 and had hoped to be at the celebration in his honor when the society met in Boston the following year. An unexpected medical situation prevented me from attending. Leaving Boston to officiate at a family member's wedding, Dungan suffered a heart attack, and in being transported from one hospital to another, he died in transit.

Two of my colleagues were enlisted for the project as well as Winthrop Brainerd (b. 1936), a Catholic priest on the staff of St. Matthew's Cathedral in Washington, D. C. This project lost its focus when C. S. Mann died in October 1996 and my two colleagues began devoting their scholarly efforts to their volumes in the Ancient Christian Commentary series and the Concordia Commentary series.

Work I intended for the New Testament project appeared as *Discourses in Matthew*. Having a chance to exchange views across traditional denominational lines with a common purpose in putting the New Testament books in the perspective for which they were written and in which the church received them was stimulating in a way that I had not experienced before and have not experienced since then.

The five years after 1984, during which I could have devoted my efforts to the study of the Gospels, were taken up by the obligations of being the academic dean. Administration and the pursuit of scholarship mix together like oil and water, but I was also faced with defending myself against accusations leveled by a man who thought himself to be a theologian.[8] This made pursuit of Gospel studies nearly impossible. Had I not taken the position of academic dean, I could have given full attention to study on the Gospels and perhaps would not have suffered the trauma brought on by the accusations. If the past can be known only partially, so also the past does not allow for reruns.

As the Concordia Commentary series began to evolve, I had good reason to think that I would be invited to be a contributor. Former students thought that the assignment to do Matthew would come my way. It did not. A pungent moment came for me when a photograph of those chosen as authors of the Concordia Commentary Series appeared in the *Reporter*. Pictured among the contributors were Dean Wenthe, William Weinrich and Arthur Just, colleagues with whom I shared a similar approach to the Gospels. Just and Weinrich were associated with me in the soon-to-be defunct New Testament catechesis project. That photo was the signal

---

8. For more information on these charges and their effects, see Excursus XIV: Waldo Werning. 277 ff.

that I would not be asked. In his Luke commentary,[9] which he dedicated to me and others, Art mentioned that he had learned his perspective on gospel interpretation from me. I never approached Wenthe, who was then an associate editor of the series for the New Testament, about being included, but when I mentioned to Bill that I had heard nothing about my participation, he urged patience with the implication that an assignment would be on the way.

If an assignment to do Matthew was not forthcoming, then certainly one on James would be. It did not happen. The author of the Matthew commentary also expressed a debt to me in the forward, and as it has been reported, he also often does in his classes in St. Louis. This appreciation did not translate into an invitation to be included in the project.

---

9. Arthur A. Just Jr., *Luke*, Concordia Commentary (St. Louis, MO: Concordia Publishing House, 1996).

Chapter Five

THE EARLY YEARS IN SPRINGFIELD

≥•

After departing Rockville, Connecticut, with tears and regrets for having to leave such a wonderful congregation, we headed off to our Pocono cabin for the rest of the summer to prepare for the first academic year at Concordia Theological Seminary, which began in September 1966. Left behind was the eight-passenger wagon provided for us by the congregation, and in its place was a much smaller Ford Falcon station wagon, bought from my parents' Jewish neighbors, the Hermans, on Ditmas Avenue. This took our family, now seven with the birth of our youngest son, Peter, on May 3, 1966, to Springfield. The Opel station wagon we drove in Germany was a second car until it broke down in the summer of 1969 in the Poconos. We thought that a broken drive shaft was beyond repair, but in subsequent summers it was sighted being driven by workmen.

On the way I had the joy of changing my first flat tire—three times! Three new tires had to be purchased on the way, mostly on the Pennsylvania Turnpike. The car had only been driven eight thousand miles and had spent most of the time in my parents' garage, which the Hermans had rented from them, and the tires had become a little mushy.

Delpha Preus, the wife of seminary president J. A. O. Preus, took care of the children as we moved into the house on West View Drive. In April, just before Peter was born, I made an extra trip to our new home city to purchase a building lot, and when we arrived in late August an eight-room house was waiting for us. For the first two years our neighbors did not include us in their frequent social gatherings. It could be that the Midwesterners have a bias about Easterners, especially the city variety, which we were. Springs and falls are warmer for longer periods in Central Illinois than they are out East, and we became accustomed to sitting outside on the driveway as the children, ours among them, went up and down the street. Soon the neighbors would bring their chairs to our driveway, and from this the deepest of friendships developed. We had barbecues in the summers and had parties in the paneled basements in the cold months.

Twice we took cruises together. Never again would we have so many friends among the neighbors.

These neighbors really meant something to us when things at the seminary were not going so well. They provided a group in which the events in the synod and seminary could be for the moment forgotten. They were the Birkes and the Curtises. Opposite us lived Walter (1920–1995) and Hattie (1920–2006) Putnick, who always managed to come across the street when I was about to engage in some dangerous behavior in fixing the house or working on the lawn.

The men who were members of the National Guard stationed at the Springfield airport offered to get me on board as a chaplain with the rank of a major, a tempting offer which I am not sure they could deliver, but with our children still young, I wanted to spend my extra time with them. In the long falls I would take our sons out to Camp CILCA, owned and operated by several Lutheran organizations about five miles north of the airport, to go swimming in the lake. I would find a place to set up a chair and read, while they jumped off the diving board and swam. In retrospect it was all idyllic. Had the seminary remained in Springfield, we would have been content for the rest of working lives.

Four new men were called to the seminary, and three accepted. John Frederick Johnson (1922–2009), Kenneth Ballas and I were installed at the opening service on the Sunday following Labor Day in 1966 by the then Central Illinois District president Lewis Niemoeller. John Warwick Montgomery (b. 1931) was called to teach dogmatics and historical theology, but declined. He had been a guest lecturer and had used the campus apartment of James Weis (1936–2017), an instructor in the department of historical theology. He would have been qualified to be the chairman of the department of historical theology, but that position was occupied by Erich Heintzen (1908–1971). Montgomery, then at the Lutheran seminary in Waterloo, Ontario, Canada would then go to Trinity Evangelical Divinity School in Deerfield, Illinois, a school founded by the Evangelical Covenant Church, a small denomination which equivocated on baptizing infants. Trinity was heavily endowed by the lay persons involved in the rising Evangelical movement of the 1960s and continues to boast a premier faculty and expanding student bodies.

In 1963, J. A. T. Robinson's (1919–1983) *Honest to God*,[1] with its radical views on God and the world, and the "God is Dead" theology came on

---

1. John A. T. Robinson, *Honest to God*, SCM Paperbacks (London: SCM Press, 1964).

center stage. Montgomery had successfully engaged its leading proponent Thomas J. J. Altizer (b. 1927) in a debate in the University of Chicago chapel. Then there was another encounter with Martin Scharlemann, who had spoken of the Bible as having errors and no errors. Some years later, Montgomery went to Melodyland School of Theology in Anaheim, California. Though at that time he did not have a permanent resident position in a Missouri Synod congregation or institution, he remained in contact with Jack and Robert Preus. Later he became a professor at Concordia College in Milwaukee.[2]

Documents accompanying my call to the seminary gave me a primary responsibility to teach dogmatics with a secondary one in the New Testament. Montgomery was to be the first ranked addition to the department of systematic theology. When he declined the Springfield call, my sole responsibility was the first three courses in dogmatics—prolegomena and Scriptures, God and creation, and Christology, which up to that time had been divided into one course for the person of Christ and another for his work. I never saw the syllabi for these two courses, but it seemed unusual or even untenable that Christ's person could be presented without his work. This reflected a "from above" theology which began with God and worked down to the lesser doctrines. It was also the approach of Karl Barth, and its similarity to the classical approach may have been one reason for its being uncritically accepted by some in the Missouri Synod.

Kenneth Ballas, a fellow 1960 graduate from the St. Louis seminary, took over the Greek and New Testament responsibilities which I was originally to share in. John Frederick Johnson—not to be confused with John Franklin Johnson (b. 1947), later president of the St. Louis seminary and the River Forest College[3]—also taught dogmatics, specializing in contemporary theology. He also had responsibilities in seminary administration with attention to recruitment and publicity. Later he would become the associate academic dean in 1971 when Lorman Petersen reassumed this position after being acting seminary president.

The entering classes in those years numbered around 120 to 130. Still in effect then was the synod rule that all students from non-synodical colleges, which included Valparaiso University, come to Springfield. Some students were acquainted with critical views of the Bible, and much of the lecture period was spent explaining its discrepancies with secular

---

2. Now Concordia University Wisconsin, located in Mequon, Wisconsin.
3. Now Concordia University Chicago, located in River Forest, Illinois.

sources and among the biblical records themselves. Inerrancy was the topic of the day. Department chairman Howard Tepker (1911–1998) directed me to Berkhof's dogmatics[4] for lectures. Quizzes were administered almost daily.

A word must be said about Howard Tepker. With his gentlemanly ways, white hair and glasses, usually dressed in neutral gray suits, he was seen as a kindly, older gentleman. Even if he was not a theologian in the sense of pioneering new thoughts and analyzing, he presented the synod's theology to each new generation of pastors. He was highly regarded by members and staff on the synod's Commission on Theology and Church Relations. Note should be made that he had been chosen as one of three coeditors of what was then called The International Lutheran Dogmatics[5] with Ralph Bohlmann as editor of the series. Kind and fair was the image he projected. For Tepker's assistance I am grateful.

At the time, conservative-minded theologians in both Lutheran and Evangelical traditions were facing what they saw as a common enemy in what were proving to be the destructive conclusions of higher criticism. Evangelicalism had an accomplished leader in Carl F. H. Henry (1913–2003), founder of *Christianity Today*, a then biweekly popular theological periodical, read by many concerned with developments at the seminary. At the time, I did not recognize Lutheran and Reformed distinctions other than the obvious Christological and sacramental ones. In this, I probably was like most of my Missouri Synod contemporaries. While I was in Rockville, Henry offered me an editorial position, and later I wrote articles on infant baptism, Christ's ascension and objective justification for the publication.

For his work on the views of the seventeenth-century Lutheran theologians, *The Inspiration of Scripture*,[6] Robert Preus was well received in Evangelical circles which were led by Carl Henry and Kenneth Kantzer

---

4. Louis Berkhof wrote twenty-two books during his career. His main works are his *Systematic Theology* (1932, revised 1938), which was supplemented with an *Introductory Volume to Systematic Theology* (1932, which is included in the 1996 Eerdman's edition of *Systematic Theology*), and a separate volume entitled *History of Christian Doctrines* (1937). And the book is *Systematic Theology* (1932, revised 1938).
5. After over thirty years in production, this project was published as Samuel H. Nafzger et al., *Confessing the Gospel: A Lutheran Approach to Systematic Theology* (St. Louis, MO: Concordia Publishing House, 2017).
6. Robert D. Preus, *The Inspiration of Scripture: A Study of the Theology of the Seventeenth Century Lutheran Dogmaticians* [2nd ed.] (Edinburgh: Oliver and Boyd, 1957).

(1917–2002). It took several years for me to see that Lutheran and the Reformed approached doctrines in different ways, something which was clarified for me by William C. Weinrich, later academic dean, who joined the faculty ten years after I did. Neoorthodoxy had made its appearance at both of synod's seminaries, and once again using the older theological categories was an improvement of sorts over the classical liberalism of the early twentieth century.

Writings by Karl Barth, Emil Brunner, Paul Tillich (1886–1965) and Rudolph Bultmann were influencing synod theologians, but with little if any critical response apart from reasserting the doctrines of biblical inspiration and inerrancy. Sputtering toward its end in the 1960s was the older liberalism, whose prominent leader Harry Emerson Fosdick (1878–1969) was then still alive. Decades before he had gone head to head with Walter A. Maier I, the famed Lutheran Hour speaker. Fosdick, then in his nineties, had written a piece for *The Readers' Digest* on his finding God on the lake at his Maine vacation retreat.

Part of my educational philosophy is having the students look at the materials to come to their own conclusions, and there is no better place to start than with an article by the renowned spokesman for the old liberalism. Not all students are comfortable with this approach and prefer to be given the answers with the questions. Much teaching in dogmatic and also biblical theology in both seminaries consisted in the instructor reading from the same set of notes year after year. This preserved, so it was probably thought, the traditional orthodox teachings of the church. It also did not prepare the next generation of ministers to recognize and respond to new and sometimes erring doctrines. With the death of Franz Pieper in 1930, Missouri's premier theologian, this is exactly what had been happening for the Missouri Synod in the years leading up to the fateful 1970s.

That first academic year was very demanding having to prepare for three new courses at the seminary and survey courses on the Old and New Testaments in the fall and spring semesters at the University of Illinois in Champaign-Urbana.[7] Like many new instructors my lack of knowledge and breadth was compensated for by being tough on the students—at least in their opinion. Robert Preus brought this to my attention one Sunday afternoon in the spring of 1967. Along with his family he had come from St. Louis to Springfield to visit his mother, widow of the late governor of Minnesota, who lived in a Presbyterian retirement

---

7. For more information on the University of Illinois classes, see Excursus IV: College Courses at the University of Illinois—Champaign, 107 ff.

home near our home. Many times we would pick her up and drive her to the seminary. Always the gentleman, Robert Preus let me know that my teaching would improve if I took things a little easier. For this advice along with many other things I remain in his debt.

I was glad when the first year of seminary teaching had come to an end and breathed a sigh of relief. Kudos, flowers and congratulations would have been in order, at least so I thought, but having survived without my lack of knowledge being detected was its own reward. Today new faculty additions are given a light load for one or two quarters in order to prepare their lectures, but teaching is a technique learned over a period of time.

After meeting Hermann Sasse at the San Francisco convention in July 1959, I again saw him in the spring of 1965, when Sasse was invited to give a lecture at Concordia, Bronxville, by its president, Albert Meyer (1905–2000). I attended, and after the lecture I drove Sasse to JFK. The next time I saw him was at the Springfield seminary in 1967. When I learned of this visit, I proposed that the faculty award him an honorary doctor's degree. Given Sasse's advanced age, I was concerned that he might not be able to return to the United States again.

Jack Preus arranged for the faculty to award the degree, probably without board approval, and it was conferred upon Sasse during a regular chapel service held at Immanuel Church, which was at the east end of the campus. Since this was an impromptu situation, a doctoral gown to fit him could not be found, so only the doctoral hood with the seminary colors was placed over his suit. It was the last time I saw him.

When asked to contribute an essay to a festschift in his honor, I declined since other obligations pressed in. It is something that I still regret. After a tragic death in a fire in his Adelaide, Australia apartment, Hermann Sasse as a theologian has continued to rise in stature. Like Walther and Pieper he is referenced now often in Missouri Synod theological discussions. As with the writings and view of most heroic figures, he became immune to critical analysis. Once on the liberal side of the origins of the Bible, he is now revered for his revival of classical Lutheranism.

To make dogmatics more accessible to seminary students, I undertook in the summer of 1967 the collection and translating of the Latin phrases in Pieper's *Christian Dogmatics*. From my father I had inherited the Baier-Walther *Compendium*,[8] a nineteenth-century dogmatics book written in Latin, his seminary dogmatics text book.

---

8. Johann Wilhelm Baier, *Joh. Guilielmi Baieri Compendium Theologiae Positivae: Adjectis Notis Amplioribus, Quibus Doctrina Orthodoxa Ad [paideian]*

This was replaced by Pieper's dogmatics written in German, *Die Christliche Dogmatik*,[9] of which an English translation was made a few years before I enrolled in the St. Louis seminary in 1955. By then hardly any seminary students, all of whom had taken several years of German or Latin in the synodical school system, had a working competence in either language. Latin phrases embedded in Pieper's dogmatics were retained in the English translation, but often without translation or explanation.

In that summer, I went through the three volumes of Franz Pieper's *Christian Dogmatics*, writing every Latin term and phrase and providing a translation on a card. Matters were complicated by having the same phrase appear with additional words added. Personal computers still lay in the future, and writing and the sorting had to be done by hand. When some years later Baker Book House asked me to do something similar, including also Latin phrases from the classical Reformed theologians, I immediately declined. That task was undertaken by the renowned Reformed scholar Richard A. Muller from Calvin Seminary. His work is as much a theology as it is a glossary and can be used only with some caution because some of the classical Lutheran phrases are misinterpreted. Mine was strictly a glossary and I soon learned that I was not made to engage in such detailed work.

A Latin Ecclesiastical Glossary for Francis Pieper's Dogmatics[10] found takers in the seminaries of the synods of the former Synodical Conference. Pieper's *Dogmatics* is not as prominent as it once was in the teaching of dogmatic theology and the use for such a glossary has drastically diminished. To the uninitiated, theology set forth in Latin phrases may seem anachronistic, but they serve as the shorthand for the history of theology. Without these phrases theological discussion would become unnecessarily expanded. Knowledge of these Latin phrases expedites theological discussion.

Some professors began their seminary classes with prayer. For some years, I have used the Nicene Creed in Latin, the one to which we are bound by our allegiance to the Lutheran Confessions. Students thus have a direct contact with a document in the words to which they are bound. Through repetition they actually become thoroughly acquainted with the phrases

---

Academicam Explicatur Atque Ex Scriptura S. Eique Innixis Rationibus Theologicis Confirmatur, Editio Auctior Et Emendatior. ed. (Sancti Ludovici: Ex Officina Synodi Missouriensis Lutheranae; Luth. Concordia-Verlag), 1879.

9. Franz Pieper, *Christliche dogmatik*, 3 vols. (St. Louis, MO: Concordia Publishing House, 1917).
10. David P. Scaer, ed. *A Latin Ecclesiastical Glossary: F. Pieper's Christian Dogmatics* (Springfield, IL: Concordia Seminary Print Shop, 1967).

so that may can recite the creed in Latin from memory. With a curtailed dogmatics curriculum, we recite the Latin creed only on occasion.

Seminary students are no longer required to have knowledge of German or Latin, but the glossary has served to keep alive at least for a generation or two those phrases in which Lutheran theology was done. My turning down a request from Baker Book House to provide a more extensive Latin theology dictionary was not only motivated by no desire ever to engage in such an arduous work again—after all, life has only so many years—but by that time I was doing theology more and more from a biblical perspective. *A Latin Ecclesiastical Glossary* was under my copyright since the year 1978. Before 1968, it was not copyrighted. In the last years in Springfield, I learned that without informing me, a person in the business office was working on obtaining a copyright for himself. To avoid facing a sticky issue, I obtained the copyright.

A close personal connection with Jack and Robert Preus did not translate into any seminary or faculty appointments. The old guard in the systematics department—Clarence Spiegel (1896–1990), Fred Kramer, Otto Stahlke (1906–1992), Howard Tepker, Harry Huth (1917–1979) and Eugene Klug (1917–2003)—had remained in place in my first eight years at Springfield.

In December 1975, Kurt Marquart came from Australia to Springfield, and so until my tenth year at the seminary, I remained in age the junior department member. Because of Robert Preus's great respect for Marquart's intellectual abilities and confessional commitment, he emerged as the seminary theologian. His *Anatomy of an Explosion*[11] provided a record of the events leading up to the Seminex walkout of February 1974, though he had no part in these events, and returned to the United States nearly two years after the main events had occurred. His was not an eyewitness account, but a post mortem assessment.

Marquart, Tepker, and Klug were recognized as the LCMS theologians and were the seminary's representatives on the Commission on Theology and Church Relations (CTCR). Disillusioned with events in the Missouri Synod, Harry Huth had left the seminary in the summer of 1969 and was not there for the critical years that followed. When Jack Preus was elected synod president in July, he was not able to reverse his decision to leave the faculty. After Robert Preus's election as seminary president in 1974, Huth

---

11. Kurt E. Marquart, *Anatomy of an Explosion: Missouri in Lutheran Perspective*, Concordia Seminary Monograph Series, no. 3 (Fort Wayne, IN: Concordia Theological Seminary Press, 1977).

returned as professor of the Lutheran Confessions to the seminary, which was by then in Fort Wayne. He died a few years later.

Students from the earlier years stand out in a greater relief than those from later years. John Kieschnick, a school teacher, had the educational expertise to help me with grading for the three years he was on campus. Now a retired pastor from a Houston congregation, he recalls that Dorothy and I attended his marriage to Jack Preus's secretary. And at the 2004 synod convention, he was elected to the CTSFW[12] Board of Regents, of which he was chosen vice chairman.

Grading students is its own science, and later, as academic dean, I learned that each instructor has his own philosophy so that grading can be so complex that it hardly measures a student's academic ability. Poor student grades are often caused by an instructor's less than fully confident teaching approach. Also, in my first class of students were William Hoesman (b. 1940), later president of the Michigan District, and Gerald Kieschnick, later president of the Texas District and now a former Missouri Synod president (from 2003–2012).

Many of those students from those first years have died and perhaps most are retired. At thirty years of age in 1966, I may have been younger than many, perhaps most of the students. For the first twenty years, I had the distinction of being the youngest member of the department of systematic theology. Even in my eighties, it is hard to accept that my comparative youth has disappeared.

John Frederick Johnson was forty-four and had come from a teaching position on the Concordia Milwaukee faculty. Clarence Spiegel was sixty-four. With white hair, he looked every bit the patriarch. An emotional man, he no longer preached in chapel-fearing that he might break down in the morning. He lived well into his nineties and he is remembered with his wife Gertrude (1900–1989) for their graciousness.

Otto Stahlke was on sabbatical in 1966 and had turned down a call to Concordia Edmonton, Canada, a school founded by the LCMS and now no longer belonging to the Lutheran Church—Canada, to teach German. His wife Esther (1906–2006), a distant cousin of mine, was active with the Concordia Historical Institute and the seminary, and passed away in January 2006, a few months before her one-hundredth birthday. Howard Tepker was department chairman.

---

12. Concordia Theological Seminary—Fort Wayne. The abbreviation began as the internet domain name for the seminary and, in recent years, was adopted as the official abbreviation for the institution.

Until the removal of Robert Preus from the seminary presidency in 1989, department meetings were held in the members' homes. Howard and his wife Rosalie (1911–1997) were the most hospitable. Harry Huth, recognized as an authority on the Lutheran Confessions, handled lectures in this area. During these first years the systematics department was the most formidable one.

Jack Preus was amiable and approachable and in this he stood out from other men who held similar high positions. In the years before his election to the synod presidency in July 1969, Jack was making contact with district presidents who had concerns about developments at the St. Louis seminary. He may have been running for office, but only because few would have also been willing to serve. There was no overt campaigning on the campus. Jack was accessible to all, and the spirit of the faculty and students were at an all-time high. In the following years, the faculty would see many changes. Arthur Graf (1912–2004), a brother-in-law of Edgar Krentz, later associated with the Seminex movement, had been teaching evangelism and thought it was time for him to return to a congregation. This family, like others, was split over developments at the St. Louis seminary in the mid-1970s. George Dolak (1903–1968), a New Testament professor had represented the old Slovak synod (now SELC District), died, and his work was taken up by Ken Ballas.

Gerhard Aho (1911–1988) had the same relationship to the National Lutheran Church, the Lutheran synod of Finnish origin that had been in fellowship with Missouri. Aho's father was born in Finland and had translated a Finnish hymn found in *The Lutheran Hymnal*. The elder Aho was a very short man. He received an honorary degree from the seminary. It was the only time I saw him.

Like his father, Gerhard had a literary mind and was, until the time of his death in 1988 by cancer, a well-liked and respected professor of homiletics. Many were the late afternoons I spent in the faculty lounge in Springfield and in his office in Fort Wayne. He had been brought up in the Upper Peninsula of Michigan and learned English as a second language. His first visit to Finland was for him like a journey home, though he had never been there. His death was the loss of a dear friend to me.

Sometime before Jack Preus took over as synod president, pastoral representatives of the National Lutheran Church, as the Finnish Lutheran synod was known, stopped over in Springfield to see Aho on their way to St. Louis to arrange merger into the Missouri Synod with then president Oliver Harms. In the faculty lounge, they expressed their hesitancy about this course of action they were about to take. For years after the amalgamation into the Missouri Synod, pastors of the old Finnish synod arranged annual gatherings.

Taking another course of action, the Slovak synod maintained its separate identity as the SELC District. Amalgamation means the loss of ethnic identity, but forty years later descendants of these ethnically organized churches have at best only an intellectual awareness of their roots. So the question of which is the better route to take is moot.

Erich Heintzen was editor of *The Springfielder*, originally a student paper, which Jack Preus had turned into a theological journal. In 1968–1969, Jack Preus appointed me an associate editor under Heintzen, and upon his retirement I became the editor. Business was conducted for the *Springfielder* by Heintzen coming down to my room to ask for an opinion about an essay, and after I assumed the job, things changed little.

Eugene Klug was the seminary's resident Luther scholar, and his many essays on Luther prompted Heintzen to ask if our colleague was a bit obsessed with him. Since 1969 I have held the editorship, with a gap of five years when I was replaced with colleague Heino Kadai (1931–1999) by then-seminary president David Schmiel.

For the first years, I had written articles which Jack had disseminated in various venues. For this reason I may have been given the editorship. Occasionally someone would write pointing out a typographical error. Among the more noteworthy was Martin Marty. In return, I had the pleasure of showing him that in writing what was purported to be an obituary in the *Christian Century* for the St. Louis faculty, he had gotten the dates wrong by ten years—but who's counting?

The 1974 St. Louis seminary faculty walkout made the continued publication of the time-honored *Concordia Theological Monthly* impossible. A skeleton faculty of four or five could not handle a monthly publication. Since our seminary was moving from Springfield to Fort Wayne, we had the chance of publishing under the name of the *Concordia Theological Quarterly*. For good or for bad, I made this decision unilaterally. The opportunity was too good to miss, and it fit perfectly the name of our seminary, "Concordia Theological Seminary." When they began their journal, the St. Louis seminary took for itself the name *Concordia Journal*.

Martin Naumann was well positioned by brothers and cousins in the ministry in other synods beside Missouri. On one occasion he had brought his cousin Oscar Naumann (1909–1979), president of the Wisconsin Evangelical Lutheran Synod (WELS) (1953–1979), onto the campus. In being introduced to me in an out-of-the-way location, he shied away from me. Not ten years had passed since Wisconsin's break with

Missouri, but it was apparent that the social connections between the synods were damaged beyond repair.

Even though I knew Martin Naumann for less than six years before he died, he remains in my mind as big as life. Beneath his self-deprecating reference as "the Lord's ploughboy" was a sharp mind. Though we were thirty-five years apart in age, we were often in each other's company—he was just plain interesting. Confessional theologians are sometimes called *Zitat Theologen*, citation theologians, for their penchant for quoting others regarded as authorities. Naumann was confessional, but he spun things out of his mind spontaneously without quotations. In the pulpit, seemingly unprepared, he was magnificent. His home was the site of annual parties for which he was able to find a willing and probably unreimbursed caterer. During Springfield days, the faculty and wives had potluck suppers off the campus on the third story of the YWCA. Naumann was the best act in town at these affairs. He died on Good Friday in 1971 in his Luther-like study, hours before he was to preach.

Later seminary presidents opened these occasions to lay and clerical staff persons, and something of the spontaneity and free exchange of ideas among colleagues was lost and never recovered. Sometimes faculty members need to be with one another to hash things out without others looking over their shoulders. Still alive in 1966 and often in attendance at the faculty potlucks was the widow of Walter Albrecht (1885–1961), a professor of dogmatics at Springfield and translator of Pieper's *Christian Dogmatics* in English and author of its index. She was an aunt by marriage to Eugene Klug and would come with Gene and wife Dorothy to the faculty occasions. During the Bolshevik revolution she fled with her parents, who had been part of the Czar Nicholas's court, to the hardships of rugged farm life in western Canada. A woman now of limited means, she carried herself with aristocratic character. In seeing the motion picture *Nicholas and Alexandra*, she was able to point out the anachronisms.

Eugene Klug, who at forty-eight suffered his heart attack in the academic year 1965–1966, lived a disciplined life. Later he would undergo open heart surgery and went on to receive a Doctor of Theology degree from the Free University of Amsterdam. His receiving it at age fifty-four was a testimony to his discipline as a scholar and his overcoming a continuing life-threatening situation. In some British and European universities, writing a dissertation followed by an examination was the chief and in some cases only requirement for the degree. For his degree, Klug compared Luther's and Martin Chemnitz's doctrines of the Scriptures, though on several occasions he intimated that the Dutch faculty did not agree with his conclusions. He did not elaborate. He died at age eighty-four in Fort Wayne in June 2003. I was a pall bearer, and he was buried from St. Paul's in Fort Wayne.

Eugene Klug had been a full-time instructor at University of Illinois at Champaign, sponsored by the LCMS board for college and university work. Following in his uncle Walter Albrecht's footsteps as a professor of dogmatics, he accepted a position in dogmatics at the seminary in 1958, a year before Jack Preus, Howard Tepker and Warren Wilbert (1927–2016) joined the faculty. When he began his work at the seminary, the position at the university was made part time, which allowed him to keep it.

Also a good friend in the first seminary year was Fred Precht (1917–2003), dean of the chapel and director of the seminary chorus. He had led choir tours with Lutheran House speaker Oswald Hoffmann to Europe at a time when travel to Europe was not as common as it is now, and he was well liked by faculty and students. Fridays would find us in the faculty lounge in the darkening evening hours hashing through the events of the past week and our own foibles and those of others.

Fred had come to the seminary around 1940 at age twenty-four and was a legitimate source of how things really were in the past. For example, I learned that when he came to the faculty, the seminary's real authority rested in the faculty and that under Walter Baepler (1893–1958) it passed to the president. He was the source of all kinds of bits of information. Jack Preus had come to the seminary as a New Testament professor during the presidency of Baepler, who had gotten to know him at meetings of the old synodical conference, which was in its twilight hours.

Walter Baepler was followed by George Beto, president of Concordia in Austin,[13] the capital of Texas. A forward thrust took place in 1959 under the administration of Walter Baepler with the calling of Jack Preus, Warren Wilbert, Eugene Klug and Howard Tepker. These men were academically credentialed or were in a position to acquire the degrees necessary for seminary accreditation. The drive toward accreditation begun by Walter Baepler was advanced by George Beto and Jack Preus. The seminary with the reputation for being the practical one was matching its sister institution in St. Louis in academic requirements. Springfield seminary presidents Walter Baepler, George Beto and Jack Preus knew the institution would have to shed its image as the practical seminary to remain viable in a world that was becoming more academic-degree conscious.

---

13. Now known as Concordia University Texas.

St. Louis had received accreditation for its Doctor of Theology (Th.D.) program in 1963 and would upgrade its Bachelor of Divinity (B.D.) degree to a master of divinity degree (M.Div.) about 1972 under its president, John Tietjen. Around 1966, Springfield was accredited by the American Association of Theological Schools, as it was called then, in awarding the B.D. degree. Fort Wayne again followed St. Louis is upgrading B.D. to an M.Div., but required two additional on-campus courses for previous graduates to obtain it. LCMS president Gerald Kieschnick was one of those who took this option. Even at that time, as now, this requirement of two courses seemed unreasonable and was an overreaction from a seminary determined to assert its academic credentials.

At that time, to acquire the Bachelor of Divinity (B.D.) degree, graduating students were required to write a thesis, which is no longer required. Now required, Hebrew was optional and taken by roughly half the student body when I arrived. These theses often approached the caliber and length of Ph.D. theses, and compared with what is now being written in schools of higher education often exceeded them. Full length B.D. theses had been dropped in my St. Louis seminary days and replaced by papers about twenty to thirty pages in length, which were no longer preserved in their library.

The Springfield seminary library cataloged its students' theses. This requirement may have deterred some students from coming to Springfield, but in nearly every case they were examples of academic excellence, sometimes approaching three hundred pages in length. Fourth-year students would choose a topic in the fall term and grudgingly begin their research. By the winter they were entrenched in their work and captivated by what they were discovering. This exercise developed in the students the mindset for research and the ability to bring it into a cohesive, intelligible unity. No longer required for graduation, this may be a case where a step backward in re-instituting the extended thesis would be a step forward.

As president of a school in Austin, the Texas state capitol, George Beto became a player in Texas politics and was appointed by its governor to the parole board. When he came to Springfield, the capital of Illinois, the opportunity to serve in the same capacity did not elude Beto. Appointment required legislative approval preceded by committee hearings.

As a character witness, Beto called on Jack's father, the former governor of Minnesota, J. A. O. Preus I (1883–1961). Beto and Jack had similar political talents and not unexpectedly they became friends. Jack served as the acting academic dean just before Beto returned to Texas and was chosen then as acting president. After leaving Springfield in 1962, Beto headed up the entire Texas penitentiary system. A building bears his name. Beto received an honorary Doctor of Divinity degree from St. Louis seminary at the Wichita Convention in 1989 where I saw him for the last time. Advanced in age and no longer associated with a synod institution, he was largely ignored by the delegates.

By the end of the 1966–1967 school year, Fred Precht had been offered the position of the executive secretary of the newly formed Commission on Worship, Liturgics and Hymnology,[14] matters to which more attention was being given. Jack Preus was determined to keep Fred on the faculty and offered him an assistant for teaching his courses, directing the choir and arranging chapel services. He was then in his mid-fifties and was approaching thirty years of service at the seminary. Fred had ties in Springfield through his wife, who entered state Democrat politics and later had become an assistant to the Republican Speaker of the Illinois House. She was also an executive with the state highway commission.

After he turned down the appointment to the Commission on Worship so that he could remain at Springfield, he did not receive the assistant Jack Preus had promised. So when an offer to head up a fund-raising endeavor for the synod came, he accepted and moved to St. Louis. I greatly missed our long conversations. The last time I saw him was at the 2001 convention at St. Louis; he was in his eighties and had trouble walking. He was as dapper as ever. His eyes lit up when he saw me and memories of past good times could not extinguish the reality that we would not see each other again.

To fill the gap Fred Precht left, Jack Preus contacted Walter C. Buszin (1899–1973), a liturgical and Bach scholar and longtime St. Louis seminary professor. Over two other submissions, Jack followed Buszin's recommendation in choosing Daniel Reuning. Dan was a longtime Bronxville and seminary classmate, friend and pastor of St. Paul's, New Hartford, Connecticut, not far from where I served as pastor in Rockville. So he arrived in Springfield in September 1968, less than one year before Jack became synod president.

One anecdote needs recording. After approval by the Board of Regents, teaching candidates for the seminary need to be examined and found acceptable by the four electors: the resident district president, the synod president, a representative of the regents and a representative of the Board for Higher Education. For my interview the only elector present was Lewis Niemoeller, both as district president and member of the regents.

---

14. Referred to hereafter as the Commission on Worship.

For his interview, Dan Reuning had the privilege of actually having synod president Oliver Harms present. With the difficulties arising at the St. Louis seminary, care had to be exercised in adding new seminary faculty members, and at least for Harms, liturgics was a sensitive area where caution had to be exercised.

Since there were accounts going around that some St. Louis professors had doubts about the historical character of Genesis 1–3, Harms asked Dan about his position on these chapters. According to folklore, he responded that he accepted the synod's position without detailing what that was. As the synod president, Harms would be supposed to know what that position was, and so this issue was not pursued.

Within a little over a year, Jack would replace Harms as synod president. In that interview two things came to light. Harms's attendance at an interview for one called to teach liturgics may have indicated an underlying distrust of anyone having an interest in worship. For some, "Romanism" is the ultimate evil. Secondly, Dan's reference to the synod's position extends the discussion on what this was. The interviews with the St. Louis faculty in the 1970s uncovered that these chapters in Genesis were seen as myths conveying theological truths.

I knew Reuning since he enrolled in what was our junior year of high school at Concordia Bronxville. In the first year of the junior college he organized the Gloria Dei Choir, which sang at the Village Lutheran Church, the college church, across the street from the main college campus. At eighteen years of age he was directing the most advanced repertoire, including works by Handel. In succeeding Precht, he took charge of the seminary choruses.

Most memorable was presentation of a work by Heinrich Schütz (1585–1672) in the rotunda of the Illinois state capitol in which, by placing sections of the choir at various levels, he was able to attain a variety of tone qualities. Daily chapel services in those years took place either at Immanuel on the eastern edge of the campus or in the chapel located on the second floor of the old classroom building. Under Reuning's deanship, a monthly communion service began to be conducted in the field house to accommodate the campus community. Leavened loaves of bread prepared by students' wives replaced the traditional wafers.

During one service, Huth and Klug were seen leaving the service for a reason that now escapes me, but probably because of their objections to a communion service on campus. Campus communion services presented for some, and in some cases still do, a problem for an older Missouri Synod theology, which sees the congregation as the only legitimate expression of the church. Now such services are common at synod colleges and church conventions. When Dean Wenthe became seminary president in 1996, monthly services gave way to weekly ones with the custom in place of having parish pastors conduct them. Now faculty and staff members also preside, and days on which major festivals fall are also celebrated with the Divine Service.

Liturgical innovation had begun in those days, and each student was required to write a liturgy, a practice from which Reuning later distanced himself. With a regular group of worshipers in place every day of the week, seminaries and colleges were ideal for introducing new liturgies and hymns.

The *Worship Supplement*,[15] a red, soft-back hymnal, had a version of the Apostles' Creed which substituted "he went to the dead" for "he descended to hell." This change like others was exacerbated by the changing conditions and theological turmoil at the St. Louis seminary. When this version of the creed was being used, a group of students, one of whom was Klemet Preus (1950–2014), clustered together, and in place of the offending word "dead" said a loud "hell."

When the seminary moved to Fort Wayne, Reuning was responsible for placing the baptismal font at the rear of the chapel and reorienting the pews under the organ balcony. Dan Reuning remained a prominent figure in seminary life until he retired in 1999.

In the spring of 1969, Jack Preus urged me to apply for the AAL John W. Behnken Postdoctoral Fellowship. When I received it, I had forgotten that I had applied for it and had to make plans to go Heidelberg for the summer semester. Dorothy was left at home with the five children, who came down with the measles just after I left. Peter Brunner (1900–1981), the great confessional scholar, was no longer teaching, but was available for conversation, as was Edmund Schlink (1903–1984) who was still lecturing. My residence in Heidelberg was in a hotel overlooking the Church of the Holy Ghost at the cost of the equivalency of two dollars a day.

One day in a lecture hall with about five hundred students, he spotted me and introduced me. The radicalization which had taken over American universities had come to Germany in a more extreme form. In the seminars, students would dominate the first two sessions in choosing which topics were to be discussed for the semester. These debates were conducted by the students standing on the desks, and in some cases it seemed as open though warfare would break out in the seminar rooms.

---

15. Lutheran Church—Missouri Synod, *Worship Supplement* (St. Louis, MO: Concordia Publishing House, 1969).

One day in waiting long for a trolley car, I found out that the students had sat down on the turnstile downtown, and so I went by foot to the main train station. Germany in 1969 was not the one I had left seven years before in 1962. No longer did the professors choose their successors, but lower rank faculty members and sometimes students were enfranchised. Something similar was instituted in St. Louis, so that a representative body consisting of nearly all engaged in seminary life had a voice in how that institution was run.

There are a few footnotes to the summer of 1969. Robert Preus was using his sabbatical year to pursue a second doctor's degree, one in theology at the University of Strasbourg, located on the Rhein. It was not far from Heidelberg by train. My visit was postponed by one week, since Preus was taking his examination on the dissertation, later published as the second volume of *The Theology of Post-Reformation Lutheranism*.[16] He was a very prolific writer and had the manuscript in hand before leaving for France with his family. During one of our back and forth visits between Springfield and St. Louis, where he taught on the seminary faculty, I had mentioned to him that he should submit the manuscript as a dissertation. This is what he did.

Matters at the university were expedited by his friend John Warwick Montgomery, who, having received a university doctor's degree from the same institution, had become a fixture there. He had given the Preus family the use of his apartment. At this writing, Montgomery still conducts his week-long apologetic seminars in Strasbourg. Since Preus had passed the examination, the festive weekend was made more so by the confirmation of his son Peter (b. 1955), now a retired LCMS pastor. The sermon and service were in French and a reception followed in the Preus apartment.

Descendants of Robert and Jack's father, J. A. O. Preus I and his brothers, constituted a remarkable group of churchmen, scholars and entrepreneurs. In spite of ideological differences, they understood themselves to be one family. A letter by a renowned professor in apologetics written to Concordia Publishing House and frequently appearing in *Christian News* speaks of that summer. "I thought back to a time in Strasbourg years before, when Robert and I invited a visiting Missouri Synod professor to dine with us at a fine restaurant, and the professor arrived in the dress of a lumberjack and displayed all the characters of the typical 'ugly American.'" This professor is not identified and I take solace that I

---

16. Robert D. Preus, *The Theology of Post-Reformation Lutheranism* (St. Louis, MO: Concordia Publishing House, 1970–72).

am not the culprit, since coming from New York I am not sure how lumberjacks dress, but their hazardous occupation deserves our respect. For the record, a classic photograph of Robert Preus is one of him dressed in a Pendleton plaid shirt, wearing boots, reading the second chapter of Luke in his home on Gunflint Lake on the Minnesota-Ontario boarder.

Also present that weekend was Dan Preus (b. 1949), later synod vice president, for his brother Peter's confirmation. Michael Rogness, a son of one of Robert Preus's cousins, then studying in Strasbourg, was also there. Dan Preus invited me to join him and two students from the theological school in Oberursel, where he was studying to accompany them in his Volkswagen to Norway. In Oslo we stayed with a physician and his wife, each of whom was a cousin to Jack and Robert Preus. The water in Oslo fjord was warm, and I and a German student, long since a pastor, swam out close to the shipping lanes, a frightening experience.

On the day I was checking out of the hotel for good at the end of the summer semester, a letter dated July 1, 1969, came from Jack saying that I had been promoted to associate professor. It was a godsend, a kind of insurance policy, since the synod was headed for what some may regard as its most tumultuous times. Dorothy, back in Springfield, had received a phone call from Jack with the same news.

Jack was under no obligation to do this, especially since after three years only a renewal of the contract was customary. In retrospect, his being elected synod president would have looked like a sure thing to others, but to him it did not. If this happened, he would be content to teach the New Testament and courses in Greek and Latin at a synodical college. Since I had worked on any number of projects for him, he may have wanted to secure my position on the faculty. Professors without tenure can be removed when another administration takes over. Seminary catalogs beginning with the one for 1970–1971 listed me as an associate professor.

At the end of July, and lasting much of August, Dorothy joined me for a three-week tour through Germany, France, Switzerland and Italy. We were in Florence when the American astronauts landed on the moon. We escaped the hot Italian summer that day by drinking gin and tonics in an air-conditioned lounge of an upscale hotel.

Jack Preus was elected synod president in July 1969. News of this came to me in a phone call from Wilhelm Oesch. The other news was that the synod had declared fellowship with the American Lutheran Church, an alliance that was doomed from the start, and that women would be full participants in congregational voter's assemblies. With Jack in St. Louis, the board appointed Lorman Petersen, then academic dean, as acting president.

Fred Kramer, translator of Martin Chemnitz's four-volume *Examination of the Council of Trent*,[17] had been academic dean until the end of the 1966–1967 academic year and honored with a pair of binoculars at the graduation ceremonies. Somehow God's faithful servants are not appropriately recognized. Kramer held that position along with that of registrar. Together with a secretary he was virtually the entire administration. Until the seminary moved from Springfield, he remained an active professor in the department of systematic theology.

---

17. Martin Chemnitz, *Examination of the Council of Trent*, trans. Fred Kramer, Chemnitz's Works, 4 vols. (St. Louis, MO: Concordia Publishing House, 2007).

Excursus IV

COLLEGE COURSES AT THE UNIVERSITY OF ILLINOIS — CHAMPAIGN

Upon arrival at the seminary in the summer of 1966, a part-time position at the University of Illinois was offered to me, probably because the other members of the department of systematic theology were twenty to thirty years older than I was. Going to Champaign on Monday afternoons was a way of keeping my head in the real world, if it is really so that seminaries are not part of the real world. During the years 1966 to 1976, life on college campuses went through drastic changes. In these years the peace movement that rose in reaction to the Vietnam War and the civil rights movement changed the world we knew.

At thirty years of age, the life on a college campus in 1966 was one I knew and could still feel a part of—jackets, ties, white shirts. Winter semesters began after Labor Day and ended at the end of January. Spring semesters ran from February to the end of May or even early June. After the riots which afflicted many schools, this university and others adjusted the fall semester so that it ended before Christmas, and so the spring term concluded at the end of April or early May, that time of the year when campus riots took place. Students preparing for final exams are less likely to participate in protest movements.

During the riots, the commons of the Champaign campus, which was modeled after the colonial Williamsburg, Virginia, restoration, was trashed. Bulls' blood was poured over the card catalogs. One night as I was preparing to drive back to Springfield, students surrounded by armed soldiers blocked the road, which made passage out of Champaign difficult. It would almost seem that in this environment, religion courses would go by the wayside. After the dust subsided, my classrooms could not contain the students desiring to take the course. Inexplicably a conservative mind had taken hold of students that could be seen in Evangelicalism, a back-to-the-Bible movement, which would become a formidable force in the Missouri Synod with its conservative theology.

Some students in colleges and seminaries identified themselves as charismatics, and so the synod, like the rest of American Christianity, had to address a new situation. A ten-minute break was allowed in the two-hour evening course. At times, a ten-minute break during evening religion classes at the University of Illinois often turned into a half hour of discussion with refreshments provided by the wife of Ray Eissfeldt (1912–2000), the campus pastor.

Lutherans were enrolled in the course, but most were Evangelicals; some atheists and occasionally Jewish students were in the mix. Eissfeldt was most cooperative in providing classroom space at the University Lutheran Chapel and recruiting students from his flock for this university credit course. His Christmas letters showed a pride in his attachment to the St. Louis seminary and his support for its president, John Tietjen. Eissfeldt was as "Missouri" as anyone was, but fissures later to form cracks in the body politic were beginning to show.

We were good friends, and he may have been instrumental in my being invited to make a ten-minute presentation at the Central Illinois District pastoral conference in the Champaign area some time before 1974. My assignment was addressing relations among Lutheran synods, an issue that was not as decisive as the historical-critical method as the major reason for differences among the synods. This was not what the convention planning committee wanted the pastors to hear, but with events developing at the St. Louis seminary, this was a message the church had to hear.

Present as the major speaker at that same gathering was St. Louis Old Testament professor Alfred von Rohr Sauer, a man with deep roots going back into the founding of the Wisconsin Synod. He came under the influence of the younger and more dashing Norman Habel (b. 1932), who was the lead Old Testament scholar at St. Louis for the new theology. After it was over, one student, who was present, called to my attention that Sauer constantly and frequently referred to me as "Mr. Scaer." Sauer had a doctor's degree from the University of Bonn, but in spite of prestigious credentials was not a particularly striking lecturer or scholar. By the 1970s he was walking in Scottish attire around the campus with an oversized shillelagh. He had adopted a different persona from the one I knew in my seminary days.

Weekly Monday trips to Champaign from our home on West View Drive were made in a 1962 Oldsmobile purchased expressly for this purpose. Interstate 72 was not even a twinkle in the eye of federal highway planners, and so the trip, a little less than two hours, was made northeast up US 54 to Clinton and then to Illinois State Route 10 east to Champaign. WLS out of Chicago provided the music to accompany an occasional cigar. For some years, my passengers included my colleagues John Frederick Johnson and Richard Schultz during the year he was elected seminary president. Both were taking graduate courses, but did not finish the programs for a doctor's degree. Robert Schaibley (b. 1946), now retired from the ministry, and John Sippola (1923–1982), later son-in-law to Johnson, who was a scion of pastors in the National (Finnish) Lutheran Church and is now a retired ELCA minister, were at times fellow travelers.

In my first years, Gerhard Aho was in residence for his Ph.D. in Champaign, and I would meet him for supper. Sometimes it was supper with several of the Evangelical students in the class. Conversations sooner or later came to infant baptism, a doctrine that stood at complete odds with the decision theology of Evangelicalism, which called upon hearers to accept Jesus as their personal Savior.

Each week before classes began, I had supper with some of the students, who nearly in all cases were non-Lutheran. Jewish students asked me for letters of recommendation. Richard Olderman, a Jewish student from New York, was signed on as an instructor at Columbia University. There was something closer to reality in the university classes than in a seminary class where the faith is passed on to those who already have the faith.

As my years came closer to forty, returning home near midnight and then having to get up early the next morning made the trip to Champaign more of a burden, but these Monday nights opened a window into a life which was decisively different from the one at the seminary. What happened at Champaign, Illinois, from the fall of 1972 to the fall of the next year might have gone unnoticed, were it not for a file of letters, articles and reports recording the events. By themselves these events were not all that significant, but just as I had been removed from teaching the regular dogmatic courses at the seminary, a full-court press was underway to remove me from my part-time teaching position at the University of Illinois that I had undertaken in September 1966.

In the 1972–1973 academic year, a double-headed thrust came to remove me from these courses. One came from the council of the University Lutheran Chapel and the other by the university whose newly formed department of religious studies argued that the survey biblical courses sponsored by church bodies including the LCMS through its Central Illinois District were not appropriate. Financial support for the Lutheran courses was supplied by the district missions commission, which had taken over from the now-defunct LCMS Commission on Colleges and Universities. It was argued that courses sponsored through the religious foundation were so similar to those offered by the university's new department of Religious Studies that they would no longer be needed.

Just one year prior to the disruptions at the St. Louis seminary that would lead to that faculty's walkout in 1974, attempts to remove me as an instructor at the University of Illinois arose from the chapel board. The allegations made against me were totally unfounded and false, but also hurtful. It happened this way.

In the fall of 1972, Pastor Ray Eissfeldt had received written notice from the College of Liberal Arts and Sciences that Religious Foundations were to submit course outlines along with the credentials of the instructors, but he had kept this information from me. He also began proceedings with the council of the chapel to discredit me as an instructor.

On Monday, November 20, 1972, at five-thirty PM, Steven Thomas informed me that unfavorable allegations about me had been brought to the attention of the church council at the two previous meetings, Sunday, October 15, and Sunday, November 19.[1] These allegations were introduced by Arden Grotelueschen (1940–1995),[2] who took the lead in the discussion. It was alleged that I did not teach the Old Testament from the viewpoint of the New Testament[3] and that my behavior was unacceptable. This was supported by only one incident, in which a girl broke down and cried. Deborah Elliott, the girl in question, had heard me say that God had chosen Israel, and she had come to the realization that God had chosen her, the Lutheran view. She realized that she had not chosen God, the Arminian view. Deborah had identified herself as "a non-denominational

---

1. Official minutes indicate that the meeting was conducted on Sunday, November 18 at 4 PM, but reference to a calendar will probably show it was the nineteenth. My notes indicate that I was informed of its proceedings on Monday, November 20, which date I used in future correspondence and notes.
2. Grotelueschen was son-in-law to Rudolf Haak, who had replaced Lewis Niemoeller in 1970 as Central Illinois District president one year after J. A. O. Preus left the presidency of the Springfield seminary to be elected LCMS president. Haak, who was favorable to developments in the St. Louis faculty under Tietjen, defined the historical-critical method as praying and then grammatically reading the Bible. This definition was the classical position of the synod and did not even come close to methods then being employed by the St. Louis seminary faculty. Haak was more naïve than he was deceptive, but he was in the pocket of those supporting new directions in the synod.
3. This is the proper critical way, but at no time did Grotelueschen have any real knowledge about what I was saying in class, though nothing prevented him from attending at any time.

Christian" and remained a member of the class throughout the fall term and enrolled for the spring semester course in the New Testament.

As for the church council, the lead witness on what happened in class was not present at the council meeting and could not be counted on to provide the testimony the members needed to remove me. Grotelueschen, associate professor of educational psychology at University of Illinois and a non-student member of the church and vice chairman of its church council, informed fellow council members that his father-in-law, Central District president Rudy Haak (1919–1999), had told him that I was always a troublemaker. Grotelueschen also referenced Martin Maehr (1933–2017),[4] who said I showed the same negative patterns as a seminary student.

That same day, November 20, 1972, about one hour after hearing about the council's actions, assistant pastor Joel Nickel, listed as "Pastor Joel" in the council minutes, appeared at seven o'clock PM class. His appearance in my class gave credence that the report the student had given me was accurate. Nickel was unaware that I knew the reason for his presence, since the council had not officially contacted me about their discussions. I welcomed and introduced Nickel to the class and asked him to join us for the usual social hour at eight o'clock PM midway through the two-hour class. He took copious notes.

At approximately nine o'clock PM, when I had put my coat and gloves on and was ready to leave the building, Nickel asked me to come into Eissfeldt's study. His tone, that of superior to an inferior, indicated that this was a not an invitation for a friendly chat. Since Eissfeldt, Nickel and Grotelueschen had not told me the reason for the conversation, I did not have their advantage of being prepared for their agenda.

Eissfeldt sat at his desk, I in the chair nearest the closed door and Nickel in the chair against the wall opposite the door. Nickel led off the conversation and was the lead interrogator for the next hour. In later reading the minutes of the November 20, 1972, minutes, I learned that he and Eissfeldt had been designated as my interrogators. Matters of concern were not having enough mimeograph materials for the students. What happened was that the duplicator broke down and the secretary was delayed in getting the work done.

---

4. Maehr, a member of the LCMS ministerium and formerly a professor at Concordia Senior College, was then professor of educational psychology at the University of Illinois. He had joined the university Lutheran church in January 1973.

What came as a surprise was Eissfeldt asking if it would be alright with me if Nickel taught the course in ecumenical theology that was offered under the title Church and World Relations with other instructors from the other religious foundations. Eissfeldt had arranged for this course to be offered on Tuesdays and not Mondays, and so he said I could not be there. He also said he had checked out Nickel's participation in the course with Sister Agnes Cunningham, who he said had devised the course. This was not true at all and I reminded Eissfeldt that I had devised the course for the 1968–69 academic year to be taught by Lutheran, Episcopal, Baptist and Jewish clergy, and that I was the instructor of record. For the first two years the courses attracted students, but by the spring semester of 1971–72 only two or three students enrolled. Conducted at first on Monday afternoons, Mr. Bright, the Baptist, and Father McElroy, the Episcopalian were frequently absent.

Often Father Andres, the Roman Catholic, and I were the only instructors present. In April or May 1972, I wrote a letter to the dean of the College of Arts and Sciences that, with a deteriorating appeal, the course should no longer be taught. On the basis of the letter, Eissfeldt claimed that I was responsible for the course's failure. Nothing could be further from the truth. I had originated and organized the course and attended all sessions.

My letter describing a failed situation was put forth as self-incriminating evidence. Nickel said that teaching was a new area of ministry for him for which he was ready. At the time Eissfeldt had already made arrangements with the College of Liberal Arts for Nickel to teach the course and was waiting for university approval.

Reports of my classroom demeanor were brought into that evening's conversation, even though Eissfeldt and Nickel never mentioned that they had already discussed this at the November council meeting and maybe also at the September or October ones. Then they brought up the matter of Deborah Elliott, who was overcome with emotion when she realized that God has chosen her.

This was the last salvo that evening, and both Eissfeldt and Nickel conceded they had no direct reports of anything wrong in my classes, and Eissfeldt went on to say that he had acted on second-, third- and fourth-hand reports. How a fourth-hand report is distinguished from a third-hand one is beyond me. Had he approached me directly, he could have avoided bringing a matter to the church council, for which he admitted there were no substantive reports. Nickel said he found nothing wrong with my teaching, but said that it was his right to contact students directly.

Nickel had approached Steven Ackerman. He probably did not know that Ackerman had requested from me a letter of recommendation for a position on *The Washington Post*. In approaching Ackerman, Nickel had gone to the wrong person. Ackerman, who was Jewish, apparently was not only not overly offended at my teaching, but liked it! Nickel would have been welcome to come to as many of my classes as he wanted, but he never came again.

Eissfeldt and Nickel informed me that there might be difficulties in continuing to offer courses at the University, a strange comment indeed, since Eissfeldt had already arranged for Nickel to teach the course in ecumenical theology. Eissfeldt also knew at the meeting but never told me that the university Board of Trustees had overruled the Faculty and Dean of the College of Liberal Arts and Science in its denying credit to the religious foundation courses and that such courses would continue to offer academic credit.

When I mentioned the high attendance in support of my continuing the biblical survey courses, Grotelueschen responded that this was because of the Jesus movement, but this did not account for the Jewish students in the class. I could have mentioned that my course attracted more students than those offered by other foundations, but I did not. Events on that Monday happened in the space of four and a half hours, from five-thirty PM, when I was informed of what was going to happen, until the end of the meeting, ten o'clock PM.

I decided to look for someone to advise me. In looking for a counselor, I could not look to my colleagues for advice. Seminary president Richard J. Schulz had received an honorary degree of Doctor of Divinity from Tietjen at the St. Louis seminary's commencement exercises in 1970, and academic dean Lorman Petersen, in being denied the seminary presidency by Jack Preus, found an ally in Tietjen. Associate academic dean John Frederick Johnson, who had driven thousands of miles with me over many years from Springfield to Champaign and whom I counted as a friend, had cast his lot with Schulz and Petersen in opposing Preus.

At this time, approximately one-third of the Springfield seminary faculty was favorable to developments on the St. Louis faculty under Tietjen and another third were neutral. A sympathetic colleague with the wisdom to give sage advice was hard to come by.

It is likely that a student at the University Lutheran Church had informed E. J. Otto (1914–1987), pastor of Our Redeemer in Quincy, Illinois, of my situation at the university. After the 1973 convention, he assumed the chair of the St. Louis seminary board, he would play a crucial role in dealing with the seminary walkout in February 1974, but in the fall of 1972, differences on the St. Louis board had not surfaced. Over the next few years, during my negotiations with the University of Illinois's dean of the College of Arts and Sciences and conversations with Eissfeldt and the church council, I was often on the phone with Otto on how to proceed. Half the time I was in a frenzy as to how to proceed, and in each of our phone conversations, he was able to grasp the problem and provide a solution.[5]

On December 17, 1972, the church council received a report from Eissfeldt and Nickel that I was innocent of all allegations. Eissfeldt did not inform the council that, for financial reasons, he had requested the District Board of Directors that I be relieved of my position and be replaced by Nickel. Not once did Eissfeldt tell me of any of his correspondence or meetings with the district board, its mission commission and its staff. Grotelueschen was not present at the December meeting, and at that time the council had not received word that from the College of Liberal Arts certifying Nickel as an instructor. At the time I was the only one recognized by the university to teach it.

There were other improprieties. The district mission commission, which had the responsibility for college and university work, did not have prior knowledge or authorize the November 20 meeting with me, but it is not improbable that Grotelueschen and his father-in-law, district president Haak, were in consultation previous to the October meeting. After the November 20, 1972, meeting, it was evident that attempts by Eissfeldt, Nickel and Grotelueschen to remove me from teaching the biblical survey courses would continue, and I began making contact with the district and its officials, not knowing which of them might have been involved in discussions with Eissfeldt and Grotelueschen.

In the 1972–1973 school year, the fall semester terminated at the end of January. Student attendance at the December chapel council was predictably low. Morale among the students at the campus Lutheran chapel was low and the annual Christmas caroling party had to be cancelled for lack of participation. At the same time, the seminary academic dean, Lor-

---

5. James C. Burkee references his interview with a supposed conservative laymen who said that E. J. Otto was myopic, autocratic and "had no use of laymen." *Power, Politics, and the Missouri Synod* (Minneapolis, MN: Fortress Press, 2011), 147, 229, n. 305. Others, including members of his congregation, saw things differently. Without our frequent phone conversations, I would have lost my position in Champaign. Though a Tietjen supporter, Eissefeldt stayed with the Missouri Synod.

man Petersen, told me that my article "The Law-Gospel Debate"[6] in the December 1972 *The Springfielder* was disturbing, the same word used of me in the Champaign discussions. Grotelueschen's father-in-law, Rudy Haak, as district president, was a member of the seminary board, and it is difficult to rule out collusion with the seminary's academic dean, Lorman Petersen.

In a February 18, 1972, letter to the district missions commission, in care of Kenneth Markworth,[7] I reported of my work as an instructor for the Survey of the New Testament course, in which twenty-six students were enrolled.[8] Two of these students were applying to the seminary. The outreach accomplished in this course might well be the envy of what later LCMS campus programs were able to do. My letter also explained the situation of Nickel teaching the course in ecumenical theology.

On February 5, the first day of the spring semester, I learned that the chapel council was endorsing certain persons for synod-wide positions. A few weeks later E. J. Otto had received and shared with me a note from a student with the same information. Raymond Eissfeldt claimed to have received an official word from "the District" that Central Illinois District churches were to nominate Oswald Hoffmann and R. Haak for the offices of president and vice president respectively of the LCMS. Such a claim was made before the church council of the University Lutheran Church in Champaign at a regular meeting in January 1973. The Church Council followed such action.[9]

Jack Preus, who had been elected synod president in July 1969, was facing his first reelection, and Oswald Hoffmann, Lutheran Hour Speaker, was the favored opponent. Rudolph Haak was never a serious contender, but by putting forth his name, Preus would be deprived of an additional nomination as a candidate. On February 20, 1972, E. J. Otto presented the letter to the district mission commission which contacted the chapel

---

6. David P. Scaer, "Law Gospel Debate in the Missouri Synod," *Springfielder* 36, no. 3 (December 1972): 156–71, http://www.ctsfw.net/media/pdfs/scaerlawgospeldebate.pdf.
7. Markworth at the time was on the board of directors of ELIM (Evangelical Lutherans in Mission), which would be the core for the AELC (the Association of Evangelical Lutheran Churches), the catalyst in the formation of the ELCA.
8. LCMS-6; ALC 3; Lutheran-1; Methodist, Episcopal, Congregational, Roman Catholic, Christian each had 1; Disciples of Christ and Catholic each had 2. Three said they had no religion and four did not express a religious preference.
9. Letter from E. J. Otto to Ken Markworth (February 22, 1973).

council. This evoked an immediate response from the chapel council's president and vice president, students Dennis P. Cluver and Arthur R. Traugott. In a letter dated February 26, 1973, they claimed that the pastors, Eissfeldt and Nickel, had impressed upon the council its responsibility in making nominations and that, "At no time did Rev. Eissfeldt instruct council members how to vote." Added was that no one "felt that Rev. Eissfeldt was influencing our choice of synodical nominations."

What they felt Eissfeldt had done and what he had actually done are two different issues. Sent along with the letter was a summary of the half-hour council meeting in which Hoffmann and Haak were nominated. The letter to the district commission was not sent by the council but by two of its officers and did not deny that Eissfeldt or Nickel and not the students had brought up the names of the two nominees. For several reasons, it is unlikely that the signatories composed this letter. The one student did not demonstrate the skills needed for such a tightly organized letter, and the other had just joined the church. Striking is the feigned shock of the third paragraph that Otto had not consulted the council with such allegations. "It would seem to us, that in the spirit of Christian love and brotherhood this should have been brought to our attention first." Of course the council had not brought up matters before its November 1972 meeting.

From 1966 until the end of the 1972 fall term, I had been on the most cordial terms with Pastor Eissfeldt and his wife, who was the chapel secretary and an important part of that ministry. I was often in their home, which was attached to the chapel, and several times for dinner. After my vindication, if that is what it was, Eissfeldt and Nickel were as scarce as hen's teeth on those December Monday evenings when I was there to teach the classes. After this episode I expected that the 1972–1973 academic year would be my last at the University of Illinois, but it was not.

In the spring term of 1973, Nickel participated in the ecumenical theology course. Nine were enrolled with seven showing up for the first class on February 6. By the next week, February 13, seven had dropped the class, leaving only two enrolled, and only one was attending. A telephone call campaign was begun to induce the dropouts to return. Teaching the course were an Episcopalian and Spanish-speaking priest and Nickel, who at the start of the course had not been credentialed. Rabbi Feld and Mr. Bright, the Baptist participant with whom I had worked, no longer had interest in the course. All these things I had explained in a letter in the spring of 1972 that was brought up as evidence that I was undermining the course.

With Eissfeldt's wife going through the last stages of cancer, things at the chapel in the spring of 1973 were depressing. Nickel was not seen around the chapel and was questioning his role there and was preparing a stinging letter to E. J. Otto. Limited funds required conserving electricity by turning off lights. This added to the gloom. Maehr, who cooperated with Grotelueschen in accusing me, but who at the time was not a member of the church, finally joined.

In spite of budgetary concerns, funds were found for the out-of-town guest speakers who came for Saturday lectures and Sunday Bible classes. Carl Graesser, who a year later joined in the St. Louis seminary faculty walkout, lectured on February 18. Others scheduled were David Schuller (who would soon become an executive with the Association of Theological Schools), and Walter Wolbrecht, assistant to synod president Oliver Harms, and Jack Preus (who would soon begin a short stint as president of the Lutheran School of Theology in Chicago). While their names appeared in the church bulletins with the appropriate titles as "Dr." or "Prof." mine appeared simply as "Scaer."

Grotelueschen and Maehr had prepared a letter dated October 10, 1972, to all synod school principals, questioning LCMS president J. A. O. Preus's investigation of the St. Louis seminary. As of February 6, 1973, the church secretary had not mailed the letter but was preparing to do so. During the 1973 spring term, Eissfeldt put his arm around me and said we have to have dinner—all this after trying to maneuver me out of my position. While Eissfeldt was expressing concern for me, a student shared with me that Eissfeldt told him I was a "legalist."

After the College of Liberal Arts and Science had established its Department of Religious Studies, they wanted to end the arrangement in having the Religious Foundations offer courses for university credit.[10] In March 19, 1973, Assistant Academic Dean W. R. Feyerharm wrote me a letter that the Old and New Testament survey courses had been denied credit for the next academic year. In connection with this decision I was interviewed by *The Daily Illini*.[11] According to the article, the university board of trustees at its May 1972 meeting had overruled the previous college administration request to stop giving credit to the Religious Founda-

---

10. Credit Courses in Religion were sponsored by the Institute of Religious Studies, consisting of the Baptist Foundation, B'Nai B'Rith Hillel Foundation, Episcopal Foundation, Lutheran Student Foundation and the University Lutheran Chapel and Student Center. The ecumenical course was listed in 1971 in the institute's folder as Church World Relations (A Survey Course in Comparative American Religion) (90584).
11. Dana Jones, "Some Religious Courses Denied UI Credit Status," *The Daily Illini* (March 24, 1973), 3.

tion courses, but had allowed the college to set guidelines and conduct staff review. Failing to meet this standard, the religious foundation courses would be denied credit.

In the fall of 1972, Eissfeldt had heard of this decision and received the guidelines but had not shared them with me. When I received the March 1973 letter from the assistant dean, ten months had already passed and with little more than two months remaining in the term, there was only so much I could do. With guidelines in hand, Eissfeldt had proceeded to get Nickel credentialed as an instructor in my place for the course in ecumenical theology.

Upon receiving the guidelines, I went directly to the dean of the College of Liberal Arts and Sciences, Robert W. Rogers, with syllabi and a *curriculum vitae*. When news surfaced that the Lutheran foundation biblical survey courses would no longer be allowed credit, letters from alumni were sent to the university Board of Trustees chairman Earl Hughes. When Eissfeldt and Nickel heard that the district board was going to petition the university board of directors, they wrote a letter on April 3, 1973, to the district board urging them not to do it.

Since Eissfeldt had not be able use his church council to remove me for poor class performance or financial reasons, he supported the college intentions to deny the courses credit, as his letter to the district board shows. However, a letter was sent by the district and seems to have been a major factor in having the university board overrule the college's decision to cancel the religious foundation courses. LCMS Lutherans constitute a significant percentage of Illinois residents.

The College of Liberal Arts acquiesced to the trustees' decision. The courses could continue,[12] but under different names. Syllabi and instructors had to meet university guidelines. The biblical survey courses under the names of Old and New Testament were last given in the 1973–1974 academic year and were replaced by "Luth 032 and Luth 033 Biblical Interpretations according to the Perspectives of the Lutheran Confessions," one course offering two credits in each semester. Their being listed in the university Time Table gave notice of the courses to all students. They were offered in connection with the School of Humanities within the College of Arts and Sciences.

---

12. Letter of May 7, 1973, from Earl M. Hughes, President of the Board of Trustees of the University of Illinois to Mr. William Ford (May 7, 1973; d. 2016) and letter from Dean Robert W. Rogers to Mr. William Ford (June 8, 1973).

Along with the formal correspondence with Board of Trustees from myself and district boards, I had a number of informal meetings with dean Robert W. Rogers and assistant dean William Feyerharm. Several times I arrived at Champaign early on Monday afternoons and went unannounced to the office of Dean Rogers, who received me most cordially. This was also true of Dean Feyerharm. They were hardly antagonistic to me or my program. My meetings with the two deans were a factor in their continuing to let me teach. I do not know with whom Eissfeldt had meetings in arranging to have Nickel teach, but his name never came up in our conversations.

Our courses with titles that included these words, "According to the Perspectives of the Lutheran Confessions," did not have the drawing power of the biblical survey courses, which simply were listed as Old and New Testaments. While the phrase "Lutheran Confessions" has a definite meaning for Lutherans, it is hardly recognizable to others and was an obstacle to student enrollment.

In the end, Eissfeldt and the college won their case. My moving to Fort Wayne was one of several reasons, maybe divine ones, for stopping the program. One item not included in the documentation may have also been a factor in discontinuing these courses. Sometime between 1970 and 1972 William "Bill" Schoedel's courses "Ancient Israel and New Testament" were seen as overlapping mine and were put forward as a reason for cancelling them. In one of my meetings with Dean Rogers, Bill Schoedel was present. Our meeting in the spring of 1973 was not significant and I continued to teach there until 1976.

In his May 5, 1976 letter to Arthur Kuehnert, who had replaced Haak as district president, Eissfeldt reported that the church council recommended cancelling the Lutheran courses. Among the reasons were declining enrollment, the university's restrictions and my move to Fort Wayne. Champaign was less than one hundred miles from Springfield, but Fort Wayne was at least two hundred miles. A round trip of four hundred miles every week was a less affordable expenditure in time, and I lost the spirit for fighting for a cause in which I could no longer be involved. A copy of the letter was sent to me, but Eissfeldt, as in the past, had not discussed any of this with me. Signed by "Dr. Esther Portnoy, clerk," the letter includes the following: "We are truly grateful to Dr. Scaer, and to the CID for the financial support of the credit course for many years, making possible an extended outreach to both Lutheran and non-Lutheran students concerned with Biblical interpretation."

Today campus-based churches probably no longer have the relationship that Eugene Klug (1950–1966) and I (1966–1976) had at the University of

Illinois. We have lost a foothold into the lives of university students which will likely not soon be recovered. In my last trip returning from Champaign to Springfield in the 1962 Oldsmobile, I mused over the Mondays in those ten years I had spent there. So far as teaching, they were probably the best, because the biblical message had to be presented not only to dyed-in-the-wool Lutherans and other Christians but to non-Christians.

Eissfeldt's world changed with the February 1974 St. Louis faculty walkout. His wife died before I ended my tenure, and he later remarried. On the few occasions we saw each other, we reminisced about good times in Champaign. Things were successful for both of us there. He was not a mean man, but the only explanation for his actions was the influence that the St. Louis faculty and its supporters had over him.

Eissfeldt was a synod man, and the synod to him, as it was for others, was St. Louis. Soon after the events of 1972–1973, Nickel left the University Lutheran Chapel. The church council was wrong to have entertained allegations which they could have determined by themselves to be false. The accusers had fabricated them. If it were not the report from the students, I would have had no prior knowledge of what was in store for me at the November 20, 1972 meeting with Eissfeldt, Nickel and Grotelueschen. With his father-in-law as district president at that time, Grotelueschen was the point man. It is a small story, but it reflects a tension endemic at that time to the synod at large.

During the last years of teaching at the University of Illinois, I made the trip to Champaign by myself listening to the synod's broadcasting company KFUO, which had reports on the seminary situation and the stances that district presidents were taking in the controversy between the St. Louis faculty majority and its board, which had removed Tietjen as seminary president in February 1974.

Excursus V

LUTHERAN WORLD FEDERATION (LWF) AT ÉVIAN

ə❦

My selection by Jack Preus as an LCMS representative to the 1970 Fifth Assembly of The Lutheran World Federation (LWF) depended not on what I could add to the mix, but was a reaction to St. Louis professor Herbert Mayer making an arrangement with Concordia Publishing House to attend the meeting at its expense.

I had been close to Jack in my first three years at the seminary, his last three as its president (1966–1969), but I was not part of his inner circle. In my appointment as editor of *The Springfielder* in 1968, my position was roughly parallel to Mayer's association with Concordia Publishing House, but not really. In being given the assignment to attend Évian, I was told to write a report for publication that appeared as *The Lutheran World Federation Today*,[1] a title not of my choosing. "The Lutheran World Federation at Évian" would have been better. Even if agreement could not be reached on justification at the 1963 Helsinki Assembly, that convention was the last serious theological one. Évian marked the first of the LWF conventions that would give priority to social issues, so the title as *The Lutheran World Federation Today* would be as embracive as it would be prophetic of where the LWF was headed.

São Paulo was chosen as the first site for the meeting, but to protest alleged human rights abuses in Brazil, the location was changed to Évian-les-Bains, France, on the south shore of Lake Geneva. With just short notice to accommodate such a large gathering, arrangements for the location of an alternative meeting place were left in the hands of a travel agency. Customarily the resident pastor, *pastor loci*, is asked to preach and celebrate communion, but since Évian had no Lutheran congregation, a Lutheran pastor from Strasbourg officiated and a Catholic parish lent its

---

1. David P. Scaer, *The Lutheran World Federation Today* (St. Louis, MO: Concordia Publishing House, 1971).

edifice. A Reformed congregation invited LWF delegates to use its building for prayer and to attend its Sunday services. A resolution proposed by Lutheran Church in America president Robert Marshall (1918–2008) condemning the Brazilian regime was passed, to which Karl Gottschalk, president of the Evangelical Lutheran Church in Brazil, delivered a scathing rebuttal. He soon left the convention. A representative of a Brazilian Pentecostal church followed suit.

A special airfare required my being in Europe for two weeks, out of which ten days were spent at Évian. Since the overt reason for my attendance was writing an account, I carried a clumsy portable typewriter—1960s typewriters were all like that—whose weight became more obvious in running through airports and as I climbed up a steep hill to the bed and breakfast where lodging was assigned. Being at the lower end of the pecking order, this residence was the one most distant from the convention center.

Prestigious churchmen stayed in hotels nearby the convention center. I took copious notes and came back with LWF official releases from which I wrote my narrative. The typewriter was not used at all and should have been left at home. In those days New York's JFK was the eastern debarkation for transatlantic flights. Upon arriving at JFK, I was paged to the first class lounge. A St. Louis travel agent had arranged a first-class seat for the price of an economy ticket. No such luxury was arranged for the return flight. In the JFK first-class lounge was Luther Seminary professor Roy Harrisville (b. 1922), a member of the Evangelical Lutheran Church, predecessor church to the ELCA.

Harrisville had coauthored with Carl Braaten a book promoting Bultmann's method of demythologizing the Gospels.[2] Having heard my name, he greeted me and asked if we could sit together on the flight over to Geneva. His radical critical views about the Gospels did not suggest that this was going to be an overly pleasant trip. To my great surprise, he told me how he no longer held to those views. Arriving very early on a Sunday morning in Geneva, we spent some more hours together waiting for the van to take us to Évian. Harrisville offered a German theologian some assistance with his baggage as he boarded the van. This courtesy was ungratefully and unpleasantly rejected, and sitting back of the theologians, my fellow traveler responded with expressive facial expressions during the ride to Évian. Harrisville was brought up with Jack and Rob-

---

2. Carl E. Braaten and Roy A. Harrisville, *Kerygma and History: A Symposium on the Theology of Rudolf Bultmann* (New York: Abingdon Press, 1962).

ert Preus. I never saw him again after that, but as the ELCA adopted increasingly more radical positions, he and his son were less welcome in official ELCA circles.

When the LWF delegates began discussing making changes in its constitution to accommodate LCMS concerns, I went out of the hall to look for Jack Preus and found him standing at the coffee bar. He thought it best not to participate. Later LCMS second vice president Theodore Nickel did. Some of my time in Évian was spent with Max Löhe (1900–1977), president of the Lutheran Church in Australia, one of whose predecessor bodies, the United Evangelical Lutheran Church of Australia, had withdrawn from the LWF to accommodate the Evangelical Lutheran Church of Australia, which had opposed LWF membership.

The Lutheran Church of Australia still wrestles with LWF membership, which has been made more complex with a sizable part of its membership wanting to ordain women. Löhe like myself was an advisory delegate, and so we did not have the obligations of the regular delegates. Also time was spent with Nickel, whose nick name was "Slug," and his wife. A man of immense energy, he could run through a castle, leaving the rest of us at the entrance.

At Évian, the LWF would no longer understand its members as being in a voluntary association of Lutheran churches, but began to understand its members as one church. Altar and pulpit fellowship among its member churches now would be assumed. Gustaf Wingren (1910–2000) argued that the Seventh Article of Augsburg Confession required church fellowship wherever the gospel was preached, a theme which he addressed at the LWF's commission on theology in the previous year.

Delegates at Évian heard how Lutherans should give up their provincialism and join with the Union, Reformed and other Protestant churches. A resolution was passed to assist Lutheran churches in Germany into a union with the Union churches that were amalgamations between Lutheran and Reformed churches, going back to 1817 and 1830. What then lay in the future is now history, with Lutheran churches in North America and Europe in full fellowship with Reformed bodies.

Professor Heinz Eduard Tödt (1918–1991) delivered the keynote address arguing that Luther's question of one's getting right with God, the classical Lutheran doctrine of justification, had been replaced by how men can get along with each other. So the assembly's sub-theme was secular ecumenism. In the 1960s and 1970s Bultmann was the theologian at center stage, and appropriately, keynote speaker Tödt followed suit by claiming Jesus did not understand himself to be the Son of God.

The tone was already set in the opening sermon by Marc Lienhard (b. 1935), no mean Luther scholar, who said the church's role was a secular one in working for the improvement of society. This went beyond the usual meaning of ecumenism of how one church works with another. Now it was the church working with the world. Call it secular ecumenism.

Cardinal Willebrands (1909–2006), the Vatican representative, told the LWF assembly that Lutherans should be just as saddened by Luther's sharp attacks against the pope as he was. I am not so sure that Pope Benedict XVI (b. 1927) would ask for this. Renaissance popes were first-class scoundrels, especially those who excommunicated Luther and declared him an outlaw. Since Lutherans have come to something of an accommodation with Rome in the *Joint Declaration on the Doctrine of Justification*,[3] the rhetoric has been lowered an octave. Students invited by LWF president Fred Schiotz (1901–1989), also then ALC president, to participate in the assembly showed their lack of appreciation by rising from their seats and placing their backs to him as he spoke.

In an official program, the youth sang "You're a Grand ol' Pig" against the backdrop of the American flag. Things outside the assembly hall mirrored events happening in America. Évian was a Lutheran "Woodstock" in France. Much of the Évian agenda was spent on world hunger, which contrasted with the gourmet tastes of the delegates, who ate in lavish, high-priced restaurants. This was world Lutheranism in 1970.

What happened at Évian was a result of the LWF's fourth assembly in Helsinki in 1963, where the delegates could not agree on justification. If agreement was not possible on the cardinal Lutheran doctrine, then seeking agreement on other important doctrines were doomed. Dr. Max Löhe and Bishop Bo Giertz (1905–1998), delegates to earlier conventions, reminisced about the original intentions of the LWF, and had hoped that the Missouri Synod would join the LWF to ally themselves with conservative delegates to save it. They admitted that this would have been a last-ditch effort.

To keep expenses down, Jack Preus arranged for the LCMS representatives to share an oversized cab on the return to the Geneva airport. Sitting next to the driver was LCMS mission director Micky Kretzmann, whose oversize, Jack said, made him look like Buddha.

At its publication my *The Lutheran World Federation Today* was generally ignored in the LCMS, but caused a stir in LWF circles. Paul C. Empie

---

3. *Joint Declaration on the Doctrine of Justification* (Grand Rapids, MI: W. B. Eerdmans Publishing Co., 2000).

(1909–1979), General Secretary of the United States, National Committee of the LWF, wrote an article in *Lutheran Forum*, to which I responded. In a review in *The Lutheran Quarterly*,[4] Hans Schwarz (b. 1939) took sharp exception to what I had written about Évian. His review and response to *The Lutheran World Federation Today* was biting. He said I was lacking in "basic honesty and objectivity in describing [the LWF's] assembly at Évian."

Then followed personal correspondence with these theologians and LWF General Secretary André Appel (1922–2007).[5] Letters went back and forth for two years in assessing what had transpired at Évian in 1970. At least I had the satisfaction that if my voice of one crying in the wilderness did not change anyone's hearts, at least it was heard. It should be republished; it would be as apropos now as it was fifty years ago.

Ralph Bohlmann (1932–2016) wrote the only positive review of my *The Lutheran World Federation Today*. He agreed with my assessment that the Evian was a disaster for confessional Lutheranism. He concludes, "If

---

4. Hans Schwartz, "The Lutheran World Federation Today," *Lutheran Quarterly* 24, no. 2 (May 1972): 215–17.
5. In his letter of October 29, 1971, Andre Appel provided a three-page, single-spaced typewritten critique of my observations of the July 1971 LWF convention. He writes that I did "not at all take into account of the evolution that took place between the Assembly proper and the time of the publishing of the report." On December 1, 1971, I responded that my task was giving a report on Évian and not the aftermath, which was impossible, as the manuscript was sent to Concordia Publishing House in September. Appel took issue with my observation that the LWF, which had been weakened at its fourth convention in Helsinki in its inability to come to an agreed view on justification, was further weakened in Évian. He wrote that "God can use the weaknesses of servants in strengthening his work." To this I responded that "we cannot use this as an excuse for endorsing these weaknesses and not strengthening what needs to be strengthened." He also took note of my observation "that the Lutheran churches are less concerned with the individual and his personal salvation, and more with the social, political and economical orders" and directed me to an essay by Professor Ishida from Tokyo delivered to the LWF's executive committee in June 1971. In response I wrote to Appel, "I read with much joy the essay of Professor Ishida of Tokyo. Here is a document that can set the church in the right direction." Yes, indeed, but the essay was delivered in June 1972, almost one year after Évian, to an elite and small audience. This ended our correspondence. I did not supply LCMS president Jack Preus or anyone else with copies of this correspondence. At this time Jack had other things on his mind, like the situation at the St. Louis seminary that would come to a head in two years.

Dr. Scaer's analysis is correct, confessional Lutheranism must find a way to accept his concluding challenge to fill the theological vacuum left in world Lutheranism in Évian." Enough said. Nothing I had ever written before or after received such notoriety from outside of the LCMS, but this did not last long. Not enough copies of *The Lutheran World Federation Today* were sold to require a reprint. Royalties were negligible. Its cover was so unattractive as to suggest that it was made out of recycled paper that had already been rejected by another printer.

In 1975 or 1976 I attended a meeting in the Seminex facilities in the old alumni hotel of St. Louis University. In the darkly lit entrance at the elevator, a seminary student sat reading *The Lutheran World Federation Today*. Did he know I was coming, and if so, was this for my benefit?

With the disruption at the St. Louis seminary coming in 1974 and our seminary's moving from Springfield to Fort Wayne in 1976, the LCMS had other things on its mind, and *The Lutheran World Federation Today* was put on the back shelf and forgotten. I had written it only because I was asked. In the long haul, it might be of limited value. In going through the files nearly forty years after the event, this book may have historical value in appraising what happened in Évian in 1970 and where the LWF was then and where it would go from there. In a strange sort of way the book was prophetic of what most of Lutheranism is today.

With the passing of time, the LWF, like the National Council of Churches, USA, has become increasingly irrelevant. There are some happy postscripts. Marc Lienhard, who addressed the Évian assembly on collaboration with the world, has since written *Luther, Witness to Jesus Christ*,[6] a Christological masterpiece.

Also, I visited twice with Hans Schwarz. Sometime after 2010, I met him at a joint meeting of the American Academy of Religion and the Society of Biblical Literature, and he was eager to speak with me. He suggested that my *Lutheran World Federation Today* and the extant responses might be the topic of a scholarly paper.

Meeting Schwarz in person for the first time could have been a problem for the both of us. He had been a professor at Capital Seminary in Columbus, Ohio, but in the restructuring which resulted in the formation of the ELCA, he had to resign and reapply for essentially the same position at the same seminary, but now named Trinity Lutheran Seminary. Rather than applying for a position which he understood as his own,

---

6. Marc Lienhard, *Luther's Witness to Jesus Christ: Stages and Themes of the Reformer's Christology* (Minneapolis, MN: Augsburg Publishing House, 1982).

he returned to Germany to teach systematics at the University of Regensburg. Some of his enthusiasm for the recent directions in Lutheran endeavors had cooled.

Now, over forty-five years after its publication, *Lutheran World Federation Today* has come to the attention of Albert Collver III, assistant to LCMS president Matthew Harrison. At the 2018 Symposium on the Lutheran Confessions, Collver cited it as an accurate description of the LWF.[7]

---

7. Albert B. III Collver, *Ethical Tensions within World Lutheranism*, 41st Annual Symposium on the Lutheran Confessions (Concordia Theological Seminary, 2018), *https://video.ctsfw.edu/media/Ethical+Tensions+within+World+Lutheranism/0_qtafiufs/86967941.*

Excursus VI

JOHN TIETJEN, JOHN DAMM AND SEMINEX

҈

Over the years, I saw John H. Tietjen on several occasions, but never had a conversation with him, and so there could be no reason to include him among past remembrances, but his *Memoirs in Exile* brought about a change of mind. His selection as president of Concordia Seminary in St. Louis literally weeks before the synod convention that elected J. A. O. Preus brought to a head differences in the LCMS that had been simmering beneath the surface. His importance occurred to me only on the 1997 Thanksgiving weekend, when I was sent as the faculty representative to the funeral of Donald Deffner, whose last academic assignment was at Fort Wayne as a visiting professor, heading the Doctor of Ministry program.

On the evening before the committal, I was seated with Don's widow, Corinne (1927–1998), in his study, recalling over martinis the good times both Dorothy and I had with them during his years at Fort Wayne (1988–1997). Corrine noticed that I was looking at Tietjen's *Memoirs* on the shelf and offered it to me along with any of the other books I wanted. Only Tietjen's *Memoirs* fit in my airplane carry-on. Tietjen's *Memoirs* was only being transferred from one shelf to another, to sit untouched for twelve years more before it caught my attention a month after the ELCA convention decided to bless same-sex unions and allow committed homosexuals into the ministry. CORE, a dissident ELCA group protesting ELCA actions, met in Fishers, Indiana, on September 27–28, 2009. Since Tietjen had seen himself as a factor in the formation of ELCA, his memoirs took on new importance.[1] Modesty was not his strong suit.

John Tietjen's *Memoirs in Exile* provides a chronology from his election as seminary president on May 19, 1969, to the closing of Seminex on December 31, 1987. Helpful as the chronology is, it should have begun sometime in the 1950s when the future seminary president and his

---

1. Tietjen, *Memoirs in Exile*, 315.

dean, John Damm, were roommates at the St. Louis seminary dorm.[2] Twelve years after graduating from Concordia Seminary, he had become its president.

On the road to the top, he had the good sense to decline calls as pastor of several congregations, as the executive of a Lutheran high school in Queens, NY, as a writer for curricular materials for the LCMS Board of Parish Education, as chairman of Valparaiso University's theology faculty and even as a professor at St. Louis. Things just happened to fall in his favor—or did he learn that he was chosen to make a change in the LCMS? Then in 1969 came the St. Louis seminary presidency or, as he puts it, "to carry out new responsibilities as leader of a major institution of a changing church body."[3]

His life's work would be to safeguard whatever changes were already in place at the seminary and to advance them in the LCMS. He came close to his goal, but in his own words his failure gave birth to the ELCA. Unknown is just when Tietjen became aware that his life's goal was to bring the LCMS into the modern era or who was his inspiration. It could have been during seminary days or already in college at Bronxville. He did not acknowledge his own political maneuvering. It was all divine. In his memoirs he speaks of his wife Ernestine's (1925–2015) distaste for the politics of his opponents at the 1971 Milwaukee convention that brought his career in LCMS closer to its end. In preparation for that convention, Tietjen convinced Peter Mealwitz (b. 1935), a classmate and friend of mine from Bronxville and St. Louis days, to remove his name as candidate to the St. Louis seminary board, to allow the election of the wider-known William A. "Bill" Buege (1902–2002).[4]

In September 1957, after my summer vicarage in Jackson Hole and Dubois, Wyoming, I sat in on the English District Metropolitan New York-New Jersey Circuit conference meeting in the Laurel Room of Pocono Crest, used for guests staying at Forest Lodge. Chairing the conference at the old Lutherland resort was my father.

Present was John Tietjen who was the assistant pastor of Grace, Teaneck, New Jersey, under Pastor Theodore Beiderwieden (1908–1981) in 1954 and became pastor of Calvary in Leonia, New Jersey, in 1956. Both were English District congregations. Also present were August Brustat (1905–1990), Armin Moellering (1919–1998) and John Damm, Tietjen's

---

2. Tietjen, *Memoirs in Exile*, xiii–xv; 9.
3. Tietjen, *Memoirs in Exile*, 11–12.
4. Tietjen, *Memoirs in Exile*, 71–72.

longtime friend and for two years a roommate at the seminary. He was then co-assistant pastor at Grace, Teaneck, where he began serving in 1951.

After Seminex was deployed, that is, dissolved, Damm returned as pastor to Teaneck and preached a sermon that led to my cousin Margaret Caemmerer Schulze and her ELCA clergy husband leaving the ELCA and joining the Catholic Church. Head pastor in the 1950s and 1960s was George Beiderwieden. Damm's assistantship to Beiderwieden allowed him the time to earn the M.A. degree in 1952 and a Doctor of Education degree in 1963 from Union Theological Seminary in conjunction with Columbia University.[5]

Beiderwieden, Damm and Tietjen, at one time all pastors in Teaneck, were widely known for their liturgical interests. My father mused whether they thought they were the only ones who knew how to pray, a question that would be appropriate for all who have this inclination. Essayist for that September 1957 conference was a young professor from Mount Airy, the LCA seminary in Philadelphia. He began by noting that though "Away in a Manger" was popularly attributed to Luther, this Christmas favorite had American origins, probably in Pennsylvania. This introduced the view that the reputed authors of some biblical books may not have been the real ones, a view that was about to catch on in St. Louis.

After the conference I took the Delaware, Lackawanna and Western Railroad from Pocono Summit back to St. Louis for the fall term, traveling as far as Buffalo with English District president Hugo Kleiner, who invited me to join him for dinner, a luxury no longer provided by the railroad. During that academic year, 1957–1958, my schoolmate and later colleague Kurt Marquart would vicar for President Kleiner. Then from Buffalo it was the Nickel Plate to St. Louis for my third seminary year.

John Damm's degrees credentialed him to follow Arthur Repp as Tietjen's academic dean at St. Louis. While at Leonia, Tietjen obtained a doctor's degree from Union Seminary in New York[6] for his dissertation, "The Principles of Church Union Espoused in Nineteenth Century Attempts to unite the Lutheran Church in America."[7] This made him the ideal candidate to head up the publicity department for the Lutheran Council in America and to become seminary president in 1969 to fulfill

---

5. Tietjen, *Memoirs in Exile*, 9, 213.
6. See Tietjen, *Memoirs in Exile*, 9.
7. John H. Tietjen, "The Principles of Church Union Espoused in Nineteenth Century Attempts to Unite the Lutheran Church in America," 1959.

LCMS president Oliver Harms's goal of bringing Lutherans in America into one church.[8]

In the LCMS tradition of men being called to particular ministries, Tietjen says he was passive in his being assigned a vicarage in New York, his being called to two New Jersey congregations, his service as public relations director for the Lutheran Council, USA and then to the St. Louis seminary. He saw all these as divine actions in which he had no part. Such modesty is expected from LCMS pastors desiring higher church posts and is generally expressed by saying that "I did not seek the job," but of course they did.

From one incident that touched my father deeply, there is reason to reassess Tietjen's self-conscious modesty. In the New York Metropolitan Circuit of the English District was a protocol that delegates to LCMS conventions alternated between pastors and laity between the New York and New Jersey sides of the Hudson River. Politicking had not yet become a widespread synodical pastime. For the 1962 Cleveland convention, a pastor from the New York side of the Hudson River was to be the delegate, and my father was next in line and looked forward to going. Pastors on the New Jersey side of the Hudson garnered enough votes to switch the alternation, and Tietjen was chosen as the delegate. My father had not encountered this kind of political maneuver in his previous thirty-five years in the circuit and was crestfallen. Five years later he died. He would not go to another convention. Time had run out. When I told this account to Rudy Ressmeyer, later Atlantic District president, then an ELCA bishop, he said that it could not have happened. But it did.

In 1967, John Tietjen and Armin Moellering were present for my father's funeral at Trinity of Flatbush, Brooklyn, NY, the one congregation he had served for the entire forty-three years of his ministry. In two years, Tietjen would be St. Louis seminary president, and Moellering would be appointed by Jack Preus four years later to the Fact Finding Committee that would interview Tietjen and other faculty members in response to reports of their false teaching circulating in the synod.

After Tietjen's removal, Moellering would join the Concordia Seminary faculty. The family of Trudy Moellering (1924–2010), his wife, had a vacation home on Rockaway, and during their summer holidays attended my father's church during the sparsely attended summer months. Moellering preached the funeral sermon. Tietjen was in the congregation. In four years they would be facing off against one another.

---

8. Burkee, *Power, Politics, and the Missouri Synod*, 89.

St. Matthew's in Manhattan was the jumping off point for higher academic degrees for St. Louis seminary students who were seen by that faculty as having promise for leading the LCMS in a new direction. Among them was John Tietjen. This congregation boasted in being the oldest Lutheran congregation in America, but this was done by Christ Lutheran Church assuming the charter of the older and now declining congregation of St. Matthew. Its pastor, Alfred Trinklein, a conservative man, may not have been aware of how he and his congregation were being used to advance the new theology by providing seminary students and recent graduates a place to earn advanced degrees at New York institutions.

Not many pastors have the pleasure of having such academically inclined students to assist them in their congregational duties. Trinklein served as Atlantic District vice president for New York and received an honorary degree of Doctor of Divinity from the St. Louis faculty, but it would be hard to see what exceptional service he had performed other than giving a place where the new leaders of the LCMS could find a launching pad. Damm and Tietjen were vicars at St. Matthew's in New York under the tutelage of Trinklein. Other noteworthies were the Old Testament scholar Ralph Klein (b. 1936), peace activist Art Simon and Walter Bouman, a leader in bringing about ELCA fellowship with the Episcopal Church in America, for which he was awarded an honorary doctor's degree from that church's General Theological Seminary.[9]

In upper Manhattan, St. Matthew's sanctuary and parsonage occupied the same building that has given way to a high rise apartment.[10] In the spring and my final semester at Concordia College in Bronxville (1955), I was in the Trinklein parsonage and visited also with his part-time assistant pastor Oswald Hoffmann, who headed the LCMS publicity bureau in New York. Later Hoffmann became Lutheran Hour speaker and would move to St. Louis. In retirement in the 1960s, Trinklein moved opposite the post office in the Pocono Pines where we were already summering. When he saw me come on the bicycle to pick up the morning mail,

---

9. See Burkee, *Power, Politics, and the Missouri Synod*, 28. However, Oswald Hoffmann was not a vicar at St. Matthew's, as Burkee says.
10. *The Lutheran Annual* gives the founding date of St. Matthew's as 1664, the year the Dutch surrendered Manhattan to the English, who were more receptive to Lutherans. Leading the congregation is the Rev. Peter A. Deebrah, whom I knew through our seminary's distance education leading to ordination program. Born in India, he has equipped himself in Spanish to minister to a congregation drawn from a changing neighborhood.

he would come over to talk about church matters. He was an avid reader of *Christian News*, whose editor had been his member. At that time Valparaiso University had acquired Pocono Crest, and Trinklein, like others, had hoped that the Lutheran heritage that was there in the founding of Lutherland in 1925 could be continued.[11]

Tietjen's election on May 19, 1969, as president of Concordia Seminary was not welcomed by everyone and was a factor leading to the July convention election of Springfield seminary president J. A. O. Preus as LCMS president and to the faculty walkout in 1974.[12] There was something messianic in how Tietjen saw himself. How else is anyone to interpret the following? "Yet I am convinced that God, who raised Jesus from the dead, worked through institutional death and transfiguration to produce the ELCA."[13] He followed this by putting a positive spin on the faculty walkout in February, 1974, and the formation of Seminex and interpreted them as major factors in the formation of the Evangelical Lutheran Church in America (ELCA) in 1986. In his mind, his election to and the removal from the presidency of Concordia Seminary and the formation of Seminex with his assuming its presidency were all part of the *Heilsgeschichte* that was destined to give Lutheranism a new direction. Changes made at the St. Louis seminary before he assumed the presidency in 1969 would remain intact at Seminex. This was his self-understood destiny that he was determined to fulfill. He saw his selection as Concordia Seminary president as on a par with Jack Preus's election to the LCMS presidency. Of course, it wasn't.

Preus was chosen by an entire church body. A seminary president was chosen by four electors—the presidents of the LCMS and Missouri District, the chairperson of the board of higher education and the board of regents, each with one vote. Harms, the LCMS president, favored Tietjen, so he claimed. His predecessor Alfred O. Fuerbringer had tendered his resignation as seminary president in 1969, knowing a different set of electors might be in place after the July convention, and only a president of their choosing would keep things in place.

---

11. See Excursus I: Lutherland and the Poconos, 13 ff.
12. See Burkee, *Power, Politics, and the Missouri Synod*, 88–89. Before the term of the incumbent seminary president Alfred O. Fuerbringer had come to an end, Academic Dean Arthur Repp called a faculty meeting together to begin the process of choosing a new president. This was to assure that a seminary president would be in place who would foster the theological goals advocated by the faculty.
13. John H. Tietjen, *Memoirs in Exile*, 341.

John Tietjen, John Damm and Seminex

Things worked out as Fuerbringer and his academic dean, Arthur Repp, had planned, and Tietjen was in place as seminary president just weeks before the LCMS convention. Jack Preus's election as LCMS president by a vote 522 to 438 could have only been a repudiation of what was being taught at St. Louis. It was not inevitable even to Preus that he would be elected LCMS president.

No matter what the result of the 1969 convention would be, it would be a life-changing event for Jack Preus. It was also for Tietjen, the LCMS and the St. Louis faculty. Shortened tenures first as president of Concordia Seminary and then Seminex provided Tietjen with the death motif that messiahs must suffer in behalf of others. His selection as bishop of the ELCA Chicago Metropolitan Synod was a temporary resuscitation, the kind that Lazarus may have experienced. It did not last long before he had to die again.

My closest contact with Tietjen, as if it were face to face, came by my reading transcripts of Jack Preus's fact-finding commission of the St. Louis faculty. It happened in this way. In the late spring of 1971, a request came from Jack Preus through Howard Tepker, then chairman of the department of systematic theology, and longtime member of the LCMS Commission on Theology and Church Relations, to assist him in evaluating the transcripts of the interviews by Preus's Fact Finding Committee with the St. Louis seminary faculty. These interviews began on December 11, 1970, and ended in early April 1971. At the time I did not know who the committee members were and how the interviews were conducted.[14]

I set aside for reading and analyzing the transcripts the second floor bedroom of our home on 2304 Westview Drive in Springfield. It was a day and night job done on a portable manual typewriter, which brought on a case of pneumonia that laid me up for the summer months.

Howard Tepker and I worked as a team in evaluating the St. Louis faculty transcripts. I did the analysis and writing and he proofread them. Tepker was not known as an analytical or creative thinker, but he did check out my evaluations with the transcripts and made no changes. He agreed with me on every point. On the title page of the evaluations ap-

---

14. Tietjen, *Memoirs in Exile*, 36. Members were Paul Zimmerman, president of Concordia College, Ann Arbor, MI; Karl L. Barth (b. 1924), later St. Louis seminary president; H. Armin Moellering, New Jersey pastor in the same circuit as Tietjen, a few years before, Paul Streufert, LCMS fourth vice president, and Elmer Foelber (1892–1987), editorial staff, Concordia Publishing House.

pears this title: "Confidential Appraisal of the Faculty Interviews, Concordia Seminary St. Louis, Missouri, June 22, 1971." The word *Confidential* was in upper case with double underlining.

As we moved from Springfield to Fort Wayne in 1976 and to another house in 1978, the transcripts moved with us, but for reasons of space, they were eventually disposed. Carbon copies of my evaluations were kept, with the possibility that they might be of some value later. My evaluations were delivered to the committee by Tepker, who agreed with them. Nothing was heard positive or negative from Jack Preus or Paul Zimmerman (1918–2014) about my evaluations, so I still do not know whether they were of any use or not.

When I read Tietjen's *Memoirs in Exile* on September 19, 2009, and compared them with my own analyses, the similarities were striking, but this has never been confirmed by the committee's chairman Paul A. Zimmerman, who lived into his 90s and often visited his son, Tom Zimmerman, who is my neighbor on the Fort Wayne campus.

A separate evaluation was made for each faculty member and arranged alphabetically according to his last name, beginning with B and ending with W. Before reading Tietjen's *Memoirs in Exile*, something I did for the first time in September 2009, I thought that my evaluations might have been unnecessarily critical, but in reading them thirty-eight years after I had written them, they appear to be right on target.

In his *Memoirs in Exile*, Tietjen summarizes the faculty view. "They [the faculty] affirmed the inspiration of the Scriptures, but they insisted that inspired Scriptures were authoritative because of their gospel content."[15] Andrew Weyermann (1930–2003), brother to Tietjen's wife Ernestine and a close confidant, said, "When people want to throttle you with facticity [sic!] and inerrancy, you have to insist on the gospel meaning in the facts as more important than the facts themselves. Only the gospel saves, not the historical facts."[16]

Bluntly put, the Scriptures are true in their accomplishing what God intends. Historicity is secondary to meaning. The truthfulness of the biblical events depends on their being accepted. What has been traditionally accepted as historically true, such as Jonah's stay in the whale or large fish, may be parabolic.[17] The Scriptures are probably historically true in what they report but not necessarily so. Whether an event is his-

---

15. Tietjen, *Memoirs in Exile*, 36–43.
16. Tietjen, *Memoirs in Exile*, 55.
17. Tietjen, *Memoirs in Exile*, 129.

torically true is an exegetical question to which scholars will and can give various answers.

My evaluations of the interviews may have had value in providing background of how individual faculty members stood on this or that issue. Professors not engaged directly in biblical subjects were willing to say that what the Bible says about historical and geographical matters might be in error, even though for them they had found no errors. Responses to questions about the historicity of the virgin birth saw its value in giving it a place in Christian doctrine apart from the question of whether it happened or not. Another professor with a conservative reputation, a faculty member since 1954 and a confidant to LCMS president Harms, held that the gospel is the first arbiter of the true doctrine and that the Scriptures play a secondary role, a response surfacing in other interviews. Some held that the existence of Adam and Eve is not a doctrine, but the interviewers failed to follow up with a question whether they were actual people.

One professor held that differences about whether or not Jesus walked on the water was not decisive for church fellowship. A professor professing belief in Jesus' resurrection would allow a student not to believe in it. This is not the place to rehearse evaluations made in 1971. These transcripts have been published and should be consulted to see how far the LCMS had fallen under the sway of destructive historical-critical methods.[18]

Some interviews were more extensive than others, but remarkably one is not that different from another. Tietjen was present for all the interviews, so as interviews progressed, he and those who were already interviewed could share their experiences with those who were still to be interviewed. This may account for the similarity of the responses. An often-used response to the question of whether an event reported in the Bible had actually happened was that the working of the gospel on the hearer was the important thing, and so the question remained unanswered.

At that time and later, I wrote essays about the law and gospel as a method of biblical interpretation.[19] Without referencing the transcripts or my evaluations, they were factors in how I developed my position. The seminary faculty approach can be characterized as a Lutheran form of neoorthodoxy that allowed for Rudolph Bultmann's radical position that

---

18. Paul A. Zimmerman, *A Seminary in Crisis: Inside Story of the Preus Fact Finding Committee* (St. Louis, MO: Concordia Publishing House, 2007), 241–91.
19. David P. Scaer, "The Law Gospel Debate in the Missouri Synod," *Springfielder* 36 (December 1972): 156–71. "The Law Gospel Debate in the Missouri Synod Continued," *Springfielder* 40 (September 1976): 107–18.

the gospel did not depend on biblical history and for Barth's evasion of historical questions. There is hardly an interview in which this Lutheran form of neoorthodoxy does not appear, but the position is so sophisticated that it must be asked whether each one who espoused it had come to this conclusion by himself. It was a philosophical rather than biblically defined method. It is likely that some faculty members were committed to the principle, while others had to be rehearsed and still others were repeating often-heard clichés.

The faculty majority received wide scholarly support from outside the LCMS, but their position was customized for a Lutheran audience and was hardly characteristic of Reformed, Catholic and even other Lutheran scholars. The law-gospel paradigm as an exegetical principle is hardly found in other scholarly circles. Seminex theology was provincial to the point of being even downright parochial, a Rube Goldberg (1883–1970) production cobbling together the Lutheran clichés of law and gospel, Bultmann's method of demythologizing and Barth's ignoring of history. Some in the synod supported the method associated with Tietjen but could not define it. Rudolph Haak, who defeated Lewis C. Niemoeller as the president of Central Illinois District in 1970, and was himself defeated in 1974, described the faculty's method of biblical interpretation as doing a grammatical study of the biblical text and praying. It would be difficult to locate this definition in the faculty transcripts.

When the 1971–1972 school year began, Lorman Petersen, who had been the seminary's acting president (1969–1970) after Jack Preus's election as LCMS president, returned to his former position as academic dean, and a pro-Tietjen seminary administration was put in place in Springfield. With survival as the first thing on my mind, events in St. Louis were secondary, and so I entirely put the evaluations of the faculty interview transcripts out of my mind.

Tietjen had established alliance with Springfield president Richard J. Schulz, who formally took office in September 1971. Regular meetings were held between administrators and faculty of both seminaries in order to curtail the influence of LCMS president Jack Preus, whose supporters would be marginalized, a story told elsewhere. So in this sense Tietjen was a factor in my service at the seminary. Had he not become the St. Louis seminary president, life at the Springfield seminary would not have taken the turn that moved the school to Fort Wayne.

The February 19, 1974, faculty and student walkout at Concordia Seminary—St. Louis led to the formation of the Association of Evangelical Lutheran Churches (AELC) on December 3–4, 1976, with about 250 congregations instead of the anticipated twelve hundred. One of these congregations was Trinity of Flatbush in Brooklyn, NY, of which my grandparents, Gustav and Lydia Zimmermann, were founders, and my father was pastor (1924–1967), and where I grew up. Another was Trinity, Rockville, Connecticut, now located in Vernon, Connecticut. My life was formed in Trinity of Flatbush and my ministry in Trinity, Rockville.

On an October 2012 visit to Brooklyn, I chanced in on a meeting of the elders of the Flatbush congregation there to learn that a Sunday in April is set aside each year to honor their pastor who died in April, 1967, and that pastor was my father. All that is left are once-sweet memories made bitter by the ambitions of men who had new plans for their synod. I am not alone in these feelings. Many former LCMS pastors now in the ELCA say that their joining this synod was the worst decision they ever made. Happily, some have returned.

In the formation of the ELCA, John H. Tietjen claims a part. "The branch growing out of the root of the felled tree was in full bloom. The Evangelical Lutheran Church in America was a reality." As 2009 was drawing to an end, the wood of that reality called the ELCA began to splinter. Without Tietjen, all these things may have nevertheless taken place, but more than anyone else he was the lynchpin. Like the keystone in the arch, his removal brought the entire enterprise to collapse. Just as things did not go so well for him at Concordia Seminary, they did not go so well for him at Seminex, and he found himself in conflict again, but not with a synod president, but with the faculty who gave up their positions at Concordia Seminary to support his presidency there.[20]

---

20. Tietjen, *Memoirs in Exile*, 282–284. For years after Seminex was disbanded, Edward Schroeder remained in St. Louis and shared his concerns in *Thursday Theology*, which was electronically available. In issue 593, sent out on October 22, 2009, entitled "Memories, Memories—of Crossings, of Seminex," Schroeder describes events at Seminex a little more than a year after the school was founded. "May Massacre 1977. Seven colleagues—contracts not renewed." On this issue the faculty was divided. Some argued that a shortage of funds demanded it, and others said "'During a time for confessing you can't throw anyone under the bus.'" At the same time a controversy arose about running the school. One group favored a plan put forth by Robert Bertram used by the Dominicans since the thirteenth century that "The decision-makers shall be the consequence-takers, and the consequence-takers shall be the decision-makers." In other words, the faculty, students and the board of directors would all have a hand in administering the community. Schroeder reports, "But Tietjen was unhappy with it. Not his style of leadership. For him and others Bob's [Bertram's] collaborative model was just too

Even then his troubles did not come to an end. In the Epilogue of his *Memoirs in Exile*, he tells that after being elected bishop of the newly formed Chicago Metropolitan Synod of the ELCA on July 5–6, 1987, he found himself in exile again.[21] Was it something he had done? Or was it just who he was? He doesn't say. It is hard not to detect a pattern. Some in the ELCA wished that February 19, 1974, had never come.

A haunting question is what Tietjen's reactions would have been had he lived to experience the 2009 ELCA decisions on homosexuality. Very good friends and supporters of Tietjen have taken serious exception to these actions, and some have taken part in the formation of the North American Lutheran Church and the protest group known as CORE, protesting the 2009 ELCA decisions on homosexuality, which are at the base of the disruptions in this church. Since what is now the public position of the ELCA on homosexuality was already being taught in St. Louis during Tietjen's tenure, he would have had every reason to see that his vision had been fulfilled.

These views may have already been present in these synods constituting the ELCA, but they were publicly being advocated in the St. Louis classrooms. Working from an historical perspective, one can speculate about how different subsequent events would have been, if Tietjen had accepted Preus's overture at the end of 1973 to resign as seminary president and take another position.[22] Perhaps some or even most of the forty-five professors would have remained in their positions, Seminex would not have been formed and the several hundred students who joined the breakaway seminary would have been ordained into LCMS congregations. At this writing, some wounds still have not healed. All the evidence points to Tietjen as a deeply committed ideologue determined to politically advance his agenda regardless of the consequences for himself or others.[23]

---

cumbersome, and piece by piece it was dismantled." In 1984, Seminex left St. Louis for Chicago, and by joining with the Lutheran School of Theology in Chicago in 1987 it ceased to exist. Several causes came together to accelerate the events between the choice of Tietjen as seminary president in 1969 and Seminex's cessation in 1987, but those affected most, pastors and congregations that came into the ELCA as a result of the faculty walkout in 1974, may be asking themselves if things would have turned out differently if Tietjen had not been chosen. Something in his style of leadership may be known only to those who worked with him.

21. Tietjen, *Memoirs in Exile*, 239–241.
22. Burkee, *Power, Politics, and the Missouri Synod*, 146.
23. George C. Heider, former president of Concordia University in River Forest,

During the spring term of 1974, I was asked to teach at Concordia Seminary, and so one day I drove from Springfield to offer two classes. Some of the Seminex professors, like Fred Danker, whom I knew, still could be seen on campus, but I never saw Tietjen. The last time I saw him was at a LCUSA sponsored meeting at a University Club of St. Louis University where Seminex had taken its operations. It was probably 1975, since Seminex has been formed in 1974 and the seminary in Springfield had not moved to its Fort Wayne campus. This would happen in 1974.

By then, Seminex was operating on a shoestring budget, and instead of the more formal fare associated with such occasions once offered on the 801 campus, Tietjen came into the room where the conference was with a plate of cheeses and crackers brought from home. He was not part of the conference. As he entered, discussions continued and no one turned around to look. Gone were the days when Tietjen could use his public relations talents to attract the press to Lambert Field airport upon his return to St. Louis from the New Orleans convention in July 1973, or when he could he lead a walkout of students and faculty on February 19, 1974, programmed to bring the LCMS to its knees. His charisma was gone.

A permanent resurrection for Tietjen would come in his claiming a part in establishing the ELCA, a denomination that embraced the LCA, the ALC and the AELC remnant he led out of the LCMS. The formation of the ELCA resembled a metaphorical and not a real resurrection, the kind some of his faculty attributed to Jesus. The ELCA had been cobbled together overlooking issues that divided the constituent synods. Tietjen provides no reason why he can refer to these transforming events in one place as a resurrection and in another as a transfiguration, but a clue may

---

and then chairman of the department of theology at Valparaiso University, holds that the decisions of the 1973 LCMS New Orleans Convention that led to the 1975 Anaheim convention closing the senior college in Fort Wayne college and moving the Springfield seminary to that campus as "power politics at its most raw and brutal" level, as "amply and irrefutably demonstrated" by Burkee. George C. Heider, "Reflections on Half a Century of Being Lutheran," *The Cresset* 79/3 (Lent 2016): 46–47. With additional research Burkee would have learned that Tietjen was working with high-placed Springfield administrators and professors to bring this seminary into the St. Louis orbit. Heider's article was first delivered as a tribute at the inauguration of Daniel Gard, a professor at the Fort Wayne seminary, as president of Concordia University in River Forest. Some present questioned its appropriateness for this kind of occasion.

be found in Rudolph Bultmann's program of demythologizing: transfiguration, resurrection and ascension were all metaphors that Jesus was glorified. Tietjen saw himself as vindicated in the formation of the ELCA, but behind the glitter of his dreams some saw something darker in what he had accomplished.[24]

---

24. See Carl E. Braaten, "The Crux of Christianity's Case: The Resurrection of Jesus,' in *A Report from the Frontlines—Conversations on Public Theology: A Festschrift in Honor of Robert Benne*, ed. Michael Shahan (Grand Rapids: W. B. Eerdmans Publishing Co., 2009), 23–34. Robert Benne, "The Trials of American Lutheranism," *First Things* 213 (May 2011): 21.

Chapter Six

THE SCHULTZ PRESIDENCY

When Jack Preus was elected president of the Missouri Synod, the board of Regents appointed Lorman Petersen, then academic dean, as acting president; it was generally thought that Lorman Petersen, when he became acting seminary president in July 1969, would be retained as seminary president. Another possible candidate was Jack's brother, Robert, but Jack, one of the four electors, may have thought that choosing his younger and only brother would bring complaints of nepotism.

To the surprise of many, including the man chosen for the job, the electors chose Richard J. Schultz, an articulate professor in Christian education with a fine mind for philosophical issues. His election took place around December 1969. Though Schultz was elected as president in December, he wanted to finish his academic work at the University of Illinois leading to a doctor's degree for the remainder of the academic year before assuming the presidential duties on July 1, 1970.

During the spring semester of 1970, he had driven with me to Champaign every Monday afternoon, and we had the opportunity for long conversations. He had already been elected seminary president, but had not assumed office, and spoke of how he would conduct this position. Once he remarked that, if he had a problem with a professor, he would take him out to lunch rather than confronting him in his office.

For good reasons Schultz was thought to be a Preus man. Jack Preus had called him to the faculty and cast one of the four votes for his election as president. Schultz had also presented a lecture with a conservative tone to a joint meeting of the seminary faculties and district presidents meeting in the last years of Oliver Harms's presidency, which was recognized as brilliant even by those who did not share his views.

Richard Schultz was installed as president the following fall at Trinity in downtown Springfield. Prominent in attendance was O. P. Kretzmann, now Chancellor of Valparaiso University. Corpulent and blind and assisted like an aged prelate by Dan Brockopp, dean of the university chapel, he was a figure of Missouri's grand past. In the procession Jack alone was not academically attired. Not pretentious in matters of ceremony, he wore a business suit.

When Schultz took over his presidency, he appointed Lorman Petersen to his former position as academic dean, and according to all appearances the real power was in Petersen's hands. Petersen left for Greece on yearlong sabbatical, and Fred Kramer took over as academic dean, a post with which he was familiar and shaped, until Petersen assumed that position again around July 1971. Robert Preus set aside any thoughts of his own in becoming president, but I suspect that he might have been disappointed. He sometimes visited us in Springfield, and on one occasion I arranged for him to visit Schultz after his election as president and before his installation, probably in the spring of 1970. In this meeting at Schultz's house, Preus recommended the name of Dean Wenthe for Old Testament, a suggestion which was taken, and Wenthe came to the seminary in the fall of 1970.

Division in the Missouri Synod became evident in the election of John Tietjen[1] as St. Louis seminary president in June 1969. Soon a pro–St. Louis faction was forming within the faculty. But they had joined together more out of personal discontent than common ideology. Motivations for discontent were as varied as those who joined themselves together. Tietjen's ascendancy to better things may have been seen as a highway to better things for everyone. Contacts began to be made by members of the St. Louis faculty and meetings between certain faculty members were held at the Gardens restaurant on US 66 in Litchfield, the midway point between the two seminaries. Arrangements for one meeting were made by John Frederick Johnson, who had become the associate dean under Petersen.

It cannot be overlooked that in June 1970, one year after Tietjen had become St. Louis seminary president, the seminary awarded Schultz its sole honorary degree of Doctor of Divinity at its graduation ceremonies. Schultz never received the doctorate in education for which he was studying at the University of Illinois—Champaign. It may be coincidental that he had no kind words for the conservative movement which, in spite of any of its failings, had been a factor in electing Jack Preus synod president, who in turn, had made him seminary president. Unknown at the time Schultz was honored by the St. Louis seminary was that its faculty was planning to award the same degree to several dignitaries of the Lutheran World Federation, which was meeting in St. Louis in the summer.

---

1. See also Excursus VI: John Tietjen, John Damm and Seminex, 129 ff.

Before one meeting with the St. Louis faculty, John Frederick Johnson hosted a social hour at his house, which was virtually around the corner from ours. Later we drove the fifty miles or so to Litchfield. On one occasion, a proposal was made that the seminaries combine their theological journals. I was the editor of one of these. I responded that I would like to be the editor of the combined journal. Those present assented.

In 1971, Lorman Petersen returned to the deanship with a power he did not even have as acting president. Soon it began to appear as if Petersen was receiving advice from those associated with the Tietjen administration at the St. Louis seminary, which by then was operating as a separate entity in the synod in response to Preus's concerns about that school.

Dean Wenthe, who had joined the faculty the year before, had received a call to a congregation just to the northeast of Springfield and was urged by Petersen to take it. During the Schultz presidency, Walter A. Maier II, Wenthe and I did not receive the salary increases that our colleagues did.

Along with what amounted to a salary reduction, my teaching assignments would soon be changed. Now I would be teaching Lutheran Confessions I, and my previous assignment in the basic three courses in dogmatics would be taken away. I do not remember the meeting with Petersen, but in a memo of February 24, 1972, which he placed in my file, he claims that he told me that in the place of Clarence Spiegel, by then retired, and Harry Huth, who had left in 1969, I would become what he called a "specialist" in confessions. This reassignment was done without any previous discussion or consultation or input from me about what amounted to be change in my original assignment to the seminary in 1969 to teach dogmatics and New Testament.

Another topic of discussion contained in the memo was my continuing as editor of *The Springfielder*. Petersen's memo has the following: "I [Petersen] informed him [Scaer] that this would also limit some of the teaching which he could otherwise do, but agreed that he should stay as Editor." Remarkably, Petersen assumed the right to appoint the editor, a privilege which belongs to the seminary president, which was Schultz. It was obvious that Petersen, now given full reign by Schultz, was intent on removing me from the classroom.

Another sentence rings true to what might have happened at that meeting. He concludes the memo with this sentence: "We also spoke but made no conclusion, of having Scaer team-teach with someone in Exegesis in the area of Hermeneutics." Professors who have fairly predictable teaching assignments no longer have time to engage in research and writing to the extent I had. The Petersen memo to himself of February 24,

1972, was inexplicit in stating that I was being relieved of courses entitled Revelation and Scripture and God and Creation and that I would have one section of Christology.

Preparing lectures on the Lutheran Confessions would be time consuming. Yet this assignment opened a new door for me. Over the years since then, I have offered any number of essays on them. The previous Confessions instructor, Harry Huth, had taught the confessions according to doctrinal topics, that is, he would look for confessional citations supporting a particular doctrine. Rather than looking at the document as a whole, this method was akin to the *sedes doctrinae* approach to studying the Scriptures. Separate passages were singled out to prove a doctrine. Ironically, it resembled the form criticism in which scholars attempted to identify the community origins of verses in the Synoptic Gospels. In both cases the documents were not approached as historical totalities.

According to students, Huth's triglot, the German, Latin and English version of *The Book of Concord*, published by Missouri Synod,[2] was color coded according to doctrines. My first interest was in the Apostles' Creed, which I traced back to earlier creeds and back into the New Testament documents to locate creedal formulas there. Lutherans are committed to the Scriptures and the Lutheran Confessions, but this phrase as it stands is open to misunderstanding, as the Reformed theologians point out, and so in need of explanation. The Reformed have confession-like documents, but these are open to revision. Lutherans do not put the confessions on the same level as the Scriptures, though commitment to both sets of documents can easily give this impression.

At this time, Fred Danker of the St. Louis Seminary retained for his entire life a well-deserved reputation as a New Testament scholar. He had written that the Nicene Creed was a philosophical document, a commonly held view. This led me to show the words and phrases from the church's two oldest creeds were taken from the Scriptures. In designating creedal formulas in the New Testament documents, my approach was form-critical, in that the church in its documents had preserved different kinds of literary forms among which were creeds.

With this understanding, that the Apostles' and Nicene Creeds and their predecessor creeds were an assimilation of biblical phrases, the word *and* between the words "the Bible and Confessions" had less meaning. So,

---

2. F. Bente, ed., *Concordia Triglotta: Die Symbolischen Bücher Der Evangelisch-Lutherischen Kirche, Deutsch-Lateinisch-Englisch*, trans. W. H. T. Dau and F. Bente (St. Louis, MO: Concordia Publishing House, 1921).

in a sense the creeds, which are the basic documents of the Lutheran Confessions, preceded the writing of the Bible. A continuous line can be drawn from Jesus to recognizing the creeds in the form we have them now. This assignment in the Lutheran Confessions, which was not given out of a completely good motive by the administration, allowed me to study the historical circumstances of the sixteenth-century documents which defined Lutheran doctrine.

Though I approached this task with some resentment, I became familiar with the *Book of Concord* and have since written several scholarly articles and one popular book on it.[3] Knowledge of the Lutheran Confessions has proven to be extremely useful in interpreting Article Five of the *Augsburg Confession*, about which great division remains in the church over whether the word *ministry* refers to the good works and responsibilities of all Christians or whether it applies to the office of the ministry.

During this period, I was also assigned a seminary course in the Epistle of James, an idea which could have hardly been my choice since, with its supposed doctrine of justification by works, this book was recognized as of limited value by Luther and has not been a favorite with Lutherans. Having limited knowledge of James, students took turns in presenting papers. After a while it seemed that James had the same doctrine of justification of faith as did Paul, but that he looked at it from the Day of Judgment, the same perspective as it was found in the Synoptic Gospels, especially Matthew.

The seminar on James met in an out-of-way classroom in an empty dormitory, but nevertheless attracted a full house. From these seminars I was led to write *James the Apostle of Faith*, a title that indicates its contents. It was the Lord's brother and not Paul who first laid down the dimensions for the doctrine of justification, which at the same time was the center of Christian doctrine and remains a major cause of division.

---

3. David P. Scaer, *Getting into the Story of Concord: A History of the Book of Concord* (St. Louis, MO: Concordia Publishing House, 1977); David P. Scaer, "Sanctification in the Lutheran Confessions," *Concordia Theological Quarterly* 53, no. 3 (July 1989): 165–81, *http://www.ctsfw.net/media/pdfs/scaersanctification.pdf*; David P. Scaer, "Augustana V and the Doctrine of the Ministry," *Lutheran Quarterly* 6, no. 4 (1992): 403–23; David P. Scaer, "The Augsburg Confession, the Apology, the Smalcald Articles and the Treatise on the Power and Primacy of the Pope, and a Few Extra Thoughts on Hoefling," in *The Office of the Holy Ministry*, ed. John R. Fehrmann and Daniel Preus, Luther Academy Lecture Series 3 (Crestwood, MO: Luther Academy, 1996), 130–49; David P. Scaer, "Rediscovering the Treatise as Ecumenical Response," *Concordia Theological Quarterly* 64, no. 4 (October 2000): 338–44.

Another seminar undertook a critical study of *The Common Catechism*,[4] a joint Protestant-Catholic endeavor to provide a faith on which all good Christians might agree. Nothing came of this ecumenical endeavor, and the book is never mentioned in theological journals—and for good reason: no student probably even remembers that seminar.

Students are expected to take notes during the lectures. What was usual was that some were taking notes only at certain times. To keep the students' attention, professors, especially this one, make what an outsider could only consider as an outrageous statement. Hyperbole is a way of making the point, which will less likely be forgotten. The Gospel of Matthew is full of them. Very few people have followed Jesus' admonition to cut off the hand and take out the eye. His threat to destroy the temple was misunderstood and led to his execution.

At the present time there are several collections circulating among former students, now pastors, of sayings collected from my lectures. Some of these sayings do seem out of bounds and are unrecognizable to me as my own, but I cannot deny ownership. Within the situation in which they were first spoken, they had meaning and provided the humor to keep the class attentive.

Several times I noted that some students were transcribing these off-the-cuff remarks and not material of the substantive lectures. In these cases, I would go over to the student's desk and repeat what I said, asking them to transcribe these words accurately for those to whom they were reporting. At times the academic dean could be seen listening outside the door. In these cases I would go the door to open it wider and stand there and repeat what I said. This was my response to the general harassment.

One day, without announcement, Sam Goltermann, executive secretary of Board of Higher Education, showed up in my classroom on the second floor of Wessel Hall. From time to time, friends on the Board of Control would ask if they could sit in for the lectures, and they still do, and I welcome this. However, I do not recall any board member, especially the Board of Higher Education, making an official visit. The course was God and Creation, and I provided him with an English Bible and a Greek New Testament and asked him to participate in the class discussion.

All this took place on the second floor of Wessel Hall across from the faculty offices. Springfield provided a compact campus which was lost in moving to Fort Wayne. Before and after classes in Wessel Hall profes-

---

4. Johannes Feiner, *The Common Catechism: A Book of Christian Faith* (New York: Seabury Press, 1975).

sors were easily accessible in their offices. All during the day students were more likely to come in and talk, and many close friendships between professors and students were made. In Fort Wayne, faculty offices were located in what were the dormitories of the Senior College away from the north and south classroom buildings, and so students no longer passed the faculty offices.

Almost three years after my promotion to associate professor, in the spring of 1972, a contract came through the postal service, as I remember, dated July 1, 1969. Copies of the contract along with a diploma of vocation are in my files at the academic dean's office. In being issued a contract, a number of irregularities were involved, but the bottom line was to provide cause for my removal. Richard J. Schultz signed the diploma of vocation as the proxy for Jack Preus, who had been out of that office for nearly three years. Dated July 1, 1969, it had been prepared in the spring of 1972. Beneath Schultz's signature are these words: "In behalf of President J. O. [sic!] Preus May 4, 1972."

Back-dating a document may well be illegal, especially in the case of what pretended to be a legal contract. Schultz was listed as the "Executive Officer" of the Board of Regents, signing in the place of J. A. O. Preus, though he would only assume that title no earlier than September 1970. An associate professorship in 1969 carried with it tenure. Later the synod would change this policy so that faculty rank was not necessarily connected to tenure.

Jack Preus, for whom Schultz substituted his own signature, may have had no knowledge of the transaction and may have never issued such a contract to anyone else who had been promoted to associate professor during his presidency. It could be that I was the only one who had received tenure along with a contract up to that time in any of the synod's schools. Most of the contract contained the details which can be found in a contract offered to a untenured professor. Listed were the obligations which were expected and assumed of all faculty members, such as teaching according to the seminary course loads, counseling students and preaching in chapel. Spelled out was the line of authority which made me responsible first through the academic dean to the president and then the board. This line of authority exists in all schools, but is not spelled out by contracts for tenured professors. The fly in the ointment is paragraph 7: "It is further agreed that the party Of [sic!] the second part shall be entitled to annual vacation with pay for three weeks, as approved by the Administrative [sic!] of the seminary." In a memo to himself, dated May 10 1972, Lorman Petersen noted that according to the synod handbook, I would have tenure on July 1, 1974. He knew that I had received tenure from Jack Preus on June 1969, and so it seems that he might have had questions about the legitimacy of having me sign the contract.

This simply had never been done before. There was period of two years between when the contract was given to me to sign and the end of the Schultz-Petersen administration. I informed Robert Preus, then on the St. Louis faculty, and some Springfield seminary board members about the contract and that I did not sign it.

Taken all together—no salary increase, being deprived of the courses for which I was called and had taught for six years, and a back-dated contract which was perhaps bogus—were good reasons to see that the administration would prefer to see me leave. A good biblical reason for not signing is that after the gospel is given, the law is not reimposed. Schultz's contract was exacting a price from me for my tenured position, something which I had already received when Jack Preus was seminary president.

Many anxious days and nights were spent on figuring out how to deal with the situation, and doing nothing proved to be the best. I realized that my seminary teaching days might come to an end. Schultz and Petersen were obviously working in collusion, and Johnson, whom I considered a friend since we joined the faculty in 1996, remained silent to my requests for explanation. There was no one in the administration or on the faculty to whom I felt I could turn for advice on what to do with the contract. Had I signed it, I would have tied a stone around my neck, and the administration and future ones could find cause for my removal. At the time, all this was a real blow. One thing for sure was that the administration was working to curtail my contact with the students and my theological influence.

Around 1972, three new additions to the faculty were made: Wickenkamp in speech, Milton Sernett in ethics, and Jon Diefenthaler in historical theology, who later was and is now Southeastern District president. All were credentialed with Ph.D.'s. I was on good terms with all of them.

Schultz invited me to lunch during the 1972–1973 school year. He was a two-Manhattan man at that lunch, and in attempting to engage in the most courteous behavior I joined him. Nothing of that meeting is remembered, perhaps because of the two Manhattans, but I do remember that during the confessions class that followed that afternoon, the thoughts in my mind had a difficult time emerging.

A similar occurrence followed a party on our back porch for seminary students getting married in the summer following the same school year. Present were Tom Hackett (b. 1949), John Fehrmann and either Klemet or Dan Preus, maybe both. It was a jovial Friday evening, perhaps too jovial. At the other end of the phone, whose ring interrupted the festivities, was Richard J. Schultz, asking me to come to a meeting in his office. When I responded that I could be there the next morning, a Saturday, he said that he would be out of the office for the next week and only then I could see him.

Administrators have used this tactic of delay to create anxiety and destroy the confidence of their subordinates. Whatever fun remained for that evening was over for me, and I faced about ten days of waiting to find out what Schultz wanted. On Monday or Tuesday morning I went for an eight o'clock meeting in the Spenser-Werner administration building, built during the presidency of Jack Preus. At this hour he was in no condition to conduct an interview and nothing happened. Whatever was on his mind on that Friday night was not on his mind that morning.

A preview of the meeting in Schultz's office happened in the faculty lounge after I had preached in chapel. In the presence of other professors, Lorman Petersen and Mark Steege (1906–1997), professor of homiletics, were criticizing me, but they were not agreed on my infraction. Petersen was censuring for content and Steege for my pulpit demeanor, not that he could adequately hide his humility. Steege agreed with my content. So it was not unlike the Pharisees and Sadducees who opposed Paul but could not agree on the reasons for their opposition.

There was still an even more formal occasion in which I was called before a committee of faculty members in Schultz's office for how I conducted myself as a professor. There was little more than their complaints about my preaching and dealing with students. Lorman Petersen was not present, but his handprints were all over the room. Now, I was not informed ahead of time that anyone else would be there, but on arrival Martin Luebke (1917–2008), the registrar, Mark Steege, Raymond Surburg (1909–2001), reputed conservative Old Testament professor, and John Frederick Johnson were in the room. When I mentioned that my preaching could not be that bad, since the students liked it, Luebke responded that I was like Walter A. Maier I of the Lutheran Hour in creating a personal following. What did that mean?

In spite of my homiletical weaknesses, some former students in recent years gathered my sermons into a published volume entitled *In Christ*.[5] Those in the president's office that day I counted as friends, including

---

5. David P. Scaer, *In Christ: The Collected Works of David P. Scaer, Lutheran Confessor* (Sussex, WI: Concordia Catechetical Academy, 2004).

Martin Luebke, with whom I chatted often in the faculty lounge, and Raymond Surburg, with whom I shared a commitment to conservative theology. No one dressed more immaculately than Mark Steege, who for many years served as the pastor of Holy Trinity, an African-American congregation, south of the seminary campus.

According to the students, Steege taught that preachers were to spare their congregations, who were already believers, from hearing the preaching of the law. This was one of several unusual aberrant understandings of sanctification which surfaced in a church body which claimed to be confessional.

I did not think that approaching John Frederick Johnson about these actions would do any good. John was fourteen years older than I was, and we had come onto the faculty together and lived in the same neighborhood and had been guests in each other's homes. In plain language, we were friends. But now as the associate academic dean, when he could have influence with Petersen in regard to my dilemma, our friendship meant nothing. All this happened in the spring of 1972.

In my consternation, I sat evenings outside our home at 2304 West View Drive thinking of what to do. This extended, and for me, depressing episode had some positive advantages in my theological journey. Class schedules for the years 1972 through 1974 will probably show that I taught Lutheran Confessions I five times during the regular school year and once during the summer. Lutheran Confessions II was never assigned to me.

During the Petersen-Schultz administration, elections in faculty meetings hinged on how those in the middle voted. In those years the seminary faculty generally divided itself into three factions, liberal, conservative and those in the middle, each with roughly ten votes at the faculty meetings. Outcomes of some faculty resolutions depended on all those supporting them to be present for the voting. Often this did not happen.

On more than one occasion what looked like certain outcomes failed because this or that faculty member left the room before the vote was taken. Typical reasons for leaving were dentist appointments or providing transportation for their children. No one can know for sure if the course of events would have in the long run been changed if these colleagues had been present to vote, but it does call to mind that certain positions require that we put personal and family matters to the side.

William F. Meyer, who later became administrative assistant to Ray Martens (b. 1933) at Concordia Austin[6] and then president of the Concordia

---

6. Now known as Concordia University Texas.

University system, had been called in 1969 to teach Old Testament before Jack Preus left. Also part of this new group was Victor Bohlmann, brother to the executive secretary of the commission on theology, and later synod president Ralph Bohlmann. Meyer was the son of a conservative Lutheran pastor who supplemented his income by farming, and so Bill was a hands-on kind of guy. Seminary salaries were meager, and so Bill contracted to paint houses. When Petersen learned about this, he asked him to stop.

During a presentation at one Monday faculty study meeting, Erich Heintzen died. Since Mondays would take me to the University of Illinois, attendance at faculty meetings scheduled for that day often found me absent. In the midst of a lecture, he sat down, put his head on the table and died. No faculty member knew how to give artificial respiration. A previous heart attack had made him cut back on his activities.

At the LCMS New Orleans Convention of 1973, Jack Preus received the go-ahead to look more deeply into the situation of the St. Louis seminary. Gene Klug, now in his mid-fifties, was the conservative hero of that convention. I came across seminary president Richard Schultz in the library in August 1973, complaining about the conservatives and how he would prefer a congregation to the seminary presidency. Before the end of the year, perhaps with the premonition that Tietjen would be suspended as St. Louis seminary president, he took a call in the pine barrens of southern New Jersey. It was only a few years before he was at the St. Louis seminary.

In December 1973, John Tietjen was deposed as seminary president. His removal by the board of regents was the cause for the students walking off in protest and then the overwhelming majority of the faculty supporting them by also leaving their positions. One does not have to look behind the curtains to see that this was not a revolution from the bottom up, but was carefully orchestrated for months before the events took place.

The situation at the St. Louis seminary was desperate for several reasons, not the least of which was that, in February of 1974, forty-five professors left their positions and the majority of the student body walked off the campus in protest. Only five professors remained. This situation was enough to put the seminary's accreditation by the American Association of Theological Schools, now the Association of Theological Schools, in jeopardy. Had that happened, district presidents, congregations and pastors supporting the faculty majority and their theological positions would have good reason to reinstate them along with John H. Tietjen as president.

What held the seminary together at least as a viable corporate entity were the five professors who remained at their posts and so came to be called the "Faithful Five," a title that did not come from heroic admiration but was likely contrived to give the impression of an embattled remnant, which of course they were. Listed as the "Faithful Five" are Ralph Bohlmann, Martin Scharlemann, Richard Klann, Robert Preus and Lorenz Wunderlich.

Klann was Teutonic in his lectures and was not that fuzzy kind of a guy that students come to love. Wunderlich was dependable but hardly creative. Martin Scharlemann was appointed interim president, a factor in keeping the seminary operating after the 1974 faculty walkout. During the 1974 spring terms he was harassed by his former colleagues and his health was destroyed by, among other things, persistent and disruptive late night phone calls. On April 15, he resigned from nervous exhaustion.[7]

Robert Preus, as academic dean, assumed the reins and continued teaching. In a matter of weeks, even days, he had to put in place enough professors to cover the courses listed in the academic catalog that were left without instructors. This was a kind of theological Dunkirk in reverse. To keep the St. Louis seminary running, some of us at Springfield were called upon to help. Concordia Seminary, St. Louis remained a viable institution and did not lose its accreditation for which Tietjen's supporters had worked for. In addition to the regularly assigned three courses in Springfield, I had taken on an extra elective. Then there was the biblical survey course in Champaign. Added to this were two New Testament courses at St. Louis which were taught in the morning and the evening of one day.

During the summer, full-time professors were called, and things were humming at the opening service of the fall term with Ralph Bohlmann as president. In an encomium to Bohlmann, his successor as Executive of the Commission on Theology and Church Relations writes, "Dr. Bohlmann was one of five members of the faculty who did not leave the seminary." He omits that when asked by Scharlemann and Robert Preus to teach just one class, he refused. Those months from February through May in 1974 were crucial for the survival of the St. Louis seminary.[8]

Destructive higher criticism had been a reason for concerns with the St. Louis seminary, but the students who remained did not seem to have a

---

7. Scharlemann was the first to lay out what purported to be a defense of the new theology and then led the opposition to it. Though John H. Tietjen was replaced by Scharlemann as seminary president, his *Memoirs in Exile: Confessional Hope and Institutional Conflict* (Minneapolis: Fortress Press, 1990) provides dates and meetings in which Scharlemann was involved. The index provides the references (367). One may also see Frederick Danker, *No Room in the Brotherhood* (St. Louis, MO: Clayton Publishing House, 1977).
8. Samuel H. Nafzger, "An Ecomium for Ralph Arthur Bohlmann: The Passing of a Leader," *Concordia Journal* 42, no. 4 (2016): 285.

minimum knowledge of this or the issues. Some students were also taking courses from the faculty majority which had formed Christ Seminary in Exile, known as Seminex, and so they had a double enrollment.

So tales were brought from Seminex to "801," as the synod campus came to be known, but there was no way of telling whether information was flowing in the opposite direction. For those who were counting, that was a total of seven courses. At age thirty-eight this was still possible for me. With a skeleton faculty and a few stragglers as students, the St. Louis campus was like a ghost town, almost as if a napalm bomb had been dropped.

That year I was the speaker for the Lutheran Brotherhood banquet for the St. Louis graduating class at a downtown St. Louis hotel. My jokes were constructed to fit the anxious times, and notes from that time are probably irretrievably lost. Late that summer I received a letter about how inappropriate my remarks were. Little did I know that the waiters were Seminex students. Visiting professors participated in the graduation procession on the St. Louis campus. Presidential addresses were given by Robert Preus and Ralph Bohlmann, who was chosen as acting president. He would soon be chosen as full-time president. Martin Scharlemann, who had taken over right after Tietjen had been removed, was slowly regaining his health but would be asked by Bohlmann to move out of his campus house.

A number of attempts to award Scharlemann the honorary degree of Doctor of Divinity failed to get a majority of the Fort Wayne faculty. Shortly before he died, it happened. Support for Scharlemann was led by his former students now serving on the CTSFW faculty, who were aware of his courage. Among them were James Voelz and William Weinrich, and Dean Wenthe and Robert Preus, who had served as Scharlemann's academic dean, also supported the move. I did, too. Past differences were not an issue. A faculty minority led by a widely respected Old Testament professor opposed the effort. It did not matter; Scharlemann was soon dead.

As 1974 approached, I did mention to Jack Preus my situation and said that it would be helpful if he could appoint me to synod committee. Public assassinations can be troublesome for the perpetrators. He appointed me to the agenda committee of the *The Lutheran Book of Worship* entrusted with preparing a rite of ordination. Its chairman was a professor of the American Lutheran Seminary in Dubuque, Iowa, whose name escapes me. At the first meeting, Kenneth Korby (1924–2006) put himself forward as the committee secretary and was as much a controlling force as the chairman.

Meetings were held either in Chicago or Minneapolis and were my first encounter with a Lutheran woman clergy person. The first woman to be ordained in the United States was on the committee and at our first meeting was attired in a black cocktail length dress with a clerical collar topped by a red jacket. My memory generally has no room for how others attired themselves, but she was the first female uniformed Lutheran pastor, and this may have been as much a problem for her as it was for me.

About a half century has passed since Lutherans in our country have ordained women pastors, but an inauguration of new practice requires that the traditional uniforms for the male clergy would have to be adjusted for the fairer sex. After she led the devotions, I asked the chairman that she not be allowed to do this again. It was not an issue whether a woman could lead a devotion, but she was doing it in the capacity of a pastor, an office which the Missouri Synod did not allow to be given to or exercised by women. After much discussion with the executive secretary, who may have been Eugene Brand (1913–2002), the chair acceded to my request.

In the evenings the male members of the committee gathered in hotel rooms, and pastors of the synod to which she belonged did not invite her. My assignment was to prepare a paper on what the Bible said about lay ministry. About this the Bible said nothing. This paper remains in my files, but the chance of its being discovered grow less with the years.

Even if I were to see the ordination service in the agenda used by the ELCA, I would scarcely be able to see if it matched what the committee prepared. I do remember that the chair said that the service could speak at the beginning of the rite of what the candidate was about to receive and at the end of the service about what he had received, but pinpointing the moment in which the candidate did receive something in ordination could not be part of the service. Just what the motive for this was I do not know. Was it the anti-clericalism of Upper Midwestern Lutheranism, or was it the influence of neoorthodoxy, which was hesitant in tying transcendental reality to an historical moment?

As I remember it, no one on the committee had an in-depth knowledge of the doctrine of ordination and its history, and so our preparation was somewhat amateurish. Later I would write an extended essay on ordination, which was received with various levels of enthusiasm, and my participation on this committee was probably a factor in this endeavor.[9]

Henry Eggold, a longtime homiletics professor who projected the image of a classical Missouri Synod minister, took up the reigns of the acting seminary presidency of Springfield in January 1974. Eggold was in the middle

---

9. David P. Scaer, *Ordination: Human Rite or Divine Ordinance?* (Fort Wayne, IN: Concordia Theological Seminary Press, 1978), http://www.ctsfw.net/media/pdfs/ScaerOrdinationHumanRiteorDivineOrdinance.pdf.

of the road in the Missouri Synod as anyone could be. He was a well-liked longtime professor of homiletics and trusted by all. He was an institution. Inhaling the smoke from his pipe brought on the lung cancer that caught up with him in Fort Wayne. He became progressively weaker, going from a cane to the wheel chair, and then unable to leave his bed. Jogging around the campus and the surrounding neighborhoods, I would stop in and see him as he neared his end. He was buried from Concordia Lutheran Church in Fort Wayne, and I was a pall bearer. My car, which was in the funeral procession to the new Concordia Cemetery, failed to start. Embarrassed, I left the car in its place as the procession lined up and hopped into another car.

Facing the district presidents in the spring of 1974 was the certification of seminary graduates for the ministry, which is their usual responsibility, but some wanted to include students who had done nearly all of their theology study at Concordia Seminary, St. Louis, but were receiving their diplomas from Seminex. Calls were typically distributed at the end of April to allow the graduates to make plans for setting up their ordination services and moving their families to the locations where they were assigned. In what could only have been seen then and now as a power play, enough district presidents were able to stymy the entire process so that students who remained enrolled at Concordia Seminary, St. Louis, and Concordia Theological Seminary, Springfield, were not assigned calls.

In a few weeks matters were worked out, but at that time parents, relatives and friends of the Springfield graduates had to change their travel plans. The call service in Springfield was canceled and the campus was filled with not only distraught but disappointed graduates and relatives—some at a high cost. Air travel then was still an expensive item and some had invested a good portion of their money to attend an event that did not take place. Among those who came were the parents of James Keurulainen (1947–2014), now the deceased president of the New England District. Students who had studied for four years were deprived of receiving the position of pastor, for which they were trained. In this there is a spiritual loss. Along with this is the financial loss for travel and for delay in assuming their new positions. Since the district presidents had failed to carry out their responsibility according to the timetable in place for placing graduates, they should have been individually and collectively held responsible for the additional costs incurred. Of course, this did not happen.

Henry Eggold continued to handle most of the president's duties in Springfield until Robert Preus came back from his summer home on Gunflint Lake on the Minnesota-Ontario border in August 1974. The fall faculty forum, which initiates the school year, was held in a downtown hotel. Norbert Mueller, who had been a member of the Commission on Theology and Church Relations as a parish pastor, was retained as the faculty representative.

Invited to participate in Preus's inauguration in the field house was the St. Louis faculty. When a reciprocal invitation to process with the St. Louis faculty in the inauguration of its president some months later did not materialize, it began to be evident that the good spirit that held the conservative movement together was becoming unglued. This was a precursor of bad days ahead.

During the Springfield years, we rented our house out for the months we were in the Poconos. The extra income was appreciated. One summer, we rented our place to the director of Concordia Historical Institute, who was teaching a summer course. Rental for a month was about $150. From that amount he deducted the days he did not occupy the house. He was conservative not only theologically, but financially. He had the use of our house for $35. In another incident, upon returning in the summer of 1974, our tenants had not left and we spent the night in a dorm and went over to the president's house to visit with Robert and Donna Preus.

After the trials of the Schultz-Petersen administration, Eggold's acting presidency was a happy and welcome relief. On the night of the Robert Preus election several board members, including its chairman, Harold Olsen, were cheery and spoke to me by phone me from his home with the news that better days were in store for me, including being included in the salary increases to keep up with inflation.

The next two years, 1974–1976, saw the exodus from the faculty of Lorman Petersen, Victor Bohlmann, William F. Meyer, John Frederick Johnson and Jon Diefenthaler. Milton Sernett went on to Syracuse University. Wickenkamp became president of the LCMS Southeastern District. Ray Martens was chosen as the president of Concordia Austin.

Esther Stahlke, wife of Professor Otto Stahlke, was involved in synod and seminary affairs as much as anyone and spoke often of Johnson's return to the faculty. It would happen in the cases of Huth, Schultz and Wenthe, who interrupted their seminary teaching careers with a return to the parish. In the case of Johnson this did not happen. Well into his eighties, he remained a frequent theological lecturer in his Florida retirement. His daughter, Charlene, who babysat for our children, married John Sippola, who traveled with me on occasion to Champaign and is now a retired ELCA pastor.

Excursus VII

ROBERT DAVID PREUS

ಶಿ

Robert David Preus was born to then Minnesota Governor Jacob A. O. Preus I and his wife, Idella, on October 16, 1924. He and his older brother, Jacob A. O. Preus II, were descended from a long line of Lutheran pastors, reaching back into seventeenth-century Norway. Confirmed in an LCMS congregation in Chicago, Robert Preus went to Luther College in Decorah, Iowa, an institution of the Evangelical Lutheran Church (ELC), which later merged into the 1960 American Lutheran Church.

He chose to study theology at Luther Seminary, also an ELC institution, where his uncle Herman A. Preus III (1896–1995) was on the faculty. While the name "Preus" came to be associated with the Missouri Synod, the name is well known in ELCA circles. During World War II students were accelerated through college and seminary, and so Robert was able to complete both phases of his education before his twenty-fourth birthday.

In his last year at Luther Seminary, he took exception to the synergistic doctrine of election taught by George Aus (1903–1977),[1] and he transferred in his final year to Bethany Lutheran Seminary in Mankato, Minnesota, a school of the Evangelical Lutheran Synod (the little Norwegian synod, as it is stilled called). Along with pastorates in East Grand Forks, North Dakota, and Cambridge, Massachusetts, he was able to obtain a Ph.D. from Edinburgh University (Scotland), where Thomas F. Torrance (1913–2007), the most prominent British neoorthodox theologian at the time, considered him the best student he ever had.

I first met Robert Preus when he arrived at Concordia Seminary in the fall of 1957. He joined the St. Louis faculty as an assistant professor in philosophy with the confidence derived from significant personal achievements. His predecessors in that position, Paul Riedel[2] and Donald Meyer

---

1. David W. Preus, *Two Trajectories: J. A. O. Preus and David W. Preus* (Minneapolis, MN: Lutheran University Press, 2015), 42.
2. I was present at Riedel's committal in New Jersey, where he had been a pastor in the English District. My father, as circuit visitor, conducted the service. Paul Riedel's brother Robert was the Atlantic District regional

(1926–1956), had both passed away. On the day of his installation in September 1957, I introduced myself to him. I felt an immediate kinship with him, which lasted until he died November 4, 1995.

During the two years we were both on campus (1957–1958; 1959–1960), I did not have Robert Preus as an instructor in the undergraduate program. That came later in graduate school (1962–1963). I was often in his company, especially at his home and benefitted from his clarity of thought. His sons, Daniel, Klemet, Rolf (b. 1953) and Peter, who were children at that time, later were students at the Springfield/Fort Wayne seminary. Even later, Rolf's sons were in my classes at CTSFW (Concordia Theological Seminary—Fort Wayne), as was Hans Fiene (b. 1980), a son of Robert's daughter, Solveig Preus Fiene (b. 1957).

By 1960, it became evident to seminary president Alfred Fuerbringer and academic dean Arthur Repp that Preus's prestigious university credentials did not translate into support for the latent Lutheran version of neoorthodoxy which, unformed as it was, was emerging within the faculty as the wave of the future.

Robert Preus led the handful of professors in opposing the new theology and, more than anyone else, Robert Preus turned the LCMS around.[3] His leadership was later recognized by Evangelicals who were facing similar challenges in their own traditions. The Southern Baptist Convention, which had fallen under the same theological spell that had overtaken the St. Louis faculty, used the same approach to recapture their seminaries.

At some point in the 1956–1957 academic year, I was alerted to Robert D. Preus's *The Inspiration of Scripture*, his published doctoral dissertation on the views of the seventeenth-century Lutheran dogmaticians on that doctrine.[4] I may have received a copy from Arne Pettersen, a benefactor of conservative students. Preus's clear explanation of doctrine attracted me, as did that of the methods of these old theologians, though later I came to view his detailed dissection of how inspiration took place as going beyond what the Biblical documents said about themselves.

---

vice president for New England when I served Trinity, Rockville, Connecticut (1962–1964). For ordaining Seminex graduates, he was removed by Jack Preus as president of the newly formed New England District.

3. See Robert D. Preus, "Current Theological Problems Which Face Our Church." This unpublished paper demonstrates Preus's mastery of the primary issues facing the LCMS as it entered the decade of the 1960s. It is a remarkably insightful piece.
4. Robert D. Preus, *The Inspiration of Scripture: A Study of the Theology of the Seventeenth Century Lutheran Dogmaticians* (Edinburgh: Oliver and Boyd, 1955).

At this time, I did not distinguish between what Lutheran theologians said about this or that doctrine and how it might have been presented in the biblical documents themselves. Seeing the Scriptures and what the classical Lutheran theologians say about them as synonymous is widespread in the synod. This is not without problems for preaching and theology.

While I was preparing my doctoral dissertation, Robert Preus was at first assigned as a reader. Later he was replaced. He may have been present for the defense of my dissertation for receiving the Doctor of Theology degree from Concordia Seminary in 1963. This association was instrumental in my being called as assistant professor to Concordia Theological Seminary, Springfield, Illinois, in the spring of 1966. Regular contacts with Robert Preus resumed when I arrived at Springfield in 1966. Robert and his wife Donna were always good company. Dorothy and I remained very good friends with them.

On February 14, 1974, the faculty of Concordia Seminary in St. Louis, following the majority of the seminary's students, walked off the campus in protest. The die was cast and there would be no turning back.

On that day, Martin Scharlemann, as acting president, and Robert Preus, as acting academic dean, took over the administration of the seminary in what was a very tense situation. Many of the protesting students and faculty remained in campus housing and, in the case of the faculty, in their campus homes and offices. Like divorces, these matters are never clear-cut, and it takes weeks, even months, to rub off the rough edges.[5]

Martin Scharlemann and Robert Preus assumed the responsibility of the reconstruction of the seminary faculty. Soon Scharlemann resigned as acting president and Robert Preus took his place. However, Preus never received any recognition from that seminary. Since many district presidents and other church officials had supported the St. Louis faculty majority, Robert Preus had good reason to distrust some church officials. This left him to depend on his intuition.

First impressions counted with him, and he regarded past friendships highly. This resulted in such anomalies as having Robert Hoerber (1918–1996), called to the St. Louis seminary from Westminster College in Fulton, Missouri, as a Greek professor, even though later on it surfaced that he found nothing wrong with the ordination of women. Preus put a high mark on his being hospitably received and enjoyed being taken out

---

5. Lawrence R. Rast Jr. "Reflections on Social and Theological Factors Leading to the Walkout," *Concordia Theological Quarterly* 80 (2016): 195–215.

to lunch. In one case, hearing what he considered a good sermon one time led to a man being called to the seminary. It did not turn out well.

When Robert Preus became president of the Springfield seminary in 1974, Dorothy and I saw less and less of them. But when we did get together we had the best of times. I received no special appointments, and so my relationship with Preus was social and theological. He was accessible, and I took any opportunity to bring my ideas to his attention. In Springfield, for the Lorman Petersen years, I was in survival mode. Robert Preus's first years were peaceful and allowed some writing. I had access to Robert, just as I had access to his brother Jack during my first three years at the seminary. After Robert Preus was dismissed in 1989, I never presumed to have that privilege with his successors, with whom those kinds of informal conversations are factors in keeping abreast of seminary affairs.

Someone once asked me at a public meeting to explain my close relationship to Robert Preus. My answer, as much as I can remember it, was that Preus felt closer to me on a human, emotional level, but he saw in Kurt Marquart a theologian who best represented his views.

Robert Preus's dependence on intuition also opened the door to his calling some conservative pastors, who were less than qualified in other important areas, to the Fort Wayne seminary. They formed a core that later—in a remarkable and noteworthy act of betrayal—actively worked to remove him or were sympathetic to those who did.

Robert's brother Jack had worked more within the system and relied on the advice of church officials and sought for their approval on names proposed for assignments to the seminary. Robert's failure to check on the past records of those whom he nominated for faculty positions cannot be discounted as a factor leading to his downfall. Preus's management style opened the door to those driven by pure ambition, but who also harbored jealousies over his theological acumen and personal charisma.

There is no doubt that I would have continued as academic dean (1984–1989) as long as Robert Preus was seminary president, simply because I got things done. However, in the last years of his presidency, I was kept out of some important policy decisions. Only after the decision and deed were done did I learn of them.

The synod seemed to be in good hands with J. A. O. Preus as synod president and brother Robert D. Preus as seminary president. It did not appear then that things could possibly go wrong—but they did. In conversations with others, I have discovered that I was privy to very little concerning the events leading up to Preus's dismissal from either his side or from the perspective of his opponents.

Before the May 19–20, 1989, board meeting at which Robert Preus was asked to retire, red flags were going up that he was in trouble. Twice, once in the winter and then again in May, the board met in executive session, in which only its members were allowed to be present. Its minutes are recorded on a colored paper that only the members may see. Preus's exclusion should have indicated trouble for him. If he was aware of it, it did not seem to bother him.

Then there was a letter from Howard Tepker to Indiana District president Reuben Garber (1929–2001) with a copy to board member Ray Mueller (1929–2007).[6] I do not know if Ray Mueller shared the letter with Preus, and if he did, Preus likely dismissed the seriousness of it. Confidence in one's own ability to handle adverse situations often evolves into overconfidence that makes one vulnerable.

Another red flag that might have been missed is the board of regents' handbook, adopted in March 1989. It had the provision that the seminary president may be retired after fifteen years of service or the year in which he reaches sixty years of age. Seventy was listed as the age of retirement in the 1973 and 1986 editions of the handbook of the synod's Board for Professional Education Services, which at the time had supervision of the synod's colleges and seminaries. This change in the regent's handbook would give them reason for retiring Preus.[7]

From my own contacts with him, Robert Preus did not seem to have an inkling of the disaster that was in store for him on May 20, 1989. He had survived past conflicts, and in his mind, there would have been no reason that he would not also survive this one, but in carrying out the plot to remove him, synod president Ralph Bohlmann, board chairman Ray Joeckel and President Garber proved to be superior. Joeckel and Preus had proved to be friends in each donating half of the moneys for the extension to the president's house on campus so that it could be used for social occasions. There was no reason for Preus to be suspicious of Joeckel's intentions.

Robert Preus was officially removed as president after a court hearing in September 1989 and his return to that position by LCMS convention action in July 1992 was even in his own eyes only a formality. Academic dean Walter A Maier II did not let him teach any courses, a policy continued by Preus's successor, David Schmiel, who was installed in April 1993 as president. Robert and Donna removed their residence from Fort Wayne in April 1994 to a suburb of Minneapolis.

---

6. For details of this and other events leading to Robert Preus's retirement, see chapter 9: "The 'Retirement' of Robert Preus," 259 ff.
7. Preus vs. Board of Regents (March 19, 1991), 5.

Preus's removal from the presidency was not a black-and-white issue of liberals taking revenge on conservatives. Some of his opponents and those watching the debacle from the sidelines were recognized in the synod as conservative, but in some cases they were lacking theological acumen. Other opponents were thinking along "Evangelical" lines in seeing little value in the liturgy and substituting informal Bible study for theology. It cannot be overlooked that because of the man Robert Preus was, he was seen as a threat to the status quo that existed in the synod headquarters. They were the synod establishment with family ties reaching back into the synod's history. Some faculty members were driven by envy, ambition and jealousy. Robert was recognized as a theologian even outside of the Missouri Synod. Simply put, he was well liked in a way his opponents were not.

At the July 1995 convention Ralph Bohlmann was not retained as synod president and slowly faded in importance. He died some twenty years later, and during that time he left little of theological accomplishment behind. Robert Preus left a written theological legacy, which was preserved by his admirers, and his progeny who followed him into the ministry of the church from which he was for a time excluded by Bohlmann.

In October 1980, Jack Preus had announced via a letter to the synod that he did not intend to stand again for the LCMS presidency. He retired to Arkansas and died in August 1994 at age seventy-four. Robert died a little more than a year later, in November 1995, at age seventy-one. Whereas Jack's last years were comparatively uneventful, Robert's were not. In the five and a half years between the night of May 20, 1989, when board chairman Raymond Joeckel and Indiana District president Reuben Garber asked for his resignation and his death on November 4, 1995, Preus aged dramatically. His vigorous, youthful appearance was replaced by the face of an old man. His erect frame became more and more bent over, his hair turned a stark white, and his face became drawn. One could see death creeping up on him.

On the afternoon of Saturday, November 4, 1995, Robert was out walking with his wife, Donna, in what was a daily ritual for them. Robert, being overcome with chest pains, they started to return home. A registered nurse noticed his difficulty and drove them home. She wanted to take him to the emergency room. Coming into the house, he collapsed. When the emergency medics came, he was already dead. That night Don and Corinne Deffner and I were invited to Barbara (1947–2015) and Bill Weinrich's home for dinner. In coming to the door, Bill told me the news. The champion of confessional Lutheranism was gone. A six-hundred-mile drive from Fort Wayne to Minneapolis was a good reason not to attend the funeral, but our lives had so intertwined that this was for me an impossible option.

Bill Weinrich, who had already been chosen to become acting president in place of David Schmiel, rented a large Cadillac, which provided transportation for his wife Barbara, Dan (b. 1954) and Annette (b. 1960) Gard, and myself. Trudy Behning, Robert's longtime secretary, found a ride in a van arranged by Richard Resch, who brought the seminary's Kantorei to sing at the funeral.

Upon arriving at the church during the visitation, I was ushered immediately into the room reserved for the family, whom I had known since September 1957, when Robert was installed as assistant professor at the St. Louis Seminary. I was overcome by seeing the man who had changed the course of the Missouri Synod lying in the casket with perhaps more life in his face than he had in those depressing years following his dismissal as seminary president and exclusion from the synod.

Seminary president David Schmiel and academic dean Alan Borcherding asked to speak to the assembled mourners at the service in behalf of the seminary. Those who would not let him teach and were responsible for his decision to move from Fort Wayne to the Minneapolis area now wanted to speak at the funeral. Seminary regent David Anderson (1931–2017) informed them that if either showed up at the church, they would be removed from the premises.

Before the service, Douglas Judisch showed the family a resolution passed by the faculty on Monday, November 8, noting Preus's contribution to the seminary. Seated about two-thirds down from the front of the church on the left side, I could see the funeral director close the lid of the coffin.

Seeing Robert's face for the last time is permanently etched in my memory. So forceful was his personality, that his face and personality are still impressed in the minds of those who knew him. Brother Jack had died the summer of the previous year at age seventy-four, and so a death for Robert at seventy-one was not out of the ordinary. Each had lived his threescore and ten, but the thought lingers that fighting his removal from office and the charges brought against him first by Waldo Werning (1921–2013) and synod president Bohlmann had brought Preus to an early grave.

Bill Weinrich was slated to bring faculty greetings, but this role fell to Douglas Judisch, who was thought to be the faculty representative. Later he apologized to me as the one who should have brought the seminary's greetings, but this honor rightfully belonged to Bill Weinrich. Seated toward the rear of the crowded church, Bill Weinrich could not come forward to share his prepared tribute. On the fateful Saturday of Robert's death, acting president Bill Weinrich was on the phone with Preus arranging for him to resume teaching at Fort Wayne. In his remarks, St. Louis seminary president John Franklin Johnson noted that Robert had begun his teaching career at that seminary and that his last teaching assignment was there. Since all the church's pews were filled and its aisles so narrow, some of the congregation had not left the building before the committal began in the adjacent cemetery. By the time I reached the grave, the committal service was nearing a conclusion.

The night before, Carl Volz (1933–1998), Robert's colleague at the St. Louis faculty and then a professor at Luther Seminary, now deceased, came to pay his respects. At the committal David Preus (b. 1922), cousin to Robert and Jack, stood at distance with his wife on the dirt road at the cemetery's edge. Once, in passing through an airport before the 1974 walkout, I had seen David Preus meeting with Missouri Synod dissidents. As its president, David Preus brought the American Lutheran Church into a merger with the Lutheran Church in America (LCA) and the Association of Evangelical Lutheran Churches (AELC), the breakoff Missouri group formed around the Seminex faculty, to form the Evangelical Lutheran Church in America (ELCA), a decision he later privately regretted. In the merger the LCA was the majority church, and so, come the elections of the newly formed church, David Preus would no longer be ALC church president. Titles like Theologian in Residence are given to the runners-up.

Many students entering the seminary now have no idea who Jack and Robert Preus were, but each shaped the Missouri Synod as none of their contemporaries or successors have. Jack's place in synod history has been documented with one account balancing the other.[8] Robert Preus's removal in 1989, along with the denial of calls to his alleged thirty-two student supporters in 1992, had repercussions in the convention that year in replacing Ralph Bohlmann as synod president with Alvin Barry (1931–2001).

---

8. Lawrence R. Rast Jr., "J. A. O. Preus: Theologian, Churchman, or Both?" *Concordia Theological Quarterly* 74 (January 2010): 57–72; James E. Adams, *Preus of Missouri and the Great Lutheran Civil War* (New York: Harper & Row, 1977); Paul A. Zimmerman, *A Seminary in Crisis: The Inside Story of the Preus Fact Finding Committee* (St. Louis, MO: Concordia, 2007); Paul Devantier, *Warrior of God, Man of Peace: The Life and Times of J. A. O. Preus* (St. Louis, MO: Lutheran Church—Missouri Synod, 1995).

It seemed a surface crack in the body politic that at the 2001 convention, the synod chose Texas District president Gerald Kieschnick over Fort Wayne seminary president Dean O. Wenthe by the slimmest of majorities. The Preus name still carried weight. At the same convention Daniel Preus was elected first vice president, which not only recognized his accomplishments, but also honored his father.

Those who voted for Matthew Harrison as synod president in 2010 and again in 2013 may not have known that Robert Preus was the first advisor of Harrison's master of sacred theology thesis and that when Preus was removed, I was chosen in his place. Harrison sees himself as a disciple of Robert Preus; he knows Preus's writings and is committed to Preus's views. Historical memory fades, but the theological legacy of Robert Preus does not.

Robert Preus is buried in the church cemetery of St. John's in Maple Grove, Minnesota, where his son-in-law, Steven C. Briel (b. 1949), was pastor before his retirement. His death sent shock waves through the synod, and with the passing of the years his fame has not diminished.

Chapter Seven

EARLY YEARS OF THE ROBERT PREUS PRESIDENCY

❧

Robert Preus would soon add others to the faculty. Douglas Judisch had finished his residency at the University of Edinburgh. Kurt Marquart, who was serving a congregation in Queensland, Australia, came back in December 1975. Of all the faculty members, he was the closest to Preus theologically. Alvin Schmidt came from Lenoir-Rhyne College in North Carolina. Later William C. Weinrich, who was finishing his work at the University of Basil, and James Voelz, soon to receive his Ph.D. from Cambridge, joined the faculty.

Howard Tepker, chairman of the systematics department, was chosen as academic dean, a position he would hold from 1974 to 1979, when he was replaced by Wilbert Rosin (b. 1923), then president of Concordia College Milwaukee. Tepker had been a pastor of St. John's, Beardstown, Illinois, on the Illinois River when he joined the faculty in 1958, the same year as did Jack Preus and Warren Wilbert. By chance both of us had received the Doctor of Theology at the same graduation ceremony on June 4, 1963, at Concordia Seminary, St. Louis. At the same ceremony my uncle Ernest Scaer, the last president of Concordia College in Oakland, received the honorary Doctor of Divinity degree, which could easily be considered a compensation for synod's closing the school. He had served that school for about forty years, sometimes as interim president. Before my coming to the seminary then in Springfield in 1966, I did not really know Tepker. After the turmoil of Petersen's tenure as academic dean, Tepker's five-year tenure was a welcome relief.

Later, as academic dean, I attended a seminar of the Association of Theological Schools (ATS) and learned that this position was a recent innovation at seminaries, and there is no one way to define this position. The position of academic dean is what that person makes it. Arthur C. Repp was the longtime academic dean at the St. Louis seminary, including during my student days, and defined it as an influential position. His successor, John Damm, was instrumental in putting forth his onetime co-pastor at Grace Teaneck, New Jersey, John Tietjen, as St. Louis seminary president, and played a leading role in the majority faculty walkout in February 1974.

Howard Tepker served as academic dean for the seminary the last two years in Springfield and the first three in Fort Wayne. It was expected that tensions between seminary and senior college faculties would exist during the one year (1976–1977) we shared the Fort Wayne campus. To Tepker's credit, they did not. Having graduated from St. Louis seminary in 1936, he was probably sixty-two when he assumed the position, and at the end of five years he was ready for giving up the position. At Fort Wayne he often could be seen leaving the campus at noon for the rest of the day. Al Schmidt, who had an interest in academic protocol, wondered how a person in this position could carry out that office's responsibilities with a schedule that ended the day at lunch time. The reason was that Preus made many of the decisions often left to the Academic Dean.

Allen Nauss stayed on as dean of students and Martin Luebke as registrar. In addition to finding faculty replacements, Robert Preus's other order of business was moving the seminary out of Springfield, whose proximity to an equally conservative seminary one hundred miles to the south might give a good reason to combine the schools. Having a more conservative seminary in Springfield than the seminary in St. Louis may have been one reason that the synod was able to go through the crises of the 1970s. The synod managed to stay together after the St. Louis majority faculty walkout. The 1975 Anaheim Convention was the last hurrah for the Seminex faculty.

Since Seminex theology no longer posed a threat, and for all appearances, Missouri's old conservative theology had been revived, two complementary problems had to be addressed. Neither the Seminex theology or the conservative theology which opposed it have been analyzed. Seminex theology was absorbed into the Evangelical Lutheran Church in America, where its proponents were leaders in introducing this church's more radical programs. That was not an issue for the Missouri Synod. An issue for the Missouri Synod was defining and retaining confessional theology.

In the years preceding and following the 1974 walkout of the faculty majority of Concordia Seminary, St. Louis, opponents of the new theology conducted seminars throughout the Missouri Synod. Its opponents were known as conservatives and centered their opposition around any method of interpretation that cast doubt on the historical character of the events the Bible reported.

But differences that were as old as the synod remained unresolved, such as the doctrine of the ministry. Even when Missouri and Wisconsin synods were in fellowship with each other, they still did not see eye to eye on this issue. The view of the Wisconsin Synod that the ministry is a deduction from the universal priesthood was one of the arguments put forward in ordaining women. Those who placed the origin of the ministry in Christ and the apostles were said to be followers of Wilhelm Löhe and J. A. A. Grabau (1804–1879) and often called sacerdotalists. The genius of both Jack and Robert Preus was directing the energies of those who differed with one another to the common good of unifying the synod.

Such differing theological approaches were not productive when the synod had to face higher critical methods in interpreting the Bible and the ordination of women ministers. In the former case, the synod's theologians were unprepared, and in the latter case some opposed the practice of women pastors only with Bible citations. Others saw that opposition to ordaining women required arguments that were integrated into a fully informed doctrine of the ministry.

With the laity playing a prominent role in the controversies leading up to 1974, the view for some was confirmed that the congregation possessed the ultimate authority in exercising the office of the keys. This was a common view in the synod long before then. As a seminary student, I had written a paper for a pastoral theology class taught by *Lutheran Witness* editor Otto Sohn (1894–1969) in which I argued that since lay people had the keys, they could baptize, preach and celebrate communion. Sohn agreed they could preach and baptize but not celebrate communion. Though my argument was judged to be wrong, it seemed as logical then as it does now. Later this argument from the priesthood of believers provided one argument among others for ordaining women, but in the 1950s none of the Lutheran church bodies in America had come to this conclusion. They soon would.

The liturgy used in the synod's congregations recognized the pastor as Christ's and not the congregation's representative in forgiving sins, but an assumption arose that he was acting by the authority of the congregation and appeared in the synod's edition of Luther's *Small Catechism*. This view that the pastor was the congregation's representative was promoted in pastoral theology classes by Norbert Mueller, who would later serve as its interim president.

The view that a congregation forgives itself through the pastor not only lacks biblical support, but involves a strange circular action in which members of the congregation forgive themselves. Each side of the debate, to which there were several nuances, referenced Walther's *Church and Ministry*,[1] but in the actual church life the vast majority of the synod's congregations, in spite of how one stood on the issue, pastors and congregations worked in harmony with one another. Just as there will always be overbearing pastors, so there will always be congregations that regard their pastors as employees. Paul's Epistles testify to the tension.

Theologically eye-opening for the synod were the ordinations, first for Herman Otten in 1959 and twenty-five years later for Seminex candidates in 1974. It seems that, together with their district president supporters, John Tietjen and John Damm believed that many congregations would rise to their defense, support the "exiles" and like ancient Israel they would return.[2] The first name given to their school was Concordia Seminary in Exile. For legal reasons it was changed to Christ Seminary in Exile. Part of the strategy was offering Seminex graduates as pastoral candidates to as many churches as quickly as possible after the walkout under the guise that they were "St. Louis seminary graduates."[3] Since most congregations call pastors serving other congregations, most congregational officers likely lack familiarity with the operations of the synod and how new candidates are placed into their first congregations.

Otten and the Seminex graduates boasted calls and authorizations for their ordinations from congregations. In response, the synod made authorization by the Council of Presidents acting on the advice of the theological faculties necessary for ordination, but this was a bylaw and not a doctrine. An appointment to a sub-committee of the *Lutheran Book of Worship* to prepare a rite of ordination for its agenda provided me an op-

---

1. C. F. W. Walther, *The Church and the Office of the Ministry, the Voice of Our Church on the Question of Church and Office: A Collection of Testimonies Regarding This Question from the Confessions of the Evangelical Lutheran Church and from the Private Writings of Orthodox Teachers of the Same*, ed. Matthew C. Harrison, trans. John Theodore Mueller (St. Louis, MO: Concordia Publishing House, 2012).
2. Tietjen himself makes this point in *Memoirs in Exile*, 252.
3. See the opinion of the LCMS Commission on Constitutional Matters of March 23, 1974, which states: "It is with sincere regret that the Commission is unanimously constrained to rule that under the bylaws of the Synod the aforementioned students cannot be declared eligible for placement in the ministry of The Lutheran Church—Missouri Synod. They will not 'have completed the prescribed courses of study and have received a diploma from one of the Synod's seminaries' (Bylaw 4.15 a. I); they will not 'have received endorsement by the proper faculty' (4.15 a.2); they will not be 'graduates of an authorized synodical institution or approved synodical training program.'"

portunity to delve into the matter. In being assigned the topic of the ministry of the laity, I could find no biblical or confessional support for this.

What was said about the pastor in the ordination liturgy did not correspond with synod teaching that the ministry is derived from the congregation. The issue still plagues us. So, in 1977, without any particular audience in view, I volunteered an ad hoc essay entitled "Ordination: Human Rite or Divine Ordinance?"[4] Intended only for discussion for those who were willing to give up their free time to come and listen. Without my knowledge or direction it found its way into the seminary print shop and then the bookstore and into the hands of Clyde Nehrenz, a Cleveland layman, who brought the matter in an overture to a synod convention.

In spite of a seminary board resolution that it no longer be sold, it continues to make the rounds, though I have never presented it again or been invited to do so. No formal and informal response was ever made, and so no opportunity was given to respond to its critics. In any event, its views did not define me. One wonders about the royalties, if rather than being bootlegged, it had been copyrighted.

With the removal of the Seminex threat, fissures would appear among those who previously saw themselves united. The AAL banquet for seminary graduates in 1976, the last year the seminary was in Springfield, was particularly festive, especially with John Warwick Montgomery, a friend of Robert Preus, as speaker. He was not the first speaker at this kind of occasion to read a chapter from a book he had written or from his dissertation. This would happen at least once more with another speaker. It did not dampen the high spirits, but then again it did not ignite them.

Jack Preus had been given synod permission to remove district presidents who continued to ordain Seminex graduates. Reprieves were given to those who had done this, but promised not to do this again. Robert Preus appointed me as the seminary's representative to the synod's 1975 Anaheim convention, and I had my first occasion to speak on the floor of a synod convention, and it was in regard to a theological point. I was appointed to serve on committee three, which customarily handles theological matters, but I played only a minor role.

THE SEMINARY MOVES BACK TO FORT WAYNE

As the Anaheim convention wore on, my desire to leave early came to the attention of Paul Zimmerman, who admonished me to stay to the

---

4. David P. Scaer, *Ordination: Human Rite or Divine Ordinance?* (Fort Wayne, IN: Concordia Theological Seminary Press, 1978).

end, but as an advisory delegate without vote and little or no chance to speak on the floor again, I took an earlier flight back to Allentown, Pennsylvania. Upon arrival back in the Poconos, I was met with the news that the seminary would be moved from Springfield to Fort Wayne, a decision made by the convention in the closing minutes. Conservatives could unite behind a proposal to close the Concordia Senior College in Fort Wayne, which was made redundant by turning the synod's junior colleges into four-year institutions, a process which now has raised most to university status with graduate programs. A separate motion followed to move the seminary from Springfield to Fort Wayne. It garnered votes from a different alignment of delegates, including Indiana District delegates, to pass. By dividing one motion into two, Jack Preus showed his political skill.

The seminary's move to Fort Wayne was not without controversy. After all, Concordia Senior College was going to be displaced from the campus it had occupied since 1957. One story that has persisted was that the synod lost money in the move. As late as 2001, twenty-five years after the seminary was in Fort Wayne, a former district president, then on the synod's commission on theology, spoke of how much the move cost the synod.

This is the story: the Springfield campus was sold to a local investor, who in turn leased the property to the State of Illinois for an institute training guards for the state's penal institutions. I know the financial details and will only say here it more than covered the costs. This was a kind of irony, since seminary president George Beto during his tenure as president served on the state's parole board, after which he left to head up the Texas state penal system in 1962.[5]

The cost of moving students and faculty were minimal. Students enrolling in the first year in Fort Wayne (1976) and students returning from their vicarage received no funding for their moves. Those who had completed their first seminary year, and so would be second year students on the Fort Wayne campus, were given a stipend. Moving expenses for faculty members were covered by the synod with the understanding that they picked up packing boxes in the seminary gymnasium and pack up their own belongings. Refrigerators and freezers were to be empty of food. Movers would pack up fragile china and crystal. So far as I know, only one colleague did not comply, and open jars of mustard and mayonnaise made their way to Fort Wayne. The spring and summer of 1976 saw a mass migration of seminary faculty and students from Springfield to Fort Wayne.

---

5. Horton and Nielsen, *Walking George: The Life of George John Beto*.

On the Saturday before Holy Week many professors hurried to Fort Wayne to make housing arrangements for the coming year. Some intended to occupy houses vacated by Concordia Senior College professors leaving for other opportunities. Others bought houses and had new houses constructed. Walter A. Maier II and I were in the latter group and found ourselves living in the Pine Valley neighborhood about four miles north of the campus. Eugene Klug found a house closer to the seminary, but it was not the one he wanted.

One episode involving two now-deceased colleagues needs preserving. On a beautiful sunny Easter morning, April 18, 1976, outside of Trinity Lutheran Church, the kind of a day that made one think that maybe leaving Springfield might not have been the best decision, several of us who had been in Fort Wayne the previous week were talking about the housing arrangements we had made. Eugene Klug spoke of how he had made a bid on a house which within hours had been topped by a higher bidder, and so he lost the house. As the conversation proceeded it came out that Raymond Surburg, who was also part of this conversation, had been that higher bidder and had purchased the house.

The night before we left in June 1976 for Fort Wayne, the neighbors gave us a farewell party with gifts to remember them. We have never forgotten them. By then stepson Rick Nehring, as Fred was then known, was in the navy and stepdaughter Pamela Nehring at the University of Illinois. With three sons, ages fifteen, thirteen and ten, we had room in the station wagon for Robert Preus to look the situation over in Fort Wayne.

Our house on West Wind Place in Fort Wayne was under construction, and we spent two nights with my mother's cousin Henry Meyer (1912–2006) and his wife, Frieda (1911–2006), on Muldoon Road. My grandmother, Lydia Zimmermann, had grown up on a farm on St. Mary's River south of town and had been a member of the prominent Fort Wayne Trier family. The Scaers had come from further up the same river in nearby Convoy, Ohio. My grandfather, Charles Scaer (1858–1928), had taught at Tri-State College,[6] north of Fort Wayne, and took the train to Hillsdale, Michigan, to attend church where he met my grandmother, Hanna Morlock (1865–1951). So in a sense it was a homecoming of sorts, but it was soon evident to others as it was to me that home was New York.

Coming to the seminary at the age of thirty, I was close to the average age of some students and much younger than many. Since travel by the interstate was not as convenient as it is now, we entertained students who

---

6. Now Trine University.

could not go home for the Christmas holidays. These parties expanded into one each term right up until we moved onto the Fort Wayne campus in 2006. In Springfield, Saturday night parties were held in our garage with students and wives. They were great fun.

In colder weather in Fort Wayne the garage parties ceased, but we continued with Sunday afternoon gatherings until age caught up with us. I can safely say—I can add dogmatically say—that no other faculty spouse in the last half century or even in the entire seminary history entertained as much as Dorothy did. She did this without any assistance from the seminary. And she must be "well attested for her good deeds, as one who has brought up her children, shown hospitality, washed the feet of the saints, relieved the afflicted, and devoted herself to doing good in every way" (1 Tm 5:10). Students, now pastors, remember those halcyon days.

We sold our house on West View Drive in Springfield, Illinois, without benefit of a real estate agent in a matter of days after we put a notice in the classified section of the newspaper. Proceeds were used to build a new home in Fort Wayne that was ready to move into when we arrived at the end of summer in 1976. During the fall of 1977, I preached several times in Berne, Indiana, where a member was a furniture manufacturer from whom we bought a couch for the family room. It proved too large, and at a Christmas party I suggested that the room be expanded. To this my wife Dorothy responded that rather than enlarging a room on an existing house, we would build an entirely new house—and we did.

Property was bought from Elmer Macke on 1912 Brandywine Trail about a mile away, and construction began on Memorial Day weekend in 1978. We read through several books with housing plans, and Dorothy chose one for which we sent sixty dollars for the plans and visited various outfitters for the lighting, the dry wall, kitchen cabinets and lumber. One contractor, Wally Borchelt (1930–2012), provided plumbing, heat and air conditioning and electricity.

Our new home had about four thousand square feet and had a stucco and cedar exterior. It had fifteen rooms counting the vestibule, the laundry and storage rooms, the glassed in porch and the balcony overlooking the living room with its sixteen foot high ceiling. Later the balcony was a hit with grandchildren, who dropped down objects into the room below. There were two brick fire places, one in the family room and the other in the living room. My study was on the third floor with a window giving a view of the neighborhood. Shelves lined the 460 square foot room. Another study over the garage served as the office for handling bills and writing checks. So many pleasant memories are associated with 1912 Brandywine Trail. Our daughter Pamela married Richard Witham in the living room in January 1986, and a wedding reception for our son Stephen and his wife Beth was held on June 18, 1988.

One of the parties after the January symposium put about two hundred attendees in the house. Here we entertained Robert and Donna Preus, George (1924–1989) and Helen Kraus and Don and Corinne Deffner. Having reached our seventies, Dorothy and I began to desire smaller quarters. In August 2006, we let these desires come true, and so we moved into 5 Tyndale Place on the seminary campus in October. A weak housing market that was becoming weaker kept the house on the market until August 2007.

THE FIRST YEARS IN FORT WAYNE

For the 1976–1977 academic year, Concordia Theological Seminary occupied the same campus as Concordia Senior College. This was not the first time that the seminary had shared a campus with another synod institution. Here is how it happened the first time.

The Missouri Synod was the result of several different German groups joining into one church. The Saxon pilgrimage to the state of Missouri was under the leadership of Martin Stephan (1777–1846) and later C. F. W. Walther. The largest group of churches was a part of the general migration of Germans looking for a better life on the frontier of Indiana, Michigan, and Ohio. A third group was a colony of men sent by Wilhelm Löhe to the Saginaw Valley of Michigan. Löhe and his associates sent funding, students and faculty to establish the Fort Wayne seminary.

In 1861, to avoid the conscription of its students into the Union side in the Civil War—or as it was known in the South, the War between the States—the seminary moved from Fort Wayne to St. Louis to share the quarters with the synod's other seminary, with C. F. W. Walther serving as president of both institutions. Missouri was a slave state but did not join the confederacy. Had the seminary stayed in Fort Wayne, its students could have been drafted into the Indiana regiments.

When a campus became available in Springfield, Illinois, and given to the synod by Trinity Lutheran Church in Springfield in 1875, the seminary moved again, where it remained for a little over a century. Abraham Lincoln (1809–1865) had served the institution which had occupied that campus. Today the phrase "the Fort Wayne seminary" is so common that its Springfield stay is remembered only by those who studied there, and the youngest of these have passed the age of retirement. By moving to any other city, the seminary's tradition could have been easily lost, but by returning to the city where the seminary had been founded there in 1846, its earliest history was revived.

Eero Saarinen (1910–1961), the famous twentieth-century Finnish-American architect who designed the Senior College campus, named its buildings by their function. A seminary committee was tasked with renaming the buildings, with seminary president Robert Preus making the final determinations. One set of buildings was named for early church fathers, another for Reformation-era theologians, still another for the theologians of Lutheran Orthodoxy and a fourth section for deceased faculty who had served in Springfield. Street names remained the same, with Luther Drive, a mile long, connecting the east entrance on North Clinton with the south one on St. Joe Center Road. Other street names retained the names of English Bible translators William Tyndale (1494–1536), Myles Coverdale (1488–1569), and John Wycliffe (1320–1384), whose views on the Lord's Supper were closer to Calvin's than Luther's. Luther's statue, whose design was suggested by Martin Naumann, a professor in Springfield, was brought to Fort Wayne and now stands guard over those entering from North Clinton.

The classroom buildings were renamed for the seminary's founders. The north classroom building was named for Wilhelm Löhe, who remained in Germany, and the south classroom building for Friedrich Wyneken (1810–1876), pastor of St. Paul's Lutheran Church in Fort Wayne and Zion Lutheran Church in Friedheim (Decatur), Indiana, the mother churches of Lutheranism in the old Northwest. From there he traveled on horseback throughout Northern Indiana, Northwestern Ohio, Southwestern Michigan and into Illinois as far as Chicago. He also served as the second synod president and the pastor of parishes in Baltimore, St. Louis and Cleveland. The auditorium was named for Wilhelm Sihler (1801–1885), the seminary's first president.

During the first years in Fort Wayne, connections with the Löhe established congregations in the Michigan District, especially with the St. Lorenz in Frankenmuth, were celebrated. Fort Wayne was not the seminary's adopted city, but after over a century's absence in St. Louis and Springfield, had come home. With some faculty members not moving to Fort Wayne along with the gradual and ordinary changes that any institution experiences, the seminary's composition changed and the Springfield years faded into memory.

Some older professors resented that Jack Preus, an outsider transplanted from the little Norwegian Synod, as the Evangelical Lutheran Synod was known, could become seminary president in only four years

(1958–1962) and then synod president in nine years (1969). Now they resented his brother Robert Preus for taking the seminary out of Springfield to Fort Wayne. Like all brothers, Jack and Robert Preus had their differences, but were seen by those within and without the Missouri Synod as almost one person. Some outside the synod confused one with the other. But within the Missouri Synod an irrational dislike for one often carried over to the other.

Walter Wente (1894–1992), an uncle by marriage to my father's sister Pauline (1894–1982), was Concordia Senior College's first academic dean and remained on the faculty until its closing in 1977. In my visits to him in the Lutheran Homes on South Anthony, he was adamant that the Missouri Synod would be better off without any Preus. Ironically some dyed-in-the-wool conservatives harbored the same thoughts. At the heart of the jealousy were the charismatic personalities of men who were in every inch of their fiber the best of scholars and pastors in whatever synod they served.

With no direct knowledge of the Lutheran scene in America, European theologians sometimes would add to the mix David Preus, last president of the American Lutheran Church, who unlike his Missouri synod cousins, was a proponent of women's ordination. Five or even six generations of the descendants of Herman Amberg Preus (1825–1894), a mid-nineteenth-century Norwegian immigrant pastor, still serve as pastors throughout American Lutheranism. Preus is a pan-Lutheran name.

With the seminary coming on campus in September 1976 and the Senior College getting ready for its last year, the tensions were less than what might have been ordinarily expected. Herbert Bredemeier (1911–2001), who had been with the college from the beginning in 1957 and held various positions including dean of administration, began the second of his own two years as college president and retained his office in the administration building. He was the last president of the Senior College. Seminary president Robert Preus had his office in what would later become the registrar's office on the second floor of Loehe Hall. Decisions about the campus remained with the Senior College and chapel services were divided between the two communities.

For chapel services, three days were allotted to the seminary faculty and two to the senior college faculty, and attendance remained high. Both communities extended invitations to each other's social and academic functions, and I made it a policy to attend as many as I could. Memorable was the college's final graduation. Held outdoors on the upper plaza, the backdrop was the north side of Kramer Chapel. More events were scheduled by the senior college, whose student body was mostly unmarried.

In preparing for one Friday sermon, I noted the pericope scheduled for Monday's service to be conducted by the senior college. Dyed-in-the-wool Missourians handle Biblical texts predictably. To add a little spice to chapel life, I preached on the text on Friday that was appointed for the following Monday and gave it an uncustomary interpretation. Sure enough and not unexpectedly, Monday's sermon began with a refutation of mine.

In my first high school year at Concordia Bronxville, I had come to know one senior college professor, Harold Haas, a specialist in psychology. He had done his vicarage as a resident counselor and teacher of religion in 1949–1950. His intense training in the synodical catechism forced us to learn Bible passages, many of them which are still with me. An awkward situation with my uncle Walter Wente was ameliorated by my wife Dorothy's constant concern for him after my aunt Pauline passed away. To come to the senior college, Uncle Walter had given up his position as academic dean at St. John's College in Winfield, Kansas, a school where my grandfather Charles Scaer was one of the founding professors and my father and aunts and uncles attended. The family name Scaer was embedded in the St. John's story, but I was viewed as an outsider to that tradition.

The 1953 Houston convention had made the decision to build the Senior College. Construction began in 1955 and was sufficiently completed in time for the first entering class in 1957. The Wentes arrived in Fort Wayne in 1956 and lived on the campus of the old junior college on Maumee Avenue, which was being sold to Indiana Institute of Technology, a flourishing and expanding college in well-appointed buildings on the same location opposite the Lutheran Cemetery on South Anthony Boulevard.

In my visit to Winfield at Thanksgiving 1955, my first year at the seminary, Walter Wente took exception to another uncle, his brother-in-law Richard Caemmerer's support for the senior college and expressed his total displeasure with what he thought was academically unfeasible. In less than a year, Walter, whose massive memory and intelligence were proverbial among colleagues and students, was in Fort Wayne setting up the curriculum. Long after the college's closing he spoke glowingly of the curriculum and its faculty. Pauline would continue providing without charge piano lessons to children of the Senior College professors, and they would become as much fixtures in Fort Wayne as they were in Winfield.

Relations between us were strained, but formal. Pauline and Walter came to the confirmation dinner for our son Stephen in the spring of 1977, but did not attend the service, which conflicted with a farewell service in the chapel for the Senior College faculty, which would soon be dispersed. Having sold their home on Colony Drive, virtually adjacent to the campus, they moved into an apartment in the Lutheran Homes. In a few years, Pauline died and Walter moved into a single room. My wife Dorothy would visit him weekly and sometimes take him downtown to L. S. Ayres department store, the old Wolf and Desauer's, for lunch, where he would often enjoy a gimlet. Since the Lutherans Homes are more than a half an hour away from where we lived, my visits were monthly. Uncle Walter's inexhaustible memory provided for the two hours of conversation. All his former students had a story about him.

Disenchanted with the Missouri Synod's change of direction, he joined Gethsemane Lutheran Church, opposite the campus, a congregation that left the synod for the newly formed Association of Evangelical Lutheran Churches, but for all practical purposes, he was a member of the Missouri Synod congregation which worshiped in the chapel of the Lutheran Homes. His extensive library, which would have made a fine addition to the seminary collection, was given to an art colony run by my now-deceased cousin Richard Caemmerer Jr. in the state of Washington. Upon returning from a driving trip with a former senior college colleague, Walter was saddened that his books were in scattered order and exposed to the elements in the uninsulated wooden building.

Valparaiso University received the bulk of his and my aunt's estate. Seminary students doing their field work at the Lutheran Home spent hours listening to his stories which, if they had been recorded, would have been a history of the Missouri Synod in itself. Others students needing help with Greek were privately tutored by him. All in all a remarkable man, but one whose last years were caught within the tragedy which the Missouri Synod was in those days.

He missed his wife Pauline very much and kept photos around to remind him of her. He reminisced about their bus trips with the choir of St. John's College, which she directed, and about their trips to Europe with another aunt and uncle, Margaret and Bill Scar. Even after Pauline had died, he would travel to Stuttgart, Germany, and sit at a coffee house in the main square. On a less strenuous trip to Chicago, he would sit in the lobby of the Palmer House listening to the instrument of the day, which was usually a piano.

A long life was not his desire, but as he got into his mid-nineties, he made one hundred his goal. Since our summers are spent in the Poconos, I saw him in May 1992 for what was the last time—and he knew it by saying a last farewell that neither Dorothy nor I was ready to accept. An announcement came at the synod Pittsburgh convention in July 1992, in which Alvin Barry replaced Ralph Bohlmann as president, that he had died. Like the funeral for my aunt, Pauline Scaer Wente, the service for him was held in the Lutheran Homes chapel by the Missouri Synod chaplain. A closely related synod had been divided, often right down to families, but these lines did not in every case reflect doctrinal differences.

Another story is an incident at a presentation in late winter 1976 at Emmaus Lutheran Church in Ridgewood, New York, located near the old Lutheran Cemetery, now All Faiths Cemetery, right on the line dividing the New York City boroughs of Brooklyn and Queens. There had been gatherings that alerted synod members to the problems at the St. Louis seminary before the February 1974 walkout for some years, with some congregations still considering leaving the synod for the newly formed Association of Evangelical Lutheran Churches (AELC), a group that would be the catalyst for formation of the ELCA.

After my presentation, Pastor Arthur Steinke (1908–1997), father of Paul (b. 1937) and Peter Steinke (b. 1939), schoolmates from Bronxville and now synod pastors, told the assembly that there were "two doctors in house." His first reference was obvious to me, but before he identified the second one, I instinctively knew that it was Walter Brunn (1897–1979), pastor of Good Shepherd Lutheran Church, not far from Trinity of Flatbush, my father's church, in Brooklyn.

Problematic was that a letter intended for a layman in Pittsburgh awarding him an honorary Doctor of Laws degree was erroneously sent by Preus's secretary to a pastor with the same name in Brooklyn. In being asked to write the letter to Walter Brunn, she assumed it was a pastor and looked for his name and address in the synod's *Lutheran Annual* and wrote to Pastor Walter Brunn that he had received the honorary doctor of divinity degree. I was totally chagrined by the situation and headed off to a small room in the church basement, so that at the end of the gathering I would not have to face Pastor Brunn as he left the church. Since I was not involved in the sending of the letter, I was not absolutely sure of what had happened.

Afterwards some of the clergy and their wives assembled in the apartment over the parsonage garage, where Jack Leininger (1903–1990), a retired pastor helping out with the congregation, lived with his wife. My mother, now a pastor's widow of about eleven years, was also there. When I relayed my concerns that Pastor Brunn may not have been the "Walter Brunn" chosen by the Springfield faculty for an honorary degree, the group broke out in laughter that lasted at least fifteen minutes. Each year Brunn arranged a dinner dance in his own honor in his congregation and had plans already underway for a similar occasion for his receiving the honorary degree.

It was a Friday night and I put in a collect call to Robert Preus back in Springfield. Phone calls then were expensive and when Preus was asked by the operator if he would accept the charges, he cried out, "Who?" It was certain that an error had occurred. Both men were descendants of a nineteenth-century German Confessional Lutheran pastor, also called Walter Brunn, who sent pastors over to help the fledgling Missouri Synod. They were probably second or third cousins, but whether they knew each other is another matter. The Walter Brunn of Pittsburgh was an executive with the Heinz Corporation of fifty-seven varieties fame, including ketchup, and had played a role in organizing conservatives.

I remember the moment of embarrassment as if it were yesterday, Jack Leininger saying to Pastor Brunn on the phone, "We have Dave Scaer here and he thinks that there might have been a mistake." Leininger played the hero in letting Brunn know how things really were. Those assembled in the apartment above the garage belonged to my parents' vintage, and so we were more than good friends. Whatever embarrassment was attached to the situation was overcome by an evening of hilarity. These occasions seem fewer and farther between.

Our friendship with Alvin Schmidt and his wife Carol began in his joining the faculty then in Springfield in 1975. During the spike in gasoline prices during the later years in Fort Wayne, we shared rides to and from the seminary. His is a friendship I have renewed on several occasions, including his fiftieth Springfield seminary class reunion on the Fort Wayne campus on May 18, 2013, and his offering of a lecture at the seminary's annual symposium.

Since the seminary would remain in Springfield for less than a year after he joined the faculty, it was agreed that he would live in rental property. Then in moving to Fort Wayne he would live in a campus house until he purchased a home. When Al did this, Preus reported to the board that Al had acted without permission. In his own defense, Al produced a letter from Preus in which such permission was given. This was reason enough for bad blood between two men who were essentially conservative in outlook.

Since faculty members of Concordia Senior College were living in the on-campus homes, not many were available to the seminary faculty at its arrival in 1976. Most had to buy their homes immediately. In being allowed to live on campus before purchasing a home, Al was given a privilege not given to others. This was not all. Allegations about Schmidt supporting women's ordination emanated from his classrooms chiefly through the ears and mouth of Jack Cascione, who had endeared himself to Preus.

Al Schmidt resigned from the faculty and for almost two years lived in Fort Wayne waiting for a position at Illinois College in Jacksonville, a town about fifty miles west of Springfield. After leaving the faculty, he began regularly to attend pastoral conferences and conferences with conservative theological causes, often as a lecturer. His writings are found in and endorsed by *Christian News* as are those of Jack Cascione, his student nemesis in his seminary teaching days. On August 11–14, 2013, he was a featured speaker at Camp Trinity in New Haven, Missouri, along with Rolf Preus, Robert Preus's third son, a pastor in Montana.[7]

---

7. Schmidt's books include *The Menace of Multiculturalism: Trojan Horse in America* (Westport, CT: Praeger, 1997), *The Great Divide: The Failure of Islam and the Triumph of the West* (Boston, MA: Regina Orthodox Press, 2004), *The American Muhammad: Joseph Smith, Founder of Mormonism* (St. Louis, MO: Concordia Publishing House, 2013), and *How Christianity Changed the World* (Grand Rapids, MI: Zondervan, 2004).

Excursus VIII

A TALE OF TWO DOGMATICS SERIES

༄༅

Sometime before 1973, Robert Preus, I and others met to discuss a new dogmatics at Ralph Bohlmann's off-campus St. Louis home with the intent that he and Robert Preus would head up the series. At the time, Bohlmann was on leave of absence from his St. Louis professorship to serve as executive secretary to the LCMS Commission on Theology and Church Relations, an appointment made by synod president J. A. O. Preus. In 1974, Jack supported Bohlmann as president of the St. Louis seminary and as his successor as synod president in 1981.

Robert Preus and Bohlmann adhered to the old theology of the synod and were out of step with the St. Louis faculty majority, especially in regard to higher-critical methods of biblical interpretation, and agreed that Pieper's *Christian Dogmatics* needed updating. With Bohlmann assuming the presidency of the St. Louis seminary and Robert Preus the presidency of Springfield, both in 1974, each pursued the task on his own so that there would be two dogmatics books and not one. Bohlmann as synod president could count on Concordia Publishing House. His dogmatics was to be called *The International Lutheran Dogmatics*, but later was published as *Confessing the Gospel: a Lutheran Approach to Systematic Theology*.[1] Robert Preus's dogmatics would be known as the *Confessional Lutheran Dogmatics*.

Preus saw no difficulty in having more than one dogmatics textbook alongside the one the synod would sponsor. Preus would have to locate his own funding. Bohlmann's dogmatics would be subjected to the synod's doctrinal review process. Doctrinal review resembles the local Roman Catholic system of a bishop giving his imprimatur or *nihil obstat* in finding nothing contrary to orthodox doctrine in a book. Synod doctrinal reviewers are anonymous, and their rejection of manuscript for doctrinal reasons was subject to appeal to the five-member doctrinal review commission on which the first reviewer might be a member.

---

1. Samuel H. Nafzger et al., *Confessing the Gospel: A Lutheran Approach to Systematic Theology* (St. Louis, MO: Concordia Publishing House, 2017).

Robert Preus was not comfortable with this procedure, but he had others read manuscripts for doctrinal content before accepting a manuscript for publication. The need for a new dogmatics arose partly from the rise of neoorthodox theology that had found a receptive hearing in the St. Louis seminary. Franz Pieper's *Christian Dogmatics* had served and still does as the synod's only dogmatics, but it did not address neoorthodoxy and the issues of the nineteenth century if a difference was less relevant.

John Theodore Mueller (1885–1967) wrote an abridgement of Pieper's *Christian Dogmatics* that was published under the same title and was used at the synod's colleges and seminaries.[2] Since it presented the classical Lutheran theology, but did not engage other theological positions, it was not a dogmatics text in the traditional sense. To celebrate the LCMS centennial in 1947, the synod published *The Abiding Word*,[3] a three-volume collection of doctrinal essays by various authors, delivered as convention essays at previous district conventions. But it also was not a dogmatics text.

Production of a new dogmatics raised the question of whether it should be the work of a single theologian or a combined effort of several theologians. Both Bohlmann and Preus would follow the example of *The Abiding Word* in using multiple authors, but each would go about organizing his dogmatics differently. Historically, doctrinal statements were prepared by one person and then tweaked and adopted by church council or convention and then accepted as binding. Dogmatics texts were the works of individual theologians, not synods.

A multi-authored two volume *Christian Dogmatics*[4] appeared in 1984 at the same time Preus and Bohlmann were mulling over prospects for a new dogmatics for the synod. Its editors, Carl E. Braaten and Robert Jenson (1930–2017), had written many of its sections and others had authored some sections. Pieper's *Christian Dogmatics* was written by one man, but it was commissioned and unanimously received by two synod conventions, and so in the opinion of some it enjoyed a special authority in the synod.

---

2. John Theodore Mueller and Franz Pieper, *Christian Dogmatics: A Handbook of Doctrinal Theology for Pastors, Teachers, and Laymen* (St. Louis, MO: Concordia Publishing House, 1934).
3. Theodore Ferdinand Karl Laetsch, ed., *The Abiding Word: An Anthology of Doctrinal Essays*, 3 vols. (St. Louis, MO: Concordia Publishing House, 1946).
4. Carl E. Braaten and Robert W. Jenson, eds., *Christian Dogmatics*, 2 vols. (Philadelphia, PA: Fortress Press, 1984).

Since half the delegates at the conventions that authorized the German and English edition were laymen, it is unlikely that they or most pastors before voting on the matter ever read it. Part of the genius of the Missouri Synod was that it had a position on any number of topics, and it was assumed that all its pastors held to it. So, in a sense, Pieper's dogmatics in reasserting the commonly held belief would be little more than reshuffling of the deck. Many of the synod's later problems might have been averted, if after Pieper, others had written dogmatics to engage newer theologies as they arose and to engage each other. Historical studies and collections of essays had appeared in the synod but did not qualify as dogmatics texts.[5]

Orthodoxy that is seen as a theological monolith does not encourage restatements required by the new theologies. Both the Preus and Bohlmann dogmatics would have their own control system over the contributions. Bohlmann's dogmatics would have the advantage of the synod's doctrinal review by anonymous censors to identify unacceptable views. As a student of classical Lutheran Orthodoxy whose theologians had written over twenty dogmatics in the seventeenth century, Preus saw no difficulty in having more than one dogmatics text available to confessional Lutherans.

Its title, Confessional Lutheran Dogmatics, implied that its foundation would be the historic sixteenth-century Lutheran Confessions. Pieper had made use of the confessions, but this was not a prime focus for him. As the Preus series evolved, it was evident that some writers would more closely adhere to the confessional outline than others.

---

5. Robert D. Preus set out to write a comprehensive study of classical Lutheran theology, but completed only two volumes, *The Theology of Post-Reformation Lutheranism* (St. Louis, MO: Concordia Publishing House, 1970–1972). In the mid-1980s, Concordia Publishing House offered Preus a staff position to complete the work, which he declined. These qualified more as historical rather than dogmatical theologies. Essays by Arthur Carl Piepkorn are being gathered into four volumes, but the topics are selective, reflecting his interests. The first volume was published twenty years after his death, *The Church: Selected Writings of Arthur Carl Piepkorn*, ed. Michael P. Plekon and William S. Wiecher (Dehli, New York: ALPB Books, 1993). Three following volumes will be entitled *The Sacred Scriptures*, *The Lutheran Confessions: Ministry and Church* and *Worship and the Christian Life*. While Piepkorn's writings, like Preus's, will be a valuable theological contribution, in his lifetime he did not compose a comprehensive dogmatics. If Pieper answered the question of why Lutherans are not Reformed, Piepkorn answers the question of why Lutherans are not Roman Catholics. The afterword in the first and now only published volume is contributed by Richard John Neuhaus, who later was ordained a Roman Catholic priest (293–298).

Though the project had been discussed as early as the 1970s and may have been a topic of discussion between Bohlmann and Preus earlier, specifics about which direction the projects should go were not made clear. As the Preus project was being hatched, Kurt Marquart and I met with Robert Preus in his seminary office. Bill Weinrich and John Stephenson, who may have been on campus at this time, may have also from time to time attended.

Discussions centered not on concepts but editorial copy details such as using upper or lower case for *incarnation, resurrection* and *baptism.* In my estimation this was fruitless, since copy editors make these decisions and then make the necessary changes. Out of a sense of frustration, I left more than one meeting before its formal conclusion. Simplicity suggests that all words except names should be lower case, as is customary in critical writings and also in the oldest surviving New Testament documents. As the documents were submitted, agreement on the theological content was more often assumed than discussed.

Ralph Bohlmann's *Confessing the Gospel* was constructed according to building blocks: scriptural foundation derived from both the Old and New Testaments, confessional witness, systematic formulation, historical and contemporary developments, and finally implications for life and ministry. Its encyclopedic layout resembles *Religion in Geschichte und Gegenwart*[6] in which a topic is subdivided with a different author for each section. In some cases a single author did the entire topic.

In the more than forty years since the project was laid out, Samuel F. Nafzger, longtime executive with the synod's commission on theology, and at his retirement in 2010, assistant to the synod president for ecumenical matters, replaced Bohlmann as editor. Since the 1990s David Lumpp, a professor of Concordia College in St. Paul, Minnesota, continued to assist.

Because Bohlmann had initiated an investigation of the Fort Wayne seminary in 1984, Preus and Marquart did not respond to an invitation to participate in *Confessing the Gospel.* Howard Tepker, as an associate editor, participated as a contributor, as did Eugene Klug.

Weinrich and I accepted. In the initial stages of the project, I was called to a meeting in St. Louis with synod president Ralph Bohlmann and

---

6. Kurt Galling and Hans von Campenhausen, eds., *Die Religion in Geschichte und Gegenwart; Handwörterbuch für Theologie und Religionswissenschaft,* 3, völlig neu bearbeitet Aufl. (Tübingen,: Mohr, 1957)—and its English translation: Hans Dieter Betz, ed., *Religion Past and Present: Encyclopedia of Theology and Religion* [4th ed., English ed.] (Leiden ; Brill, 2007).

William F. Meyer, a friend and former Springfield colleague, then president of Concordia Publishing House. After waiting at the Best Western Motel across the street from the International Center for an entire afternoon, Bill came across the street to tell me that he and Bohlmann had met and decided the crucial matters and my input would not be needed.

In those days air travel was more flexible, and I was soon on the way in the motel van back to Lambert Field for the flight to Chicago and on to Fort Wayne. Bohlmann was the editor-in-chief. Associate editors would be Nafzger, John Franklin Johnson, then St. Louis academic dean, soon to be seminary president and finally president of Concordia University Chicago, and Tepker, retired Fort Wayne seminary professor and formerly chairman of its department of systematic theology and academic dean.

I was assigned twenty pages in the Bohlmann dogmatics on the confessional segment of the Christological locus. Compared to the more extensive assignments of well over one hundred pages given others, I was given a bone. My section was completed by the fall of 1987, when opposition on the faculty to Preus was taking form. Shortly thereafter, Tepker informed me that the editors were so pleased with my confessional Christological contribution that they asked me to write the locus on anthropology, a more significant contribution of one hundred pages. They had found the contribution of the first author unacceptable, and I asked for and was given a copy of the rejected manuscript and proceeded to carry out the assignment.

I now know that when *Confessing the Gospel* appeared in print, my contribution on anthropology did not appear. About this time (1987–88) Howard Tepker had begun advising Waldo Werning in charging me with a false Christology. The December 1995 *Reporter* reported that *Confessing the Gospel* would be available by mid-1997. It finally appeared in 2017!

This was reason enough for me to write on December 15, 1995, to Concordia Publishing House president Steve Carter (b. 1941), former seminary colleague, to ask about the status of the project and the fate of my two contributions. My letter was referred to Earl H. Gaulke (1927–2013), vice president for its editorial division, who on January 25, 1996, wrote me that the dogmatics project has already been ten years in the making and that I would soon see the galleys for my articles. He also said that John Franklin Johnson was doing the editorial work for my longer locus and that a remuneration scale was being put in place. None of this will come to pass since my contributions have been cut. In enquiring about my anthropology manuscript, Nafzger said that the project had undergone a complete revision and that my work would not be included.

For his Confessional Lutheran Dogmatics, Robert Preus, like Bohlmann, did not think that one man could or should produce an entire dogmatics, since no one had the breadth of knowledge or time to accomplish this. Pieper was able to accomplish this, since his classroom lecture notes had been transcribed into his dogmatics. In the Preus dogmatics, one and not several writers would be responsible for one topic or locus, each or several loci appearing in its own volume.

Contracts given to the first the contributors specified the number of pages. Contributions were intended to complement gaps in Pieper's dogmatics. Rather than being books, these were to be extended essays described as *fascicles*, a term used in the initial discussion. As with any dogmatics, Pieper's style did not lend itself to updating. This might be possible in preparing a history of doctrine, but not a dogmatics text. In 1986, Robert Preus laid out thirteen sections or topics, specifying page length and authors:

1. Prolegomena (110 pages)—Kurt Marquart (deceased; now reassigned to Roland Ziegler)
2. Scripture (75 pages)—Robert Preus (deceased; now reassigned to Jack Kilcrease)
3. God [The Trinity] (100 pages)—William C. Weinrich (reassigned to Carl L. Beckwith, completed and published as *The Holy Trinity*)[7]
4. Creation—Richard Klann (75 pages); (manuscript declined; deceased; now reassigned to Albert Collver)
5. Anthropology and Sin—Richard Klann (75 pages); (uncompleted; deceased; now reassigned to Detlev Schulz)
6. Person of Christ—David Scaer (75 pages); (completed and published as *Christology*)[8]
7. The Work of Christ and Justification—Robert Preus (75 pages); (uncompleted; deceased)
8. Means of Grace and Pneumatology—David Scaer (100 pages); (completed; published with Law and Gospel as *Law and Gospel and the Means of Grace*)[9]

---

[7]. Carl L. Beckwith, *The Holy Trinity*, Confessional Lutheran Dogmatics 3 (Fort Wayne, IN: Luther Academy, 2016).

[8]. David P. Scaer, *Christology*, ed. Robert Preus, Confessional Lutheran Dogmatics 6 (Fort Wayne, IN: International Foundation for Lutheran Confessional Research, 1989).

[9]. David P. Scaer, *Law and Gospel and the Means of Grace*, Confessional Lutheran Dogmatics 8 (St. Louis, MO: Luther Academy, 2008).

9. The Christian Life—Richard Klann (100 pages); (deceased; now reassigned to Gifford Grobien and retitled Life in Christ)
10. Church and Ministry—Kurt Marquart (75 pages); (completed; published as *The Church and Her Fellowship, Ministry and Governance*)[10]
11. Baptism—David Scaer (75 pages); (completed; published as *Baptism*)[11]
12. The Lord's Supper—(75 pages); Lowell Green; reassigned to John R. Stephenson (completed; published as *The Lord's Supper*)[12]
13. Eschatology—(100 pages) John Franklin Johnson; reassigned to John R. Stephenson (completed; published as *Eschatology*)[13]

This kind of project comes with the hazard that the writers will not meet the deadlines or will fail to submit anything at all. Accepting the task is easier than doing it. In preparing the contracts, Robert Preus acknowledged that it was unlikely, even impossible, for the contributors to follow his original outlines. "I wonder if my inclusion of topics may be incomplete or distorted in many cases." He followed this up by saying each author was "to construct [his] own more detailed outline of those chapters assigned to [him]."[14]

At the start of the Confessional Lutheran Dogmatics series project, I was involved in reviewing submissions by other contributors, and my recommendations about publishing were accepted by Preus. Stephenson soon became Preus's right hand man as copy editor. At the funeral of Robert Preus on November 7, 1995, John Stevenson offered his services to Robert's son Daniel Preus to succeed Robert as editor-in-chief of the Confessional Lutheran Dogmatics series.

John Franklin Johnson's involvement as associate editor in the Bohlmann dogmatics may have been his reason for declining the section on

---

10. Kurt E. Marquart, *The Church and Her Fellowship, Ministry, and Governance*, Confessional Lutheran Dogmatics 9 (Fort Wayne, IN: International Foundation for Lutheran Confessional Research, 1990).
11. David P. Scaer, *Baptism*, ed. John R. Stephenson, Confessional Lutheran Dogmatics 11 (St. Louis, MO: Luther Academy, 1999).
12. John R. Stephenson, *The Lord's Supper*, Confessional Lutheran Dogmatics 12 (St. Louis, MO: Luther Academy, 2003).
13. John R. Stephenson, *Eschatology*, Confessional Lutheran Dogmatics 13 (Fort Wayne, IN: Luther Academy, 1993).
14. From the private correspondence between David P. Scaer and Robert D. Preus.

eschatology in the Preus series. Preus assigned to Stephenson the volume on eschatology, the last locus in the series, since he had done such a splendid job on the festschift for Robert Preus as the copy editor. In 1990, he took the assignment of the volume on the *Lord's Supper*.

In a letter that predates the issuing of contracts, Robert Preus explains that together all the essays were to comprise no more than 1100 pages, and for editing Stephenson would receive $1100, that is, a dollar a page. Preus remained as the general editor, and on July 17, 1986, he signed his contract as both publisher and author for the volumes on Scripture and the work of Christ and justification. At Preus's death on November 4, 1995, he had not completed the assignment. From May 1989 until he died, Preus was literally fighting for his life in church, ministry, and seminary. Kurt Marquart completed his volume on church and ministry, which argued for the synod's traditional position as outlined by its first president, C. F. W. Walther. It soon went to a second printing and enjoys a continued popularity.

Somewhere along the line, probably in 1989 or 1990, International Foundation for Lutheran Confessional Research as the publisher was replaced by Luther Academy, whose officers have chosen replacements for some of the original contributors. According to the original contracts, each contributor was to be paid $20 a page, not for each published page. Only $10 a page would be paid for a late submission. Acceptance or rejection was in the hands of the general editor. Two rejected manuscripts had earned their writers $750.

My Christology lectures had moved away from the scholasticism of Lutheran Orthodoxy to a grappling with the theological and historical character of the gospels, and that formed the basis of the Christological volume that was the first in the series to be published. Having written my doctoral dissertation on baptism in nineteenth-century German theology, and having already written an extensive essay of the biblical doctrine of baptism for the Southern California District in April 1967, I had also a grip on this topic.

Still unknown was the reason that Robert Preus chose me for volume eight on the means of grace and pneumatology, which included the law and the gospel. At that time, Waldo Werning filled my mailbox with threatening correspondence, and the editors with Luther Academy were less than fully pleased with my loose writing style. These topics were not of particular interest to me, and up to that time I had not been assigned seminary courses on them. I simply did not want to do volume eight, and several times I asked Preus to reassign these topics to someone else, but he consistently refused, by saying, "Dave, I know how you write and I like it."

My colleague Cameron MacKenzie described my writing style as a stream of consciousness, which is undoubtedly accurate, but in self-defense it might be close to Franz Pieper's self-admitted conversational style. Style belongs to who a person is. In the spring or summer of 1990, I sent my baptism manuscript off to Robert Preus, who forwarded it on to Stephenson.

When the Luther Academy staff thought of replacing me, I remembered that Robert Preus had said that I was the one for the job. To say that writing this volume took forever is no exaggeration. Ironically, *The Law and the Gospel & the Means of Grace* more than any other volume would bring the series to the attention of scholars outside the synod, including those in Europe.

My *Christology* volume is and will most likely remain the shortest volume in the Confessional Lutheran Dogmatics series, because, in comparison with the remaining volumes, it was noticeably shorter, the goal Robert Preus originally set for each volume. Paul McCain, former president and now publisher for Concordia Publishing House, was at work in his final undergraduate year (1987–1988) in editing the *Christology* volume and continued on the project into the next year as a graduate assistant for the department of systematic theology. Books printed in a series by multiple authors tend to become more complex as one volume follows another and second and third editions appear. This was the case with the Confessional Lutheran Dogmatics series. More complex than my *Christology* volume were Kurt Marquart's work, John Stephenson's volume and my books on *Baptism* and *Law and Gospel and the Means of Grace*. More complex theological works are bound to lose the lay readership, a group Preus wanted to include. Here his goal was compromised.

My *Christology* in its first printing sold two thousand copies, but with a new general editor succeeding Preus it appeared that my remaining two volumes might not see the light of day. For me this was a sensitive issue. After Concordia Publishing House had published my *James: the Apostle of Faith*, which went through two printings, it had rejected for doctrinal reasons my *Sermon on the Mount: The Church's First Statement of the Gospel*.[15]

A similar fate seemed to be waiting for my *Baptism* and the *Means of Grace* volumes at the hands of the new general editor of the Confessional Lutheran Dogmatics series. Writing is its own misery, not because of the compensation or the lack of it, but writing is an investment of time, mental and emotional energy that can only be rewarded by its being published.

---

15. See also Excursus XI: The Sermon on the Mount: The Church's First Statement of the Gospel, 241 ff.

Robert Preus spoke annoyingly of his spending "literally scores of hours on the first Scaer manuscript [Christology]" and not having "the time to do it on this second one."[16] My literary felonies include solecisms, which Preus defined as unfinished sentences. He was displeased that I did not write with the same precision as Kurt Marquart and John Stephenson and that editing my work required too much money. Of course it could be mentioned that the *Christology* volume was providing the funding for the seed money for their volumes.

Apart from this, Robert Preus and I knew that Kurt Marquart and I did theology differently. Preus wrote with precision. I rambled and then gathered the rambling into a composite whole. Noteworthy is that Preus takes exception to my position in the baptism volume that the unborn can have faith *in utero*, a view which he finds speculative, and he instructed Stephenson to look for "other speculative *theolegoumena*." In light of the church's opposition to abortion, faith of the unborn is now considered less speculative.

Robert Preus, Kurt Marquart and John Stephenson did theology from the perspective of the seventeenth century, and I was doing it more and more from a biblical perspective. Stephenson took Preus's assignment to look for unsubstantiated *theologoumena* seriously, and as general editor he continued to scrutinize my two remaining manuscripts on *Baptism* and *Law & Gospel and the Means of Grace*. He wrote to me that he would approve the baptism manuscript only after a major rewriting, and that as the general editor, he and not Dan Preus would have the final say.

When the baptism volume appeared in time for the seminary's January symposium in 1999, it would be the section that Robert Preus found to be speculative that received much attention, especially to a young mother who had been active in confessional Lutheran circles and had recently given birth to a stillborn child. In the same letter in which he raised concerns about my positions, Preus mentioned Stephenson's endorsement of Richard Klann's manuscript on creation with the proviso that only a little work in the footnotes was required for its publication.[17] I found a document on creation written with an obsession for refuting evolution sufficient reason for its rejection. Preus told Stephenson he would follow his advice, but he took mine. Klann's manuscript was not published.

After Robert Preus died, the officers of Luther Academy reexamined the original contracts along with other documents outlining the project,

---

16. Robert Preus, letter to John Stephenson, August 21, 1990.
17. Robert Preus, letter to John Stephenson, August 21, 1990.

and finding them unworkable wrote new contracts for the contributors to sign. I did not sign. My *Christology* was published before Robert Preus died, but with a new editor in place the fate of my two remaining volumes hung in the balance. Writers experience satisfaction in seeing their manuscript in print, but rejection comes with the turf.

Sometime in 1996, I provided an updated version of the *Baptism* manuscript to John Stephenson and Dan Preus. Stephenson faxed a blistering critique, also admonishing me for not sharing my manuscript with Kurt Marquart and Bill Weinrich, a strange request since Kurt Marquart had not shared his manuscript with me and Bill Weinrich had no manuscript to share with me.[18] Stephenson said "that no small amount of revision and reworking is called for" before it could be used as a textbook in our circles.

In rewriting the *Baptism* manuscript I was to consult with Marquart and Weinrich and was to do the same with the one on the means of grace. Only then was it to be forwarded on to Stephenson. Stephenson had wanted me to be like him. A touch of hubris might be found in this sentence: "... that we must strive ... to subordinate the idiosyncrasies of the several members of the writing team to the subject matter with which we have to deal. Care must be taken to do justice to both the appropriate freedom of an individual and the rightful prerogatives of the editor."

In other words, what Stephenson writes and thinks is the objective standard of what is acceptable. Any deviations are quirks and he will decide which is which. After all this, Stephenson, on November 19, writes wishing me and Dorothy a happy Thanksgiving Day. Amazing!

In accordance with Stephenson's wishes, I shared the baptism manuscript with Art Just and Dan Preus, both of whom liked it. When I shared this information with Stephenson, he replied, "Please share your Baptism MS as a matter of urgency with Prof. Kurt Marquart, who unlike Dr. Just, is a cowriter involved in the Confessional Lutheran Dogmatics project. Kurt will be expecting to receive a copy of your MS on his return from Detroit."[19] Stephenson and Marquart critiqued each other's manuscripts. They did not share theirs with me, though I was expected to share mine with Marquart. Stephenson was defining orthodoxy not only for himself but for me.

In January 1999, two years after Stephenson's scathing critique, Luther Academy published *Baptism* in the Confessional Lutheran Dogmatics se-

---

18. John Stephenson, fax to David P. Scaer, November 12, 1996.
19. John Stephenson, letter to David P. Scaer, December 5, 1996.

ries. A reprint edition came out in 2003 for 3600 copies in print. It has been translated into Latvian and Spanish.

Stephenson's critique of *The Law and the Gospel & the Means of Grace* was similarly devoid of appreciation. Daniel Preus, who had succeeded his father as publisher, took a more favorable view toward the baptism manuscript and arranged for John Maxfield to act in the place of the general editor, John Stephenon, as editor for *Baptism* and also to serve as the copy editor. I was told that this volume would be reviewed for publication by Dan Preus and John Maxfield, who now was appointed as its special editor for this volume.

Stephenson told Maxfield that "the board is not able to approve this portion of the proposed volume for publication without substantial revision."[20] From the rest of this letter it seems he was referring to the entire manuscript. There were the usual suggestions about length, repetition and reworking the introduction and topics needing further development.

Since the manuscript for *Law and Gospel & the Means of Grace* had been written over a period of about ten years, I was able to update my arguments. These critiques reinforced in my mind that each theologian does theology in his own way, a perspective that was not shared by my critics.

Stephenson's five-page critique, single spaced in some parts, issued although he supposedly was no longer the editor of my volume, was not intended to be seen by me, but had been accidently sent to me in a packet of materials and called for a reworking of *Law and Gospel & the Means of Grace* manuscript. Discovering and reading it was comparable to my first reading of Waldo Werning's doctrinal charges being leveled against me. It was a déjà vu experience. He was repeating what he had done in calling for a rewriting of the manuscript on baptism. Among his requests was answering Volker Stolle of the Oberursel seminary in Germany, who allegedly asserted that the law and gospel foists a foreign category on the Bible, and he found my application of law and gospel to theologians prior to Luther and even to Luther himself inappropriate.

Already on the first page of his critique, Stephenson found me to be "a full-fledged Barthian." In the following, Stephenson was at his eloquent best: "Scaer rides a personal hobbyhorse with his ridiculous claim that the Sermon on the Mount is gospel, not law . . . . [Stephenson's dots] Let him propagate this nonsense without subsidy from the Luther Academy." Accusations of Barthianism appear throughout his critique. "If this Barthian drivel is published by the Luther Academy, I have a problem being

---

20. John Stephenson, letter to John Maxfield, April 30, 2004.

your editor! ... [Stephenson's dots, again] What does Kurt [Marquart] have to say about this?"

On page five, Stephenson takes exception to my seeing our love for God as synonymous with faith. Rolf Preus, who would also serve as a reader, came across Stephenson's remarks and responded.

> I think this is a wonderful book. Scaer's comments on the gospel as fulfilled law and the ramifications this has for the life of the Christian are valuable. The way Scaer brings the law into service of Christology is also very good. I think I may have more regard for Scaer's view of the Sermon on the Mount as gospel than Stephenson does.

When Luther Academy was formed, I was one of the four incorporators with Robert Preus, Wilhelm Petersen, a former president of Bethany Seminary, Mankato, Minnesota, and Kenneth Hagen (1936–2014), a retired professor for Luther studies at Marquette University. As much as I can remember, Marquart was not there. Apart from the one meeting in which the academy was formed, I did not attend any more meetings and was not consulted.

Dan Preus spoke of the rift between myself and Stephenson, but the weight of our differences rested on his shoulders, since he wrote the critiques on my work. I was not asked to respond to anything he wrote, nor have I taken it upon myself to do so. Only when *Law and the Gospel & the Means of Grace* was months away from going to the press was I made aware that he recommended against its publication.

For the next three years, especially in the summer of 2007, I was in frequent conversation with John Maxfield and his wife, Jennifer, who is a professional copy editor, in order to meet the deadline of having this volume ready for distribution at the seminary's January 2008 confessional symposium.

Scholarly writings are never successful in the way other books are. In speaking about one of Jaroslav Pelikan's books, my Pocono neighbor Rudy Ressmeyer remarked it would only sell about 1500 copies. In preparing to publish the Confessional Lutheran Dogmatics, Robert Preus noted that academic writings in Europe are never supported by their sales and have to be subsidized. Within the range of scholarly works, my three contributions to the series have exceeded expectations. There is a sense of satisfaction that they received positive attention from outside the synod, but in the case of the last two books this satisfaction came with the cost of time and frustration in part due to the general editor.

Excursus IX

SYMPOSIA ON THE LUTHERAN CONFESSIONS

ತಿ

In 1977, Robert Preus wrote to Eugene Klug that January 4–6, 1978, had been set aside for convocation with the theme "Lutheran Confessions in the Contemporary Church."[1] Preus goes on to say that Waldo Werning had already agreed with Klug that his topic would be "Confessional Emphasis on Law and Gospel for Our Day," a forty-five minute lecture to be delivered on January 4.

The format of these occasions, now called symposia, has changed little. Sometime in the 1980s, I began organizing these events, but Preus's letter shows that Werning originated these popular annual events, which were first called Congresses on the Confessions. In previous years, these large gatherings of laity and pastors, which were organized by Werning and Alvin Wagner to alert lay people to the synod's doctrinal problems that culminated in the February 1974 St. Louis seminary walkout, were called *congresses*, and the term was carried over to the seminary's first symposia.

Confusion about what these first gatherings were intended to be can be gleaned from an addendum from the minutes of the January 7, 1980, meeting of the seminary's administrative council, in which Preus himself writes, "Who is in charge of the Congress on the Confessions? One person should coordinate the entire program so people know to whom to go for information. The Chairman of the Systematics department [Eugene Klug] will be asked to head up future programs, and delegate responsibilities in various areas as he sees fit."[2] Werning, who thought he should be the point man, had been sidelined.

The date of the first symposium, so soon after the New Year, proved to be a disaster in terms of attendance. When the seminary attempted to begin a liturgical symposium in the spring, spearheaded by Dan Reuning, it experienced a worse fate, because it intruded into Lent.

---

1. Robert Preus, letter to Eugene Klug, October 10, 1977.
2. Minutes of the Seminary Administrative Council, January 7, 1980.

For years, the liturgical symposium remained part of the confessional symposium. It was later relocated to each November by Arthur A. Just Jr. and Richard Resch, and is now sponsored by the Good Shepherd Institute.

I was not one of the speakers in the first few years, probably because Robert Preus saw other colleagues as more steeped in the Lutheran Confessions than I was. I can't argue with that. The first gathering in January 1978 was really more like "a congress" with some sessions opening with rousing hymn singing accompanying the organ in Sihler Auditorium. In a few years these gatherings were called *symposia*, and theologians and scholars from outside of the Missouri Synod were invited. Robert Preus had initially put the symposium in Werning's hands, but it soon came to be seen as a function of the systematics department.

After one symposium, probably in the 1982 spring term, Academic Dean Wilbert Rosin called Eugene Klug and myself into his office about things which he said had fallen through the cracks. As we were novices in arranging convocations that would bring hundreds onto the campus, glitches could be expected and were not uncommon. In spite of careful organization, things do not work out the ways they should. Klug responded that he would not be spoken to in this way and stormed out of the office. An issue was made out of a non-issue, and whatever problem existed could have been easily fixed. For several minutes I sat stunned with Rosin in his office.

By this time, the nuts and bolts of running the symposium had fallen into my hands. Symposium financial matters were handled by the business office. Participating lecturers, in making their own travel arrangements, were conscientious in keeping down the costs of air travel. There were some exceptions. A Yale Divinity School professor included in his travel expenses the taxi fare from New Haven, Connecticut, to LaGuardia Airport and the cost of having someone live in his home while he was gone. Another lecturer came from Australia across the Pacific and returned via England and Europe, visiting relatives and friends along the way. Such expenses strained the symposium budget and threatened future ones. To provide a secure financial basis for future symposia, Robert Preus established a special account, of which I was the executive, to which I paid casual attention.

In time Preus asked Wally Degner (1925–1998) to put together an exegetical symposium. At first it began at noon on Tuesday, the day before the confessional symposium began. Now it begins early on Tuesday, and that department invites others to give papers at smaller sectional groups. Once in an address to the faculty, synod president Ralph Bohlmann spoke of the faculty being more open to those outside of the synod. In response, I called attention to the seminary's annual January confessional symposium that has invited speakers from virtually all of the major Christian traditions—Roman Catholic, Russian and Greek Orthodox, Episcopalian, Presbyterian, Reformed and Methodist. No other synod institution has been as open to hearing and exchanging views with others as the annual January Symposium on the Lutheran Confessions of Concordia Theological Seminary.

In time, several other groups scheduled ad hoc meetings and gatherings on campus and nearby hotels. Publishers and vendors of liturgical supplies set up their booths. When Christmas becomes a lost memory in the cold of mid-January, Fort Wayne has become a favored destination. That's how Robert Preus planned it.

During the trying days that began with Preus's removal as president, his supporters made the January confessional symposium their rallying point, and each one attracted ever larger crowds, and for the 1993 symposium tensions had reached a peak. During his tenure as interim president, Norb Mueller had the authority to remove me from organizing the symposium. Had he done that, a growing outcry over what was happening at Fort Wayne might have become louder.

At the heart of the symposia were the banquets that were as orchestrated as they were spontaneous. Anyone who attended was "fair" to be roasted. Norb Mueller, the interim president for three symposia (1990–1992), was not known for his sense of humor, and there would be a price to pay for a misplaced word. At the time of the 1993 symposium, Mueller had been sidelined to director of placement and Stelmachowicz was chief executive officer. Robert Preus was ending his term as president in name only and on sabbatical.

On the afternoons prior to the Thursday evening banquet, I would sketch out the programs. Sometimes books with titles corresponding to the personalities of the speakers, guests and professors were ceremoniously presented to them. Guests and lecturers from other countries would stand for the playing of their country's national anthem. Songs, religious and secular, were sung that fit the characters of faculty and guests. Some symposium attendees came with the hope that they would be the next victim. These were great occasions whose hilarity has not been matched in the increasingly somber years.

With the seminary in administrative transition, the 1993 symposium banquet provided relief for the bad things that happened and were about to happen at the seminary. As one pastor said, we could not have survived those days without them. That year hymns were chosen to match the character of guest presenters and faculty, something that had been done at previous banquets.

Leading the singing was Peter Bender, a pastor from Wisconsin with a talent for music and soon to be known synod-wide for his catechetical interests. For Eugene Bunkowske (1935–2018), "I Have Decided to Follow Jesus" was sung. His reaction to the spoof was not known, but a colleague and longtime friend and two Fort Wayne area pastors, all three former students, rose from the table and walked out of the banquet. Actions speak louder than words.

In a subsequent conversation, I brought up the matter and my colleague said after four years I was giving the impression that I was "directing the tanks right into the middle of my opponents," who supposedly included Bunkowske. He said that he and others were amazed that I had gotten away with as much as I had for so many years, and they were was astounded how Robert Preus had provided protection for me. Out of office now for three and a half years, Preus had been in no position to provide protection for me or anyone else, including himself. Never identified were who "the others" were. Whatever Werning had given me I had deserved, so he said. For what I had done, I was told, I would never receive vindication from the faculty, in his view. In a real sense he was right.

Now a word about roasting. Often used at formal occasions, it delivers its message so persons with differing views can remain on friendly terms with one another. The annual White House Press Corps dinner in April used to be such an occasion. President Ronald Reagan (1911–2004) and United States House Speaker Tip O'Neill (1912–1994) were well versed in roasting one another. Anyone concerned about theological differences I might have with others needed only to consult what I have written. Symposium banquets are not the place to look for how one theological perspective differs from another, but in light of the dire things that were happening, it would have been as good a time as any other to put the cards on the table.

At the thirty-first annual Symposium, St. Louis seminary professor Charles Arand began his January 18, 2008 lecture by congratulating its organizers, calling it the gold standard for such convocations.

Excursus X

QUEST FOR AN ADVANCED DEGREE PROGRAM

Robert Preus was easily the most recognizable name in world confessional Lutheranism, and because of his defense of biblical inerrancy he also had a heroic image among Evangelicals, who were replacing the older liberalism as the face of Protestantism. In the synod he was a popular figure who attracted students to the seminary and found the funds for seminary expansion. Often forgotten is that at the time of his dismissal by the board, with Robert Preus as president the seminary was approaching an endowment so large that tuition could be eliminated.

Sometime before I became academic dean in 1984, the Master of Sacred Theology degree (S.T.M.) was put in place. For Robert Preus, the next step was the Doctor of Theology (Th.D.) program, a task that partially fell to me. Originally it was agreed or at least thought that the St. Louis seminary would continue with the Th.D. program, which was a research degree with attention to evaluating original sources, and that Fort Wayne would offer the doctor of ministry (D.Min.), a professional degree that was given on the basis of a project carried out by pastors generally in their own congregation.

Board for Higher Educational Services director Michael J. Stelmachowicz often referred to a meeting of this board in which a promise was made to then St. Louis seminary president Karl Barth for that seminary to offer the D.Min., and with that promise St. Louis began to offer the program leading to a D.Min. A division of labors with one school offering the Th.D. and the other the D.Min. was no longer in effect, and so steps were made at Fort Wayne to put a Th.D. program in place.

Fort Wayne's Th.D. initial proposal numbered eight type-written double-spaced pages, and the program had four parts: New Testament, Ecumenical Church Creeds and Confessions, the Confessions of the Sixteenth Century and the Post-Reformation Era to the Present. Proficiency in Greek, Latin and German had to be demonstrated before being admitted. Competence in a modern language other than German was also required. Along with the seminary's own faculty, off-campus instructors would be involved. Among the twenty names proposed were Lewis Spitz (1923–2000), John Warwick Montgomery, John Stephenson, Kenneth Korby, Gottfried Martens, Kenneth Hagen and Ulrich Asendorf, all notable lights in Lutheran circles in the concluding decades of the twentieth century. Proposed were formal relations with other academic institutions: Concordia Seminary, St. Louis, Marquette University, School of Theology at Notre Dame, Lutheran School of Theology in Chicago and Trinity Evangelical Divinity School, Deerfield, Illinois.

Thirty years later, relations with most of these schools would be untenable. This proposal was made when the churches supporting those institutions were at a different place. Suggested were thirty-eight different courses. Even by today's standards the proposal was avant-garde, and its language requirements are hardly matched by any other institution.

In the end, the Fort Wayne proposal was rejected by the Board for Higher Educational Services. In its place, plans were being put in place to offer the Doctor of Missiology (D.Miss.) degree, a program that fit with Robert Preus's interests in missions that would fit within the context of confessional Lutheranism even in those churches not in formal fellowship with the Missouri Synod. To advance this vision, Preus had called to the faculty Eugene Bunkowske, a missionary in Africa, who had a doctor's degree, and Robert Newton, who was working toward a degree at Fuller Theological Seminary in Pasadena, California. Preus saw an opportunity to expand the Doctor of Missiology program by entering into a joint program with the then recently established and now defunct Oswald Hoffmann School of Missions at Concordia University at St. Paul, Minnesota. Representing the seminary in making these arrangements was Eugene Bunkowske.

Before seminary courses could be given by Oswald Hoffmann School of Missions, approval had to be given by the Association of Theological Schools, the seminary's accrediting agency. Since the Oswald Hoffmann School of Missions offered its program to college graduates, and the Fort Wayne seminary's program was for those who had graduated from the seminary and served in some capacity in mission, the program's accreditation was denied.

I had not been involved in setting up the jointly offered program and was not aware of how advanced negotiations between the two schools were, but as the academic dean I was responsible and had the task to inform the co-signers at the university in St. Paul that the agreement had to be broken. This was not an ideal situation and I faced the task with trepidation. As I recall, a meeting with the university administrators took place in the winter, and I traveled to St. Paul on Saturday and on Sunday conducted Bible class and preached at University Lutheran Chapel, where I stayed with John T. Pless, the campus pastor. Separate meetings were scheduled for Sunday afternoon, first with the university's academic dean Loma Meyer (1928–2014) and then college president Alan Harre, now retired from the presidency of Valparaiso University.

Meyer was not especially pleased that the agreement had to be broken, and for over two hours asked how the seminary could go into an agreement that it could not keep. Though I was not involved in the agreement, I was held responsible. The meeting with Harre was more cordial, but only slightly so.

There were lessons here to be learned. In instituting new programs, any school, including a seminary, has to inform and involve the entire faculty and then present it to all the supervising agencies including its own board, the synod's oversight authorities and the accrediting agencies. Those involved in devising the program, and this includes the academic dean, should finalize the arrangements. This was not done, and the result was ill will with a sister synodical institution. There are many situations which we do not want to relive. The meeting in St. Paul was one for me.

Later the seminary would change the Doctor of Missiology (D.Miss.) degree's nomenclature to the Doctor of Philosophy (Ph.D.) in Missiology. In spite of the letters Ph.D., it did not require the rigors traditionally associated with this degree. Not long after, St. Louis changed its nomenclature for its research degree from Th.D. to Ph.D. and added more requirements.

The report on "New Program Proposals" was sent by BHES staff member R. [Rudy] C. Block on May 15, 1987, to college and seminary academic deans. Robert Preus sent a memo to dean of graduate studies Dean Wenthe, William Weinrich and myself, calling for a meeting to take immediate steps for "an early advent of a Th.D. program in Confessional Studies."[1] A graduate faculty would be made up of these professors: Heino Kadai, William Weinrich, Robert Preus, Kurt Marquart and Eugene Klug. Preus proposed having John Stephenson and still another member join the faculty. In the same memo he said that Richard Muller (1928–2016) could help in Reformed and Calvinist studies.

Robert Preus wrote Michael Stelmachowiscz trying to overcome previous BHES objections to calling Steven Briel, son of seminary business manager Al Briel and his own son-in-law.[2] He added the names Walter A.

---

1. Robert Preus, letter to Dean Wenthe, William Weinrich and David Scaer, October 22, 1987.
2. Robert Preus, letter to Michael Stelmachowiscz, February 23, 1988.

Maier III, son of a faculty member, and Charles Manske (1933–2015), the founding president of Christ College in Irvine, California. In the same letter he asked to plead his case directly to the BHES and also to ask them for permission to collect funds for "a five million General Endowment for the Seminary."

Stelmachowiscz replied that the proper paper work had not been done for the Th.D. degree and held up the example of previous seminary degree applications for the Doctor of Missiology degree (D.Miss.) presented by Eugene Bunkowske.[3] He also informed Preus that special fund drives could only be allowed by the LCMS board of directors. Two paragraphs in the letter recalled that the BHES rejected Briel in 1984 and claimed that Preus's attitude in 1988 was sufficient reason for not reconsidering Briel.

Stelmachowicz did say that he would poll the board on granting Preus's request to attend the next meeting of the BHES on April 21–23 at Ann Arbor. Ironically, in a year and a half, the BHES allowed Walter A. Maier III to join the faculty in spite of his father's newly acquired position as academic dean, and Briel went on to serve on the BHES, the board that had previously rejected him.

Robert Preus informed Stelmachowicz that since he would be out of the country on a lecture tour, I would address academic concerns about the Th.D. program and that Norb Mueller would speak to financial matters.[4] In a letter written on March 10, 1988, Stelmachowicz wrote Preus that by a mail ballot vote the board had rejected Preus's request for a personal appearance before it and repeated his concerns contained in the previous letter. Preus responded on April 6, 1988, that Norbert Mueller was at work on an endowment fund to support the program and that I had been in contact with William Baumgartner of the Association of Theological Schools and Rudy Block to expedite initiating the Th.D. program.

On March 9, 1988, I drafted a letter to Stelmachowicz that was never sent, addressing some of the concerns he raised between him and Preus, which in rough form is still in my files. In a few months my focus was directed to charges brought against me. Preus's requests for new faculty, including Briel and Stephenson, were rejected.

Robert Preus's dream of a Th.D. in Confessional Studies was to be pursued by the Dean Wenthe and Lawrence Rast administrations. In the fall of 2018, this dream was realized with the inauguration of a Ph.D. in Theological Studies.

---

3. Michael Stelmachowiscz, letter Robert Preus, February 26, 1988.
4. Robert Preus, letter to Michael Stelmachowiscz, March 6, 1988.

Chapter Eight

THE ERA OF GOOD FEELING

❧

At the beginning of the Robert Preus presidency, contentment reigned in the faculty and there seemed to be little concern about which professors had administrative positions. Preus was interested in getting the finest academic credentialed men on the faculty. Douglas Judisch helped out with the *Concordia Theological Quarterly*. James Voelz was soon to get his Ph.D. from the University of Cambridge (UK) and William C. Weinrich had a doctor of theology from the University of Basel. New faculty members Norb Mueller and Kurt Marquart joined Howard Tepker as the faculty's representatives on synod's Commission on Theology and Church Relations. With his vast reservoir of theological and secular knowledge, Kurt Marquart provided Robert Preus with a wide breadth of references in performing the theological responsibilities given the president.

C. George Fry (b. 1936) had been a member of the ministerium of the American Lutheran Church (ALC) before its merger into the ELCA. An article in *Christianity Today* on Islam as a heresy of Christianity was reason enough for me to recommend him to Robert Preus for a faculty position. His classroom and chapel lectures made him a popular professor. After leaving the seminary, he continued his colorful career by teaching at St. Francis College, now a university in Fort Wayne, and resuming membership in the ministerium of the ALC as it was incorporated into the ELCA. Later he would present himself as bishop of a small denomination.

Albert Garcia (b. 1947) was a member of the systematics department and handled the seminary's burgeoning but not long-lasting Hispanic program, which slipped out of the hands of Fort Wayne to St. Louis. He went on to teach in the department of theology of Concordia University—Wisconsin in Mequon and wrote his doctoral dissertation for Carl Braaten. Garcia was the compiler of the essays and editor for a festschift in Braaten's honor. Al is one whom I counted as a friend then and still do.

As time went on, I was no longer teaching dogmatics from its basis in sixteenth- and seventeenth-century classical Lutheranism, as that had been handed down to our generation by Franz Pieper. Now I was thinking more in categories outlined in the Gospels. At meetings of the systematic department, Robert Preus made the point that a student taking the Christology course from Kurt Marquart and a student taking the same class from me were taking two different courses. He even went so far as to suggest that two courses be given in the place of one. Preus might have been saying that he wanted me to be like Marquart or that he found both approaches indispensable. Like Pieper, the synod's premier theologian, Marquart had no degree beyond the Bachelor of Divinity awarded to St. Louis seminary graduates. The ATS required that all faculty members with few exceptions have doctor's degrees.

Since the seminary was newly accredited, Robert Preus, with board pressure, required Kurt Marquart to obtain at least a master's degree, which he received from Western Ontario University in London, Canada, where he spent a sabbatical year with his family. For this degree, a still-unpublished extensive paper was required but not a dissertation. Like Pieper and Harry Huth, who taught the Lutheran Confessions during the seminary presidency of Jack Preus, Marquart was self-taught.

In spite of his preference for Marquart's approach, Robert Preus completely supported my approach as it was expressed in *The Apostolic Scriptures* and *What Do You Think of Jesus?*, whose publication with Concordia Publishing House he arranged. Later he assigned me three volumes in The Confessional Lutheran Dogmatics series of which he was the editor.

More than anyone else I knew, Preus encouraged others in their scholarly endeavors and did all within his power to provide them opportunities. His receiving a Ph.D. from the University of Edinburgh before his thirtieth birthday remains a model to others. While Preus encouraged my theological approach, he preferred those who followed the classical model of the sixteen- and seventeenth-century theologians and Pieper.

As it turned out, the unity among synod conservatives in their concern for historical biblical Christianity was coming apart. Thomas N. Olsen as president of the National Evangelical Lutheran Conference invited me to preach at an October 30 Reformation service in 1983 at St. John's Lutheran Church in Clifton, New Jersey, with a presentation to follow.[1] Weak attendance may have indicated that theological issues behind the February 1974 St. Louis seminary walkout had become less pressing. Nearly ten years had passed.

Olsen wrote, "Our speakers for our past service have been Dr. Martin Scharlemann, Dr. J. A. O. Preus, Dr. John Warwick Montgomery,

---

1. Thomas N. Olsen, letter to David Scaer, May 15, 1983.

Dr. Robert Preus, Dr. Walter A Maier, Dr. Paul A. Zimmerman, Rev. E. J. Otto, Rev. Philipp Giesler, Dr. Waldo A. Werning, and last year Dr. Walter A. Maier again." These names, except Giesler's, are likely to be found in any account of events leading to the walkout and elsewhere in this narrative. Differences among those who were opposed to the Seminex theology were already emerging.

Walter Maier II and the Preus brothers did not see eye to eye on the doctrine of justification. Montgomery found wider acceptance among Evangelicals then he did in the LCMS. Werning would soon bring charges against me for saying that all theology was Christology.

THE ASSOCIATION OF CONFESSIONAL LUTHERAN SEMINARIES (ACLS)

In August 1980, I was sent by Robert Preus to a gathering of professors from Lutheran seminaries at Oberursel, Germany. There I delivered at essay on baptism and the Lord's Supper translated into German for delivery by Wilhelm Torgerson. This essay was later published and received a positive review in the *Theologische Literaturzeitung*.[2] Another attendee, Gottlieb Wachler, a pastor from East Germany, who brought it to the attention of my systematic department chairman Eugene Klug, was less than pleased with it.

Manfred Roensch (1930–2001), a professor of historical theology of the seminary of the Independent Evangelical Lutheran Church (SELK) in Oberursel, had obtained funds for the meeting from *Spiegel* publisher Axel Springer (1912–1985), a member of Jobst Schöne's St. Mary's congregation in Berlin. It would be almost another ten years before the wall dividing the two Germanys would fall. During the meeting Roensch proposed forming The Association of Confessional Lutheran Seminaries with him serving chairman and I as secretary. Roensch and I, as the executive committee, drew up a protocol in contacting potential members, arranging for funding from the LCMS and SELK, and laying groundwork for another meeting, including a theme.

The Oberursel meeting lasted six days, from Monday to Saturday in late summer 1980. Usually funds could hardly be acquired for a meeting of such length, but they were. According to the minutes of a meeting held in Cambridge, England (UK) from September 6–9, 1982, the 1980

---

2. David P. Scaer, "Baptism and the Lord's Supper in the Life of the Church," *Concordia Theological Quarterly* 45, no. 1–2 (January 1981): 37–59, http://www.ctsfw.net/media/pdfs/scaerbaptismandthelordssupper.pdf.

Oberursel meeting was considered the first meeting of the ACLS and the Cambridge meeting the second.

While I do not have a record of the attendees to the Oberursel meeting, the minutes of the Cambridge meeting list the following as attending: Karl Barth (St. Louis), Ron Feuerhahn (1937–2015) (Cambridge), J. Gamaliel (India), Wilbur Kreiss (France), Hans-Lutz Poetsch (Germany), Manfred Roensch (Germany), David Scaer (Fort Wayne), Gottlieb Wachler (East Germany), E. Weber (South Africa), Rudi Zimmer (Brazil), Detlaff Lehmann (Canada), Glen Zweck (1935–2014) (Cambridge) and George Pearce (chairman of Evangelical Lutheran Church of England). Pearce gave a history of the International Lutheran Conference (ILC), whose previous two meetings were held in Cambridge in 1963 and 1966. Discussion assumed that the ACLS would step into the shoes of the ILC, but would not take up fellowship issues among the churches.

According to the minutes at least eleven papers were presented. Upon the request of the delegates, Roensch and I were asked to prepare "A Statement of Purpose for the Association of Confessional Lutheran Seminaries." Eight goals were set forth: (1) sharing of information, (2) exchange of professors and students, (3) meetings to discuss common issues, (4) assisting each other in research projects, (5) exchange of periodicals and lectures, (6) exchange of curriculums, (7) exchange of teaching methods and textbooks, and (8) exchange of standards for graduation. The group also decided that a newsletter could carry out some of these goals, and seminaries might help one another with textbooks. Dates for meetings were to be announced as soon as possible. Minutes of the Cambridge meeting contain a detailed account of the discussions.

A third meeting was held at Concordia Lutheran Theological Seminary in St. Catharines, Ontario, Canada, on September 17–20, 1985. Eleven essays were presented, and both Roensch and I were retained as chairman and secretary respectively. Along with delegates from Canada and the USA, professors from seminaries in Germany, South Africa, Korea, New Guinea, France, Hong Kong, Brazil, England, India, and Argentina were present. The group decided that regional meetings for seminaries be conducted for Europe-Africa, Asia, and North and South America.

In September 1989, the group was dissolved at a meeting of ILC in Korea. As the ACLS secretary I was there for no other purpose than to watch its demise. It was revived by synod president Alvin Barry with Ron Feuerhahn as coordinator.

Four years passed between the 1985 meeting in St. Catharines and the 1989 ILC meeting in Korea. With the removal of Robert Preus as Fort

Wayne seminary president in September 1989, the seminary situation was desperate, as was mine, with doctrinal charges being leveled against me and my removal as dean. About forty years have passed since the idea of the ACLS was hatched, and after 1989, I was never involved again. ACLS goals are now being carried out by Al Collver, an assistant to LCMS president Matthew Harrison. It was a vision set in place in August 1980.

WIL ROSIN'S TENURE AS ACADEMIC DEAN

My close association with Robert Preus may have been behind his bringing Wilber Rosin, Howard Tepker's replacement as academic dean, to our home on 1912 Brandywine Trail in Fort Wayne. There had been no talk of Tepker's retirement, and so it was with some surprise that Robert and Jack Preus showed up unannounced at our door one evening in the spring of 1979 with Wilbert Rosin, who was introduced as the next academic dean. His wife, Dorothy (1925–2010), was the daughter of Lewis Spitz Sr. (1895–1996), who had come out of retirement to teach in 1974 after the faculty majority left their positions vacant.

Robert Preus was also interested in bringing onto the faculty Wil's son, Robert Rosin (b. 1951), who was doing his doctoral work in Reformation studies at Stanford University under his uncle, Lewis Spitz Jr., brother to Dorothy Rosin. Wil Rosin did not think that a dean's son should serve on the same faculty, and the younger Rosin, Robert, soon accepted a position at the St. Louis seminary, from which he is now retired.

Wil and Dorothy Rosin bought a home in Paper Mills Bluff, to the south of the campus on the other side of St. Joe Center Road. Rosin had been the president of Concordia College, Milwaukee. It had been a school of less than three hundred. After Rosin left, the college moved to a campus belonging to order of Catholic sisters in Mequon on the shores of Lake Michigan. Under the presidencies of first John Buuck and then Patrick Ferry, it grew to a student body of about four thousand. Jack Preus may have thought that it was time for changes at Concordia Milwaukee and maybe at the Fort Wayne seminary also.

Wil was a take-charge academic dean, more in line with the style of Lorman Petersen, whose association for me was less positive. Certain things that happened during Rosin's three-year tenure as dean became well known. After having been the de facto president and academic dean at St. Louis in the spring of 1974 and then assuming the presidency of the Springfield seminary in 1974 and supervising its move to Fort Wayne, Robert Preus was looking forward to a sabbatical in the fall and winter terms of the 1980–1981. This left Rosin as the acting president of the seminary, with full presidential authority given him by the seminary board of regents.

Having served just recently as president of Concordia College, Milwaukee, as seminary interim president, he was ready to take on similar responsibilities at the seminary during Preus's sabbatical absence and proceeded to recommend to the board Dan Bruch and Steven Carter for faculty positions. Bruch and his wife, as well as his high school daughters, were associated with feminist causes, including the ordination of women.

Bruch eventually took a position at Concordia College, St. Paul, Minnesota, and has since passed away. Carter would later become president of Concordia Publishing House. Trudy Behning, as the president's secretary was told by Rosin not to be in contact with Robert Preus about seminary developments during his sabbatical (August–December 1981).

In the seminary's fall term, Robert Preus taught at Luther Seminary in Adelaide, Australia. At the invitation of its principal, Henry Hamann, he also delivered the graduation address. Later Hamann would come as a visiting professor to Fort Wayne several times. In the winter term, Preus had gone to his newly constructed house on the American side of Gunflint Lake, Minnesota, to write.

Previously the Preus family had spent summers in cabins on the Canadian side, which were uninhabitable in the severe winters and could be inaccessible due to the rough ice of the frozen lake. Upon returning from his sabbatical, Preus took umbrage at what had happened during his absence. Heino "Hank" Kadai, professor of historical theology since 1960, asked me why, upon returning to the campus, Preus had not spoken to Rosin, whose offices were side by side. Typically Preus cut off contact with those with whom he had disagreements. Hank must have thought that I was privy to some inside information, but I wasn't.

In spite of Rosin's request to Trudy Behning that she not make reports to Preus during his sabbatical, he must have known of seminary happenings. Other college and seminary presidents away on sabbatical have kept their hands on developments at their institutions. Then there's the precedent of Luther, who left his refuge in the Wartburg to return to Wittenberg when things under Andreas Karlstadt (1486–1541) got out of control. Heads of organizations like pastors of congregations are rarely given the privilege of being away from their responsibilities without incurring problems. Regular flights connect the down-under continent with North America. Gunflint is only a day's drive from Fort Wayne.

Relationships between the heads of organizations and subordinates present their own challenges. Subordinates are susceptible to criticism from their superiors for not acting decisively; but, on the other hand, taking decisive action also opens them up to censure. Academic Dean Tepker left most decisions up to Preus. Rosin did things differently.

An unexpected change in an administration is never without its own trauma, and it would be no different in this case, with Wil Rosin vacating the post of academic dean. As I was walking back to Jerome Hall from Loehe Hall and passing by the visitors' parking lot, I saw Rosin carrying his books out from the administration building to a faculty office building. My experience with Petersen had taught me to respect the office of academic dean, and so observing Rosin carrying boxes of his own books was a jolting experience. This was a task for the maintenance staff.

A letter from board secretary David G. Ebeling informed the faculty "that, effective June 1, 1982, Dr. Wilbert Rosin will no longer serve as Academic Dean of CTS" and that "This decision ought not be construed as a mark whatsoever against the Christian character, the morality, or the professional competence of either Dr. Rosin or Dr. Preus."[3]

Wil Rosin continued on the faculty as professor of historical theology until he accepted a position in the editorial division of Concordia Publishing House. Dorothy Rosin's brother, Lewis Spitz Jr., presented guest lecturers at Fort Wayne twice and remained on good terms with Robert Preus. His second lecture on his view of Lutheranism may have been his last, and I deeply regret that duties as academic dean prevented me from attending.

For those like myself who did not know the pre-history of this letter, it was enough to shock the nerves. This was precursor of a troubled future for the seminary. Until 1988, Rosin remained on the faculty, his last four years coinciding with my first four years as academic dean. He did not question my credentials in my holding an office as he once did, and in our conversations he did not discuss with me what transpired between him and Robert Preus.

A tinder bed for discontent is laid when professors at seminaries are not fully credentialed. Synod bylaws limit faculty positions to men who have served as parish pastors. Martin Luebke, the registrar along with Barbara Whalen, later Mark Steege, the librarian, and Warren Wilbert, one-time athletic director, were not seminary graduates and hence had not been pastors. None of them had doctorates. Seminary students studying for the parish ministry take notice of professors without this experience. They also soon become aware of those who are not academically equipped.[4]

---

3. David G. Ebeling, letter to the faculty of Concordia Theological Seminary, May 30, 1982.
4. Some students took exception to having the seminary librarian, Barbara Steege,

After his removal as academic dean, Wilbert Rosin told student body president Charles Gieschen that the board of regents was so under the control of Robert Preus that it did not know the real situation on campus and asked him about dissent among the students. There wasn't any. Gieschen kept Rosin's typewritten memorandum from that meeting.

RICHARD MULLER'S TENURE AS ACADEMIC DEAN

Richard Muller, who replaced Wil Rosin as academic dean, had not served as a pastor and was without a doctor's degree. He had come to the seminary to prepare for entrance into the synod's ministerium by colloquy, fulfilling the residency requirement by studying one year for the master of sacred theology degree, which he never acquired. He had acquired a master of divinity degree from the explicitly conservative Calvinist Westminister Seminary and had entertained Robert Preus in his Valley Forge home after he lectured in the vicinity. When the position of registrar was vacated by Martin Luebke, who was a parochial school teacher, it was offered to Muller, who agreed to accept it with the condition he would be made regular faculty member with an appointment to the department of systematics.

Robert Preus informed me that in becoming registrar, Muller's request for assignment the systematics department, of which I was chairman, would be granted. On several grounds I opposed this, including that he had never been a parish pastor and had no theological degree beyond the Master of Divinity degree. Preus assured me that his appointment to the department was a formality and that he would do no teaching. After years later in his appointment as academic dean, Muller told Preus that he would accept it only on a temporary basis.

Richard Muller's choice as academic dean was a surprise to everyone and was probably made necessary because at the end of the 1981–1982 school year, there was little time for deliberations to fill the vacancy left by Wil Rosin in the academic dean's position. So Robert Preus thought he had no other options. Lowell Fein, who had served on a submarine and claimed expertise in the computerizing of the seminary, took over as registrar. Fein later aligned himself with those who worked to remove Preus from the presidency.

Seminary life was pleasant under Richard Muller who handled the administrative functions of the academic dean's office with great skill. He

---

who was not theologically credentialed and not allowed by the synod to be a pastor, certify them for the ministry.

had to endure Rosin's reminders that he was not qualified for the position. After the two years, Muller was happy to head to the classroom to teach dogmatics, something which Preus had said would not happen.

His having gone to a strict Calvinist seminary had a reverse effect on Muller and gave him an aversion to the Reformed position on the Lord's Supper, which he called the doctrine of the "real absence." Preus noted that Muller's book acquisitions were nearly all from Reformed publishers like the Presbyterian and Reformed Publishers in Phillipsburg, New Jersey, and urged him to read Lutheran books.

In the aftermath of the St. Louis faculty walkout, some conservative Lutherans came to think that in the doctrine of biblical inspiration they shared a common foundation for doing theology with the Reformed. Classical seventeenth-century Lutheran theologians saw things entirely differently, and if it were not for the doctrine of the Trinity, they would not have recognized the Reformed as Christian.

One department colleague, greatly admired throughout the synod, said that while Zwingli had the word, Lutherans had word and sacraments. Of course, Zwingli did not even have the word. Even some of the synod's brighter lights could not grasp that Lutherans and the Reformed lived in two different worlds, beginning with what each believed about God.

At the end of Richard Muller's term, the post of academic dean had to be filled again. Robert Preus tossed several names around for the position of academic dean, most prominently Samuel Nafzger, then secretary, later called executive director, of the LCMS Commission on Theology and Church Relations. Nafzger had been the assistant to Ralph Bohlmann in that position and then became his successor, when Bohlmann followed Jack Preus as synod president. As a member of that commission, Preus knew him, and at that time every one of its members was almost by definition conservative.

MY TENURE AS ACADEMIC DEAN

At age forty-five years and with his experience on the commission, Nafzger would have been a perfect fit for the job. In a car ride to St. Louis for a meeting, probably with its faculty, Jim Voelz proposed my name to Robert Preus. By the end of the trip, Preus offered the position of academic dean to me, and I took it. And so it happened that I was the dean from July 1984 to September 1989.

At the same time, the spring of 1984, synod president Bohlmann announced his appointment of a six-member committee consisting of district presidents to investigate alleged unrest at the seminary. This was a matter with which I did not want to get involved, and so I changed my mind about the appointment. Preus offered the position to Eugene Bunkowske, a St. Louis seminary classmate, who would in 1989 be elected a synod vice president. Bunkowske accepted Preus's offer.

I began to suffer pangs of conscience for running away from what could be a difficult situation, and so I approached Al Wingfield (1933–2018), Robert Preus's assistant, to intercede with Preus that I was ready to accept the position. During my tenure as dean I participated in all the board meetings, with the exception of one in the winter and another in the summer of 1989 at which Preus was removed from office.

Phyllis Saunders, secretary to the previous deans, served as the real powerhouse and kept me up to date on my responsibilities as dean and arranged the calendar. She continued with my successor, Walter A. Maier II. For the first two years I had the assistance of Richard Muller as associate academic dean, and for the third and fourth years Douglas Christian, a graduate student, helped. Then fourth-year student Larry Rast, later seminary assistant academic dean, then academic dean and now seminary president, provided some assistance in the fifth year. He claims that I would come into the dean's office in the afternoon, offer a few loud complaints and leave. Any frustration about the academic dean's position was fueled by my desire to be in the classroom and teach. A history of the seminary and seminaries in general may show how the president's job as the chief teacher developed into being the chief fund raiser, and that the academic dean became less and less involved with teaching and more with administration.

Several things were initiated during my tenure. Responsibility of assigning classes was transferred from the academic dean to the department chairman in consultation with its members. This was a departure from the years in Springfield, when a letter, sent in early August from the academic dean, then Lorman Petersen, informed the faculty of their course loads for the coming year. One professor's contract was not renewed for lack of academic credentials. Had this criterion been applied across the board, others also should have left. Many were called with the understanding that they would get their doctorates.

This is an acceptable policy if their residency or course work for the degree had been completed. Then there was the stipulation that professors have some parish experience. These criteria were routinely ignored. Some never had been full-time pastors of congregations and others served without receiving their doctorates. Two had their doctor of ministry degrees, which is more of a professional than an academic degree, and their dissertations matched neither the length nor the caliber of a full-length term paper. Four faculty members, perhaps more, had not even served regular vicarages under the continued supervision of a parish pastor. One professor used his sabbatical to build kitchen cabinets.

Sadly, some faculty members were judged by the students as incompetent. Addressing this question after they had been called to the faculty was like locking the barn door after the cow was stolen. In contract renewal and tenure, I adopted a procedure that each professor had to provide two letters of evaluation, one from a colleague and another from outside of the campus. In one case this produced some interesting results.

Another task of the academic dean is to advise the president on acquiring new faculty and retaining and promoting current members. Ideally, names come from the department members through its chairman to the dean, and then the president who presents the candidate to the board.

In several instances I objected to certain candidates because they did not meet the requirements of having or being close to obtaining an advanced degree and parish experience. Hank Kadai never served a parish and was ordained only after he had served for some years on the faculty in Springfield—and then under pressure by Robert Preus. Jim Voelz served as assistant pastor at Zion in Fort Wayne, and Bill Weinrich had a long and distinguished career as a chaplain in the air force national guard. Others who had not served a congregation were John Saleska (1929–2017) and Richard Muller, both of whom were widely respected as Bible class teachers among the laity. According to current nomenclature Barbara Steege, Warren Wilbert and Martin Luebke were commissioned ministers, and thus had not been parish pastors.

During St. Louis seminary days, a course in sermon delivery was offered by a lay speech teacher. Amazingly no one saw the discrepancy in having a man teach future pastors how to preach who had never cared for a congregation or stood in the pulpit of a congregation for whose spiritual care he was responsible. Behind this mentality might be the idea that one general rule was applicable for any and all public speaking, and preaching was no different. Often heard as established canon was Aristotle's (384–322 BC) dictum that every speech had three parts. Somehow my own productions either got hung up on one point or went without form from one point to another.

Standards for faculty members may have been so unworkable that they could not be applied in each case. In any event, requirements set down by synod convention are widely ignored. Today the youngest graduating seminary student is rarely less than twenty-six years of age, but more likely twenty-seven. Four years of residence are required for most doctoral degrees, and then five years of parish experience are expected. If all works according to plan, a pastor could be called as a seminary professor no earlier than thirty-six years of age. Tenure could come first in his mid-forties.

During my tenure as dean I do not recall making any recommendations for new faculty members, and if there were any, they were not acted upon. Robert Preus wanted to bring on Robert Newton, a missionary in the Philippines, who did not then have the academic qualifications as prescribed by synod protocol. To get around this obstacle, Preus gave Newton a one-year contract and then renewed it for another year and then had him appointed assistant professor for two years.

Bob Newton had made a positive impression on Preus, who gave him two successive one-year contracts followed by a two-year contract as instructor, a position he was hesitant to accept. Waldo Werning, who still had hopes of obtaining faculty status, encouraged him to accept the position by telling him that he was their hope for the future. He accepted. My concerns were ignored.

With Robert Newton's love for missions and evangelism, Robert Preus thought that he could tolerate certain church growth principles. Newton had a master's degree from Fuller Seminary, where the method had been developed and where Werning was recognized as an authority in its application. Church growth principles emphasized individual Christian responsibility as it was promoted by late sixteenth- and early seventeenth-century pietism, in which the clergy were functionaries or enablers in assisting each believer to use his innate authority. Those who saw the ministry as established by Christ in the apostles were seen as the opponents of these principles and had to be eliminated or their roles minimized.

At the seminary, Newton would play a significant role until Dean Wenthe became president in April 1996. In 1989, Norb Mueller appointed Newton to the synod's Committee for Pastoral Ministry to take the place of Wenthe. He served on the faculty committee for recommending candidates for seminary president (1992–1993), and he put forth the name of David Schmiel as permanent seminary president. Mueller appointed him as vice president for certification, in which position he targeted liturgical students for counseling. His rise from staff member to faculty with the title of vice president was mercurial.

Bob Newton at first did not think himself qualified, but then was convinced by Waldo Werning, who told him to join the faculty. This was similar to the calling of Gene Bunkowske, a classmate of mine from St. Louis days. He had a doctor's degree but also declined the first and second call. Preus persisted and Gene accepted the third time around.

At the board meeting at which Bob Newton's name was presented as an assistant professor, the name of Tom Acton was also put forth and rejected. Initial appointment to the seminary requires the approval of the electors, who endorse the board decisions. The four electors then were the synod president, the chairman of the Board for Higher Education Services, the Indiana district president or any representative of these three, with the regents casting one vote. Electors also choose college and seminary presidents. Today, a district president chosen by the college of district presidents and the synod praesidium takes the place of the area district president as a seminary elector.

Newton and Acton had met with the electors and were found to be doctrinally acceptable. Both were waiting in the president's house on campus to learn their fate, but while Newton was offered the post of an assistant professor, Acton was not.

Another indication of approaching foul weather was the rejection of John Stephenson as assistant professor in systematic theology. Stephenson had gone out of his way to meet Robert Preus at a lecture in England and impressed him with his commitment to Scripture. With a master's degree from Cambridge and a Ph.D. from Durham, he was too good to be true, the kind of scholar that enhances any seminary's credentials.

Two obstacles stood in the way of bringing him on the faculty: he had no seminary training or parish experience. Seminaries provide ministers in the United Kingdom and Europe, but theological education is also provided by universities, and so Stephenson had the necessary academic prerequisites, especially with a doctor's degree, for which he wrote an impressive dissertation which far exceeded what 90 percent of the faculty had written, but was not a seminary graduate. Stephenson also taught at Concordia College, Moorhead, Minnesota (1982–1983), and was provided a vicarage by teaching at the seminary until his assignment to Escarpment Lutheran Church, Lewiston, New York, through colloquy in 1985.

I set forth Stephenson's credentials (B.A., M.A. Oxford; theological diploma, Cambridge; Ph.D. Durham) along with recommendations of Eastern District president Arnold Krompardt.[5] So certain was his appointment to the seminary as an assistant professor, that I wrote to Robert Preus, his assistant Norb Mueller and business manager Gary Satterfield, that Stephenson should be assigned an office in Jerome Hall.[6]

---

5. David Scaer, letter to Robert Preus, November 16, 1987.
6. David Scaer, letter to Robert Preus, Norbert Mueller and Gary Satterfield, November 16, 1987.

Things looked good for a time. Stephenson was voted an assistant professorship by the regents, but failed to get the electors' approval. Only the regents cast their one vote for him. Synod president Ralph Bohlmann was present to cast his vote along with those of Indiana District president Reuben Garber and of Board for Higher Education Services against him. Even if Garber would have voted to approve, Stephenson's cause would have been lost.

Born, raised and educated in England, Stephenson had all the intelligence and wit associated with his countrymen. He had also translated a large theological tome by Wolfhart Pannenberg (1928–2014), who was the rage at that time as a theologian of history, from ponderous German into English. One misstep stood in Stephenson's way, an albatross from around his neck that could not be untied. It had to do with the Lord's Supper.

Receptionism is a view of the Lord's Supper that the bread is Christ's body first at the moment of the communicant's receiving it with his/her mouth. Gene Klug supported this view as Luther's with a quotation from the Reformer. In checking out the reference, John Stephenson discovered that this was not Luther's view, but Luther was quoting Zwingli's receptionist view of the Lord's Supper, so he could not look to Luther for support. His wit in pointing out the error made things worse. With an abject apology Stephenson expressed his regrets to Klug, but the dye was cast and opposition to Stephenson could not be undone. In retrospect, it seems as if Bohlmann's opposition to Stephenson was directed more at Robert Preus than Stephenson, who was crestfallen in learning his fate.

I continued to press Stephenson's cause. I suggested to Preus that having Stephenson lecture at the January 1989 winter symposium, and in the following two weeks in the intensive winter session.[7] His talents became known to Concordia Lutheran Theological Seminary in St. Catharines, Ontario, where he was later called.

With Acton and Stephenson not being approved by the electors, Robert Preus might have sensed that he and the seminary were already under siege. So the appropriate action for him would have been to bring men onto the faculty who would remain loyal to him, if he was asked to stand down from the presidency. This he did not do. It was all or nothing, and when September 7, 1989, rolled around it was closer to nothing.

During my tenure as academic dean, Norbert Mueller, then assistant to the president, asked for my support in having senior administrative officers being given the designation of vice president. My title would have

---

7. David Scaer, memo to Robert Preus, February 2, 1988.

been vice president for academic affairs, a designation already in vogue in institutions of higher learning. This had no appeal to me at all and I flatly refused.

THE GATHERING STORM

A letter to the Board of Regents supporting Robert Preus appeared on May 24, 1984, containing a petition. The petition was signed by James W. Voelz, who seems to have circulated it, Arthur A. Just Jr., James Bollhagen, George Kraus, William C. Weinrich, G. Waldemar Degner, Raymond Surburg and Otto Stahlke.

The May 24 petition claimed that differences among the faculty were being addressed and expressed confidence in the Preus presidency. These names represented about 80 percent of the faculty. Howard Tepker declined to sign the letter and added that if Preus lost his job, he would be well taken care of. Tepker was showing his colors.

At that time a letter written in the previous spring from synod's Board for Higher Education Services surfaced, requesting Preus's retirement. Walter Kaiser, a member of that board, claimed Ralph Bohlmann was the letter's real author.

In an address to the faculty on May 26, Ralph Bohlmann told us that he had asked Wil Rosin to resign from the faculty. To resolve faculty difficulties, Bohlmann proposed a faculty committee of "gray heads"—Aho, Tepker and Klug—to mediate.

Soon after, the faculty met again to iron out difficulties. Klug read a letter from Tepker that Professors Mark and Barbara Steege, Allen Nauss, Martin Luebke and George Fry had left the faculty with ill will. Added to those who were discontented would be Dan Bruch, Al Schmidt, and Albert Garcia. Also Rosin, Tepker and Klug were less than fully supportive of Preus.

In July 1984, a letter outlining unresolved faculty issues was sent to Robert Preus by Howard W. Tepker, Warren N. Wilbert, John W. Saleska, Stephen J. Carter, Randy Shields, Eugene F. Klug, Edgar Walz (1914–2003) (who was not technically a faculty member), Walter A. Maier II, and Waldemar Degner.[8] The letter refers to a report Preus had made saying "reconciliation was not yet reached with Professors Bruch, Garcia, Rosin and Schmidt." It also said that, as of that June 30, Bruch was no longer on the faculty.

---

8. Howard Tepker, Warren Wilbert, John Saleska, et al., letter to Robert Preus, July 1984.

On the next page of the letter the names of these aggrieved professors are listed again with that of George Fry, whose name was in parentheses, who was also not on the faculty. Signatories urged Robert Preus to "accept President Ralph Bohlmann's offer to provide a committee whose purpose will be to assist the seminary in the difficult task of bringing about reconciliation between you and these men."

A strange and unplanned turn of events aggravated the situation.[9] This is how things played out. In a letter to Gladys Suelflow (1924–2008),[10] Robert Preus was less than fully complementary of Ralph Bohlmann's administration as president of the St. Louis seminary and that of his successor, Karl Barth. He also requested her to provide an update on what was taking place there.

As the wife of a St. Louis professor and director of the Concordia Historical Institute, she was well placed in synod circles. She had been on staff at the St. Louis seminary and was now secretary to Pastor Arlo Janssen, an executive at the International Center, the synod's headquarters in Kirkwood, Missouri, a St. Louis suburb. During a day off from her job, her replacement did not notice that a letter from Preus was addressed to Gladys Suelflow and not to her supervisor, Arlo Janssen, whose mail she was tasked to open. In reading the letter, she realized it was personal and asked Janssen what to do. He advised her to tell Gladys Suelflow and inform Bohlmann and Barth.

When Robert Preus learned about his letter falling into the wrong hands, he made an apology to Bohlmann, which he accepted. Bohlmann pointed out to Preus that Gladys Suelflow "was not in a position to supply him with accurate information." He also "explained to [Preus] his procedural error in contacting an employee about her present (and past) supervisors' actions." When Preus brought up the letter's concerns to the Fort Wayne seminary board of regents, Bohlmann said he began having second thoughts about the sincerity of Preus's apology.

As if this was not enough, a letter Robert Preus wrote to Herman Otten, editor of *Christian News*, was mistakenly placed in an envelope addressed to Bohlmann, who rightly assumed its contents were intended for publication.[11] Preus had photocopied material from a Lutheran Church in America publication and mailed it to Otten. It had already been available

---

9. Ralph Bohlmann, letter to the Concordia Theological Seminary Board of Regents, July 20, 1984.
10. Robert Preus, letter to Gladys Suelflow, February 7, 1984.
11. Robert Preus, letter to Herman Otten, January 31, 1984.

to readers of that publication and was of no significance and by anyone's standard not confidential. It was hardly more than filler for the newspaper's columns. Since Otten's seminary days, Preus had befriended him and advanced his quest for certification into the synod ministerium and from time to time supplied him bits of information from news sources available to him for publication. Preus called the incidents surrounding the letter that fell into Bohlmann's hands a "bizarre occurrence."

Ralph Bohlmann thought otherwise. He called it "a much more serious matter than the former item [the letter to Gladys Suelflow]" and called on the seminary's regents to deal with the two incidents that reflected Preus's poor judgment. Bohlmann says these concerns about Preus's letter should "not be confused with our current efforts to bring an end to the polarization and erosion of confidence in the seminary administration."[12] He goes on to say that "Doctor Preus himself constitutes one of the poles of a polarized faculty." While claiming not to connect the dots, this is exactly what Bohlmann did.

When the fall term in 1984 turned into the winter term, things had quieted down and would remain quiet for the next few years. A visit of the six district presidents to interrogate the faculty was not disruptive. Some of my hesitancy in taking over as academic dean was that my teaching and time to write would be curtailed by administrative duties.

In November 1984, Robert Preus sent a report to the regents which listed the dates on which meetings from May 25 through November 12 were to be held to iron things out with his opponents. "The four" professors opposing Preus wanted their accusations against him to be validated.[13] These meetings with "the four," one with Norbert Mueller and another with Indiana District president Elwood Zimmermann (1919–2006), "were totally nonproductive."

EDDIE BALFOUR AND THE BUSINESS OFFICE

After the summer of 1985, having completed one year as academic dean, I was drawn into a case in which Eddie Balfour and Warren Wilbert were the chief players. In the summer of 1984, having come to Fort Wayne to enroll in the seminary, Eddie Balfour said he was offered the position of "the director of computer services for the seminary," which was part of the business office. He had held a similar position at Concordia College in

---

12. Ralph Bohlmann, letter to the Concordia Theological Seminary Board of Regents, July 20, 1984.
13. Robert Preus, letter to the Concordia Theological Seminary Board of Regents, November 16, 1984.

Portland, Oregon, and had a letter of recommendation from its president. Had he not enrolled in the seminary as a student, he could have accepted a position similar to the one he had at Portland for twenty dollars an hour, a fair wage now and an extremely good one in 1984.

A bit of a tiff developed when Red Schnell, who then was in charge of seminary computer matters, learned that Eddie was offered a position to work with computers. In the same summer, along with Business Manager Gary Satterfield and Robert Preus's assistant Al Wingfield, Eddie attended a meeting to prepare for tying the seminary's computer system into the one at Concordia Teachers College in River Forest under the direction of a certain Dennis Witte. Eddie determined that the cost for the River Forest connection was about three times that charged the largest corporations.

Throughout the summer, relations between Eddie on one side and Satterfield and Wingfield on the other had their high and low points, and their verbal exchanges were often heard throughout the administration building, as could be attested by the secretaries. In his new position, Balfour had access to the seminary's finances and claimed to have discovered irregularities. He said that the business office was skimming money off the top.

What should a new student do who sincerely believes that the institution in which he has just enrolled has staff who are guilty of financial malfeasance? Eddie Balfour contacted dean of students John Saleska, who in his position was entrusted with student problems. According to Balfour, Saleska said he could not go to Robert Preus with these things. Soon after meeting with the dean of students, Balfour received a phone call from Warren Wilbert, who told him, "I know everything," and urged him to contact synod president Bohlmann. Eddie Balfour claimed that Wilbert kept phoning him up to ten or twelve times. He called so often that Eddie's wife, Marie, said she came to recognize Wilbert's voice before he identified himself.

During the course of these phone conversations, which took place in August and early September 1984, Wilbert told Eddie that the phones of Seminary professors Robert Collins, John Saleska, Harold Zietlow (1926–2011), and Melvin Zilz (1932–2005) were being tapped. Soon after, John Saleska had arranged to have Balfour meet General Gerhardt Hyatt (1916–1985) outside the chapel at the opening service on September 19.

General Hyatt was a former Army chaplain, and now a synod vice president. To coordinate the work of both seminaries, Ralph Bohlmann appointed Hyatt to both seminary boards, each numbering nine members. Ironically Balfour would later become well known as a member of synod's board of directors, having been first appointed through the recommendation of board member attorney Christian Preus (b. 1959), Robert Preus's fifth son, and then retained by election in 2004. In the summer of 2006, *Christian News* began proposing Balfour's name for first vice president on a ballot with Wallace Schulz as president.

Eddie Balfour later provided a detailed account of that late summer 1984 meeting. He had not attended the opening service, but arrived after it was over and met Hyatt outside of the chapel. Accompanied by Eddie's wife, Marie, they went to Luther Hall, whose interior is described as "pitch dark," and they sat in the room's left-hand corner. When Eddie said he did not like to sit in dark rooms, Hyatt asked him not to turn on the lights. By chance, during the meeting, Al Wingfield came in and Eddie said, "I'm real scared."

According to Balfour, the meeting with Hyatt lasted a half hour, during which Hyatt asked pointed questions. When asked by Hyatt whether there was any hanky-panky going on the business office, Eddie responded, "It could be a possibility." He also told Hyatt that the business office was sloppy and that he was upset that one of the seminary's auditors was appointed as the comptroller. Eddie reported this meeting with Hyatt to Wilbert, who responded, "Everyone who falls into disfavor with President Preus disappears."

There are some sidebars to the Wilbert-Balfour-Hyatt episode. Before this meeting I was not privy to what was going on. By chance as I was leaving the 1984 opening service, I saw Saleska introducing Balfour to Hyatt on the northwest outside corner of the chapel and could not help remembering that an incoming student was being introduced to a synod vice president. One year later, I learned that the meeting had been arranged by Wilbert.

At a placement meeting on November 10, 1985, a few loose ends came together on what was happening. Wilbert told Eddie that if he "went to Preus's office, there is nothing that can save you," and Harold Zietlow said "Something is morally wrong here and it is coming to a head." Eugene Klug may have also had known about these allegations, because he told Eddie, "You have had it with the business office, and it is coming to a head."

Balfour was caught between contradictory advice of whether or not he should tell church authorities of what he thought was taking place in the business office. Had he kept things to himself, nothing would have come of it, but now synod president Ralph Bohlmann had become involved.

To get to the bottom of things, Robert Preus called a meeting for September 11, 1985, held in the then regular faculty meeting room on the ground floor of Loehe Hall. As the academic dean, I was present as one who had not been involved in order to hear all sides and to learn what really had happened. If something was amiss, actions were to be taken. Present were Robert Preus, Al Wingfield, Arthur Just, Walter Maier II, Attorney John Walda, Warren Wilbert, Harold Zietlow, Business Manager Gary Satterfield, seminary student Eddie Balfour and his wife, Marie. A series of events that began in early August 1984 came to light. At the heart of the turmoil were conversations, nearly all by phone, between Balfour and Wilbert. In giving his account of his September 1984 meeting with Hyatt, Balfour reasserted that it was arranged by Warren Wilbert. Eddie Balfour's allegations of financial wrongdoing proved to be baseless, and he retracted his accusations about the business office. Reports of a tapped phone were proven to be bizarre.

This is not the end of the story of Eddie Balfour. During his fourth and last year at the seminary, Balfour worked in the hospital where Professor George Kraus approached death and provided extraordinary care for this dying professor. He became close to Helen Kraus, George's wife, and is now the retired pastor of Redeemer Lutheran Church in Cape Elizabeth, Maine, where she attends and where her husband was once pastor.

Eddie Balfour received his call into the ministry to Trinity Lutheran Church in the Bay Ridge section of Brooklyn, New York, in the evening of the same April day in 1989 on which the morning funeral service for George Kraus was held. Since the LCMS's Council of Presidents was on campus for the evening call service, the chapel was filled that morning to capacity for the funeral.

Helen Kraus, George's widow, asked that Norbert Mueller participate as an officiant. Norbert saw himself as a close friend to George, and Helen thought it was the right thing to do, though as the placement director he would ordinarily not have had a part. Following the call service, a medical doctor who knew Eddie gave a party for him at an Italian restaurant in the east central part of town.

There was a personal price to pay for this Balfour incident. A rift developed between John Saleska and his longtime friend and colleague Harold Buls (1920–1997), who strongly supported Robert Preus. Both had served at St. John's College, Winfield, Kansas, and after Buls came to the seminary (1969), he had recommended Saleska to Robert Preus. Until he died in September 1997, Buls yearned for the old friendship with Saleska to be restored. Robert Preus lost an ally and a friend in Saleska, who may have acted in good faith in arranging for Balfour to meet Hyatt, the synod president's representative. Saleska remained as an associate professor in offering courses in pastoral counseling and English Bible and remained a favorite among the students.

Administrators at that time received a stipend in addition to their regular salaries. Saleska's stipend as the dean of students remained in place, and so he received more pay than other professors of the same or similar rank. Preus did not have the heart to remove the stipend for work he was no longer doing. This might have been handled internally without embarrassment to anyone.

John Saleska was replaced as dean of students by Randy Schroeder, who rose quickly through the ranks from student to dean of students. Schroeder's field work assignment was counted as fulfilling the vicarage requirement, and the requirement that faculty members be parish pastors was waived. Randy was working for a Ph.D. in counseling, and alongside his duties in counseling students, he had a private practice, sometimes using his seminary office for consultations. Upon retirement, John Saleska left Fort Wayne for Concordia University in Mequon, Wisconsin, where his son-in-law, Patrick T. Ferry, is president.

Both John Saleska and Randy Schroeder were without regular parish experience, and for a dean of students, this was a problem since the one responsible for the welfare of students studying for the pastoral ministry should have been a pastor. Yet Saleska was known to have a pastoral heart and was well liked by all.

DOCTRINAL DISPUTES AND CONTROVERSIES

Differences on the doctrine of the ministry took on serious proportions for me in the fall of 1984 at a presentation at Peace Lutheran Church in Beaverton, Oregon, where Walter A. Anderson was pastor. Such seminars were remnants of the 1960s and 70s and were continued to keep the issues of those days in the forefront. In this case, concerns about biblical history were replaced by the church and ministry question, even though this was not the announced topic of the seminar. Captured on videotape was my presentation, part of which was my response to the question to whom did Jesus give the keys.

My answer dogged me for the next four years, but was no more than a restatement of Matthew 16:18–19: "And I tell you, you are Peter, and on this rock I will build my church, and the powers of death shall not prevail against it. I will give you the keys of the kingdom of heaven, and whatever you bind on earth shall be bound in heaven, and whatever you loose on earth shall be loosed in heaven."

Ernest Schulze, who, four years later, in a letter identified himself as the questioner, may have had an underlying motive in asking the question. Had I known the group's intentions, I would have declined the invitation or would have answered the question differently. Perhaps I should have detected what was in store for me in recognizing that the committee that picked me up at the airport had definite views.

That Saturday morning of the presentation, I went jogging in the foggy, wet countryside and came down with a fiercely bleeding nose that refused to stop, but it was the two leaders of the afternoon seminar that made that day really memorable. Issues from those days are preserved in correspondence exchanged in the summer of 1988, the beginning of my last year as academic dean.

F. W. "Rick" Kortum, a self-proclaimed conservative, threatened to bring charges against me on the basis of the 1984 Beaverton, Oregon presentation on the office of the ministry.[14] A meeting on January 20, 1988, between myself and the Reverend Walter Anderson, representing the Beaverton group, including Kortum and Schulze, found that Kortum's charges were without merit. This did not prevent Kortum from writing to each Fort Wayne seminary board member, stating that nothing had been settled in Anderson's January conversation with me and asking for board action. He wrote, "A videotape is available to establish the accuracy of these concerns."[15]

He argued that any reconciliation supposedly accomplished at the January 20, 1988, meeting should be reevaluated, since the pastor representing the Oregon group was carrying too heavy a burden, whatever that meant. He also alleged that my responses at the Beaverton meeting were "condescending," "arrogant," "flippant," and he repeated his accusation that Jesus giving the keys to Peter was false doctrine.

To back up his accusations in the letter, Kortum sent Robert Preus a videotape of the Beaverton presentation for the regents to review. Preus did not look at the tape but gave it me, but I only viewed enough of the tape to recognize that I was a lot younger-looking then. When the board reviewed the tape, some fell asleep and others were bored.

To that charge, another was added that I had criticized Theodore Schubkegel's (1948–2014) lexicon in its not distinguishing between λαλέω as divine speaking and λέγω as ordinary speaking. Robert Preus responded to Kortum that his description of my presentation was his own and that my saying that Jesus gave the keys to Peter was not a denial of a congregation's rights. He also added that it was perfectly alright for me to take exception to Theodore Schubkegel's lexicon.

---

14. F. W. Kortum, letter to Robert Preus, July 12, 1988.
15. F. W. Kortum, letter to Concordia Theological Seminary Board of Regents, September 12, 1988.

Ernest Schulze followed up, identifying himself as the questioner at the Beaverton meeting.[16] Four years later it was obvious that the question was a setup into which I naively walked. Schulze had again reviewed the tape to substantiate my alleged aberrations. In addition Schulze wanted me to respond to what Lenski (1864–1936) had said on Matthew 16:19 and John 20:23 in his commentaries, which were widely used in the synod and for some pastors were the only ones they possessed.

I set forth the position which I believe is recognizable as that of the synod. "My reference to Peter's receiving the keys was almost a direct quotation of Matthew 16:18. John 20:22–23 gives the keys to all the apostles. Both Peter and the apostles stand for the entire church. The clergy hold the keys as a trust for the congregation . . . I have never held or taught that any pastor possesses the authority in and of himself."[17] Schulze never replied.

After my correspondence with Ted Schubkegel, he acknowledged that my interpretation of λαλέω as "special prophetic utterance" was correct. He wrote to Kortum asking him "to bury the hatchet" with me.[18] Schubkegel also wrote Preus, "Please forgive me if I have contributed to your grief," with copies to me, Elmer Steenbock (1925–2016) and *The Loyal Lutheran*. Also on the same date he wrote me, "Forgive me. I'll try to be a better Greek student." He wrote to Rick Kortum, "Sometimes it is necessary to eat crow. This is one of those occasions."[19] So far as I was concerned, things were coming to a happy and long overdue conclusion. On all counts there was vindication.

However, I was now faced with formal charges from Waldo Werning, who got hold of some of the Beaverton papers with the intentions of including them in charges against me, but since they proved baseless, he found other ones. This story is told elsewhere.[20] Charges against the St. Louis faculty in the 1960s and 70s had opened Pandora's Box. Anyone who disagreed with anyone else had reason to bring formal charges.

Shortly thereafter, the controversy over ministry sprang up again, but closer to home. Colleague G. Waldemar ("Wally") Degner heard about a lecture I gave before it appeared in the *Concordia Theological Quarterly* entitled "The Validity of the Churchly Acts of Ordained Women."[21] Re-

---

16. Ernest Schulze, letter to Robert Preus, September 23, 1988.
17. David Scaer, letter to Ernest Schulze, October 3, 1988.
18. Ted Schubkegel, letter to Rick Kortum, September 28, 1988.
19. Ted Schubkegel, letter to Rick Kortum, October 3, 1988.
20. See Excursus XIV: Waldo Werning, 277 ff.
21. David P. Scaer, "The Validity of the Churchly Acts of Ordained Women," *Concordia Theological Quarterly* 53, no. 1–2 (January 1989): 3–20.

sponding both critically and positively to "The Validity of the Churchly Acts of Ordained Women" were P. R. H. [Paul R. Hinlicky] and L. K. [Leonard Klein] in the Advent 1990 issue of *Lutheran Forum* in an opinion piece entitled "Professor Scaer's Tactics."[22] They agreed with me that a functional view of the ministry is not an adequate basis for ordaining women, since it would allow all to be ordained. In using this argument, the ELCA had at that date failed "to give a sound theological rationale for the ordination of women."

Hinlicky and Klein, however, did take issue with me that the ordination of women would lead to a feminine view of God. Since ELCA liturgies have come to speak of God as "Mother" with the feminine pronouns "she" and "her," the argument has already been proven and need not be rehearsed, but it has value in showing that how we think of the ministry has consequences for how we think about God. The writers claim that the title of their opinion piece, "Professor Scaer's Tactics," is a pun on "scare tactics." Family members have had to endure this less-than-amusing attempt at humor.

To his credit, Leonard Klein would later support J. A. O. Preus in his removal of district presidents who allowed for the unauthorized ordination of Seminex graduates, the issue that led to the formation of the Association of Evangelical Lutheran Churches (AELC) and eventually the ELCA. More telling is that he has since then been ordained a priest in the Roman Catholic Church, a denomination that has been persistent in disallowing the ordination of women priests. In writing this opinion piece, neither Hinlicky nor Klein had come up with biblical, historical and theological support for the ordination of women. This led Klein into the Catholic Church, and Hinlicky remains with the ELCA.

Wally Degner did not find it appropriate for my lecture to appear in print.[23] He responded to a Preus December 1 memorandum in which he "announce[d] a change in mode of handling the paper by Dr. Scaer and of dealing with the issue of woman 'pastors' and the validity of their 'services.'" Wally recounts how after one night of not being able to sleep, he got up and put into eight points "to reply to a few of the tumultuous assertions in the paper.

1. Spiritual priesthood of believers denied.
2. Ordination is sacramental in nature and essence.

---

22. Paul R. Hinlicky and Leonard R. Klein, "Professor Scaer's Tactics," *Lutheran Forum* 24, no. 1 (February 1990): 5.
23. Waldemar Degner, memorandum to Robert Preus, December 3, 1988.

3. Either ordination or call is necessary.
4. A pastor being 'a projection of the incarnate life of Christ' implies denying this feature to the laity.
5. A functional view ministry allows for ordaining women.
6. Ministry is derived from the creed's second and not third article.
7. Ministerial acts by women pastors are null and void.
8. Indiscriminate and poorly defined use of gnosticism."

Wally argued that Robert Preus should not accept such errant views of the ministry just "for the sake of attacking the female pastor." Arguments against ordaining women must be based on the "*sola scriptura* principle," which he said mine were not but his were.

Wally then listed false arguments against ordaining women that he never said were mine. "All the fine talk about 'theology of gender,' 'language of Caanan,' 'Athena vs. Zeus,' 'I in the name and the place of,' etc. are unimportant in determining the will of God." For the record, these views were more likely those of my colleagues than they are mine.

In support of the *sola scriptura* argument that Degner claimed as his own, he refers to the eight *Gutachten*, opinions offered by the seminary's department of exegetical theology, without listing them. First, they say that "the Word alone must impel us to know and to do God's will." Then he quotes Luke 16:31, "If they will not hear Moses and the Prophets, they will not be persuaded even if someone rose from the dead."

Then Wally argued that in chromosomes "there is only a 2.2 percent difference between genders." Two final paragraphs are a potpourri. One person "was going to give a half million to Fort Wayne, then chose St. Louis and then gave one million to Fort Wayne." Then he said he read in *Christian News* a letter from an unnamed colleague that voters' assemblies were unimportant and *voilà!* the seminary lost a generous donation, "because we were not sensitive to the honor and duty of the spiritual priesthood entrusted to every believer in the Lord's church."

Wally Degner was content with the argument that the Bible forbade women pastors—period—and found further theological elaboration, at least the kind I offered, as aberrant doctrine. In being driven by emotion, Degner attributed to me the views of others. Not only were his views jumbled up, but wrong, and could even be used to support the ordination of women. What is noteworthy is that he could not see that the ministry belongs to Jesus Christ, the subject of the creed's second article.

His was a blind spot of some proportions. Even the functional view of the ministry saw the minister doing the things Christ did—preaching, baptizing and administering the Lord's Supper. His chromosome argument was either bizarre and/or he was agreeing with the supporters of the ordination of women that inherent differences between men and women were insignificant in keeping women from the ministry. In holding that the "Word," understood as spoken vocables apart from the incarnation was the determinative factor in doing theology, he was a caricature of the Missouri Synod. He agreed with Preus on justification, the doctrine on which the church stands or falls, but this did not prevent him from working to remove Preus from the presidency less than six months later.

Nothing came of the disjointed memo. Eight months after he had written the memorandum detailing his sleepless night over an unacceptable doctrine of the ministry, Degner aligned himself with Walter A. Maier II in removing Preus as president. Until that time Degner vehemently disagreed with Maier II's doctrine of justification. Degner's dreams of entertaining hopes of succeeding me as an academic dean disappeared at the dawn. Maier II succeeded me, and Degner had to settle for biblical department chairman.

Though at the time I was not computer competent, I worked unsuccessfully to introduce a uniform computer system for the faculty. Robert Preus was not enthusiastic about this. Until my tenure, the academic dean assigned classes. On December 21, 1988, for the first time, the department heads met with the academic dean to make these assignments. Following the example of Indiana University, classes were extended from fifty to fifty-five minutes, and all began on the hour, e.g., eight o'clock AM, nine o'clock etc. This allowed for a full hour for chapel and coffee hour and a ten-week term. A long-term calendar of faculty committees and activities was also put in place, but this was done without the advantage of computers. Having prepared the seminary's self-study, I was asked by the Association of Theological Schools to serve on its visitation committees for other seminaries.

THE BOHLMANN INVESTIGATION

Ralph Bohlmann's faculty investigation by six district presidents was announced in the spring of 1984 and took place on February 19–21, 1985, during my first academic year as dean. Each professor was interviewed by two district presidents, one of whom read from a set of prepared questions and the other who recorded the professor's responses.[24] This format was

---

24. Notification of the interview came on a January 25, 1985 memo from R[alph] A. B[ohlmann] to the following: Gerhard Aho, James Bollhagen, Eugene W. Bunkowske, Stephen J. Carter, Robert H. Collins, G. Waldemar Degner,

determined by Bohlmann, who chose the interrogators and framed the questions. Interchange between the interrogators and the professors were not allowed. No witnesses or counselors were allowed in the room.

Transcripts of these interviews, to the best of my memory, were never made available. Professors could not check on the accuracy of their recorded responses. Some saw this as a fishing trip to uncover misconduct or false teaching, but none was found. This episode may serve as a reminder for future church leaders that this kind of investigation where a third party was not allowed to serve as witness to what really happened had all the marks of the infamous star chambers in which the English king could try suspects without legal counsel.

Robert Preus, who had been on the St. Louis faculty when his brother Jack had sent in a committee under the chairmanship of Paul A. Zimmerman to question the faculty, was convinced that Ralph Bohlmann had modeled this investigation after that one. In the 1971 investigation of the St. Louis faculty, John Tietjen as seminary president was present, and each professor was allowed to review the transcript for accuracy. Thirteen years had passed since then. Besides Robert Preus, no one on the Fort Wayne faculty had firsthand knowledge of the 1971 investigation. Memories of what happened from 1969–1974 in St. Louis had already faded.

In support of Preus, a petition was circulated by Norbert H. Mueller, dated May 14, 1984. It spoke of the seminary's success in enrollment, finances and morale, all of which was attributed to Robert Preus's leadership, his popularity with the students and the confidence in the church. This was so, but this did not count for much. Confidence on the faculty had begun to erode. Names on the petition in the order in which they signed were Norbert H. Mueller, myself, Douglas Judisch, Kurt Marquart, James W. Voelz, Albert B. Wingfield (who had no faculty status), Daniel G. Reuning, Dean O. Wenthe, Richard E. Muller, Gerhard Aho, George Kraus, Harold H. Buls, Cameron A. MacKenzie, W. G. Houser, Robert H. Collins and Eugene Bunkowske. This was a bit more than half of the faculty, but was not unanimous.

Albert L. Garcia, William G. Houser, Douglas Judisch, Arthur Just, Eugene Klug, Heino O. Kadai, George R. Kraus, Cameron A. Mackenzie, Kurt E. Marquart, Walter A. Maier, Norbert H. Mueller, Richard E. Muller, Robert D. Preus, Daniel G. Reuning, Wilbert H. Rosin, John W. Saleska, David P. Scaer, Alvin J. Schmidt, Randall W. Shields, Otto F. Stahlke, Raymond F. Surburg, Howard W. Tepker, James W. Voelz, William C. Weinrich, Dean O. Wenthe, Warren N. Wilbert, Albert B. Wingfield, Harold H. Zietlow and Melvin L. Zilz.

1985 ACCREDITATION VISIT

Former Senior College biology professor Melvin Zilz, who was in charge of seminary campus administration, was to organize the seminary self-study necessary for maintaining accreditation with the Association of Theological Schools (ATS) and the North Central Association (NCA). A few years before, Zilz had drawn the ire of pastors and parents of seminary students by sending a letter to students who were in financial arrears to the seminary that he would give their bills to a collection agency. This incident occurred a few days before the great Fort Wayne flood of 1982.

On the way with Robert and Donna Preus to see *Amadeus* at Embassy Theater, as we were driving through downtown streets soon to be flooded, I informed Preus of the impending explosion on campus. For the record, Dorothy and I sat in the balcony, and Robert and Donna in the more preferable seats to the front in the lower auditorium. Zilz was required to send letters of apology. In 1984, Preus felt he could no longer entrust the accreditation task to Zilz and passed it on to Richard Muller, who had a degree in education, had been the academic dean and now remained as my associate in that office.

After a while, Muller turned Preus down because of the pressure connected with the project, and in the fall the ball was tossed into my lap. He was fifty-six at the time. I was forty-eight. Not having a penchant for things administrative, my mood was not happy. Alvin Schmidt had worked two years in preparing the accreditation report with accompanying documents for the ATS. It appeared that neither Preus nor most of the faculty had seen the report before it was passed on to an ATS committee, who rejected it.

As I undertook this task in September, the seminary had been plagued by more problems. In preparing the report, the faculty was divided into committees to assess and evaluate various aspects of the seminary—academics, student life, finances, and physical facilities, administrative operations especially with the board, faculty qualifications and spirit. Procedures for the self-study to maintain accreditation had changed, and my supervision of the process in 1984 did not prepare me for being a chairman of a sub-committee in preparing a report on academic matters in 2000.

Today self-study procedures have changed again and become more complex, partially because of the necessity of assessing of student performance instituted by U.S. President Bill Clinton (b. 1946). Today assessment is an ongoing process with data collected at the end of each term. One faculty member now holds the title dean of assessment. We are forever having to take our pulse.

Art Just, age thirty-one in 1984, had just come on the faculty as an assistant professor in the pastoral department with a responsibility for homiletics. This position had been offered first to William Thompson, who was Guido Merkens's (1927–2012) successor at Concordia Lutheran Church in San Antonio. Having to face fulfilling a vacant position time in the summer of 1984, Preus turned to Arthur, a 1980 seminary graduate, who in his four years as a pastor in Middletown, Connecticut, had earned a master's degree from the divinity school of Yale University.

Like his father, Art was also a "Yalie." More than anyone else, Art saw me through the quagmire of maintaining accreditation. Art received his baptism of fire into the working of the seminary, which would stand him in good stead for the rest of his seminary and synodical career. There was no other choice but what could be seen as an iron-fisted approach with my colleagues, since something had to be on paper by the beginning of spring term of 1984–1985. Many committees had to work over the Christmas break. Making this process more difficult was that the previous years had seen conflicts in those who held the positions of academic dean and dean of students. This gave reason for dissonant professors to cause further division.

Any of this could be reason for jeopardizing accreditation or requiring that the process be repeated in a few years. According to the time table for maintaining accreditation, the ATS team came in the middle of the next school year, 1985–1986, and when all was said and done, it gave the seminary a clean bill of health. Al Schmidt said that some, perhaps most, of the materials in the self-study were contained in the report he had prepared and that was rejected. Since I did not chair any of the subcommittees that dealt with the original materials and had not compared our report with his, I cannot say whether this is so, but I do suspect it is. Committees were under time restraints to put something down on paper, and they probably took whole sections over from Al's work. If this is so, then mention should be made of his work. Something in his report may have put the administration in an unfavorable light. I don't know.

Apart from the report to the scheduled visit of the ATS team, the seminary requested that the association make an assessment of the seminary. Sent on September 15–17, 1985, were Jean-Marc Laporte of Regis College and Marvin J. Taylor, recently retired as associate director of the ATS.

On the afternoon of September 24, 1985, Taylor spoke to me about their visit, and in the course of the conversation said he and Laporte found that our self-study "was quite good." We had presented the seminary faculty problems without assessing blame or attempting to cover them up. The report noted that some faculty members found that in my preparing the document, I had cut myself off from most of the faculty members and had relied on two or three close associates. Their concern was with my conclusions, not how I had arrived at them. Another conversation with Taylor took place Thursday, September 26, 1985, in regard to charges made by a certain faculty member. Taylor laid out the procedure:

1. Lay the charges out in writing or stop making them.
2. Determine the truth by a hearing, if the charges are denied.
3. Due process is required.
4. Evidence must be laid out before arriving at a conclusion.

Details of this conversation may have played a factor in the case of Warren Wilbert leaving the faculty.

Accrediting teams follow a set procedure in their visits. Before leaving the campus, they present its findings to the president, but continued accreditation is left to the boards of the accrediting organizations and not to the visiting team. Here Robert Preus jumped the gun by sending out a public relations announcement that, on the basis of the visitation report, the seminary had maintained its accreditation. Since his administration had been put under pressure from both the outside and inside the seminary, with many others on the faculty, he was relishing in this accomplishment—and why not?

In May 1986, Robert Preus provided a lavish celebration on the porch of his Fox Chase home for those who had worked on the self-study, among whom was Norbert Mueller. On that day the world was our oyster—or so we thought. Memories of that bright spring day under the trees are firmly fixed in my mind, but soon dark clouds would appear on the horizon. Seeds of the upheaval had already begun to sprout, and more seeds were still to be planted. In riding my bike by the house on Fox Chase, my thoughts often go back to that happy day in May 1986, a day that lasted only for a moment.

PLANNING A SABBATICAL

In the summer of 1986, I had been at the seminary twenty-years and had no sabbatical relief from teaching in that time. My summers served as sabbaticals in the Poconos to write. After coming to Fort Wayne, I applied again several times for the AAL John W. Behnken Post-Doctoral Fellowship and, for a second time, finally succeeded in receiving it for the fall term of 1986. Factors in being awarded the fellowship were recommendations from Bo Reicke (1914–1987) of the University of Basel and William R. Farmer of Perkins School of Theology at Southern

Methodist University. Both had challenged the majority scholarly view that Matthew and Luke were dependent on Mark and the "Q" document. And on this I was in agreement with them.

A generous fellowship made it possible for me and Dorothy to go to Europe, a trip which was enhanced by our son Peter studying with a Stamford University extension program in Rome. With the accreditation behind me and things at relative peace at the seminary, the stars were in their right order. Robert Preus also wanted to be away during the same term and asked me to postpone my sabbatical leave until the spring so that I could take over as acting president during his absence. Fall is a better time than spring to visit Europe, especially when your son is in Rome. At fifty years of age, I was not prepared to adjust my plans, especially since Preus had often traveled abroad and had taken a sabbatical just five years before. His absence from campus had contributed to the situation at the seminary which had now just been resolved.

An ominous sign for Preus was the election of Melvin Bredemeier to the seminary board by the July 1986 Indianapolis Synod convention. Even though ten years had passed since the seminary moved from Springfield to replace Concordia Senior College on the Fort Wayne campus, resentment remained in the community that still had close ties to the displaced faculty.

Herbert Bredemeier, Mel's father, had deep Fort Wayne roots and was the last president of Concordia Junior College, which was closed when the synod established Concordia Senior College in 1957 on the outskirts of this city. He joined that faculty and served as the dean of administration, and after the synod at its July 1975 convention in Anaheim, California, closed this school too, he was the president for its final year (1976–1977), the seminary's first year on the same campus. This kind of situation gives birth to personal animosities, and little was done to overcome them. During the subsequent years I often visited with Bredemeier in the seminary dining room, who often expressed the wish that on some personnel matters, Robert Preus would have asked for his advice.

Robert Preus was not prone to do that. The election of the son of the last president of senior college to the seminary board had in itself predetermined consequences for Preus. In a nine-member board, one member could be the point of successful opposition. Indianapolis, where the synod convention was held, was a two-hour drive from Fort Wayne, and somehow Preus had hitched a ride there.

When Melvin Bredemeier was elected, Preus began to challenge Bredemeier's election by the synod to the board on the grounds that he had solicited support for the position by using the official stationery of the Fort Wayne National Bank, of which he was a vice president. This matter may have been brought up to the board itself. If I was there, I have no memory of it. In any case, discussion of Bredemeier's suitability for the position with him present in the meeting hardly engendered unity of purpose. Gasoline was poured on the fire when Preus transferred the seminary's account from the Fort Wayne National Bank to another institution. Not only could Preus not count on the support of Bredemeier, but the election of John Wiebe, another layman, to the board on the first ballot, would also eventually undermine Preus remaining as president.

Wiebe, an investor in Nebraska shopping malls and a personal friend of the Preus family, was elected to the board on the first ballot with 523 votes. When, for family reasons, he thought he could no longer serve on the board, he resigned, and I was present when the board accepted his resignation. He was not. Somehow I was sitting near enough to Robert Preus to tell him that accepting his resignation would be disastrous. With eight members on the board, his opponents were better positioned to remove him from the presidency—and they did in July 1989.[25]

THE SEMINARY DURING THE PREUS AND SCAER SABBATICALS

Since I would be on sabbatical in the fall, the substitute for Robert Preus for the fall quarter had not been resolved when I left for the Poconos. One evening I received a phone call from then graduate dean Dean Wenthe, who had taken his wife, Linda, to the Cafe Gennel to celebrate their wedding anniversary. Also in this upscale, well-known and now unfortunately closed restaurant were Robert Preus, Al Wingfield, Norb Mueller and their wives. Wingfield had taken a position with a Lutheran high school association in the Detroit area and recommended to Preus that Norb Mueller replace him as assistant to the president. It was a double celebration: a farewell for Wingfield and a welcome for Mueller.

Norb Mueller had been a pastor at the prestigious St. Paul's Lutheran Church in Ann Arbor, Michigan. His reputation as a conservative pas-

---

25. Poor organization among Preus supporters may have been a factor in Mel Bredemeier's election to the board. Wiebe on the first ballot got an outright majority, with Bredemeier acquiring 495 votes and Roy Guess, a longtime conservative favorite, with 426 ballots. On the second ballot, Bredemeier acquired 456 votes and Guess 393. On the third ballot with only two candidates remaining, Bredemeier got 603 votes and Guess 460. Tallying the totals, fewer delegates, particularly those who supported Wiebe, took part in the second and third ballot.

tor, earned or not, was reason enough for Robert Preus to call him to the seminary to teach pastoral theology in 1974, and then for him to become director of placement. Preus had given me no prior notice of Norb Mueller's appointment. When asked for a reason for taking this kind of action without prior notification or consultation, Preus would typically say that circumstances allowed him no other option.

Robert Preus had a supreme confidence in his own ability to make decisions. This was not and would not be the first time he did not consult others. Consultation even with those who disagree is not without value. As assistant to the president, Norb Mueller had his office right outside of Preus's, but soon discovered that he had a greater claim to the title than to its obligations. He did not live up to Preus's expectations, but this was not the first time this happened with Preus.

For the degree of doctor of ministry, Norbert Mueller wrote a dissertation on lay ministry to the aging for a theological school in Dayton, Ohio. During Preus's absence from the campus, Mueller took the position of acting president seriously and soon was having himself called the interim president.

For one seminary occasion, he asked chapel dean Dan Reuning to list his title in the service folder as interim president, since he would only have this title for a few more months. In three years he would have it for thirty-four months. While I was gone in Europe, Gerhard Aho was fighting his last battle against cancer and died during the Thanksgiving break shortly after I returned. His funeral service was at Peace Lutheran Church in Fort Wayne, where Luther Strasen was pastor. As the academic dean, I would normally represent the president in his absence. When I presented this to Norb Mueller, he asserted that he was in charge—and so he was.

Before the fall 1989 term ended, Norbert Mueller was arranging for three new faculty members to come on board who would be not be Preus men when it came to faculty organization elections. With Mueller adding three members to the faculty before the end of the 1989 school year and the board failing to support two men Preus proposed, Preus was fast losing faculty support.

RANDY SCHROEDER AND THE OFFICE OF DEAN OF STUDENTS

Randy Schroeder's tenure as dean was described by some students as a "regime." He was intent in getting things done, a quality which Robert Preus admired. Along with the position of dean of students, Randy kept the job of financial aid director. This could be interpreted as a conflict of interest, and it was. Those in the dean's favor would more likely receive a higher grant in financial aid—at least it was seen this way. At its September 1987 meeting, the board awarded Randy an additional stipend for holding two positions at one time.

I wrote to Robert Preus opposing the additional stipend and his advancement to assistant professor on the grounds that he lacked pastoral experience.[26] In a letter copied to Robert Preus, Norbert Mueller and me, Randy complained about having to arrange meetings of students with faculty in their homes after the orientation banquet for new students. This custom was as old as Springfield days. Though my memo was addressed to Preus, Preus supposed that it was intended for the board and asked me to withdraw it.[27] Preus wrote that he did "not want in [my] records anything that suggests that the academic dean opposed in writing for the record an action of the Board of Regents." He then goes on to speak about the relationship that he, Norb Mueller and I should have with the board.

According to Robert Preus, the board initiated a promotion for Schroeder and an additional stipend. Soon Schroeder made problems for Preus that would continue even after he was relieved of the seminary presidency, but that was not at issue at this time. Had protocol been followed, Preus as the executive should have said that he would take under advisement any offer from the board and return it with a recommendation to the board.

A Wyoming pastor wrote Robert Preus on how he was fired by Randy Schroeder from his gymnasium job on allegations of complaints that he refused to substantiate.[28] He also spoke of students brought into the dean's office and accused of wrongdoing and threatened with expulsion. One student claimed that Schroeder had entered his room without prior knowledge or permission looking for evidence of wrongdoing.

On June 27 1989, Robert Preus thanked the pastor for writing so frankly and assuring him that he would look into the matter. This did not and could not happen, since Preus soon would be removed from office. These unhappy days for students lasted until Bill Weinrich assumed the acting presidency and Randy Schroeder was relieved of his position as dean of students. He did stay on faculty for some years after this and was well received as an instructor in counseling by the students.

---

26. David Scaer, letter to Robert Preus, September 15, 1987.
27. Robert Preus, memo to David Scaer, September 21, 1987.
28. A Wyoming pastor, letter to Robert Preus, June 15, 1989.

Excursus XI

THE SERMON ON THE MOUNT

The Church's First Statement of the Gospel

This excursus is named after the title of my book published by Concordia Publishing House in 2000. On the road to its publication, my approach to the Gospels clashed with the traditional one. Teaching the first course in dogmatics led me to believe theology had to be derived not only from the understanding that the Scriptures were inspired by the Holy Spirit, but had to involve Christ as their content and origin. This connection was made in 1 Peter 1:10, 11: the Spirit who had inspired the Scriptures was no other than the Spirit of Christ who spoke through the prophets. To take the argument further, both biblical inspiration and Christology had to be grounded historically in Jesus' choosing of his apostles.

Christology, the teaching about Christ, had to be grounded first in what he said about himself and how these teachings were preserved in first oral form and then in writing. All doctrines were about Christ. Without a historical foundation in the man Jesus, Christianity lapses into Gnosticism. Apart from the successes and the failures of the three searches for the historical Jesus, Christian doctrine, especially what the church said about Jesus, had to be grounded in revelation taking place in history. Revelation cannot be detached from history, an approach popular in twentieth-century neoorthodoxy.

Addressing these issues gave birth first to my book *The Apostolic Scriptures*; as the title suggests, authority for the New Testament is derived through the apostles. After that came *What Do You Think of Jesus?*, a popular Christology whose views were expanded in the first published volume in the Confessional Lutheran Dogmatics series.[1]

An avenue into how the Gospels could be understood was opened to me in an assignment to teach the Epistles of James, which bore an uncanny re-

---

1. David P Scaer, *Christology*. A third reprint edition appeared in 1993, but there might have been others.

semblance to the Sermon on the Mount. This resulted in my commentary, *James the Apostle of Faith*, which soon appeared in a reprinted edition. My interpretation of James was noticeably different from Luther's, who had called it the Epistle of straw. As is evident in the title, James had first to do with faith and works, which provided the evidence upon which God's judgment on the last day was made. Most scholars followed the Reformer in seeing that it was little more than a collection of wisdom sayings, and like him some held that the sayings were collected in disarray. A common conclusion was not only that it was at odds with Paul, but was written to counteract his teaching on justification by faith. However, it appeared to me that this should be reversed and that Paul used James to his advantage. James had been misunderstood because his language was measured against Paul's Epistles and not the Gospels, especially the Sermon on the Mount.

Both the Sermon on the Mount and the book of James had in mind persecuted Christians who lived in and around Jerusalem. With that on my mind, I immediately set to writing a commentary on the Sermon on the Mount, and with the James commentary in its second printing, had good reason to believe that it would be accepted for publication by Concordia Publishing House. If one was not dependent on the other in some way, each had drawn on the same oral traditions. Themes, vocabulary and theology, especially in regard to an impending judgment, were similar. William T. Simmons, Concordia Publishing House's professional books developer, confirmed my expectations.

> The reviews are all in regarding your manuscript, and I am happy to say they are quite positive. As one highly regarded reviewer states: "According to my judgment, this study and presentation on the Sermon on the Mount will be an important contribution which will present a solid Lutheran interpretation, which is not at the present available to the Christian public." Our consensus is that you have another winner here, Dave. Following receipt of final draft which incorporate the comments listed below, I will recommend to top management for publication."[2]

The manuscript was on the fast track to publication. Not only would *The Sermon on the Mount: The Church's First Statement of the Gospel* be added to *James the Apostle of Faith*, but future offerings might also be favorably received. As the reviewer noted, it would "present a solid Lutheran interpretation," an assessment similar to one made by a reviewer of a well-known Evangelical publishing house.

---

2. William T. Simmons, letter to David Scaer, June 17, 1985.

Yet it was turned down by the synod's Commission on Doctrinal Review and, ironically, for the same reason offered by the Evangelical reviewer. I had "Lutheranized" what was nearly universally held as law.

Both Lutherans and Evangelicals, who stand in the Reformation tradition, agree that the Sermon on the Mount is chiefly law and not gospel. They disagree on whether that law can be fulfilled. For me, the Sermon on the Mount was chiefly gospel and reflected how the early church received it. In the opinion of the synod's commission, I had broken with the majority of half a millennium of Lutheranism that the Sermon on the Mount was law. In the manuscript's being rejected, the commission had come down on the side of tradition. That was not a very Lutheran thing to do.

Doctrinal review might seem to some to be a relic of a bygone age, but organizations including corporations and churches must protect the core principle that holds them together by disallowing the dissemination of writings that challenge their reasons for existence. Core positions can be found in what are now called mission statements, and for a church they are their confessions and traditions, commonly held beliefs and practices some of which may not have been formally adopted. Writings of some theologians referenced over the years are a factor in what is allowed and disallowed.

Thus it is not unusual that the LCMS has a process of doctrinal view to preserve church teaching. Roman Catholics have a process of review. By placing the Latin words *nihil obstat* after the title page, the reviewer declares that he finds that the book contains nothing contradicting church teaching. It does not disallow other views. It only affirms that the work does not contradict. This process is in keeping with the LCMS's first constitution that one purpose was publication of orthodox materials.

Today this process is generally carried out with a two-tiered review of manuscripts submitted for publication to the synod's Concordia Publishing House. First, a manuscript is screened by the publisher's own doctrinal reviewers. An accepted manuscript is passed along for confirmation to the five-member Commission on Doctrinal Review appointed by the synod president. Upon receiving a manuscript, the commission gives it to one of a panel of anonymous reviewers who have also been appointed by the president. Should that reviewer find it acceptable, he returns it to the commission to forward it to Concordia Publishing House for publication. If it is found not acceptable by the reviewer, the author has the right of appeal, and together the author and the reviewer, who remains anonymous to the author, engage in a discussion to readjust what that reviewer finds unacceptable.

Should writer and reviewer remain at odds, the matter is forwarded to a review panel of two or three of the commission's own members for a final determination that cannot be appealed. My manuscript on the Sermon on the Mount had passed doctrinal review at Concordia Publishing House, but was rejected twice by the anonymous reviewer and finally by the Commission's review panel.

Notification of rejection was attached to a memo dated October 22, 1986, by Commission chairman John E. Meyer. Without major revision, the review panel concluded that "it would cause a considerable amount of confusion in LCMS congregations and perhaps even give serious offense to many of our pastors, since it frequently takes positions that are opposed to those traditionally held in our midst. "

These words carry more weight than what might appear at first glance. Putting aside concrete arguments for or against the manuscript's theological acceptability, it was rejected because it broke with what was perceived as what many pastors held. In other words, it broke with synod tradition, even though one reason for its rejection was its dependency on early church tradition. Tradition that was acceptable in the manuscript's rejection was found unacceptable in its arguments. Let it be said that reference to such early church documents as the *Didache* was only collaborative and not fundamental to the arguments offered. Four years after the manuscript was rejected, it was found acceptable and published, but without reference to its rejection by the review panel.

At the beginning of its report, the review panel attempted to show that it had been evenhanded in pointing out that the green, red and blue colors used by the doctrinal reviewer in marking the manuscript were unclear. Also the anonymous reviewer exceeded his authority in correcting the spelling and grammar, a task properly left to the publisher's copy editors.

After the gratuitous first page, the remaining four set forth the review panel's agreement with the anonymous reviewer's assessment of the manuscript, e.g., that the manuscript lacked "explicit references to the doctrine of inspiration" and it had not taken the Scriptures at face value. Historical content was subordinated to the editorial purpose of the evangelist, and I was giving "the impression that the text is the product of merely human thought and experience." Matthew is pictured as a writer who shaped the teachings of Jesus. "The author tends to suggest that the early church fathers and tradition authenticate the Gospel of Matthew." Well, they do. A general criticism is that the manuscript "goes beyond the clear meaning of the text." Reference to the Lord's Supper in the Fourth Petition asking for daily bread is wrong. Also unacceptable is any Eucharistic interpretation of the miraculous feeding of the five and four thousand, especially John 6. The Sermon on the Mount cannot be Christological because "It has been the view of Lutheran theologians since the time of the great Reformer himself that the Sermon on the Mount is law preached to the Christian." A reference to Luther's *Sermons on John 6–8*[3] settled this matter. Such a far sweeping conclusion is amazing!

At one point, the manuscript is faulted for "pictur[ing] Matthew as an editor who not only applied Jesus' doctrine to second-generation Christians, but as one who *shaped* Jesus' doctrine. This goes beyond the way in which Luther and the Lutheran Confessions use the writings of the early fathers" (italic is underlining in original). Then the panel notes that Luther saw the sermon as a law preached to Christians. This is amazing. In the eyes of the panel Luther's view is acceptable—Jesus preached the sermon to Christians—even though the crowd that first heard the sermon were hardly Christians. Yet it is unacceptable that Matthew preached the sermon to second-generation Christians. To prove this thesis, the panel references Luther, the Confessions, and commonly held opinions, but does not exegetically engage the arguments offered. The panel takes exception to the higher righteousness (Matthew 5:20) as Christ's righteousness and not as law.

A major reason for the panel's rejection of the manuscript is the view of Luther and Lutheran theologians who saw the Sermon as impossible law. These differences are brought up in the manuscript itself, so the anonymous reviewer and the review panel had their work done for them. Because the law's exhortations are seen as unnecessary in doing good works, the manuscript was said to deny the third use of the law.

In line with this critique, the manuscript has "a tendency to confuse the law and the gospel." This is weasel language. Here logic is offended. If the traditional view is that the Sermon on the Mount is law and the alternative view is that it is gospel, this is not a confusion of the law and the gospel. The critique of the law's third view indicates that the anonymous reviewer is at home with the Reformed view of the third use that the law's threats are a factor in doing works.

At this writing, the anonymous reviewer remains anonymous. We do not know if he or any members of the panel read the manuscript in its published form and reevaluated their decisions. Anonymous writers invite their readers to hypothesize their identity. For nearly two thousand

---

3. Martin Luther, *Sermons on the Gospel of St. John: Chapters 6–8*, American ed., Luther's Works 23 (St. Louis, MO: Concordia Publishing House, 1959), 3–4.

years scholars have been trying to figure out who wrote Hebrews. In this case, the anonymous reviewer is a member of the commission and so can offer his input twice. This seems unlikely, since he is not unfamiliar with biblical studies. The extreme irony is that the reviewer found the arguments against accepting the manuscript in the manuscript itself as the writer set them forth. If the critique is original, then it is unlikely that he was a member of the commission, since none of its members were particularly qualified in this area. In this case, he would have been a member of a seminary faculty who, in the quake of the events of 1974, saw himself as preserver and defender of the church's faith. Also unknown is which two or three members of the commission comprised the review panel that wrote the final report and if the remaining two or three members read it before it was mailed by John E. Meyer, the commission chairman. In the course of negotiations, I had several congenial phone conversations with Meyer, and he does not seem to have had a hand in writing the report.

Listed as the other four members of the commission were Arthur Graudin, professor at St. Louis; Jerald C. Joersz, at that time assistant to Samuel Nafzger, executive director of the synod's Commission on Theology and Church Relations; John W. Klotz, with a Ph.D. in biology, who left the Fort Wayne Senior College for a professorship at the St. Louis seminary and Howard Tepker, the Springfield-Fort Wayne academic dean (1974–1979). He had retired as professor in 1985. They had been appointed by Ralph Bohlmann and were solidly entrenched in synod teaching.

Art Graudin joined the St. Louis faculty shortly after the 1974 walkout and had the degree of doctor of religion, though what this degree entailed was not widely known. Jerry Joersz specialized in refining the synod's position on fraternal organizations. They were conservatives in every sense of the term, but whether they thought things through theologically is another matter.

Fourteen years passed between the time the manuscript was rejected and when it was published in 2000 as *The Sermon on the Mount: The Church's First Statement of the Gospel*. If it is any value in Bible classes and preaching, then the agony of rejection was worth it. In a more nearly perfect world it would have served as the first chapter of *Discourses in Matthew: Jesus Teaches the Church*, which was published in 2004. Authors suffer their own peculiar frustrations: in my case not being asked to write a commentary on Matthew, as many of my students thought, and in another case facing the rejection of a manuscript. It does not come close to losing one's child, but in a way it does.

Excursus XII

WARREN WILBERT

❧

When Jack Preus became Springfield seminary president, he not only wanted professors with doctrinal conviction, but professors who were theologically competent. Warren Wilbert had neither a formal seminary education nor an accordingly advanced degree for teaching seminary courses. He had brought talents to the seminary which shortly would be of limited value.

Until the 1950s, both St. Louis and Springfield provided a college curriculum as a prior requirement before continuing in courses leading to a theological degree. With college curricula, both seminaries had athletic programs with full-time directors. At the St. Louis seminary Coach Eldon Edward "Pete" Pederson (1914–2012) was legendary for his basketball and baseball teams. Some of his photographs show the teams on which the editor of *Christian News* played (1952–1957). After 1957, the St. Louis seminary no longer offered college courses, and the class entering in the fall of 1958 had already completed college at Concordia Senior College in Fort Wayne. More and more students were married, and their average age was higher than that of traditional four-year colleges.

Baseball fell out of vogue, but not basketball. Warren Wilbert was called to the Springfield seminary to head the physical education program that was playing a lesser role in seminary life. He had a master's degree in education and was a commissioned, but not an ordained, minister. Jack Preus advised him to make himself available for an assignment in the synod where his talents could be put to better use. Wilbert's response was remarkable. He said that just as Jack was educated as a Greek professor and not as an administrator—Jack was president now—so Wilbert argued that he could assume teaching responsibilities for which he was not retained. Rejecting Jack's hint, Warren Wilbert continued to offer courses in parish education which were, in the opinion of the students, less than spectacular.

In faculty meetings, Wilbert often referred to that proverbial arrogant minister as having a "Herr Pastor" mentality. In his mind, he assumed that other people were immune to the sin of hubris and only pastors were arrogant. Wilbert, who was not linguistically trained, did not realize that in German the word *Herr* is placed before one's profession, including waiters, bakers, butchers, professors, etc. Not using *Herr* in addressing any professional is considered impolite.

Hardly into my first year as dean, I became aware of stirring in the department of pastoral theology, of which Wilbert was a member. At one-twenty PM on November 26, 1984, I phoned Wilbert to ask for a copy of a report of approximately forty pages in length that was being circulated among its members. Warren Wilbert with Steven Carter and Arthur Just had prepared the report and was circulating it. In my asking for the report, he responded that I would get a copy on Monday, December 3. So that I would not have to face it cold, I replied that I would like to see it before the meeting.

Wilbert denied my request saying the report was only for the department members. I replied that the academic dean is a member of all departments. He answered, "That's stretching it a bit much." Typically academic deans have the proceedings of the department at their disposal. When I told him that as academic deans, Wilbert Rosin (1979–1982) and Richard Muller (1982–1984) attended meetings of all departments, he said that no more copies of the report were available and that I was free to make a photocopy of Gerhard Aho's copy. As academic dean, I did not usually attend department meetings. Richard Muller, who had become associate dean, attended in my place, but I received transcriptions of the minutes of meetings to keep up on what was going on.

Shortly after the Eddie Balfour incident,[1] Robert Preus called for a meeting with Warren Wilbert at which Wilbert spoke of his father's cancer and his own heavy burden. Preus told Wilbert that he had no other choice but to recommend to the regents that he should seek another position. To this Wilbert responded that he was reluctant to act on this recommendation after having twenty-seven years of successful teaching. Preus advised Wilbert that a change in position would bring him a new lease on life. No conclusion was reached, and Wilbert remained on the faculty.

Soon after, Board of Regents chairman Raymond N. Joeckel wrote to Warren Wilbert, who had been on the faculty since the fall of 1958, that "As of December 1, 1985, you will be on sabbatical leave and relieved of all classroom and administrative responsibilities to the seminary."[2] Ini-

---

1. See Eddie Balfour and the Business Office, 326–334.
2. Raymond Joeckel, letter to Warren Wilbert, November 8, 1985.

tialed at the bottom of the page was "geb," initials of Getrude "Trudy" E. Behning, secretary to Robert Preus.

That was not the end of the story. Warren Wilbert left Fort Wayne as suggested by the board of regents and took a professorship at Concordia College, Ann Arbor, Michigan, and remained there until he returned to Fort Wayne to retire.

Excursus XIII

OBJECTIVE VS. SUBJECTIVE JUSTIFICATION

ào

While biblical inspiration and authority was foundational for Pieper's *Christian Dogmatics*, Franz Pieper was absorbed with the doctrine of objective justification throughout his three volumes. Also known as universal justification, it distinguished the Missouri Synod from other synods as no other doctrine in the second half of the nineteenth century and the early twentieth century did. At the heart of the doctrine was that God justified the entire world in the resurrection of Christ. The contrary position was that faith made justification or forgiveness effective, and hence justification was not prior to faith, a position that has reappeared in the theologies of Gerhard Forde, Steven Paulsen and James Nestigen.

Missouri's position on justification reflected its 1880s controversy with the Ohio Synod, which held that God justified people in view of their final or persevering faith, abridged in the Latin phrase *intuitu fidei*. Missouri's first controversy was resolved by breaking fellowship with the Ohio Synod. Another one arose in the 1900s, and this time it led to breaking fellowship with the Norwegian Evangelical Lutheran Synod. Later the Norwegian Evangelical Lutheran Church left the Synodical Conference and joined two other Norwegian synods to form in 1918 the Norwegian Lutheran Church in America, which in 1946 took the name the Evangelical Lutheran Church. The reconstituted church allowed the belief that God predestined believers on account of their faith, a position the Missouri Synod found unacceptable.[1]

---

1. Doctrinal agreement on predestination reached by three ethnic Norwegian synods in 1912 is called the Madison Agreement. At its center was a statement accommodating opposing beliefs on predestination that up until that time had separated the three churches. They "agreed to reject all errors which seek to explain away the mystery of election either in a synergizing or a Calvinizing manner, in other words, every doctrine either on the one hand that would deprive God of his glory as the only Savior or on the other hand would weaken man's sense of responsibility in relation to the acceptance or

Another factor was the Ohio Synod's leading exegete, R. H. C. Lenski, who wrote a multi-volume Bible commentary that was found on the shelves of many of the Missouri Synod's pastors and determined how the Scriptures were interpreted in their preaching and Bible classes.[2] Lenski's denial of objective justification was found in his commentary on Romans. Opponents of seeing justification only as subjective see it as nothing other than synergism, the issue which was at the heart of the Lutheran Reformation protest against Rome. Since God justifies all humanity by raising Christ from the dead, justification is universal and, as an act of God and not of man, is objective. By faith justification becomes a reality for the believer and is called subjective.

At the end of the Great War, different understandings of justification may have been introduced as a Protestant virus by making English for all practical purposes the official synodical language. Matters have been made more complex by discussion among New Testament scholars that the reference to faith in the Pauline passages used by the Reformers to advance their doctrine of justification may refer not to the faith whereby Christians are justified, but the faithfulness of Christ. It is also arguable that in certain passages the word faith refers to what Christians believe, known in Latin as *fides quae*.[3]

Logically, the phrase *subjective justification* can only have meaning if there is objective or some other kind of prior justification. Remove "objective" from the justification equation, then subjective justification becomes nothing other than sanctification, God's work within the sinner to make him a believer. That is the Roman Catholic position. If subjective justification completely defines God's justification of the sinner, then Christ can be seen as the cause of justification, but not the one who completes it. This can only be done by faith. If this is so, all theology is not Christology.

Charles Evanson (1936–2018), pastor of Redeemer Lutheran Church in Fort Wayne, who later taught for many years students for the ministry in Latvia, remarked that the doctrine that distinguishes one church from others presents the most problems for that church. Rome wrestles with papal infallibility as the Anglicans struggle with apostolic succession.

---

rejection of grace." Any idea that man could on his own accept grace was synergism that was not mollified by the Madison Agreement, which rejected synergism but allowed a synergistic option.

2. Lenski, R. C. H., *The Interpretation of the New Testament*, Columbus, OH: Wartburg Press, 1934–1966.
3. For my own views on justification, readers can consult my *James the Apostle of Faith* and *The Sermon on the Mount: The Church's First Statement of the Gospel*.

Baptists cannot agree on the age of accountability. Justification by faith may very well be the albatross around the Lutheran neck.

At its 1963 Helsinki convention, the Lutheran World Federation attempts to come to agreement on justification failed. Lutheran and Catholic agreement in the *Joint Declaration on the Doctrine of Justification*[4] has proven to be more illusory than real. So it is not surprising that any Lutheran church, including the Missouri Synod, should be immune from dissent on this issue.

David W. Preus provides a perspective on the two Preus brothers, Jack and Robert, and their adherence to the doctrine of predestination.[5] All three Preus's were descendants of Herman Amberg Preus I, a founding pastor of the Norwegian Evangelical Lutheran Church in America in 1843. He was an admirer of the doctrinal stance of the Missouri Synod's first president, C. F. W. Walther,[6] especially on justification and predestination.

Influential on Jack and Robert was confirmation instruction received from a Missouri Synod Chicago area pastor where their father, J. A. O. Preus I, was a Lutheran insurance company executive after he had served as governor of the state of Minnesota. I often heard Robert speak of his three-year confirmation instruction and of how he would walk to the church on Saturday afternoons to announce for Communion. David Preus describes this very personable and conservative pastor as having made a permanent impression on Jack.[7]

Herman Amberg Preus III (1896–1995), an uncle to Jack and Robert, supported the union of the three Norwegian synods in 1917 and spent most of his ministry as a professor at Luther Seminary in St. Paul, Minnesota. Here Jack and Robert received their theological education and experienced firsthand the theological differences between their uncle, H. A. Preus III, who steadfastly held to the old doctrine of predestination against George Aus, who held that God predestined those whom he knew would come to faith.

David Preus recalls, "Some [Luther] seminary students delighted in stirring up classroom controversy between Professor [H. A.] Preus and

---

4. Catholic Church and Lutheran World Federation. *Joint Declaration on the Doctrine of Justification* (Grand Rapids, MI: W. B. Eerdmans Publishing Co., 2000).
5. David W. Preus, *Two Trajectories: J. A. O. Preus and David Preus* (Minneapolis, MN: Lutheran University Press, 2015).
6. David W. Preus, *Two Trajectories*, 35–36.
7. David W. Preus, *Two Trajectories*, 15.

Professor George Aus, who equally defended the second predestination form [God elected those who he knew would believe.]"[8]

For Jack Preus and Robert Preus, predestination was not simply another doctrine, but the one that defined them. For David Preus, their cousin, differences over predestination mattered little. "The theological controversy over predestination that had been so prominent in the first generations of Preus pastors had been largely forgotten until the appearance of Jack and Robert Preus in the fourth generation."[9]

As a seminary student David lived with Jack and his wife Delpha while Jack was studying for his doctor's degree at the University of Minnesota. At the time, Delpha was recovering from polio, and David would help with the household chores. Robert was a vicar in a neighboring congregation, and he and his wife Donna often came to visit, and the topic of conversation was predestination.

What David says about these conversations speaks for itself. "I liked both Jack and Robert and was interested in their theological discussions, even though I wondered how they could get all worked up over some theological disagreement as mystery-laden as predestination."[10] David Preus was not only a cousin, but close friend to Jack and Robert.[11] He was present at the funerals of both Robert and Robert's widow, Donna Rockman Preus.

The controversy over subjective justification and over the theology of Walter A. Maier II goes back in the Missouri Synod to 1965, when Jack Preus had the board of Concordia Theological Seminary call him to the Springfield faculty. In the four years which followed, during which Jack continued as president, it is unlikely that he did not know Maier II's positions. The students did!

In the conservative renewal that anticipated the suspension of John Tietjen as seminary president and the majority St. Louis faculty majority walkout in February 1974, Maier II had been elected a synod vice president as a conservative favorite. Some who thought that Jack Preus was not acting quickly enough in resolving the St. Louis situation put forth Maier II as their choice for synod president to replace Jack. After the situation at St. Louis was resolved, Maier II remained a viable alternative for synod president.[12]

---

8. David W. Preus, *Two Trajectories*, 42.
9. David W. Preus, *Two Trajectories*, 43.
10. David W. Preus, *Two Trajectories*, 16.
11. David W. Preus, *Two Trajectories*, 16–17.
12. For another account of this see Burkee, *Power, Politics, and the Missouri Synod*, 175–176.

Maier II's lectures on Romans were the source of seminary legends. Students had transcribed them, and at last count three different versions existed—something like Luther's lectures. Since his lectures were the same year after year, students would read one or more of the transcriptions as Maier II lectured. All this anecdotal information, including that Maier II held to only subjective and not objective or universal justification, was common knowledge among students and faculty. Once or twice I got hold of library copies of these notes and his dissertation in attempting to get to the bottom of the concerns about his position. This proved futile, perhaps because I did not have the fortitude to wade through these materials. I was not asked to be a member of the faculty committee assigned to handle this matter and was a bit befuddled by the final solution.

Support for Walter A. Maier II as synod president cannot be ruled out as a reason for Jack Preus asking his brother Robert to handle Maier II's doctrine of justification. Relations between the Preus brothers were not without their rough spots. Yet both Robert Preus and Jack Preus could not accept what they saw as the denial of objective justification by both Walter Maier I and his son Walter Maier II. His views also became an issue in September 1989 with the calling of Walter Maier III, whose views were seen by some faculty members as virtually identical with his father's view. Neither understood this doctrine according to traditional Missouri Synod definitions.

For the Preus brothers, this was not a minor issue. Jack Preus was not the only one to look into the issue. Ralph Bohlmann also did. The inability of the Missouri Synod once and for all to bring this matter to a conclusion may partially lie in that the Missouri Synod had long been "Protestantized" in an Arminian direction.

Apart what anyone thought about the doctrinal controversy, the name "Walter A. Maier" as the speaker of the Lutheran Hour was a symbol of what to many were the Missouri Synod's golden days. Here was a potentially deadly potion of historical, theological, political, emotional and family issues.

At the time of the faculty's conversations with Maier II, Robert Preus looked for support and found it among conservative friends in the Evangelical movement who admired him for his defense of biblical inspiration and inerrancy, including several faculty members of Westminster Seminary—Escondido, California, with its renowned Reformed scholar Michael Horton (b. 1964). Preus must have been aware, but chose to ignore that the Reformed see objective justification as a component of their doctrine of election, but it was hardly universal in scope as Lutherans have historically held it.

Several faculty members who were at odds with Maier II's views saw certain kinks in the traditional position because it saw each individual rather than humanity as a totality being justified. It came across like this:

1. Each person was held responsible for Adam's sin, the doctrine of original sin.
2. Then he was justified before the world began, the doctrine of objective justification.
3. Being born into the world, he was again made accountable for original sin.
4. He came to faith and was justified, the doctrine of subjective justification.

On several occasions, Maier II had expressed to me his disappointment that the faculty did not get embroiled in theological issues in a scholarly way, and I have every reason to believe that he would have been willing to have the faculty engage in a more detailed analysis of his position. When a theological issue becomes entangled with other issues, however, it is too late for the kind of scholarly objectivity which, if it does not solve problems, at least lays them out.

Complicating matters was that Maier's position may have been held by those who thought of themselves as conservatives in working for a change at the St. Louis seminary. *Christian News* editor Herman Otten factored into Jack Preus's election as synod president and had supported Robert Preus in his attempt to be retained as the Fort Wayne seminary president. Otten had written his master of sacred theology thesis on the Lutheran Hour speaker's social views and maintained a personal connection by inviting his widow, Hulda Maier (1890–1986), and then his son Walter II to speak at inaugural events at Camp Trinity in New Haven, Missouri.

Robert Preus came to Walter Maier II's defense, not because he believed that his position was tenable, but because Maier II's position was being challenged by Jack Preus for what Robert Preus thought were political reasons. He may have also resisted what he considered his brother's interference in seminary matters. Had Jack been so concerned with Maier II, he could have handled this matter when he was Springfield seminary president. Family, personal and theological factors were intertwined.

Equally tragic was that in the matter of justification, John Saleska stood with Robert Preus to the point of his being angry for not solving the question of objective justification once and for all. Saleska was reported to be upset with Robert Preus because he did not "go all out to get Walter A. Maier II."

At the time when the faculty was engaged in this issue, I supplied a one-page article to *Christianity Today* entitled "The Two Sides of Justification,"[13] to lay out the problem to a wider Protestant audience who had gotten wind of the controversy. On two occasions, perhaps more, Wallace "Wally" Schulz, first as a Lutheran Hour speaker and then as synod second vice president, told me that in this essay I was not at my stellar best. Since he last reminded me of this in my office sometime in 1999 or 2000, nearly twenty years after the essay was written, it was obvious he did not approve of what I had written. It may also show that Maier II's views were representative of a large group in the Missouri Synod, even those who saw themselves and were seen as conservatives.

All this came up again. According to the synod rule students not receiving placement within one year of graduation are required to undergo an interview before being certified for the ministry. Waldemar "Wally" Degner and Harold Buls were assigned to interview Walter Maier III, who had finished his Ph.D. residency at Harvard and was slated for a teaching position at Concordia River Forest, now Concordia Chicago.

Up to this point, Harry Buls and Wally Degner had been vehement and vocal opponents of Maier II's position. While Buls remained firm in his support of Robert Preus, Degner had made common cause in removing Preus as president and had good reason to believe that he might be appointed academic dean in my place. Walter Maier III's interview raised the same concerns about the son that they had with his father.

Walter III's appointment to the faculty would assure that what the faculty once unanimously saw as an aberrant doctrine on justification could be perpetuated for another generation. Harry Buls was not able to come to terms in how the Preus brothers had handled Maier II's position on justification, which was also espoused by the son. Personal distress about the matter led Harry Buls to an earlier than expected retirement that allowed him to teach in Russia and Africa.

A faculty committee came up with a solution for the impasse with Walter Maier II based on 1 Timothy 3:16, a hymn which speaks of Jesus being justified in the spirit, that made it applicable to the doctrine of justification—an interpretation I found a bit contrived. Apart from how it was

---

13. David P. Scaer, "The Two Sides of Justification," *Christianity Today* 25 (June 26, 1981), 44.

understood, it was acceptable to Maier II and received nearly unanimously with one dissent by the faculty with the understanding that Maier II would not teach Romans again. Once Maier II was appointed academic dean, no one expected this resolution would be enforced. Ray Surburg, a still reserved Old Testament professor, did not support the resolution. Personal reasons trumped theological ones.

Chapter Nine

THE "RETIREMENT" OF ROBERT PREUS

Whatever issues the board had with Robert Preus were easily balanced by record student enrollments and record financial support. With synod officials asking Preus to retire, the ambition of friends would become the overriding factor in removing him as seminary president. Probably in the late fall or early winter of 1988, Norbert Mueller became aware that some board members were intent on removing Preus. Mueller most likely had put himself forth to succeed him.

Opposition to Robert Preus began to coalesce in April 1988. Early one morning, I received a frantic telephone call from Art Just that the academic dean's secretary, Phyllis Saunders, was in tears. When I rushed over to her office, I discovered that Gary Satterfield, the business manager, had chewed her out for not getting to work at eight AM. I tried to intervene with Satterfield by telling him that Phyllis generally came to work about eight-twenty, and that she often worked during the lunch hour and stayed late to keep up with the work of the dean's office. Had she been recompensed according to an hourly scale, she would have been underpaid.

Satterfield continued the tirade he had started with Phyllis and informed me that he, and not I, set policy at the seminary for the secretaries. Gary had a colorful vocabulary and was heard down the hall by Trudy Behning, secretary to Robert Preus, who was out of town. It is hard not to think that Satterfield at that time was unaware of Norb Mueller's hopes to be the interim president, and in a new administration he would exercise even more authority than he did with Preus. These events are recorded in a memo to Robert Preus. Under current administrative procedure, the secretary of the Academic Dean is responsible to him and not the business manager.

In my tenure as academic dean I attended nearly all board meetings. However, for the February 1989 meeting, scheduled in St. Louis in conjunction with a joint meeting with its board, Preus said that he would present the academic dean's report and thus I was not to go. As what was destined to be the fateful May 20 meeting drew near, I was kept at arm's length from what was going on. At that February meeting in St. Louis, the board went into in an executive session during which Norb Mueller was invited to testify on Preus's fitness to remain as seminary president. I became privy to his testimony years later.

In November, board chairman Raymond Joeckel wrote Robert Preus that Rodney Otto of Kentwood, Michigan, now retired, had brought charges against him and me.[1] His charges had to do with *Affirm*'s endorsement of Robert Preus for synod president. Preus wrote to Joeckel[2] that he had already replied to Otto.[3]

Robert Preus shared the correspondence with John Heinz, Otto's Michigan District president. Preus noted that his name had already been removed from the masthead, but he would stand by what *Affirm* had done in the past. Preus added, "Dr. Scaer will have to speak for himself on this issue." I do not recall that I ever did.

Faculty members serve not only on editorial boards of their seminaries and synod, but also the boards of other publications. Over the years my name has appeared on the mastheads of *Christianity Today*, *Modern Reformation*, *Logia* and *The Bulletin of Biblical Research*. In the past I had written for *Affirm*, as I had written for *Lutheran Forum* and *Christianity Today*, and had never thought that contributing to any periodical involved political alliance.

Slamming today means being switched from one telephone company to another without being asked. The term might apply to my name being included on the masthead of *Affirm*. This may have happened when John Klotz was president of the organization, but I have never been a member of anything resembling a political action group in synod and have never been pushed or suggested for an elected position.

Around the May 1989 graduation, Jim Voelz, who joined our faculty in the fall of 1976, took a position at the St. Louis seminary in New Testament studies, offered by its president, Karl Barth. Later Preus admonished me for not urging Jim to stay, but I had in fact written him a letter that he was playing an important role in Fort Wayne. I received no response. Preus also wrote Voelz saying he was playing the most vital role at the seminary. In 2015, Jim Voelz took up residence in Fort Wayne again, but formally remained on the St. Louis faculty.

In May of 1989, Howard Tepker wrote to Indiana District president Reuben Garber, "It is common knowledge that tension on campus has

---

1. Raymond Joeckel, letter to Robert Preus, November 30, 1988.
2. Robert Preus, letter to Raymond Joeckel, December 7, 1988.
3. Robert Preus, letter to Rodney Otto, November 22, 1988.

not lessened over the last five years and that morale continues to be low."[4] Enclosed in the letter were eight documents on the following subjects:

1. tensions existing for five years;
2. attempts of faculty members to contact the board, most likely the efforts of Warren Wilbert;
3. May 26, 1984, board guidelines for the faculty;
4. visitations organized by the synod president beginning five years ago;
5. a visit by "six prominent and respected churchmen";
6. a board-authorized visit by three district presidents;
7. the visit by a committee of the Association of Theological Schools; and
8. failed efforts at reconciliation.

Strictly speaking, these were not eight separate points. Point 1 is an introduction and points 4 and 5 are the same. The "six prominent and respected churchmen" of point 5 were district presidents. Howard Tepker sent all this to the board less than two weeks before the May 20, 1989, board meeting, during which Garber and board chairman Ray Joeckel would ask Preus to retire.

The letter's literary style with its enumeration and duplication of items to exaggerate the charges has an uncanny resemblance to Waldo Werning's style. In 1989, Tepker at seventy-six years belonged to the typewriter generation and probably had not transitioned to the computer. Nevertheless the letter is computer generated with Tepker writing his name and a short note to the board on the first page.

For the first years of my ministry, May 20 was remembered each year as the day of my ordination at Trinity Evangelical Lutheran Church of Flatbush in 1962. After 1989, it was remembered as the day on which Robert D. Preus was asked by the board chairman and district president to step down as the president of Concordia Theological Seminary. What is offered here is how I remember experiencing that time.

Earlier in the week, Monday, May 15, through Wednesday, May 17, I was attending a meeting of the Evangelical Theological Society held at Trinity Evangelical Divinity School in Deerfield, Illinois, north of Chicago. I delivered a paper in response to Os Guinness (b. 1941), a widely respected Evangelical leader who had proposed a moral coalition involving

---

4. Howard Tepker, letter to Reuben Garber, May 8, 1989.

Christians with other religionists. Historical boundaries among Christians were regularly transgressed by Evangelicals, but I pointed out that placing Christians with non-Christians was *testimonium paupertatis*, an admission that the Evangelical task in providing a united front against the old liberalism had failed. Os Guinness was proposing that a moral or ethical agenda take the place of one that saw the defense of the historical character of the Bible as primary. My "Response to Os Guinness" was printed in *Evangelical Affirmations*,[5] edited by the brain trust of the Evangelical movement, Carl F. H. Henry and Kenneth Kantzer, both former editors of *Christianity Today*, friends and admirers of Robert Preus. Guinness was not too happy with me.

For this conference, I was appointed to a committee that met each day at six AM with the task of preparing a statement acceptable to Seventh-Day Adventists allowing them membership in the society. It failed. Hell plays too prominent a part in Evangelical preaching to allow for the Adventist belief that unbelievers were annihilated. This was probably the last time I saw the former editors of *Christianity Today* Carl F. H. Henry and Kenneth Kantzer, who have a well-earned place in the Evangelical pantheon.[6] Both were knowledgeable in what Lutherans believed and made every attempt to incorporate our beliefs into Evangelical definitions.

When some years later Evangelicals and Catholics Together was formed as an ecumenical alliance among Christians to recognize common beliefs and points of disagreement, Lutherans were excluded. Perhaps one day those in this group may explain this, but it might be that the Evangelical Lutheran Church in America (ELCA), the majority Lutheran group, had become so mainline in its theology that it had no definite position from which to negotiate. On the other side, the LCMS may have been seen as so entrenched in its own historic position that it could not engage in these kinds of open discussions. As the central figure of the five faculty members who remained at the St. Louis seminary after the majority walkout in February 1974, Robert Preus may have been perceived as so entrenched in his own theology that he was not open to listening to or participating with non-Lutherans.

Those who knew Robert Preus knew this was untrue. None of those who worked for his removal as seminary president and so to advance

---

5. David P. Scaer, "Response to Os Guinness," in *Evangelical Affirmations* (Grand Rapids, MI: Acadamie Books, 1990), 457–97.
6. David P. Scaer, "Carl F. H. Henry: A Tribute to an Evangelical Theologian," *Concordia Theological Quarterly* 68:2 (April 2004): 155–156.

themselves in position were his match intellectually, academically or in the pulpit. He combined confessional commitment with a broad knowledge of theology. In the four and half years between when he was removed as president in September 1989 until he moved from Fort Wayne in April 1994, students gathered around him in the commons after chapel. Robert Preus was worth listening to. Both Preus brothers, Jack and Robert, had magnetic and charismatic personalities, characteristics lacking in their detractors.

Robert Preus had roots in what would become the American Lutheran Church, and for his defense of biblical inerrancy he was a respected figure in Evangelical circles. His ecumenical credentials were more expansive than any of his colleagues, and more than anyone else, he had the name recognition outside of the Missouri Synod. From time to time he would appear at the meetings of Evangelicals, and thus it was no surprise that he put in an appearance on May 17, 1989, at the meeting at Trinity Seminary in Deerfield, Illinois. Preus had coordinated his obligations with visits to family, friends and supporters of the seminary, and for that meeting was probably staying with Ruth (b. 1963), his youngest daughter's family in the Chicago area.

As he walked about during that one day at the conference, he was greeted by his admirers. It did not seem possible that in a few days one of the giants of twentieth-century Lutheranism would be toppled from the post of seminary president and for a time removed from the synod that owed him a debt for its survival. A greater debt was owed him by the seminary and even by the faculty and staff who opposed his continuation at Fort Wayne.

When I became academic dean, the baccalaureate service was made separate from the graduation exercises. Before that they comprised one service. Relatives and friends staying with the students were often confined to close living quarters, and events scheduled during the day would give them a chance to get out of the house and to get acquainted with the campus. A whole day of activities began with the morning baccalaureate service, followed by an afternoon organ recital, a reception on the plaza, and finally the six o'clock graduation itself in the chapel with the altar covered over. Flags of the nations from which the foreign students had come were hung from the choir loft in the back of the chapel. Following the graduation exercises, cookies, coffee and punch were set out in the plaza.

The 1989 commencement exercises took place on the evening of Friday, May 19, at the end of the same week at which we had been at the conference in Deerfield, Illinois. It was an important day for Robert Preus, since his son Daniel, now a pastor and later synod first vice president (2001–

2004) and then a vice president at other levels was receiving his master of sacred theology degree, and a family reception had been planned for him in the Preus home in Fox Chase, a subdivision adjacent to the campus. Preus was delayed coming home by a couple of hours.

Board chairman Ray Joeckel, an oil man from Colorado, whose brother and nephew were synod pastors, and Reuben Garber, president of the Indiana District, had asked Preus to meet with him in his office after graduation. Previously Preus had been asked by the synod's Board for Higher Education Services to step down, but he had no inkling that the seminary board would ask him to retire.

That same day, May 19, a meeting of the seminary board was held at the Lincoln National Bank, where board member Melvin Bredemeier was a vice president. Since the board went into executive session, Preus was not present. Just minutes after the meeting began, Bredemeier left the room and returned with a formally prepared resolution in hand for board consideration that Preus should be honorably retired as president. According to the decision of the Commission on Appeals, the resolution "shocked three or four BOR [board of regents] members because they had no prior notice thereof although it was clear that BOR members Joeckel, Garber and Bredemeier, knew in advance what was in the resolution."[7] That evening, Preus was informed by Joeckel and Garber of the board's attempt to retire him, a motion that garnered four votes in favor, three votes against and one abstention.

Trudy Behning called me the next morning, Saturday, May 20, to inform me that the academic dean's report that was scheduled for about nine or ten o'clock would be delayed until the afternoon, and that news from the board was not good. Her tone of voice indicated that a critical period awaited Preus which would have ramifications for the seminary. Since grim faces were the order of the day when I arrived, I can only assume that the vote had already been taken. For the eight-member board, five constituted a majority.

In 1992, the motion to retire Preus was ruled unconstitutional by the Commission on Constitutional Matters, but that decision had no force on that day in May. The Commission would rule one could be retired, but not for cause, which in this case was given as faculty dissension. Voting for retiring Robert Preus were Reuben Garber, Ray Joeckel, Melvin Bredemeier and August Mennicke, the synod first vice president, appointed by Ralph Bohlmann. Those voting against the resolution and so in support

---

7. Preus v. Board of Regents, 3.

of Preus continuing as president were William "Bud" Fehl (1922–1992), David Anderson and Don Kirchner. Abstaining was teacher Richard J. Bultemeyer, a Fort Wayne resident. A ninth board member, John Wiebe, a mall developer from Iowa, had resigned the previous year, claiming that family matters prevented him from attending meetings. Considering that Preus was removed less than four months later, that resignation contributed to his downfall.

In the same resolution removing Preus, Norbert Mueller, his administrative assistant, was named the interim president. So it appears that the action had to do not only with his removal, but providing an entirely new direction for the seminary.

Since Robert Preus had been under surveillance by synod authorities at least since the spring of 1984, resignation of a board member favorable to him would prove to be costly. Somehow Preus did not do the counting. In handling this kind of situation, the board majority would have advanced their agenda if they had asked only for his retirement in one resolution and only then put forward a second resolution making Norb Mueller the interim president. Putting both items into one resolution confused matters. It showed that board members opposed to Preus were ready to put a new administration in place, and that Norb Mueller was complicit in an action to become seminary president, a position he had long desired for himself.

Robert Preus had originally designated his assistant Norbert Mueller as the faculty delegate to the July 1989 Wichita Convention, but then chose to send him to the Philippines. Mueller already at this time knew of the proposal of some members to remove Preus at the May 19 board meeting. How Robert Preus was unaware of Mueller's ambition is a good question. His second choice for faculty representative was Robert Newton, but then Preus sent him off to a conference in Finland.

My being the third choice for Wichita might indicate my place on Robert Preus's totem pole. I asked Preus about how the academic dean could be outranked in being chosen to represent the seminary. He responded that he knew that the first two choices would be unable to go. Each had accepted the appointment to Wichita and in accepting the other assignment turned Wichita down. In physical space, Preus was a hair's breadth away from the desk of the one desiring his position, but he was either unaware of it or thought that he could handle any situation.

As usual, I left for the Poconos after the May graduation. On July 1, I flew from the Lehigh Valley Airport to Wichita to attend the synod convention. August Mennicke's description of the upcoming convention

Sunday morning service as a "barn burner" was a sufficient reason for walking to a church nearby the hotel.

My memories of the Wichita Convention were colored by the conviction that a significant change was in store for the seminary, and that my future there would be in jeopardy. President Ralph Bohlmann preached at the opening service, which was conducted in an almost completely darkened convention hall. A spotlight focused on the officiants, with Bohlmann in the front each time as they proceeded to and from the stage, which served as the altar space.

August Mennicke, who was reelected first vice president, had voted for Preus's removal in May, but the other vice presidents, Robert Sauer (1921–2013), George Wollenberg (1930–2008), Walter Maier II and Eugene Bunkowske, could be counted on as Robert Preus's friends to support him. Preus had brought Bunkowske on to the seminary faculty and thought of him as its future president. Sauer had been Jack Preus's assistant during the Seminex situation, in which Robert Preus was the key figure in the St. Louis faculty minority that kept the seminary open. Several times each day during the Wichita convention, I was on the phone providing updates to Wenthe back in Fort Wayne on what at every moment was a collapsing situation.

At the convention, two faculty members, Walter A. Maier II and Eugene Bunkowske, would be elected synod vice presidents, and as members of the praesidium they would be able to influence the seminary board in reversing actions to retire Robert Preus—at least Preus and others thought this. Preus had helped Maier II through the controversy on objective justification, saved his position at the seminary and his place in the ministerium. Bunkowske had been called three times to the seminary at Preus's recommendation, and he, like Maier, was counted on to support Preus. It did not work out this way. Both had something to gain through Preus's retirement. As it turned out, they were among those who thought that Preus should be removed and were engaged at various times in carrying this out.

Robert Preus had been nominated to be a synod vice president, and on the basis of name recognition would have been easily elected, but, as he later told me, he declined on the grounds that he did not want to serve under Ralph Bohlmann, who for at least five years had been working to remove him. This proved to be a tactical error, since as a sitting vice president, it would have been more difficult to remove him from the seminary presidency, professorship and the pastoral roster of the synod. For the record, I was the last of fifteen nominees for one of the five synod vice presidencies and unsurprisingly not retained on the second ballot.

Two other events stand out in my mind. One delegate called attention to the number of candidates proposed for election to synodical offices with the name "Preus" or who were closely related to those who had this name. This was a death knell! Synod by-laws specify that delegates at one convention elect the nominating committee for the next convention. So that this would not happen again, the convention passed a resolution that district boards of directors each would choose one member for the nominating committee. Now district conventions do this. To keep the committee within manageable proportions, the districts would alternate every other synod convention in performing this function. Vacancies that occur between conventions are filled by nominees offered by the nominating committee. Districts with as few as fifty congregations are given the same leverage as those with five hundred. This attempt to limit the influence of Robert Preus has failed. His second- and third-generation descendants are theologically prominent in the LCMS and have been elected to high positions.

Early in the convention a leading synod feminist from the Atlantic District came to the microphone. Before she began to speak, I knew instinctively what she was going to say. *The Concordia Theological Quarterly*, of which I was the editor, had published an article by a now former colleague which contained the following: "The author rejects any idea that woman is morally or spiritually inferior to man. Nor does he mean to imply that woman is intellectually or physically inferior."[8] Of course, these sentences could be taken to mean the exact opposite of what they say, and they were. So, those who were opposed to the ordination of women were made out to be male chauvinists. Her reading this disclaimer to the delegates had the desired effect. In proofreading the essay for publication, I had removed it because I knew the impression it would give. But the assistant editor, who had authored it, put it back in the copy that went to the printer. When it was read to the delegates, it had the desired effect, and I was devastated. Like a bad penny, the offending statement has been referenced in other gatherings as representative of the Fort Wayne theology.

Passed at this convention was what former Missouri Synod and then ELCA pastor Richard John Neuhaus (1936–2009) would later call "the Wichita recension to the Augsburg Confession" in allowing laymen to celebrate the Lord's Supper. It is still a divisive issue, even though reversed at the 2016 Convention.

---

8. Douglas Judisch, "Theses on Woman Suffrage in the Church," *Concordia Theological Quarterly* 41, no. 3 (July 1977): 45, n. 6, http://www.ctsfw.net/media/pdfs/judischthesesonwomansuffrage.pdf.

Strict regulations for changing airline tickets were not in place in 1989, and so I headed out to the airport one day earlier to return to the Poconos on another airline. Then a ticket on one airline was legal tender on another; 9/11 would change all this. When I arrived at the airport, I learned that an important issue—I don't remember what it was—had come up, and I returned to the convention and found another place to spend the night, and then took the original return flight. Things were bad, and they were going to get worse before the summer was over. Reuben Garber was given the task of assuring a board majority would vote for Preus's retirement.

On May 21, the seminary board of regents set another meeting for July 28, the last Friday in the month, which coincided with the last day of the annual ten-week summer Greek program. Classes are conducted on campus after graduation from the end of May to the end of July, when the seminary maintenance staff begins preparing the buildings for the fall. When the meeting began, the Greek students were already leaving, and for all practical purposes the campus was empty. Robert Preus had requested that I return from the Poconos for the board meeting to meet with him and Wenthe on Thursday.

He opened the board meeting with a devotion. The calling of two professors in Old Testament, Daniel Gard, a pastor of a rural congregation in Indiana, later president of Concordia University Chicago, and Walter A. Maier III, an assistant professor at Concordia River Forest, were the only items that Preus placed on the agenda. Both Dan Gard and young Walter Maier III were sons of Lutheran pastors. Gard's father was an ELCA pastor. While his father was still in that synod, Dan left it for the Missouri Synod because of what he saw in it as its increasing doctrinal aberrations. Gard and Maier III were added to the faculty by a unanimous board vote.

Such swift action was taken by the board so that it could proceed to other things that were more important for them that July morning. Having taken this action, the board went into executive session with only board members present and minutes kept on colored papers which are not disseminated. Advisory members, including the president as executive officer of the board and his advisors, of which I was one, were dismissed.

On the night before the meeting, I had dinner with Dan Gard at Ernie's Steak House, located then in the shopping mall near our home in the Pine Valley development. Dan was in the process of receiving his Ph.D. from Notre Dame for a dissertation on the Old Testament books of Chronicles, which, through his research, I found to be a fascinating topic. First and Second Kings brought out the worst of the kings of Judah and Israel, the southern and northern kingdoms. Chronicles put a more positive twist on things. In one Bible existed two somewhat different perspectives on the same events.

Walter A. Maier III not only came with credentials from Harvard, but with a name long made famous by his grandfather, the Lutheran Hour speaker, and father, who was a synod vice president. Synod regulations required that only those who had been parish pastors be called to the seminary teaching positions, though in the case of others this rule had not been followed. Arrangements were made with Concordia Lutheran Church, Fort Wayne, for Maier III to serve for three years on a part-time basis on the pastoral staff. Robert Preus assumed that calling Walter Maier III to the faculty would assure that Maier II's support could be counted on. Preus had discussed bringing the youngest Maier years before.

On that fateful day, I returned to my office in Jerome Hall, from which I viewed the upper plaza between the chapel and dining hall and the steps leading down to what after Robert's death would be called the Preus Plaza. Somehow I learned that, during that meeting, Robert and his attorney were in the dining room alone, where I then joined them. Somber moments were turning into darker hours as Preus waited for what he knew was going to be his inevitable fate. According to what was learned later, the board voted throughout the day and could not get around a 4-3-1 stalemate until late in the afternoon.

Five votes constituted a majority, and teacher Richard J. Bultemeyer was the only holdout standing in the way of the necessary majority of five votes. Bultemeyer's daughter was getting married the next day, a Saturday, and a rehearsal dinner was scheduled for that Friday evening. As the afternoon wore on, this family occasion became more important to him. Late in the afternoon, Indiana District president Reuben Garber asked and was given the privilege of offering a prayer, assumedly asking for God's will to be done in the board coming to a quick decision in the Preus matter.

Immediately after the prayer, a motion to recess was made and passed, and Garber went outside and privately took Bultemeyer aside. When the recess was over, Bultemeyer supplied the fifth vote for the majority requiring Preus to retire. After Preus learned that he was removed as seminary president by retirement, he phoned Bohlmann asking for his help in retaining his position.

Unknown to Robert Preus, Bohlmann's secretary was listening in on the phone conversation and taking notes, from which a typewritten transcript was made. In asking Bohlmann for counsel and aid, Preus also did not know that Bohlmann was hardly a neutral referee in the dispute but was working with Joeckel to remove him. The decision of the Commission on Appeals refers to the decision of the Commission of Adjudication that "He (Preus) contacted President Bohlmann who offered no help or relief."[9] Here the ruling of the Commission on Appeals can speak for itself. The "Draft of Telephone Conversation, July 28, 1989"[10] was typed and the original notes thereafter thrown away.[11] In other words there was no original evidence of what was said in the phone conversation.

Following the corporate model, Preus was allowed to remain in office for a few weeks to put his matters in order. Elected as Indiana District president in the summer of 1988, in that one year Reuben Garber was key in removing Preus from office. He did not create the events that brought this about, but he brought them to a conclusion.

Anticipating health problems, Garber did not stand for office in 1991 and was followed by Timothy Sims, who though not a board member played a key role in seminary president Dean Wenthe not being elected synod president in 1987. When health problems did not develop for Garber, he later had second thoughts about not standing for office. Perhaps there were other health problems, and he died soon thereafter.

Synodical regulations required that one board member be a commissioned minister, a fluid category that included parochial school teachers and directors of Christian education. Bultemeyer, who held the latter position, was at that time moving into a newer home in Fort Wayne and later retired in Florida. Since Bultemeier held out for so long in not casting his vote to remove Preus, it seems that he was not fully convinced it was the right thing to do.

News of his dismissal was brought to Robert Preus in his office assumedly by Garber and Joeckel, who said, "Robert, you are now retired." Preus who was the young David against the Goliath in the Seminex controversy in 1974, had been taken down by a coalition of those whom he counted as friends as well as by his own inattentiveness to what was happening around him. Former successes and his personal stature in the synod may have led him to believe in his own invulnerability. His removal created a corporate trauma among his family and friends and for the seminary community.

---

9. Preus v. Board of Regents, 3.
10. Preus v. Board of Regents, P. Ex. 11.
11. Preus v. Board of Regents, 3.

The Preus home had always been a haven of hospitality, but what was appropriate now that he knew that his days as president were numbered? Board members who had supported Preus went to his house for supper, and he went out and bought Chinese. This was as good as anything else. As Butlemeier celebrated his daughter's wedding at the rehearsal dinner, one wonders what was going on in his mind.

To get the most reasonable price, my air trip back to the Poconos was scheduled for Sunday, but with nothing else to be done, I took a chance to go standby on Saturday. This allowed me to attend services at The Lutheran Church of Our Savior in Mount Pocono, where the Sunday reading follows the three-year series. Series C prescribed Ecclesiastes 2:18–19 as the Old Testament lesson for that Eleventh Sunday after Pentecost:

> "I hated all my toil in which I had toiled under the sun, seeing that I must leave it to the man who will come after me; and who knows whether he will be a wise man or a fool? Yet he will be master of all for which I toiled and used my wisdom under the sun. This also is vanity." (RSV)

Whenever the three-year cycle comes around with this reading, the events of the last week in July 1989 come to mind. Preus and Joeckel provided their personal funds for the expansion of the president's house on campus to accommodate more guests at seminary social occasions. During the Preus administration, he had accumulated sufficient funding to abolish student tuition, and for this purpose he had donated a farm in southern Indiana to the seminary. Without too much imagination, Norb Mueller, Preus's successor, can be found in the words of Solomon.

Robert Preus left an indelible mark on the seminary that those who knew him will never forget. What happened that Friday afternoon should not have been unexpected, but it was for me. I was as much at a loss about the future as was anyone else. Summers were used for research and writing projects, and for my own satisfaction I would like to recall what projects were underway during those trying months of the summer 1989, but I cannot. Looming in front of me was the revival of Waldo Werning's charges brought against me in September 1988 that had been dismissed three times, once by a faculty committee, then the entire faculty and finally the board. This also hung over my head that summer.[12]

The removal of Dr. Robert Preus from the presidency of Concordia Theological Seminary, Fort Wayne, Indiana, was done on the basis of the claim of the Board of Regents to have the authority to retire a president.

---

12. For details of these struggles, see Excursus XIV on Waldo Werning. 277 ff.

Faculty and staff were assured that it was done without any theological or political motivation. The board action found a reason for their action in the turmoil on the campus between faculty and staff, as it noted in its July 28, 1989 resolution to retire Preus.

The faculty was neither questioned nor consulted about this. One could hardly expect student participation in such a decision, and there was none, but in light of events of the next three years, the students liked Preus and would have preferred him as president to ham-fisted Norb Mueller. He was not well liked.

In August, board member William H. B. Fehl Jr. wrote me from Beaumont, Texas, where he was pastor.[13] "Bud," as he signed the letter, was one of three board members voting against Preus's retirement. At the age of about forty-four Fehl came as a student to the Springfield seminary in 1966, the same year I came on as an assistant professor. He had been a widower with adult children and had married a lovely gal named "Vi" with whom he had two children. Since he came to campus for board meetings, we remained in contact. Fehl reported that he did not vote with the board majority to remove Preus, but now he supported that decision. Preus had threatened the board and had brought his attorney into the board meeting. Fehl concluded that this was a classic case of stress and asked me to intervene with Robert Preus, whose further actions in his view would hurt the seminary. Quite bluntly Fehl wrote that "[Preus] is the problem."

Since Preus was already in Gunflint and I was in the Poconos until leaving for Korea, I was never able to carry out Fehl's suggestions. Preus had already written me saying that he had been too harsh with me when I pointed out where things could have been done differently, and it was less likely that I could influence him now.

Synod boards serve until the end of August following the triennial convention. In September, the board was reconstituted and Fehl would no longer be a member. Two six-year terms were allowed for service on the board, and according to the 1989 *Lutheran Annual* Fehl's term was up in 1989. I never saw him again. His August letter was the last.

Bud Fehl had sided with the conservative cause and was a mild man, so there is little reason to doubt his assessment. Like others Fehl seemed to be unaware that what had happened was not about Preus but about a wholesale reorganization of the seminary administration that would lead it away from its conservative direction that Preus had attempted to put in place.

---

13. William H. B. Fehl Jr., letter to David Scaer, August 1, 1989.

Preus fought to retain and then regain the seminary presidency not only for himself but for the sake of the institution and what it had come to represent to others both positively and negatively to those in and outside of the synod.

For ambitious colleagues, Robert Preus was an obstacle in putting in place a more "moderate" agenda. Faculty acquisitions and appointments made by his successor proved him right. Fehl did not grasp the complexity of the motives behind the board action in removing Preus, and so in the same letter he wrote that he hoped that I would stay on as dean and be a leavening factor. Not only would this not happen, but it had already been decided that I was also marked for immediate removal from the deanship and then gradual extinction from the faculty. Notice of Bud's death came in an obituary in the *Lutheran Witness*. I intended to write his widow. Good intentions do not always materialize.

At the end of August, at Ralph Bohlmann's invitation, I attended the meeting of the International Lutheran Council, a counterpart to the Lutheran World Federation, of confessional Lutheran churches, with which the Missouri Synod was affiliated. Since I was on the East Coast, I chose to fly out of JFK in New York City on August 24 with a stop first in London, where I stayed with Jonathan and Cheryl Naumann, and then on to Hong Kong, where I spent a few days with Joan and Louis Jasper, who was engaged in the deaf ministry there in Macau.

Historic Hong Kong had been signed over by the British to the Peoples Republic of China, but the formal handing over of the operations by the British was a few years away. On the Fifth Sunday in Pentecost, I preached on Luke 14:1, 7–14, the appointed gospel in the three-year series, at the Church of All Nations. This pericope speaks about taking the lowest seat at a wedding to avoid the embarrassment of being asked to step down from a higher seat to make room for a more important person.

After the service, an American diplomat's wife who had the responsibility for seating arrangements at formal dinners spoke of the reality of this story. Embassy diplomats attending social occasions make sure that they are seated in a place appropriate to their rank. This is not so easily resolved. Some New Testament scholars hold that the Bible has to be adjusted to speak to the modern man. In this case it needed no adjustment.

That afternoon Bruce Betker, pastor of the Hong Kong church, took me around the city. Timothy Yip, a former seminary student who had found his way into a charismatic church, looked me up and showed me around the city. One evening we had dinner in a restaurant away from the center of town, where I was the only Caucasian. Fellow diners looking at me attempted to politely keep their amusement to themselves. As I later learned, this was during a festival to commemorate the dead, and to them I resembled a ghost.

Then it was on to Singapore where Edmund Lim, a seminary graduate, was second to the bishop of the Lutheran synod in that city-nation. He arranged for me to preach in the Protestant seminary, and we visited the Evangelical seminary. For several evenings he arranged for me to speak on the gospel of Matthew at his crowded church. An opponent of women's ordination, he had to leave that synod and come to Fort Wayne, where he ministered to a Chinese congregation. Now Lim is serving a congregation in Indianapolis. Seoul was the last stop. Since I had no responsibilities at the International Lutheran Council, there had to be a reason for my being there, but I had not been told in advance what that was.

Synod president Ralph Bohlmann wanted to dissolve an international association of confessional Lutheran professors that I had helped form at the Lutheran seminary in Oberursel, Germany. Since its founding in 1980 the group had met in Cambridge, England, and St. Catharines, Ontario, Canada. At the Seoul meeting my concerns were for the Fort Wayne seminary and my own future and not the continuation of this organization. My presence may have been to lend a degree of legality to its demise, though it really did not matter. When Al Barry was elected synod president replacing Bohlmann, he appointed Ron Feuerhahn of the St. Louis faculty to reorganize it, and since then regular meetings have been held. I was not involved. Minutes for the nine years of the first organization remain in my files.

In Korea, I learned that one should stay away from mini-bars in hotel rooms. Opening a small bag of peanuts was a costly mistake, and nowhere in Seoul could I find an exact replacement. A lavish dinner with gifts for the guests was given with Dr. Won Sang Ji presiding. The Korean church president arrived in a chauffeur-driven car and was met with a carpet literally rolled out into the hotel. After the dinner he and his brother, a St. Louis seminary dogmatics professor, Dr. Won Yong Ji, complimented each on the other's successes. This may be an Oriental custom.

At start of the meeting, Dr. Bohlmann huddled the Missouri Synod delegates together by themselves and asked them not to speak about the Fort Wayne situation. It might have been because those who supported Preus's removal for whatever reason were less than fully confident that the board's July action would stand.

The rest of the summer Robert Preus spent at his home on the American side of Gunflint Lake, around which he, his brother Jack and their children had cabins. To counter Bohlmann's delay tactics, Preus filed a complaint with the Allen County Circuit Court that he was being deprived of access to the synod's "ecclesiastical courts and that all of the defendants (synod, Bohlmann, Walter Rosin, Richard Schlecht, Roland Hopmann, James Groh, Gene Schnelz and Norbert Mueller) were '... working in concert as agents of synod ...' to deprive Preus from timely access to the Synod's adjudication system."[14] Preus filed a complaint for a declaratory judgment that the synod's commission on appeals had delayed in giving him a hearing, and this delay would allow the seminary board to choose a replacement for him as president. Of course they did. Preus was turning sixty-five on October 16, though the date set by the board for his removal was probably sometime in August.

A few weeks of breathing space may have been gained, but in the end it mattered little. An attorney, appointed by a circuit judge for a short duration, suspended the board's action, and a court hearing was set for September 12. The court held that the board had acted within its rights in removing Preus.

On the Tuesday that Preus lost his case in court, I telephoned John Warwick Montgomery, who was a longtime friend of the Preus brothers and who had turned down a position on the faculty in 1966. Montgomery, who had gained notoriety as a theologian, also had a law degree and might be able to provide some light on this situation. Nine AM in Fort Wayne was seven AM in California, and a phone call later in the morning would have been preferable.[15] So it was reported, he phoned the court house and later interrupted proceedings.

It was becoming more and more evident that Bohlmann and Norb Mueller were working hand in hand to make sure Preus would never regain his position. At the same time Preus was working to be reinstated to his position as president through the synod's system of adjudication, Bohlmann was working to delay this by attempting to put in place an informal five-member reconciliation committee.

---

14. Walter Rosin, Richard Schlecht, Roland Hopmann, James Groh, and Gene Schnelz were most likely members of the synod's Commission on Constitutional Matters, which had delayed in handling Preus's request on whether the actions taken against him were in line with the bylaws. Norbert Mueller was keeping the board and the faculty in the dark about the actions Preus was taking. "Preus v. Board of Regents", 9. Schlecht was president of the Michigan District and Walter Rosin Secretary of Synod and brother of Wilbert Rosin, who was removed by Preus as academic dean in 1982.
15. In 1989, Indiana did not participate in Daylight Savings Time. So, during the summer, Fort Wayne was on the same time as Chicago.

Bohlmann appointed board members Donald Kirchner and David Anderson to present Preus's cause, and for the board he appointed its chairman Ray Joeckel and Atlantic District president David Benke, who was not a board member. Should these accept their appointments, the four would then choose a fifth member. Kirchner and Anderson declined. Had they accepted, the committee of reconciliation would have been deadlocked in choosing the fifth member, and Preus's case would have been further delayed, which was Bohlmann's ultimate goal, if all else should fail. So even if Preus was vindicated, a new seminary president would have already been in place, and Preus would be prevented from recovering his position.

Ralph Bohlmann's next tactic in forming a committee of reconciliation was asking the synod's board of directors to nominate forty-one names out of which six would be chosen. Each one of the six would choose one of themselves and an alternate, and the two with the most votes would choose a third member. Bohlmann had assumed the role of a judge.

On December 19, 1989, Bohlmann reported that Henry Koepchen, Arnold Kuntz and Wilbert Sohns would constitute the reconciliation committee.[16] The Commission on Appeals notes in its ruling that Bohlmann, who said he would not participate in the committee of reconciliation, had become a participant in choosing its members. Should the reconciliation efforts fail, the case could be taken up by the synod's Commission on Appeals, an outcome Bohlmann worked to prevent or at least delay.

---

16. Preus v. Board of Regents, 7.

Excursus XIV

WALDO WERNING

☙

Waldo Werning had been an important figure in the conservative movement leading to the election of Jack Preus in 1969, and was appointed to the synod mission board, of which he was chairman, but his appointment did not continue.

Robert Preus wanted to bring Werning to the seminary faculty to teach evangelism and stewardship, but was prevented by the board of regents. He was offered a staff position to the seminary advancement department in 1976, and like other staff members, he could not teach regular seminary courses. It is not unlikely that Werning was assured by Preus of full faculty status in the future, but in some cases promises are implicit. Werning was not academically credentialed, but still continued to work toward the goal of being a full-fledged faculty member. However, his staff obligations were gradually reduced until he was relieved of any staff status at the end of the 1987–1988 academic year.

Seminary course schedules list the courses Werning offered. For example, a memo from Richard E. Muller, the associate academic dean, shows that Waldo would teach Stewardship Theology in all three terms in the 1985–1986 school year. This arrangement, covering over ten years, gave Werning reason to think that he would soon become a full-fledged faculty member. Waldo played a significant role in seminary life, and Robert Preus acted upon his recommendations on who would be called to the faculty.

Something that might border on the bizarre occurred in the fall of 1982. Academic dean Richard Muller[1] notified the faculty of a visit to the campus by Dr. Earl S. Perrigo (1942–2010), a physician, of Toledo, Ohio, arranged by Waldo Werning. It would take place on November 5 and 6, a Friday and Saturday, and Perrigo would speak on health issues of smoking and weight loss.

As it turned out, the visit involved more than lectures. Accompanying Dr. Perrigo were a physiologist with a Ph.D. and a nurse to give the facul-

---

1. Richard Muller, memos to the faculty, September 22, 1982 and September 29, 1982.

ty and their wives physicals including stress tests. As many as sixty people may have undergone the procedure. The then faculty meeting room on the ground floor of Loehe Hall looked a like a clinic. One memorable event was Harold Zietlow passing out on the tread mill and quickly recovering. Eye-opening was the discovery of high blood pressure inherited from my father. We were told that all these services would be without charge. Later we learned that this was all charged to the synod's health plan. This may have affected what the health plan would allow in the future.

Those of us who did not receive a clean bill of health—and that was everyone, so it seemed—made two-hundred-mile round trips to Perrigo's Toledo office to address our maladies. I had become obsessed with the numbers of my blood pressure and was phoning his office regularly to report the figures. Distance between Fort Wayne and Toledo made for an impossible situation, and I switched for a few years to a Fort Wayne cardiologist who was wondering why an out-of-town physician was treating so many people in Fort Wayne. Since the blood pressure episode, I, like the rest of an aging humanity, began to see a family physician biannually and now only annually. In retrospect, I became annoyed by the process, but Eugene Klug's wife, Dorothy, a registered nurse, reminded me, without the traveling clinic I might have remained ignorant of the high blood pressure.

Waldo Werning over time became an issue for me, Robert Preus and the board of regents. Since he was a staff member and not a faculty member, I notified him that he had improperly attended a joint seminary faculty meeting with St. Louis. In response, he boasted of his success in bringing those who disagree with him down to his terms. This was nothing else than a threat that characterized much of his correspondence to me and others. Here are a few excerpts:

> In my life, I've had to deal with various people in high Synodical office and Synodical Boards and have not hesitated doing what my conscience compels me to do on the basis of the Word of God. When my determination was tested, individuals and boards have themselves painted in a corner. I have gotten a favorable ruling from the Synod's Board of Judication [sic!] and also a private letter from Synod's President (asking for forgiveness) in the past year. Cleaning the slate has given good relations again and I believe given the parties joy in their life, assurance that other people in Synod would not be treated the same way. I wish only joy and happiness in your work for you.[2]

---

2. Waldo Werning, memo to David Scaer, January 4, 1987.

It is hard to avoid the conclusion that Werning was intent on my removal long before he brought his formal charges. Only one year after I became academic dean, Werning began asking students in my classes to gather information from the lectures which might be used against me. Bradley Smith (b. 1961), a 1988 seminary graduate, informed me that Arthur J. "Art" Bode regularly reported on me to Werning. Outside the chapel on October 12, 1987, without mentioning Werning, I asked Bode about his supplying material about me to others and whether this was the Christian thing to do. He replied that as a student, he was without rights and so could not speak to me directly. Several times he had been requested to gather information on me. When I asked him to justify his behavior, he replied that it was a the duty of Christians to correct one another.

Werning began having questions about my article "Sanctification in Lutheran Theology"[3] and approached me directly and by letters. This was followed by a letter dated September 1, 1988, to the board of regents, without a copy to me, questioning my fitness and claiming that I had no faith.

In the summer, Werning had informed Robert Newton and Eugene Bunkowske that he was going to bring charges against me. Bunkowske had told Jim Voelz, who in turned informed Robert Preus. At the annual faculty Labor Day picnic in 1988, Preus then informed me of Werning's impending suit against me. During the previous year or so, Werning had been writing letters to me, and since that year I was without an assistant in the academic dean's office, I had let the matter slide.

Robert Preus told me that Werning was serious and would not be put off. Hoping to avert this and looking for a peaceful solution, I phoned Werning and arranged to meet him for lunch on Tuesday, September 6, at the Town Hall restaurant in the Canterbury Green shopping center on the southwest quadrant of St. Joe and St. Joe River Roads. After lunch with an amiable conversation, he handed me the charges in a sealed envelope. Werning had sent another copy of the charges in an envelope postmarked the same day, September 6, to my summer address in the Poconos.[4] At its

---

3. *Concordia Theological Quarterly* 49 (April–July 1985): 181–95, http://www.ctsfw.net/media/pdfs/scaersanctificationinlutherantheology.pdf.
4. Synodical bylaws governing charges required that they not be shared until the matter is resolved. At the time I was not versed in these matters and did not ask Werning about his having told Newton and perhaps others. Four colleagues knew of the charges against me before I did. In these cases, Waldo claimed that persons he consulted were his "confidants," and other cases brought into adjudication may show that he found himself justified in doing this. Confidants were never named or numbered.

September 26, 1988 regular business meeting, the faculty passed a resolution that my article "Sanctification in Lutheran Theology" "neither contains nor promotes any false doctrine." This should have been the end of it, but it was not.

Before September 7, 1988, a day that would be remembered for the misery it brought on me, Werning had approached my colleagues Harold Buls, Otto Stahlke and Waldemar Degner to join him in bringing charges against me on the basis of a faculty essay, but they refused. At a faculty meeting on December 5, 1989, Harry Buls told of Werning's soliciting my colleagues to join him in his charges against me. At center of the meeting was an essay that later appeared as "The Relation of Matthew 28:16–20 to the Rest of the Gospel."[5] It argued that the Gospel's last four verses were not a later addition, but were written by the evangelist. Spoken to the eleven disciples, they established the ministry, hardly a radical view, as it was held by the classical Lutheran theologians of the sixteenth and seventeenth centuries. It also part of the synod's rite of ordination. An opposing and widely held view was that these words gave all Christians the ministry. This was called the Great Commission.

Customarily, Waldo Werning went after his victims with his understanding of Matthew 18 that all that was required was to make an accusation and then in the second step to bring two or three others to testify that the accuser made his accusation to the one accused. Werning said he was taking the second step of Matthew 18 with me and bringing two or three witnesses to confront me with transgression.[6] Matthew 18:16 requires that the accuser find one or two other people who agree to the accusations as witnesses. Werning took the passage to mean that his accusation was valid if he made it in the presence of others. Werning's consultants were those whom he consulted before bringing the accusation to the alleged offender. Werning boasted that his "confidants" were highly placed and regarded synodical and district officials. While he never divulged their identity or their number, he gave good reason to assume that some were members of the praesidium and Fort Wayne faculty, among whom was certainly Howard Tepker.

In a two hour and fifteen-minute meeting in my office, he took exception to my January symposium lecture.[7] My sins were my saying all theology was Christology and my canceling his courses for the coming

---

5. Concordia Theological Quarterly 55 (October 1991): 245–67, http://www.ctsfw. net/media/pdfs/scaerrelationofmatthew.pdf.
6. Waldo Werning, memo to David Scaer, August 11, 1988.
7. Waldo Werning, memo to David Scaer, August 11, 1988.

academic year. Waldo Werning concluded that my holding that all theology is Christology was reason enough to charge me with having a defective doctrine of the Trinity. Robert Preus, who had defended me on this Christological statement, was fighting for his life as president and as a member of the faculty and synod. I felt more alone and defenseless than ever. The faculty had spoken in my defense, but that voice became muted. Noticeably silent was the St. Louis seminary faculty or any of its members. Had a praesidium member or that faculty or one of its members affirmed the orthodoxy of my Christological statement, charges against me would have come to a screeching halt. No one in St. Louis said anything.

The formal charges came right after Labor Day. Werning expressed his regret that "his conscience compelled [him] to bring charges against [me] before the LCMS Commission on Adjudication." The same note says that he "is not sending copies of the documentation [to me] because you [I] have shared Matthew 18 [sic] and attempts at private communication with whatever public you [I] chose." Werning adds this classic sentence: "I do not want to put any temptation before you to continue that practice."[8]

His argument completely reversed the meaning of the passage that protects the accused by requiring others to attest to the alleged offense. His misunderstanding of Matthew 18 was reason enough to dismiss his entire enterprise against me and raise questions of his remaining in the synod.

Colleague Dean Wenthe circulated a petition, dated September 22, 1988, supporting me. A few months later, twenty-one faculty members put their signatures on a petition in support of Robert Preus. Wenthe garnered twenty six signatures for me. Signing the petition were Dean Wenthe, Richard Muller, Walter Maier II, Jan Case, Jim Bollhagen, Marty Stahl (b. 1949), Cameron Mackenzie, Randy Schroeder, Don Deffner, Hank Kadai, Dan Reuning, Art Just, Jim Voelz, Bill Weinrich, G. Waldemar Degner, Kurt Marquart, Bob Newton, Doug Judisch, Harold Zietlow, Harold Buls, Bill Houser and John Saleska.

A faculty committee consisting of Eugene Bunkowske, Norbert H. Mueller, Daniel Reuning, Bill Weinrich and Dean Wenthe reported to the board that I was not guilty of Werning's charges, and they attested to my character and doctrine. On the basis of this report and faculty action on September 26, the board of regents on November 12, 1988, said Werning's case against me was closed.

In this particularly dark time of my life, September 14, 1988, I received an encouraging letter from Cameron MacKenzie, written when he heard

---

8. Waldo Werning, memo to David Scaer, August 23, 1989.

Preus's announcement that concerns about me had been brought to the regents.

> This indeed is unfortunate and unfair. I, for one, but I know I speak for many, appreciate very much the time, work, and thought you have put into your office; and your dedication to this school and its students is obvious to all. I also appreciate the encouragement you have given to me to complete my degree and to all the faculty to make our school a first class theological and academic institution. I hope that the present difficulties will not discourage you, and I pray that God will uphold you as you carry out His work.

Another letter came from Don Deffner.

> It grieved me Saturday at the end of the faculty meeting to hear someone had made some negative comments about you. This is just a note of personal support for you personally, and in appreciation for the aggressive leadership you have been giving the seminary as academic dean.[9]

Art Just wrote to Preus:

> As Academic Dean, Dr. Scaer provides the faculty with both pastoral and scholarly leadership. He is keen on the pursuit of excellence for himself and the faculty, supporting in every way possible so that we might carry out our task to the best of our abilities.

Then Art adds that the coming year (1988–1989)

> ... promises to be the best one yet under his leadership because of his efforts in shaping this faculty to be the finest seminary faculty in the world.[10]

The next day, Dean O. Wenthe wrote Preus that I bring "a crisp theological vision that combines both orthodoxy and creativity... David Scaer is doing a great job as Academic Dean. You and the board can be proud of him."[11]

In a November 12, 1998 resolution, the board of regents incorporated part of the memo from Preus that "presents in a loving and truthful manner both the evident blessings God has given to the Church through his servant, Dr. David Scaer, along with *his occasional shortcomings* ... "(Italics added.) In the face of formidable charges, support for me was remarkable, and it was a relief to know that my shortcomings were occasional though not specified. It looked as if a bad episode was behind me. I was wrong.

---

9. Donald Degner, letter to David Scaer, September 11, 1988.
10. Arthur A. Just Jr., letter to Robert Preus, September 11, 1988.
11. Dean O. Wenthe, letter to Robert Preus, September 12, 1988.

By himself, Waldo Werning would not have been a significant factor, but he would become a rallying point for those working for a change in the Fort Wayne seminary. Some of the names on the petition supporting me would soon work to remove Preus, but opposition to him had not jelled.

THE WERNING CHARGES IN THE LCMS COURTS

In summer of 1988 Ray Schkade,[12] the executive director of the Texas District, wrote me asking about Waldo Werning's status at the seminary and, in the same letter, questioned Robert Schaibley's qualifications to teach courses in practical theology.[13] Schkade sent a follow-up note asking for a response.[14] He also complained about having non-Lutherans speak on the campus, probably a less-than-oblique reference to the annual January Symposium on the Lutheran Confessions.[15] Robert Preus thought that Schkade was using Waldo Werning for his purposes. Preus says of Schkade that "he is one mean person" and refers to Werning's character assassination of me and his poisoning of Werning's mind.

Preus instructed me to write to Schkade that "Dr. Werning is highly respected by Dr. Preus and Waldo has a very prominent place in the teaching of the Seminary, especially since he is not a faculty member." At this time, Preus was unaware of Werning's motives or that Schkade might be serving Werning's purposes. I wrote Schkade that Schaibley had a master of theology degree from Trinity, Deerfield, Illinois, and was pursuing a Ph.D. at Purdue University and was thus qualified to teach, but in the meantime he asked to be relieved of teaching seminary responsibilities for health reasons and to complete his work at Purdue.[16]

By May 1988 the seminary board had decided that Werning would no longer be teaching. Werning interpreted his termination as his being "placed on Emeritus status beginning September 1, 1988." No such action was taken by the board, but if it had, Werning would have had the privileges of a faculty member without the responsibilities.

---

12. In a December 31, 1987 memo, Waldo had wanted me to apologize to Schkade "for the offense which he took at your statements in your presentation in Texas."
13. Ray Schkade, letter to David Scaer, July 25, 1988.
14. Ray Schkade, letter to David Scaer, September 20, 1988.
15. Robert Preus, memo to David Scaer, January 29, 1988.
16. David Scaer, letter to Ray Schkade, September 26, 1988. A year later, in December 1989, when I was no longer academic dean, Pastor Schaibley would assist me in preparing responses to charges formally made by Werning in September 1988.

Waldo Werning brought formal charges against me in September 1988.[17] He claimed that my statement "all theology is Christology" amounted to heresy. Our theologians knew that Lutheran theology is christological in its content in a way that Reformed and Arminian theologies are not. A solution to my dilemma would have been my citing *The Brief Statement*,[18] but this thought only came to me twenty years later.

Luther and the Lutheran theologians had said some of the same things in some of the same language about Christology that I said. Charges leveled against me were so trivial in that the accuser had a faulty understanding of the Trinity and Christ. The charges were serious in that the intent was to remove me from the deanship and the seminary. Begun was a politically motivated process, and at no point was the conversation with Werning theologically informed. Eugene Klug knew this and only called it off in December 1989 when he or his superiors concluded that Werning had no grounds to stand on.

A person with real theological concerns would have seen my statement in the light of what I had written elsewhere. This controversy, which began in earnest in 1985, would take four years to come to a tentative end in 1989, but only in 1992 was it announced that a satisfactory conclusion was reached after faculty review. Thus it took seven years to resolve the matter.

With so much and so many important things to do, this was for me a huge waste of time. Behind Waldo Werning's charges was a man with a bitter spirit for not having been offered a faculty position and then being slowly eliminated from his seminary staff position. Refusing later to let Robert Preus sign my agreement with him of December 19, 1989, shows his goals were not theological. Werning could not have advanced as far as he did and for as long as he did without the backing of others who for their own reasons wanted to rid the seminary of Preus. I was collateral damage.

This Christology controversy also played itself out on the pages of *The Reporter*, the synod's official publication. It also was chronicled in the widely circulated and, for some, the influential *Christian News*, which printed Werning's charges against me—just four days after he had handed them to me.[19] Electronic communication was still in its infancy. Per-

---

17. His story is told in his book Waldo J. Werning, *Making the Missouri Synod Functional Again* (Fort Wayne, IN: Biblical Renewal Publications, 1992).
18. Evangelical Lutheran Synod of Missouri, Ohio and Other States, *Brief Statement of the Doctrinal Position of the Missouri Synod* (St. Louis, Missouri: Concordia Publishing House, 1932).
19. *Christian News*, September 11, 1989.

haps they were hand delivered to *Christian News*, but more likely they were sent by priority mail.

The Reporter informed the Missouri Synod's rank and file that I had been accused of false doctrine, when in fact I had been found innocent by the seminary's faculty and board. "Werning, now a private stewardship consultant, has charged Scaer, currently acting chairman of the seminary's systematic department with false teaching and other violations."[20] Readers were left to their own imaginations to determine what the false teaching and alleged violations were. This was never done, since afterwards *The Reporter* never informed its readers that the charges were bogus.

Waldo Werning claimed that he pleaded with the editor not to print the document with the charges against me before he gave them to me, but unanswered is how *Christian News* got the charges. One of his confidants might have done it. His doctrine of "confidants" let things be brought out in the public without, in his mind, offending the procedures of Matthew 18 of speaking first to the accused.

The front pages of its November 13, 1989, issue of *The Reporter* featured an article about Preus and me. It stated that Waldo Werning had "charged Scaer ... with false teaching and other violations." An article like that could not have appeared without the foreknowledge of synod president Ralph Bohlmann, and if it did, he had the obligation to rectify matters. Signs of a conspiracy began to emerge.

The synod's handbook holds that if a charge is made public before adjudication has taken place, the charge is to be dismissed, but in giving the charges to *Christian News*, Werning had done just that. I had been tried and found guilty in print before the entire Missouri Synod, and a retraction was never made. Werning had found an accomplice in the editor of *Christian News*.

In the Missouri Synod, charges are filed with the Commission on Adjudication and, upon request, reviewed by the Commission on Appeals. At first I did not consider the charges Werning had filed against me with the synod's Commission on Adjudication to be that serious. Werning was habituated to filing charges on most anyone with whom he had a disagreement. This was not atypical for him. He handed me the charges on the Tuesday following Labor Day 1989, almost a month after he filed them with the commission. By sharing them with Eugene Bunkowske before giving them to me, he already had invalidated his case against me. When confronted with having broken the synod rules in sharing his charges with

---

20. *The Reporter*, November 13, 1989.

others, he argued that he was not responsible for what others did with the information he had given them. Around this time Voelz and Bunkowske were interested in language and collaborating on some kind of linguistic project. When confronted, Bunkowske denied he was one of Werning's confidants, but Werning claimed he was. Bunkowske's association with Voelz meant the news got to Preus and then to me.

As all these things were happening, I wondered to myself why one of Werning's confidants did not rein him in, unless they were using him for their own purposes. It was coming to light that Howard Tepker and Erich Kiehl (1920–2012), hailed as stalwarts in the cause for conservative theology in the synod during the 1970s, were among Werning's confidants.

Within two weeks after charges asking for my removal were leveled against me, twenty-four of my colleagues, nearly 90 percent of faculty, signed a petition saying they "recognize no sufficient reason for calling into question either the competency or suitability of our colleague." They affixed their names in this order: Dean O. Wenthe, Richard E. Muller, Walter A. Maier II, J. C. Case, James Bollhagen, Martin R. Stahl, Cameron A. MacKenzie, Randall Schroeder, Donald L. Deffner, Heino Kadai, Eugene Bunkowske, Daniel G. Reuning, Arthur A. Just Jr., James W. Voelz, William C. Weinrich, W. Degner, Kurt Marquart, Norbert H. Mueller, Robert Newton, Douglas Judisch, Harold Zietlow, Harold H. Buls, W. G. Houser and John Saleska. If there was a conspiracy at this time, it hadn't reached into the faculty.

The only full-time professor not signing was Melvin L. Zilz. Emeriti professors Eugene Klug, Howard Tepker, and Raymond Surburg did not sign (they may not have been asked), but at this time Klug and Tepker were already closely aligned with Werning. Buls was retired and signed. Names on the list included those who in previous petitions had supported Robert Preus, and even a few who had called aspects of his presidency into question.

This near-unanimous faculty support may have indicated that in the face of the accusation about my competency as dean, I was found to be evenhanded in the conduct of my office. Also boding well for the future was the positive response on November 3, 1988, to my report on the seminary from Rudolf C. "Rudy" Block, director of curriculum services for the synod's Board for Higher Education Services.

During the fall term of the 1988–1989 year, a faculty committee, the faculty, a committee appointed by the regents and the regents themselves found the charges leveled by Werning against me were not justified. Yet the charges were resurrected in December 1989, and an accommodation for all parties concerned was found, but by that time Robert Preus had been replaced by Norb Mueller as an interim president, and I was replaced as dean by Walter A. Maier II.

In the fall of 1989, Waldo Werning continued to barrage me with accusing letters, and in desperation I approached Norbert Mueller to get him off my back. Werning's letters were countless and long, and each raised more issues. At this point, Ralph Bohlmann wrote a letter to Norb Mueller to bring peace in this matter, and so Mueller wrote Werning, asking him to abridge his charges.[21] Mueller appointed a committee of "gray heads," meaning that age brought the wisdom needed to resolve differences. Howard Tepker, John Saleska and Eugene Klug, the chairman, were Mueller's "gray heads." Inclusion of Tepker, a Werning advisor and confidant, was the first signal the committee of "gray heads" was stacked and I would be subjected to a kangaroo court. At my request, Tepker was removed from the committee.

Denied was an additional request to remove the committee chairman, Eugene Klug. In response to my request to remove Klug, Norbert Mueller told me point blank that I was not going to choose the committee to examine me, but it did look like my accuser Waldo Werning had been given this privilege. As originally constituted, the committee consisted of two members who were convinced supporters of Werning and one sympathizer. Appointed in place of Tepker was Cameron Mackenzie, whom Werning found acceptable.

For a moment, let's consider the circumstances. What the faculty found unacceptable in Werning's accusations against me on several occasions a year earlier was made the basis of my having to defend myself. Waldo, who had been the accuser, was now the judge, making the accusations and determining the legal process. I was being tried for things of which I had been exonerated.

Cameron MacKenzie sent a memo to Walter A. Maier II asking him to inform *The Reporter* that "the Faculty on one occasion did review a Scaer article charged as heretical and found that it did not contain false doctrine."[22] MacKenzie added that he was "willing to write as a faculty member but perhaps a more formal response if required," i.e., a faculty statement would be a counterweight to what the article in *The Reporter* claimed. A copy of MacKenzie's letter was sent to Norbert Mueller, who wrote on the bottom of a photocopy, "WAM called Cameron in response

---

21. Norbert Mueller, letter to Waldo Werning, November 29, 1989.
22. Cameron MacKenzie, memo to Walter A. Maier II, November 17, 1989.

to this memo:[23] "We must first find out Waldo's charges vs. Scaer before sem administration can defend Scaer."

Both Maier II and Mueller knew very well what Werning's charges were, and that they had been dismissed by the faculty. A year before both Mueller and Maier II voted to support the faculty resolution that found Werning's charges against me to be baseless, and Norb was even a member of the committee that brought the resolution to the faculty. Now they remained silent and did not step forward with not only what they knew, but what they had agreed to.

Nothing about my vindication appeared in *The Reporter*. It was hard for me not to think that the seminary administration of Mueller and Maier II and highly-placed synodical officials were in collusion. What was a minor blip on the screen in December 1988 took on huge proportions. Mueller wanted to be on the winning side, and now that was highly placed officials on the praesidium.

Norbert Mueller soon wrote a letter to Werning and me with copies to Klug, Mackenzie and Saleska that they had been appointed "to expedite the informal reconciliation process" and that "we could joyfully clear this whole matter before the Christmas holidays."[24] The only meeting was held on the afternoon of December 4, 1989, in Luther Hall, with Klug, Saleska, Mackenzie, Werning and myself present and Norbert Mueller opening with prayer. In medieval England and Europe a chaplain was provided for the accused before his execution. Here was something resembling the Star Chamber. On leaving the room before the conversation began, Mueller explained that this was "not a judicial proceeding," which Klug in fact soon allowed it to become.

Several times during the meeting, Werning insisted that his issues against me had to be settled by January 1990, but he did not give any reasons for this. Before leaving the room, Norbert Mueller repeatedly made the point that any report issuing from this meeting would not be used in any future procedures. Cameron MacKenzie made the point that we had come together as friends, but the occasion resembled an inquisition. Klug said that the meeting would not go beyond three-thirty or four o'clock.

As soon as the meeting began, Werning began to distribute a printed list of questions which I was supposed to answer. I objected to this, since

---

23. Walter A. Maier II, phone conversation with Cameron MacKenzie, November 21, 1989.
24. Norbert Mueller, letter to Waldo Werning, November 29, 1989.

I could put myself in a position of self-incrimination. This was neither a meeting of friends nor a conversation as Mueller had promised.

Eugene Klug said he saw no problem with Werning distributing written questions. I responded I would leave the room if Werning were allowed to distribute the questions. This procedure was all too similar to a department meeting in Howard Tepker's home where Klug wanted me to defend my essay "Baptism and the Lord's Supper."[25] After some thought on that evening, I said would respond to someone else's critique, but I would not say anything more than what I had written. In that case, Richard Muller and Tepker reported at the next meeting that nothing wrong was found in the essay.

Now at this meeting, I did agree to answer Werning's prepared questions as he read them. Even this was totally unfair and unethical in having the accused present evidence against himself, but this is the procedure Klug allowed. As the accuser, Werning was obligated to present his case against me. This was not mine to do. It became evident minute by minute that his claim to have confidants in high places was not empty boasting—and the high places were really high. It is likely that synod president Bohlmann was kept abreast and provided counsel.

The first question was a setup for incriminating myself. I deliberately responded with long answers. Werning caught this and said that I was trying to run the clock out, which I was. My other choice was to put my neck into Werning's noose, which he began tightening four years before and which he would continue to do long after this meeting was over. When I questioned Werning, he responded that he was asking the questions and I was not. Does anyone know a case, at least in American law, where the accused is not allowed to question the prosecution's witnesses? I knew what the psalmist meant when he felt like a bird in the fowler's net.

After each of my answers, Werning came back with another question to which MacKenzie asked Werning, "Why aren't Scaer's answers good enough for you?" He also asked Werning whether "Scaer was a heretic," to which Werning responded no. Mackenzie asked Werning "Then what are you looking for?" Eugene Klug entered the conversation by saying that the "all theology is Christology" statement was "exclusive," "ill worded," "an overstatement" and "a misstatement," but never explained why. Waldo Werning responded that the Christology statement must be rejected as

---

25. David P. Scaer, "Baptism and the Lord's Supper in the Life of the Church," *Concordia Theological Quarterly* 45, no. 1–2 (January 1981): 37–59, http://www.ctsfw.net/media/pdfs/scaerbaptismandthelordssupper.pdf.

"untenable." Klug responded that it was "peculiar" and "exclusive." Klug was giving all the signs that he also was a Werning confidant, which he was, and which I already knew.

When Cameron MacKenzie asked for the clarifications from Werning, he was challenged by Werning for daring to ask him a question. In one of my responses I used the word *perichoresis*, a term used in Christology and in Trinitarian theology to describe how the divine and human natures exist within one another and how one person of the Trinity is within and is accompanied with the other two. So the statement that "all theology is Christology" does not exclude the Father and the Spirit. Waldo Werning did not know what *perichoresis* meant and complained that I had introduced a theological term into the discussion. This word *perichoresis* was what the debate was all about, and Werning did not know this word was used to describe interrelation of Christ's human and divine natures in one person and of the interrelation of the persons of the Trinity, e.g. John 14:10–11, "Do you not believe that I am in the Father and the Father in me? The words that I say to you I do not speak on my own authority; but the Father who dwells in me does his works. Believe me that I am in the Father and the Father in Me."

The meeting that was to go only to three-thirty PM had gone to five-thirty. Seeing that we were getting nowhere, Eugene Klug called the now three-hour meeting to a halt. We would not go through the dinner hour. John Saleska did not participate in the discussion, as I remember, but shook his head in disbelief as Werning kept firing the questions. Saleska had pain all over his face when Werning in his questioning went after me. Mackenzie often pleaded for fairness, thus indicating that the procedure was anything but fair. Never was there any indication that Saleska was in collusion with Werning, but his silence was of no help or comfort to me.

Should it be asked why I do not remember the questions or did not take notes, the obvious answer was that my life was literally on the line. My mind was too busy coming to terms with the questions and then answering. No recorder was present for a trial that was advertised as a conversation. I was without counsel. In his *Making the Missouri Synod Functional Again*, Werning, who provides data of all kinds from August 1988 to December 1989, makes no reference to the December 4 meeting.[26] Klug did recognize that after about three hours nothing was accomplished, and this may be the reason that I received a phone call from him in two weeks.

---

26. *Making the Missouri Synod Functional Again*, 207–243.

Around eight o'clock AM on December 19, 1989, I received a phone call at home from Klug that Waldo Werning wanted to conclude matters between us with an agreement. For the first part of the morning, negotiations were conducted by phone. My ignorance of the circumstances that brought this arrangement about shows how naïve I was. In retrospect, this was no chance happening, but Klug and Waldo had connived it in consultation with Norb Mueller, and it may have been that Ralph Bohlmann thought the whole scheme up. Waldo Werning and I remained at our homes each speaking separately with Klug by phone, who was in his office on the third floor of Jerome Hall. At midday I came over to my seminary office, which was a few steps down from Klug's office, to more easily facilitate the writing of an agreement.

During the day, I was in contact by phone with Robert Schaibley, the pastor of Zion Lutheran Church in Fort Wayne, a former student and now my advisor. Art Just provided inestimable help. His office was located on the third floor directly across from Klug's and so also up the stairs from mine. Weinrich, whose office was also on the third floor diagonally across the hall from Klug's, was counseling a student and entered the conversation from time to time.

Since my professional life was at stake, I kept hoping that Weinrich would have provided more direct help. In late afternoon, after an agreement had been hammered out, Weinrich came into Klug's room, read it and said "we are not going to sign this." Just was counseling a mediating position in the Christology statement. Not so Weinrich. Of course, he was not legally involved as I was, but he felt that he was involved in the theological issue. In the face of Weinrich's forcefulness, Werning backed down—big time.

I agreed to and Werning accepted the following: "Any attempt to make Christology preliminary to theology, or even its most important, but not *its primary, central core in the light of which all articles of faith are interpreted*, is a denial of Luther's doctrine and effectively destroys the Gospel as the message of a completed atonement."[27] The italicized section replaced "... its only part." And so Werning was "satisfied that no exclusion of the Trinity was intended or suggested in the original wording."[28]

Having been vindicated now for a third time, or was it fourth or fifth time, that night I went home a relieved man. This meeting was not billed as a follow-up to the December 4 meeting, but Mackenzie and Saleska, as participants in that meeting, were called in later in the day.

---

27. Emphasis original.
28. In his *Making the Missouri Synod Functional Again* Werning speaks of the

At first I thought that perhaps Klug and Werning had run by chance into one another, since they lived scarcely a block apart, but things rarely happen by chance. Another plausible explanation was that continued action against me leading to my exclusion from the seminary and synod would impede the board's attempts to keep Preus from regaining the seminary presidency. Attempts to marginalize me would continue right through the end of Norb Mueller's administration in July 1994.

Another scenario for calling the December 19 meeting was that Eugene Klug may have thought that I had been beaten up enough and persuaded Werning to back off. But Werning kept harassing me with direct conversations and letters for years. Klug had been the relentless hammer at the New Orleans convention, which had brought Tietjen and St. Louis seminary faculty majority to its knees in July 1973. A determined person, he could use his talents in any situation, and this may have been the case with his dealing with Werning. Since Ralph Bohlmann had been involved in matters since the time he announced an investigation of the seminary in May 1984 up to Preus's dismissal in 1989, there would be no good reason not to conclude that he had his reasons for bringing the Werning matter to a conclusion.

A day after signing the agreement, we headed to New York to see my mother, then seventy-nine and living in Douglaston, New York, in an apartment next to my aunt's. Few trips could have been happier than that one.

Following his custom, Robert Preus had left Fort Wayne for Gunflint Lake, Minnesota, for the Christmas-New Year's Break (1989–1990). Waldo Werning had now brought charges against Preus for his defense of my Christological statement. When Robert Preus heard of my settlement with Werning, he phoned me in Fort Wayne to see how he could sign it. Werning would not allow it. This shows the matter was not really a theological issue but a political one for Waldo.

My discovery of what was happening behind the scenes calls for a reevaluation of the two December 1989 meetings with Werning, both involving Eugene Klug as a mediator. I do not recall Norb Mueller at any

---

December 19, 1989 agreement, but not of the meeting or its circumstances (243). At the end of the meeting Schaibley and Weinrich noted that Werning had conceded my position that all theology is Christology: "I was satisfied that no exclusion of the Trinity was intended or suggested in the original wording." Werning adds, "The statement I [he] signed was far from satisfactory, but since it took Dr. Scaer a long time to come this far, I felt that he would have the good will to change his view and I forgave him."

time saying that the reconstituted seminary board had rescinded the decision of the previous board in dismissing Werning's charges against me. Now it appears in arranging a meeting with me and Werning on December 4 that Norb Mueller had anticipated the board allowing Werning to reinstate his charges against me. It is not unlikely that he may have already placed it on the board's agenda for its December 14 meeting.

Since the December 4 meeting with Werning failed to have the desired outcome, Mueller contacted Klug to clear things with me on December 19, 1989, one day after the board passed a formal resolution that let Werning charge me once again. Naively, I thought Werning may have had a change of heart, but it is more likely it had been maneuvered by Mueller in collaboration with Klug and Werning.

Though Waldo Werning and I came to an accommodation, he continued to use colleagues, administrators and students to pursue his case against me. One day in 1990, in the coffee hour in the dining room following the chapel service, student Charles Brooks introduced himself to me. Before then I did not know him. This later proved to be entrapment in which he would report to Werning what I would say about him. Brooks told me that the files of the synod adjudication of Preus were in the library and that he would be happy to accompany me to the library to show me where they were. He went behind the checkout desk to retrieve the papers, which were not the synod adjudication papers, but Preus's civil case against the seminary in Allen County court from September 1989.

In looking through the papers, I told Brooks that everything in the file had been public knowledge for a year. Brooks then said that he was so incensed about how Preus was handled and that in his behalf he would cause disruption on campus. I advised him against it. The next day, Brooks found me and thanked me for my advice. Brooks then reported my conversation with him to Werning, who then came to my study on October 31, 1990, about eleven o'clock AM, to confront me with things which I had supposedly said to Brooks. He stood in the hall and I stood in my office.

Waldo was speaking from notes and at the same time was taking notes. When asked about his note-taking, he replied that this was a good thing. Werning asked me to explain why Bob Schaibley said that he, Werning, had bullied me into signing the December 19, 1989 document. Waldo was known for and admitted to making threats to those who did not give him what he wanted.[29] According to Werning, I replied that I was not ac-

---

29. The Association of American Lutheran Churches (AALC), a break-off group from the old American Lutheran Church with less than a hundred

countable for what others said and hence I was unable to offer an explanation.[30] Werning wanted to meet with me and Brooks. My first reply was no. Then I said I would do it and continued to say that Werning had damaged me and my family and that he continued to be intent in catching me saying something he could he use against me. Waldo retorted that he was the one victimized. Dan Gard, whose office was up the stairs, heard the entire conversation.

During the October 31, 1990 conversation, Waldo Werning said that I had shown Brooks the December 19, 1989 document we had signed. This was categorically untrue. I did not carry the document around and had not shown it to anyone, though it did have the character of a public document. My meetings with Brooks were outside the chapel and the library, in public places, not in my study. In working to get me to revise the Christological statement that all theology is Christology, Werning had no difficulty in sharing the document with those he wanted to impress. He allowed himself to share the document with others, but did not allow me this same privilege, even though I had not done it. It is likely that Werning, in discussing the document with Brooks, had showed it to him.

The meeting Werning wanted with himself, me and Charles Brooks never took place since Brooks was dismissed from the seminary for misrepresentation on his seminary applications discovered by registrar Lowell Fein. Brooks had been a member of the Lutheran church south of Manchester, New Hampshire, but rarely attended, since he was the organist at the Congregational Church in Amherst, a typically beautiful New England town. He was an accomplished organist and had listed a doctor's degree from an English university in music, which was later

---

congregations, established fellowship with the LCMS and located their office in Augustine Hall on the seminary campus. Shortly after establishing fellowship with the LCMS, it held a convention at which Werning was the speaker. Financial arrangements had not been established, and the fee submitted by Werning was so exorbitant that it withdrew its invitation to him for the next gathering, something it had already agreed to. One day its president, who knew of how Werning had dealt with me, approached me about the matter. Werning was threatening a suit if the AALC did not follow through in having him address the next convocation. Its president asked me if I knew of any way of getting Waldo off his back. I did not.

30. Werning, *Making the Missouri Synod Functional Again*, 243. Werning sheds some light on who bullied whom. In his adjudication hearing, Preus said in the presence of Schaibley that Werning had bullied me into signing the December 1989 document. Bullied or not, as mentioned, Preus wanted to sign on to the document. Waldo wanted me to meet with him and Brooks.

discovered not to award this degree. Other matters may have led to his dismissal. He was discontinued from the seminary and was accepted into Trinity Seminary in Columbus, Ohio.

It is likely that Brooks had been recruited by Werning to introduce himself to me and engage me in conversation to get me to say that Werning was the cause of campus disruption. He reported our conversation back to Werning, who seems to have advised him to thank me. Werning admitted to conversations with Brooks.

While Werning's complaints against me were withdrawn at our December 19, 1989 meeting, his complaint against Robert Preus had to wait until March 15, 1990, to be resolved. Before the Commission on Adjudication convened the hearing in Chicago, Werning requested and received a postponement. Preus had brought his attorney with him from Fort Wayne to Chicago, so he was not only responsible for the attorney's hourly fee from the time he left his house until he returned, but he also had to pay for his airfare. There are no one-day round trip discount fares to Chicago.

A second meeting was set up for April 26–27, 1990, in Fort Wayne. In August 1990, the Commission on Adjudication found that the charges against Preus were without merit. Its decision refers to the testimonies of Wally Degner and Robert Newton made before the Commission on Adjudication, which vindicated Preus of breaking the Eighth Commandment in regard to Werning.

Since neither party to the case was satisfied with the outcome, the case went to the synod's Commission on Appeals which, in a January 17, 1991 ruling that found Werning's charges against Preus baseless, so Werning's request for a rehearing was dismissed. Of interest to me was that in the commission's ruling, it took note that both the faculty and the board had exonerated me of Werning's charges before the two meetings with Werning took place in December 1989, and so they were unnecessary. In other words I had gone through an unnecessary torture.

In determining whether Preus spoke disparagingly of Werning, the Commission on Appeals took note of an incident recorded in the report of the Commission on Adjudication that supposedly happened at a seminary faculty meeting on April 17, 1989. Here is how it was reported: "Dr. Waldo [sic!] Degner, a witness called by Werning, testified that in that meeting, Preus referred to Werning in a way that Degner guessed characterized Werning as a "fly in the ointment." Preus allegedly also called Werning "a lame duck."

Robert Newton, also called as a witness for Werning, did not have an opinion on whether the faculty resolution censuring Werning was right or wrong. Of particular interest to me what that in its July 17, 1991 ruling, the Commission of Appeals found that seminary board's reopening of Werning's charges against me were out of order.[31]

The Commission on Appeals makes a classic understatement concerning the case: this "is hardly deserving of hearing by an adjudication commission of the LCMS." Newton, another witness called by Werning, offered testimony that did not advance Werning's case against Preus. Robert Newton held that Matthew 18 was not to be invoked in a faculty member defending himself, as Werning claimed. He went on to say that the thirteen faculty members voting for April 1989 resolution supporting Robert Preus were not guilty of violating the Fourth Commandment, as Werning claimed. The Commission on Appeals also took note that Werning, who was concerned about others following the procedures of Matthew 18, had himself not followed them. It would have been nice if *The Reporter* would have mentioned this. It did not. Preus wrote to the seminary faculty and board and, among others, to Howard Tepker and Erich Kiehl with the news that the Commission on Appeals had vindicated him and had refused to entertain an appeal by Werning.[32]

WALDO WERNING AND *MAKING THE MISSOURI SYNOD FUNCTIONAL AGAIN*

By 1992, Werning's charges against me should have been a dead issue, but they weren't. He continued to be relentless in his long, single-spaced letters with their accusations that comprised much of the contents of his book *Making the Missouri Synod Functional Again*. In the spring of 1992, Waldo Werning sent copies of the book to each of the delegates to the synod convention in Pittsburgh. Kurt Marquart sent Waldo a scathing twelve-page critique on June 22, asking him to correct his errors and informing him that he would share this letter with anyone who asked about it.

The convention began on July 11 and ended on July 19. On the very next day, July 20, 1989, Werning wrote me that he "was sorry that it was necessary to share the problems about you [me] and others in my [his] book. These are actions which still are serious offenses which need to be

---

31. "A resolution by a reconstituted Board of Regents dated December 14, 1989, declaring that the Werning/Scaer matter was not closed since it was being dealt with in the adjudication process, was deemed for comment by the SCA [Synod Commission on Appeals]. Such belated resolution must be questioned as to its timeliness and also its correctness."
32. Robert Preus, letter to Concordia Theological Seminary Faculty, Board of Regents et al., April 6, 1991.

erased." He claimed that he "received hundreds of comments of appreciation about the book, and only at the Convention I have [he had] heard about seven or eight people of the mean 'Confessional Lutheran' political machine accuse and attacked me [him] illogically without evidence."

His claim was that others had given him more evidence to substantiate his concerns about me. His last sentence was a less than lightly veiled threat. "If you don't like them in print, you might want to consider changing your speech and actions. Grace and peace in our Lord Jesus Christ! Yours in Him, 'Waldo' [signed]. Waldo J. Werning."

He apparently was not satisfied with our agreement reached in December 1989 and was going to prolong his attacks. His writing this on the day after the convention showed he was confident that a newly organized seminary administration headed by Michael Stelmachowicz could be used to his advantage—and he was right.

During the subsequent years, Werning sent a barrage of letters with some of the same allegations as found in his book. Answering each one of the allegations would have taken a lifetime, but one claim about my sponsoring a party is of note and was a complete fabrication, as he admitted to Walter A. Maier III, whose father had been serving in my place as academic dean. Werning's allegations were so egregious that I read a statement at a faculty meeting disclaiming them as totally false with the hope that my colleagues would conclude that the entire book was not only mean-spirited, but more importantly fundamentally untrue and should be dismissed. All the while, Werning was being invited by some colleagues into their classes as a guest lecturer.

Making matters worse was that Werning's book was recommended before the 1991 synod convention by Michigan District president John Heins and Pacific Southwest president Loren Kramer to their convention delegates. Along with a gratis copy, they sent a letter that delegates should consult it to know what was really happening at Fort Wayne. Later Kramer and I both served on the synod's Commission on Theology and Church Relations. This might have led to some tense moments, but it never did.

Hardly two weeks after the January 1993 symposium, Gene Bunkowske with Paul Jackson, a seminary librarian, approached me after a faculty meeting, at about five-twenty PM, to arrange a meeting to bring peace within the faculty in regard to Werning. Nothing was said about who would participate. Since handling the Werning matter would be the subject of the meeting, he would likely be there to pursue old and additional charges against me so that I would repent. If not, there might be reasons to remove me.

When I told Jackson that I was wary of still another meeting with Werning, he asked me how long I would keep hate in my heart. Though he framed his words as a question, Jackson was making an accusation. In turn I asked him how he knew what was in my heart and I assured him that I did not have hate in my heart toward anyone including Werning. Turning down my offer of a meeting on a Wednesday at four PM, Bunkowske agreed to a Friday meeting at the same time.

In another conversation outside the placement and vicarage offices on the mezzanine in Wyneken Hall, I said to Bunkowske that Werning had published his accusations against me in his book and then he had widely circulated it. Bunkowske responded that he had experienced other forms of pain. To this I responded that he had not been formally charged. When I informed Bunkowske that Jackson said that I had hate in my heart, he replied, how could I blame him, since I had instigated the situation.

On the same day that Bunkowske and Jackson proposed their scheme to me, I told a longtime friend and younger colleague how distraught I was about having to relive the situation of being accused again by Werning in the meeting proposed by these two colleagues. My friend told me I could not expect vindication in the Werning matter, and in an evening phone conversation he affirmed what he said in the afternoon. In his view, I was the one at fault.

Also coming to light was that Robert Newton had approached Bill Weinrich with the proposal that Newton would persuade Werning to withdraw *Making the Missouri Synod Functional Again* and that Bunkowske would propose a faculty resolution vindicating Werning. Of course this soon would happen.

With a sense of being caught between two sides, I phoned board member Ray Mueller to tell him about my conversations with Bunkowske and Jackson and asked for his advice. He said that Jackson was on sabbatical at Indiana University working on a Ph.D. in library science, and during this time he was not to be involved in faculty affairs—but he was. Ray Mueller recommended that I seek the advice of Stelmachowicz, now the seminary's chief operating officer, Indiana District president Tim Sims or board member Melvin Bredemeier. At the previous board meeting, Bredemeier and Sims had expressed displeasure with Werning. Stelmachowicz encouraged the board not to reverse its decision to keep Werning from teaching in the spring term.

In case I needed him, Ray Mueller said he would be away for the weekend and could be reached at the home of Joseph Ardy. On Wednesday, February 3, 1993, at about twelve-thirty PM, I saw Indiana District president Tim Sims in the seminary dining room and asked him for advice in handling the Bunkowske-Jackson matter, as Ray Mueller suggested. Sims had no advice to offer, but went on to say that he had been in contact with George Black, pastor of Concordia Lutheran Church in Fort Wayne, who said he had succeeded in convincing Werning not to write me any more letters. To describe what Sims called "a huge pile of letters" Black had received from Werning, he stretched out his arms to make the point. Sims did not tell me why or how Black became involved with Werning.

Now to how George Black became involved with Waldo Werning. Norb Mueller had asked Black, as pastor of Concordia Lutheran Church, where Werning was a member, and Richard Radtke, as pastor of St. Paul's Lutheran Church in Fort Wayne, where Preus was a member, to resolve Werning's charges: that Preus was guilty of unchristian behavior toward Werning and of holding to false doctrine for defending my statement that all theology as Christology.

This was the approach Ralph Bohlmann suggested to Norb Mueller to resolve Werning's concerns with me. Preus was more of a concern to Bohlmann than I was. Radtke and Black interviewed both men and found that Werning's charges against Preus were baseless. This led Werning to charge Black with false doctrine for exonerating Preus for holding that all theology was Christology, and he phoned Black to arrange for a meeting in his office on the day before Christmas. So the year was probably 1990 or 1991. Werning intended to take the second step of Matthew 18, as he understood the procedure, and to do this he said he would bring along with him Eugene Bunkowske, whom he called his confidant, as a witness. Matthew 18 requires that two or three other people had seen or agreed that a moral infraction had taken place or heard the false teaching.

When asked by George Black, Bunkowske denied he was Werning's confidant, even though Werning said he was. Black said one of them was telling the truth and the other not. This becomes important since, when asked on February 1, 1993, Bunkowske denied that Werning was consulted in the meeting he and Paul Jackson were arranging with me. At past meetings Werning made threats that he had brought some of the synod's highest officials to their knees, and he was prepared to do the same with me if I did not repent. Such repentance, Werning said, had been therapeutic for those who repented, as it would be for me.

At one meeting with Werning, Black reported that a prominent Lutheran in Frankenmuth, Michigan, a fabled place in early Missouri Synod history, the home of St. Lorenz Church and Bonner's Christmas store and Zehnder's restaurant, had approached the treasurer of Concordia Church in Fort Wayne with a gift of $10,000 with the request that it be passed on to Werning. When Bob Roegner, an executive for synod missions, heard about this, he reported that Werning had done the same thing with him, but he also refused on both moral and legal grounds. George Black told the visitor from Frankenmuth that this was money laundering, in this case, to get tax deduction for a contribution. When Werning was confronted, he repented and went on to ask Black to repent of finding nothing wrong with the statement that all theology is Christology. In these meetings with Black and Radtke, Robert Preus apologized to Werning, if any way he had sinned against him. Werning accepted Preus's apology with the stipulation it be made public. As the years have passed, many others were accused by Werning of unchristian behavior and false teaching have come forward to tell of their experiences. They made peace with Werning from the fear that their ministerial careers would come to end.

It seems unlikely that Bohlmann was directly instructing Werning, but in the case of myself and Preus, he did nothing to dissuade Werning from his disastrous acts. Werning did serve the purposes of those who wanted to dispose of Preus and me, and so only when things got out of hand was it necessary to rein him in. What is more telling is that Norb Mueller told Black and Radtke not to tell anyone else that Werning's charges against Preus were baseless. Had that been revealed, the regents would have had one less reason for removing him, and Preus could have been returned to office. Then Norb Mueller would have had no other choice but to retire.

On Wednesday, February 3, at about four-fifteen PM, I stopped in at Stelmachowicz's office to alert him to what was happening, to seek advice from anyone I could. Stelmachowicz said that he was aware of the Jackson-Bunkowske initiative in arranging a meeting with Werning. In reply to my asking Bunkowske if he had met with Werning in proposing a meeting with me, he replied his last contact with him was about a month or two before the proposal was made. This turned out not to be so.

From the beginning Waldo Werning was in on the plan proposed by Bunkowske and Jackson. For the record, at the March faculty meeting, Stelmachowicz allowed a resolution to go through, removing the faculty's April 1989 censure of Werning.

Waldo Werning continued to be invited by some colleagues into their classes as a guest lecturer and remained in good social standing with them. Werning had won the day. He did not retract his book. It would have mattered little if he had; the damage in my case had been done.

Chapter Ten

INTERREGNUM

~

THE NORBERT MUELLER INTERIM PRESIDENCY

In the summer of 1989, my position as academic dean presented a problem to me. I consulted Father Baumgartner, an executive with the Association of Theological Schools, who helped with the renewal of our accreditation in 1984–1986 and whom I had come to know quite well. He assured me that when the president of an institution is removed, it behooves the academic dean to remain to provide continuity and stabilization.

In the summer of 1989, Daniel H. Fienen (b. 1952) of Holdrege, Nebraska, had raised the issue of women's ordination again.[1] At issue was my article on the validity of pastoral acts performed by women.[2] Earlier, in late August or early September 1988, Ralph Bohlmann, in a casual encounter, brought the matter up with me but without pursuing it. To summarize my argument: women's ordination should be viewed within the context of the feminization of a church. This has since proven to be the case with the ELCA and other LWF churches. Fienen reported that he had brought the matter up to the pastors in his circuit and said that he would represent me in sharing my responses to him made in a phone call that I initiated and later with the circuit.

It is a strange procedure for the accuser to take a kind of deposition in representing the accused to those before whom he made the accusations. Only in later correspondence was it learned that he had copied his letter to Nebraska District president Eldor Meyer (1929–2010), LCMS president Bohlmann's cousin. I would receive two more letters from Fienen, the first dated September 21, explicitly copied to Meyer, and circuit counselor Russell Sommerfeld, later district president, and the second dated September 29, 1989.

---

1. Daniel H. Fienen, letter to David Scaer, August 9, 1989.
2. David P. Scaer, "The Validity of the Churchly Acts of Ordained Women," *Concordia Theological Quarterly* 53, no. 1–2 (January 1989): 3–20, http://www.ctsfw.net/media/pdfs/scaervalidityofordainedwomen.pdf.

I explained to him that Gnostics had ordained women and promoted a feminized theology, and that the correlation could not be overlooked. I have never taught that ordination is a factor in making sacraments valid. I explicitly declined his offer to have him represent my views and said that I would be happy to meet with the pastors in his circuit. No response followed. Nothing came of it.[3] Whatever I wrote on these matters was for a discussion which never occurred. Reports from the synod's St. Louis headquarters surfaced that the "validity" article was the talk of the town, but no one approached me about it. Later Fienen expressed his views on women lectors in the *Concordia Journal*.

Over the years, the LCMS has moved closer to the Wisconsin Synod position on the ministry without formally adopting it. For tax purposes, and then for some theological reasons, pastors, teachers, directors of Christian education and others are lumped together as professional church workers for district conferences. *The Lutheran Annual* has two categories for ministers: minister-ordained and minister-commissioned. Biblically the term *minister*, in the formal sense, is reserved for apostles, and then the pastors who assumed their task of preaching the gospel. For some this distinction was lost. Two of my essays were the first in the synod to oppose the ordination of women and were included in an anthology of essays on the topic edited by synod president Matthew Harrison.[4] "The Validity of the Churchly Acts of Ordained Women" was not.

During much of the time between the board's July 1989 meeting and the opening of the school year, I was in the Poconos and Korea and had no direct knowledge of what was transpiring on campus. Later it came out that a shadow cabinet to replace Robert Preus administrators was being put in place. When Preus's case against the board was dismissed by the court, Norbert Mueller took over his position and moved into the president's office.

When the last classes of Concordia Senior College were taught in the spring of 1977, Robert Preus had moved into the vacated office of college president Hebert Bredemeier. Those passing through the second floor of the administration building could poke their heads in to see him. On or off the job, Preus was always ready to talk.

---

3. David Scaer, letter to Daniel Fienen, October 9, 1989.
4. "May Women Be Ordained as Pastors?" and "The Office of the Pastor and the Problem of the Ordination of Women Pastors," in *Women Pastors? The Ordination of Women in Biblical Lutheran Perspective*, ed. Matthew C. Harrison and John T. Pless (St. Louis, MO: Concordia Publishing House, 2009), 227–264. An expanded edition has been printed.

As the assistant to Robert Preus with a desk right outside the president's office, Norbert Mueller was well located and had the time to think how things should look after taking over for the man he once served as assistant to the president. How the office space was configured by Preus and Mueller was indicative of how different they were. Norbert Mueller reconfigured the entry space to the president's office with walled partitions so that it was no longer accessible and the president's desk was no longer visible from the hall.

That summer, Jim Voelz's courses had to be reassigned, and as academic dean, I informed registrar Lowell Fein that the class Principles of Biblical Interpretation (PBL) should be assigned to Art Just, who had just received his Ph.D. from the University of Durham, England. This discipline is also known as hermeneutics. My memo was effectively countermanded. Here is how this happened.

In the seminary structure, Dean Wenthe, as graduate dean, held the position just below the academic dean. While I was still on the return trip from Korea, Walter Maier II intervened. He wrote Wenthe that "a number of professors of the Exegetical Department expressed their concern" with having Just teach this course.[5] Maier II refers to himself and Wally Degner as "department heads," who had met with Norb Mueller to assign the course to Degner. Wenthe was deputized to inform Just that he would not be teaching the course.

Art Just is reported to have been unhappy with the change, but was willing to acquiesce. Wenthe was to phone me in Korea. Norb Mueller gave an order that the change be made immediately to accommodate student registration on Friday, September 8, 1989.

Other members of the exegetical department were also consulted, but not named. Members at that time were Douglas Judisch, Ray Surburg, James Bollhagen and Dan Gard, though it was unlikely the latter two had been consulted. Wenthe was not consulted and was informed after the fact.

At the time, Wally Degner was head of the exegetical department. Maier II's concerns with objective justification had made it difficult for him to hold this position. Oddly, in the memo Maier II refers to himself and Degner as "department heads," which can only mean that in a new administration one or the other would be department chair. It seems credible that both Maier II and Degner were told that each could be a candidate to replace me as academic dean, and the one not receiving the

---

5. Walter A. Maier II, memo to Dean Wenthe, September 8, 1989.

appointment would be the department chairman. At the time of the memo, the appointments had been neither made nor gone to the board for approval.

Walter Maier II was usurping the authority that was still mine as academic dean to make, and he was intent that Art Just should not teach biblical interpretation. This was a matter I discussed with Baumgartner of the ATS. I did not return from the meeting in Korea until the night of Sunday, September 10, the day of the opening service.

During the previous week, the one following Labor Day, the seminary went through its usual opening activities including the two-day faculty forum, campus picnic, the Saturday night banquet, September 12, welcoming entering students and the opening service, events over which Robert Preus presided with his usual aplomb. According to all reports, everything went smoothly, but beneath the surface a new regime had their plans in place to take over the seminary.

Arriving Sunday night, September 13, on the plane from Chicago to Fort Wayne was Ray Joeckel, board chairman with whom I had been on the friendliest terms in connection with the board meetings, which I regularly attended. Just three years before, the seminary, after some especially difficult times, had been accredited, and common challenges brought us together. On the flight from Chicago, Ray made no attempt to sit with me, though this was possible. A previous sign of things to come may have been an incident in the previous February.

In going to San Francisco from Salt Lake City, I was delayed for a full day in Denver, where Joeckel lived. Several attempts were made to reach him by phone from the Denver airport, which got no further than his secretary. One cannot help be suspicious in retrospect. Later it came out that during this time, synod president Bohlmann had visited Joeckel at his winter home in Florida.

When Joeckel arrived in Fort Wayne, Norb Mueller was there to meet him and I asked if I could hitch a ride with them to save my wife Dorothy the trouble of coming out to get me. After a two-week trip and a long plane ride from Korea, I was exhausted, but more exhaustion would follow in the next days and months.

On September 18, six days after Preus was removed from office and six days before four board member terms expired, a board conference by telephone was held without the participation of the newly elected board members, in which they were entitled to participate as advisory members. None of the newly elected members had been notified, so their participation was not possible.

This was an illegally held meeting, and its decisions would not be binding, even if the retiring board members were unaware of or uninformed about synod bylaws. In the six days after taking office, Norbert Mueller was in a hurry to make the changes before his actions could be questioned. Another irregularity in this telephone conference was that changes in administrative personnel proposed by Mueller had not been included on the agenda given to the board before the phone conference.

While it may have been shared with board members who had consented to Robert Preus's removal, it was not shared with those who opposed this. Mueller was not letting anything stand in his way for his plans for the seminary.

On Tuesday, September 19, news was floating around the seminary that I would be replaced as academic dean. Still in the position of academic dean, I met with Norb and Jan Case at a meeting that had already been scheduled in regard to the seminary self-study, for which I was still responsible. At this meeting, Norb told me that student tuition was being raised. I responded that was not in the best interest of the seminary, especially with a surplus of $150,000 on hand.

Early on September 20, I received a phone call that I was about to be officially relieved of the position of academic dean. When I told my son Peter, who was living at home at the beginning of his second seminary year, he responded, "Every dog has its day." Absolutely true. This was my day.

A meeting with Norb to inform me of my removal had been scheduled for September 29, but with the news already out, Mueller pushed up the date to September 20. I went to my seminary office expecting that the guillotine was soon to descend, and as anticipated Mueller showed up at my door at ten-thirty AM. During the meeting I asked Mueller whether Waldo Werning's request to the board to remove me was a factor in my removal. He said it was not.

During our meeting Norb asked me about spending summers in the Poconos. This may have been an issue with other faculty members too. My response has always been that what I had written was evidence enough to how I spent my time. A formal letter of removal from the post of academic dean was dated September 22 and received on September 25. He said that every president has to have his own men in the administrative posts, and my being relieved as the academic dean did not reflect on how I had carried out the office. How things can radically change so quickly!

The seminary world was changing rapidly. In September, Norbert Mueller assembled a new team. Gary Satterfield as business manager and Randy Schroeder as dean of students were retained. William C. Weinrich replaced Dean Wenthe as dean of graduate studies. Don Deffner, a good and longtime friend of Robert and Donna Preus from their days at the St. Louis seminary, was replaced by Melvin Zilz as department of pastoral theology chairman. Zilz did not have a full seminary education and never served as the sole pastor of a congregation. Walter A. Maier II replaced me as academic dean. Mueller had sided with Robert Preus in his defense of Satterfield. Schroeder had been nominated by Preus for his position as dean of students. Alliances never are permanent.

Walter A. Maier II's appointment as academic dean was with the understanding that it would be temporary—at least so he told me. During the Preus administration, the regents had turned down his nomination of Steven Briel for a professor of Old Testament on the grounds that he was his son-in-law. Now they were allowing the academic dean's son, Walter A. Maier III, to take the Old Testament position on the grounds he would be under the supervision of the newly appointed department chairman, G. Waldemar Degner, and not his father.

Norb Mueller informed Dean Wenthe on September 25 that all appointments were temporary, and hence the word *acting* was placed before each. The word *acting* was the rhetoric of the day, but what was temporary soon became permanent. Wally Degner would stay on as chairman of the exegetical department.

Robert Newton stayed on as vicarage director and Randy Schroeder as dean of students. During the passing of time, what seemed at first to be disconnected incidents looked more and more like a well-orchestrated scheme. A great deal of anxiety arose among those who were sitting on the sidelines. We were informed that the new arrangement would last only until matters were sorted out.

Part of the board's agreement with Robert Preus in dismissing him was that the election of a successor would not take place until his case was heard. In the next two years, Norbert Mueller made several attempts to have the faculty elect a presidential search committee. With a new president in place, Preus's attempts at reinstatement as president would be moot.

Mueller announced his administrative appointments to the student body in the Wednesday, September 27, 1989, edition of the *Daily Bulletin*, commonly now called *Blue News*, because of the color of the paper on which it was printed.

Since I had been charged with false doctrine in September of 1988 and the accuser would not let it rest, I thought to make myself as publicly accessible as possible. Any execution would be public and not by private assassination. If Robert Preus could be so easily removed, then my removal would be even easier. Some words of Jesus have a wider applicability: "A servant is not greater than his master. If they persecuted me, they will persecute you." So they did and so they would do. These were lonely days, and as the next years wore on, they would become even lonelier.

I continued as editor of the *Concordia Theological Quarterly*, but I did not see the dangers that lay ahead. Others also attempted to put the best construction on things. During these times Bill Weinrich stayed on good terms with both Robert Preus and Norb Mueller and had invited them separately over to his house for dinner. Only later did he and others come to terms with what was really involved in the administrative changes.

My last official day as academic dean was September 30, though Walter A. Maier II was already exercising the duties of this office weeks before. Since the good that men do is often interred with their bones, I prepared a full report of my years as academic dean, July 1, 1984, through September 30, 1989, and on May 1, 1990, I forwarded it to the board of regents for its end-of-academic-year meeting through my successor, Walter Maier II.

He made no acknowledgment of its receipt. When I asked him about it, he seemed mystified and said he did not know it was for the board. It was specifically and clearly addressed to the board. Since the Waldo Werning matter and others were occupying my time, I did not pursue the fate of the report, and so I do not know whether or when it reached the regents to be included on its agenda or in its files.

Jan Case was preparing a report of the governance and administration of the seminary in the spring of 1990, in which he made reference to Gerhard Aho and Dean Wenthe as deans of graduate studies in past years, but no reference to my service as academic dean, though I had held that office until September 30, 1989. I wrote to him, listing what had been accomplished during my tenure, to which came no reply.[6]

When David Schmiel announced his resignation as seminary president, I supplied a copy to the Presidential Search Committee. What I had done as dean was being erased from the seminary's corporate memory by the Mueller administration and by Waldo Werning's persistent challenges. A written report does not guarantee a place in history, but it helps to deter future fabrications. During my tenure as dean, the thesis requirement for the M.Div. was eliminated. We had no choice, since prospective students would choose the easier route offered at St. Louis. Greek, Hebrew and biblical knowledge tests were waived for students from the

---

6. David Scaer, memo to Jan Case, April 24, 1990.

synod's colleges. Hebrew was added as a required course with only pass and fail options. The seminary received visits from the synod's Board of Higher Education Services and two combined visits from the Association of Theological Schools and the North Central Association, for which I led the preparation and writing of the self-study.

As these administrative changes began to unfold in the 1989–1990 academic year, it was evident that Norbert Mueller did not understand himself as a caretaker officer of the board. He was there to stay—or so he thought. These changes were executed without the consultation or request of the faculty and created a climate of fear and suspicion among both the faculty and students. Mueller did this under the pretense that he wanted to surround himself with men with whom he felt comfortable working.[7]

When I was terminated as dean, I was promised a full year's salary increment of $2000. In relieving men of their office, Robert Preus followed the same policy. One telling moment came during the first week after my release from the position of academic dean. Upon returning to my office after chapel, I found Seminary Comptroller Mike Caudill leaving my office. He had entered the office with a pass key and detached the special telephone administrators had and replaced it with an ordinary one. One phone is as good as another, but one wonders if I could have been informed beforehand about this.

With the computer now widely used, seminary administrators no longer dictate letters, a talent that was common in the 1980s, which I had never mastered as academic dean. When I told the administration that I used the typewriter as editor of the *CTQ*, I was informed that I was to use the dictating machine and give the tapes to Trudy Behning. Walter Maier II, my successor as dean, informed me that the academic council turned down my request to retain the typewriter, and that I was to turn it over to security by October 17.[8] That typewriter was soon useless. With the coming of computers, this was a moot issue, but one does not have to read between the lines to see what was going on. As dean I had a pass key to all seminary doors. Perhaps it was a coincidence that Mueller had all the locks changed.

In September 1989, Trudy Behning, longtime secretary to Robert Preus, was replaced in the president's office by Dorothy McGill, who had served as secretary to Norbert Mueller in the placement office. Trudy had begun her service as a secretary at Concordia Senior College and remained to

---

7. *Reporter*, October 2, 1989.
8. Walter A. Maier II, memo to David Scaer, October 15, 1990.

serve the seminary when it returned to Fort Wayne. Trudy was placed in charge of the secretary's pool. Under Dean Wenthe, she was returned to her former position as administrative assistant to the president. At the May 2013 graduation, she received the Miles Christi Award, the only honor given by the seminary that year.

There were also major changes in the seminary's academic program. Students in the seminary's colloquy program were now required to spend seven and not six quarters in residence. This action was undertaken without consultation of the faculty or the board. Such a change may be considered a breach of contract. It was a breaking of a good-faith understanding and fundamentally altered the colloquy program in making its requirements nearly equal to that of the regular Master of Divinity program. It would give the St. Louis seminary, which required only six quarters, an advantage in recruiting students for its programs.

Normally changes in seminary programs are first deliberated on by the faculty, accepted by it and then proposed to the Board of Regents for adoption. In comparison with what was required by the St. Louis faculty, this was a way of sinking our program. Before these things began to happen, I as the academic dean contacted the Association of Theological Schools concerning what was about to happen. It advised that, when a president is removed against his will, because of the inevitable disruption, all other officers should stay in place. This was not happening at the Fort Wayne seminary.

As soon as he was interim president, Norb Mueller changed the titles of several seminary officers. Walter A. Maier II was now known as seminary vice president for academic affairs. He already was a synod vice president. Gary Satterfield, who had been appointed as head of the business administration, was pleased with the administration change. He became vice president for administration. Norbert Mueller then began to call new members to the faculty who would not be supportive of Robert Preus's cause to regain the presidency. In my new role of five days as acting chairman of the systematics department, I sent our nominations to Walter A. Maier II, now the interim academic dean.[9]

Our department proposed three names: Charles Robert Hogg, Martin Noland and John Stephenson, none of whom were asked to come for an interview. Hogg was then working on his Ph.D. at Indiana University on a fellowship whose holder was then determined by our seminary, a strange arrangement that has been dissolved, with each institution divid-

---

9. David Scaer, memo to Walter A. Maier II, October 5, 1989.

ing the estate that supported the fellowship. He is now a priest in the Russian Orthodox Church. Martin Noland would go on to become director of Concordia Historical Institute and is now a pastor in California. John Stephenson remains as professor at the seminary in St. Catharines in Canada. In a memo, Robert Preus asked me why the department had not put forth candidates. We did and they were ignored.

Asked to be interviewed were Richard Shuta and Alan Borcherding. There was an interview with a third candidate that I do not remember. Interviews were held in Maier II's office with myself as acting department chairman and Eugene Klug, former chairman, and Norb Mueller.

Gregory Lockwood, a pastor in Australia who got his doctor of theology degree in New Testament studies from St. Louis, also came for an interview in January 1990 and was called. I was not involved in his interview, but, as he was walking around the campus, on the day of his interview, I introduced myself and provided some information about how these interviews were conducted. He would be asked about John 6 and its Eucharistic interpretation. Calling a professor from Australia and bringing his belongings including a grand piano involves some expense and raises the question of whether a stateside candidate was available.

At first Lockwood was quite at home with the professors on whom Norb Mueller could count on for support. He became less enamored with the Fort Wayne situation and returned to Australia, where he joined the theological faculty in Adelaide and became an ardent opponent of the ordination of women in a church body that was then and still is divided on this issue. Since his daughter married a seminary graduate, now a synod pastor, he returns to the United States, and we have opportunity from time to time to visit with him and his wife.

Also called at this time to teach New Testament was Lane Burgland, who would take over in a few years as dean of the chapel after Dan Reuning. Burgland took over the interim pastoral duties at Faith Lutheran Church in nearby Churubusco, where he still serves.

In January of 1990, an episode took place that was made more serious by the administration than it really was. For the annual confessional symposium, we ask the bookstore manager, who in that year was Marcie Hess, to order books written by our speakers for purchase. This is a courtesy to the guests, who have an additional opportunity to sift through the ideas of the speakers by reading their books. Speakers like this too, because theological books rarely make the bestseller lists.

For the January 1990 symposium, the bookstore had been asked to order copies of the Anchor Bible Commentary on Mark by my good friend,

C. S. Mann. Come the time of the symposium, the books were not there. When I inquired about this, the bookstore manager explained that the staff had not found the book in the usual listings.

My response was that in such a case, someone on the staff should have contacted me for information. For the record, the Anchor Bible Commentary series has been around for years and is well known among biblical scholars and pastors. The bookstore manager informed Walter A. Maier II, my successor as dean, about what she considered my alleged ill behavior. He in turn called me into his office about the incident, and I apologized directly to her, and she accepted.

A matter like this should have ended there, but it did not. She had the last word by writing to me, accepting my apology and asserting that she and her staff "run a competent operation in the Bookstore, and that our staff is very helpful and cooperative; therefore it is a discredit to us and to the Seminary when we are not treated in a professional manner and respect."[10]

Disrespect of her staff was a matter of opinion, but their running a competent operation is another matter. If the staff were as cooperative as her letter claims, she would have contacted me when she could not find Mann's book. The staff did not look in the right place. All of this was and remains of no importance, except for the fact that after she accepted my apology directly from me, she wrote down her description of the account in a letter sent to me with copies to Maier II and Satterfield.

Copies of letters are put in one's files to be used to create a paper trail which can lead to one's dismissal. One cannot dismiss the suspicion that she may have been advised by someone in the administration to take this action. Maier II, the academic dean, and Satterfield, the vice president for business affairs, were copied. Its language was the legalese of a seminary administrator. Poorly hidden beneath the surface was a threat that I was under surveillance.

During Norbert Mueller's interim presidency and the David Schmiel administrations, Robert Preus faced four challenges: regaining the seminary presidency, defending himself against charges by Waldo Werning,[11] reinstatement into the synod ministerium, from which he would shortly be removed because of charges from the praesidium, and retaining his position as seminary professor. All this took a toll on Preus. His face showed a man who aged almost overnight, and his erect posture stooped.

---

10. Marcie Hess, letter to David Scaer, January 30, 1990.
11. See Excursus XIV: Waldo Werning, 277 ff.

My work with the seminary accreditation shortly after my taking over as dean was noted by the Association of Theological Schools, and in 1990 I was asked to serve on accreditation teams to St. Vladimir's Orthodox Seminary in Crestwood, New York, Garrett-Theological Seminary, a Methodist school, and Seabury Theological Seminary, an Episcopal school in Chicago. There was another school in Jackson, Mississippi whose name I have forgotten.

For St. Vladimir's I was teamed up with a classical Social Gospel professor in the style of Rauschenbusch (1861–1918), with whom I got along famously. Strangely, at this school the professor of liturgics was not a priest. A woman served on the faculty but absented herself for decisions belonging strictly to the clergy, an arrangement that might meet everyone's concerns in the Missouri Synod. There I met my colleague Kurt Marquart's famous step-cousin John Meyendorff (1926–1992), then the seminary's president and the leading American theologian for Orthodoxy. His office was more that of a priest than an administrator.

On the day we were there, a student sermon resembled more of a poorly delivered lecture on baseball. Later Meyendorff embraced the student for his sermon. I am not so sure that a student in similar circumstances in our synod would have received such kind treatment. There was something here to learn.

For the visit to Garrett-Evangelical Theological Seminary I was team chairman, a task that merited a letter of commendation on August 1, 1990, to Norb Mueller, then seminary interim president, with a copy to me. Leon Pacala wrote. "His careful assessment and judgments provided the basis for the accrediting actions of the Commission. We are indebted to Dr. Scaer for serving so ably in these roles and commend him for it." These positive remarks stood in sharp contrast to what was and would be appearing in print about me in the Missouri Synod. Theology and not administration was my forte, but I could rise to the occasion and got satisfaction for a job well done. After those four visits to other seminaries, none followed.

In March or April 1991, when Norb Mueller had served about eighteen months as interim seminary president, he felt sufficiently secure in this position to call me into his office to ask me and Kurt Marquart to resign from the *Affirm* editorial board. Policy at the magazine was never made in consultation with me. Since faculty members, as I did, served in similar positions with other publications, his request was as unusual as it was ironfisted. My first article for *Affirm* was "The ALC Issue—Still Unresolved" (April 12, 1976), and my last one was "Christians United in Christ?" (June–July 1989). *Affirm* had been set up as a conservative voice in the LCMS.

Shorter articles attract a wider readership. This was also true of the Theological Observer sections in *The Springfielder* and the *Concordia Theological Quarterly*, which attracted more readers than the longer, more extensively argued major articles. Articles in *Affirm* were not volunteered but requested by the editors, who were recognized leaders in the synod's conservative wing. Contents of my articles were generally taken from longer ones, and like other ones in this periodical, were to inform the laity of current issues.

I sent my letter of resignation to its editor-in-chief, John W. Klotz, with a copy to Tom Baker, in which I mentioned that I had never been involved in its editorial policies, but I would continue to support its aims, especially in upholding the synod's policy in not ordaining women.[12] Kurt Marquart's and my resigning from *Affirm* received no publicity in the usual channels, but it should have been a sign that those seen as favorable to Robert Preus were being intimidated.

THIRTY-TWO CANDIDATES DENIED CALLS

One happening in the academic year 1991–1992 will long be remembered by thirty-two students who did not receive calls to congregations in April 1992, as did their classmates and nearly all the St. Louis graduates. At the beginning of that school year, two years had passed since Robert Preus was asked to retire, and he remained a much beloved man. Now Norb Mueller had students seen as Preus supporters in his sights.

Norb Mueller was quite open in his determination that students he deemed Preus supporters would not receive calls. Plans for what happened in April were laid at least half a year in advance, and on several occasions Norb Mueller announced to members of the student government that he was going to do something to the students who he thought still supported Preus. Among those students was Rick Nuffer, now retired vicarage placement director and emeritus professor.

These students were aware of the sensitive situation on campus that year and deliberately decided to remain neutral and uninvolved. The student body president made every attempt to work with Norb Mueller.

---

12. David Scaer, letter to John Klotz, April 8, 1991. Klotz, who had taught biology at Concordia Senior College, Fort Wayne, was recruited for the St. Louis faculty as one of the replacements for the Seminex faculty. His appointment as editor of *Affirm*, to which I contributed articles, testified to his conservative credentials. He was a member of the Commission of Doctrinal Review that had rejected for publication my *Sermon on the Mount: The Church's First Statement of the Gospel* in 1986.

Similarly, class president Steve MacDougall created a class consensus not to be involved in issues between Robert Preus and Norb Mueller. There were no pro-Preus rallies of the kind that supported John Tietjen in January and February 1974 leading to Seminex. Norb was not a person to fool around with. Nothing stood in Mueller's way, and he carried through with his threat.

Randy Schroeder was the dean of students appointed by Robert Preus to replace the much beloved John Saleska. Jan Case had been called to the seminary on the recommendation of George Kraus to succeed him in the area of specialized ministries to the disabled and was appointed by Mueller to follow him as director of placement. Directors of vicarage and placement were treated by the students with God-like fear. In this case it was more like divine-like wrath.

Early each spring, committees from each seminary meet with representatives from the council of district presidents to present the names of those being offered for the synod's ministry and to make preliminary placements in calling congregations. In the spring 1992 meeting, the names of the thirty-two students were never presented by the committee representing the Fort Wayne faculty!

Kurt Marquart, whose courage remains his everlasting tribute, asked Randy Schroeder about this, and to this Schroeder responded with indignation that Marquart was challenging the committee's integrity—which he was, and it happened to be true.

At that time, students wishing to play intramural basketball organized themselves into teams of seven. One day, Jan Case's wife saw the team on which my son Peter played walking to the gym and remarked loud enough for them to hear her, "There go those confessional guys." To make that kind of reference, a person would have to know who these students were and what was going to happen to them. She could have only known this from her husband. The hit was on!

Their fate had become a topic of table conversation in the homes of those who would be involved in depriving the thirty-two students of calls in April 1992. In deference to her remark, the team called themselves "Those Confessional Guys" and used the abbreviation TCG, letters that appeared on pins and clothing. This was not a self-appellation, but one given them and which they happily bore.

With great pride, Professor Richard Muller wore those letters in the lapel of his coat. Of the seven members of the team, only one of the six eligible for calls received one. My son Peter was not eligible for a call until 1996, when he was assigned to Emanuel Lutheran Church in Arcadia, Indiana.

Before it was known that the committee, with Norb Mueller's involvement, had not presented the names to the placement committee consisting of district president and professors of both seminaries, it was said that there were not enough calls. That was a lie! Their names were deliberately not submitted. This is a prime case for statistical analysis.

What is the statistic possibility that five out of six members eligible for calls of one team would not get calls when approximately one hundred were distributed? The second notable incident is that Pat Boomhower (b. 1949), who was Norb Mueller's student informant on my activities, was called as an assistant to Guido Merkens at Concordia Church in San Antonio—a real plum! It was to this church that its pastor considering calling me as his successor in April 1989 and where our son David married Nancy Skul of La Vernia, Texas, in October 1988. Boomhower later was pastor in Lombard, Illinois, and is now retired.

Things at the seminary had been going from bad to worse. With Robert Preus gone as president, student enrollment and contributions declined. To offset the shortfall, tuition was raised and scholarship funds were plundered to make up the difference. Mueller did not have the charisma that made Jack and Robert Preus so well-liked by the students.

In retrospect there were signs that some students would face difficulty in being certified. In his role in placing graduates in their first call to a congregation, Robert Newton told the faculty that he examined them on the basis of Walther's *Church and Ministry*.[13] This was irregular. Two faculty members, one chosen by the student and his advisor, interview the student and forward their decision to the faculty through the director. The director of placement has no role in the theological interview with the students.

Formal conversations take place also before vicarage. All through their seminary days students are being informally certified by individual faculty members, but no faculty member, including the placement officer and any member of the placement committee, has the privilege or right to conduct a theological interview of any student on his own. When a theological problem is perceived, the student's original interviewer or advisor is told.

Newton informed two faculty members that as the director of placement he had the authority from the district presidents to examine any student. When asked about this authority, he could not provide as a

---

13. C. F. W. Walther and Matthew C. Harrison, *The Church and the Office of the Ministry, the Voice of Our Church on the Question of Church and Office: A Collection of Testimonies Regarding This Question from the Confessions of the Evangelical Lutheran Church and from the Private Writings of Orthodox Teachers of the Same* (St. Louis, MO: Concordia Publishing House, 2012).

source any official resolution from the Council of Presidents or the name of any district president. The director of placement was attempting unilaterally to identify students with what some considered sacerdotal views on church and ministry.

Several cases are worth relating. Newton once informed the faculty he was going to discipline seminary student Charles Hudson for using the phrase "high altar." Paul Strawn, was informed in the spring of 1992 by dean of students Randy Schroeder that he would not be certified for the ministry unless he took a psychological exam. Fearing it could be used against him, he refused and pursued doctoral studies on Martin Chemnitz at the University of Marburg in Germany and later became pastor in Spring Lake Park, Minnesota.

During these days some students were notified that they had to make appointments with Jan Case, Bob Newton and Randy Schroeder concerning unspecified infractions, but then had to wait for days to learn the specifics. I knew this tactic, since seminary president Richard Schultz had used it with me back in Springfield. Unspecified charges are intended to create anxiety. Alan Borcherding, soon to become academic dean, was a master in writing threatening memos to me and other colleagues. There were other cases in which students were put at a disadvantage by this tactic.

Then there was the case of a member of John Pless's University of Minnesota campus congregation, who had taken a couple of my off-campus extension courses. Jodi Rinas was found psychologically unfit by the certifying committee of the Minnesota South District, thus being denied admission to the Fort Wayne seminary. He went to St. Catharines, and after graduating, he enrolled in our seminary's Master of Sacred Theology degree program. For that one year, he was my graduate assistant and has now served several congregations in Canada. His wife, Lorraine, is Canadian, and so they found a more comfortable environment to serve north of the border.

For some years Art Just, Bill Weinrich and I had held meetings with the now late C. S. Mann, author of *Mark*[14] in the Anchor Bible Commentary series, and Winthrop Brainerd, a Roman Catholic priest in the Diocese of Washington, D. C., assigned then to St. Matthew's Cathedral and now is assumedly retired. Our project was viewing the New Testament documents as catecheses. The project was abandoned, but my part appeared in *Discourses in Matthew: Jesus Teaches the Church*, chosen by the

---

14. C. S. Mann, *Mark: A New Translation with Introduction and Commentary*, 1st ed., vol. 27, The Anchor Bible (Garden City, NY: Doubleday, 1986).

Association of Theological Publishers as one of the best books in the year of its publication. Sometimes we met in Fort Wayne or Maryland, but the weekend before call day 1992 we had met in Washington and stayed in the dormitories of the Catholic University. We returned to Fort Wayne Sunday night by car.

Monday morning began as an ordinary day, or so so it seemed. After chapel services we discovered that thirty-two fourth-year students had been notified by a sheet of paper with their names placed on the glass wall outside of the office of the secretary of the director of placement that they would not receive their calls—no explanation! Adding to their humiliation, they were not being allowed to process with the students who were getting their calls, as was the seminary custom.

Each year some students may not receive calls because appropriate ones have not been found, but they process with the other students into the chapel. Each one is notified to allay that he will not be called soon. No other service in the chapel is filled with such anticipation. When the calls are distributed, students also receive the good wishes of the seminary and synod presidents and the chairman of the council of presidents. Participation in the service would not be allowed to these thirty-two students.

Upon learning of this, I approached Norb Mueller as he entered chapel before the regular morning service to ask that even if the thirty-two students were not receiving calls, at least he would let them process with those for whom calls were designated. He responded that he would have to ask Jan Case, the director of placement, but he would have to support Case's decision. I also approached and pleaded with academic dean Walter Maier II, who responded he could do nothing about this, but it is highly likely that he, like Mueller, knew of what was going to happen and did not object to what Case had planned.

Then students going to graduate school ordinarily participated in the procession. This was an issue that touched Dorothy and me, since our youngest son, Peter, who had been admitted into the Ph.D. program of Notre Dame, would be excluded from participating in the procession. After thinking my request over, Mueller wrote me that, as interim president, he was committed to stand behind and would not countermand the decision of the director of placement, Jan Case, which allowed only those receiving calls to process.[15]

Ironically, those receiving calls and those not receiving calls both numbered thirty-two. Everyone, including myself, was absolutely stunned by

---

15. Norbert Mueller, letter to David Scaer, April 30, 1992.

the lack of compassion of the ham-fisted Norbert Mueller. These thirty-two students without calls would be allowed to enter the chapel before the service began and sit in rows reserved for them behind those receiving calls. Among them was my son Peter. These students accepted their humiliation with good grace. With no prior notice, parents and other family members of these thirty-two students, who had invested time and money to come for the service, were flabbergasted.

This was of course *déjà vu*. Eighteen years before in the spring of 1974, all of the graduates of the Springfield seminary were held hostage by the council of presidents, who delayed giving them calls until the Seminex students received them. This time the administrators, who had interviewed the students and been their teachers, put the knife in. Poignant in my memory are students, their wives and their families, walking around the Springfield campus in May 1974 stunned, some crying, wondering what they had done to deserve such treatment.

Was the act of not submitting the names of the thirty-two students for placement in the synod ministry done for revenge, jealousy or political advancement? Probably all three, but one is bad enough. In three months, notice was given that the students would receive calls by July 14, but the damage had been done and done big-time. Each of those thirty-two students was faced with unexpected financial burdens for having to remain in Fort Wayne for several more months. Without calls there would be no salaries and parsonages. Those who rented in Fort Wayne had already given notice of termination to their landlords and in some cases had to find other lodgings. Others and some wives had given notice to their employers to terminate their employment, since they thought they would be leaving Fort Wayne in May or June. These students were stuck with additional months of rent and loss of wages.

If they never had received calls, down the tube would be four years of seminary education including a year of vicarage, the cost of the education including the living expenses, the forfeited salaries of four years, which would have been theirs if they entered the world of ordinary employment or remained in their jobs, and the physical and emotional strains of moving entire families from their homes to and from Fort Wayne.

One wonders if those who in any way were responsible for this think about this or have any remorse about their actions. It is certain that their remorse has not resulted in compensating the students for this evil and financial deprivation which these seminary administrators inflicted upon them.

A moderate estimate of their financial loss would be, at that time, between two thousand and five thousand dollars. The honorable and moral thing to do would have been for members of Mueller's administration to apologize and make restitution to the students out of their own pockets, but honor is as much a lost virtue as is repentance for the evil done to others.

A side note. Under date of May 3, 1992, our son Peter's twenty-sixth birthday, my wife, Dorothy, addressed a letter to "Dr. Mueller" with copies to Jan Case, Walter Maier II and board chairman Rusty Roetman, in which she wrote the following:

> It is with deep regret that I am compelled to express the pain and anguish experienced by myself and the parents and family of half of the graduating students [on] call night. My husband urged you to change your mind about permission to process with their classmates behind the cross of their Savior. It was ultimately your decision. To deny them this honor was to dishonor them. An apology to all the students and their families would be a first step in showing good faith towards them. If calls are received, the student should be placed without waiting for the July 14th meeting.

No reply was received from Norb Mueller. No surprise there. When the wife of a senior member of Norb's administration, to whom the letter was addressed, learned of Dorothy's note, she responded, "Dorothy will get over it." How she got to see the note, we don't know, but Norb probably shared it with his top lieutenants. That's fine—and for the record, Dorothy did not get over it. Neither did I.

The call service was held on April 27. Jan Case's memo taped to the window began with this opening paragraph. "As anticipated, there is a shortage of calls for the Spring Placement Service 1992. I can assure you that each assignment was prayerfully weighed by those involved in the placement process. The following men will __NOT__ be extended a call on April 30, 1992." (underlining original)[16]

Unclear is what was meant by "prayerfully weighed," since the names of the students were presented by the Fort Wayne faculty representatives only after the assignments were made, if they were presented at all. There were twenty-six M.Div. students and six colloquy students for a total of thirty-two listed below the notice.[17]

---

16. Jan Case, memo to the Concordia Theological Seminary Student Body, April 27, 1992.
17. Alms, Paul Gregory; Bishop, Daniel John; Dreyer, John M.; Dumperth, Dale Allen; Farnsworth, Kenneth Walter; French, David Ray; Hinrichs, Kenneth Nelson; Hodel, David Kurt; Johnson Sr., James Robeli; Kaiser, Paul Matthew; Kettner, Michael Allen; Koch, Mark Andrew; Love, Mark W.;

Dean Wenthe advised the students not receiving calls to remain calm. He reasoned, and perhaps properly so, that the Mueller administration was hoping that depriving the thirty-two students of their calls would cause them to protest by walking out of their classes. This would give the administration an excuse to discontinue them from the seminary and remove them as candidates for the ministry. Perhaps they had in the back of their minds the hope of instigating a student walkout approximating the St. Louis seminary one in February 1974.

On the same date, April 27, John Heins, Michigan District president, and David Buegler, Ohio District president, as representatives for the Council of Presidents, addressed a letter to 1992 candidates that they "regret that of this date we remain short of sufficient calls to place the entire 1992 class." Another placement of candidates would be scheduled for July 14. Noteworthy in the letter is this sentence: "Therefore, this lack of calls should not be explained in any other way than the Lord's providence in the life of the church."

It is theologically true that God as the creator is responsible for all things, but missing was that God does not work directly but through agents, and in this case the agents were the faculty placement committee. It seems that the district presidents assigned to work with the faculty committee were aware that the thirty-two would not receive calls until those calls that were available were assigned. Divine providence works through evil but is not responsible for it.

By April 30, 1992, nearly three years had passed since the board of regents removed Robert Preus as president. During this time the Mueller administration suspected without firm evidence that Preus was involved with a group of confessional students. In the winter quarter of 1992–1993 Dean of Students Randy Schroeder inquired of one student about Donna Preus serving breakfasts on Saturday mornings to organize these students. Schroeder also gained access to student Rodney Dunker's room, and shortly thereafter, Dunker was suspended. More than half a year was spent in laying out the plot to deprive students who were thought to be Preus sympathizers of their calls. Such infractions were not dealt with, and the injustices remain unaddressed.

> MacDougall, Steven Alan; Power, Gregory John; Rogers, Mark Konrad, Rosenkaimer II, Robert Ron; Schedler, Walter John; Schoessow, Daniel Ray; Schwiesow, Wayne William; Thomas, Craig Brooker; Thompson, Gregory Noel; Vaughan, Timothy Bryan; Walter, Jody Roger; William, Jeffrey Baxter. Colloquy: Andresen, Ronald M.; Jaeger, Ralph; Kipp, David; Schurle, Darrell W.; Staweicki, Gary T.; Woolery, Wayne M.

The thirty-two students deprived of their calls graduated in the usual style after receiving their diplomas at the May 1992 graduation. Some students had Robert Preus add his signature to their diplomas where Mueller had signed as interim president. On a rare few certificates I added my signature over that of my successor's signature as academic dean. This all happened in 1992, and these students still display with pride their seminary diplomas. They are also reminders of an evil which was never undone and still waits to be remedied even in a minimal way.

A compromise decision made at the Pittsburgh convention of the LCMS that summer returned Robert Preus to the presidency of the seminary with spiritual but not administrative oversight. This created a moment of confusion on the campus, where plans were being put in place for a July service providing calls for the thirty-two students. Some of these calls, maybe most of them, had been available for the spring call service but had not been presented by the committee to the district presidents.

For the summer, Daniel Gard had temporarily taken the place of Daniel Reuning as dean of the chapel, who was on sabbatical. Just how what happened in Pittsburgh would have an effect in Fort Wayne was uncertain. What was definite was that Norb Mueller was no longer interim seminary president and deprived of the authority of this office.

This was how it all played out in Fort Wayne. The call service had been planned by Bob Newton, director of placement. He had invited a local pastor to preach. Preus was "restored" with spiritual oversight, but administrative and academic oversight was assigned to Michael Stelmachowicz. Before leaving Fort Wayne for the synod convention in Pittsburgh, Robert Preus told Dan Gard that if he was restored, then he would preach for the call service, and Gard advised Newton of Preus's decision. So when Preus was restored as the synod convention came to end, he phoned Dan Gard and expressed his desire to preach for the call service and advised Newton of the same. It was the last sermon he preached there.

On the morning of the service, a note was placed under Gard's office door from Newton that he was resigning as placement director and letting him know that the preacher assigned for the service would not be there. Since nobody else was on campus with the final authority, Dan Gard called Dan Reuning to ask him to serve as officiant. Gard asked Bollhagen to take the role of the placement director in the service to read the names of the graduating candidates and the places to which they had been assigned.

Since a bulletin for the service was already prepared, it had to be revised to take note of those who were now participating. Bob Newton's secretary had called in sick and her computer was locked. Dan Reuning,

Dan Gard and Trudy Behning, who had served as Preus's secretary during his tenure as president, took an existing copy of the bulletin and cut and pasted the names of those who were now participating in the service.

Gary Satterfield, the vice president for business affairs, who served with both Robert Preus and Norb Mueller, refused to have it printed on campus. Dan Gard then took the cut-and-pasted hard copy to an off-campus printer, paid for the printing out of his own pocket and picked the new ones up on the way back to the chapel for the service. They were quite literally "hot off the press," i.e., still warm.

Robert Preus preached and Jim Bollhagen sorted through calls so that they could be given out in alphabetical order. Afterwards Preus wanted to go to the office he had occupied as president and was now his again, but a student security guard prevented him from entering. Dan Gard begged Robert not to leave the campus, but the next day he was on his way to his place on Gunflint Lake on the Minnesota-Ontario border. Gard and others feared that without Preus exercising the limited authority he was given, things under Michael Stelomacowisz could become worse than what they were before—and they were.

Norb Mueller returned to the campus from the Pittsburgh Convention, but not as interim president. This did not prevent him from expressing his displeasure with Dan Gard. Norb was described as "very, very unhappy" with Gard, but this was not unexpected. He was a man of heavy temper.

Dan Gard had had a prior tense moment with the seminary administration. He had come to the Fort Wayne seminary as junior faculty member in the summer of 1989 along with Walter Maier III. When his three-year contract came up for renewal, the Mueller-Maier II administration did not act on the renewal until two weeks before it expired. According to the rules, an instructor requiring renewal would be informed six months and preferably one year before its expiration on whether or not his contract would be renewed. This allows the instructor time to locate another place in church service. A renewal of the contract given only two weeks before its expiration creates an unnecessary and well-calculated anxiety.

When this manuscript appears in print, more than a quarter century will have passed. Some of those thirty-two students may no longer be in the ministry, but the vast majority are and will have served well and with honor.

The successors of the Mueller administration remembered this event well. For example, in the 2008 spring placement, there were not enough calls for those eligible from St. Louis and Fort Wayne. In the 1992 placement, all of the St. Louis candidates were placed. In 2008, the available calls were proportionately divided between the two seminaries. Those not receiving calls were acknowledged and personally greeted in front of the chapel altar by LCMS president Gerald Kieschnick and seminary president Dean Wenthe, and Kieschnick promised them calls as soon as they were available. The congregation assembled in the seminary chapel showed their support for these students with applause. This was not the case in 1992!

ROBERT PREUS VINDICATED AND RESTORED TO OFFICE

The Missouri Synod's 1992 Pittsburgh convention replaced Ralph Bohlmann as president with Alvin Barry. It held out the promise that things would be turned around at the Fort Wayne seminary and that Robert Preus would be returned as president. The synod's Commission on Appeals had ruled that the regents had overstepped their authority in removing him, and that he should be returned to office. However, the regents were determined that this would not happen.

Before the convention convened, Robert Preus also had been exonerated of un-Christian behavior, of which Ralph Bohlmann and the synod praesidium, which included two of Preus's colleagues, synod vice presidents Eugene Bunkowske and Walter Maier II, had accused him. Robert Sauer, also a member of the praesidium, a runner-up for the synod presidency, an ally and a friend of Preus, also signed the charges against him. It was also common knowledge that Bohlmann played a part in having the regents retire Preus, and so this was another reason for Bohlmann not retaining the synod presidency. Another factor in convention events was the outrage that thirty-two seminary graduates were denied calls into the ministry, a wrong that would be soon rectified by their receiving calls back in Fort Wayne before the convention adjourned. During his nearly three-year tenure as interim seminary president, Norb Mueller had overplayed his hand in his determination to rid the seminary not only of Preus but his alleged student supporters.

Throughout the convention, mediators shuffled back and forth between the board of regents and Preus to overcome the impasse. As the convention neared its end, an agreement was reached that he would regain the presidency until April 1993 with the operative functions of the office being exercised by Michael Stelmachowicz, former president of Concordia Teachers College in Seward, Nebraska, and longtime executive with the synod's Board for Higher Education. Central to these negotiations was Henry "Hank" Koepchen, a longtime friend of mine, then chairman of the synod's board of directors.

THE STELMACHOWICZ-PREUS INTERIM PRESIDENCY

Until Stelmachowicz arrived in August, Walter A. Maier II was left as the top seminary administrator. A mild-mannered man with years of experience as executive with the synod's Board for Higher Education, Stelmachowicz exercised the powers of the seminary presidency to their fullest. Walter A. Maier II in a memo informed me of my reappointment as systematics department chairman and specifically said that it had Stelmachowicz's approval. Preus was not mentioned. He had been vindicated, but was out of the mix.

Two months after being reinstated as president, Preus was again the odd man out. Robert Preus asked the Board of Regents for a sabbatical and it was granted. After December, the buffer that Preus could have provided for some faculty members was no longer there.

Michael Stelmachowicz appointed the now former interim president Norb Mueller to his former position as placement director. This was hardly any consolation for the students, who were fully aware that during Norb Mueller's interim presidency in the previous April thirty-two students did not receive calls into the ministry.

I do not remember the exact date of Mueller's complete retirement from seminary service, but sometime in the spring of 1993 he moved to Texas, where he served the district in ministerial allocation. Norb was given a farewell seminary reception, but no formal faculty farewell. Often farewells for faculty are given in Luther Hall accompanied by a few speeches and refreshments.

There were many good reasons for my not attending, but Eugene Klug saw me on the upper plaza outside the dining room and asked whether I was going to attend. I was put on the spot. Knowing what Mueller did to Preus and the thirty-two students, I did not want to go, but with Klug having seen me, I went. Retribution was in vogue.

Norb thanked the service staff, the secretaries and ground and maintenance crew who filled the room—a command performance—and stated that he could not have done the job as president without them. He did not thank the faculty, some of whom were noticeably absent. Few of us leave noticeable impressions on the face of the world in which we live. Some leave even less.[18]

---

18. Norbert H. Mueller died January 10, 2013, and was buried from Zion Lutheran Church in Dallas, Texas. His obituary listed his coming to the seminary in 1976 and the various positions he had held, including professor of systematic and pastoral theology, faculty secretary and director of field work and vicarage

From 1990 through 1995, I was among those faculty members who were bypassed for regular salary increases set to match inflation that were given others. In the same meeting in which Norbert Mueller told me that I was being replaced as dean by Walter A. Maier II, he told me that my salary increment would be continued to the end of the year. This may have been done to prevent my rocking the boat of a fragile administration that was uncertain of its faculty support, but in a few weeks, it was firmly entrenched. Continuation of the salary increment came at the price of my not receiving the cost-of-living salary increase during the remainder of Mueller's three-year-term that was given to other faculty members.

When Michael Stelmachowicz became the executive officer of Concordia Theological Seminary, there was legitimate expectation that the salary discrepancy could be addressed. In a memo to me on October 1, 1992, Stelmachowicz conceded that I had not received a salary increase for three years, and that he "saw no reason, therefore, to continue the practice of omitting some faculty or staff members from annual salary adjustments." He also informed me that I would receive a two-percent raise which, would be retroactive to July 1, 1992, the beginning of that fiscal year.

I wrote Walter A. Maier II a memo with a copy to the regents about my exclusion from regular cost-of-living salary increases. "Each year we are told the seminary has limited funds. Still proportionately substantial increments have been made for others. For four years I have received no increment and been left in a position which is not commensurate with my senior status or my academic contributions."[19] Here the reader can do the math. Add these three years under Norb Mueller to the three years in the Schulz-Petersen administration (1971–1974) and add to the three years of the Schmiel administration (1992–1995), and the total comes to nine years

---

and candidate placement. Since he retired in 1993, the occasion marking this event took place in the spring of that year. In April of the following year, 1994, Robert D. Preus moved from Fort Wayne to a Minneapolis suburb, and so both men around whom the seminary was polarized were in a position of one not seeing the other. Two weeks after Mueller's death, the seminary held its Annual Symposium on the Lutheran Confessions. Some of the thirty-two students deprived of calls in the 1992 spring placement were there. Mention of his then-recent death evoked little response. His obituary listed memorials to Lutheran World Relief and Zion Lutheran Church, the congregation of which he was last a member. The seminary where he served seventeen years, three of which as assistant to the president and nearly three as interim president, were not mentioned. At his funeral, the seminary was not represented.

19. David Scaer, memo to Walter A. Maier II, April 18, 1994.

of being passed over for a raise given to other faculty. This was for me a replay of my years in the Schultz-Petersen administration in Springfield.

At the 1992 Pittsburgh convention, Robert Preus had hoped to remain as a professor, but this was not made part of the agreement. Walter A. Maier II, who continued as academic dean, did not allow Preus back into the classroom, a policy continued later by Maier II's successor, Alan Borcherding. Since he could not resume teaching, in his frustration Preus moved from Fort Wayne five months later in April 1994.

Since the moving van removed the furniture from his residence in Fox Chase, a development adjacent to the seminary campus, Robert and Donna spent that last night in Fort Wayne with us at 1912 Brandywine Trail. On return visits they stayed with Richard and Kay Muller (1926–2010). The man who had literally saved the St. Louis seminary after the faculty majority walkout in February and given the Springfield seminary a new lease on life by bringing it to Fort Wayne in 1976, was, in effect, exiled. Not allowed to teach, he was not going to stay. It is hard not to think that was not a factor in bringing on his death a year and a half later on November 4, 1995, several weeks after his seventy-first birthday.

In place of a vigorous confessional spokesman, here was a man whose hair had turned white, his complexion no longer robust but gray, and whose once erect posture was bent over. If his opponents had intended to destroy him, they had succeeded.

Selection of a new president involves a faculty-elected committee which at the initial level evaluates the nominations put forth by the synod congregations and offers its choices to the electors. A spirit of optimism accompanied its work, and the person of choice was Jonathan F. Grothe (b. 1941), formerly executive secretary with synod's Board for Higher Education for seminaries and at that time president of Concordia Lutheran Theological Seminary in St. Catharines, Canada.

Bob Newton put forth the name of David G. Schmiel, who at that time was executive for synod's Board for Higher Education and previously president of Concordia Ann Arbor, Michigan.[20] He was a largely unknown factor to the faculty. Surprisingly, members of faculty of Concordia Ann Arbor, who had served under him as president, sent letters to the seminary faculty committee opposing his candidacy. At its founding by synod's Anaheim convention in 1975, one year after the 1974 St. Louis faculty majority walkout, Ann Arbor was intended to be the crown jewel among the synod's liberal arts colleges. Under Schmiel's administration

---

20. Now known as Concordia University Ann Arbor.

enrollment declined and faculty discord arose. Very rarely, if ever, are negative letters of this kind sent by members of one faculty to another. His selection as seminary president by the four electors seemed remote.

Interviews with the finalists were spaced out on two days, and on the second day, the electors with all the regents met for a preliminary discussion. Then the regents were sequestered without the district president representative, who casts his own vote as an elector. The regents will cast its one collective vote. Then this one vote is tabulated with those of the other three electors to determine the seminary president. When a majority of three for one candidate is not reached, the process with discussion is repeated. This can be a day-long process and is sometimes unsuccessful. Most regents anticipated several ballots and were taken by surprise when on the first ballot David Schmiel was supported by three electors: synod vice president Robert King (1922–2016), David Buegler, the district president representative, and the chairman of synod's Board for Higher Education.

Board members who had cast their one vote for another candidate were surprised that Schmiel was elected and stunned that it happened on the first ballot. In office as synod president for only six months, Alvin Barry was open in his opposition to Schmiel and was so confident that he would not be chosen that he sent Bob King in his place. At this time Barry's wife was undergoing cancer therapy, and he was permitted by synod by-laws to send a vice president as an elector. Barry also had not been present to cast a vote at the election of the president of Concordia University in River Forest, Illinois, and lived to regret that outcome. This was not the first or the last time when synod leaders were required to balance serious family and church obligations against one another, and too often devotion to family wins out.

When Robert Preus heard what happened, he said that Barry should have contacted the other electors before the meeting to assure a happier outcome. In several elections of the president of synod's other institutions of higher learning, Barry's recommendations had been ignored, and this might have been the case, even if Barry had been present to vote. Grothe was the faculty's favorite candidate for president, and it was thought he was a shoe-in, but his sympathies at the time of the election for the St. Louis faculty majority that walked out in 1974 were largely unknown.

Chapter Eleven

THE SCHMIEL PRESIDENCY

ક્ષ

With the seminary chapel undergoing renovations, David Schmiel was installed as seminary president on Sunday afternoon, April 18, 1993, in the scarcely filled historic St. Paul's Lutheran Church. Generally only the faculty, ordained staff, students and their families attend such an occasion. Enthusiasm for Schmiel was limited. Seminary administration officials suggested to the secretarial, maintenance and kitchen staffs that they attend—and they did. A suggestion by the vice president for business affairs could be very persuasive.

As the faculty marshal, I sat for the service in the chancel next to David Schmiel. From there I could see Robert Preus sitting with the faculty, most of whom he had brought to the seminary, in the front pews on the lectern side of the church. They were in every sense his faculty.

With chief administration officer Stelmachowicz having put the Waldo Werning matter to rest, Schmiel was given a clean slate to put his agenda in place, which included keeping Robert Preus off the teaching schedule, curtailing my responsibilities with the intent of removing me and arranging for the sale of the campus, a big order for anyone, as it proved to be for Schmiel. As with other events in the previous ten years, others were coaching him. David Schmiel would serve a little more than two and a half years. Robert Preus had begun to accept the fact that he would not return to the presidency and that seminary president Schmiel and Academic dean Alan Borcherding would not allow him to teach.

David Schmiel saw his election as president as a mandate to close down the seminary. Papers later discovered showed that negotiations had been undertaken to sell the property to the Towne House, a retirement home, adjacent to the campus's south boundary. During the Schmiel administration, physical improvements were made to the campus, but enrollment had fallen, with an incoming class of under forty students, as had financial contributions. Receptions for the graduates and their families are held on the outdoor mezzanine. For the first time baskets for voluntary contributions were put out to collect monetary donations. The wife of a prominent member of Schmiel's administration described it as tacky.

At first David Schmiel presented himself as a good old boy and said he was concerned with faculty and would have one-on-one meetings with each one, but at the same time came ominous signs of changes. My turn came at a morning meeting in my study on May 10, 1993, not even one month after he had been installed as president, when he came to my office to assure me of his good will.

He arrived a little late, which is expected for administrators. He took off his coat and hung it up in the closet left over from senior college dormitory room days. I took the opportunity to express my concerns.

The Werning conflict, a matter which had been officially going on for nearly five years and less formally for eight years, was taking a toll on me.[1] One sure sign that Schmiel was going to have a less-than-positive relationship with me was his sharing a photocopy of a memo from Earl E. Haake, executor director of LCMS Worker Benefit Plans, written to William F. Meyer, director of the Board for Higher Education, with a copy to Schmiel and others. It contained this sentence: "The one name I have heard over the years is Dr. David Scaer, as one who is very emphatic that pastors should get out of Social Security."[2]

Years before, I had informal presentations on how students as future pastors were allowed to have portions of their salaries designated as untaxable housing allowance and the advantages and disadvantages of belonging to Social Security, from which they as clergy could opt out. Before coming to the seminary, some students had been in the work force long enough to accumulate enough quarters to qualify for a Social Security pension. Others had the advantage of receiving these benefits through their wives' employment. During Rosin's deanship (1979–1982), I desisted when I learned that some district presidents disapproved.

Haake mentioned me in his memo to Bill Meyer, but never contacted me directly. If Haake had, he would have learned that I had not given any advice in the last ten years. How convenient that the matter surfaced when Schmiel became seminary president. Here was another item to be put in my file that could be used to remove me. Completely false is Haake's statement that I was "one who is very emphatic that pastors should get out of Social Security." The words "very emphatic" made the statement untrue.

---

1. See Excursus XIV: Waldo Werning, 277 ff.
2. Earl E. Haake, memo to William F. Meyer, February 23, 1993.

A managed pension, even if it is federally managed, is the best possible option for some students.

Strange how some things will change. A professional financial planner advised graduating students in the spring of 2006 to opt out. Unless Social Security is adjusted, only the date of its collapse is uncertain. Several pastors, including colleagues, have appreciated my thoughts on the matter.

Schmiel replaced me as systematics department chairman with Alan Borcherding in 1993. One year later, in July 1994, Al Borcherding replaced Walter A. Maier II, who had reached seventy, as academic dean. At first Borcherding was quite outspoken about those colleagues who were less fully committed to objective justification, but later pushed his concerns aside. He liked being alone, but met socially on Friday nights with Lane Burgland, Robert Newton and Jan Case to identify "troublesome" students. Ironically, these gatherings were held at 5 Tyndale Place, later my campus address. Another member of the group remained on the faculty.

From the time Alan Borcherding came onto the faculty in fall of 1989, in the first year of Mueller administration, we often discussed theological matters, and I had considered him a friend. Borcherding had a fine mind, was trained in philosophy and well versed in historic classical Lutheran sources. We were on good terms with each other, and he had very strong views about one junior member in the exegetical department whose star was fast ascending.

David Schmiel's coming on as president changed that. Within four years of joining the faculty, Borcherding was not only the chairman of the department of systematic theology, but the academic dean, and David Schmiel was using him to establish a paper trail to provide reasons for my removal. Schmiel had already brought my name up to the board in my eventually being removed from the editorship of the *CTQ*. Coming in with a file filled with letters of complaints and poor evaluations would be all that would be necessary for the *coup de grâce*.

In appointing Borcherding as academic dean, Schmiel held that since he had been serving as the vacancy pastor of Holy Cross in Fort Wayne, he was closer to the pastoral ministry than I was. Borcherding was the junior member of the department of systematic theology and not pastoral theology. His service as a vacancy pastor had little or nothing to do with qualifications for being the systematic department chairman.

Little notice was made of my being discontinued as department chairman. Kurt Marquart, who had joined the faculty in December 1975 and who had already served in that position, could have resumed that position. Not uncommon in some institutions is the rotation of positions. Nothing could or should be read into my not being reappointed department chair were it not for Waldo Werning's years long campaign to remove me first from the academic deanship and then the faculty. I was getting closer to the edge of the precipice. To survive these ever bitter times, I requested and received a sabbatical leave for the fall and spring terms in the 1994–1995 academic year, and thus I would teach in the winter term.

Just as during the Schulz-Petersen administration, students and others had sought to entrap me. One year had passed since Norbert Mueller gave serious consideration to the false charges against me. Schmiel also announced that he would set things straight in regard to the doctrine of the ministry and to the chapel's liturgical practice, and so he set aside the 1994–1995 academic year for faculty study meetings on these topics. Again, it looked like the administration was looking for causes to remove me and others.

In April 1994, on behalf of the faculty program committee, Walter Maier III came to my study to ask me to give a paper on the ministry on the grounds that I was known around the campus for this doctrine. At this time I was deprived of any faculty position and craved the attention that such an assignment would give me, and so I accepted.

As with Eugene Klug's request to explain—really defend—an essay on Baptism and the Lord's Supper[3] I had given in 1980 at a systematics department meeting, any rational person would recognize this as entrapment. Since I had extensively written on the subject, especially in connection with the ordination of women, my colleagues were free to respond, an opportunity they had not taken for about twenty years. After first accepting Maier III's invitation, the next day I declined. I did not want to write on a subject about which I had already written, and I wanted to finish my work on Preus's Confessional Lutheran Dogmatics,[4] to which I had now been assigned three volumes. Maier III asked Marquart to deliver the paper, which he did.

Not content with my refusing to offer a paper, Borcherding sent a memo in November 1994 personally inviting me to participate in the discussion on ministry, but recognizing that during a sabbatical I was not under obligation to attend. Borcherding's memo assured me of his and Schmiel's good will, all this in the face of my being deprived of depart-

---

3. David P. Scaer, "Baptism and the Lord's Supper in the Life of the Church," *Concordia Theological Quarterly* 45, no. 1–2 (January 1981): 37–59, http://www.ctsfw.net/media/pdfs/scaerbaptismandthelordssupper.pdf.
4. See Excursus VIII: A Tale of Two Dogmatics Series, 185 ff.

ment chairmanship and annual raises given to most of the faculty. Promises of the administration's good will sounded even hollower in the light of other events.

On May 9, 1994, Schmiel asked me to use my sabbatical six months to teach in Novosibirsk, Russia, and said he would additionally toss in another six months in the winter term. I had several times taught in Siberia, really in every season of the year, and was well acquainted with our seminary's work there. I was literally and figuratively being exiled to Siberia. This meant I would be out of the country and away from the campus for one entire academic year and in no way able to prevent attempts at my being removed. Someone would have to take my place and I would have become expendable. I declined. It was becoming clear that Schmiel would use any means including faculty study meetings to find cause to remove me. Schmiel had an aggressive agenda for his tenure as seminary president.

When Robert Preus had left the presidency, the seminary had a surplus of one million dollars, which during the interim and Schmiel administration was transformed into a one-million-dollar debt, some of which probably was needed to meet federal requirements to make the campus handicap accessible. Professors residing on campus would be given a monthly stipend of $275 and be required to sign a contract to rent the campus housing at an unspecified amount. When some attorneys challenged the legality of the contracts in court, this action was later rescinded. Students and faculty were asked to make phone calls to acquire funding for the seminary. A typical response was, "I don't know what is happening at Fort Wayne, but I am not going to give any money." During the Preus years the entering class averaged around one hundred. Now with Schmiel the number was under fifty—or was it forty? Financial problems for the seminary came as soon as Robert Preus was removed as seminary president. Michael Stelmachowicz, then executive for Board for Higher Education Services, said that the board stood ready to provide the extra funds.

To cover the shortfall, the campus daycare center for children of seminary students whose wives had to work to support their husbands was closed down. So student wives who took care of the children were deprived of wages, and students with children had to make off-campus arrangements for them. Students with children on campus used to pick them up at the daycare center and take them to chapel and did this again during the lunch hour. This was no longer possible.

Rent was charged by the administration for the food and clothing bank where students had received these items without charge. The food and clothing bank is now a nearly 175-year-old institution, begun by Wilhelm

Sihler's wife, Susanna (1829–1918), and August Craemer's (1812–1891) wife, Dorothea (1817–1884). It marshalled donations from congregations near and far to help with the expenses of students. It continued when the seminary moved to St. Louis, where C. F. W. Walther's wife, Emilie (1812–1885), joined Dorothea in the effort. The tradition continued when the seminary moved to Springfield, Illinois, and returned to Fort Wayne. So the food and clothing bank tradition continued and strengthened. The rent charges put the effort of generations of Lutheran laity at risk.

One account is worth relating. During the Schmiel years, student Chris Esget was about to enter the chapel only to discover that the Lutheran Women's Missionary League was about to conduct a service, and he had a change of heart and for his own reasons turned around. A woman, later identified as the league's president, asked the student for his name, which he was not required to give, but he did so, to his detriment. She carried through with her threat to report him to Robert Newton. In attempting to correct the situation, the student apologized to Newton, who informed student Esget that he was not in the business of forgiving. The student had to undergo a series of discussions. He is now pastor of a thriving congregation near the nation's capital and came to serve as a synod vice president.

On May 10, 1994, Richard Resch, who had been on staff as the seminary kantor since 1977, was informed that his salary would be cut in half with no medical insurance. When Schmiel was asked about Resch's dire financial situation, he responded that Resch had made arrangements with St. Paul's Lutheran Church in Fort Wayne to pick up the shortfall. This was slightly ingenuous, since Resch and not Schmiel made these arrangements with St. Paul's, and only after Resch had been informed that his salary was cut. Waldo Werning took credit for removing Resch, whose electives Maier II had urged students not to take. On May 21, 1994, Dan Reuning was informed that he would be replaced as chapel dean by Lane Burgland. Reuning fought his removal and the lettuce began hitting the fan. Dan was not going to take this sitting down and prepared a lengthy document on the illegality of his being removed. It came to naught.

With Resch given half-time status, two courses, Baptism and Eucharist, Church Year and Hymnology, were dropped, breaking with a long seminary tradition. Eugene Bunkowske saw liturgics as an obstacle to mission work, and so courses offered by both Resch and Reuning had to go. Schmiel was carrying out his stated intent to have less formal daily services in the chapel.

Of course, I am more familiar with the circumstances surrounding my discontinuation as editor of *Concordia Theological Quarterly*. At that same,

May 9, 1994, meeting with Schmiel in his office, in which I declined his offer to spend a year in Russia, I told him I would like to and could continue as editor during my sabbatical. Weinrich had done this as graduate dean, and I as academic dean in the fall of 1986, so my request was not unusual. Even as I write this, professors on sabbatical continue with administrative responsibilities.

On Wednesday, May 18, Schmiel attended the *CTQ* meeting, as he had other meetings, and said nothing about my being relieved of the editorship. Official notification that I would be replaced as editor by Heino "Hank" Kadai came in a memorandum five days later.[5] However, I did not see it until September 3, 1994. During the summer, my mail is taken out of the pigeonhole faculty mailbox and forwarded by the faculty secretary to me in Pocono Pines. Schmiel's letter was placed on my desk by someone who had a key to my office. There it sat and thus it was not forwarded.

Mail is put into faculty mailboxes, and in certain cases, like mine, it is forwarded to a temporary address. Schmiel could claim that he informed me at the end of the school term of my being replaced as editor, but by putting it on my desk I would not have the letter in hand for another three and a half months, and thus I did not know of its contents. Cleaning personnel have access to faculty offices, and administrators have a master key to let themselves in, but this is never done except for cause, as when a professor dies.

Schmiel may be the only one who knows who came into my office. It had to have been him or someone deputized by him. Peter Bertram (b. 1955) was the first to inform me later that I was removed. Schmiel had written him that I had been removed as editor.[6] Others had heard about the contents of the letter or even seen it, but not me. By rehearsing the dates, Schmiel's scheme can be seen. Wednesday, May 18, the *CTQ* editorial committee met, with Schmiel present met. Thursday was the last day of classes, and graduation took place on Friday, May 20. Dorothy and I left campus on May 22 for the summer. On May 22, Schmiel wrote a memo that I had been relieved of the editorship and placed it in my office. Totally ingenious!

During my first tenure as editor (1969–1994) I had initiated the Theological Observer section of the *CTQ*, which was well received because of the brevity of its contents. At the September 1993 faculty meeting, Schmiel informed us that he had brought up my performance as editor as an issue to

---

5. David Schmiel, memo to David Scaer, May 23, 1994.
6. David Schmiel, letter to Peter Bertram, July 1, 1994.

be addressed by the board of regents. A memo from academic dean Walter A. Maier II called my attention to the same matter, but without specification. During the 1993–1994 academic year, Schmiel attended all the *CTQ* meetings, at which I explained that the editorial committee works toward a consensus in choosing the articles to be published. If a minority of the members had scruples about a certain article, their wishes were honored and an article was not published. Articles by faculty were generally accepted with little debate. It is after all a faculty journal.

Though the seminary president is *ex officio* member of the editorial committee, his predecessors had rarely attended. They received reports on which articles were selected and declined. In the year in which Schmiel attended all the meetings, he never mentioned anything negative to me about my editorship. At the May 18, 1994 *CTQ* meeting, Schmiel made no mention of his discontent or plans to replace me, though two days later he recommended to the regents at their May 20–21 meeting that I be replaced with Hank Kadai.[7]

All this information was in Schmiel's May 23 report of the board meeting that was given to the faculty in September. On the same day, May 23, Schmiel complained to Dan Reuning that the *CTQ* articles were always about "the ontic relationship between Christ and the priest," which he labeled a "Grabauism," a belief that he said he was going to correct at faculty study meetings. He did not specify which articles put forth the views he found unacceptable, either at the editorial meetings or by memo.

A furor broke out in some 1994 district conventions about my being removed as editor and Reuning as dean of the chapel. At this time I had still not seen Schmiel's memo to me. Since reports from these conventions had discrepancies, there was good reason to think that these were unsubstantiated rumors. Synod vice president Robert King, as president Al Barry's official representative, told several district conventions that I was removed from the editorship because of my sabbatical. King also said that Schmiel

---

7. David Schmiel, memo to David Scaer, May 23, 1994. "Since I have been unable to contact you by phone, either at your office or at your home, I will do so by this memo. I wanted to notify you personally that the Board of Regents in its meeting on May 20 and 21 decided to ask Professor Heino Kadai to edit the *Concordia Theological Quarterly* during your sabbatical year. The editorship will then be reviewed." Since a president's reports to the board are prepared days or even weeks before the board's meetings, it is probable that the president had already made his decision and written the memo at the time of the *CTQ* meeting on May 18. The memo appears to suggest that Kadai was only given an interim appointment.

was content with my performance as editor and that after my sabbatical I would be returned to that position. It is unlikely that King made up this story, but rather this was the version supplied by Schmiel to the board.

Two pastors, both named Christiansen, said that Northern Illinois District president and seminary classmate Theodore Laesch (b. 1935), now deceased, had told his fall pastoral conference that Schmiel had told him that Reuning and I were content with our removal from our positions. This could not be true, since I did not know anything about it, and had I known, it would be even more untrue, if that were possible.

On October 29, 1994, I phoned Laesch from Chicago to determine what Schmiel had said and left a message on the answering machine, to which his wife returned a call with the promise that he would contact me. He never did, and so in his case it could not be determined who was responsible for this false report that I was content in being removed. Later it came out that Schmiel had provided information about our being removed to the district presidents and our being satisfied with the decision. Schmiel had written a letter to Michigan District president John Heins, presumably sent to other district presidents, that I was removed as editor because of my sabbatical, and in any event, it was a good time to make a change.

Walter A. Maier II came closer to the truth when he told the Minnesota South District convention that "the seminary did not like the way Scaer was running the *CTQ*." All this should be pieced together. Schmiel had determined to remove me as editor, and when he reached this decision, he only informed me in a memo placed on my desk by someone who entered my office without my knowledge or permission. Two synod vice presidents and two district presidents had or were giving conflicting stories about my removal.

Heino "Hank" Kadai, my replacement as editor of the *CTQ*, a 1960 Springfield graduate, had been on the faculty since 1960 and received the master of sacred theology and doctor of theology degree from Concordia Seminary, St. Louis. Regarded as a scholar with an extensive library, he had to his written credits the editorship of a collection of Herman Sasse's essays, but little if anything else. Schmiel did not and could not say, as he said about Borcherding, that Kadai was closer to the pastoral ministry, since he had never served a congregation, and at his death it was difficult to determine to which congregation he belonged. He had never served a parish, and only in coming to Fort Wayne was he ordained at Preus's insistence.

During his first years at the seminary, Kadai was friends with those whose contracts would not be renewed during the presidency of Jack

Preus. Among them was Richard "Dick" Jungkuntz (1918–2003), later appointed executive secretary of the Commission on Theology and Church Relations by then synod president Oliver Harms, a decision made on the basis of an essay on baptism Harms heard.

As the lines began to be drawn in the Missouri Synod, this group was seen as liberal. Hank remained in good standing with the administrations of Richard Schultz, Robert Preus and now Schmiel. Hank and his wife, Lois, were the most gracious of hosts at their Christmas parties, to which I and Dorothy were invited when I was academic dean. Writing from a perspective of thirty years later, all this now seems like ancient history. A faculty member is available for appointment to any administrative post and committee but without permanent claim to any one. Removal as academic dean, department chairman and editor of the *CTQ* is all part of seminary life, and a change in positions can be expected by every faculty member. A faculty member is called to teach.

I wrote to academic dean Alan Borcherding and registrar Lowell Fein about my offering two New Testament courses and having my name no longer listed as professor of New Testament in the seminary catalog.[8] Alan Borcherding wrote to Dean Wenthe, "Our files indicate that Dr. Scaer was called only to the Systematics Department, but his most recent contract stipulates that he should teach elsewhere 'as needed.' If Dr. Scaer wishes to teach NT courses he would be doing so in response to the Exegetical Department's expression of need, not as a right granted by his Diploma of Vocation."[9] It goes without saying that Borcherding declined my request to teach New Testament courses, very carefully noting that his files indicated that I had no right to teach New Testament.

My original call document and contract of March 31, 1966, specifically says that I was to teach "Seminary courses assigned to [me] in Systematic Theology and in New Testament Theology." This document was on file in the academic dean's office when Borcherding wrote his memo. Borcherding was making use of a bogus 1972 contract backdated to July 1, 1969, on which then seminary president Richard Schultz affixed his signature as the surrogate for Jack Preus, who was seminary president in 1966.[10]

On the basis of my original call document of April 1966, academic dean Lorman Petersen had assigned me a course in the Epistle of James and then Matthew, and so he recognized my position as a professor in New Testa-

---

8. David Scaer, memo to Alan Borcherding, November 1994.
9. Alan Borcherding, memo to Dean Wenthe, November 2, 1994.
10. For details of this contract, see the discussion in an earlier chapter.

ment. Alan Borcherding and seminary president Schmiel were claiming that I had no call to teach New Testament, but the original documents showed otherwise. My signature was missing from the backdated documents, as every board member at that time (1972–1974) and he also knew.

In all his memos Borcherding assured me of his good will, as did Schmiel, but there were reasons to think otherwise. My arguments for maintaining my position as an instructor in New Testament are contained in documents in my seminary files. At the bottom of one memo to Borcherding, I wrote, "Galatians 3:17: The law does not annul a covenant previously ratified by God." By ignoring the 1966 document, this is exactly what happened.

A personally devastating episode occurred when academic dean and acting department chairman Alan Borcherding came to give me an evaluation. During my first years on the faculty, I have no recollection of being given a formal evaluation. Evaluations are intended to be cordial so that the professor can see himself the way that others do, and if needed, to make adjustments. Now at the end of every course an instructor is subjected to intense evaluations by the students.

As academic dean, I evaluated the department chairmen, who in turn evaluated his department's members. This amounted to an informal conversation in which the professor speaks about his teaching load, articles and books written and future plans. The interviewer makes the evaluation based on ten to twenty criteria, e.g., scholarship, social skills, intelligibility. In one case an instructor was not renewed for lack of scholarly literary production, though if others were measured by this criterion, they would also have to leave the faculty. One cause for non-renewal or non-advancement is failure to obtain the necessary advanced degree for his position or lack of parish experience. Professors with tenure, especially older ones, were often not evaluated, but now they all are.

At age fifty-eight, with twenty-eight years on the faculty, third in seniority, I might be considered exempt from an interview, or at least it would be more of a formality, or at least a collegial conversation. With Alan Borcherding, it was not. An appointment was made for the afternoon, but after chapel I saw him and said that if he was free for the next hour, ten forty-five AM, I would be available, and he assented. A free full afternoon is always good for tackling bigger projects—why not have the interview in the morning?

It was an overcast day. After coffee in the commons, I went back to my office in Jerome Hall to wait for Alan at eleven o'clock. When eleven-twenty AM approached and he had not shown up, I suspected something was up and began to worry that something sinister was in store. I was right. When he came in my room, more than a half hour past the appointed time, he handed me his evaluation. For each category—hospitality, getting along with students, honesty, integrity—there are ten rankings with "10" as the highest and "0" or "1" being the lowest. On his evaluation of me, certain categories were not marked at all, and items like getting along with students a "5" or lower was given. I was stunned! Also, again without counsel and not being able to sift through this vicious attack on my character, I said, "Alan, I am writing down everything you say," and I proceeded to take notes on a large yellow legal pad.

He ripped the evaluation sheet off the desk and said he was going to continue the evaluation in the afternoon, a bizarre situation to say the least, and I went with him over to the dining room for lunch, because in these kinds of situations every attempt should be made to avoid an explosion whose damage cannot be undone. Then I went home and told Dorothy. It was a miracle I did not wreck up the car. Later in the same afternoon, Alan Borcherding came to my room, now for the second time in the same day, and gave me an evaluation in which I received "8s" in every category.

My being deprived of various positions and teaching assignments was part of a plan to remove me from the faculty, and an unfavorable evaluation from the academic dean would be reason enough to put the final nail in the coffin. Schmiel followed Norb Muelller's tactic in filling my file in the dean's office with unfavorable memos. As an administrator, he knew the importance of a paper trail in getting rid of a professor. Probably Schmiel planned to meet with Borcherding later that day before my afternoon scheduled meeting with him. Since Alan had assented to meet me right after chapel, Schmiel had met with him right away. Borcherding was doing Schmiel's dirty work.

Most likely, a strategy meeting with David Schmiel accounted for Alan Borcherding coming late to my office for the eleven AM meeting. Either Schmiel wanted to tell Alan how to fill out the evaluation sheet and conduct the meeting with me, or Alan was uncertain on how to do this and asked Schmiel for advice. The evaluation was a masterpiece with some items left blank, e.g., honesty. That ought to kill anyone's future chances to remain in the job. As mentioned, Alan was caught off guard when I told him I was taking notes of what he said. He did not expect this. Not knowing how to handle this, he grabbed the evaluation from my desk. After we had lunch together, he probably consulted Schmiel for a second time.

My receiving all "8s" on the second evaluation was ingenious. Again it seemed that Schmiel had coached him: "8s" were not good enough to be great and not low enough to be bad; "7s" would also have done the trick. Later on, Borcherding sent a memo asking how details of our meeting had come to appear in the October 1994 edition of *RALI News* and concluded with these threatening words, "I do expect a response from you."[11] I never did. As mentioned above, after having lunch with Borcherding, I did go home to discuss with Dorothy what was a looming crisis that was emerging from an evaluation that was about to be placed in my file, providing a reason to dispose of me. This followed the example of Alan Borcherding himself, who did not reply to several requests to look into Waldo Werning's charges against the department of systematic theology, of which he was the chairman.

Alan Borcherding's dilemma in interviewing me partially resulted in the muddling of his administrative functions. Since the department chairman was also the dean, he had no one to consult but himself. Since consulting oneself may not be too productive, he had to consult the president.

During the Schmiel administration, 1993–1995, many of the newer faculty members held multiple committee assignments. Walter Maier III was at the same time a member of the following faculty committees: nominations, academic policies, the degree of the master of sacred theology, faculty concerns, faculty hearings, faculty programs, library advisory and certification and placement. He was also appointed as assistant dean of students. On the certification and admissions committees, Maier III could play a role in determining the suitability of students for the ministry.

Lane Burgland, nominated to the faculty by Norb Mueller, held eight positions. Lane Burgland's replacement of Dan Reuning as dean of the chapel caused many letters of protest from alumni. Richard Muller, who protested the continued involvement of Waldo Werning in seminary affairs, held one committee assignment, as did Kurt Marquart—Library Advisory Committee. Dan Reuning and I had none. The only position left to me was the ceremonial post of faculty marshal, which in November 1995 President David Schmiel suggested that I give up. What is implicit is often clearer than what is explicit.

During Norb Mueller's interim presidency, I continued to handle the annual symposium, and Schmiel affirmed this. Popularity of the symposia and their financial success, including sales in the seminary bookstore, may have been one reason for my being retained, that in a time of declining seminary income. Had they been stopped, it would have called atten-

---

11. Alan Borcherding, memo to David Scaer, November 2, 1994.

tion to the synod clergy, especially Fort Wayne alumni, that something was seriously amiss at the seminary.

In November 1994, about seven months into the Schmiel administration, Trudy Behning phoned to tell me that the account for annual confessional symposium had been abolished and no charter for it could be found. Transferred out of what we thought was a symposium account to the general fund was approximately $50,000, established by grant by the late Herman Fink Sr., owner of a tool and dye factory in Connecticut. Learning that he had terminal cancer, he gave this amount to underwrite the symposium, which then was in its infancy. The fund's purpose was to provide additional funds to the registration fees to cover unanticipated shortfalls.

For seventeen years I served as the symposium account officer and signed requisitions, but prior to Trudy's phone call, I was not told that the fund was being merged into the seminary's general operating budget. These funds could be used to cover the shortfalls during the Mueller and Schmiel years. All this I shared in a letter to board member Raymond Mueller with a copy to Walter Dissen.[12]

With no record on file about the donation of Herman Fink Sr. to the seminary to underwrite the seminary's annual Symposium on the Lutheran Confessions, I often wondered if such a donation had actually been given. What I knew, I had been told by Robert Preus. It seems unlikely that my recollection of such detail was inaccurate. For this fund I was the account executive in distributing the funds, even though others prepared the requisitions which I signed.

In June 2011, I attended the installation of Matthew Rasmussen at St. John's, Hazleton, Pennsylvania, a church that had been served during the vacancy by Ronald Fink (1937–2014), Herman Fink Sr.'s son, a former Atlantic District president and pastor. At the reception following the service, I could not resist asking Ron whether he had any memory of a donation his father had made to the seminary—and he did. Without a letter or other documentation, nothing about the funding of a symposium account can be known for certain, but at least that part of the story could be verified.

Concerns raised by Bob Newton came to light when Donna and Robert Preus received a visit from David Anderson, a seminary board member, and his wife on the evening of May 19, 1995, six years minus a day after Preus was asked to step down as seminary president. Anderson had spoken at a Chicago meeting dealing with doctrinal differences among faculty members in a prepared paper, which then came up for discussion

---

12. David Scaer, letter to Raymond Mueller, December 11, 1995.

at the seminary's next board meeting. Waldo Werning had been coaching Newton from the time he came to the seminary, and so Newton's charges were similar to Werning's. This close association between Werning and Newton seemed to have continued for some time.

On the next day, Robert Preus wrote to Bob Newton about what Dave Anderson told him.[13] When the topic of faculty teaching came up at the meeting, Bob Newton, who was attending the meeting in his position as placement officer, remarked that Robert Preus "had allegedly allowed Dr. Just and Dr. Gard to teach a doctrine that denied the third use of the Law, and... had allowed Dr. Scaer to teach false doctrine." In parentheses in his letter describing the conversation, Robert Preus adds that Dave Anderson did not remember whether Bob Newton provided the specifics about my views.

Robert Newton had gone on to say that if Dave Anderson had any doubts about Newton's allegations, then he "should talk to his 'idol' [i.e., Robert Preus] and check this out." Robert Preus goes on to say that he "will be very pleased to be investigated by anyone for my [his] doctrinal position and my [his] conduct as president." Then Preus added, "Let me assure you and all who receive this letter than [sic] I am totally unaware of Prof. Gard or Prof. Just denying the third use of the Law or Prof. Scaer teaching false doctrine on any point."

Preus also told Bob Newton that both he and Dave Anderson are convinced that if there are doctrinal differences on the faculty, they should be brought up to the LCMS 1995 convention, floor committee five, scheduled for Memorial Day Weekend, chaired by English District president Roger Pittelko (b. 1932), which was then only a few days away. If Preus had gotten anything wrong, he asked Bob Newton to respond by Sunday, May 28. Newton responded with copies to all those accused and David Schmiel that Dave Anderson did not get things right.

"In short, Rev. Anderson's report of my conversations in the board meeting, as you have described them in your letter, is grossly inaccurate, as was the paper that he delivered in Chicago. Thus I would not recommend using Rev. Anderson's report of the Board of Regents' meeting when you address Convention Floor Committee 5."[14]

This drew an immediate response from Anderson in which he questioned Newton's integrity.[15] After the meeting, according to Anderson, Newton

---

13. Robert Preus, letter to Robert Newton, May 20, 1995.
14. Robert Newton, letter to Robert Preus, May 23, 1995.
15. David Anderson, letter to Robert Newton, May 25, 1995.

had said these things in the presence of Raymond Mueller, another board member. Mueller corroborated Anderson's account. Ray Mueller stated that after Paul Krumm, newly appointed vice president for seminary advancement, made his report, "Newton made his remarks to the board about Preus and the professors teaching false doctrine without naming them."[16] Ray Mueller then went on to say that he joined the conversation in which Newton named the three professors—Scaer, Just and Gard—to Anderson.

Bob Newton's charge about Dan Gard could hardly be correct, because Gard was called at the same meeting in which Preus was fired. Gard had only begun to teach after Robert Preus was removed, and so it was impossible that Preus was in a position to tolerate Gard's alleged false doctrine or that he protected him. Then Ray Mueller added that Newton "had never been called by the Holy Spirit to serve a congregation in these highly anti-clerical times in this country." In parentheses, Ray Mueller adds: "Bob, I add this only to jar your memory regarding that conversation between Anderson, yourself, and myself." Newton's claims made at the seminary 1995 spring seminary board meeting strongly resembled Werning's accusations against me for false doctrine in 1988 and against Robert Preus for covering it up in 1989.

Synod president Alvin Barry was asked by its 1995 convention to appoint a committee to look into the situation at the Fort Wayne seminary. To prepare for the committee's visit, I prepared a written account in which events were listed chronologically. I do not remember my interview, how I used the written account, who the interviewers were or whether I supplied them with copies. I don't remember even if an interview took place.

At the end of the July 1995 synod convention, my former student, colleague and longtime friend Art Just called me from his summer home in New Hampshire to share his best wishes with me. The graduates from the Springfield and Fort Wayne seminary played a major role, if not the major one, in bringing about the astounding results in the synod elections, especially on who was elected as Fort Wayne regents. Art added that these pastoral delegates had been my students in a special way. These pastors had shown themselves to be leaders, and a trend was set in place that would carry into the next election in 1998.

I told Art that celebrating might be premature, since things can quickly change from one situation to another. Sobriety rather than elation in the face of success is sometimes the best attitude, especially in light of disappointments which each succeeding year had given me.

---

16. Raymond A. Mueller, letter to Robert Preus, May 26, 1995.

Shortly after the 1995 synod convention, David Schmiel announced that he was retiring from the presidency. Robert and Donna Preus, now living in Minnesota, returned to Fort Wayne on Labor Day weekend and were guests of Richard and Kay Muller. For Preus, the first order of business was putting in place a skeleton administration to take over after Schmiel's administration came to an end. A meeting took place at Dan Reuning's home on the evening of Labor Day. Though Robert Preus was not allowed to teach, he was still a faculty member and allowed to attend meetings, and so he attended the annual Fall Faculty Forum on September 5.

As soon as Preus entered Luther Hall, everyone, even his detractors, rushed up to greet him. It was almost as if Lazarus had come back from the dead, and in sense it was. Robert Schaibley, pastor of Zion Lutheran Church and an advisor in my case with Waldo Werning, thought that Schmiel knew he had failed in his mission to close down the seminary and was planning to leave soon. I was too close to the situation to make the kind of observation that can sometimes only be made from someone outside.

Sometime in the summer of 1995, Schmiel, who had been in office for barely two years, decided to retire. A report that he had already submitted his resignation at the May board meeting was never denied. Another factor leading to Schmiel's retirement was a spreading discontentment with the seminary administration expressed in letters to him written in the summer of 1994. Among the letters was a lengthy one by the pastor of Grace English Ev. Lutheran Church and School in Chicago, a later seminary professor, John G. Nordling, under date of July 14, 1994.

Under his photograph in the 1995–1996 seminary yearbook was this inscription: "Schmiel, David G., President (until Nov. 27, 1995)." On the same line under the photograph of William C. Weinrich were these words: "Acting President (as of Nov. 27, 1995)."

At this Fall Faculty Forum, Robert Preus was being greeted by those who had so shamefully treated him. David Schmiel, still the seminary president, chaired the meeting, but he might as well not have been there. He had become incidental—not even a side attraction. Preus was center stage. His old familiar charisma was still there. People's motives are only known to themselves, but Preus was brought down by the jealous ambition of those less talented than he was.

In the ensuing theological discussion of the meeting, David Schmiel spoke with the authority that the office as president gave him, and for the faculty the matter was settled, at least until Preus rose to speak. He spoke, no one responded. Preus had provided an answer to the theological question, and everyone remained silent. Nobody in the room was a match for him.

On the following Sunday he kept a speaking engagement in Peoria, Illinois, and he did not attend the seminary's afternoon opening service on the Sunday following Labor Day. Had he attended the service, he would have been the star, and Schmiel would have been pushed further back into the shadows where he had placed himself.

Several years later, I listened to the tape of Preus's Peoria lecture, which was in the possession of the late Arthur A. Just Sr., the father of my colleague Arthur Just. Even on the tape Preus's great style came through. Both he and brother Jack had a knack in speaking to the laity which even those who make a profession out of playing to the crowds cannot match.

On October 29, 1995, I preached for the Reformation service in the Quad Cities of Illinois and for a small cost added Buffalo as a second destination on the airplane ticket to attend a symposium in honor of Hermann Sasse at Concordia Lutheran Theological Seminary in St. Catharines, Ontario, Canada. Robert Hogg, then a professor at St. Catharines, invited me to stay at his home. At the banquet on the final evening, October 31, 1995, Preus and I sat together. Incidentally this was the day on which the Quebec electorate narrowly defeated a proposal to break away from Canada.

On November 1, a Wednesday, Hogg drove Preus and me to Buffalo Airport. This would provide an opportunity to discuss with him my manuscript for the volume on the *Law and the Gospel and the Means of Grace* in Confessional Lutheran Dogmatics, the series of which he was the editor. We both had long waits for our planes, but then discovered our flights originated from different terminals. The discussion over dogmatics did not take place. This was the last time I saw him. On the afternoon of Saturday, November 4, Robert Preus died while out walking with his wife, Donna.[17]

When one administration at a synodical seminary institution is about to replace another, the Board for Higher Education conducts a "transit audit." Before the one that took place on December 1, 1995, in anticipation of Schmiel's retirement, I do not remember participating in one. Since hardly a month had passed since Robert Preus had died, not much attention was given to the December visit. Members of the audit team were Eugene Krentz (b. 1932), who as president of Concordia University, River Forest,

---

17. For the details of Robert Preus's death and funeral, see Excursus VII: Robert David Preus, 159 ff.

Illinois, had urged students planning to attend Fort Wayne to consider St. Louis; Ed Trapp, a layman who had served on several synod boards and was supportive of Norbert Mueller and Schmiel; and Ralph Reinke, one time president of Concordia University, Seward, Nebraska, and Concordia Publishing House, was a third member of the exit team.

Before he died, Robert Preus claimed that Reinke was intent on closing the Fort Wayne seminary. He also said that Schmiel, who was Ralph Bohlmann's and Michigan District president John Heins's choice for seminary president, had the same mission. Schmiel denied allegations that he discouraged Ann Arbor students from attending Fort Wayne. Bill Meyer, friend and former colleague at Springfield, was present with the visiting committee as executive of the Board for Higher Education. In their report, the team said that it "made a conscientious effort to interface with the faculty, student and support personnel." "Further contact with faculty was facilitated by a 'social hour' on Thursday."

Embarrassingly, only four or five faculty members showed up at the social hour, at which time Bill Meyer told me that not one professor had taken the opportunity to meet individually with team members in the designated offices. It later was discovered that no notification of the team's visit was made in the weekly faculty news or by individual or collective memos.

David Schmiel hosted the team and Alan Borcherding was given the responsibility for publishing in the faculty news the opportunity for individual faculty members to visit with the team. Team members waited for faculty members to come for the interviews in offices in the tunnel connecting Loehe and Wyneken halls.

With both Schmiel leaving campus and Christmas break coming only days after the "transit audit," the team's visit was soon forgotten. Schmiel and Borcherding were responsible for the faculty not knowing about the team's visit and presence on campus. Announcing an official visit by synod teams does not simply "fall between the cracks." In spite of an announced November 27, retirement date, Schmiel was staying on as president supposedly until the end of the year.

There was one last somber occasion, the annual Christmas dinner. Robert Preus's death less than seven weeks before contributed to the dark spirits of some faculty. On the morning of the day Robert Preus died, he spoke by phone with Bill Weinrich about coming back, but he would not. That night the dining room for the faculty Christmas dinner was unusually dark, producing a macabre atmosphere. Lacking were laudatory and good-natured roasting speeches typical for such occasions. In place of the customary carols, David Schmiel asked the guests to accommodate him by singing songs from his childhood. They were unknown and not received well. To lead the singing, Schmiel introduced Dan Reuning as "the campus musician," almost as if he were a medieval troubadour performing for the lord of the manner.

In the corner separating the dining area from the end of food line sat Schmiel and his closest advisors. David Schmiel left the campus unnoticed and unannounced. So secretive was it that interim president Bill Weinrich was unsure when he was to assume his duties.

From at least 1984, or maybe before then, until 1995, there were unidentified persons outside of the seminary directing how certain faculty members were to be treated, and if necessary, released, and who was to be called. It seems unlikely that Norb Mueller was the sole perpetrator of his decisions, and David Schmiel never had his heart in the seminary. Reflection on the seminary's history especially in the 80s and 90s may serve as a deterrent to those who are contemplating sacrificing principle for ambition and as a comfort to those whose ministries are afflicted and challenged by those who pose as fellow saints and pilgrims on the way but are not.

These years were for me a story of survival. In writing of these things I became aware of dangers which when they were encountered did not seem so ultimate, but were in fact intended to be so. There were many happy moments which provide the light under which the less pleasant things are only shadows.

AFTER THE WHIRLWIND: THE WEINRICH INTERIM

The four months before the election of a permanent president, for which position William Weinrich appeared as the faculty's choice, did much to change the direction and complexion of the seminary. With Dean Wenthe in tow as the acting academic dean, Weinrich was ready to initiate changes. He went into the offices to relieve Bob Newton of his position as director of placement and Randy Schroeder of his position as dean of students. During his tenure as director of placement, Newton kept files with detailed notes, especially on those students who held to what he considered "high church" beliefs on the ministry. Before he left Fort Wayne, it was reported that he spent hours shredding them. Notes taken in the course of duties performed in the service of an institution belonged to the seminary and were not privately owned papers.

I was returned as the chairman of the systematics department. Dan Reuning was back as dean of chapel. As if born with a permanent condition of immunity, Hank Kadai remained as chairman of the department of historical theology and the editor of the *CTQ*, though his meager bibliography had not been expanded. His reputation as a scholar was reflected in his library rather than by what he had put down on the printed page.

Randy Schroeder remained at the seminary, but was relieved of his post as dean of students. Before Dean Wenthe left the presidency, Schroeder's contract was not renewed. After being replaced by Alan Borcherding as academic dean, Walter A. Maier II kept the title of vice president, but as assistant to seminary president Schmiel. He remained as full-time professor before going on modified status.

Other professors who were prominent in the Mueller-Schmiel administrations left. Lane Burgland became pastor of Faith Lutheran Church, in Churubusco, Indiana, hardly half an hour from Fort Wayne. He had already been serving as vacancy pastor. I have seen him from time to time. He is greatly loved by his congregation.

Alan Borcherding became first an assistant executive on the synod's Board for Higher Education, then director and later assistant director of university services and then interim president of the Concordia University System. Now he is on the staff of Concordia Seminary, St. Louis.

Jan Case, who was placement officer and directly involved in thirty-two graduating students not receiving calls, became assistant to the Southern District president and is now a pastor in New Orleans. Bob Newton took a parish call in California and soon after became president of the California-Nevada-Hawaii District, a position to which he was reelected several times.

A memorial service for Robert Preus was held on January 19, 1996, during the January confessional symposium, whose character bore the impress of his theology. My sermon for that occasion was printed in *Logia*[18] and reappeared in an appendix of *Doctrine is Life: Essays on Justification and the Lutheran Confessions*,[19] one of two volumes in which Preus essays were collected by his son Klemet, now deceased. Carrying the crucifix in the procession was Jim Hogg, who after leaving the synod and being reinstated through the intervention of seminary president Dean O. Wenthe, severed his ties again and is listed as the bishop of the (Lutheran) Diocese of North America.

One particular incident stands out. It has to do with a particularly good photograph of Robert Preus, which now appears on the covers of

---

18. David P. Scaer, "Commemoration Sermon for Dr. Robert D. Preus," *Logia* 5, no. 3 (1996): 9–10.
19. Robert Preus, *Doctrine Is Life: The Essays of Robert D. Preus on Justification and the Lutheran Confessions* (St. Louis, MO: Concordia Publishing House, 2006).

both volumes of *Doctrine is Life*. It should have been put on the cover of the service bulletin for the memorial service and available for display in the chapel narthex. I asked Gary Penner, who handled public relations, to bring the photograph to the narthex of the chapel. He refused. Penner soon left the seminary's employ for other employment in Fort Wayne. It is hard to avoid the conclusion that his loyalties were still with those who prevented Robert Preus from returning to the seminary.

With Robert Preus's death and his family present, the symposia banquet could have easily become a wake, but before the banquet, Donna took me aside and said that Robert would want no change in how these banquets were conducted. We took her admonition seriously. Of course humor can deliver serious messages. Previously banquets were held in the seminary dining room, which was found to be too small for the ever-increasing attendance. This would be especially so for the symposium that would follow Preus's death by less than three months.

Thus, for the January 1996 confessional symposium, the banquet was held in the newly renovated Johnny Appleseed dining room of the Coliseum, Fort Wayne's primary indoor arena, just a five-minute drive from the seminary. Donna Preus, Robert's widow, received sympathetic well-wishers, among whom were Gene Klug and Walter A. Maier II and their spouses, a moment that was both somber and joyful.

Bill Weinrich phoned Martin Taddey (1932–1996), who was only days away from death, to inform him that the faculty had awarded him the honorary degree of doctor of divinity. Taddey, pastor of Trinity Lutheran Church in Palo Alto, California, who had a reputation for conducting the church service with magnificent liturgical detail and was in every way committed to confessional Lutheranism, was as gracious as ever in receiving the degree and never at a loss for humor.

Arrangements were made so that banquet guests could hear Bill Weinrich's conversation with Taddey. Martin died on one of the following Sundays right as the *Nunc Dimittis*, the liturgical piece concluding the Holy Communion, was sung in the church adjacent to the parsonage. It was as if he planned it—or was it by divine design? Marty would have had it no other way. A few years before, I arranged with Taddey to preach seven sermons on Good Friday afternoon in exchange for sleeping accommodations for myself and my wife. We had not visited California before and thought this a good way to do it.

One way or another, symposium matters fall into my hands, but the announcement that my colleagues were preparing a festschift for me took me by complete surprise. Its title *All Theology Is Christology* was not only an affirmation of friendship, but of my theology, for which both Robert and I had been accused of false doctrine. Editors were Dan Gard, Art Just, Dean Wenthe and Bill Weinrich. I took this as a happy vindication. Soon a festschift was planned for Kurt Marquart and published before mine was.

Weinrich remained as interim president until July 1, 1996, when he took over as academic dean, a position he held until December 2006, when he was followed by Lawrence Rast Jr., Wenthe and Weinrich had been classmates at the St. Louis seminary and ever since have remained very good friends. Bill has not been hesitant in giving advice, and Dean had never a deaf ear in receiving it.

On the evening of Labor Day in 1995, it became evident that my days of influence in a reconstituted seminary administration would never happen. Since I was no longer part of the mix, I left a small informal gathering at the Reuning's house. As I headed for the front door, my old friend Art Just followed me and urged me to stay, but the handwriting was on the wall. It could not be erased. Even before the five years I served as dean, I was frequently in the president's office to discuss any number of things and to toss in my two cents. Now as my sixtieth birthday approached, striving for administrative influence would be fruitless.

It seemed as if I was forgotten, and I shared my deep sense of abandonment with Art Just, Bill Weinrich, Dean Wenthe and Matthew Harrison, then pastor of Zion Lutheran Church, where we were members. I also spoke with Paul McCain, then an assistant to synod president Al Barry. He told me in November 1995 that people "either hated or loved me," and that he was not among the haters, but made it clear that there would be no appointment. Someone had Robert Preus's ear and had advised him not to use his influence to return me to the deanship.

Seeing this all evolve from the middle of 1994 through 1995 was disheartening, but in retrospect it let me devote the following years to writing. Attending meetings, part of the academic dean's duties, was not my cup of tea. For the record, I received high marks as academic dean from the regents for organization, and I served on accrediting teams for the Association of Theological Schools for four seminaries.

Chapter Twelve

THE WENTHE AND RAST PRESIDENCIES

ॐ

During the initial balloting in April 1996 for seminary president, Bill Weinrich could garner no more than two votes of the three needed for election. Two electors were content in having no permanent president put in place, but synod president Alvin Barry was also an elector, and unlike his absence at the election for Schmiel, was present for this one. He insisted that a president had to be elected. Dave Anderson, the regents' chairman, and a last holdout for Weinrich, saw the handwriting on the wall and switched his vote to Dean Wenthe.

A fifteen-year period of contentment was ushered in at the seminary. Dean Wenthe's personal skills prevailed over any remaining differences in the faculty, which dissipated almost overnight. There would be no more petitions written to boards outside of the seminary from faculty groups with Wenthe as president. We could do theology again.

When Wenthe took over in 1996 as president, photos and pictures of his predecessors were removed from the second floor of the administration building. One president could not be removed without removing the others. Toward the end of Wenthe's tenure, pictures were put up again. Missing was Mueller's. His three years as acting president did not qualify him as a permanent sitting president. Under Preus's photo were the dates 1974–1993. He had not been the real president after September 1989, but appearances are often adjusted.

One of the first things Wenthe did was to memorialize Jack and Robert Preus, both of whom had been seminary presidents, by naming the lower outdoor area by the side of Wyneken Hall "Preus Plaza," though it is rarely referred to by this name. This signaled the end of the Preus era that had so defined the seminary since 1958 when Jack joined the faculty then in Springfield. Students who entered the seminary after 1989 have not had direct contact with Robert Preus. At this writing I remain the only full-time faculty member who served during the administration of Jack Preus.

Things changed for me when Wenthe became president. At the death of our good friend Donald Deffner, I was sent by Wenthe as the seminary representative to his funeral in California. He and his wife, Corinne, were our dear friends, especially after September 1989, when Preus was in virtual exile from the seminary.

Donald Deffner had taught homiletics and directed the doctor of ministry program after retirement until he died. Don had left the St. Louis faculty several years before the 1974 faculty walkout to take a position at Pacific Lutheran School of Theology, an LCA seminary in Berkeley, California, in anticipation of improved relations between the LCMS and the LCA, a goal of the administration of Oliver Harms, LCMS president (1962–1969).[1]

Another reason for leaving St. Louis was to avoid the anticipated turmoil that was already coming to a head in the late 1960s. With the St. Louis seminary faculty walkout in 1974, rapprochement between the two synods became remote, and Deffner's place on the faculty of Pacific Lutheran Theological Seminary no longer served the purpose for which it was intended. With a majority of the faculty leaving their positions on the St. Louis faculty in 1974, positions had to be found for those who were not assigned to Christ Seminary in Exile, Seminex. *Deploy* and *deployment* were words added to the vocabulary of Seminex faculty who had to find positions elsewhere.[2]

---

1. Burkee, *Power, Politics, and the Missouri Synod: A Conflict that Changed American Christianity*, 71. Harms's immediate goal was fellowship with the ALC, but at that time ALC and LCA fellowship was on the verge of being consummated.
2. Taking up position at Berkeley were the biblical scholars Carl Graesser, Everett Kalin and Robert H. Smith (1932–2000) and the homiletics professor George Hoyer. Graesser had taught me Hebrew, and during my first two years at the seminary I saw him at Luther Memorial Church, where David Schuller was pastor before being called to the seminary. Hoyer was my first professor in homiletics, whose father Theodore Hoyer was sitting next to my grandfather Charles Scaer when he died after speaking to the Kansas District Convention in 1928. George Hoyer's wife was a granddaughter of Franz Pieper. His sister was married to Martin Scharlemann. Hoyer's wife, also a Pieper granddaughter, was sister to Rudolph Ressmeyer, Atlantic District president at the time of the 1974 seminary walkout. I saw George Hoyer, brother-in-law to Ressmeyer, at the July 7, 2008 funeral of Virginia Ressmeyer (1927–2008), wife of Rudolph Ressmeyer and sister of Robert Werberig, also a St. Louis and Seminex seminary professor. At the reception following the service at Faith Lutheran Church in Blakeslee, Pennsylvania, Hoyer and I talked amicably. It was as if the events of the intervening years had not happened.

To make room at the ELCA seminary in Berkeley, California, Deffner was relieved of his position. Finding himself too young to retire, he contacted Robert Preus to see if he could be of use in Fort Wayne. During their St. Louis days, the Preuses and the Deffners had been good friends, and Deffner was made a visiting professor at Fort Wayne, being paid by the course hours taught.

Don Deffner was committed to his work and was in his office in Jerome Hall by six AM, if not earlier. Smoking was forbidden in public places on campus, and so Don enjoyed his cigars beyond closed doors. Besides teaching homiletics, he served as chairman of the department of pastoral theology and was the director of the doctor of ministry program.

He was greatly loved by the students, and a portrait of him with an oversized Anglican clerical collar and large pectoral cross hangs in the tunnel connection between Wyneken Hall and Loehe Hall. Don would teach for the fall and spring terms and remain in California for the winter, where he had been professor at the Lutheran School of Theology in Berkeley.

When preaching and teaching obligations took me to California, I would stay at their place, and often Dorothy came along. In May 1997, Corinne was diagnosed with cancer, and at first Don was determined to finish the final weeks of the spring term, but soon he went to her side. Within weeks Don was diagnosed with terminal cancer, though he kept this to himself. All during the summer, I phoned him at home and other times in the hospital and each time found him in the high spirits out of which saints are made.

For lodging during Don's funeral, I slept on the couch in the den as the family filled the rest of the house. In spare moments, Corinne and I went into Don's study, sometimes with a martini, to reflect on his illustrious career and their happy moments. My words at the service were well received, and I felt I was back in the club. Slightly more than six months later Corinne succumbed to cancer. Though many years have passed, Dorothy and I still feel the gap left by their deaths, and it has never been completely filled. From 1989 through 1994 it was not only a matter of losing position at the seminary and being slandered in print, but some close friendships did not remain as firm. For some colleagues the future was better attached to more rising stars.

In 2001, the traditional faculty Labor Day picnic was dedicated to thanking Wenthe, following his near election as synod president, for his work as seminary president. A few humorous gifts added a note of levity to a solemn time in his life. Wenthe took the results of the convention election gracefully and continued successfully as seminary president, working cordially with Jerry Kieschnick, who was chosen as synod president. In the following nine years, he never expressed regret or resentment. Early in 2011, he announced his retirement at the end of the academic year, and the process of finding his successor was put in place.

On May 21, 2011, Lawrence R. Rast Jr., a former student of mine and graduate assistant in the academic dean's office, was chosen as his successor and immediately took over the reins.

Excursus XV

COMMISSION ON THEOLOGY AND CHURCH RELATIONS

ॐ

Not until 1998 with my selection by the faculty to the Commission on Theology and Church Relations (CTCR) did I have a significant part in the public theology of the Missouri Synod. My efforts were directed to the lecture hall and the writing of articles and books, and determining the influence of one's individual efforts on others is subjective. Actions and resolutions taken by church conventions and commissions have an immediate measurable result.

In the Missouri Synod, official doctrinal statements are generated by the CTCR and passed on to the synod's conventions for approval. Until 1962, this task had belonged to the St. Louis faculty, but with a growing distrust of some of its professors, the CTCR was created to perform these tasks. Since its inception, changes have been made in how its members were chosen, but its basic framework as representing various aspects of the synod has remained the same.

Members consist of seminary faculty members, parish pastors, one commissioned minister, one college theology professor, and lay persons. They are chosen by synod convention, the synod president, the council of presidents, and seminary faculties. The intended result is to show how the synod, that is, its pastors and congregations, think in regard to certain issues. CTCR resolutions represent the deliberate consideration of its members, but they are not binding on consciences. Only after they are presented to the synod and adopted by the convention are they recognized as official statements of what the synod believes and teaches. Their binding nature on LCMS members remains a debated issue. Even *A Brief Statement*, prepared by Franz Pieper and adopted by unanimous vote of the synod convention, does not have the status of the Lutheran Confessions, but it is still regarded as the synod's official position.

During my first years at the seminary, senior members of the systematics department, Howard Tepker, Eugene Klug, and Harry Huth represented the faculty on the commission. When Robert Preus became president, he along with Norb Mueller and Kurt Marquart served. Mueller, while still pastor of St. Paul's, Ann Arbor, Michigan, was a member as a pastoral representative chosen by the convention. He was chosen by the faculty as its representative when he came to Springfield in 1974. My first association with the commission was to fulfill a request for a paper entitled "Problems of Inerrancy and Historicity in Connection with Genesis 1–3."[1] A plausible reason for its rejection was that it did not fit into customary ways of synodical thinking.

With Robert Preus out of the seminary presidency in 1989, Norb Mueller and Walter A. Maier II were chosen as the faculty representatives to the CTCR, even though it was widely known that Maier II held to a view on justification that was widely criticized. During the Mueller, Stelmachowisz and Schmiel administrations (1989–1995), the faculty was represented by Cameron MacKenzie and Greg Lockwood, who had recently come from Australia. Those who felt uncomfortable with these administrations promoted the election of professors who were not explicitly attached to Robert Preus but still could articulate traditional Lutheran views. At that time, I had been on the faculty for a quarter of a century. I had a more extensive and diverse theological bibliography than any of my colleagues. Even though I had been cleared of charges of false doctrine, my even being considered for any faculty position, especially one on the CTCR, was remote.

As the Schmiel administration came to an end in December 1995, I was without faculty committee assignment or administrative position either by appointment or election. In September 1988, faculty appointments and elections were my least concern. Even if, after December 1989, my removal from the synod became less probable, my removal from my teaching position became more probable. This left such a lasting impression on me that even after Dean O. Wenthe's election as president in April of 1996, I lived with the fear that bad times would return. For years I lived in a survival mode.

As a result, it came as a complete surprise when Bill Weinrich informed me in April 1998 that I and Marquart would be candidates for the CTCR to fill vacancies left by Maier II and Mackenzie. Things did not proceed smoothly, since Jim Bollhagen and Doug Judisch had been

---

1. David P. Scaer, "Problems of Inerrancy and Historicity in Connection with Genesis 1–3," *Concordia Theological Quarterly* 41 (January 1977): 21–25, http://www.ctsfw.net/media/pdfs/scaerproblemsofinerrancy.pdf.

placed in nomination from the floor. Each faculty member had two votes, one for each of the two positions, and Marquart garnered a majority on the first ballot.

Jim Bollhagen, Douglas Judisch and I remained on the second ballot, and on the third ballot only Judisch and I were left. Even though the vote tallies were not reported, I was probably elected by one vote. In surveying those present at the meeting, it did not seem that there were enough votes for my election, and I did not expect it.

Since coming to the faculty at the end of 1975, Marquart was the favorite of the traditionally conservative members, and at his death in September 2006, he had served longer than anyone else since the commission was established. Highly placed professors who had benefitted in the Mueller, Stelmachowicz and Schmiel administrations had little reason to support me, but one of them probably found the alternative candidate was less attractive. After thirty-two years on the faculty I was on the commission. I was not the only one who was shocked.

The commission has sixteen members who, when they are not meeting together in plenary, are divided into three subcommittees. Some members serve for six-year terms and others like seminary professors for three-year terms, so the membership is partially changed every three years. Continuing members maintain their positions in the subcommittees. Newly elected and appointed members fill in the positions left vacant. Both Marquart and I took seats on the subcommittee for theology and I was chosen as chairman, a position I held for my nine-year tenure.

Usually the commission's first meeting is held in September after the synodical convention. For whatever reason, it was postponed until November 18–21. At the election for the officers of the commission at its first meeting it soon became apparent that the CTCR was evenly divided. On the first ballot for chairman were Texas District president Gerald Kieschnick and Scott Murray, a Houston, Texas pastor. At the time, Kieschnick was being proposed as an opposition candidate to Alvin Barry for the post of synod president. Weinrich, the seminary's academic dean and also President Alvin Barry's appointed member, was absent, and Kieschnick defeated Scott Murray by a vote of eight to seven.

In 2000 Kieschnick was a frequent speaker at district conventions and was introduced to the delegates not only as president of the Texas District but chairman of the CTCR, and so he was theologically credentialed to be elected by the slimmest of majorities over Fort Wayne seminary president Dean Wenthe as synod president in 2001. As chairman, Kieschnick was eminently fair in the conduct of the meetings and never used his position as chairman to dominate the debate. When he was challenged by Kurt Marquart on several occasions, he stepped down from the chair and handed over the gavel to vice chairman Scott Murray.

At the beginning of our tenure on the commission, previously seated members had been warned by the commission's executive that Marquart and I would be obstacles to the commission's work. One member, a circuit judge from Michigan, was overheard saying to a staff member, "Those Fort Wayne guys are not as bad as you said they are." Even when there were differences of opinions on the commission, the most cordial relations existed.

Probably over these years I had more differences with Marquart than with anyone else on the commission, something that defied the stereotype that Fort Wayne theology was monolithic. On resolutions on which differences among the members could not be immediately resolved, executive director Sam Nafzger worked to delay passage in order to attain the highest degree of unanimity possible. Unresolved during my tenure were differences on the proposal *Male and Female in the Image of God*, and another, *Lay Teachers of Theology*, an issue that remained on the commission in other forms.

Nathan Jastram, synod president Alvin Barry's appointee to the CTCR as a college professor of theology, was the writer of *Male and Female in the Image of God*. For a commission document, it was excessive in length and overly documented, which may have been one reason for its not being adopted. As a rule, longer documents present more opportunities for dissent, and so the chances of adoption decrease in proportion to a document's length. At least this is my theory. Jastram, who has one of the finest minds in the synod's system of higher education, had arranged all created things on a scale, and within this scale placed man and woman at the top.

President Al Barry had died in March 2001. During a hospitalization in Florida, Barry, who had been fighting cancer, had come down with an infection from which he did not recover. His death came three months before the July 2001 LCMS convention. Present for the May meeting for adoption of the Jastram proposal were Bob Kuhn (b. 1937) and Bob King, who succeeded into the offices of president and first vice president and were advisory members of the commission. Texas District president Gerald Kieschnick had been put forth as a candidate for synodical president at the 1998 convention. He had been serving as the representative of synod's college of presidents to the Commission on Theology and Church Relations, and so he was a known figure in synod circles.

As chairman of the CTCR, other district presidents gave him the opportunity to address their conventions in 2000. Before Barry had died, Kurt Marquart made several references to Kieschnick's drive to the presidency at CTCR meetings chaired by Kieschnick. Kieschnick, always the gentleman, never responded to personal challenges from fellow commission members.

Bob King had strongly supported passage of *Male and Female in the Image of God*. An obstacle to taking action on the *Image of God* document was Marquart's objections to a proposal recommending the synod establish fellowship with the Evangelical Lutheran Church of Latvia. This discussion absorbed the remainder of the time. A recommendation for fellowship with the Haitian Lutheran church, strongly supported by Marquart, went through quickly and received unanimous endorsement at the synod convention.

Having to adjourn by three o'clock on Saturday, April 28, the clock was ticking. A synod convention generally acts on the recommendation of the commission, and with the 2001 convention scheduled for July 14–20, it was only weeks away. Resolutions had to be in the hands of the convention committees for its meetings by May 25–28. Kurt Marquart had deep concerns regarding a church that had fellowship arrangements with other Lutheran churches and its membership in the Lutheran World Federation. Latvian churches operate with an episcopal system of church government and not a congregational one. As a loyal son of C.F.W. Walther, Marquart had still another reason to object, and so he prolonged the discussion, but finally fellowship with Latvia was recommended by the CTCR to the synod for adoption. Marquart also had concerns about the Evangelical Lutheran Church of Siberia, which also had an episcopal system with a permanent bishop at its head. On a teaching assignment to Siberia, he had worked to convince its members to adopt the Waltherian congregational model of the LCMS. Now the clock had come down to the last few minutes before three o'clock, and little time was allowed for *Male and Female in the Image of God*, which appeared to have enough support from the members for passage.

Before a vote could be taken, the three o'clock deadline for adjournment had come and the document could not be acted upon. Technically, the hour of adjournment could have been postponed, but set air travel arrangements and the cost of readjustment made this unfeasible. Had the Latvian matter not been drawn out, the Jastram paper on the *Image of God* would have come up for a vote and passed, largely because of the hearty support of synod vice president King.

In September, the CTCR membership was reconstituted with presidential appointments no longer in the hands of the deceased president Alvin Barry, but his elected successor Gerald Kieschnick, and *Male and Female in the Image of God* was rejected. Marquart expressed regret that at the May meeting no time was left for its passage, but his prolonging the discussion on fellowship with Latvia at that meeting was a factor, maybe the main reason for its not coming to a vote.

Support or rejection of *Male and Female in the Image of God* cannot be understood simply as a conservative/liberal matter. In tracing the progression from simple creatures through complex ones to man, some conservatives saw in it an evolutionist scheme. It was printed in the *Concordia Theological Quarterly* (*CTQ*),[2] and none of its readers wrote to say that they had understood the essay in this way. This was the last thing in the mind of its author.

From the perspective of those favoring a greater role for women and thus allowing fellowship with churches that favor the ordination of women, e.g., the Evangelical Lutheran Church in America, the document was a death-knell of their hopes. Though through the *CTQ* it received a wide circulation, the article's impact might have been greater had it been adopted by the commission. What surfaces is the inability of like-minded persons to agree that some things are more important than others and then to adjust the means of attaining the goals reckoned as the more important. Those who opposed *Male and Female in the Image of God* found an ally in the member who ran the clock out for them in not opposing the Latvian fellowship and its archbishop. Marquart's principles!

Rejection of the essay allowed synod president Kieschnick to call for an ad hoc convocation at which prominent synod feminists were invited to express their views, though commission members were told that this would not be done. A commission with a different makeup during the presidency of Matthew Harrison was finally able to settle the issue, on which most of the synod members already agreed.[3] Expenditures in additional time and money were as unnecessary as they were enormous. Irony lurks everywhere.

---

2. Nathan Jastram, "Man as Male and Female: Created in the Image of God," *Concordia Theological Quarterly* 68, no. 1 (January 2004): 3–96.
3. Lutheran Church—Missouri Synod, Commission on Theology and Church Relations, *The Creator's Tapestry: Scriptural Perspectives on Man-Woman Relationships in Marriage and the Church: A Report of the Commission on Theology and Church Relations, The Lutheran Church—Missouri Synod* (St. Louis, MO: Lutheran Church—Missouri Synod, 2010).

While fellowship with the Latvian church limped through the 2001 synod convention with opposition, fellowship with the Haitian church was accepted unanimously. At last report, the Haitian church was facing difficulties. It has proven to be a weak sister church. Latvia had happier results.

A funeral service for Al Barry was held in the St. Louis seminary chapel. It was as much a gathering of the major players for the synod's July convention. Wenthe, who had successfully walked a tightrope in Fort Wayne as its president for six years, was seen as an ideal candidate, and had been advised by synod secretary Raymond Hartwig to avoid right-wing groups. Kieschnick, on the other hand, traveled to New Haven, Missouri, to meet with *Christian News* editor Herman Otten, who became convinced of Kieschnick's biblical commitment. Wenthe was seen by some conservative operatives as "high church," which he was not.

In the spring faculty elections, Bill Weinrich was elected in my place as the faculty representative to the CTCR. Should he be chosen as synod president in July, Wenthe said I would be his appointment to the group. So certain was Wenthe's election as synod president that the faculty virtually *en masse* went to St. Louis for the convention, something that was duly noted by district presidents supporting Kieschnick. Wenthe led on the first three ballots, but on the fourth ballot Kieschnick won by nineteen votes—or was it seventeen? A switch of a handful of votes would have made the difference. Other candidates collectively garnered a majority of the votes in the second and third ballots. More delegates were against him than for him. Already on the first ballot, Wenthe's loss was inevitable. Wenthe's election was thought to be such a certainty that it caught his supporters off guard.

Daniel Preus's election as first vice president was another piece in the puzzle. He was the oldest son of the late Robert D. Preus. The younger Preus was the true favorite of the conservatives. Except for the election for president, the conservative proposed candidates took the remaining elected positions. Several forces had been working against Wenthe.

Indiana District president Tim Sims had written a letter to his district delegates to the synod convention that Wenthe had done such a marvelous job as seminary president that he should remain in that position. On that account Kieschnick should be elected synod president. This letter may have provided Kieschnick with the ten votes needed for his election. Kieschnick also was the overwhelming favorite of most of the district presidents. Against such opposition this makes Wenthe's close showing all the more remarkable.

Though it never was made explicit, there was an underlying resistance to Wenthe among some conservatives that surfaced in *Christian News* issues before the convention. The straw breaking the camel's back came with an issue that was placed in bulk at seven PM on Saturday in the lobbies of the hotels in downtown St. Louis housing the convention delegates. Balloting for president was scheduled for Sunday morning, the next day.

Prominently featured in *Christian News* were articles by Jack Cascione questioning Wenthe's commitment to Messianic prophecy. With only twelve hours between the time the delegates read Cascione's article and the balloting, no chance for refutation was possible. This was a low blow that deprived Wenthe of the synod presidency. After the election Atlantic District president David Benke (b. 1946) said that Kieschnick should thank *Christian News* for his election. In the back of the convention floor Weinrich told Cascione, "Look what you have done."

After that, Cascione was removed from the synod when his congregation left, and the editor of *Christian News* expresses wonderment why he remains uninvited to certain events and the newspaper is not distributed at our seminary, though it is available. Even if he did not know, many others do.

Jack Cascione graduated from the seminary's two-year alternate route program for ordination. He had come to the seminary with a master's degree in fine arts from Indiana University and gave himself wholeheartedly to causes close to Robert Preus's heart. Foregoing receiving the M.A. degree to which he was entitled, Cascione, after ordination, enrolled in other seminary courses and eventually received the standard M.Div. degree. This also impressed Preus.

A Fort Wayne faculty member, later transferred to St. Louis, arranged for Cascione to make a presentation at the prestigious Society of New Testament Studies for his book that assigned numerical value to the letters of the Greek alphabet in the Book of Revelation. In conversation with Cascione, I noted that standard Greek texts of the New Testaments were a compilation derived from various manuscripts and that these compilations and the texts from which they were derived differed from one another. I asked if his scheme of assigning a mathematical value to the alphabet would work on other texts.

Adoption of *Lay Teachers of Theology* was also a matter of timing, but more importantly, its approval reflected the synod's position on the ministry. In its 1998–2001 term, the commission received a request on whether laity could teach theology in the Concordia University System. Had the commission handled the request in that term, it would have said no. By postponing to the 2001–2004 term, a positive answer was assured. Without first addressing the question of what constitutes the teaching of "theology" and what does not, this resolution could be seen as a step leading to ordaining women, since both male and female laity would be allowed to teach theology.

At its 1969 convention, the synod had allowed women to participate in the governance of congregations by their becoming members of voters' assemblies. Since synod's congregations had the ultimate authority in choosing pastors and in owning property, women could be seen as having a supervisory role of the pastors of the congregations to which they belonged. Sociologists point out that churches allowing women to participate in local congregational governance will later allow them to be fully authorized ministers. Would the Missouri Synod be an exception? So far it has been.

Another question is whether voters' assemblies are biblically ideal, or whether the synod's founding fathers simply adopted a model widespread in their adopted country. European churches did not have voter's assemblies, but congregational churches had governed themselves in this way since the first settlements in New England in the 1600s. Typically LCMS Lutherans argued that congregational autonomy and self-governance was the ideal Luther wanted but never was able to achieve in sixteenth-century Germany.

For the members of synod, only the position of the local parish pastor had a biblical mandate. All other church positions were auxiliary to that office. Whatever was said about the ministry in the Bible was applicable only to the congregation and its worship services and not to other church-related institutions like elementary schools, high schools, college and seminaries, so the argument went.

According to the resolution that passed, ten members voted in the affirmative. Women would not be allowed to preach from the pulpit, but they were not prohibited from lecturing on theology in synod-sponsored institutions, including seminaries. Of the remaining six members, four clearly voted in the negative, including Marquart and myself, and two seemed to vote the same way.

Without further clarification, there is rhyme and reason not to allow women to teach theology. Historically, Missouri Synod theologians held that only parish pastors were ministers in the New Testament sense, and so it required that those holding seminary teaching positions and posts of synod and district president and vice presidents also had to be pastors of congregations or qualified to be such. Walther, Wyneken and Pieper were pastors of St. Louis congregations, and Schwan was a pastor of a Cleveland church, even if he only occasionally carried out ministerial duties there. For centuries in the Catholic Church, cardinals residing in Rome were pastors of churches in that city or in Asia Minor, where Christianity was long extinct. So the synod practice was not idiosyncratic.

In the commission's opinion, what the Bible said about ministers serving congregations did not apply to educational institutions, and so lay persons could teach any subject. Theology was seen simply as another subject in the curriculum. A century ago, ordained ministers comprised the majority of all positions at the synod's high schools and junior colleges, roughly the equivalent of the German gymnasium, and all positions at its seminaries. This gradually changed so that now the teaching staffs of the colleges are predominantly lay people—some not Lutheran or even Christian. Rarely does an ordained pastor teach courses like history, English, biology or the humanities, though up to the middle of the last century this was common.

Nomenclature also underwent a subtle change. What was now more frequently called "theology" and "theology courses" at the synod's universities were called—at least in the first century of the synod's existence—"religion" and "religion courses." "Theology" used to refer to the education that students studying for the ministry received. Courses teaching Lutheran doctrine and the Scriptures in the high schools and colleges were called religion courses. Now we hear of non-ordained persons, often with only a college degree, teaching theology at the high-school level. These teachers of theology are not, or should not be, seen as theologians in the traditional sense.

There is a practical side to the question that remains unaddressed. Pastors with four years of seminary education are qualified to serve as high school teachers and perhaps in some cases college teachers. Those with a bachelor's degree or in some cases only a one- or two-year degree in religion, whether they be men or women, are not trained to the extent pastors are, who are actually trained to read the Bible in its original languages. While the opponents see this as a step in the direction of women's ordination by allowing lay women to teach theology, an equally disturbing issue is that the distinction between clergy on one side and laity on the other was being eroded.

This issue could have been resolved, if certain courses in the curriculum had been labeled as secular, e.g. the teaching of Hebrew and Greek, the biblical languages, and of German and Latin, the languages of the Lutheran Confessions. These could have been seen as secular courses that would allow for lay teaching. However, the resolution gives a blanket approval to lay persons teaching any theology or religion course at any level in the synod's higher education system. The resolution did not distinguish teaching theology at a seminary or a college, and so presupposes that what happens at one institution is what may happen at another. Students accustomed to having women lecture on theology will be prepared for seeing them in pulpit preaching.

Also at issue is whether the word *church* only covers what happens in the regular church service or whether it also applies to what happens in a seminary. Getting this question straight would require an unraveling of a century and a half of synod history, and this is not likely to happen.

Also at work in the *Lay Teachers of Theology* resolution was a cultural factor in transforming the gymnasium model of German education that corresponds to the four years of high school and the first two years of college into the American system, which makes the four high school years preparatory for four years of college. To accomplish this, the four high school years were dropped and the remaining institutions became four-year colleges that now comprise the Concordia University System.

Their curriculums are heavily weighted on the side of secular courses leading to business and professional degrees. They recruit and attract non-Lutherans and even non-Christians. Lutherans enrolled in these colleges no longer constitute a majority, and those preparing for professional church work are a decreasing minority. While theology is required for graduation, it has become less significant in shaping the academic environment. On that account the proponents of *Lay Teachers of Theology* had their eye on allowing women to teach theology at the synod's two seminaries.

With Gerald Kieschnick taking over as synod president in place of the deceased Alvin Barry in 2001, Weinrich was not reappointed to the commission, and so he was in a position to allow his name to stand for election as the faculty's representative to the commission. As the academic dean, he had an advantage in attracting more votes from the faculty than I did, and he replaced me. Marquart was easily reelected.

Synod rules allow for only three successive terms on the commission, and so Weinrich was ruled ineligible to serve, and I was returned by the faculty in a special election in September 2001. Due to the system of balloting, Marquart, Weinrich and I all received a majority of the votes cast, but Charles Gieschen worked to have another ballot. During the second triennium, I was the chairman of the subcommittee on theology and was involved in writing and editing the documents. My fingerprints are all over two documents in particular, *The Lutheran Understanding of Church*

Fellowship[4] and *Guidelines for Participation in Civic Events.*[5] A long time can elapse between the time the commission accepts a request for a theological opinion to its final adoption. A subcommittee can offer a resolution only to have it turned down by the full commission or returned to the subcommittee where it originated or its chief author. Often a second or a third author is chosen to prepare the document.

This is what happened with *The Lutheran Understanding of Church Fellowship*, for which I was asked to prepare the first draft. Upon its rejection, it was assigned to Marquart and again rejected. Then it fell into my lap again. He may not have been present for that meeting.

One morning after chapel, he let me know that he was less than happy with my being chosen. This time my draft was accepted by the commission, with Marquart in agreement. A few days later, again after chapel, he expressed his appreciation and at the same time was amazed that all had assented to it.

Every institution is by definition a political one, and so the commission has its own political life. Staff members do not vote, but with offices in the synod office building in St. Louis, they are in a position to influence which documents will be discussed and who will elect its officers. In the 1998–2001 triennium, support for *Lay Teachers of Theology* was lacking, and to assure its passing it was delayed by the staff to 2009.

Then there is the matter of consistency in the application of the rules. Upon his retirement from his congregation, commission secretary George Dolak was ruled ineligible to continue as a member, since it was said this position required an active pastor, not emeritus pastor. On the other hand, Orville Walz (b. 1939), who had been appointed by Kieschnick (2001–2004), in his role as a college professor, was reappointed as a member to fill the position reserved for an active member of the clergy (2004–2007). Walz was not an active pastor. If the rule concerning retiring Dolak had been applied to Walz, he would not have been allowed to hold that position. In addition, he may have never served as a parish pastor.

During my first triennium on an evenly divided commission with Kieschnick as its chairman and Alvin Barry as synod president, production

---

4. Lutheran Church—Missouri Synod, Commission on Theology and Church Relations, *The Lutheran Understanding of Church Fellowship: Study Materials* (St. Louis, MO: Lutheran Church—Missouri Synod, 2000).

5. Lutheran Church—Missouri Synod, Commission on Theology and Church Relations, *Guidelines for Participation in Civic Events: A Report of the Commission on Theology and Church Relations of The Lutheran Church—Missouri Synod* (St. Louis, MO: Lutheran Church—Missouri Synod, 2004).

of *The Lutheran Understanding of Church Fellowship* was an accomplishment worth noting. Elected in 2001 as synod president, the commission's chairman, Gerald Kieschnick, was able to exert more influence. Loren Kramer, appointed by synod president Kieschnick, was serving his first term on the commission and on the first ballot was elected chairman. Kieschnick appointee Orville Walz and Peter Hess, a Cleveland attorney, were elected vice chairman and secretary respectively. As chairman of the subcommittee on theology, I remained a member of the executive committee and became well acquainted with them.

Even though the 2001 convention chose Kieschnick as synod president, it did not support those who were associated with him for other positions. Loren Kramer, the popular former president of the Pacific Southwest District, stood for election as a candidate for synodical vice president, synod board of directors and the St. Louis seminary board of regents and lost. He was Kieschnick's man for the commission on theology.

Though I had opportunities to ask Kramer why he proposed that the delegates from his district to the 1998 synod convention read Waldo Werning's *Making the Missouri Synod Functional Again*, I did not. When Werning's name came up, we all kind of laughed, though for me, who he was and what he did could never be a laughing matter.

I thought I was ineligible for a third term, but in the spring of 2004, Weinrich phoned to remind me that a faculty meeting was in session (I had forgotten about it), and I would be a candidate for the seminary's representative for the third term. Marquart and I continued as the faculty representatives, but while I was chosen on the second ballot, his election came with the third ballot.

In six years things had changed. The third term was less eventful, and after serving nine years, it is not difficult to see why term limits are put on terms of church service. My experiences with the commission members were all positive, though I must admit my frustration when staff members dominated the discussion.

For me the last meeting was April 15–19, 2007, with the evening of the eighteenth set aside for a dinner noting the service of those leaving the commission. On April 27, 2001, my retirement from the commission had already been noted with a plaque given to those who serve on synod's board. Now I would receive another one. The one hangs on my home office in Fort Wayne and the other in our Pocono summer home.

The length of these farewell occasions can be tiring. I turned down the option of giving lectures in Japan to attend the last meeting, though I had doubts about whether this was the right choice. At the evening celebration, executive director Sam Nafzger had the job of saying nice things about each retiring member. When he came to me, he said that I was the member that provided the unity of the commission for making it as productive as it was. I had never thought about it in quite that way, but these words do reflect how I wanted to see my place in the synod.

For the sake of peace we can never forego speaking frankly and honestly with each other, but without impugning the motives of those who do not agree with us. Only by laying our cards on the table can we see where we agree and from there work to work out our disagreements. On some issues, Sam and I did not see eye to eye. We worked through some of them and on some we probably still disagree. Disagreement on *Lay Teachers of Theology* was based on a more fundamental disagreement on the ministry that was endemic to the synod's theology since its founding, and it was not up to us to resolve it. My years on the commission in working through theology was a far cry from those years when I was being accused of false doctrine, where my accuser allowed for no discussion.

GLOSSARY

801 ✦ Concordia Seminary—St. Louis campus in Clayton, Missouri.

ALC ✦ American Lutheran Church. Later merged with the AELC and LCA to form the ELCA.

ATS ✦ Association of Theological Schools

AELC ✦ Association of Evangelical Lutheran Churches. A schism of the Lutheran Church—Missouri Synod congregations, formed after the LCMS rejected liberal methods of interpreting Biblical texts.

Association of Evangelical Lutheran Churches ✦ *see AELC*

BAG(D) ✦ Frederick W. Danker et al., *A Greek-English Lexicon of the New Testament and Other Early Christian Literature*, 3rd ed. (Chicago: University of Chicago Press, 2000).

Bethany Lutheran Seminary ✦ The Seminary of the Evangelical Lutheran Synod

BHES ✦ Board for Higher Education Services. Supervised the Concordia University System and the seminaries until it was phased out by the 2011 Convention of the Synod.

Bronxville ✦ *See Concordia Collegiate Institute.*

Central Illinois District ✦ A regional division of the Lutheran Church—Missouri Synod.

Christ College (Irvine, California) ✦ *See Concordia University Irvine*

Christ Seminary in Exile ✦ *See Seminex*

Commission on Worship, Liturgics and Hymnology ✦ *see Commission on Worship*

Concordia—Austin ✦ *See Concordia University Texas*

Concordia Collegiate Institute ✦ *See Concordia College New York.*

Concordia College New York ✦ Formerly known as Concordia Collegiate Institute, it is located in Bronxville, New York.

Concordia University Chicago ✦ Formally Concordia Teachers' College, located at various times in Fort Wayne, Indiana, Addison, Illinois and now in River Forest, Illinois.

Concordia University Irvine ✦ Formally known as Christ College.

Concordia University Texas ✦ Formally known as Concordia College—Austin, it is located in Austin, Texas.

Concordia University Wisconsin ✦ Formally Concordia College—Milwaukee and located at first in Milwaukee, Wisconsin. Now located in Mequon, Wisconsin.

CTQ ✦ Concordia Theological Quarterly—The faculty journal of Concordia Theological Seminary, succeeding its former title *The Springfielder*.

CTCR ✦ Commission on Theology and Church Relations. An elected board of the Lutheran Church—Missouri Synod that provides official theological opinions on topics of interest to the church and answers theological questions directed to them.

CTSFW ✦ Concordia Theological Seminary—Fort Wayne. The nickname by which the former practical seminary is now known. First used as the seminary's official internet domain name.

Der Deutsche Evangelisch-Lutherische Synode von Missouri, Ohio und anderen Staate. ✦ See Lutheran Church—Missouri Synod

ELC ✦ Evangelical Lutheran Church (Norwegian). Later merged with the American Lutheran Church (ALC).

ELCA ✦ Evangelical Lutheran Church in America. A merger of the American Lutheran Church, the Lutheran Church in America and Association of Evangelical Lutheran Churches. This church body is the largest and most theologically liberal of American Lutheran Churches in the twenty-first century.

ELS ✦ Evangelical Lutheran Synod

English Synod (English District) ✦ The English Evangelical Lutheran Synod of Missouri and Other States was founded by English speaking Lutherans, generally from the Tennessee Synod, who were in complete agreement with the doctrine and practice of Der Deutsche Evangelisch-Lutherische Synode von Missouri, Ohio und anderen Staate (now known as the Lutheran Church—Missouri Synod). The German synod felt it needed to operate in German as long as possible in order for its members to have full access to the literature of the Lutheran Church and to protect them as much as possible from the influences of the many non-Lutheran denominations and religions. So, while it rejoiced that English-speaking Lutherans wanted to join their fellowship, it encouraged them to form a separate church body. The English synod mirrored its name and structure and subscribed to its doctrines. It was finally admitted into the German Evangelical Lutheran Synod of Missouri, Ohio, and Other States in 1911 as a non-geographical district. In 1917, the Synod dropped "German" from its name. For a history of the English District, see John H. Baumgaertner, *A Tree Grows in Missouri* (Milwaukee: Agape Publishers, 1975).

Evangelical Lutheran Church in America ♦ *see ELCA*

LCA ♦ Lutheran Church in America. One of three church bodies that merged to form the Evangelical Lutheran Church in America

LCMS ♦ See *Lutheran Church—Missouri Synod*.

Little Norwegian Synod ♦ See *Evangelical Lutheran Synod*

LWF ♦ Lutheran World Federation, a communion of Lutheran Churches generally made up of liberal church bodies worldwide.

Lutheran Church—Missouri Synod ♦ A federation of confessional Lutheran congregations organized in 1847 by three groups of German confessional Lutherans who settled in the American Midwest. One group was made up of Saxons led by Martin Stephan and later C. F. W. Walther. They formed a a colony like other nineteenth-century utopian movements, settling in Perry County and St. Louis Mission. Another were from a variety of Lutheran territories and settled in Indiana, Ohio and Michigan for economic reasons under the pastoral care of F. C. D. Wyneken and Wilhelm Sihler. The third group were mainly Franconians sent by Wilhelm Löhe as a mission to Native Americans in the Saginaw Valley of Michigan. Among the middle group were the ancestors of David Scaer. This church body grew rapidly and led American Confessional Lutheranism until the middle of the twentieth century. It was originally called Der Deutschen Evangelisch-Lutherische Synode von Missouri, Ohio und andern Staaten, and adopted its present name in 1947.

Missouri Synod ♦ See *Lutheran Church—Missouri Synod*

NCA ♦ North Central Association.

NCC ♦ National Council of Churches.

Preus, Jack ♦ Jacob A. O. Preus II, eleventh President of Concordia Theological Seminary (Fort Wayne, St. Louis, Springfield, Illinois, F. Wayne) and President of the Lutheran Church—Missouri Synod during the Biblical inerrancy controversy of the 1960s and 1970s

RF ♦ See *Concordia University Chicago*

River Forest ♦ See *Concordia University Chicago*

Seminex ♦ The institution formed by the 1974 faculty majority of Concordia Seminary, St. Louis, Missouri, who went on strike ("walked out") to protest the suspension of Dr. John Tietjen as President. At first, it was formally named Concordia Seminary in Exile and later Christ Seminary in Exile, and was commonly known by the conflation as Seminex. At the founding of the ELCA, the institution disbanded and some of its faculty and staff moved to other seminaries of the new church body.

Synodical Conference ✦ From 1872 to 1967, a fellowship of confessional Lutheran church bodies, including the LCMS and WELS.

ULCA ✦ United Lutheran Church in America was formed by a merger of the synods belonging to the General Synod, General Council and the United Synod of the South. These included the oldest Lutheran church bodies in America and represented the "American Lutheran" movement, which adapted Lutheran theology and practice to the culture of the United States. Later it merged with several other church bodies to form the Lutheran Church in America, which later merged into the ELCA.

The Walkout ✦ To protest the suspension of Dr. John Tietjen from his post as President of Concordia Seminary, St. Louis, the majority of the student body and faculty went on strike, walking out of the campus.

INDEX

A

Ackerman, Steven ✦ 113
Acton, Thomas ✦ 219–220
Aho, Gerhard (1911–1988) ✦ 96, 109, 221, 232n, 233, 239, 248, 307, 410
Albrecht, Walter (1885–1961) ✦ 98–99
Alms, Paul Gregory ✦ 319n
Althaus, Paul II (1888–1966) ✦ 53
Altizer, Thomas J. J. (b. 1927) ✦ 89
Anderson, David (1931–2017) ✦ 165, 265, 276, 342, 343–344, 343n, 353
Anderson, Walter ✦ 227–228
Andres ✦ 112
Andresen, Ronald M. ✦ 320n
Appel, André (1922–2007) ✦ 125
Arand, Charles ✦ 202, 387
Ardy, Joseph ✦ 298
Aristotle (384–322 BC) ✦ 217
Arndt, William (1880–1957) ✦ 28, 29n
Asendorf, Ulrich ✦ 204
Aus, George (1903–1977) ✦ 159, 253–254

B

Baepler, Walter (1893–1958) ✦ 99
Baker, Tom ✦ 313
Balfour, Eddie ✦ 223–225, 226, 248
Balfour, Marie ✦ 226
Ballas, Kenneth ✦ 88–89, 96
Barry, Alvin (1931–2001) ✦ 166, 182, 210, 274, 323, 327, 336, 344, 351, 353, 359–363, 367–368
Barth, Karl (American Pastor) (b. 1924) ✦ 138, 203, 210, 222, 260
Barth, Karl (Swiss Theologian) (1886–1968) ✦ 21, 22, 23, 27, 30, 50, 81, 82, 89, 91
Bauer, Walter ✦ 28n
Baumgaertner, John H. ✦ 372n
Baumgartner, William ✦ 122, 206, 301, 304
Beckwith, Carl L. ✦ 190

Behning, Trudy ✦ 59, 165, 212, 249, 259, 264, 308, 322, 342
Behnken, John (1884–1968) ✦ xvii, 13, 28, 36–38, 40–41, 103, 236
Beiderwieden, George ✦ 131
Biederwieden, Theodore (1908–1981) ✦ 130
Bender, Peter ✦ 202, 402
Benke, David (b. 1946) ✦ 276, 364
Bertram, Robert ✦ 139
Bertram, Peter (b. 1955) ✦ 335
Betker, Bruce ✦ 273
Beto, George (1916–1991) ✦ 67, 99–101, 174
Bishop, Daniel John ✦ 319n
Black, George ✦ 299–300
Block, Rudy C. ✦ 205–206, 286
Blumenkamp, Edwin (b. 1929) ✦ 65, 67
Bode, Arthur J. ✦ 279
Bohlmann, Ralph (1932–2016) ✦ 90, 125, 153–155, 163–166, 182, 200, 215, 220–225, 232–233, 236, 255, 264, 266, 269–270, 273–276, 285, 287, 289, 291–292, 299–300, 301, 304, 323, 347
Bohlmann, Victor ✦ 153, 158
Bollhagen, James ✦ 221, 232n, 281, 286, 303, 321–322, 358–359
Boomhower, Patrick (b. 1949) ✦ 315
Borchelt, Wally (1930–2012) ✦ 176
Borcherding, Alan ✦ xv, 165, 310, 326, 329, 331–332, 337–341, 347, 349
Bouman, Herbert J. A. (1908–1981) ✦ 28, 38
Bouman, Walter ✦ 133, 421
Braaten, Carl (b. 1929) ✦ xvi, 122, 186, 207, 389
Brainerd, Winthrop (b. 1936) ✦ 85, 316
Brand, Eugene (1913–2002) ✦ 156
Brauer, Fritz ✦ 72
Bredemeier, Herbert (1911–2001) ✦ 179, 237, 302

Bredemeier, Melvin ✦ 237, 238, 264n, 298
Bretscher, Paul (1921–2016) ✦ 53, 416
Briel, Steven (b. 1949) ✦ 167, 205–206, 306
Bright ✦ 112, 116
Brinkel, Karl ✦ 60
Brockopp, Daniel Carl (1934–2016) ✦ 143
Brooks, Charles ✦ 293–295
Brown, Ada ✦ 6
Bruch, Dan ✦ 212, 221
Brunn, August (1895–1994) ✦ 68
Brunn, Walter (1897–1979) ✦ 182–183
Brunner, Emil (1889–1966) ✦ 21, 27, 30, 91
Brunner, Peter (1900–1981) ✦ 103, 410
Brustat, August (1905–1990) ✦ 130
Buchheimer, Louis (1897–1988) ✦ 30
Buchheimer, Paul (1915–1999) ✦ 30–31
Buege, William A. (1902–2002) ✦ 130
Buegler, David ✦ 320, 327
Buls, Alfred (b. 1925) ✦ 64
Buls, Harold (1920–1997) ✦ 64n, 226, 233, 257, 280, 281, 286
Bultemeyer, Richard J. ✦ 266. 269, 270
Bultmann, Rudolf (1884–1976) ✦ xi, 21–22, 27, 30, 55, 77, 80, 83, 91, 122–123, 137–138, 142, 419, 421, 425
Bunkowske, Eugene (1935–2018) ✦ 202, 204, 206, 216, 218, 233, 266, 279, 281, 285–287, 298–300, 323, 334
Burgland, Lane ✦ 310, 331, 334, 341, 349
Buszin, Walter C. (1899–1973) ✦ 101
Buuck, John ✦ 211

C

Caemmerer, Dorothy Scaer (1905–1996) ✦ 25, 50
Caemmerer, Richard (1904–1984) ✦ 19, 25, 29, 35, 41, 49–50, 180
Caemmerer, Richard R. II (1933–2016) ✦ 25n, 181
Calvin, Jean (1509–1564) ✦ 56, 58, 178

Carter, Steven (Stephen) (b. 1941) ✦ 189, 212, 221, 248
Cascione, Jack ✦ 184, 364
Case, Jan ✦ 281, 286, 305, 307, 314, 316–317, 319, 331, 349
Caudill, Mike ✦ 308
Christian, Douglas ✦ 216
Christiansen ✦ 337
Clinton, Bill (b. 1946) ✦ 234
Cluver, Dennis P. ✦ 116
Cobo, Albert (1893–1957) ✦ 31
Coiner, Harry (1912–1992) ✦ 63
Collins, Robert ✦ 224, 232n, 233
Collver, Albert III ✦ 127, 190, 211
Coverdale, Myles (1488–1569) ✦ 178
Craemer, August (1812–1891) ✦ 334
Craemer, Dorothea (1817–1884) ✦ 334
Cullmann, Oscar (1902–1999 ✦ 23
Cunningham, Sister Agnes ✦ 112

D

Damm, John (b. 1926) ✦ 48, 129–131, 133, 170, 172
Daniel, Theodore A. "Ted" (1920–2008) ✦ 30
Danker, Frederick (1920–2012) ✦ 28, 141, 146
Deffner, Corinne (1927–1998) ✦ 164, 177
Deffner, Donald (1924–1997) ✦ 28, 62, 129, 177, 281, 282, 286, 306, 354, 391
Degner, Waldemar "Wally" (1925–1998) ✦ 200, 221, 229–232, 257, 280–281, 286, 295, 303, 306
Dewey, Thomas (1902–1971) ✦ 4
Diefenthaler, Jon ✦ 150
Dissen, Walter ✦ 342
Dodd, C. H. (1884–1973) ✦ 45
Dolak, George (1903–1968) ✦ 96, 368
Dorn, Paul ✦ 66–67
Dreyer, John M. ✦ 319n
Dumperth, Dale Allen ✦ 319n
Dungan, David L. (1936–2008) ✦ 84–85
Dunker, Randy ✦ 320

E

Ebeling, David ♦ 213
Eggold, Henry "Hank" (1917–1982)
  ♦ xv, 156–158, 410
Ehlen, Arlis (1931–2016) ♦ 33n
Eissfeldt, Eleanor (1916–1973) ♦ 116, 120
Eissfeldt, Raymond (1912–2000)
  ♦ 108, 110–120
Elert, Werner (1885–1954) ♦ 53, 57–58
Elliott, Deborah ♦ 110, 112
Elliott, John (b. 1935) ♦ 61
Empie, Paul C. (1909–1979) ♦ 125, 399
Ervin, Bob (1931–1964) ♦ 15
Esget, Christopher ♦ 334
Evanson, Charles ♦ 252
Ewenson, Andy ♦ 65

F

Farmer, William (1921–2000) ♦ 83, 84, 237, 421
Farnsworth, Kenneth Walter ♦ 319n
Fehl, William "Bud" (1922–1992)
  ♦ 265, 272–273, 319n
Fehrmann, John ♦ 150
Fein, Lowell ♦ 214, 294, 303, 338
Feld ♦ 116
Ferry, Patrick T. ♦ 211, 227
Feuerhahn, Ronald (1937–2015)
  ♦ 210, 274
Feyerharm, W. R. ♦ 117, 119
Fiene, Hans (b. 1980) ♦ 160
Fiene, Solveig Preus (b. 1957) ♦ 160
Fienen, Daniel H. (b. 1952) ♦ 301–302,
Fink, Herman Sr. ♦ 342
Fink, Ronald (1937–2014) ♦ 342
Foelber, Elmer (1892–1987) ♦ 135n
Forde, Gerhard O. (1927–2005) ♦ 251
Fosdick, Harry Emerson (1879–1969)
  ♦ 91
French, David Ray ♦ 319n
Frincke, Herman (1912–2010) ♦ 17
Froehlich, Charles (b. 1927) ♦ 26
Fry, C. George (b. 1936) ♦ 207, 221–222, 422
Fuerbringer, Alfred O. (1903–1997)
  ♦ 26–27, 35, 37, 50, 134–135, 160

G

Gamaliel, J. ♦ 210
Garber, Reuben (1929–2001) ♦
  163–164, 220, 260–261, 264,
  268–270
Garcia, Albert (b. 1947) ♦ 207, 221, 233n
Gard, Annette (b. 1960) ♦ 165
Gard, Daniel (b. 1954) ♦ A165 D141n,
  165, 268, 294, 303, 321, 322n
  343–344, 351
Gaulke, Earl H. (1927–2013) ♦ 189
Geiseman, O. A. (1893–1962) ♦ 13
Giertz, Bo (1905–1998) ♦ 124
Gieschen, Charles ♦ 214, 367
Giesler, Philipp ♦ 208–209
Goltermann, Sam I (1926–2004) ♦
  73, 148
Gottschalk, Karl ♦ 122
Grabau, J. A. A. (1804–1879) ♦ 171, 330
Graesser, Karl (b. 1929) ♦ 26, 47, 70,
  72–73, 117
Graf, Arthur E. (1912–2004) ♦ 26n, 96
Graham, Billy (1918–2018) ♦ 49
Graudin, Arthur ♦ 246
Green, Lowell ♦ 48, 191
Griesbach, Johann Jakob (1745–1812)
  ♦ 84
Grobien, Gifford ♦ 191
Grotelueschen, Arden (1940–1995) ♦
  110–111, 113–115, 117, 120
Grothe, Jonathan F. (b. 1941) ♦
  326–327
Grueber, John Andrew Henry
  (1877–1959) ♦ 40, 42
Grumm, Arnold H. (1893–1959) ♦ 36
Guebert, Alex (1895–1986) ♦ 49
Guinness, Os (b. 1941) ♦ 261–262, 408

H

Haak, Rudolf (1919–1999) ♦ 110n, 111,
  114–116, 119, 138
Haake, Earl ♦ 330
Haas, Harold (1925–2013) ♦ 10, 180
Habel, Norman (b. 1932) ♦ 108
Hackett, Tom (b. 1949) ♦ 150

Hagen, Kenneth (1936–2014) ◆ 197, 204
Hallcher, Fred (1908–1997) ◆ 68, 70
Hallcher, Martha (1901–1991) ◆ 68
Halter, Howard (1907–1975) ◆ 48
Hamann, Henry ◆ 212
Handler, Klaus ◆ 58
Hanser, Carl Johann Otto (1832–1910) ◆ 69
Harms, Herman A. (1889–1978) ◆ 36
Harms, Oliver (1901–1980) ◆ 28, 38, 73, 96, 102, 117, 132, 134, 137, 143, 338, 354
Harre, Allen ◆ 205
Harrison, Matthew C. ◆ 127, 167, 211, 302, 351, 362, 417
Harrisville, Roy (b. 1922) ◆ 122
Hartwig, Raymond ◆ 363
Heider, George ◆ 140n
Heins, John ◆ 297, 320, 337, 347
Heintzen, Erich H. (1908–1971) ◆ 88, 97, 153, 410
Hengel, Martin (1926–2009) ◆ 83–84, 411
Hengstenberg, David ◆ 80
Henry, Carl F. H. (1913–2003) ◆ 90, 262
Hess, Marcie ◆ 310, 311n
Hess, Peter ◆ 5369
Heuchert, Lawrence (1924–2014) ◆ 67
Higgins, Eugene (d. 1948) ◆ 7
Hinlicky, Paul R. ◆ 230
Hinrichs, Kenneth Nelson ◆ 319n
Hinz, Frederick (1926–2009) ◆ 64
Hodel, David Kurt ◆ 319n
Hoerber, Robert (1918–1996) ◆ 161, 425
Hoffmann, Oswald (1913–2005) ◆ 13, 15n, 19, 99, 115–116, 133, 204
Hogg, Charles Robert ◆ 309, 346
Hogg, Jim ◆ 349
Horton, Michael (b. 1964) ◆ 255, 412, 418
Hoesman, C. William (b. 1940) ◆ 95
Houser, William ◆ 233, 281, 286

Hoyer, George (1919–2011) ◆ 26, 49, 354n
Hoyer, Theodore (d. 1928) ◆ 354n
Hudson, Charles ◆ 316
Huegli, Albert (1913–1998) ◆ 19
Hugh, Earl ◆ 16, 118
Hummel, Horace ◆ 34, 36, 400
Huth, Harry (1917–1979) ◆ 94, 96, 102, 145–146, 158, 208, 357, 410
Hyatt, Gerhardt Wilfred (1916–1985) ◆ 224–226

J

Jackson, Paul ◆ 297–300
Jaeger, Ralph ◆ 320n
Janssen, Arlo ◆ 222
Jasper, Joan ◆ 273
Jasper, Lewis ◆ 273
Jastram, Nathan ◆ 360–361, 362n
Jenson, Robert (1930–2017) ◆ 186, 426
Jersild, Paul ◆ 62
Ji, Won Sang ◆ 274
Ji, Won Yong (1924–2013) ◆ 274
Joeckel, David ◆ 41
Joeckel, Raymond ◆ 163–164, 248, 260–261, 264, 270–271, 276, 304
Joersz, Jerry ◆ 246
Johnson, James Robeli, Sr. ◆ 319n
Johnson, John Franklin (b. 1947) ◆ 189, 191
Johnson, John Frederick (1922–2009) ◆ 88–89, 95, 109, 113, 144–145, 150–152, 158, 166
Jones, Holland "Casey" ◆ 22
Judisch, Douglas ◆ 165, 169, 207, 233, 253n, 267n, 281, 286, 303, 358–359
Jungkuntz, Richard "Dick" (1918–2003) ◆ 338
Just, Arthur A., Jr. ◆ 85, 86n, 195, 200, 221, 226, 233n, 235, 248, 259, 281, 282, 286, 291, 303–304, 316, 343, 344, 346, 351
Just, Arthur A., Sr. ◆ 346

K

Kadai, Heino "Hank" (1931–1999) • H97, 205, 212, 217, 233n, 281, 286, 335, 336–337, 348
Kadai, Lois • 338
Kaiser, Paul Matthew • 319n
Kaiser, Walter • 221
Kalin, Evertt • 354n
Kantzer, Kenneth (1917–2002) • 90, 262, 406
Karlstadt, Andreas (1486–1541) • 37, 212
Kelm, Lawrence (b. 1939) • 17
Kenyon, Florence (1921–1950) • 19
Kettner, Michael Allen • 319n
Keurulainen, James E. (1947–2014) • 157
Kiehl, Erich (1920–2012) • 286, 296
Kieschnick, John • 95
Kieshnick, Gerald (b. 1943) • xvi, 95, 100, 167, 323, 356, 359–364, 367–369
Kilcrease, Jack • 190
Kinder, Ernst (1921–2016) • 53–54, 56–58
King, Robert (1922–2016) • 327, 336–337, 360–361
Kipp, David • 320n
Kirchner, Donald • 265, 276
Klann, Richard (1915–2005) • 9, 154, 190, 191, 194
Klein, Leonard • 230, 390
Klein, Ralph (b. 1936) • 133
Kleiner, Hugo (1897–1963) • 39–40, 131
Klink, Alfred (1900–1959) • 34
Klotz, John • 240, 260, 313
Klug, Dorothy • 98, 278
Klug, Eugene (1917–2003) • 94, 98–99, 102, 119, 153, 175, 188, 199–200, 205, 209, 220–221, 233n, 225, 278, 284, 286–293, 310, 324, 332, 350, 357, 410
Koch, Mark Andrew • 319n
Koenig, George C. (1894–1951) • 3
Koenig, Richard E. • 29n
Koepchen, Henry (1896–1957) • 16
Koepchen, Henry "Hank" (b. 1931) • 276, 323

Korby, Kenneth (1924–2006) • 155, 204
Kortum, F. W. "Rick" • 228, 229
Kramer, Fred (1902–1991) • 73, 94, 106, 144
Kramer, Loren (b. 1934) • 49, 297, 369
Kraus, George (1924–1989) • 221, 233, 226, 314
Kraus, Helen • 177, 226
Kreiss, Wilber • 210
Krentz, Edgar (b. 1928) • 26, 96
Krentz, Eugene (b. 1932) • 346
Kretzmann, Micky • 124
Kretzmann, Norman (1928–1998) • 70, 71
Kretzmann, O. P. (1902–1975) • 13, 143
Krompardt, Arnold • 219
Krumm, Paul • 344
Kuehnert, Arthur • 119
Kuhn, Robert (b. 1937) • 360
Kuntz, Arnold • 276

L

Laesch, Theodore (b. 1935) • 337
Laporte, Jean-Marc • 235
Lehmann, Detlaff • 210
Leininger, Jack (1903–1990) • 182–183
Lenski, Richard C. H. (1864–1936) • 229, 252
Lienhard, Marc (b. 1935) • 124, 126
Lim, Edmund • 274
Lincoln, Abraham (1809–1865) • 177
Lockwood, Greg • 310, 358
Löhe, Max (1900–1977) • 123, 124
Löhe, Wilhelm (1808–1872) • 56, 171, 177, 178
Loose, George (1920–2007) • 16
Love, Mark W. • 319n
Luebke, Martin (1917–2008) • 151–152, 170, 213, 214, 217, 221
Lueker, Ewin (1914–2000) • 59
Lumpp, David • 188
Luther, Martin (1483–1546) • 7, 37, 46, 56, 57, 58, 60, 78, 83, 97, 98, 121, 124, 131, 147, 178, 196, 212, 220, 245, 255, 284, 365

M

MacDougall, Steve • 314, 320n
Macke, Elmer • 176
MacKenzie, Cameron • 193, 287, 288, 233, 281, 286–290, 358
Maehr, Martin (1933–2017) • 111, 117
Maier, Hulda (1890–1986) • 256
Maier, Paul L. (b. 1930) • 48, 82
Maier, Walter A. I (1893–1950) • 13, 14, 32, 90, 151, 255
Maier, Walter A. II (b. 1925) • xv, 145, 163, 175, 208, 209, 216, 221, 226, 232, 233, 254–258, 266, 269, 286–288, 303–304, 306–311, 319, 322–326, 331, 334, 336–337, 349, 350, 358
Maier, Walter A. III • 206, 255, 257, 268–269, 297, 306, 322, 332, 341
Main, Robert • 45
Mann, Christopher S. (1917–1996) • 80, 84–85, 311, 316
Manske, Charles (1933–2015) • 206, 404
Markworth, Kenneth • 115
Marquart, Barbara • 67
Marquart, Kurt E. (1934–2006) • 11, 30, 32–33, 36–43, 46, 47, 66, 94, 131, 162, 169, 188, 190–195, 197, 205, 207–208, 233, 281, 286, 296, 312–314, 331–332, 341, 351, 358–362, 365, 367–369, 403, 410, 422
Marshall, Robert (1918–2008) • 122
Martens, Gottfried • 204
Martens, Ray (b. 1933) • 152, 158
Marty, Martin (b. 1928) • 36, 97
Marxsen, Willi (1919–1993) • 55, 77
Maxfield, Jennifer • 197
Maxfield, John • 196–197
McCain, Paul • 193, 351
McClean, Don • 74
McElroy (Father) • 112
McGill, Dorothy • 308
McNally, Elizabeth Scaer (b. 1931) • 3, 6, 8, 43
Mealwitz, Peter (b. 1934) • 130
Meilaender, Gilbert (b. 1946) • 26
Mennicke, August • 264–266
Merkens, Albert (1897–1980) • 37
Merkens, Guido (1927–2012) • 235, 315
Meyendorff, John (1926–1992) • 312
Meyer, Adoph F. (1899–1988) • 13, 16
Meyer, Albert (1905–2000) • 70, 92
Meyer, Carl S. (1907–1972) • 38
Meyer, Donald (1926–1956) • 29, 159
Meyer, Eldor (1929–2010) • 301
Meyer, Freida (1911–2006) • 175
Meyer, Henry (1912–2006) • 175
Meyer, John E. • 244, 246
Meyer, Lois Graesser • 19, 47
Meyer, Loma (1928–2014) • 205
Meyer, Louis J. (1886–1958) • 19
Meyer, Marie Otten • 19
Meyer, William F. • 152–153, 158, 189, 330, 347
Milke, Oscar (1913–1982) • 71
Miller, Hugh • 16
Moellering, H. Armin (1919–1998) • 130, 132, 135n
Moellering, Trudy (1924–2010) • 132
Montgomery, John Warwick (b. 1931) • 82, 88–87, 104, 173, 204, 208, 275, 427
Mowinckel, Sigmund (1884–1965) • 34
Mueller, Ewald H. (1916–1991) • 19
Mueller, John Theodore (1885–1967) • 186, 402, 410
Mueller, Norbert (1927–2013) • xv, 158, 171, 201, 206, 207, 218–220, 223, 226, 233, 236, 238–240, 259–260, 265, 271–272, 275, 281, 286–289, 291–293, 299–300, 301–315, 317–325, 331–332, 341–342, 347–349, 353, 358–359
Mueller, Raymond (1929–2007) • 163, 298–299, 342, 344
Mueller, Walter E. (1912–1971) • 69
Muller, Catherine "Kay" (1926–2010) • 326, 345
Muller, Richard A. • 93
Muller, Richard E. (1928–2016) • 205, 214–217, 233, 234, 248, 277, 281, 286, 289, 314, 326, 341, 345
Murray, Scott • 359–360, 422

N

Nafzger, Samuel ♦ 90n, 188–189, 215, 246, 360, 370
Naumann, Cheryl ♦ 273
Naumann, Jonathan ♦ 273
Naumann, Martin (1901–1972) ♦ 40, 97–98, 178
Naumann, Oscar (1909–1979) ♦ 97
Nauss, Alan (b. 1923) ♦ 170, 221
Nehrenz, Clyde ♦ 173
Nehrenz, David ♦ 26
Nehring, Frederick II (d. 1957) ♦ 48
Nehring, Frederick III "Rick" (b. 1955) ♦ 48, 64, 175
Nestigen, James ♦ 251
Neuhaus, Richard John (1936–2009) ♦ 49, 187n, 267, 399, 410
Newton, Robert ♦ 204, 218–219, 279, 281, 286, 295–296, 298, 306, 315–316, 321, 326, 331, 334, 342–344, 348–349
Nickel, Theodore ♦ 123
Nickel, Joel ♦ 111–116, 118–120, 123
Nielsen, Alma ♦ viii
Nielsen, Corrine ♦ viii
Nielsen, Paul ♦ viii
Niemoeller, Lewis (1911–1999) ♦ 73, 88, 101, 138
Nissen, Eugene (b. 1925) ♦ 14
Noland, Martin ♦ 309, 310
Nordling, John G. ♦ 345
Nordstrom, Arthur ♦ 61
Nuffer, Rick ♦ 313

O

Oesch, Wilhelm (1896–1982) ♦ 39–40, 105, 394, 410
Olderman, Richard ♦ 109
Olsen, Thomas N. ♦ 208
Olsen, Harold ♦ 158
O'Neill, Thomas Philip "Tip" Jr. (1912–1994) ♦ 202
Orchard, Bernard (1910–2006) ♦ 82, 84
Ost, Warren (1926–1997) ♦ 57
Otten, Herman ♦ 13, 37, 40–42, 46, 48–50, 52, 55, 61, 65, 245–246, 324, 374, 534
Otten, Walter (b. 1934) ♦ 44
Otto, E. J. (1914–1987) ♦ 113–117, 158, 209
Otto, Rodney ♦ 260

P

Pannenberg, Wolfhart (1928–2014) ♦ 220, 418, 426
Paulsen, Steven ♦ 251
Pearce, George ♦ 210
Peckman, Henry (1906–1988) ♦ 64
Pederson, Eldon Edward "Coach Pete" (1914–2002) ♦ 247
Pelikan, Jaroslav (1923–2006) ♦ 30, 197, 410
Penner, Gary ♦ 350
Perrigo, Earl S. (1942–2010) ♦ 277–278
Petersen, Lorman (1915–2009) ♦ xv, 89, 105, 113, 115, 138, 143–144, 149–153, 158, 162, 169, 211, 213, 216, 325–326, 332, 338
Petersen, Wilhelm ♦ 197
Petterson, Arne (1911–1999) ♦ 40–41
Pfitzner, Victor (b. 1937) ♦ 61–62
Philippi, Friedrich Adolph (1809–1882) ♦ 56, 59–60
Pieper, Erich O. (1897–1965) ♦ 72
Pieper, Franz August Otto (1852–1931) ♦ 3, 27, 46, 72, 91, 92, 93, 186–187, 190, 193, 207, 208, 251, 354n, 357, 365, 392, 402, 405
Piepkorn, Arthur Carl (1907–1973) ♦ 11, 23, 28, 187n,
Pingel, Martin (1922–1989) ♦ 15, 17
Pittelko, Roger (b. 1932) ♦ 343, 403
Pless, John T. ♦ 205, 316
Poetsch, Hanz-Lutz ♦ 210
Pope Benedict XVI (b. 1927) ♦ 124
Portnoy, Esther ♦ 119
Power, Gregory John ♦ 320n
Precht, Fred (1917–2003) ♦ 99, 101, 102
Preus, Christian (b. 1959) ♦ 225
Preus, Daniel (b. 1949) ♦ 105, 150–151, 160, 167, 363
Preus, David W. (ALC President, ELCA Bishop) (b. 1922) ♦ 166, 179, 253–254

Preus, Delpha (1917–1999) ♦ 87
Preus, Donna Mae Rockman (1925–2017) ♦ 68, 158, 175, 234, 254, 306, 320, 342, 345, 350
Preus, Herman Amberg I (1825–1894) ♦ 179, 253
Preus, Herman Amberg III (1896–1995) ♦ 159, 253
Preus, Idella (1884–1968) ♦ 159
Preus, J. A. O. I (1883–1961) ♦ 104, 159, 253
Preus, J. A. O. II "Jack" (1920–1994) ♦ 21, 22, 50, 67, 72, 73, 87, 89, 92, 94–97, 99–101, 103–105, 110n, 113, 115, 117, 121–122, 124, 129, 132, 134–136, 138, 140, 143–145, 149–151, 153, 155, 158, 159, 162, 164, 166, 173, 174, 178, 208, 211, 215, 230, 247, 253–256, 263, 266, 277, 315, 338, 353
Preus, Klemet (1950–2014) ♦ 103, 150–151, 160
Preus, Peter (b. 1955) ♦ 104, 160
Preus, Robert D. (1924–1995) ♦ 28, 36, 37, 39, 41, 43, 48, 51, 59, 62, 68, 72, 89–92, 94, 96, 104–105, 121–122, 144, 150, 154–155, 157, 158, 159–167, 169–175, 177–179, 182–184, 194, 199–202, 203–206, 207–229, 231–240, 248–249, 253–257, 259–276, 277–279, 281–287, 292–293, 295–296, 299–300, 302–311, 313–315, 320–324, 326–327, 329, 333, 337–338, 342–347, 349–351, 353–354, 358, 363, 364, 373
Preus, Rolf (b. 1953) ♦ 160, 184
Prokopy, Paul (1929–2008) ♦ 72
Puelle, John (1935–1999) ♦ 48
Putnick, Hattie (1920–2006) ♦ 88
Putnick, Walter (1920–1995) ♦ 88

R

Radtke, Richard ♦ 299–300
Rasmussen, Matthew ♦ 342
Rast, Lawrence R., Jr. ♦ xi, xii, xv, 36, 206, 216, 351, 353, 356, 398
Rauschenbusch, Walter (1861–1918) ♦ 312

Reagan, Ronald (1911–2004) ♦ 202
Rehwinkel, Alfred (1887–1979) ♦ 29, 41
Reicke, Bo (1914–1987) ♦ 237, 425
Reimann, Henry (1926–1963) ♦ 27
Reinke, Ralph ♦ 347
Rengsdorf, Karl Heinrich (1903–1992) ♦ 53–55, 61, 417, 419
Repp, Arthur (1906–1994) ♦ 36, 40, 50, 131, 134n, 135, 160, 169
Resch, Richard ♦ 165, 200, 334
Ressmeyer, Henry "Joe" ♦ 72
Ressmeyer, Rudolf "Rudy" (1924–2017) ♦ 14, 16, 18–19, 47, 132, 197, 354n
Ressmeyer, Virginia (1927–2008) ♦ 354n
Reuning, Daniel ♦ 48, 101–103, 199, 233n, 234, 239, 281, 286, 310, 321, 334, 336–337, 341, 345, 348, 351
Reuther, Walter (1907–1970) ♦ 31
Rickey, Branch (1881–1965) ♦ 8
Riedel, Paul H. (1921–1956) ♦ 29, 71, 159
Riedel, Robert "Bob" ♦ 71–72, 159n
Rinas, Jodi ♦ 316
Rinas, Lorraine ♦ 316
Rippe, Herman J. (1896–1969) ♦ 47
Robinson, J. A. T. (1919–1983) ♦ 88
Roegner, Robert ♦ 300
Roensch, Manfred (1930–2001) ♦ 209–210
Roetman, Rusty ♦ 319
Roettger, Harold ♦ 8
Rogers, Mark Konrad ♦ 320n
Rogers, Robert W. ♦ 118–119
Rogness, Michael ♦ 105, 423
Rosenkaimer II, Robert Ron ♦ 320n
Rosenkoetter, Robert H. (1918–1983) ♦ 45
Rosin, Dorothy (1925–2010) ♦ 211, 213
Rosin, Robert (b. 1951) ♦ 211
Rosin, Walter ♦ 275
Rosin, Wilbert (b. 1923) ♦ 169, 200, 211–215, 221, 222, 233n, 248, 330
Rudolf, Bruce ♦ 70

S

Saarinen, Eero (1910–1961) ♦ 178
Saleska, John (1929–2017) ♦ 217, 221, 224–227, 233n, 256–257, 281, 286–288, 290, 291, 314
Sasse, Hermann (1895–1976) ♦ xvi, 46, 53, 92, 337, 346, 387, 403
Satterfield, Gary ♦ 219, 224, 226, 259, 305–306, 309, 311, 322
Sauer, Alfred von Rohr (1908–1991) ♦ 37, 108
Sauer, Robert (1921–2013) ♦ 266, 323
Saunders, Phyllis ♦ 216, 259
Saunders, Ruth Preus (b. 1963) ♦ 263
Scaer, Beth (b. 1962) ♦ 177
Scaer, Carl (1896–1983) ♦ 46
Scaer, Charles (1858–1928) ♦ 175, 180
Scaer, David II (b. 1961) ♦ 55, 61, 64, 315
Scaer, Dorothy Nehring (b. 1931) ♦ 15, 48–49, 53, 54, 55, 64, 66, 68, 73, 74, 95, 103, 105, 129, 161, 162, 176, 177, 180, 181, 234, 237, 304, 317, 319, 335, 338, 340, 341, 355
Scaer, Ernest F. (1900–1971) ♦ 46, 169
Scaer, Hanna Morlock (1865–1951) ♦ 175
Scaer, Nancy Skul ♦ 315
Scaer, Paul Henry (1898–1967) ♦ 3
Scaer, Peter (b. 1966) ♦ 70n, 73, 87, 237, 305, 314, 317, 318, 319
Scaer, Stephen (b. 1963) ♦ 64, 177, 180
Scaer, Victoria née Zimmermann (1909–2005) ♦ 3
Scar, Margarette Scaer (1903–1991) ♦ 64, 181
Scar, William (1922–2009) ♦ 64, 68, 69n, 181
Schaibley, Robert (b. 1946) ♦ 109, 283, 291, 292n, 293, 294n, 345
Scharlemann, Martin (1910–1982) ♦ 22, 33, 34, 38–39, 46, 89, 154, 155, 161, 208, 354n
Schedler, Walter John ♦ 320n
Schnell, Red ♦ 224
Schiotz, Fred (1901–1989) ♦ 124
Schkade, Ray ♦ 283
Schlecht, Richard ♦ 275
Schleiermacher, Friedrich (1768–1834) ♦ 27n, 59, 78
Schlink, Edmund (1903–1984) ♦ 103, 423
Schmidt, Alvin ♦ 169, 170, 183–184, 221–222, 233n, 234–235
Schmidt, Edward Frank Christian (1892–1980) ♦ 44
Schmidt, Emma Pieper (1889–1972) ♦ 72
Schmidt, Norm ♦ 74
Schmiel, David G. (b. 1931) ♦ xv, 97, 163, 165, 218, 307, 311, 325–327, 329–349, 335n, 336n, 353, 358, 359
Schneltz, Gene ♦ 275
Schoedel, Walter (b. 1926) ♦ 14
Schoedel, William ♦ 14, 33, 119
Schoessow, Daniel Ray ♦ 320n
Schomburg, Del (b. 1948) ♦ 17–18
Schöne, Jobst (b. 1931) ♦ 58, 209
Schroeder, Ed ♦ 139n
Schroeder, Randy ♦ 227, 240, 281, 286, 305–306, 314, 316, 320, 348–349
Schubkegel, Theodore (1948–2014) ♦ 228–229
Schuller, David (1926–2002) ♦ 49, 117,
Schultz, Richard "Dick" (1920–2001) ♦ xv, 109, 143–145, 149–153, 158, 316, 326, 338
Schulz, K. Detlev ♦ 190
Schulz, Robert ♦ 48
Schulz, Wallace ♦ 225, 257
Schulze, Ernest ♦ 228–229
Schulze, Margaret Caemmerer (b. 1935) ♦ 19, 25, 50, 131
Schulze, Raymond "Ray" (b. 1932) ♦ 19, 25, 50
Schurle, Darrell W. ♦ 320n
Schütz, Heinrich (1585–1672) ♦ 102
Schwan, Henry C. (1818–1905) ♦ 10, 365
Schwarz, Hans (b. 1939) ♦ 125–126
Schwiesow, Wayne William ♦ 320n
Sernett, Milton ♦ 150, 158
Severn, Albert ♦ 64
Shields, Randy ♦ 221, 233n
Shuta, Richard ♦ 310
Sihler, Susanna (1829–1918) ♦ 334
Sihler, Wilhelm (1801–1885) ♦ 178, 334

Simon, Arthur (b. 1930) ♦ 37–38, 133, 425
Sims, Timothy ♦ 270, 298–299, 363
Sippola, Charlene Johnson ♦ 158
Sippola, John (1923–1982) ♦ 109, 158
Smith, Bradley (b. 1961) ♦ 279
Smith, Robert H. (1932–2000) ♦ 354n, 419
Sohn, Otto (1894–1969) ♦ 171
Sohns, Wilbert ♦ 276
Sommerfeld, Russell ♦ 301
Spiegel, Clarence (1896–1990) ♦ 94–95, 145
Spiegel, Gertrude (1900–1989) ♦ 95
Spitz, Lewis, I (1895–1996) ♦ 211
Spitz, Lewis, II (1923–2000) ♦ 204, 211, 213
Springer, Axel (1912–1985) ♦ 209
Stahl, Marty (b. 1949) ♦ 281, 286
Stahlke, Esther (1906–2006) ♦ 158
Stahlke, Otto (1902–1992) ♦ 23, 94, 95, 158, 221, 233n, 280
Staweicki, Gary T. ♦ 320n
Steege, Barbara ♦ 213n, 217, 221
Steege, Mark (1906–1997) ♦ 151–152, 213, 221
Steenbock, Elmer (1925–2016) ♦ 229
Steinke, Arthur F. (1908–1997) ♦ 182
Steinke, Paul (b. 1937) ♦ 182
Steinke, Peter L. (b. 1939) ♦ 182
Stelmachowicz, Michael (1927–2009) ♦ xv, 201, 203, 206, 232, 297–298, 300, 321, 323–325, 329, 333, 359
Stephan, Martin (1777–1846) ♦ 177, 396
Stephenson, John ♦ 188, 191–197, 204–206, 219–220, 309–310
Stolle, Volker ♦ 196
Strasen, Luther ♦ 239
Strauss, David Friedrich (1808–1874) ♦ 80
Strawn, Paul ♦ 316
Strege, Arthur H. (1927–2013) ♦ 44
Streufert, Paul ♦ 135n
Stupperich, Robert (1904–2003) ♦ 54
Suelflow, Gladys (1924–2008) ♦ 222
Surburg, Raymond (1909–2001) ♦ 151–152, 175, 221, 233n, 258, 286, 303, 410, 420

T

Taddey, Martin (1932–1996) ♦ 350
Taylor, Marvin J. ♦ 235–236
Tepker, Howard (1911–1998) ♦ 11–90, 94–95, 99, 135–136, 163, 169–170, 188–189, 207, 211, 213, 221, 233n, 246, 260–261, 280, 286–287, 289, 296, 357
Tepker, Rosalie (1911–1997) ♦ 96
Theiss, Norman ♦ 41
Thiele, Gilbert A. (1910–1983) ♦ 23, 27n
Thomas, Craig Brooker ♦ 320n
Thomas, Steven ♦ 110
Thompson, Gregory Noel ♦ 320n
Thompson, William ♦ 235
Tietjen, Ernestine (1925–2015) ♦ 130, 136
Tietjen, John (1928–2004) ♦ 16n, 26, 27, 35, 38n, 42, 48, 100, 108, 110n, 113, 114n, 120, 129–142, 144–145, 153–154, 170, 172, 233, 254, 292, 314, 374,
Tillich, Paul (1886–1965) ♦ 91
Tödt, Heinz Eduard (1918–1991) ♦ 123
Torgerson, Wilhelm ♦ 209
Torrance, Thomas (1913–2007) ♦ 159
Trapp, Ed ♦ 347
Traugott, Arthur R. ♦ 116
Trigg, Jonathan ♦ 60
Trinklein, Alfred (1902–1993) ♦ 15–16, 133–134
Truman, Harry (1884–1972) ♦ 4
Tyndale, William (1494–1536) ♦ 178

V

Van Gilder, Jean Scaer Ervin (b. 1937) ♦ 3, 6, 13, 15, 16, 18
Van Gilder, William ♦ 18
Vaughan, Timothy Bryan ♦ 320n
Voelz, James ♦ 155, 169, 207, 215, 217, 221, 233, 260, 279, 281, 286, 303
Volz, Carl (1933–1998) ♦ 166
von Harnack, Adolf (1851–1930) ♦ 21
von Schenk, Bertholdt (1895–1974) ♦ 70n, 422

W

Wachler, Gottlieb • 209–210
Wagner, Alvin • 199
Walda, John • 226
Walter, Jody Roger • 320n
Walther, C. F. W. (1811–1887) • 32, 34n, 56, 59, 61, 91, 92, 177, 192, 253, 315, 334, 361, 365, 416
Walther, Emilie Buenger (1812–1885) • 334
Walz, Edgar (1914–2003) • 221
Walz, Orville (b. 1939) • 368–369
Weber, E. • 210
Weidmann, Carl F. (1906–1980) • 10, 60–61
Weinrich, Barbara (1947–2015) • 164, 165
Weinrich, William "Bill" (b. 1945) • xv, 85, 91, 155, 164–166, 169, 188, 190, 195, 205, 207, 217, 221, 233n, 240, 281, 286, 291, 292n, 298, 305, 307, 316, 335, 345, 347–348, 350–351, 353, 358, 359, 363, 364, 367, 369, 426
Weis, James (1936–2017) • 88
Wente, Pauline Scaer (1894–1982) • 179–182
Wente, Walter (1894–1992) • 179–191
Wenthe, Dean O. • xv, 85, 86, 103, 144–145, 155, 158, 167, 205–206, 218, 233, 238, 266, 268, 270, 281, 282, 286, 303, 306, 307, 309, 320, 323, 338, 348, 349, 351, 353–356, 358–359, 363–364, 403, 404
Wenthe, Linda • 238
Werberig, Robert • 354n
Werning, Waldo (1921–2013) • 165, 189, 192, 196, 199–200, 202, 209, 218, 229, 261, 271, 277–300, 305, 307, 311, 329, 330, 332, 334, 341, 343–345, 369
Weyermann, Andrew (1930–2003) • 136
Whalen, Barbara • 213
Wickenkamp • 150, 158
Wiebe, John • 238, 265
Wilbert, Warren (1927–2016) • 99, 169, 213, 217, 221, 233, 224–226, 236, 247–249, 261

Wilken, Robert (b. 1936) • 41, 49, 423
Willebrands, Cardinal (1909–2006) • 124
William, Jeffrey Baxter • 320n
Wingfield, Al (1933–2018) • 216, 224–226, 233, 238
Wingren, Gustaf (1910–2000) • 123, 419
Witham, Pamela née Nehring (b. 1957) • 48, 54, 175, 177
Witham, Richard • 177
Witte, Dennis • 224
Wittrock, Ted (1920–2007) • 14
Wolbrecht, Walter F. (1915–1990) • 32n, 117
Wollenberg, George (1930–2008) • 266
Woolery, Wayne M. • 320n
Wuerffel, Leonard (1910–1987) • 41
Wunderlich, Loenz (1906–1993) • 28, 37, 154
Wycliffe, John (1320–1384) • 178
Wyneken, Friedrich (1810–1876) • 178, 365

Y

Yip, Timothy • 273
Young, Brigham (1801–1877) • 47

Z

Ziegler, Roland • 150
Zietlow, Harold (1926–2011) • 233n, 224–226, 278, 281, 286
Zilz, Melvin (1932–2005) • 224, 233n, 234, 286, 306
Zimmer, Rudi • 210
Zimmerman, Paul (1918–2014) • 135n, 136, 173, 209, 233, 425
Zimmerman, Thomas • 136
Zimmermann, Elwood (1919–2006) • 223
Zimmermann, Gustav (1874–1958) • 3, 7, 139
Zimmermann, Lydia Trier (1885–1982) • 6, 139, 175
Zimmermann, Maximillian (1844–1935) • 5
Zweck, Glenn (1935–2014) • 210, 408
Zwingli, Ulrich (1484–1531) • 46, 215, 220

BIBLIOGRAPHY
OF THE WORKS OF DAVID P. SCAER
by Robert E. Smith

ARTICLES

Co-authored

Arand, Charles P. and David P. Scaer. "The Porvoo Declaration in Confessional Perspective." *Concordia Theological Quarterly* 61, no. 1–2 (January 1997): 35–52. http://www.ctsfw.net/media/pdfs/porvoodeclarationinconfessionalperspective.pdf.

Sasse, Hermann. "Ecumenical Council for Practical Christianity." Translated by David P. Scaer. *Logia* 6, no. 4 (1997): 53–55. https://logia.org/scaer-articles.

A

"Abortion: A Moment for Conscientious Reflection." *Springfielder* 36, no. 3 (December 1972): 180–84. http://www.ctsfw.net/media/pdfs/scaerabortionreflection.pdf.

"Abortion, Incarnation, and the Place of Children in the Church: All One Cloth." *Concordia Theological Quarterly* 77, no. 3–4 (2013): 213–28. http://media.ctsfw.edu/Video/ViewDetails/4053.

"The Advantage of Liturgical Ruts." *Logia* 6, no. 2 (1997): 53–54. https://logia.org/scaer-articles.

"Advent 3: Matthew 11:2–15: Faith Driven to the Edge of Unbelief." *Concordia Pulpit Resources* 18, no. 1 (2008): 18–20.

"Advent 4: Matthew 1:18–25: Unbelief of a Different Kind: Infidelity of a Different Kind." *Concordia Pulpit Resources* 18, no. 1 (2008): 1–23.

"The AELC Constitution." *Concordia Theological Quarterly* 41, no. 2 (1977): 71. http://www.ctsfw.net/media/pdfs/CTQTheologicalObserver41-2.pdf.

"Against the Ordination of Women." *Lutheran Forum* 25, no. 1 (February 1991): 14.

"The ALC Issue—Still Unresolved." *Affirm* 5 (1976): 3.

"All Theology Is Christology: An Axiom in Search of Acceptance." *Concordia Theological Quarterly* 80, no. 1–2 (2016): 49–62. http://www.ctsfw.net/media/pdfs/ScaerDAllTheologyisChristology.pdf.

"'All Theology Is Christology': How Does Every Passage of Scripture Reveal Christ?" *Modern Reformation* 8, no. 5 (1999): 28–32.

"An Essay for Lutheran Pastors on the Charismatic Movement." *Springfielder* 37, no. 4 (1974): 210–23.

"An Old Piece of Paper [Magdalen College Papyrus Fragment of Matthew 26]." *Lutheran Witness* 114, no. 7 (1995): 10–11.

"An Uncelebrated Anniversary." *Concordia Theological Quarterly* 46, no. 1 (1982): 39–40. http://www.ctsfw.net/media/pdfs/TheoObserver46-1.pdf.

"Another Gloomy Advent." *Concordia Theological Quarterly* 55, no. 4 (1991): 300–302. http://www.ctsfw.net/media/pdfs/CTQTheologicalObserver55-4.pdf.

"Apostolicity, Inspiration, and Canonicity: Opinion of the Department of Systematic Theology." *Concordia Theological Quarterly* 44, no. 1 (January 1980): 46–49. http://www.ctsfw.net/media/pdfs/ScaerApostolicityInspirationandCanonicity.pdf.

"Are Confessions Archaic? The Lutheran Tradition Has Broad, Ecumenical Application." *Christianity Today* 26, no. 7 (April 9, 1982): 82–83.

"Augustana V and the Doctrine of the Ministry." *Lutheran Quarterly* 6, no. 4 (1992): 403–23.

"Authentic Endings: Matthew and Mark." *Springfielder* 39, no. 3 (1975): 130–31. http://www.ctsfw.net/media/pdfs/TheologicalObserver39-3.pdf.

B

"Baptism and the Lord's Supper in the Life of the Church." *Concordia Theological Quarterly* 45, no. 1–2 (January 1981): 37–59. http://www.ctsfw.net/media/pdfs/scaerbaptismandthelordssupper.pdf.

"Baptism as Church Foundation." *Concordia Theological Quarterly* 67, no. 2 (2003): 109–29. http://www.ctsfw.net/media/pdfs/scaerpbaptismchurchfoundation.pdf.

"Baptism: Christ Marks Us as His Own." *For the Life of the World* 3, no. 3 (1999): 6–7. http://www.ctsfw.net/media/pdfs/BaptismChristMarksUsasHisOwnDScaer.pdf.

"Baptism–Past, Present, and Future Tense." *For the Life of the World*, 6, no. 2 (2002): 7–9. http://www.ctsfw.net/media/pdfs/BaptismPastPresentandFutureTenseDScaer.pdf.

"The Beatitudes." *Higher Things* 10, no. 3 (2010): 4–5.

"Beck Bible Published." *Springfielder* 40, no. 1 (1976): 42. http://www.ctsfw.net/media/pdfs/TheologicalObserver40-1.pdf.

"Bible Passages and Principles: 'Just Not Getting It.'" *Logia* 8, no. 1 (1999): 4–5. https://logia.org/scaer-articles.

"Biblical Inspiration in Trinitarian Perspective." *Pro Ecclesia* 14, no. 2 (2005): 143–60.

"Bo Giertz and the Ordination of Women." *Lutheran Forum* 33, no. 1 (1999): 4–5.

"Body, Soul, and Spirit." *Concordia Theological Quarterly* 66, no. 2 (2002): 167–69. http://www.ctsfw.net/media/pdfs/CTQTheologicalObserver66-2.pdf.

"By What Shall We Read?" *Modern Reformation* 6, no. 5 (1997): 26–28.

C

"C. S. Lewis on Women Priests." *Concordia Theological Quarterly* 44, no. 1 (January 1980): 55–59. http://www.ctsfw.net/media/pdfs/TheoObserver44-1.pdf.

"Cambridge Highlights." *Modern Reformation* 5, no. 1 (1996): 7–8.

"Carl Braaten's Sixth Locus: The Person of Jesus Christ." *Concordia Theological Quarterly* 51, no. 4 (October 1987): 275–78. http://www.ctsfw.net/media/pdfs/TheoObserver51-4.pdf.

"A Catechism on Fellowship (Part I)." *Affirm* 8 (1980): 2.

"A Catechism on Fellowship (Part II)." *Affirm* 8 (1980): 4.

"A Catechism on Fellowship (Part III)." *Affirm* 9 (1980): 4.

"The Centennial Celebration of Lutheranism in Connecticut." *Concordia Historical Institute Quarterly* 38, no. 2 (1965): 95–101.

"A Chapel Sermon on Matthew 8:24: Reformation 1997." *Concordia Theological Quarterly* 62, no. 2 (April 1998): 145–48. http://www.ctsfw.net/media/pdfs/CTQTheologicalObserver62-2.pdf.

"Changing Churches: An Orthodox, Catholic, and Lutheran Theological Conversation." *Logia* 22, no. 4 (2013): 48–49. https://logia.org/scaer-articles.

"The Charismatic Movement as Ecumenical Phenomenon." *Concordia Theological Quarterly* 45, no. 1–2 (1981): 81–83. http://www.ctsfw.net/media/pdfs/TheoObserver45-1,2.pdf.

"The Charismatic Threat." *Concordia Theological Quarterly* 41, no. 3 (1977): 52–54. http://www.ctsfw.net/media/pdfs/TheologicalObserver41-3.pdf.

"Christ or the Bible." *Christianity Today* 12, no. 3 (November 10, 1967): 9–10.

"The Christian Family in Today's Society Viewed in a Biblical Perspective." *Concordia Theological Quarterly* 54, no. 2–3 (1990): 81–97. http://www.ctsfw.net/media/pdfs/scaerchristianfamily.pdf.

"Christians United in Christ?" *Affirm* 13 (1989): 10.

"Christmas Eve: Mark 1:15: A Time to Be Born." *Concordia Pulpit Resources* 17, no. 1 (2007): 54–56.

"Christology and Feminism." *Logia* 9, no. 1 (2000): 3–7. https://logia.org/scaer-articles.

"Church's One Foundation." *Springfielder* 38, no. 3 (December 1974): 218–25. http://www.ctsfw.net/media/pdfs/ScaerChurchsOneFoundation.pdf.

"Civil War of 1776." *Christianity Today* 20, no. 20 (July 2, 1976): 12–14.

"The Clergy as New Testament Ministers with a Proposal for Parochial School Teachers." *Issues in Christian Education* 27, no. 1 (1993): 6–9.

"Close/d Communion—2." *Lutheran Forum* 32, no. 1 (1998): 59–62.

"Closed Communion: Saying It Better." *Concordia Theological Quarterly* 55, no. 4 (1991): 302–309. http://www.ctsfw.net/media/pdfs/CTQTheologicalObserver55-4.pdf.

"Commemoration Sermon for Dr. Robert D. Preus." *Logia* 5, no. 3 (1996): 9–10. https://logia.org/scaer-articles.

"Communion Closed and Full." *Logia* 8, no. 2 (1999): 62. https://logia.org/scaer-articles.

"The Concept of *Anfechtung* in Luther's Thought." *Concordia Theological Quarterly* 47, no. 1 (1983): 15–30. http://www.ctsfw.net/media/pdfs/scaeranfechtung.pdf.

"'Concordia'—Where Did It Come From." *Concordia Theological Quarterly* 49, no. 2–3 (April 1985): 199–199. http://www.ctsfw.net/media/pdfs/TheoObserver49-2,3.pdf.

"The Conference of the Association of Confessional Lutheran Seminaries (ACLS), Cambridge, September 6–9, 1982." *Concordia Theological Quarterly* 47, no. 1 (1983): 33–34. http://www.ctsfw.net/media/pdfs/TheoObserver47-1.pdf.

"Confessional 'Reawakening' in Germany." *Springfielder* 34, no. 3 (December 1970): 228–30. http://www.ctsfw.net/media/pdfs/SpringfielderTheologicalRefractions34-3.pdf.

"Confirmation as a Sacramental Rite." *Logia* 15, no. 1 (2006): 49–58. https://logia.org/scaer-articles.

"Conflict over Baptism." *Christianity Today* 11, no. 14 (April 14, 1967): 8.

"A Critique of the Fourfold Pattern." *Concordia Theological Quarterly* 63, no. 4 (October 1999): 269–80. http://www.ctsfw.net/media/pdfs/scaercritique.pdf.

"CTQ: Coming Back to the Roots." *Concordia Theological Quarterly* 41, no. 2 (1977): 5–6. http://www.ctsfw.net/media/pdfs/CTQEditorials41-2.pdf.

"*Cum Patre et Filio Adoratur*: The Spirit Understood Christologically." *Concordia Theological Quarterly* 61, no. 1–2 (January 1997): 93–112. http://www.ctsfw.net/media/pdfs/scaerdcumpatrefilioadoratur.pdf.

D

"Das Matthaus-Evangelium Als Dokument Theologischer Ausbildung." *Evangelium/Gospel* 10 (1983): 128–48.

"David Scaer: A Reply to Leonard Klein." *Logia* 3, no. 1 (January 1994): 52–54. https://logia.org/scaer-articles.

"The Deadly Trio of Liturgical Heresies." *Concordia Theological Quarterly* 55, no. 4 (1991): 297. http://www.ctsfw.net/media/pdfs/CTQTheologicalObserver55-4.pdf.

"Death and Resurrection as Apocalyptic Event." *Concordia Theological Quarterly* 64, no. 4 (October 2000): 279–94. http://www.ctsfw.net/media/pdfs/scaerddeathandresurrection.pdf.

"The Debut of the Bible as a Pagan Classic." *Concordia Theological Quarterly* 41, no. 2 (1977): 71–72. http://www.ctsfw.net/media/pdfs/CTQTheologicalObserver41-2.pdf.

"Delay of Infant Baptism in the Roman Catholic Church." *Concordia Theological Quarterly* 68, no. 3–4 (July 2004): 341–46. http://www.ctsfw.net/media/pdfs/CTQTheologicalObserver68-3.pdf.

"The Diet of John the Baptist: 'locusts and Wild Honey' in Synoptic and Patristic Interpretation." *Bulletin for Biblical Research* 16, no. 2 (2006): 364–65.

"Dismembering the Pastoral Office." *Concordia Theological Quarterly* 41, no. 3 (1977): 56–57. http://www.ctsfw.net/media/pdfs/TheologicalObserver41-3.pdf.

"The Distinctive Spirituality of the Evangelical Lutheran Church." *Logia* 8, no. 2 (1999): 9–11. https://logia.org/scaer-articles.

"Do Lutherans Need Bishops?" *Lutheran Forum* 5 (1971): 18–19.

"Do We Need Bishops Now?" *Springfielder* 35, no. 2 (September 1971): 125–27. http://www.ctsfw.net/media/pdfs/TheoRefrac35-2.pdf.

"Doctrine and Practice: Setting the Boundaries: An Abstract Essay with Practical Implications." *Concordia Theological Quarterly* 66, no. 4 (October 2002): 307–14. http://www.ctsfw.net/media/pdfs/scaerddoctrineandpractice.pdf.

"The Doctrine of the Trinity in Biblical Perspective." *Concordia Theological Quarterly* 67, no. 3–4 (2003): 323–34. http://www.ctsfw.net/media/pdfs/scaerbiblicalperspective.pdf.

"Does the State of Israel Really Deserve Special Religious Consideration." *Concordia Theological Quarterly* 47, no. 3 (July 1983): 245–47. http://www.ctsfw.net/media/pdfs/TheoObserver47-3.pdf.

"*Dominus Iesus* and Why I like It." *Concordia Theological Quarterly* 65, no. 1 (2001): 77–79. http://www.ctsfw.net/media/pdfs/CTQTheologicalObserver65-1.pdf.

"Donald Deffner—The Preacher." *Concordia Pulpit Resources* 9, no. 3 (1999): 32.

E

"Ecclesiastical Geometry." *Concordia Theological Quarterly* 64, no. 1 (2000): 71–73. http://www.ctsfw.net/media/pdfs/CTQTheologicalObserver64-1.pdf.

"Eine Studie Über Die Charismatic Bewegung." *Evangelium/Gospel* 2 (1975): 49–63.

"Epiphany and Baptism: Christian Beliefs and Traditions Vary on This Sacrament." *Lutheran Witness* 125, no. 1 (2006): 10.

"Epistles before Gospels: An Axiom of New Testament Studies." *Concordia Theological Quarterly* 77, no. 1–2 (2013): 5–21. http://www.ctsfw.net/media/pdfs/ScaerDEpislesBeforeGospels.pdf.

"Essay for Lutheran Pastors on the Charismatic Movement." *Springfielder* 37, no. 4 (March 1974): 210–23. http://www.ctsfw.net/media/pdfs/scaerlutheranpastors.pdf.

"Eucharistic Themes in the Gospels." *Logia* 18, no. 2 (2009): 41–48. https://logia.org/scaer-articles.

"Evangelical and Catholic: A Slogan in Search of a Definition." *Concordia Theological Quarterly* 65, no. 4 (October 2001): 323–44. http://www.ctsfw.net/media/pdfs/scaerdevangelical.pdf.

"Evangelical Theological Society." *Concordia Theological Quarterly* 42, no. 1 (1978): 37–38. http://www.ctsfw.net/media/pdfs/TheoObserver42-1.pdf.

"Evangelicals and Wine—Some Things Never Change." *Concordia Theological Quarterly* 47, no. 1 (1983): 35. http://www.ctsfw.net/media/pdfs/TheoObserver47-1.pdf.

"Eyewitness Reconsidered." *Forum Letter* 27, no. 1 (1998): 6–8.

F

"Feminism: The End of the Forward Advance." *Concordia Theological Quarterly* 55, no. 4 (1991): 299–300. http://www.ctsfw.net/media/pdfs/CTQTheologicalObserver55-4.pdf.

"Few Notes on Translating the Apostles Creed." *Springfielder* 33, no. 4 (1970): 58–62. http://www.ctsfw.net/media/pdfs/TheoRefrac33-4.pdf.

"Fifteenth Sunday after Trinity: Matthew 18:15–20 (Sept. 3, 1978)." *Concordia Theological Quarterly* 42, no. 2 (1978): 172–73. http://www.ctsfw.net/media/pdfs/CTQHomileticalStudies42-2.pdf.

"Fighting for Souls: Mormons Versus Anglicans." *Concordia Theological Quarterly* 55, no. 4 (1991): 297–98. http://www.ctsfw.net/media/pdfs/CTQTheologicalObserver55-4.pdf.

"Finding a Place for the Third Use of the Law in Our Preaching." *Concordia Pulpit Resources* 25, no. 1 (2015): 3–9.

"A Formula of Agreement: A Theological Assessment." *Concordia Theological Quarterly* 62, no. 2 (April 1998): 107–24. http://www.ctsfw.net/media/pdfs/FormulaofAgreementTheologicalAssessment.pdf.

"Formula of Concord Article VI: The Third Use of the Law." *Concordia Theological Quarterly* 42, no. 2 (April 1978): 145–55. http://www.ctsfw.net/media/pdfs/scaerfcvi.pdf.

"Formula of Concord X: A Revised, Enlarged, and Slightly Amended Edition." *Logia* 6, no. 4 (1997): 27–33. https://logia.org/scaer-articles.

"Fort Wayne Seminary Sponsors ILCW Seminar." *Concordia Theological Quarterly* 41, no. 2 (1977): 70. http://www.ctsfw.net/media/pdfs/CTQEditorials41-2.pdf.

"Francis Pieper (1852–1931)." *Lutheran Quarterly* 22, no. 3 (2008): 299–323.

"From the Chapel: God Was Manifested in the Flesh." *The Cresset* 32 (1968): 17–18.

"Functionalism Fails the Test of Orthodoxy." *Christianity Today* 26, no. 3 (February 5, 1982): 90.

G

"Gnosis in the Church Today." *Springfielder* 38, no. 4 (1975): 334–44. http://www.ctsfw.net/media/pdfs/scaergnosischurchtoday.pdf.

"God as Secondary Fundamental Doctrine in Missouri Synod Theology." *Concordia Theological Quarterly* 75, no. 1–2 (2011): 43–61. http://www.ctsfw.net/media/pdfs/ScaerDGodAsSecondary.pdf.

"'The God Squad': Towards a Common Religion." *Concordia Theological Quarterly* 71, no. 3–4 (2007): 371–73. http://www.ctsfw.net/media/pdfs/CTQTheologicalObserver71-3.pdf.

"God the Son and Hermeneutics: A Brief Study in the Reformation." *Concordia Theological Quarterly* 59, no. 1–2 (1995): 49–66. http://www.ctsfw.net/media/pdfs/scaergodsonandhermeneutics.pdf.

"God's Word, Three Views, One Bible." *Concordia Theological Quarterly* 77, no. 1–2 (2013): 165–73. http://www.ctsfw.net/media/pdfs/CTQTheologicalObserver77-1.pdf.

"Great Thanksgiving of the ILCW." *Springfielder* 40, no. 1 (1976): 36–41. http://www.ctsfw.net/media/pdfs/scaergreatthanksgivingilcw.pdf.

"The Greatest Comeback Ever." *Higher Things* 4, no. 1 (2004): 5–6.

H

"He Did Descend to Hell: In Defense of the Apostles' Creed." *Journal of the Evangelical Theological Society* 35, no. 1 (1992): 91–99.

"He Died For Sins." *Lutheran Worship Notes*, no. 21 (1991): 4–5.

"He Went to the Dead." *Springfielder* 33, no. 3 (1969): 34–36. http://www.ctsfw.net/media/pdfs/SprTheologicalRefractions33-3.pdf.

"Heaven Is Not Our Home?" *Concordia Theological Quarterly* 72, no. 3 (2008): 277. http://ctsfw.net/media/pdfs/CTQTheologicalObserver72-3.pdf.

"Here and There on Theological Journals." *Concordia Theological Quarterly* 70, no. 3–4 (2006): 367–69. http://www.ctsfw.net/media/pdfs/CTQTheologicalObserver70-3.pdf.

"Historical Critical Method: A Short Historical Appraisal." *Springfielder* 36, no. 4 (March 1973): 294–309. http://www.ctsfw.net/media/pdfs/scaerhistoricalcriticalmethod.pdf.

"The Historical–Critical Method: What Is It?" *Affirm* 4 (1974): 1.

"History of Synod's Theological Controversy Now Available." *Affirm* 6 (1977): 4.

"The Holiness Quest." *Logia* 5, no. 1 (1996): 71–73. https://logia.org/scaer-articles.

"Holy Baptism's Diminishment." *Logia* 22, no. 2 (2013): 73–74. https://logia.org/scaer-articles.

"Holy Cross Day." *Concordia Theological Quarterly* 74, no. 3–4 (2010): 359–60. http://www.ctsfw.net/media/pdfs/CTQTheologicalObserver74-3.pdf.

"The Holy Spirit, Sacraments, and Church Rites." *Concordia Theological Quarterly* 70, no. 3–4 (2006): 311–22. http://www.ctsfw.net/media/pdfs/scaerdholyspirit.pdf.

"*Homo Factus Est* as the Revelation of God." *Concordia Theological Quarterly* 65, no. 2 (2001): 111–26. http://www.ctsfw.net/media/pdfs/scaerdhomofactus.pdf.

I

"I. C. B. I. Summit Report (International Council on Biblical Inerracy)." *Concordia Theological Quarterly* 43, no. 1 (1979): 45–46. http://www.ctsfw.net/media/pdfs/TheoObserver43-1.pdf.

"In Memoriam: Wilhelm Martin Oesch, 1896–1982." *Concordia Theological Quarterly* 46, no. 2–3 (1982): 241–42. http://www.ctsfw.net/media/pdfs/TheoObserver46-2,3.pdf.

"In Response to Bengt Hägglund: Did Luther and Melanchthon Agree on the Real Presence?" *Concordia Theological Quarterly* 44, no. 2–3 (1980): 141–47. http://www.ctsfw.net/media/pdfs/scaerresponsetohagglund.pdf.

"Incarnation as the Perfection of Creation." *Concordia Theological Quarterly* 78, no. 3–4 (July 2014): 153–66. http://www.ctsfw.net/media/pdfs/CTQTheologicalObserver78-3.pdf.

"The Integrity of the Christological Character of the Office of the Ministry." *Logia* 2, no. 1 (1993): 15–19. https://logia.org/scaer-articles.

"International Council on Biblical Inerrancy: Summit II." *Concordia Theological Quarterly* 47, no. 2 (1983): 153–58. http://www.ctsfw.net/media/pdfs/TheoObserver47-2.pdf.

"Is Closed Communion an Option in Today's Church?" *Affirm* 10 (1984): 5.

"Is It Lutheran to Celebrate the American Revolution?" *Lutheran Synod Quarterly* 16 (1975): 66–78.

"Is Nothing Sacred?" *Logia* 8, no. 1 (1999): 61–62. https://logia.org/scaer-articles.

J–K

"Jesus: Beginning the Conversation." *Lutheran Witness* 130, no. 1 (2011): 22–23.

"Jesus Christ Superstar." *Springfielder* 34, no. 4 (1971): 295–98. http://www.ctsfw.net/media/pdfs/SpringfielderTheologicalRefractions34-4.pdf.

"Jesus Did Not Leave—He Reigns through Us: If the Ascension Is Viewed as a Spatial Event, Its Significance Is Lost." *Christianity Today* 26, no. 10 (May 21, 1982): 24–25.

"Johann Sebastian Bach as Lutheran Theologian." *Concordia Theological Quarterly* 68, no. 3–4 (2004): 319–39. http://www.ctsfw.net/media/pdfs/scaerjsbachlutherantheologian.pdf.

"Joint Lutheran/Roman Catholic Declaration on Justification: A Response." *Concordia Theological Quarterly* 62, no. 2 (1998): 83–106. http://www.ctsfw.net/media/pdfs/jointlutheran-romancatholicdeclarationresponse.pdf.

"Jürgen Moltmann and His Theology of Hope." *Springfielder* 34, no. 1 (1970): 14–24. http://www.ctsfw.net/media/pdfs/editorjurgenmoltmann.pdf.

"Justification: Jesus vs. Paul." *Concordia Theological Quarterly* 76, no. 3–4 (2012): 195–211. http://www.ctsfw.net/media/pdfs/ScaerJustificationJesusvPaul.pdf.

"Justification: Set Up Where It Ought Not to Be." *Concordia Theological Quarterly* 80, no. 3 (2016): 269–85. http://www.ctsfw.net/media/pdfs/ScaerDJustificationSetupWhereitOughtNottoBe.pdf.

L

"The Law and the Gospel in Lutheran Theology." *Grace Theological Journal* 12 (1991): 163–78.

"The Law and the Gospel in Lutheran Theology." *Logia* 3, no. 1 (1994): 27–34. https://logia.org/scaer-articles.

"Law Gospel Debate in the Missouri Synod." *Springfielder* 36, no. 3 (1972): 156–71. http://www.ctsfw.net/media/pdfs/scaerlawgospeldebate.pdf.

"Die Lehre von Der Rechtfertigung in Der Augustana." *Evangelium/Gospel* 9 (1982): 80–94.

"The Lord's Supper: Symbol of Christian Unity." *Affirm* 5 (1975): 4.

"L'osservatore Romano." *Concordia Theological Quarterly* 63, no. 4 (1999): 301–5.

"Luther and Emergency Communions." *Concordia Theological Quarterly* 45, no. 1–2 (1981): 83–86. http://www.ctsfw.net/media/pdfs/TheoObserver45-1,2.pdf.

"Luther, Baptism, and the Church Today." *Concordia Theological Quarterly* 62, no. 4 (1998): 247–68. http://www.ctsfw.net/media/pdfs/scaerdlutherbaptism.pdf.

"Luther on Prayer." *Concordia Theological Quarterly* 47, no. 4 (1983): 305–15. http://www.ctsfw.net/media/pdfs/scaerprayer.pdf.

"The Lutheran Confessions on the Holy Ministry With a Few Thoughts on Hoefling." *Logia* 8, no. 4 (1999): 37–43. https://logia.org/scaer-articles

"The Lutheran Confessions: Stepping Stones between the Bible and Current Church Problems." *Concordia Theological Quarterly* 44, no. 1 (1980): 51–53. http://www.ctsfw.net/media/pdfs/TheoObserver44-1.pdf.

"Lutheran Hermeneutics." *Logia* 10, no. 1 (2001): 41–42. http://www.ctsfw.net/media/pdfs/ScaerDavidLutheranHermeneutics.pdf. Also https://logia.org/scaer-articles.

"A Lutheran Response to Evangelicalism: Ordination of Women." *Concordia Theological Quarterly* 51, no. 2–3 (April 1987): 103–5. http://www.ctsfw.net/media/pdfs/TheoObserver51-2,3.pdf.

"Lutheran Viewpoints on the Challenge of Fundamentalism: Eschatology." *Concordia Journal* 10, no. 1 (1984): 4–11.

"Lutheranism as Catholic and Evangelical." *Logia* 22, no. 1 (2013): 13–20. https://logia.org/scaer-articles.

"Lutherans and Anglicans Talk in Australia." *Concordia Theological Quarterly* 41, no. 2 (1977): 77. http://www.ctsfw.net/media/pdfs/CTQTheologicalObserver41-2.pdf.

"Lutherans and Episcopalians Pair off: New Ties between Two Churches Alter the Ecumenical Equation." *Christianity Today* 27, no. 2 (January 21, 1983): 20–21.

"Lutherans and Roman Catholicism: The Changing Conflict, 1917–1963." *Christianity Today* 13, no. 20 (July 4, 1969): 17–18.

"Luther's Concept of the Resurrection in His Commentary on 1 Corinthians 15." *Concordia Theological Quarterly* 47, no. 3 (1983): 209–24. http://www.ctsfw.net/media/pdfs/scaerlutherresurrection.pdf.

M

"The Man Luther: Reformer." *Lutheran Witness* 102, no. 10 (1983): 334–35.

"Man Made in the Image of God and Its Relationship to the First Promise." *Concordia Theological Quarterly* 41, no. 3 (1977): 20–35. http://www.ctsfw.net/media/pdfs/scaermanmadeimage.pdf.

"Martin Stephan: The Other Side of the Story or at Least Part of It." *Concordia Theological Quarterly* 72, no. 4 (2008): 363–66. http://www.ctsfw.net/media/pdfs/CTQTheologicalObserver72-4.pdf.

"A Matter of Doctrine." *For the Life of the World* 5, no. 2 (2001): 10–12. http://www.ctsfw.net/media/pdfs/ScaerAMatterofDoctrine.pdf.

"Matthew as a Catechism." *Missio Apostolica* 10, no. 1 (2002): 14–23.

"Matthew as the Foundation for the New Testament Canon." *Concordia Theological Quarterly* 79, no. 3–4 (2015): 233–44. http://www.ctsfw.net/media/pdfs/ScaerMatthewAsTheFoundationForNTCanon.pdf.

"May Women Be Ordained as Pastors?" *Springfielder* 36, no. 2 (1972): 89–109. http://www.ctsfw.net/media/pdfs/scaerwomenordination.pdf.

"The Metamorphosis of Confessional Lutheranism." *Concordia Theological Quarterly* 71, no. 3–4 (2007): 203–17. http://www.ctsfw.net/media/pdfs/scaermetamorphosis.pdf.

"Ministry: The Vocation That Matters Forever." *Pilgrimage* 2, no. 5 (1998): 1.

"Missouri at the End of the Century: A Time for Reevaluation." *Logia* 7, no. 1 (1998): 39–52. https://logia.org/scaer-articles

"Missouri: Not Just a State." *Logia* 8, no. 1 (1999): 70–71. https://logia.org/scaer-articles

"A Missouri Response to Ephraim Radner." *Lutheran Forum* 39, no. 1 (2005): 32–35.

"Moderate–Conservative Reports Show Difference." *Affirm* 6 (1976): 6.

"The Moderates Cry 'Legalism!'" *Affirm* 8 (1979): 1.

"Musings on the 2007 Annual Meeting of the Society of Biblical Literature (SBL)." *Concordia Theological Quarterly* 72, no. 2 (2008): 182–84. http://www.ctsfw.net/media/pdfs/CTQTheologicalObserver72-2.pdf.

N

"The Nature and Extent of the Atonement in Lutheran Theology." *Bulletin of the Evangelical Theological Society* 10, no. 4 (September 1967): 179–87.

"The New Book of Concord." *Logia* 9, no. 1 (2000): 62–63. https://logia.org/scaer-articles.

"The New International Version—Nothing New." *Concordia Theological Quarterly* 43, no. 3 (1979): 242–45. http://www.ctsfw.net/media/pdfs/TheoObserver43-3.pdf.

"No Oral Tradition: No Words of Jesus." *Springfielder* 34, no. 3 (1970): 227–28. http://www.ctsfw.net/media/pdfs/SpringfielderTheologicalRefractions34-3.pdf.

O

"The Office of the Ministry According to the Gospels and the Augsburg Confession." *Concordia Theological Quarterly* 70, no. 2 (2006): 113–21. http://www.ctsfw.net/media/pdfs/scaerofficeaccordingtogospelsandac.pdf.

"Office of the Pastor and the Problem of Ordination of Women Pastors." *Springfielder* 38, no. 2 (1974): 123–33. http://www.ctsfw.net/media/pdfs/scaerofficeofpastor.pdf.

"On the Morning After." *Concordia Theological Quarterly* 64, no. 1 (2000): 69–71. http://www.ctsfw.net/media/pdfs/CTQTheologicalObserver64-1.pdf.

"On the Nature of Confessional Subscription: An Explanation on the Action of the Missouri Synod at New Orleans in July 1973." *Concordia Theological Quarterly* 74, no. 1–2 (2010): 153–58. http://www.ctsfw.net/media/pdfs/CTQTheologicalObserver74-1.pdf.

"The One Anointing of Jesus: Another Application of the Form-Critical Method." *Concordia Theological Quarterly* 41, no. 3 (1977): 54–55. http://www.ctsfw.net/media/pdfs/TheologicalObserver41-3.pdf.

"Once More to John 6." *Concordia Theological Quarterly* 78, no. 1–2 (2014): 47–62. http://ctsfw.net/media/pdfs/ScaerOnceMoreJohn6.pdf.

"The Ordination of Women Pastors." *Logia* 12, no. 4 (2003): 25–29. https://logia.org/scaer-articles.

"Ordained Women Pastors: The Crisis in Christendom." *Affirm* 13 (1989): 2.

"The Origin of Authentic Rationalism." *Concordia Theological Quarterly* 80, no. 1–2 (2016): 133–34. http://www.ctsfw.net/media/pdfs/CTQTheologicalObserver80-1-2.pdf.

"Out of the Mouths of Babes—Almost." *Concordia Theological Quarterly* 64, no. 4 (2000): 336–38. http://www.ctsfw.net/media/pdfs/CTQTheologicalObserver64-4.pdf.

P

"Passing through Rockville, Connecticut." *Concordia Theological Quarterly* 66, no. 1 (2002): 83–85. http://www.ctsfw.net/media/pdfs/CTQTheologicalObserver66-1.pdf.

"The Patristic and Byzantine Review." *Concordia Theological Quarterly* 47, no. 1 (January 1983): 32. http://www.ctsfw.net/media/pdfs/TheoObserver47-1.pdf.

"Paul's Second Christmas: Sermon for the Second Christmas Day: Galatians 4:4–7." *Concordia Pulpit Resources* 25, no. 1 (2015): 55, 57.

"A Peaceful Church: Is It Possible?" *Affirm* 10 (1984): 2.

"Policy of an Editor." *Springfielder* 36, no. 3 (1972): 223. http://www.ctsfw.net/media/pdfs/policyeditor.pdf.

"The Pope as Antichrist: An Anachronism?" *Christianity Today* 25, no. 18 (October 23, 1981): 66–66.

Portals of Prayer 63 (2000).

"Preaching Sanctification." *Concordia Pulpit Resources* 4, no. 4 (1994): 2–4.

"The Proposed Rite for Holy Baptism—Biblically Considered." *Springfielder* 31, no. 4 (1968): 30–35. http://www.ctsfw.net/media/pdfs/scaertheproposedriteforholybaptism.pdf.

"Providing a Basis for a Civil Religion in America." *Concordia Theological Quarterly* 49, no. 2–3 (1985): 201–4. http://www.ctsfw.net/media/pdfs/TheoObserver49-2,3.pdf.

Q

"Questions and Answers about the AELC." *Affirm* 6 (1977): 3.

R

"Rast, Vehse, and Wather." *Logia* 9, no. 3 (2000): 47–50. http://www.ctsfw.net/media/pdfs/ScaerDavidRastVehseandWalther.pdf. Also https://logia.org/scaer-articles.

"Recent Research on Jesus: Assessing the Contribution of Larry Hurtado." *Concordia Theological Quarterly* 69, no. 1 (2005): 48–62. http://www.ctsfw.net/media/pdfs/scaerrecentjesushurtado.pdf.

"Rediscovering the Treatise as Ecumenical Response." *Concordia Theological Quarterly* 64, no. 4 (2000): 338–44.

"Reflections on a European Trip." *Springfielder* 33, no. 3 (1969): 15–23. http://www.ctsfw.net/media/pdfs/scaerreflections.pdf.

"Reformed Exegesis and Lutheran Sacraments: Worlds in Conflict." *Concordia Theological Quarterly* 64, no. 1 (2000): 3–20. http://www.ctsfw.net/media/pdfs/scaerreformedexegesis.pdf.

"The Relation of Matthew 28:16–20 to the Rest of the Gospel." *Concordia Theological Quarterly* 55, no. 4 (1991): 245–66. http://www.ctsfw.net/media/pdfs/scaerrelationofmatthew.pdf.

"Relationship between Liturgics and Dogmatics." *Springfielder* 35, no. 3 (1971): 197–200. http://www.ctsfw.net/media/pdfs/scaerrelationshipliturgicsdogmatics.pdf.

"Response to David Lotz." *Springfielder* 38, no. 3 (1974): 226–31. http://www.ctsfw.net/media/pdfs/scaerresponsedavidlotz.pdf.

"A Review of 'A Common Calling.'" *Concordia Theological Quarterly* 57, no. 3 (July 1993): 191–213. http://www.ctsfw.net/media/pdfs/DeptOfSysAReview.pdf.

"Rewriting the Bible in Non-Sexist Language." *Concordia Theological Quarterly* 44, no. 1 (1980): 50–51. http://www.ctsfw.net/media/pdfs/TheoObserver44-1.pdf.

"Richard John Neuhaus and the Pilgrimage to Rome." *Concordia Theological Quarterly* 55, no. 1 (1991): 43–48. http://www.ctsfw.net/media/pdfs/CTQTheologicalObserver55-1.pdf.

"The Rise and Fall of Clark H. Pinnock." *Concordia Theological Quarterly* 46, no. 1 (1982): 40–42. http://www.ctsfw.net/media/pdfs/TheoObserver46-1.pdf.

"Roman Catholic Communion Practices." *Concordia Theological Quarterly* 44, no. 1 (1980): 54–55. http://www.ctsfw.net/media/pdfs/TheoObserver44-1.pdf.

"Roman Catholic Recognition of the Augsburg Confession: What Does It Mean?" *Concordia Theological Quarterly* 43, no. 3 (1979): 243–45. http://www.ctsfw.net/media/pdfs/TheoObserver43-3.pdf.

S

"Sacraments as an Affirmation of Creation." *Concordia Theological Quarterly* 57, no. 4 (October 1993): 241–64. http://www.ctsfw.net/media/pdfs/scaerdsacramentsaffirmationcreation.pdf.

"Sanctification." *Concordia Journal* 41, no. 3 (2015): 236–49. http://scholar.csl.edu/cgi/viewcontent.cgi?article=1160&context=cj.

"Sanctification by Grace Alone." *For the Life of the World* 2, no. 3 (1998): 8–9. http://www.ctsfw.net/media/pdfs/SanctificationByGraceAloneDScaer.pdf.

"Sanctification in Lutheran Theology." *Concordia Theological Quarterly* 49, no. 2–3 (1985): 181–97. http://www.ctsfw.net/media/pdfs/scaersanctificationinlutherantheology.pdf.

"Sanctification in the Lutheran Confessions." *Concordia Theological Quarterly* 53, no. 3 (1989): 165–81. http://www.ctsfw.net/media/pdfs/scaersanctification.pdf.

"Scaer: A Second Look at Promise Keepers." *Logia* 7, no. 1 (1998): 75–77. https://logia.org/scaer-articles.

"Scaer: A View from the Pew." *Logia* 7, no. 1 (1998): 77–79. https://logia.org/scaer-articles.

"Scaer: Categorically Speaking." *Logia* 7, no. 1 (1998): 79. https://logia.org/scaer-articles.

"Scaer Replies to Empie." *Lutheran Forum* 7, no. 2 (May 1973): 29–30.

"Scaer: The Computer as Liturgical Meatgrinder." *Logia* 7, no. 1 (1998): 79. https://logia.org/scaer-articles.

"Season of Creation." *Concordia Theological Quarterly* 72, no. 2 (2008): 186. http://www.ctsfw.net/media/pdfs/CTQTheologicalObserver72-2.pdf.

"*Semper Virgo*: A Doctrine." *Logia* 19, no. 3 (2010): 15–17. https://logia.org/scaer-articles.

"*Semper Virgo*: Pushing the Envelope." *Lutheran Forum* 41, no. 2 (2007): 24–28.

"A Shot in the Arm for Confessional Studies." *Concordia Theological Quarterly* 65, no. 4 (2001): 361–62. http://www.ctsfw.net/media/pdfs/CTQTheologicalObserver65-4.pdf.

"Should Children Go to the Communion Rail for a Blessing?" *Concordia Theological Quarterly* 42, no. 2 (1978): 169–71. http://www.ctsfw.net/media/pdfs/CTQTheologicalObserver42-2.pdf.

"Should Children Go to the Communion Rail for a Blessing: A Follow-up by Helmut Thielicke." *Concordia Theological Quarterly* 46, no. 2–3 (1982): 242–43. http://www.ctsfw.net/media/pdfs/TheoObserver46-2,3.pdf.

"Shroud of Turin: Protestant Opportunity or Embarrassment?" *Concordia Theological Quarterly* 43, no. 1 (1979): 46–49. http://www.ctsfw.net/media/pdfs/TheoObserver43-1.pdf.

"The Simon Greenleaf Law Review." *Concordia Theological Quarterly* 46, no. 1 (January 1982): 42. http://www.ctsfw.net/media/pdfs/TheoObserver46-1.pdf.

"'The Son of Man'—a Euphemism?" *Springfielder* 34, no. 3 (1970): 225–27. http://www.ctsfw.net/media/pdfs/SpringfielderTheologicalRefractions34-3.pdf.

T

"That Christmass Issue Again." *Lutheran Forum* 31, no. 2 (1997): 60–61.

"The Theology and Life of Robert David Preus." *Concordia Theological Quarterly* 74, no. 1–2 (2010): 181–82. http://www.ctsfw.net/media/pdfs/CTQBookReview74-1.pdf.

"The Theology of Robert David Preus and His Person: Making a Difference." *Concordia Theological Quarterly* 74, no. 1–2 (2010): 74–91. http://www.ctsfw.net/media/pdfs/ScaerTheologyofRobertPreus74-1,2.pdf.

"Theses on the Law and Gospel." *Springfielder* 37, no. 1 (June 1973): 53–63. http://www.ctsfw.net/media/pdfs/scaerlawandgospel.pdf.

"The Third Use of the Law: Resolving the Tension." *Concordia Theological Quarterly* 69, no. 3–4 (2005): 237–57. http://www.ctsfw.net/media/pdfs/scaerthirduseresolvetension.pdf.

"Three Cheers for Hummel." *Lutheran Forum* 3, no. 11 (December 1969): 16–17.

"Tongues." *Lutheran Witness* 101, no. 5 (1982): 155.

"Towards a World Confessional Federation." *Concordia Theological Quarterly* 45, no. 1–2 (January 1981): 86–88. http://www.ctsfw.net/media/pdfs/TheoObserver45-1,2.pdf.

"The Traditions of Lent." *Lutheran Witness* 100, no. 2 (1981): 48.

"Tweaking Bishops' Noses: A Slight Retraction." *Concordia Theological Quarterly* 55, no. 4 (1991): 298–99. http://www.ctsfw.net/media/pdfs/CTQTheologicalObserver55-4.pdf.

"Twenty Years Later—Things Have Not Changed That Much." *Concordia Theological Quarterly* 74, no. 1–2 (2010): 158–59. http://www.ctsfw.net/media/pdfs/CTQTheologicalObserver74-1.pdf.

"The Two Sacraments Doctrine as a Factor in Synoptic Relationships." *Philosophy and Theology* 3, no. 3 (1989): 205–22.

"The Two Sides of Justification." *Christianity Today* 25, no. 12 (June 26, 1981): 44–44.

U

"Unfinished Business at Anaheim." *Springfielder* 39, no. 3 (1975): 126–28. http://www.ctsfw.net/media/pdfs/TheologicalObserver39-3.pdf.

V

"The Validity of the Churchly Acts of Ordained Women." *Concordia Theological Quarterly* 53, no. 1–2 (1989): 3–20. http://www.ctsfw.net/media/pdfs/scaervalidityofordainedwomen.pdf.

W–X

"Was Junias a Female Apostle? Maybe Not." *Concordia Theological Quarterly* 73, no. 1 (2009): 76–76. http://www.ctsfw.net/media/pdfs/ScaerReaserchNotes73-1.pdf.

"We Believe, Teach and Confess . . . The Return of Christ." *Lutheran Witness* 115, no. 5 (1996): 12–14.

"Werdet Ihr Nicht Essen Das Fleisch Des Menschenshones": Ein Versuch Über Johannes 6." *Lutherishe Beiträge* 10, no. 3 (2005): 139–56.

"What Next for the Missouri Synod?" *Affirm* 8 (1977): 4.

"When 'Father, Son, and Spirit' Is Better Than Triune God." *Lutheran Witness* 103, no. 6 (1984): 218.

"'With Common Consent.'" *Springfielder* 39, no. 3 (1975): 134–36. http://www.ctsfw.net/media/pdfs/TheologicalObserver39-3.pdf.

"The Woman as Pastor." *Springfielder* 33, no. 4 (1970): 1–2. http://www.ctsfw.net/media/pdfs/SpringfielderEditorial33-4.pdf.

"Women Pastors in the Missouri Synod." *Springfielder* 39, no. 3 (1975): 131–33. http://www.ctsfw.net/media/pdfs/TheologicalObserver39-3.pdf.

"Worship in Our Age: New Psalms, Stapled Foreheads." *Modern Reformation* 9, no. 3 (2000): 3–4.

Y–Z

"The Year of Concordia." *Concordia Theological Quarterly* 41, no. 2 (1977): 70. http://www.ctsfw.net/media/pdfs/CTQTheologicalObserver41-2.pdf.

"Yes, Virginia, There Is a Santa Claus." *Christianity Today* 17, no. 6 (December 22, 1972): 9–11.

Scaer, D. P. and Paul R. Harris. "Forward." In *Me and My Arrows: Family Devotion Based on the Historic Collects*, iv–x. Austin, TX: Paul R. Harris, 2010.

BOOKS

Klotsche, E. H., John Theodore Mueller, and David P. Scaer. 基督教教義史 = *The history of Christian doctrine*. Chu ban. Taibei Shi: Zhong hua fu yin shen xue yuan chu ban she, 2002.

The Apostolic Scriptures. St Louis, MO: Concordia Publishing House, 1971.

The Apostolic Scriptures. Contemporary Theology Series. Fort Wayne, IN: Concordia Theological Seminary Press, 1979.

Baptism. Edited by John R. Stephenson. Confessional Lutheran Dogmatics 11. St. Louis, MO: Luther Academy, 1999.

Christology. Edited by Robert Preus. Vol. 6. Confessional Lutheran Dogmatics. Fort Wayne, IN: International Foundation for Lutheran Confessional Research, 1989.

Church's First Statement of the Gospel. Fort Wayne, IN: Concordia Theological Seminary Press, 1993.

Discourses in Matthew: Jesus Teaches the Church. St. Louis, MO: Concordia Publishing House, 2004.

Getting into the Story of Concord: A History of the Book of Concord. St. Louis, MO: Concordia Publishing House, 1977.

Getting into the Story of Concord: A History of the Book of Concord. Fort Wayne, IN.: Concordia Theological Seminary Press, 1990.

In Christ: The Collected Works of David P. Scaer, Lutheran Confessor. Edited by Peter C. Bender. 2 vols. Sussex, WI: Concordia Catechetical Academy, 2004.

Infant Baptism in Nineteenth Century Lutheran Theology. St. Louis, MO: Concordia Publishing House, 2011.

James, the Apostle of Faith: A Primary Christological Epistle for the Persecuted Church. 1st ed. St. Louis, MO: Concordia Publishing House, 1983.

James, the Apostle of Faith: A Primary Christological Epistle for the Persecuted Church. 3rd ed. Eugene, OR: Wipf & Stock, 2004.

Kristība. Translated by Ģirts Grietiņš. Latvian edition. Rīga: Luterisma mantojuma fonds, 2011.

A Latin Ecclesiastical Glossary: F. Pieper's Christian Dogmatics, I. Springfield, IL: Concordia Seminary Print Shop, 1967.

A Latin Ecclesiastical Glossary for Francis Pieper's Christian Dogmatics. Fort Wayne, IN: Concordia Theological Seminary, 1978.

A Latin Ecclesiastical Glossary [of] F. Pieper's Christian Dogmatics. Springfield, IL: Concordia Seminary Print Shop, 1967.

Law and Gospel and the Means of Grace. Confessional Lutheran Dogmatics 8. St. Louis, MO: Luther Academy, 2008.

Ley Y Evangelio Y Los Medio de Gracia. Translated by Jose Pfaffenzeller. Buenos Aires: Concordia Seminar, 2013.

Mateo enseña a la iglesia: estructura teológica del primer evangelio. Translated by Erich Sexauer. St. Louis, MO: Editorial Concordia, 2006.

Mieux Conntaitre l'histoire de Concorde. Translated by Lyne Schmidt. St. Louis, MO: LCMS World Mission, 1999.

The Lutheran World Federation Today. St Louis, MO: Concordia Publishing House, 1971.

The Sermon on the Mount: The Church's First Statement of the Gospel. St. Louis, MO: Concordia Publishing House, 2000.

What Do You Think of Jesus? St. Louis, MO: Concordia Publishing House, 1973.

What Do You Think of Jesus? Fort Wayne, IN: Concordia Theological Seminary Press, 1999.

Scaer, D. P. and Dean O. Wenthe. *All Theology Is Christology: Essays in Honor of David P. Scaer.* Edited by Dean O. Wenthe. Fort Wayne, IN: Concordia Theological Seminary Press, 2000.

DISSERTATION

"The Doctrine of Infant Baptism in the German Protestant Theology of the Nineteenth Century." Ph.D., Concordia Seminary, 1963.

CHAPTERS

Sasse, Hermann. "Ecumenical Council for Practical Christianity: Law and Gospel (December 1936)." In *Letters to Lutheran Pastors*, edited by Matthew C. Harrison, translated by David P. Scaer, 2:504–520. St. Louis, MO: Concordia Publishing House, 2013.

Numbers

"2 Peter and the Canon." In *Mysteria Dei, Essays in Honor of Kurt Marquart*, edited by Paul Timothy. McCain and John R. Stephenson, 269–85. Fort Wayne, IN: Concordia Theological Seminary Press, 1999.

A

"Abortion: A Moment for Conscientious Reflection." In *A Christian Handbook on Vital Issues*, 231–232. New Haven, MO: Leader Publishing Co., 1973.

"'According to the Scriptures': A New Testament Precedent for a Liturgical Practice." In *Shepherd the Church: Essays in Honor of the Rev. Dr. Roger D. Pittelko*, edited by Roger D. Pittelko and Frederic W. Baue, 71–85. Fort Wayne, Ind.: Concordia Theological Seminary Press, 2002.

"Apologetics as Theological Discipline: Reflections on a Necessary and Biblical Task." In *Let Christ Be Christ: Theology, Ethics and World Religions in the Two Kingdoms: Essays in Honor of the Sixty-Fifth Birthday of Charles L. Manske*, edited by Daniel Nathan Harmelink, 299–307. Huntington Beach, Calif.: Tentatio Press, 1999.

"Article IV: Good Works." In *Contemporary Look at the Formula of Concord*, edited by Wilbert H. Rosin and Robert D. Preus, 163–70. St Louis, MO: Concordia Publishing House, 1978.

"The Augsburg Confession, The Apology, The Smalcald Articles and the Treatises on the Power and Primacy of the Pope, and a Few Extra Thoughts on Hoefling." In *The Office of the Holy Ministry*, edited by John R. Fehrmann and Daniel Preus, 130–49. Luther Academy Lecture Series 3. Crestwood, MO: Luther Academy, 1996.

B

"Baptism: Christ Marks Us as His Own." In *We Believe: Essays on the Catechism as Drawn from For the Life of the World*, edited by Scott C. Klemsz and David P. Scaer. Fort Wayne, IN: Concordia Theological Seminary Press, 2000.

"Baptist View: Christ's Presence as Memorial: A Lutheran Response." In *Understanding Four Views on the Lord's Supper*, edited by John H. Armstrong, 48–52. Counterpoints. Grand Rapids, MI: Zondervan, 2007.

"Beatitudes." In *Evangelical Dictionary of Biblical Theology*, edited by Walter A Elwell, 53–55. Grand Rapids, MI; Carlisle, Cumbria: Baker Books ; Paternoster Press, 1996.

"Blessedness." In *Evangelical Dictionary of Biblical Theology*, edited by Walter A. Elwell, 69. Grand Rapids, MI; Carlisle, Cumbria: Baker Books ; Paternoster Press, 1996.

C

"Christian Involvement in the Public Square." In *The Restoration of Creation in Christ: Essays in Honor of Dean O. Wenthe*, edited by Arthur A. Jr. Just and Paul J Grime, 211–26. St. Louis, MO: Concordia Publishing House, 2014.

"Christology: Key to Understanding the Doctrine of the Trinity." In *Who Is God? In the Light of the Lutheran Confessions: Papers Presented at the Congress on the Lutheran Confessions, Bloomington, Minnesota, April 22–24, 2009*, edited by John A. Maxfield and Jennifer H. Maxfield, 96–111. Luther Academy Lecture Series 16. St. Louis, MO: Luther Academy, 2012.

"Cultural and Theological Readjustments and the Survival of Lutheranism." In *Propter Christum: Christ at the Center: Essays in Honor of Daniel Preus*, edited by Scott R. Murray, Aaron M. Moldenhauer, Carl D. Roth, Richard A. Lammert, Martin R. Noland, Charles L. Cortrright, and Michael J. Albrecht. St. Louis, MO: Luther Academy, 2013.

D–G

"Doctrine and Practice: Setting the Boundaries." In *Contemporary Issues in Fellowship: Confessional Principles and Application: Papers Presented at the Congress on the Lutheran Confessions, Bloomingdale, Illinois, April 24–26, 2003*, edited by John A. Maxfield, 85–100. Luther Academy Lecture Series 10. St. Louis, MO: Luther Academy, 2004.

"The Doctrine of Election: A Lutheran Note." In *Perspectives on Evangelical Theology: Papers from the Thirtieth Annual Meeting of the Evangelical Theology Society*, edited by Kenneth S. Kantzer and Stanley N. Gundry, 105–15. Grand Rapids, MI: Baker Book House, 1979.

"The Doctrine of the Scriptures in the Theology of Robert David Preus (1924–1995)." In *The Theology and Life of Robert D. Preus: Papers Presented at the Congress on the Lutheran Confessions, Itasca, Illinois, April 8–10, 1999*, edited by Jennifer H. Maxfield and Bethany Preus, 47–63. Luther Academy Lecture Series 6. St. Louis, MO: Luther Academy, 2009.

"Francis Pieper." In *Handbook of Evangelical Theologians*, edited by Walter A. Elwell, 40–53. Grand Rapids, MI: Baker Books, 1993.

"Francis Pieper (1852–1931)." In *Twentieth-Century Lutheran Theologians*, edited by Mark C. Mattes, 10:17–36. Refo500 Academic Studies. Göttingen: Vandenhoeck & Ruprecht, 2013.

"Francis Pieper: His Theology and Legacy Unmatched Stature." In *The Office of the Ministry*, edited by Chris Christophersen Boshoven, 9–41. The Pieper Lectures. St. Louis, MO: Concordia Historical Institute, 1997.

"The Free Will: Confessional and Historical Perspectives." In *We Confess, We Condemn . . . : God's Will and Work in Lutheran Perspective: Papers Presented at the Congress on the Lutheran Confessions, St. Louis, Missouri, April 20–22, 2006*, edited by John A. Maxfield, 103–19. Luther Academy Lecture Series 13. St. Louis, MO: Luther Academy, 2009.

"Gerhard, Johann (1582–1637)." In *The New Westminster Dictionary of Church History*, edited by Robert Benedetto and James O. Duke, 266. Louisville, KY: Westminster John Knox Press, 2008.

"Gnesio-Lutherans." In *The New Westminster Dictionary of Church History*, edited by Robert Benedetto and James O. Duke, 272. Louisville, KY: Westminster John Knox Press, 2008.

H

"Heideberg Catechism." In *The New Westminster Dictionary of Church History*, edited by Robert Benedetto and James O. Duke, 296. Louisville, KY: Westminster John Knox Press, 2008.

"Herbert, Edward (1583–1648)." In *The New Westminster Dictionary of Church History*, edited by Robert Benedetto and James O. Duke, 301. Louisville, KY.: Westminster John Knox Press, 2008.

"Hesshus, Tilemann (1527–1588)." In *The New Westminster Dictionary of Church History*, edited by Robert Benedetto and James O. Duke, 513. Louisville, KY: Westminster John Knox Press, 2008.

"Historical Criticism: A Biblical and Contemporary Application." In *The Word They Still Shall Let Remain: The Place of the Holy Scriptures in the Faith and Life of Confessional Lutherans: Papers Presented at the Congress on the Lutheran Confessions, Bloomington, Minnesota May 4–6, 2011*, edited by John A. Maxfield, 123–34. Luther Academy Lecture Series 18. Fort Wayne, IN: Luther Academy, 2015.

"Hobbes, Thomas (1588–1679)." In *The New Westminster Dictionary of Church History*, edited by Robert Benedetto and James O. Duke, 314. Louisville, KY: Westminster John Knox Press, 2008.

"How Do Lutheran Theologians Approach the Doing of Theology Today?" In *Doing Theology in Today's World: Essays in Honor of Kenneth S. Kantzer*, edited by John D. Woodbridge and Thomas Edward McComiskey, 197–225. Grand Rapids, MI: Zondervan, 1991.

I–K

"Infants and Children in the Church: A Lutheran View." In *Infants and Children in the Church: Five Views on Theology and Ministry*, edited by Adam Harwood and Kevin E. Lawson, 81–111. Nashville, TN: B & H Academic, 2017.

"Is Reformation Theology Making a Comeback?" In *A Confessing Theology for Postmodern Times*, edited by Michael Scott Horton, 153–69. Wheaton, IL: Crossway Books, 2000.

"Johann Gerhard's Doctrine of the Sacraments." In *Protestant Scholasticism: Essays in Reassessment*, edited by Carl R. Trueman and R. Scott. Clark, 289–306. Carlisle: Paternoster, 1999.

"Jonas, Justus (1493–1555)." In *The New Westminster Dictionary of Church History*, edited by Robert Benedetto and James O. Duke, 362. Louisville, KY: Westminster John Knox Press, 2008.

"Joy." In *Evangelical Dictionary of Biblical Theology*, edited by Walter A. Elwell, 430–31. Grand Rapids, MI; Carlisle, Cumbria: Baker Books; Paternoster Press, 1996.

"Judgement as Life's Great Reality: Fourth Sunday After Pentecost: Second Corinthians 5:6–10." In *Concordia Pulpit*, 187–192. St. Louis, MO: Concordia Publishing House, 1976.

L

"Law in a Law-Less World." In *The Law in Holy Scripture*, edited by Charles A. Gieschen, 191–209. St. Louis, MO: Concordia Publishing House, 2004.

"Lutheran Publishing." In *Encyclopedia of Martin Luther and the Reformation*, edited by Mark A. Lamport, 1:467–69. Lanham, MD: Rowman & Littlefield, 2017.

"Lutheran View: Finding the Right Word." In *Understanding Four Views on the Lord's Supper*, edited by Russell D. Moore, 87–101. Counterpoints. Grand Rapids, MI: Zondervan, 2007.

"Luther's Understanding of Baptism—Grounded in the Word." In *Divine Multi-Media: The Manifold Means of Grace in the Life of the Church: Papers Presented at the Congress on the Lutheran Confessions, Bloomingdale, Illinois, April 15–17, 2004*, edited by John A. Maxfield. Luther Academy Lecture Series 11. St. Louis, MO: Luther Academy, 2005.

M–Q

"The Man Luther: Reformer." In *Who Was Martin Luther?*, 95–101. St. Louis, MO: Concordia Publishing House, 2017.

"Maurice of Saxony." In *Encyclopedia of Martin Luther and the Reformation*, edited by Mark A. Lamport, 2:507–9. Lanham, MD: Rowman & Littlefield, 2017.

"May Women Be Ordained as Pastors?" In *In Women Pastors? The Ordination of Women in Biblical Lutheran Perspective: A Collection of Essays*, edited by Matthew Harrison and John T. Pless, 3rd Revised ed., 227–52. St Louis, MO: Concordia Publishing House, 2008.

"Menius, Justus (1499–1558)." In *The New Westminster Dictionary of Church History*, edited by Robert Benedetto and James O. Duke, 428. Louisville, KY: Westminster John Knox Press, 2008.

"Neoorthodoxy." In *Encyclopedia of Christianity in the United States*, edited by George Thomas Kurian and Mark A. Lamport, 4:1608–11. Lanham, MD: Rowman & Littlefield, 2016.

"The New Jerusalem." In *Concordia Pulpit*, 113–17. St. Louis, MO: Concordia Publishing House, 1980.

"The New Translation of Luther's Small Catechism: Is It Faithful to Luther's Spirit?" In *Luther's Catechisms—450 Years: Essays Commemorating the Small and Large Catechisms of Dr Martin Luther*, edited by Robert D. Preus and David P. Scaer, 32–40. Fort Wayne, IN: Concordia Theological Seminary Press, 1979.

"The Office of the Pastor and the Problem of the Ordination of Women Pastors." In *Women Pastors? The Ordination of Women in Biblical Lutheran Perspective: A Collection of Essays*, edited by Matthew C. Harrison and John T. Pless, 2nd ed., 253–64. St. Louis, MO: Concordia Publishing House, 2009.

"The Office of the Pastor and the Problem of the Ordination of Women Pastors." In *Women Pastors? The Ordination of Women in Biblical Lutheran Perspective: A Collection of Essays*, edited by Matthew C. Harrison and John T. Pless, 3rd Revised., 253–64. St. Louis, MO: Concordia Publishing House, 2012.

"Once More to John 6." In *Teach Me Thy Way, O Lord: Essays in Honor of Glen Zweck on the Occasion of His Sixty-Fifth Birthday*, edited by Glen Zweck, 217–33. Houston, TX: Zweck Festschrift Committee, 2000.

"Peucer, Caspar (1525–1602)." In *The New Westminster Dictionary of Church History*, edited by Robert Benedetto and James O. Duke, 513. Louisville, KY: Westminster John Knox Press, 2008.

"Probleme und Nutzen des Gebrauchs nachapostolischer Quellen bei der Frage nach der Ordnung der synoptischen Evangelien." In *Einträchtig Lehren: Festschrift für Bischof Dr. Jobst Schöne*, edited by Jürgen Diestelmann and Wolfgang Schillhahn. Oesingen, Germany: Verlad der Lutherischen Buchhandlung, 1997.

"Providence." In *Baker's Dictionary of Christian Ethics*, edited by Carl F. H. Henry, 548–49. Grand Rapids, MI: Baker Book House, 1973.

"El Puntao de Vista Bautista: Un respuesta luterana." In *Cuatro puntos de vista sobre la Santa Cena*, edited by John H. Armstrong, 48–52. Counterpoints. Miami, FL: Vida, 2010.

"El Puntao de Vista Catolico Romano: Un respuesta luterana." In *Cuatro puntos de vista sobre la Santa Cena*, edited by John H. Armstrong, 144–52. Counterpoints. Miami, FL: Vida, 2010.

"El Puntao de Vista Luterano." In *Cuatro puntos de vista sobre la Santa Cena*, edited by John H. Armstrong, 85–104. Counterpoints. Miami, FL: Vida, 2010.

"El Puntao de Vista Reformado: Un respuesta luterana." In *Cuatro puntos de vista sobre la Santa Cena*, edited by John H. Armstrong, 75–78. Counterpoints. Miami, FL: Vida, 2010.

"Putting Things in Right Perspective (II Cor. 4:13–5:1)." In *Concordia Pulpit*, 181–86. St. Louis, MO: Concordia Publishing House, 1976.

R

"Reformation." In *Concordia Pulpit*, 274–79. St. Louis, MO: Concordia Publishing House, 1982.

"Reformed View: The Real Presence of Christ: A Lutheran Response." In *Understanding Four Views on the Lord's Supper*, edited by John H. Armstrong, 75–78. Counterpoints. Grand Rapids, MI: Zondervan, 2007.

"A Response to Genre Criticism—Sensus Literalis." In *Hermeneutics, Inerrancy, and the Bible*, edited by Earl D. Radmacher and Robert D. Preus, 207–16. Grand Rapids, MI: Academie Books, 1984.

"Response to Os Guinness." In *Evangelical Affirmations*, edited by Kenneth S. Kantzer and Carl F. H. Henry, 457–97. Grand Rapids, MI: Acadamie Books, 1990.

"The Return of Christ (Article 17)." In *Augsburg Today: This We Believe, Teach, and Confess*, edited by David L Mahsman, 93–98. St. Louis, MO: Concordia Publishing House, 1997.

"Righteousness." In *Baker's Dictionary of Christian Ethics*, edited by Carl F. H. Henry, 588–89. Grand Rapids, MI: Baker Book House, 1973.

"Roman Catholic View: Christ's True, Real, and Substantial Presence: A Lutheran Response." In Understanding Four Views on the Lord's Supper, edited by John H. Armstrong, 144–51. Counterpoints. Grand Rapids, MI: Zondervan, 2007.

S

"Sanctification and Baptism in Lutheran Theology." In *Sanctification: New Life in Christ*, edited by John A. Maxfield, 93–110. The Pieper Lectures. St. Louis, MO: Concordia Historical Institute, 2003.

"Sermon on the Mount." In *Evangelical Dictionary of Biblical Theology*, edited by Walter A. Elwell, 723–25. Grand Rapids,MI.; Carlisle, Cumbria: Baker Books ; Paternoster Press, 1996.

T–V

"Taufe Und Herrenmahl Im Leben Der Kirche." In *Die Eine Heilige Christliche Kirche Und Die Gnadenmittel*, edited by Manfred Roensch and Jobst Schöne, 166–89. Erlangen: Martin Luther-Verlag, 1981.

"Theology of Hope." In *Tensions in Contemporary Theology*, edited by Stanley N. Gundry and Alan F. Johnson, 197–234. Chicago: Moody Press, 1976.

"Theology of Hope." In *Tensions in Contemporary Theology*, edited by Stanley N. Gundry and Alan F. Johnson, Rev. Ed., 197–234. Chicago: Moody Press, 1979.

"Theology of Hope." In *Tensions in Contemporary Theology*, edited by Stanley N. Gundry and Alan F. Johnson, Second edition., 197–234. Grand Rapids, MI: Baker Book House, 1983.

"Third Use of the Law: Resolving the Tension." In *You, My People, Shall Be Holy: A Festschrift in Honour of John W. Kleinig*, edited by John R. Stephenson and Thomas M. Winger, 242–62. St. Catharines, Ontario, Canada: Concordia Lutheran Theological Seminary, 2013.

W–Z

"Women's Ordination: More than Bible Passages." In *Marriage, Sex, and Gender in the Lutheran Church Today*, edited by John A. Maxfield, 95–110. Luther Academy Lecture Series 22. Fort Wayne, IN: Luther Academy, 2015.

"The Word Was God: Inerrancy or Christology." In *"Built on the Foundation of the Apostles and Prophets": Sola Scriptura in Context*, edited by Tapani Simojoki, 45–62. Cambridge, United Kingdom: The Evangelical Lutheran Church of England, 2013.

Scaer, D. P. and Adolf Koeberle. "Holiness: Man's Unending Quest." In *The Quest for Holiness*. Evanston, IN: Ballast Press, 1995.

Scaer, D. P. and James A. Lucas. "Preface." In *What's That Supposed to Mean? Using the Catechism in the 21st Century*, 17–20. Lima, OH: CSS Publishing Company, 2000.

John Theodore Mueller, and E. H. Klotsche. "Theological Developments Since World War II." In *The History of Christian Doctrine*, Rev. ed., 350–87. Twin Brooks Series. Grand Rapids, MI: Baker Book House, 1979.

OBITUARIES

"Carl F. H. Henry: An Evangelical Tribute to a Theologian." *Concordia Theological Quarterly* 68, no. 2 (April 2004): 155–56. http://www.ctsfw.net/media/pdfs/CTQTheologicalObserver68-2.pdf.

"Eggold, Henry J., Th. D., D. D., 1917–1982." *Concordia Theological Quarterly* 46, no. 2–3 (April 1982): 98–100. http://www.ctsfw.net/media/pdfs/ScaerEggold.pdf.

"Harry A. Huth, DD, 1917–1979." *Concordia Theological Quarterly* 44, no. 1 (1980): 1–2. http://www.ctsfw.net/media/pdfs/HarryHuth.pdf.

"Hermann Otto Erich Sasse, July 17, 1895–August 9, 1976." *Concordia Theological Quarterly* 41, no. 2 (1977): 1–5. http://www.ctsfw.net/media/pdfs/CTQEditorials41-2.pdf.

"In Memoriam: Dr. Erich H. Heintzen." *Springfielder* 35, no. 3 (1971): 150–51. http://www.ctsfw.net/media/pdfs/SchultzInMemoriamHeintzen.pdf.

"In Memoriam: Peter Brunner: 1900–1981." *Concordia Theological Quarterly* 45, no. 4 (October 1981): 297–297. http://www.ctsfw.net/media/pdfs/TheoObserver45-4.pdf.

"In Memoriam Robert D. Preus." *Logia* 5, no. 3 (1996): 7–8. https://logia.org/scaer-articles.

"In Memoriam: Wilhelm Martin Oesch, 1896–1982." *Concordia Theological Quarterly* 46, no. 2–3 (1982): 241–42. http://www.ctsfw.net/media/pdfs/TheoObserver46-2,3.pdf.

"Jaroslav Pelikan (1923–2006)." *Concordia Theological Quarterly* 72, no. 2 (2008): 180–82. http://www.ctsfw.net/media/pdfs/CTQTheologicalObserver72-2.pdf.

"Klug, Eugene F. A., 1917–2003." *Concordia Theological Quarterly* 67, no. 3–4 (2003): 195–96. http://www.ctsfw.net/media/pdfs/ScaerDKlug.pdf.

"Kurt Marquart: Saluting a Fellow Saint." *Concordia Theological Quarterly* 71, no. 1 (2007): 86–87. http://www.ctsfw.net/media/pdfs/CTQTheologicalObserver71-1.pdf.

"Professor Gerhard Aho, Ph.D. [1923–1967]." *Concordia Theological Quarterly* 51, no. 4 (October 1987): 241–44. http://www.ctsfw.net/media/pdfs/ScaerAho.pdf.

"R. I. P. Reminiscences on an Editor: E. H. H." *Springfielder* 35, no. 3 (1971): 1. http://www.ctsfw.net/media/pdfs/SchultzInMemoriamHeintzen.pdf.

"Raymond F. Surburg (1909–2001)." *Concordia Theological Quarterly* 65, no. 4 (2001): 291–92. http://www.ctsfw.net/media/pdfs/RaymondFSurburg.pdf.

"Richard John Neuhaus (1936–2009)." *Concordia Theological Quarterly* 73, no. 2 (2009): 174–77. http://www.ctsfw.net/media/pdfs/CTQTheologicalObserver73-2.pdf.

PAPERS AND NOTES

A Response to Martin Hengel's "Probleme Des Markusevangeliums," Together with an Attempted Resolution of the Problem Caused by the Tension in Understanding Mark's Gospel as Possessing Petrine Authority but Nevertheless Dependent on Matthew and Luke as an Appendix. Fort Wayne, IN: Concordia Theological Seminary Press, n. d.

An Introduction to the Method and Practice of Lutheran Theology. Fort Wayne, IN: Concordia Theological Seminary Press, 1990.

"Anfechtung, Prayer and Resurrection," 43. Mankato, MN: Bethany Lutheran Theological Seminary, 1980.

Baptism and the Lord's Supper in the Life of the Church. Fort Wayne, IN: Concordia Theological Seminary Bookstore, 1989.

Baptism Is God's Revelatory Act to Create the New Life. n.p.: Southern California District. Lutheran Church—Missouri Synod, n.d.

Crucifixion and Resurrection in the New Testament. Fort Wayne, IN: Concordia Theological Seminary Press, 1980.

Implications of Christology for the Doctrine of the Ministry. Springfield, IL: Central Illinois District, 1991.

Kritik und Antwort auf Martin Hengels "Probleme des Markusevangeliums": als Anhang dazu der Versuch einer Loesung des Problems, das durch die Spannung hervorgerufen wird, das Markusevangelium als ein Dokument zu verstehen, das petrinische Autoritaet besitzt und dennoch von Matthaeus und Lukas abhaengig ist. Translated by Gottfried. Martens. [Fort Wayne, IN]: [Concordia Theological Seminary Press], 1980s.

Life, New Life, and Baptism. Fort Wayne: Concordia Theological Seminary Press, 1980.

Ordination: Human Rite or Divine Ordinance? Fort Wayne, IN: Concordia Theological Seminary Press, 1978. http://www.ctsfw.net/media/pdfs/ScaerOrdination-HumanRiteorDivineOrdinance.pdf.

Sanctification: A Lutheran Response to the Evangelical Movement. Hattiesburg, MS: Pastoral Conference. Southern District. Lutheran Church—Missouri Synod, 1991.

The Call and the Church Today. Hastings, NE: Nebraska District Conference, 1991.

The Doctrine of Justification and the Augsburg Confession: Essay for the Nebraska District of the Lutheran Church—Missouri Synod. Nebraska District, 1980.

"The Law and the Gospel in Lutheran Theology," 22. Evangelical Theological Society Papers; ETS-0229. Portland, OR: Theological Research Exchange Network, 1992.

The New Reality and the Church's Message. Springfield, IL: Concordia Theological Seminary, 1969.

The Problems and Benefits of Citing Post-Apostolic Sources in Resolving the Order of the Synoptic Gospels: A Proposed Solution. Fort Wayne, IN: David Scaer, 1987. http://www.ctsfw.net/media/pdfs/ScaerTheProblemsandBenefitsofCitingPostApostolicSources.pdf.

The Relationship of Pastor and Church. Fort Wayne, IN: David Scaer, 1980.

The Sermon on the Mount as Eucharistic Homily. Fort Wayne: Concordia Theological Seminary Press, 1980.

Thesis on Church and Ministry. Fort Wayne, IN: Concordia Theological Seminary, 1977.

Women in the Church. Pittsburgh, PA: First Trinity Lutheran Church, 1979.

Scaer, D. P., James L. Hoke, Inter-Lutheran Commission on Worship, and Concordia Theological Seminary. *Seminar Notes S675 ILCW Materials*. [Fort Wayne, IN]: Concordia Theological Seminary, 1977.

Scaer, D. P., and Phil. Tesch. *Study Guide for What Do You Think of Jesus?* Fort Wayne: Concordia Theological Seminary Press, 1980.

Seaman, William D., and David P. Scaer. *An Analysis of Some Lutheran Charismatic Writings: With Respect to Lutheran Theology*. [Fort Wayne, IN]: [Concordia Theological Seminary], 1978.

RECORDED PRESENTATIONS AND INTERVIEWS

1-19-96 Memorial Service for Dr. Robert D. Preus at Kramer Chapel, CTS, Fort Wayne, IN. VHS. Fort Wayne, IN: Concordia Theological Seminary, 1996.

Horton, Michael Scott., Todd. Wilken, David P. Scaer, and KFUO (Radio station: St. Louis, MO). *Hell*. [KFUO], 2002.

Integrity of a Christocentric Ministry. Audiocassette. Vol. 1. 6 vols. [Integrity Series]. Fort Wayne, IN: Concordia Theological Seminary, 1991.

Matzat, Don. "Baptism." CD. *Issues, Etc*. St Louis, MO: KFUO, 1999.

"The Moral Majority." VHS. *Morning Break*. Fort Wayne, IN: WPTA-TV (ABC), 1981.

A

Abortion, Incarnation, and the Place of Children in the Church: All One Cloth a Common Basis. Thirty-Sixth Symposium on the Lutheran Confessions. Fort Wayne, IN: Concordia Theological Seminary, 2013. https://video.ctsfw.edu/media/1_onjghjed.

Augustana V: Is It Still Useful for a Lutheran Doctrine of the Ministry? Audiocassette. Vol. 6. 10 vols. Fourteenth Symposium on the Lutheran Confessions. Fort Wayne, IN: Concordia Theological Seminary, 1991.

Advent/Christmas Preaching Seminar. 4 vols. Northville, SD: Distributed by Logia Business Office, 1998.

Altar and Pulpit Fellowship. CD. Divine Service Institute at St. Paul's. Fort Wayne, IN: St. Paul's Lutheran Church, 1996.

B

Baptism and the Lord's Supper in the Catholic Epistles. MP3. Thirty-Third Symposium of the Lutheran Confessions. Concordia Theological Seminary, Fort Wayne, IN, 2010. https://video.ctsfw.edu/media/Exegetical+-+Baptism+and+the+Lord%27s+Supper+in+the+Catholic+Epistles+-+Audio/1_rbdnybhg/86967741.

Baptism as Foundational Sacrament. MP3. Twenty-Sixth Symposium on the Lutheran Confessions. Concordia Theological Seminary, Fort Wayne, IN, 2003. https://video.ctsfw.edu/media/Confessions+-+Baptism+as+Foundational+Sacrament/1_yxdksscc/86967631.

The Beatitudes. MP3. Issues, Etc., n.d. http://www.issuesetc.org/podcast/351110209H1S2.MP3.

Biblical Studies as Culturally Driven Discipline. MP4. Twenty-Seventh Symposium on Exegetical Theology. Fort Wayne, IN: Concordia Theological Seminary, 2015. https://video.ctsfw.edu/dia/2015+Symposia+Biblical+Studies+as+Culturally+Driven+Discipline/1_zy5ydocz/86967921.

C

Church Order in the New Testament: Do Pastors Stand in the Succession of Christ and the Apostles? Audiocassette. n.p.: Evangelical Theological Society, n.d.

Christology: Key to Understanding the Trinity. Vol. 7. Luther Academy Lecture Series ; no. 16. Minneapolis, MN: Association of Confessional Lutherans, 2009.

Cum Patre et Filio Adoratur, the Spirit Understood Christologically. VHS. Vol. 4. 9 vols. Eighteenth Symposium on the Lutheran Confessions. Fort Wayne, IN: Concordia Theological Seminary, 1995.

Cum Patre et Filio Adoratur, the [Spirit Understood Christologically]. Audiocassette. Vol. 4. 9 vols. Eighteenth Symposium on the Lutheran Confessions. Fort Wayne, IN: Concordia Theological Seminary, 1995.

D–I

Death and Resurrection as Apocalyptic Event. MP3. Twenty-Third Symposium on the Lutheran Confessions. Fort Wayne, IN: Concordia Theological Seminary, 2000. https://video.ctsfw.edu/media/Confessions+-+The+Death+and+Resurrection+of+J esus+as+Eschatological+Event/1_ensqk4aw/86967571.

Do the Epistles Have to Come Before the Gospels? Thirty-Fifth Symposium on the Lutheran Confessions. Fort Wayne, IN: Concordia Theological Seminary, 2012. https://video.ctsfw.edu/media/Symposia+2012+-+Do+the+Epistles+Have+to+Com e+Before+the+GospelsF/1_416uzhbi/86967811.

Ethics as Part of a Seminary Curriculum. MP4. Fort Wayne, IN: Concordia Theological Seminary, 2013. https://video.ctsfw.edu/media/Ethics+as+Part+of+a+Seminary +Curriculum/1_ylyi4ljs/86967871.

The Evangelical and Catholic Principles in Lutheran Theology. MP3. Issues, Etc., 2013. http://issuesetc.org/?s=The+Evangelical+and+Catholic+Principles+in+Lutheran+Theology.

The First Article and the Sacraments. VHS. Vol. 5. 7 vols. 16th Symposium on the Lutheran Confessions. Fort Wayne, IN: Concordia Theological Seminary, 1993.

The First Article and the Sacraments. Audiocassette. Vol. 5. 7 vols. 16th Annual Lutheran Confessions Symposium. Fort Wayne, IN: Concordia Theological Seminary, 1993.

God the Son and Hermeneutics. Audiocassette. Vol. 2. 8 vols. Seventeenth Symposium on the Lutheran Confessions. Fort Wayne, IN: Concordia Theological Seminary, 1994.

God the Son and Hermeneutics. VHS. Vol. 2. 8 vols. Seventeenth Symposium on the Lutheran Confessions. Fort Wayne, IN: Concordia Theological Seminary, 1994.

Good Works and Sanctification in the Lutheran Confessions. Audiocassette. Vol. 3. 6 vols. Eleventh Symposium on the Lutheran Confessions. Fort Wayne, IN: Concordia Theological Seminary, 1988.

The Holy Spirit, Sacraments, and Church Rites. Twenty-Ninth Symposium on the Lutheran Confession. Fort Wayne, IN: Concordia Theological Seminary, 2006. https://video.ctsfw.edu/media/Confessions+-+The+Holy+Spirit%2C+Sacraments% 2C+and+Other+Churchly+Rites/1_ei77p9oi/86967671.

Incarnation, Children and Abortion. MP3. Issues, Etc., 2014. http://issuesetc.org/?s=In carnation%2C+Children+and+Abortion.

J–L

Justification: Set Up Where It Ought Not to Be. MP4. Thirty-Nineth Symposium on the Lutheran Confessions. Fort Wayne, IN: Concordia Theological Seminary, 2016. https://video.ctsfw.edu/media/2016+Symposia+-+JustificationA+Set+Up+W here+It+Ought+Not+to+Be/1_jgud7k5h/86967931.

Lex Semper Accusat - Really? MP4. Forty-First Symposium on the Lutheran Confessions. Fort Wayne, IN: Concordia Theological Seminary, 2018. https://video.ctsfw.edu/media/Lex+Semper+Accusat+-+ReallyF/o_lsgt00v0/86967941.

The Lord's Supper. MP3. Issues, Etc., n.d. http://issuesetc.org/podcast/532071310H1S2.MP3.

Lutheran Distinctives as Theological Substitutes. MP4. Fort Wayne, IN: Concordia Theological Seminary, 2014. https://video.ctsfw.edu/media/2014+Symposia+-+Lutheran+Distinctives+as+Theological+Substitutes/1_qgzsf770/86967901.

Lutheranism and the Charismatic Movement. MP3. Issues, Etc., n.d. http://www.issuesetc.org/podcast/192032409H1S2.MP3.

M-R

Matthew the Apostle. MP3. Issues, Etc., 2015 http://issuesetc.org/?s=Matthew+the+Apostle.

Matthew the Apostle and Evangelist. MP3. Issues, Etc., 2012 http://issuesetc.org/?s=Matthew+the+Apostle+and+Evangelist.

The Metamorphosis of Confessional Lutheranism. Thirtieth Symposium on the Lutheran Confessions. Fort Wayne, IN: Concordia Theological Seminary, 2007. https://video.ctsfw.edu/media/Confessions+-+The+Metamorphosis+of+Confessional+Lutheranism/1_xygthxs0/86967681.

Ministry Crisis in the Lutheran Church. Audiocassette. Vol. 1. 10 vols. Eighth Annual Symposium on the Lutheran Confessions. Fort Wayne, IN: Concordia Theological Seminary, 1985.

Missouri's Identity Crisis: Rootless in America. MP3. Twenty-Fifth Symposium on the Lutheran Confessions. Fort Wayne, IN: Concordia Theological Seminary, 2002. https://video.ctsfw.edu/media/Confessions+-+Missouri%27s+Identity+CrisisA+Rootless+in+America/1_oexc6dj1/86967601.

The Office of the Public Ministry: Concerning the Power of the Bishops. CD. Northville, SD: Logia Business Office, 2007.

The Ordination of Women. MP3. Issues, Etc., n.d. http://www.podtrac.com/pts/redirect.MP3/issuesetc.org/podcast/696022811H1S1.MP3.

The Ordination of Women. Audiocassette. Vol. 2. 2 vols. Winter 1977 Day of Theological Reflection. St. Louis, MO: Concordia Seminary Media Services, 1977.

Reformed Exegesis and Lutheran Sacraments: Worlds in Conflict. MP3. Twenty-Second Symposium on the Lutheran Confessions. Fort Wayne, IN: Concordia Theological Seminary, 1999. https://video.ctsfw.edu/media/Confession+-+Reformed+Exegesis+-+Lutheran+Sacraments/1_n0zbc9kf/86967561.

Responding to Liberal Proof Texts: Ecumenism, 1 Corinthians 10 and 12, Ephesians 2. MP3. Issues, Etc., n.d. http://www.podtrac.com/pts/redirect.MP3/issuesetc.org/podcast/19790204162.MP3.

Responding to Liberal Proof Texts: The Kingdom of God, Mark 10:14–25. MP3. Issues, Etc., 2015. http://issuesetc.org/?s=Kingdom+of+God%2C+Scaer.

The Role in the LCMS. CD. Lutheran Confessional Identity: What Will This Mean? St. Louis, MO: Concordia Seminary Media Services, 2000.

S–Z

Sacraments and Inspiration in Trinitarian Perspective. MP3. Twenty-Seventh Symposium on the Lutheran Confessions. Fort Wayne, IN: Concordia Theological Seminary, 2004. https://video.ctsfw.edu/media/Confessions+-+Sacraments+and+Inspiration+in+Trinitarian+Perspective/1_nzrbv948/86967651.

Summary Reflections on "The Law in Holy Scripture." MP4. Twenty-Fourth Symposium on the Lutheran Confessions. Fort Wayne, IN: Concordia Theological Seminary, 2001. https://video.ctsfw.edu/media/Exegesis+-+Summary+Reflections+on+The+Law+in+Holy+Scripture/1_8ej9vm85/86967591.

The Third Use of the Law: Resolving the Tension. Twenty-Eighth Sympoisum on the Lutheran Confessions. Fort Wayne, IN: Concordia Theological Seminary, 2005. https://video.ctsfw.edu/media/Confessions+-+Third+Use+of+the+LawA+Recolving+the+Tension/1_lncx6cgm/86967661.

Walther, the Third Use of the Law, and Contemporary Issues. MP4. Thirty-Fourth Symposium on the Lutheran Confessions. Fort Wayne, IN: Concordia Theological Seminary, 2011. https://video.ctsfw.edu/media/Symposia+2011+-+Walther+and+the+Third+Use+of+the+Law+-+Video/1_6e1zllcv/86967751.

Will the Real Luther Stand Up? MP4. Fortieth Symposium on the Lutheran Confessions. Fort Wayne, IN: Concordia Theological Seminary, 2017. https://video.ctsfw.edu/media/2016+Symposia+-+JustificationA+Set+Up+Where+It+Ought+Not+to+Be/1_jgud7k5h/86967931.

Scaer, D. P. and Edward H. Schroeder. *Is Ordination of Women Divisive of Fellowship?* Audiocassette. Vol. 1. 3 vols. New Orleans '73/Issues. St. Louis, MO: Concordia Publishing House, 1973.

What Makes a Hermeneutic Lutheran? VHS. Vol. 1. 4 vols. Hermeneutics Lectures. Fort Wayne, IN: Concordia Theological Seminary, 1999.

Wilken, Todd. *Anfechtung: Affliction in Luther's Thought*. MP3. Issues, Etc., n.d. http://www.podtrac.com/pts/redirect.MP3/issuesetc.org/podcast/632113010H1S1.MP3.

REVIEWS

"Jesus Christ: Savior and Lord." *Springfielder* 30, no. 4 (1967): 35–39. http://www.ctsfw.net/media/pdfs/ScaerJesusChristSaviorAndLord.pdf.

"Law-Gospel Debate in the Missouri Synod Continued. [Review of Paul G. Bretscher, *After the Purifying. Thirty-Second Yearbook, Lutheran Education Association*. River Forest, IL: Lutheran Education Association, 1975]." *Springfielder* 40, no. 2 (1976): 107–18. http://www.ctsfw.net/media/pdfs/ScaerLawGospelDebate-Continued.pdf.

Numbers

"Review of *365 Days with Calvin* by Joel R. Bleeke, Editor." *Concordia Theological Quarterly* 73, no. 4 (2009): 372–73. http://www.ctsfw.net/media/pdfs/CTQTheologicalObserver73-4.pdf.

A

"Review of *Acts* by Gerhard Krodel." *Concordia Theological Quarterly* 51, no. 2–3 (1987): 214–15. http://www.ctsfw.net/media/pdfs/BookReviews51-2,3.pdf.

"Review of *Adam's Fractured Rib* by Margaret Stittler Ermarth." *Springfielder* 34, no. 4 (1971): 318–20. http://www.ctsfw.net/media/pdfs/SpringfielderBookReview34-4.pdf.

"Review of *American Lutherans and Roman Catholics in Dialogue on the Eucharist: A Methodological Critique and Proposal* by Kevin W. Irwin." *Concordia Theological Quarterly* 45, no. 4 (1981): 322–23. http://www.ctsfw.net/media/pdfs/BookReviews45-4.pdf.

"Review of *Apostolate and Ministry: The New Testament Doctrine of the Office of the Ministry* by Karl Heinrich Rengstorf." *Springfielder* 33, no. 1 (1969): 54–55. http://www.ctsfw.net/media/pdfs/SpringfielderBookReview33-1.pdf.

"Review of *At Home in the House of My Fathers: Presidential Sermons, Essays, Letters, and Addresses from the Missouri Synod's Great Era of Unity and Growth* by Matthew C. Harrison." *Concordia Theological Quarterly* 74, no. 1–2 (2010): 165–67. http://www.ctsfw.net/media/pdfs/CTQBookReview74-1.pdf.

"Review of *The Authoritative Word: Essays on the Nature of Scripture* by Donald K. McKim." *Concordia Theological Quarterly* 48, no. 1 (1984): 80. http://www.ctsfw.net/media/pdfs/BookReviews48-1.pdf.

B

"Review of *Baptism and Christian Unity* by A. Gilmore." *Springfielder* 31, no. 1 (1967): 75–76. http://www.ctsfw.net/media/pdfs/SpringfielderBookReview31-1.pdf.

"Review of *Baptism: My Adoption into God's Family* by Gaylin R. Schmeling." *Logia* 8, no. 4 (1999): 57–58. https://logia.org/scaer-articles.

"Review of *Baptism: Three Views* by David F. Wright." *Logia* 19, no. 3 (2010): 49–49. https://logia.org/scaer-articles.

"Review of *Baptism Through the Centuries* by Henry F. Brown." *Springfielder* 31, no. 2 (1967): 45–46. http://www.ctsfw.net/media/pdfs/SpringfielderBookReview31-2.pdf.

"Review of *The Beginning of Dialectic Theology*, Vol. 1 by James M. Robinson." *Christianity Today* 13, no. 10 (February 14, 1969): 18.

"Review of *The Book of Joshua* by Marten H. Woudstra." *Concordia Theological Quarterly* 46, no. 2–3 (1982): 255–255. http://www.ctsfw.net/media/pdfs/CTQBookComments46-2,3.pdf.

"Review of *Born Againism: Perspectives on a Movement* by Erich W. Gritsch." *Concordia Theological Quarterly* 46, no. 4 (1982): 341–42. http://www.ctsfw.net/media/pdfs/CTQBookReviews46-4.pdf.

"Review of *By Oath Consigned: A Reinterpretation of the Covenant Signs of Circumcision and Baptism* by Meredith G. Kline." *Springfielder* 32, no. 4 (1969): 46–47. http://www.ctsfw.net/media/pdfs/BookReviews32-4.pdf.

C

"Review of *C. S. Lewis and the Search for Rational Religion* by John Beversluis." *Concordia Theological Quarterly* 49, no. 2–3 (1985): 230–31. http://www.ctsfw.net/media/pdfs/CTQBookReview49-2,3.pdf.

"Review of *Called to Freedom: Liberation Theology and the Future of Christian Doctrine* by Daneil L. Migliore." *Concordia Theological Quarterly* 46, no. 2–3 (1982): 256–256. http://www.ctsfw.net/media/pdfs/CTQBookComments46-2,3.pdf.

"Review of *The Case of Biblical Christianity* by Edward John Carnell." *Springfielder* 33, no. 4 (1970): 81–82. http://www.ctsfw.net/media/pdfs/BookReviews33-4.pdf.

"Review of *Chi Rho Commentary on James, Jude* by Henry Paul Hamann." *Concordia Theological Quarterly* 46, no. 2–3 (1982): 249. http://www.ctsfw.net/media/pdfs/BookReviews46-2,3.pdf.

"Review of *Christ in the Gospels of the Liturgical Year* by Raymond Edward Brown." *Concordia Theological Quarterly* 73, no. 3 (2009): 282–83. http://www.ctsfw.net/media/pdfs/CTQBookReview73-3.pdf.

"Review of *The Christian Faith: A Systematic Theology for Pilgrims on the Way* by Michael Horton." *Concordia Theological Quarterly* 76, no. 1–2 (2012): 186–88. http://www.ctsfw.net/media/pdfs/CTQBookReview76-1.pdf.

"Review of *The Church* by Wolfhart Pannenberg." *Concordia Theological Quarterly* 48, no. 1 (1984): 82–84. http://www.ctsfw.net/media/pdfs/BookReviews48-1.pdf.

"Review of *The Church in Experiment* by Rüdiger Reitz." *Springfielder* 33, no. 4 (1970): 83–84.

"Review of *Church, Ministry, and Sacraments in the New Testament* by C. K. Barrett." *Concordia Theological Quarterly* 50, no. 3–4 (1986): 293–94. http://www.ctsfw.net/media/pdfs/BookReviews50-3,4.pdf.

"Review of *Church, Mission, Ministry: The Family of God* by Armin W. Schuetze." *Logia* 6, no. 1 (1997): 47–47. https://logia.org/scaer-articles.

"Review of *The Common Catechism: A Book of Christian Faith* by Johannes Feiner." *Springfielder* 40, no. 1 (1976): 45–48. http://www.ctsfw.net/media/pdfs/TheologicalObserver40-1.pdf.

"Review of *Concise Dictionary of Christian Theology* by Millard J. Erickson." *Concordia Theological Quarterly* 51, no. 2–3 (1987): 218. http://www.ctsfw.net/media/pdfs/BookReviews51-2,3.pdf.

"Review of *Contemporary Celebration* by Ross Snyder." *Springfielder* 35, no. 4 (1972): 306–7. http://www.ctsfw.net/media/pdfs/SprBookReviews35-4.pdf.

"Review of *Creeds in the Bible* by Fred Danker." *Springfielder* 31, no. 1 (1967): 77–78. http://www.ctsfw.net/media/pdfs/SpringfielderBookReview31-1.pdf.

"Review of *A Critical and Exegetical Commentary on the Gospel According to Matthew*, The International Critical Commentary in Three Volumes. Volume II. Commentary on Matthew VIII–XVIII. by Dale C. Allison Jr." *Concordia Theological Quarterly* 58, no. 2–3 (1994): 188–90. http://www.ctsfw.net/media/pdfs/CTQBookReview58-2.pdf.

"Review of *The Cult of the Virgin Mary: Psychological Origins* by Michael P. Carroll." *Concordia Theological Quarterly* 51, no. 2–3 (1987): 213. http://www.ctsfw.net/media/pdfs/BookReviews51-2,3.pdf.

D–E

"Review of *A Daystar Reader* by Matthew L. Becker." *Concordia Theological Quarterly* 74, no. 1–2 (January 2010): 165–67. http://www.ctsfw.net/media/pdfs/CTQBookReview74-1.pdf.

"Review of *Death Set to Music: Masterworks by Bach, Brahms, Penderecki, Bernstein* by Paul Sevier Minear." *Concordia Theological Quarterly* 51, no. 4 (1987): 301–2. http://www.ctsfw.net/media/pdfs/BookReviews51-4.pdf.

"Review of *Die Delitzschsche Sache: Ein Kapitel Preussischer Kirchen Und Fakultaetspolitik Im Vormarz* by Karl Heinrich Rengstorf." *Springfielder* 33, no. 1 (1969): 66.

"Review of *The Diet of John the Baptist* by James A. Kelhoffer." *Bulletin for Biblical Research* 16, no. 2 (2006): 364–65.

"Review of *Easter Gospels: The Resurrection of Jesus According to the Four Evangelists* by Robert H. Smith." *Concordia Theological Quarterly* 49, no. 1 (1985): 65–65. http://www.ctsfw.net/media/pdfs/CTQBookReview49-1.pdf.

"Review of *Encyclopedia of Bible Difficulties* by Gleason Leonard Archer Jr." *Concordia Theological Quarterly* 46, no. 4 (1982): 339. http://www.ctsfw.net/media/pdfs/CTQBookReviews46-4.pdf.

"Review of *The Evangelical Faith, V 3: The Holy Spirit, the Church, and Eschatology* by Helmut Thielicke." *Concordia Theological Quarterly* 46, no. 2–3 (1982): 251–53. http://www.ctsfw.net/media/pdfs/BookReviews46-2,3.pdf.

"Review of *Exodus Theology: Einar Billing and the Development of Modern Swedish Theology*. By Gustav Wingren." *Springfielder* 33, no. 2 (1969): 59–60. http://www.ctsfw.net/media/pdfs/SprBookReview33-2.pdf.

F–G

"Review of *Faith and Understanding*, v I by Rudolf Karl Bultmann." *Springfielder* 34, no. 2 (1970): 161–62. http://www.ctsfw.net/media/pdfs/SpringfielderBookReview34-2.pdf.

"Review of *Five Gospels: An Account of How the Good News Came to Be* by John Carney Meagher." *Concordia Theological Quarterly* 48, no. 1 (1984): 79. http://www.ctsfw.net/media/pdfs/BookReviews48-1.pdf.

"Review of *The Foolishness of God: The Place of Reason in the Theology of Martin Luther* by Siegbert W. Becker." *Concordia Theological Quarterly* 46, no. 1 (1982): 89–90. http://www.ctsfw.net/media/pdfs/BookReviews46-1.pdf.

"Review of *Fortress Introduction to Salvation and the Cross* by David A. Brondos." *Concordia Theological Quarterly* 72, no. 3 (2008): 278–278. http://www.ctsfw.net/media/pdfs/CTQBookReview72-3.pdf.

"Review of *Founding Fathers: The Puritans in England and America* by John Eric Adair." *Concordia Theological Quarterly* 50, no. 3–4 (1986): 294. http://www.ctsfw.net/media/pdfs/BookReviews50-3,4.pdf.

"Review of *Four Other Gospels: Shadows on the Contours of Canon* by John Dominic Crossan." *Concordia Theological Quarterly* 49, no. 2–3 (1985): 230. http://www.ctsfw.net/media/pdfs/CTQBookReview49-2,3.pdf.

"Review of *God in an Age of Atheism* by S. Paul Schilling." *Springfielder* 33, no. 4 (March 1970): 77–78. http://www.ctsfw.net/media/pdfs/BookReviews33-4.pdf.

"Review of *The Gospel of the Lord: How the Early Church Wrote the Story of Jesus* by Michael F. Bird." *Concordia Theological Quarterly* 79, no. 3–4 (2015): 374–75. http://www.ctsfw.net/media/pdfs/CTQBookReview79-3.pdf.

H–I

"Review of *The Historical Jesus: A Continuing Quest* by Charles C. Anderson." *Springfielder* 37, no. 3 (1973): 185–86. http://www.ctsfw.net/media/pdfs/SprBookReviews37-3.pdf.

"Review of *The Historical Jesus: Five Views* by James K. Beilby and Paul Rhodes Eddy." *Concordia Theological Quarterly* 74, no. 1–2 (2010): 184. http://www.ctsfw.net/media/pdfs/CTQBookReview74-1.pdf.

"Review of *A History and Critique of the Origin of the Marcan Hypothesis 1835–1866* by Hajo Uden Meijboom." *Concordia Theological Quarterly* 60, no. 1–2 (1996): 146–47. http://www.ctsfw.net/media/pdfs/CTQBookReview60-1.pdf.

"Review of *Holy Conversation: Spirituality for Worship* by Jonathan Linman." *Cross Accent* 19, no. 2 (2011): 29–30.

"Review of *Hope and Planning* by Jürgen Moltmann." *Theology Today* 28, no. 3 (1971): 364–66.

"Review of *Horizontal Line Synkopsis of the Gospels* by Reuben J. Swanson." *Springfielder* 39, no. 4 (1976): 235. http://www.ctsfw.net/media/pdfs/SpringfielderBookReview39-4.pdf.

"Review of *How Dependable Is the Bible* by Raymond F. Surburg." *Springfielder* 36, no. 3 (1972): 227–29. http://www.ctsfw.net/media/pdfs/SprBookReview36-3.pdf.

"Review of *How Modern Should Theology Be?* by Helmut Thielicke." *Lutheran Forum* 4, no. 1 (January 1970): 27–27.

"Review of *The Hungering Dark* by Frederick Buechner." *Springfielder* 33, no. 1 (1969): 61–62. http://www.ctsfw.net/media/pdfs/SprBookReview33-1.pdf.

"Review of *In Retrospect: Remembrance of Things Past* by F. F. Bruce." *Concordia Theological Quarterly* 45, no. 4 (1981): 321–22. http://www.ctsfw.net/media/pdfs/BookReviews45-4.pdf.

"Review of *Infant Baptism in Reformation Geneva: The Shaping of a Community, 1536–1564* by Gregory K. Beale." *Concordia Theological Quarterly* 73, no. 4 (2009): 377–78. http://www.ctsfw.net/media/pdfs/CTQBookReview73-4.pdf.

"Review of *The Influence of the Gospel of Saint Matthew on Christian Literature before Saint Irenaeus* Book 1. The First Ecclesiastical Writers by Edouard Masaux." *Concordia Theological Quarterly* 58, no. 2–3 (1994): 190–93. http://www.ctsfw.net/media/pdfs/CTQBookReview58-2.pdf.

"Review of *Inspiration and Canonicity of the Bible* by Robert Laird Harris." *Springfielder* 33, no. 4 (1970): 66–67. http://www.ctsfw.net/media/pdfs/BookReviews33-4.pdf.

"Review of *Interpreting the Synoptic Gospels* by Scot McKinght." *Concordia Theological Quarterly* 53, no. 1–2 (1989): 133–133. http://www.ctsfw.net/media/pdfs/BookReviews53-1,2.pdf.

"Review of *Introducing the New Testament: A Historical, Literary, and Theological Survey* by Mark Allan Powell." *Concordia Theological Quarterly* 74, no. 1–2 (2010): 186–87.

"Review of *Introduction to the Old Testament: Hear, O Israel* by James King West." *Springfielder* 36, no. 1 (1972): 60–61. http://www.ctsfw.net/media/pdfs/SprBookReview36-1.pdf.

"Review of *An Introduction to the Theology of Rudolf Bultmann* by Walter Schmithals." *Lutheran Forum* 3, no. 1 (January 1969): 25–26.

"Review of *Is There a Synoptic Problem? Rethinking the Literary Dependence of the First Three Gospels* by Eta Linnemann." *Concordia Theological Quarterly* 59, no. 1–2 (1995): 128–29. http://www.ctsfw.net/media/pdfs/CTQBookReview59-1.pdf.

"Review of *Ist Das Nicht Josephs Sohn: Jesus Im Heutigen Judentum* by Pinchas Lapide." *Concordia Theological Quarterly* 49, no. 4 (1985): 310. http://www.ctsfw.net/media/pdfs/BookReviews49-4.pdf.

J

"Review of *Jesus and the Eyewitnesses: The Gospels as Eyewitness Testimony* by Richard Bauckham." *Concordia Theological Quarterly* 73, no. 1 (2009): 83–88. http://www.ctsfw.net/media/pdfs/CTQBookReview73-1.pdf.

"Review of *Jesus and the Gospel: Tradition, Scripture, and Canon* by William Reuben Farmer." *Concordia Theological Quarterly* 46, no. 4 (1982): 339–41. http://www.ctsfw.net/media/pdfs/CTQBookReviews46-4.pdf.

"Review of *Jesus and the Old Testament: His Application of Old Testament Passages to Himself and His Mission* by R. T. France." *Springfielder* 38, no. 1 (1974): 60–61. http://www.ctsfw.net/media/pdfs/SprBookReviews38-1.pdf.

"Review of *Jesus, Apocalyptic Prophet of the New Millennium* by Bart D. Ehrman." *Concordia Theological Quarterly* 64, no. 2 (2000): 157–58. http://www.ctsfw.net/media/pdfs/CTQBookReview64-2.pdf.

"Review of *Jesus Is Risen—Theology for the Church: The Lifework and Teaching of the Rev. Dr. Walter R. Bouman, ThD* by Walter R. Bouman." *Concordia Historical Institute Quarterly* 89, no. 4 (2016): 65–67.

"Review of *Jesus the Pharisee: A New Look at the Jewishness of Jesus* by Harvey Falk." *Concordia Theological Quarterly* 49, no. 4 (1985): 311. http://www.ctsfw.net/media/pdfs/BookReviews49-4.pdf.

"Review of *Jewish Christianity: Factional Disputes in the Early Church* Hans Joachim Schoeps." *Springfielder* 33, no. 4 (1970): 72–73. http://www.ctsfw.net/media/pdfs/BookReviews33-4.pdf.

"Review of *Johannine Christianity: Essays on Its Setting, Sources, and Theology* by D. Moody Smith." *Concordia Theological Quarterly* 49, no. 4 (1985): 307–8. http://www.ctsfw.net/media/pdfs/BookReviews49-4.pdf.

"Review of *John 1: A Commentary on the Gospel of John* by Ernst Haenchen." *Concordia Theological Quarterly* 50, no. 3–4 (1986): 299. http://www.ctsfw.net/media/pdfs/BookReviews50-3,4.pdf.

" Review of *John among the Gospels: The Relationship in 20th-Century Research* by D. Moody Smith." *Concordia Theological Quarterly* 58, no. 2–3 (1994): 235. http://www.ctsfw.net/media/pdfs/CTQBookReview58-2.pdf.

"Review of *Justification: The Chief Article of Christian Doctrine as Expounded in Loci Theologici* by Martin Chemnitz." *Concordia Theological Quarterly* 51, no. 2–3 (1987): 224–25. http://www.ctsfw.net/media/pdfs/BookReviews51-2,3.pdf.

"Review of *Justification: The Doctrine of Karl Barth and a Catholic Reflection* by Hans Küng." *Concordia Theological Quarterly* 45, no. 4 (1981): 323–24. http://www.ctsfw.net/media/pdfs/BookReviews45-4.pdf.

L

"Review of *Law, Life, and the Living God: The Third Use of the Law in Modern American Lutheranism* by Scott R. Murray." *Logia* 11, no. 4 (2002): 51–51. https://logia.org/scaer-articles.

"Review of *A Lively Legacy: Essays in Honor of Robert Preus* by Kurt E. Marquart." *Concordia Theological Quarterly* 50, no. 2 (1986): 147–49. http://www.ctsfw.net/media/pdfs/CTQBookReview50-2.pdf.

"Review of *Lively Stone: The Autobiography of Berthold von Schenk* by C. George Fry and Joel R. Kurz." *Concordia Theological Quarterly* 70, no. 3–4 (2006): 377–78. http://www.ctsfw.net/media/pdfs/CTQBookReview70-3.pdf.

"Review of *The Living Text of the Gospels* by D. C. Parker." *Concordia Theological Quarterly* 68, no. 2 (2004): 169–70. http://www.ctsfw.net/media/pdfs/CTQBookReview68-2.pdf.

"Review of *The Lord's Supper in the Reformed Tradition: An Essay on the Mystical True Presence* by John W. Riggs." *Concordia Theological Quarterly* 79, no. 3–4 (2015): 372–74. http://www.ctsfw.net/media/pdfs/CTQBookReview79-3.pdf.

"Review of *Luther and the Old Testament* by Heinrich Bornkamm." *Springfielder* 33, no. 4 (1970): 65–66. http://www.ctsfw.net/media/pdfs/BookReviews33-4.pdf.

"Review of *Luther on Conversion: The Early Years* by Marilyn J. Harran." *Concordia Theological Quarterly* 48, no. 1 (1984): 88. http://www.ctsfw.net/media/pdfs/BookReviews48-1.pdf.

M

"Review of *Mark: A New Translation with Introduction and Commentary* by C. S. Mann." *Concordia Theological Quarterly* 51, no. 4 (1987): 308–9. http://www.ctsfw.net/media/pdfs/BookReviews51-4.pdf.

"Review of *Matthew: A Commentary on His Literary and Theological Art* by Robert H. Gundry." *Concordia Theological Quarterly* 46, no. 2–3 (1982): 247–48. http://www.ctsfw.net/media/pdfs/BookReviews46-2,3.pdf.

"Review of *Matthew and the Didache: Two Documents from the Same Jewish-Christian Milieu?* By Hubertus Waltherus Maria van de Sandt." *Concordia Theological Quarterly* 69, no. 3–4 (2005): 349–51. http://www.ctsfw.net/media/pdfs/CTQBookReview69-3.pdf.

"Review of *Matthew as Story* by Jack Dean Kingbury." *Concordia Theological Quarterly* 51, no. 2–3 (1987): 226–28. http://www.ctsfw.net/media/pdfs/BookReviews51-2,3.pdf.

"Review of *Matthew's Christian-Jewish Community* by Anthony J. Saldarini." *Concordia Theological Quarterly* 60, no. 1–2 (1996): 145–46. http://www.ctsfw.net/media/pdfs/CTQBookReview60-1.pdf.

"Review of *Melanchthon: Reformer Without Honor* by Michael Rogness." *Springfielder* 33, no. 4 (1970): 75–76.

"Review of *Melanchthons Briefwechsel*, Bd 4: Regesten 3421–4529 (1544–1546) by Philipp Melanchthon." *Concordia Theological Quarterly* 49, no. 1 (1985): 67–67. http://www.ctsfw.net/media/pdfs/CTQBookReview49-1.pdf.

"Review of *Ministry in the New Testament* by David L. Bartlett." *Logia* 3, no. 3 (1994): 64–65. https://logia.org/scaer-articles.

"Review of *Ministry, Word, and Sacraments* by Martin Chemnitz." *Concordia Theological Quarterly* 46, no. 1 (1982): 90–91. http://www.ctsfw.net/media/pdfs/BookReviews46-1.pdf.

"Review of *The Myth of Christian Beginnings: History's Impact on Belief* by Robert L. Wilken." *Springfielder* 35, no. 1 (1971): 66–69. http://www.ctsfw.net/media/pdfs/SpringfieldBookReview35-1.pdf.

N–O

"Review of *New Testament Theology* by Donald Guthrie." *Concordia Theological Quarterly* 45, no. 4 (1981): 320–21. http://www.ctsfw.net/media/pdfs/BookReviews45-4.pdf.

"Review of *No Orthodoxy But the Truth: A Survey of Protestant Theology* by Donald G. Dawe." *Springfielder* 33, no. 3 (1969): 45–46. http://www.ctsfw.net/media/pdfs/SprBookReview33-3.pdf.

"Review of *Ökumenische Dogmatik: Grundzüge* by Edmund Schlink." *Concordia Theological Quarterly* 51, no. 2–3 (1987): 219–21. http://www.ctsfw.net/media/pdfs/BookReviews51-2,3.pdf.

"Review of *The Old Testament and Jesus Christ* by Claus Westermann." *Springfielder* 34, no. 1 (1970): 77–78. http://www.ctsfw.net/media/pdfs/SpringfielderBookReview34-1.pdf.

"Review of *On Being Reformed: Distinctive Characteristics and Common Misunderstandings* by I. John Hesselink." *Concordia Theological Quarterly* 49, no. 1 (1985): 65–66. http://www.ctsfw.net/media/pdfs/CTQBookReview49-1.pdf.

"Review of *On Not Leaving It to the Snake.* by Harvey Cox." *Springfielder* 34, no. 2 (1970): 162–63. http://www.ctsfw.net/media/pdfs/SpringfielderBookReview34-2.pdf.

"Review of *Options on the Atonement in Christian Thought* by Stephen Finian." *Logia* 17, no. 4 (2008): 54–54. https://logia.org/scaer-articles.

P–Q

"Review of *Pastoral Theology: Essentials of Ministry* by Thomas C. Oden." *Concordia Theological Quarterly* 48, no. 1 (1984): 84–85. http://www.ctsfw.net/media/pdfs/BookReviews48-1.pdf.

"Review of *Patterns of Reformation* by Ernest Gordon Rupp." *Springfielder* 33, no. 4 (1970): 76–77. http://www.ctsfw.net/media/pdfs/BookReviews33-4.pdf.

"Review of *Pauline Studies: Essays Presented to Professor F. F. Bruce on His 70th Birthday* by Donald A. Hagner." *Concordia Theological Quarterly* 45, no. 4 (1981): 321–22. http://www.ctsfw.net/media/pdfs/BookReviews45-4.pdf.

"Review of *The Power of the Powerless* by Jürgen Moltmann." *Concordia Theological Quarterly* 49, no. 1 (1985): 66–67. http://www.ctsfw.net/media/pdfs/CTQBookReview49-1.pdf.

"Review of *The Present-Day Christological Debate* by Klaas Runia." *Concordia Theological Quarterly* 49, no. 2–3 (1985): 229. http://www.ctsfw.net/media/pdfs/CTQBookReview49-2,3.pdf.

"Review of *The Puritan Hope: A Study in Revival and the Interpretation of Prophecy* by Iain H. Murray." *Springfielder* 36, no. 4 (1973): 326–27. http://www.ctsfw.net/media/pdfs/SpringfielderBookReview36-4.pdf.

"Review of *Preus of Missouri* by James E. Adams." *Concordia Theological Quarterly* 41, no. 3 (1977): 50–52. http://www.ctsfw.net/media/pdfs/TheologicalObserver41-3.pdf.

"Review of *Problems with the Atonement: The Origins of, and Controversy about, the Atonement Doctrine*, by Stephen Finlay." *Logia* 15, no. 3 (2006): 64–65. https://logia.org/scaer-articles.

"Review of *Protestantisches Christentum Im Zeitalter Der Aufklärung* by Friedrich Wilhelm Kantzenbach." *Springfielder* 31, no. 2 (1967): 49–50.

"Review of *Q: The Sayings of Jesus: With a Reconstruction of Q* by Athanasius Polag by Ivan Havener." *Concordia Theological Quarterly* 51, no. 2–3 (1987): 232–33. http://www.ctsfw.net/media/pdfs/BookReviews51-2,3.pdf.

R

"Review of *Reading the New Testament for Understanding* by Robert G. Hoerber." *Concordia Theological Quarterly* 50, no. 3–4 (1986): 276. http://www.ctsfw.net/media/pdfs/BookReviews50-3,4.pdf.

"Review of *The Reform of the Church* By Donald G. Bloesch." *Springfielder* 34, no. 2 (1970): 159–61. http://www.ctsfw.net/media/pdfs/SpringfielderBookReview34-2.pdf.

"Review of *Reformed Confessions: Theology from Zurich to Barmen* by Jan Rohls." *Logia* 8, no. 2 (1999): 47–48. https://logia.org/scaer-articles.

"Review of *Religion in Communist China* by Richard Clarence Bush." *Springfielder* 34, no. 3 (1970): 246–47. http://www.ctsfw.net/media/pdfs/SpringfielderBookReview34-3.pdf.

"Review of *Religion, Revolution, and the Future* by Jürgen Moltmann." *Christianity Today* 14, no. 6 (December 19, 1969): 26–26.

"Review of *The Rising of Bread for the World: An Outcry of Citizens against Hunger* by Arthur Simon." *Concordia Theological Quarterly* 74, no. 1–2 (2010): 168–69. http://www.ctsfw.net/media/pdfs/CTQBookReview74-1.pdf.

"Review of *The Roots of Anti-Semitism in the Age of the Renaissance and Reformation* by Heiko Augustinus Oberman." *Concordia Theological Quarterly* 49, no. 4 (1985): 308–10. http://www.ctsfw.net/media/pdfs/BookReviews49-4.pdf.

"Review of *The Roots of the Synoptic Gospels* by Bo Ivar Reicke." *Concordia Theological Quarterly* 51, no. 4 (1987): 255–59. http://www.ctsfw.net/media/pdfs/scaerreviewarticle.pdf.

"Review of *Rudolf Bultmann in Catholic Thought* by Thomas F. O'Meara." *Springfielder* 32, no. 4 (1969): 53–54. http://www.ctsfw.net/media/pdfs/BookReviews32-4.pdf.

S

"Review of *Sacra Doctrina: Reason and Revelation in Aquinas* by Per Erik Persson." *Springfielder* 34, no. 3 (1970): 248–49. http://www.ctsfw.net/media/pdfs/SpringfielderBookReview34-3.pdf.

"Review of *The Scope and Authority of the Bible* by James Barr." *Concordia Theological Quarterly* 45, no. 4 (1981): 319–319. http://www.ctsfw.net/media/pdfs/BookReviews45-4.pdf.

"Review of *A Seminary in Crisis: The Inside Story of the Preus Fact Finding Committee* by Paul A. Zimmerman." *Concordia Theological Quarterly* 74, no. 1–2 (January 2010): 162–63. http://www.ctsfw.net/media/pdfs/CTQBookReview74-1.pdf.

"Review of *The Sermon on the Mount* by Robert A. Guelich." *Concordia Theological Quarterly* 49, no. 2–3 (1985): 222–23. http://www.ctsfw.net/media/pdfs/CTQBookReview49-2,3.pdf.

"Review of *The Sermon on the Mount through the Centuries* by Jeffrey P. Greenman." *Concordia Theological Quarterly* 73, no. 3 (2009): 284. http://www.ctsfw.net/media/pdfs/CTQBookReview73-3.pdf.

"Review of *The Spirit of the Reformed Tradition* by M. Eugene Osterhaven." *Springfielder* 35, no. 1 (1971): 69–70. http://www.ctsfw.net/media/pdfs/SpringfieldBookReview35-1.pdf.

"Review of *Somewhat Less than God: The Biblical View of Man* by Leonard Verduin." *Springfielder* 34, no. 3 (1970): 243–44. http://www.ctsfw.net/media/pdfs/SpringfielderBookReview34-3.pdf.

"Review of *Spirit and Martyrdom* by William C. Weinrich." *Concordia Theological Quarterly* 45, no. 4 (1981): 326–27. http://www.ctsfw.net/media/pdfs/BookReviews45-4.pdf.

"Review of *Spirit, Faith and Church* by Wolfhart Pannenberg." *Springfielder* 34, no. 3 (1970): 244–45. http://www.ctsfw.net/media/pdfs/SpringfielderBookReview34-3.pdf.

"Review of *Story and Promise* by Robert W. Jenson." *Lutheran Forum* 7, no. 4 (November 1973): 39–40.

"Review of *Studies in Matthew: Interpretation Past and Present* by Dale C. Allison Jr." *Concordia Theological Quarterly* 69, no. 3–4 (2005): 357–58. http://www.ctsfw.net/media/pdfs/CTQBookReview69-3.pdf.

"Review of *Systematic Theology: Volume 1, The Doctrine of God* by Katherine Sonderegger." *Concordia Theological Quarterly* 80, no. 1–2 (2016): 188–89. http://www.ctsfw.net/media/pdfs/CTQBookReview80-1-2.pdf.

T

"Review of *Table and Tradition: Towards and Ecumenical Understanding of the Eucharist* by Alasdair I C. Heron." *Concordia Theological Quarterly* 49, no. 2–3 (1985): 228. http://www.ctsfw.net/media/pdfs/CTQBookReview49-2,3.pdf.

"Review of *A Theology of Human Hope* by Rubem A. Alves." *Springfielder* 34, no. 1 (June 1970): 83–84. http://www.ctsfw.net/media/pdfs/SpringfielderBookReview34-1.pdf.

"Review of *The Theology of Post-Reformation Lutheranism: A Study of Theological Prolegomena* by Robert D. Preus." *Springfielder* 34, no. 4 (1971): 314–16. http://www.ctsfw.net/media/pdfs/SpringfielderBookReview34-4.pdf.

"Review of *The Theology of the Gospel of Matthew* by Ulrich Luz." *Concordia Theological Quarterly* 60, no. 4 (1996): 308–9.

"Review of *Tradition: Old and New* by F. F. Bruce." *Lutheran Forum* 5, no. 9 (November 1971): 27–28.

"Review of *Traditions of Ministry: A History of the Doctrine of the Ministry in Lutheran Theology* by James H. Pragman." *Concordia Theological Quarterly* 48, no. 1 (1984): 86–87. http://www.ctsfw.net/media/pdfs/BookReviews48-1.pdf.

"Review of *The Two Natures in Christ (1578)* by Martin Chemnitz." *Springfielder* 34, no. 4 (1971): 311–13. http://www.ctsfw.net/media/pdfs/SpringfielderBookReview34-4.pdf.

U–W

"Review of *The Universal Word: A Theology for a Universal Faith* by Nels F S. Ferré." *Springfielder* 33, no. 4 (1970): 82–83. http://www.ctsfw.net/media/pdfs/BookReviews33-4.pdf.

"Review of *When the Minister Is a Woman* by Debra E. Harmon." *Springfielder* 34, no. 3 (1970): 251–52. http://www.ctsfw.net/media/pdfs/SpringfielderBookReview34-3.pdf.

"Review of *Where Is History Going?* By John Warwick Montgomery." *Lutheran Forum* 4, no. 3 (March 1970): 26–27.

"Review of *Why Scientists Accept Evolution* by James D. Bales." *Springfielder* 30, no. 4 (1967): 51–52. http://www.ctsfw.net/media/pdfs/SprBookReview30-4.pdf.

"Review of *Witchcraft in Europe, 1100–1700: A Documentary History* by Alan C. Kors." *Springfielder* 36, no. 3 (1972): 245–46. http://www.ctsfw.net/media/pdfs/SprBookReview36-3.pdf.

"Review of *Witness and Revelation in the Gospel of John* by James Montgomery Boice." *Springfielder* 34, no. 3 (1970): 238. http://www.ctsfw.net/media/pdfs/SpringfielderBookReview34-3.pdf.

"Review of *Women's Liberation and the Church: The New Demand for Freedom in the Life of the Christian Church* by Sarah Bentley Doely." *Springfielder* 35, no. 1 (1971): 73–74. http://www.ctsfw.net/media/pdfs/SpringfieldBookReview35-1.pdf.

"A Welcome Gift from Canada: Lutheran Theological Review." *Concordia Theological Quarterly* 48, no. 1 (January 1984): 72–72. http://www.ctsfw.net/media/pdfs/TheoObserver48-1.pdf.

SERMONS

"David Scaer Sermons." Concordia Theological Seminary Media Resources, n.d. http://media.ctsfw.edu/Collection/Details/100.

www.ingramcontent.com/pod-product-compliance
Lightning Source LLC
Chambersburg PA
CBHW020728160426
43192CB00006B/153